An Introduction to Language and Linguistics

Second Edition

Edited by
RALPH FASOLD
and
JEFF CONNOR-LINTON

*Hashem Asadallah
Men's Basketball
HMA125@georgetown.edu
+1 (202) 304 ▬▬▬
5465*

LING 1000

Contributors

Elizabeth Zsiga *Georgetown University, Washington, DC*
Donna Lardiere *Georgetown University, Washington, DC*
Ruth Kramer *Georgetown University, Washington, DC*
David Lightfoot *Georgetown University, Washington, DC*
Paul Portner *Georgetown University, Washington, DC*
Deborah Schiffrin *Georgetown University, Washington, DC*
Deborah Tannen *Georgetown University, Washington, DC*
Alison Mackey *Georgetown University, Washington, DC*
Natalie Schilling *Georgetown University, Washington, DC*
Michael T. Ullman *Georgetown University, Washington, DC*
Shaligram Shukla *Georgetown University, Washington, DC*
Kendall A. King *University of Minnesota*
Inderjeet Mani *Yahoo Labs*

CAMBRIDGE
UNIVERSITY PRESS

D0071386

CAMBRIDGE
UNIVERSITY PRESS

University Printing House, Cambridge CB2 8BS, United Kingdom

Cambridge University Press is part of the University of Cambridge.

It furthers the University's mission by disseminating knowledge in the pursuit of education, learning and research at the highest international levels of excellence.

www.cambridge.org
Information on this title: www.cambridge.org/9781107637993

© Cambridge University Press 2014

First published 2006
Second edition 2014
10th printing 2022

Printed in Great Britain by Ashford Colour Press Ltd.

A catalogue record for this publication is available from the British Library

Library of Congress Cataloguing in Publication data
An introduction to language and linguistics / edited by Ralph W. Fasold, Jeffrey Connor-Linton. – Second Edition.
    pages cm
ISBN 978-1-107-07064-6 (Hardback) – ISBN 978-1-107-63799-3 (Paperback) 1. Linguistics. 2. Language and languages. I. Fasold, Ralph W. II. Connor-Linton, Jeff.
P121.I58 2014
410–dc23   2013050335

ISBN 978-1-107-07064-6 Hardback
ISBN 978-1-107-63799-3 Paperback

CONTENTS

DETAILED CONTENTS

ACKNOWLEDGMENTS

The editors sincerely thank Zhaleh Feizollahi, who helped in the revision of most chapters and added many new textboxes and other content. She taught introductory linguistics courses with the first edition at several universities and applied that experience to make the second edition even more accessible and engaging.

CHAPTER 6 CHILD LANGUAGE ACQUISITION

Thanks to Donna Lardiere, Alison Mackey, and Gigliana Melzi for their many helpful comments on this chapter, and to Rebekha Abbuhl for excellent research and editorial assistance.

CHAPTER 7 LANGUAGE AND THE BRAIN

This chapter was written with support from NSF SBR-9905273, NIH R01 HD049347, and research grants from the National Alliance for Autism Research, the Mabel Flory Trust, and Pfizer, Inc. The author thanks Paul Aisen, Sherry Ash, Harriet Bowden, Stefano Cappa, Alfonso Caramazza, Jeff Connor-Linton, Antonio Damasio, John Drury, Ivy Estabrooke, Angela Friederici, Jennifer Ganger, Matthew Gelfand, Jordan Grafman, Yosef Grodzinsky, Gregory Hickok, Argye Hillis, Peter Indefrey, Edith Kaan, Amy Knight, Sonja Kotz, Alex Martin, Goldie Ann McQuaid, Robbin Miranda, Matthew Moffa, Susan Nitzberg Lott, Aaron Newman, Alvaro Pascual-Leone, David Poeppel, Brenda Rapp, Ardi Roelofs, Ned Sahin, Karsten Steinhauer, Tamara Swaab, Michael Thomas, Sharon Thompson-Schill, John van Meter, Jill Weisberg, and particularly Matthew Walenski, for useful suggestions and help in preparing this chapter.

CHAPTER 9 DIALECT VARIATION

Thanks to Philip Carter, Janet M. Fuller, Kirk Hazen, Andrea Kleene, Anastasia Nylund, Aida Premilovac, Daniel Schreier, Corinne Seals, Barbara Soukup, and Walt Wolfram.

CHAPTER 14 COMPUTATIONAL LINGUISTICS

Thanks to Jonathan Frank for comments on a draft version of this chapter.

Introduction

"History is universal and basic," a history professor said during a faculty meeting, "It's about every event that involves all people at all times and in all places." "Yes," observed his colleague from linguistics, "but how would you record and interpret that history without language?" Indeed, it is hard to imagine how there could even be history without language, without a means to pass a record of what has happened from one generation to the next through retold stories and sagas, even before written records. Much of the history (and prehistory) of the human species consists of the development and adaptation of various tools to meet a broad range of needs: think of the wheel, the domestication of animals, the steam engine, computers, and the internet. The development and refinement of these and all other tools could not have been accomplished without language.

The human capacity for self-awareness and abstract thought is facilitated by language, if not dependent upon it. The ability to transfer complex information, to discuss the meaning of events and possible outcomes of alternative actions, to share feelings and ideas – all these are impossible without language. The origins of language are shrouded in obscurity, but archaeological records suggest that communication with language emerged about 200,000 years ago. The ability of an individual to model the world for him/herself and to communicate using language was probably the single most advantageous evolutionary adaptation of the human species.

Defining language

As one can imagine, a precise definition of language is not easy to provide, because the language phenomenon is complex and has many facets. Slightly modifying a definition provided by Finegan and Besnier (1989), we might define language as a *finite system of elements and principles that make it possible for speakers to construct sentences to do particular communicative jobs*. The part of the system that allows speakers to produce and interpret grammatical sentences is called **grammatical competence**. It includes the knowledge of which speech sounds are part of a given language and how they may and may not be strung together. Grammatical competence also includes knowing the meanings signified by different sound sequences in a language and how to combine those units of meaning into words, phrases, and sentences. Grammatical competence is what allows a speaker of English to string together twenty-one sounds that sound something like "The dog chased the cat up the tree" and allows another speaker of English to understand what dogs, cats, and trees are, what chasing is, and which way is up. Further, grammatical competence is what allows these speakers of English to share the understanding that it was the dog doing the chasing and that it was the cat that went up the tree. Of course this does not apply only to English. Grammatical competence contributes similarly to comprehension in all human languages.

But people use language to do far more than just communicate the literal meanings of grammatical sentences. The sentence "The dog chased the cat up the tree" might be used to accomplish a wide variety of jobs: to narrate part of a story, to complain to the dog's owner, to help the cat's owner find his pet. The second part of the definition, "to do particular communicative jobs," refers to **communicative competence**. The most frequent "job" that people do with language is communicate with other people.

Grammatical competence is almost useless for human interaction without communicative competence. In fact, a lot of the actual use of language is not in sentences at all, but in discourse units larger and smaller than sentences, some grammatical (in the technical sense used in formal linguistics), some not. To be effective, speakers have to combine grammatical competence with the knowledge of how to *use* grammatical sentences (and other pieces of linguistic structure) *appropriately* for the purpose and context at hand. The two taken together comprise *communicative competence*. Communicative competence – the knowledge included in grammatical competence plus the ability to use that knowledge to accomplish a wide range of communicative jobs – constitutes *language*.

Universal properties of language

Over thousands of years of evolution, the human species developed a vocal tract flexible enough to produce a wide range of distinguishable sounds and the ability to perceive differences among those sounds. But most important, the human species developed the ability to use these sounds in systems which could communicate meaning. No one knows just how this happened. Perhaps mental capacities that had evolved for a variety of other adaptive purposes (like fine motor hand–eye coordination) were "re-purposed" to support a complex symbolic and communicative system. Perhaps some mental capacities are exclusively dedicated to language and evolved more gradually along with the increasing complexity of human communication. Or perhaps once they reached a certain level of neurological and cognitive complexity, the synapses of the brain "reorganized" themselves, making the development of language possible.

Although languages differ in many ways, they are all made possible by the same genetic information, they are all processed by the brain in basically the same ways, and, not surprisingly, they all share certain fundamental "design features" and structural characteristics that enable them to work the way they do. For example, although different languages use different sets of sounds, their sounds are organized and combined according to just a few principles. If there were no shared, universal features of language, we would expect the sounds of languages and their combinations to vary randomly. Instead, the sounds of languages and their combinations are limited and systematic. Likewise, all languages follow similar constraints on how they can combine words into phrases and sentences.

Understanding and explaining the properties which are universal to all languages – as well as those which vary across languages – is the fundamental job of the linguist.

Modularity

Most linguists believe that language is a modular system. That is, people produce and interpret language using a set of component subsystems (or modules) in a coordinated way. Each module is responsible for a part of the total job; it takes the output of other modules as its input and distributes its own output to those other modules. Neurolinguistic studies show that different regions of the brain are associated with different aspects of language processing and, as the following chapters show, dividing language into modules facilitates linguistic analyses greatly.

Some modules have been central to linguistics for a long time. Phonetics is about production and interpretation of speech sounds. Phonology studies the organization of raw phonetics in language overall as well as in individual languages. Larger linguistic units are the domain of morphology, the study of structure within words – and of syntax, the study of the structure of sentences. Interacting with these modules is the **lexicon**, the repository of linguistic elements with their meanings and structural properties. In recent decades, philosophers have developed the formal study of semantics (the detailed analysis of literal meaning), and linguistics has incorporated and added semantics as another module of language. Still more recently, discourse – organization of language above and beyond the sentence – has been recognized by most linguists as another important subsystem of language.

Discreteness

Each module of language deals with the characterization, distribution, and coordination of some discrete linguistic unit (phonemes, morphemes, words, phrases, sentences, utterances). **Discreteness**, another property of languages, divides the continuous space of sound or meaning into discrete units. The range of sounds that human beings can make is continuous, like a slide whistle. For example, you can slide from a high "long *e*" sound (as in *feed*) all the way down to a low "short *a*" sound (as in *bat*) in one continuous glide. But all languages divide that continuous space of sound into discrete categories, just as most western music divides the continuous range of pitch into discrete steps in a scale. Sounds that are discrete in one language may not be discrete in another. In English, for example, we distinguish [a], "short *a*," from [ɛ], "short *e*," so that *pat* and *pet* are different words. The same is not true in German, so German speakers have trouble hearing any difference between *pet* and *pat*. At the same time, German has a vowel that is like the English "long *a*," but with rounded lips, spelled *ö* and called "*o*-umlaut." The distinction between the vowel that is like English "long *a*" and this rounded vowel is responsible for the meaning difference between *Sehne* ('tendon') and *Söhne* ('sons'). This distinction is as easy for German speakers as the *pet* and *pat* distinction is for English speakers, but it is hard for English speakers. Precisely *what* is discrete varies from one language to another, but all languages have the property of discreteness.

Discreteness also shows itself in other modules of language, such as meaning. The color spectrum is a clear example. Color variation is a continuum – red shades through red-orange to orange to yellow-orange to yellow and so on through the spectrum. But all languages divide the color spectrum into discrete categories, although languages differ in how they divide that continuum into words. In some languages there are only two basic color terms, roughly meaning 'light' and 'dark'; others add red, yellow, and green, whereas still others, including English, have developed words for many more colors. Likewise, although the claim that Eskimos have hundreds of terms for snow may be overstated, the languages of Native Americans living in the far north do distinguish more kinds of snow than do languages which have developed to meet the needs of peoples living in warmer climates. Similarly, American English has a range of words for different types of automotive vehicles (sedan, sports utility vehicle, minivan, convertible, wagon, sports car, for example) related to the importance of the automobile in that culture.

Language is composed of separate sounds, words, sentences, and other utterance units. Acoustically sounds and words blend into each other. (If you have tried to learn a second language as an adult, you know how hard it can be to separate words spoken at a normal conversational pace.) Remarkably, babies only a few weeks old are able to distinguish even closely related sounds in the language of their home from each other and to distinguish the sounds that belong to the language they are learning from the sounds in other languages at a very early age. Furthermore, children in the first year or two of life learn to pick out words from the stream of speech with no instruction. The fact that we hear speech as a sequence of individual sounds, words, and sentences is actually an incredible accomplishment (and all the more incredible for how instantaneously and unconsciously we do it).

Constituency

All languages organize these basic discrete units into constituents, groups of linguistic units which allow more complex units to enter structures where simpler ones are also possible. So we can say in English, "*She* sat down," "*The smart woman* sat down," "*The tall, dark-haired, smart woman with the bright red sweater and pearl necklace* sat down." Each italicized phrase constitutes a noun phrase (which is the subject of the sentence in these examples); a noun phrase can be as simple as a pronoun as in the first sentence, or it can be made more complex by modifying the noun with adjectives and prepositional phrases. Being composed of constituents gives language a balance of structure and flexibility. Constituents can be replaced by other constituents, but you can't replace a constituent with a series of words that is not a constituent. So you can't replace *she* with *smart with the bright red sweater* ("*Smart with the bright red sweater* sat down" doesn't work). Constituents can be moved, but you can only move a complete constituent. *She is very smart* is possible and so is *Very smart, she is*, but not *Smart, she is very*.

Recursion and productivity

Being composed of constituents allows languages to be recursive. **Recursion** is a property of systems which allows a process to be applied repeatedly. In language we can combine constituents to produce an infinite variety of sentences of indefinite length. For example, coordination in English allows us to combine two or more constituents of the same type together. We can expand a short sentence like *He was tall* into longer sentences like *He was tall and strong and handsome and thoughtful and a good listener and . . .* or infinitely embed clauses to modify noun phrases, as in *This is the mouse that nibbled the cheese that lay in the house that Jack built.*

The recursiveness of language has profound implications. It means that no one can learn a language by memorizing all the sentences of that language; instead, they must learn the system for creating and combining constituents in that language. The human brain is finite, but the recursive property of language means that by learning a language we are capable of producing and understanding an infinite number of sentences. This nonfinite quality of language is due to its **productivity**. Even if one were to attempt to memorize all the sentences ever uttered, one could always add another modifier – (*A great big huge beautifully designed, skillfully constructed, well-located new building . . .*) or embed one sentence within another, over and over again (*He said that she said that I said that they believe that you told us that . . .*) through the recursive rules of the language. Since languages place no limits on the use of these recursive processes, all languages are potentially *infinitely* productive.

Productivity in language is also demonstrated by neologisms, newly coined words, which occur all throughout history and society. When people hear a word for the first time, they often ask, "Is that a word?" If they ask a linguist, the answer is likely to be, "It is now." If the novel word is formed according to the morphological and phonological rules of its language and it is understandable in context, it is a bona fide word, even if it's not found in a dictionary. Consider the word *bling*, recently coined to mean 'flashy jewelry.' It is phonologically well-formed (in English *bl* is allowed at the beginning of syllables, and the *ng* [ŋ] sound is allowed at the end). The word has caught on in the mainstream public and is now a bona fide word. Most of these spontaneous coinings – inspired by a particular context, and often labeled as **slang** – are not used frequently enough to ever make it into a dictionary, but some coinings *do* become part of the lexicon (and are included in some updated dictionaries) because they meet a new need. Coining new words is one productive process by which languages change to meet the changing communicative needs of their speakers.

The productivity of languages derives, in large part, from the fact that they are organized around a finite set of principles which systematically constrain the ways in which sounds, morphemes, words, phrases, and sentences may be combined. A native speaker of a language unconsciously "knows" these principles and can use them to produce and interpret an infinite variety of utterances. Defining and making these principles explicit is one of the goals of linguists studying grammatical competence.

Arbitrariness

While productivity in language derives from a finite set of principles which systematically constrain the ways in which sounds, morphemes, words, phrases, and sentences may be combined, language is arbitrary in its sound–meaning correspondence. With few exceptions, words have no principled or systematic connection with what they mean. In English, the first three numbers are *one, two, three* – but in Chinese they are *yi, er, san*. Neither language has the "right" word for the numerals or for anything else, because there is no such thing (Bolton, 1982: 5). Even onomatopoetic words that are supposed to sound like the noise they name – for example, words for sounds, like *ding-dong* and *click* and the sounds various animals make – are arbitrary and vary from language to language. In English, for example, a dog says *bow wow* or perhaps *woof woof*, but in Hindi it says *bho: bho:*. Greek dogs say *gav* and Korean dogs say *mung mung*. People perceive these sounds through the arbitrary "sound filters" of their respective languages, so even something as seemingly objective as a dog's bark is in fact represented arbitrarily in language.

The inventory of speech sounds used by a particular language is also arbitrary. English is spoken using only 36 different sounds (a few more or less, depending on how the English sound system is analyzed). But, as you will learn in detail in Chapter 1, the sounds used in English are not all the same as the sounds needed to speak other languages, nor are they put together in the same way. The 36 sounds of English are in turn arbitrarily represented by 26 letters, some of which stand for two or more sounds (like *g* in *gin* and in *gimp*) while other sounds are spelled in two or more different ways (consider *c* in *center* and *s* in *sender* or *c* in *cup*, *k* in *kelp*, and *qu* in *quiche*). The patterns into which words and sounds are arranged are also arbitrary. We know perfectly well what *tax* means but any English speaker knows without a doubt that there is no such word as *xat*. Adjectives go before nouns in English – so it's *fat man*; in French nouns go before adjectives, making it *homme gros*. **Arbitrariness** is a property of sign languages as well as spoken languages. Some manual signs in sign languages are iconic – they look like what they mean – but most signs give not the slightest clue to their meaning.

It's important to remember that arbitrariness doesn't mean randomness. It means that, for example, the sounds that one language uses and the principles by which they are combined are inherently no better or worse than those of any another language. Likewise, it means that the principles of one language variety (or dialect) for arranging words are inherently no better or worse than those of another. For example, many non-linguists who speak the standard variety of English believe that it is "incorrect" to use two words that express negation (referred to as *negative concord*), as in *I didn't see nobody*. However, **negative concord** is used in the standard variety in other languages such as Italian:

Giulia non ha   visto nessuno.
Giulia not has seen   no one
'Giulia didn't see anyone.'

And some nonstandard varieties of Italian use the singular negative just like standard English. This property of abritrariness in language is, perhaps, one of the most needed linguistics lessons for the general public. It means that no one language – and no one language variety in a particular society – is the "correct" way of speaking, and no group speaks ungrammatically.

Reliance on context

A corollary of arbitrariness – of association between sound sequences and meanings or in the order of words in phrases – is **duality**. Because there is nothing about the pronunciation of the word *one* (transcribed phonetically – as it sounds – it would be [wʌn]) that necessarily associates it with the numeral 1, that same sequence of sounds (but spelled *won*) can also be used to mean something entirely different – the past tense of the verb *to win* (Bolton, 1982: 5). But if the same sequence of sounds can represent different concepts in the same language, how are you able to figure out which meaning I intend when I say [wʌn]? The answer – which is as complex as it is obvious – is that you rely on its context. If I say [wʌn] *before* a noun, as in "[wʌn] dog," your knowledge of English grammar will lead you to guess that I mean *one*. On the other hand, if I say [wʌn] *after* a noun (or pronoun), as in "Mary [wʌn]," that same knowledge will lead you to guess that I mean the past tense of *win*.

Reliance on context is a crucial property of languages, not just in figuring out the meaning of words like *one* and *won*, but in interpreting the meaning of entire utterances. The meaning of a sentence depends crucially on the context in which it is uttered. That context could be the sentence or sentences that immediately precede it, or it could be the broader physical or social circumstances in which the sentence it uttered. If someone says "One," the meaning of that utterance is only clear in the context of a preceding utterance – for example, "Do you want one lump of sugar or two?" Similarly, "It's cold in here" could be a complaint, a request to close a window, or even a compliment (about a freezer, perhaps). Who or what a given pronoun (like *she, it, us,* or *them*) refers to may rely on prior sentences or the immediate physical environment. Languages rely on the connection between form (what is said) and context (when, where, by whom, and to whom it is said) to communicate much more than is contained in a sequence of words.

Variability

Although all languages share some universal characteristics, languages also differ in many ways. The language that people use varies depending on who's speaking and the situation in which they're speaking. In fact, variability is one of the most important – and admirable – properties of language. Variation (also known as difference and diversity) is the essence of information. Without variation in light frequencies, there would be no sight; without variation in sound frequencies, there would be no speech and no music. (And as we are beginning to realize, without a certain minimum level of genetic diversity, our ecosystem is threatened.) Variability in language allows people to communicate far more than the semantic content of the words and sentences they utter. The variability of language is indexical. Speakers vary the language they use to signal their social identities (geographical, social status, ethnicity, and even gender), and also to define the immediate speech situation.

People let the world know who they are by the variety of their language that they use. They reveal their geographical and social status origins after saying just a few words. People also use their variety of language to signal membership in a range of overlapping social groups – as male or female, as a teenager or an adult, as a member of a particular ethnic group. They keep their speech, often despite the best efforts of teachers to change it, because at an unconscious level, maintaining their ties to their origin is more important than any reason to change.

People also use language variation to communicate the situation and purpose in which they are talking, as well as the roles they are playing in those situations. A priest uses different forms of language during a sermon than during the social hour after a church service, playing different roles (and projecting different roles on the churchgoers he addresses). At work, people speak differently to subordinates than to superiors, and differently during coffee breaks than in meetings. Parents speak differently to their children than to other adults (or even to other people's children). The language used in writing typically differs from the language used in speaking, reflecting and communicating the different conditions under which language is produced and its various purposes.

A large part of a speech community's culture is transacted through the medium of language variation. Norms of appropriate language use help speakers to construct and negotiate their relations to each other. The unwritten and unconsciously applied rules for the various forms and uses of language can vary from one cultural milieu to another, within and between societies, and even between genders. This raises the risk of misunderstanding when speakers unknowingly are behaving according to different cultural norms, but enriches our ways of seeing the world when those differences are understood.

Language variation is also the mechanism by which languages change. The lexicon of a language changes just a bit every time a new word is coined. Its inventory of sounds, and their relations to each other, changes over time, sometimes due to migration or contact with another language, sometimes due to innovations from within its speech community (see Chapter 9). The order of words allowed in sentences can change as well (see Chapter 8). Even the prescriptive rules can change with developments in fashion or policy (see Chapter 11).

One of the consequences of language variation is that no variety or dialect of a language can be better than any other; each is simply a snapshot in the process of language change. Linguists find it analytically useful sometimes to look at language synchronically (as a fixed system), but it is a system always developing into a new system. John McWhorter (1998), arguing against the myth of a "pure" standard English, wrote:

> Any language is always and forever on its way to changing into a new one, with many of the sounds, word meanings, and sentence patterns we process as "sloppy" and incorrect being the very things that will constitute the "proper" language of the future ... What we perceive as "departures from the norm" are nothing more or less than what language change looks like from the point of view of a single lifetime.

Consider that French, Italian, and Spanish each developed from Latin and were once considered "corrupt" versions of Latin. The variety of English we now call standard is the result of a sociopolitical accident, developing from the dialect of the center of British power in the 1300s. We might be able to eliminate a lot of discrimination against speakers of

"nonstandard" varieties if more people understood that each language and dialect of a language is a coherent, and equally valid, system.

The descriptive approach

The fact that language is a universal characteristic of human beings means that all languages (and language varieties) are equal. That is, they all come from the same genetic blueprint, and they all are equally "human." Language varieties differ because over time they have adapted to the differing needs of their speech communities. Each language does things differently: some languages explicitly distinguish between several verb tenses (English marks only two); some languages organize nouns into many "gender" categories (English does not). Each language is equally "functional" at meeting the communicative needs of its own speech community. But sometimes when two or more speech communities come into contact, one group will have more power, status, or economic resources than the others. Not surprisingly, the language variety of that dominant group is often perceived as having higher status as well, especially if speaking it affords increased access to power or wealth. By comparison, the language varieties spoken by the less powerful groups often are stigmatized as "incorrect" or "bad" language.

Linguists approach language in the same way that astronomers approach the study of the universe or that anthropologists approach the study of human cultural systems. It would be ridiculous for astronomers to speak about planets orbiting stars "incorrectly" and inappropriate for anthropologists to declare a culture "degenerate" simply because it differs from their own. Similarly, linguists take language as they find it, rather than attempting to regulate it in the direction of preconceived criteria. Linguists are equally curious about all the forms of language that they encounter, no matter what the education or social standing of their speakers might be.

The fact that, in most societies, some varieties of language are perceived as "correct" while others are considered "incorrect" is, for linguists, a social phenomenon – an aspect of language use to be explored scientifically. Since "correct" language is *inherently* no better or worse than the varieties that are considered "incorrect," linguists eagerly seek to discover the reasons for the conviction that some part of language variability is superior to the rest, and to examine the consequences of those beliefs.

One consequence of these kinds of language attitudes – in which one language variety is considered better than others – is the corollary belief that speakers of "incorrect" varieties are somehow inferior, because they will not or cannot speak "correctly." Their "incorrect" language is then used to justify further discrimination – in education and in employment, for example. Discrimination on the basis of language use is based on two false propositions: that one variety of language is inherently better than others, and that people can be taught to speak the "correct" variety. However, so powerful are the natural forces that guide how a person learns and uses spoken language that explicit teaching on how to speak is virtually irrelevant. If a person is not very good at mathematics, we are probably justified in assuming that he or she did not learn mathematics in school. The same may well be true of reading and writing; if someone cannot read or write, it is likely that something went wrong with that person's schooling. But the same is not true with spoken language. A person who uses negative concord, as in *She can't find nothing*, or says *knowed* for *knew* may have received the best instruction in the rules of traditional grammar from the most skilled teachers available. However, just knowing what the rules are, or even practicing them for a few minutes a day in school, will be as effective in influencing how someone speaks as a meter-high pine tree would be in stopping an avalanche. The most powerful feature influencing spoken language is its ability to mark a person's identity as a member of the group closest to him/her in everyday life. This power trumps grammar instruction in classrooms every time.

Even the best-educated speakers of American English will not say "For what did you do that?" (which is formally correct); they'll say "What did you do that for?" Nor will they say "Whom did you see today?"; instead it will be "Who did you see today?" For exactly the same reason, a speaker of nonstandard English will say "I ain't got none," knowing that "I don't have any" is considered correct – in either case, to use "correct grammar" would make the speaker sound posh or snobbish and cost him/her the approval of his/her peers. There is an enormous disincentive to use language in a way that makes it seem that you are separating yourself from the people who are most important to you.

In fact, people who speak in close to the approved way probably did not learn to do so in school. They are just fortunate to come from the segment of society that sets the standards for correct speech. This segment of society also controls its schools – and the language variety used and taught in its schools. Ironically, when children learn to use the socially approved variety of spoken language in school, it is not from what their teachers explicitly teach in class, but rather from adjusting their speech to match the speech of the other children in the halls, on the playground, and outside of school, and thus gain their approval.

The diversity of linguistics

Unlike other linguistics textbooks, each chapter in this book has been written by a linguist who teaches and does research in that area. The field of linguistics, like the phenomenon of language which it studies, is broad and diverse, and although linguists share some beliefs – in a descriptive approach, and in the functional equality of all language varieties, for example – they differ in some of the assumptions they bring to their analyses. Some linguists – particularly those in the areas of phonetics and phonology, morphology, syntax, semantics/pragmatics, and historical linguistics – assume, to varying degrees, that the forms of language can be understood separately from their use. The chapters on these topics are primarily about language form and constitute what was considered the essential core of linguistics in the mid twentieth century. Since then, the field has expanded considerably, and this book is designed to represent that broader scope.

Today the field of linguistics studies not just the nuts-and-bolts of forms and their meanings, but also how language is learned (both as a first and second language), how it plays a central role in reflecting and creating the interactive and cultural settings of talk, how computers can be designed to deal with language, and how language is represented in our very brains. Because much of this expanded scope of the field involves intense study of people actually *using* language, some doubt has arisen about how separate grammatical and communicative competence actually are. The degree of distinction between grammatical and communicative competence is understood differently by different linguists, even among the contributors to this book.

For example, Chapter 3, "The structure of sentences," presents syntax as essentially about form, not use. Chapter 4, "Meaning," is largely about the boundary between semantic meaning (part of grammatical competence) and pragmatic meaning (part of communicative competence). A somewhat similar contrast is seen in Chapter 1, "The sounds of language," involving the boundary between phonetics (the observable and observed phenomena of pronunciation) and the more abstract phonological aspects of pronunciation systems (a part of grammatical competence).

Chapter 8, "Language change," and Chapter 12, "Writing," implicitly present both language form and communicative use, but with less concern for strict boundaries between them. The sympathies of the authors of Chapter 5, "Discourse," Chapter 6, "Child language acquisition," and Chapter 13, "Second language acquisition," are with the primacy of communicative competence. In Chapter 10, "Language and culture," we find the strongest representation of the inseparability of grammatical and communicative competence, as the author suggests replacing the terms "language" and "culture" with "language-culture" to emphasize the inseparability of language from its context.

How are we to understand these differences in emphasis? Perhaps linguists are like the blind men in John Godfrey Saxe's version of the Indian legend about the blind men and the elephant. The poem relates the story of several blind men each touching a different part of the elephant and arguing over what sort of thing they are touching. The blind man touching the tusks of the elephant has a very different idea from the one holding the tail. Perhaps linguistic research is much the same, and each linguist is "partly in the right," depending on which aspects of language the linguist is studying. Some approaches could be proceeding down blind alleys and may eventually have to be abandoned. Or perhaps someone will discover a brilliant unifying insight, like general and special relativity and quantum field theory in physics, which shows how all these approaches are related. Our understanding of the world and of human behavior has advanced in all these ways. In this book, we introduce our readers to the study of language in its current breadth and diversity of approaches – with their tensions and unresolved issues.

How to approach this book

We close this introduction with suggestions for how to approach this book. While we would like to think that all of it will be useful to everyone, language is a broad and diverse phenomenon and there are many ways to explore such a vast terrain. Different aspects of language – and linguistics – are more relevant to various other academic disciplines, and so we propose several "routes" through different territories of language.

- **General linguistics**: The sounds of language; Words and their parts; The structure of sentences; Meaning; Language change; Writing; Dialect variation; Discourse
- **Language acquisition, learning, and teaching**: The sounds of language; Words and their parts; The structure of sentences; Meaning; Child language acquisition; Second language acquisition; Discourse; Language in culture; The politics of language
- **Sociolinguistics**: The sounds of language; Words and their parts; Meaning; Language change; Writing; Dialect variation; Discourse; Language in culture; The politics of language
- **Language processing**: The sounds of language; Words and their parts; The structure of sentences; Meaning; The brain and language; Computational linguistics; Child language acquisition
- **Linguistics and other fields**: Child language acquisition; Language in culture; Computational linguistics; The politics of language; The brain and language; Writing; Dialect variation; Discourse; Second language acquisition

We have taught a multi-section introductory linguistics course for both linguistics majors and non-majors for many years, at first with other textbooks and more recently with the first edition of this textbook. Initially, we followed a "traditional" structure; starting with a shared structural foundation (Chapters 1–4: "The sounds of language"; "Words and their parts"; "The structure of sentences"; and "Meaning"), and then allowing instructors of different sections to choose among the remaining chapters according to to their expertise and interest. Several years ago, we shifted to a syllabus which integrates the structural chapters with the following chapters more directly. "The sounds of language" is followed by "Dialect variation," where many of the concepts of phonetics and phonology are exemplified in contexts that students have personally experienced. "Words and their parts" is followed by "Language change"; "The structure of sentences" is followed by "Child language acquisition" (or "Language and the brain"); and "Meaning" is followed by the chapter on "Discourse" (or "Language and culture"). This balanced sequence of topics enables students to relate the structural aspects of language to a variety of its manifestations, and leaves room for the instructor of each section to choose a couple of other chapters as well.

The companion website for this textbook can be found at **www.cambridge.org/fasold**. There you will find sound files, further reading suggestions, additional exercises and teaching materials, links, and electronic versions of key figures.

1 The sounds of language

KEY TERMS

- acoustic phonetics
- active and passive articulators
- allophone
- alternation
- articulatory phonetics
- complementary distribution
- derivation
- distinctive features
- fundamental frequency
- formant
- intonation
- manner of articulation
- minimal pair
- natural class
- obstruent
- phoneme
- phonology
- phonotactic constraint
- pitch track
- place of articulation
- sonorant
- sonority
- source-filter theory
- spectrogram
- stress
- suprasegmentals
- syllable structure
- tone
- vocal tract
- voicing
- waveform

CHAPTER PREVIEW

This chapter is about the sounds of speech. Without sound, communication can still take place –
with a nod or a wave, a photograph, or a drawing. There can even be language without sound:
those who cannot hear use languages based on manual signs instead. Yet for most of us most of
the time, getting our message across involves encoding it in sounds. Even when we write, we
use symbols that are based on speech (though sometimes not very directly).

The study of the sounds of speech can be divided into the disciplines of **phonetics** and
phonology. Phonetics studies speech sounds as physical objects. Phoneticians ask questions
such as:

- **How are speech sounds made?**
- **How do physical characteristics make people sound different?**
- **How many different sounds do languages use?**
- **How are different languages and dialects distinguished by the sounds they use?**
- **How does sound travel through the air?**
- **How is it registered by the ears?**
- **How can we measure speech?**

Phonology studies how languages organize sounds into different patterns. Phonologists ask questions such as:

- **How do languages organize sounds to distinguish different words?**
- **How do languages restrict, or constrain, sequences of sounds?**
- **What sorts of changes (alternations) do sounds undergo if sequences arise that don't obey the restrictions?**
- **How are sounds organized into larger constituents (syllables, words, phrases)?**
- **How are these patterns the same, and how are they different, across languages and dialects?**

We begin with phonetics, the study of how speech sounds are made and perceived, and then discuss phonology, the study of how a language organizes those speech sounds into a meaningful system.

GOALS

The goals of this chapter are to:

- **describe the basic anatomy of the vocal tract**
- **explain how the structures in the vocal tract are controlled to make speech sounds**
- **show how to transcribe English words using IPA transcription**
- **describe the basic properties of suprasegmental aspects of speech, and how languages differ in their use of them**
- **describe some of the physical properties of sound waves**
- **interpret some basic aspects of waveforms, pitch tracks, and spectrograms**
- **explain phonemic and allophonic distributions**
- **describe some of the most common phonological alternations**
- **introduce some of the major goals of phonological theories**

You pick up the phone and say "Hello?" into the receiver. The voice on the line responds "Hi!" and with this one syllable your brain is flooded with information. You recognize, first, the content of the message: a conventional greeting in English, distinct from the similar-sounding farewell (*bye!*), question (*how?* or *why?*), or command (*Fly!*). But you also probably recognize the identity of the person speaking, with or without caller ID, and get a sense of his or her mental state: excited, bored, happy, or angry. If you can't identify the person, you can still probably tell if the speaker is male or female, figure out whether he or she is a native speaker of English, and make a pretty good guess about where he or she is from. How can all this information be packed into a single word?

Speech sounds in fact constitute an elaborate multilevel code, to which every competent speaker holds the key. Meanings are mapped into sound sequences in the brain of the speaker, which sends commands for vocal tract movements, which produce characteristic vibrations in the air or on the phone line, which impact on the ear and auditory nerve of the listener, whose brain decodes the message, factoring out the aspects of the signal that correspond to the message and those that correspond to the characteristics of the messenger, recreating the sound sequence, and thus the meaning, that the speaker intends. This chapter is about how this process of encoding and decoding takes place in the organization, production, and perception of speech sounds.

Articulatory phonetics

The tools of phonetics

One of the biggest obstacles phoneticians face is that they can't see the objects they are studying. You can't see the tongue as it's moving around inside someone's mouth; you can't see the sound waves traveling through the air; you can't see the vibration of the fluid in the inner ear. Since ancient times, however, phoneticians have made the best use of the information they had access to, employing careful listening, measuring, modeling, and notation. In addition, more sophisticated devices have been developed within the past decades – devices such as Magnetic Resonance Imaging (MRI), sonography, and digital acoustic analysis. Figure 1.1 shows some pictures of the vocal tract as seen by these devices.

With these aids, what have we learned about how humans make and hear speech sounds?

The vocal tract

Basically, sound is vibrating air. Speaking means using your **vocal tract** (lungs, **trachea**, **larynx**, mouth, and nose) to get air moving and vibrating, and then shaping that movement in different ways. Figure 1.2 shows a diagram of the upper parts of the vocal tract.

Most speech sounds are made with air exiting the lungs; therefore, speech begins with breath. To begin to speak, you pull down your diaphragm, the big muscle that separates your chest cavity from your stomach. This enlarges the lungs, which draws air in. Then the diaphragm relaxes and the muscles around the ribs contract, slowly squeezing the lungs and forcing the air out and up the windpipe, or **trachea**.

At the top of the trachea is a little box of cartilage, called the larynx (the "Adam's apple"). Inside the larynx, two folds of soft tissue, called the **vocal folds** (sometimes called "vocal cords"), lie across the top of the trachea. If the vocal folds are held in the correct position with the correct tension, the air flowing out of the trachea causes them to flap open and closed very quickly (around 200 times per second). You can feel this opening and closing motion as vibration in your throat. Find your larynx (you should be able to feel the bump of the Adam's apple at the front of your throat), and then hum a tune. Muscles attached to the cartilages of the larynx allow you to adjust the tension of the folds, thus adjusting the rate of vibration and raising or lowering the pitch. The faster the vibration, the higher the pitch of the voice. Other muscles also allow you to draw the folds apart so that no vibration occurs.

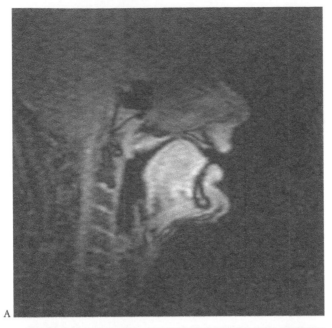

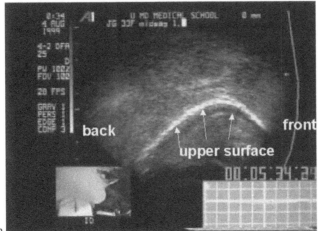

Figure 1.1 Views of the vocal tract. A. A magnetic resonance image of a mid-sagittal section (sideways slice) of the vocal tract. B. A sonograph image of the surface of the tongue. C. A digital waveform showing sound pressure variations during one second of speech. (Images A and B courtesy of Dr. Maureen Stone, Vocal Tract Visualization Laboratory, University of Maryland, Baltimore)

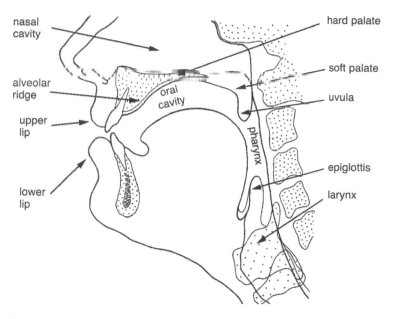

Figure 1.2 Parts of the vocal tract

Just above the larynx, at the base of the tongue, is the **epiglottis**. The epiglottis is a muscular structure that folds down over the larynx when you swallow to prevent food from going down into the lungs before it enters the passage to the stomach. The payoff for the risk of a larynx located low in the throat is an open area at the back of the mouth, the **pharynx**. The pharynx allows the tongue freedom for front and back movement. Other mammals, including nonhuman primates, have the larynx high up at the back of the mouth, connected to the nasal passages. Because they have no pharynx, chimps could never learn to talk. (This is why scientists who try to teach primates to communicate with language use gesture-based languages instead.)

Inside the mouth itself, there are many different structures – **active articulators** and **passive articulators** – that we use to shape speech sounds as the air passes through the vocal tract. The active articulators move toward the passive articulators in order to constrict and shape the air that is moving out from the lungs. Active articulators include the lips, which can be opened or closed, pursed or spread, and the tongue. What we usually see of the tongue is the small, pink tip, but it is actually a large mass of interconnected muscles that fills the floor of the mouth. Although the tongue has no bones or cartilage, different parts of the tongue can move fairly independently. The **tongue front** (including the **tongue tip** and the **tongue blade**, which extends a few centimeters back from the tip), the **tongue body** (the main mass of the tongue, also known as the dorsum), and the **tongue root** (the lowest part of the tongue, back in the pharynx), are considered separate active articulators.

The passive articulators lie along the top of the vocal tract. Run your tongue along the top of your mouth beginning behind your upper teeth. You will first encounter the **alveolar ridge**, the bony rise just behind your teeth. The **postalveolar** region arches

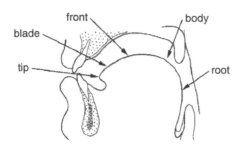

Figure 1.3 Areas of the tongue

from the alveolar ridge toward the **hard palate**, the roof of the mouth. If you curl your tongue very far back in your mouth, you can feel that the bony structure of the hard palate gives way to softer tissue, which is known as the **soft palate**, or **velum**. The velum is a muscular structure that regulates the velar port, the opening in the back of the mouth that connects the mouth and nose. When the velum is lowered, as it is for breathing and for some sounds such as [m] and [n], the port is open and air flows freely between the nose and lungs. (It's a phonetic convention to write the symbols for sounds within square brackets. See the following sections for more on phonetic writing.) When the velum is raised, as it is for most speech sounds, the opening to the nose is closed off and all the airstream is directed through the mouth. At the very end of the velum is the **uvula**, the little pink pendulum you can see hanging down in the back of your mouth when you open wide and say "ah."

Articulation

Speaking involves using the structures of the vocal tract in different ways to control and shape moving air. We can think of the speaker producing the right combinations by making "choices" about which active and passive articulators to use and about how different constrictions will be made. These choices are not conscious; they are automated from long practice, just like the muscular routines of walking or reaching. When you reach for a cup of coffee, you don't say to yourself, "OK, now contract the tricep, relax the bicep," etc. Instead, without much conscious thought you select a goal, such as "fingers to mug," and your long-practiced routines of motion execute the goal-directed movement. Speech works the same way. The movements of speech are goal-directed gestures. Each sound is comprised of a set of articulatory goals that will get the vocal tract in the right positions to make the sound you wish to make. An overall goal like "make an [m]" can be broken down into a set of subcomponents: "Close the lips," "open the velum," "make the vocal folds vibrate." These subroutines can be recombined in different ways to make different sounds, like a set of Lego blocks that can build a castle or a boat depending on the way they're put together.

The first choice is that of airstream mechanism: how will the speaker get the air moving in the first place? The usual choice is **pulmonic egressive** – that is, air moving out from the lungs. Most sounds used by most of the world's languages are pulmonic egressive.

However, it is also possible to get air moving in other ways, such as by moving the larynx up or down, or by popping little pockets of air made with the tongue against the roof of the mouth, as in clicks. (Clicks include the expression we write in English as *tsk tsk* or *tut tut*, but in some languages of southern Africa sounds such as these are incorporated into the stream of speech as regular consonants like [p] or [t] in English.) The rest of this chapter discusses only sounds that are pulmonic egressive.

The second choice is what to do with the vocal folds. Sounds produced with vocal fold vibration are **voiced**; sounds produced without vocal fold vibration are **voiceless**. If you place your finger on your larynx and produce a sustained [z], you should be able to feel the vibration, or voicing. If you switch to [s], a voiceless sound, the vibration ceases. For some sounds, as in the initial [p] in *pop*, the vocal folds are held apart far enough and long enough to allow an extra "puff of air" to exit the mouth at the end of the [p]. This is called **aspiration**. You can feel the extra release of air if you hold your fingertips an inch or so in front of your lips as you say *pop* or *pill*. Aspiration can be indicated by a superscripted *h*: [p^h].

Besides deciding what to do with the larynx, the speaker must decide whether the velum will be open or not. If the velum is open, so that air flows into the nose, the sound is **nasal** (like [m]). If the velum is closed, the sound is **oral**.

Finally, the speaker must decide which active articulator will be used to make a constriction (lips, tongue front, tongue body, tongue root), where the constriction will be made (the **place of articulation**), and what sort of constriction will be made (the **manner** of **articulation**). The various places of articulation are discussed in following sections; we turn first to the various manners of articulation.

Manners of articulation

The manners of articulation include: stop, fricative, affricate, approximant, and vowel.

If the active and passive articulators are brought together to make a complete closure, so that airflow out of the mouth is completely cut off, the manner of articulation is a **stop**. The sounds [p], [t], and [k] in English are stops. Say the word *poppa* very slowly, and note that there is complete silence, with no air exiting the mouth, while the lips are closed for [p] in the middle of the word. You may even feel pressure building up behind the lips, as air continues flowing from the lungs and has nowhere to go. This pressure is released with a slight pop, or burst, when the lips are opened. The sound [m] is a nasal stop. Even though the velum is open and air flows freely out of the nose, so that you can hum a tune while producing an [m] sound, the manner of articulation is still a stop, because the lips are completely closed, as they were for [p]. (Try pinching your nose closed for a moment while you're humming a tune, and see what happens.)

If the articulators are brought close together but not closed completely, so that the stream of air that is forced between them becomes turbulent and noisy, the manner of articulation is a **fricative**. The sounds [s], [z], [f], and [v] are fricatives. **Affricates** combine a sequence of stop plus fricative in a single sound. The sound usually written *ch* in English is an affricate. Try saying the word *achoo* as slowly as possible, paying attention to the movement of the tongue between the *a* and *oo* sounds. You first make a closure with the tongue front at or just behind the alveolar ridge, and then lower the tongue tip to let the air out through a narrow constriction slightly further back, between the tongue blade and postalveolar region.

If the active articulator moves to narrow the vocal tract, but not so much that fricative noise is created, the manner of articulation is an **approximant**. **Glides**, such as the sounds at the beginning of the words *yell* and *well*, are approximants, as are [l] and [r] in English. The *l*-sounds of the languages of the world are called **laterals**, because air flows out over the sides of the tongue. Try drawing out the initial sound in the word *lateral*. Now, without moving your tongue, take a deep breath in and out. You'll feel the air moving over the sides of the tongue. The *r*-sounds are called **rhotics**. The rhotic sounds of the languages of the world are quite varied, including quick taps of the tongue against the alveolar ridge, trills in which the tongue is set into vibration by air flowing over it, and the very odd shape of the American English [r], in which the body of the tongue is bunched up high and the tongue tip may be raised or curled backwards. (It is no surprise that non-native speakers of English have trouble with this sound.) Vowels are the most open manner of articulation. Different vowel sounds are made by moving the tongue body up or down, front or back, and by rounding or spreading the lips. During all vowel sounds, however, the vocal tract is relatively wide open, and air flows out freely. Oral stops, fricatives, and affricates together form a class of sounds called **obstruents**, because they make noise by obstructing the airflow in the vocal tract, causing a burst of sound as a closure is released or a hissing sound as the air passes through a narrow constriction. Nasal stops, approximants, and vowels (anything that's not an obstruent) form a class of sounds called **sonorants**. They make audible sounds not by obstructing the airflow, but by letting the air resonate. Sonorant sounds are almost always voiced. The vibration of the vocal folds causes the air inside the vocal tract to vibrate. If the vibration is strong enough, it produces an audible sound, like the ringing of a bell. Different vocal tract shapes (which we control by moving the active articulators) produce different patterns of vibration, which we hear as different sounds (more on this below). It is possible to produce voiceless sonorants, by moving a large volume of air through the open vocal tract. Languages like Hmong and Burmese use voiceless nasals. Listen carefully, and you'll hear that the [l] in an English word like *play* is also voiceless.

Writing sounds: transcription

Before we discuss the different places of articulation used in English and other languages, we have to consider how to write down different sounds. Descriptive phrases like "the sound at the beginning of the word *yell*" or "in the middle of *achoo*" are cumbersome. We need a **phonetic alphabet**. Writing down sounds using a phonetic alphabet is called **phonetic transcription**.

In 1888, the International Phonetic Association (based in Paris) tackled the problem of how to precisely describe any sound the members might encounter in their efforts to describe all the languages of the world. They published symbols for a new alphabet, the *International Phonetic Alphabet* (**IPA**), based on two principles:

– The alphabet would be universal. There would be enough symbols so that every sound in every human language could be represented. (As new sounds have been discovered or old sounds reanalyzed, the IPA has been revised to incorporate the new findings. The latest revision took place in 2005.)
– The alphabet would be unambiguous. Every sound would have one symbol, and every symbol one sound.

Consider how English spelling falls short on these two principles. We certainly don't have letters for the clicks of southern Africa or the sounds made in the back of the throat in Arabic. And the one sound/one symbol correspondence is constantly violated. How many ways can you pronounce the letter *c*? (Consider *each vicious circle*.) The letter *x* stands for a sequence of two sounds, [k] followed by [s] (*box* rhymes with *locks*), while the sequence of letters *sh* stands for a single sound (a fricative made with the tongue blade against the postalveolar region).

Figure 1.4 shows the IPA symbols for all the sounds discussed in this chapter, and more.

In an IPA consonant chart, place of articulation is written across the top, and manner of articulation is written down the side, so that each cell indicates a combination of a specific manner and place. Cells that are shaded gray are physically impossible combinations. If there are two symbols in a cell, the one on the left is voiceless, the one on the right is voiced.

A good place to start learning IPA transcription is with the symbols for the consonants of English, which are given in Table 1.1, along with example words in which the sounds occur. Many, though not all, of the symbols will be familiar. As you learn the definitions of the different places and manners of articulation, you should be able to combine them to figure out the pronunciations of unfamiliar symbols in the IPA chart.

As you look through the example words in Table 1.1, you'll notice that not all of the cells are filled. Some of these gaps are *accidental*: English just doesn't happen to have a word *nen*, for example, though it has similar words like *nine* and *net*. Other gaps are *systematic*: no word in English ends with the sound [h], for example. (Plenty of words end with the *letter h*, but we are concerned with sound, not spelling.) Systematic gaps will be discussed further below.

Consonants

We will organize our discussion of the consonants by active articulator and place of articulation. Generally, each articulator can move to more than one place of articulation, as shown in Table 1.2.

The lower lip can make constrictions at two different places. If the lower and upper lip come together, the sound is **bilabial**. The sounds [p], [b], and [m] are bilabials. Note that [p] is voiceless and [b] and [m] are voiced. Alternatively, the lower lip can make contact with the upper teeth to produce a **labiodental** sound. [f] and [v] are labiodentals.

THE INTERNATIONAL PHONETIC ALPHABET (revised to 2005)

CONSONANTS (PULMONIC)   © 2005 IPA

	Bilabial	Labiodental	Dental	Alveolar	Postalveolar	Retroflex	Palatal	Velar	Uvular	Pharyngeal	Glottal
Plosive	p b			t d		ʈ ɖ	c ɟ	k ɡ	q ɢ		ʔ
Nasal	m	ɱ		n		ɳ	ɲ	ŋ	N		
Trill	B			r					R		
Tap or Flap		ⱱ		ɾ		ɽ					
Fricative	ɸ β	f v	θ ð	s z	ʃ ʒ	ʂ ʐ	ç ʝ	x ɣ	χ ʁ	ħ ʕ	h ɦ
Lateral fricative				ɬ ɮ							
Approximant		ʋ		ɹ		ɻ	j	ɰ			
Lateral approximant				l		ɭ	ʎ	L			

Where symbols appear in pairs, the one to the right represents a voiced consonant. Shaded areas denote articulations judged impossible.

CONSONANTS (NON-PULMONIC)

Clicks		Voiced implosives		Ejectives	
ʘ	Bilabial	ɓ	Bilabial	ʼ	Examples:
ǀ	Dental	ɗ	Dental/alveolar	pʼ	Bilabial
ǃ	(Post)alveolar	ʄ	Palatal	tʼ	Dental/alveolar
ǂ	Palatoalveolar	ɠ	Velar	kʼ	Velar
ǁ	Alveolar lateral	ʛ	Uvular	sʼ	Alveolar fricative

OTHER SYMBOLS

ʍ	Voiceless labial-velar fricative	ɕ ʑ	Alveolo-palatal fricatives
w	Voiced labial-velar approximant	ɺ	Voiced alveolar lateral flap
ɥ	Voiced labial-palatal approximant	ɧ	Simultaneous ʃ and x
ʜ	Voiceless epiglottal fricative		
ʢ	Voiced epiglottal fricative	Affricates and double articulations can be represented by two symbols joined by a tie bar if necessary.	k͡p t͡s
ʡ	Epiglottal plosive		

VOWELS

Where symbols appear in pairs, the one to the right represents a rounded vowel.

SUPRASEGMENTALS

ˈ	Primary stress
ˌ	Secondary stress ˌfoʊnəˈtɪʃən
ː	Long eː
ˑ	Half-long eˑ
˘	Extra-short ĕ
ǀ	Minor (foot) group
‖	Major (intonation) group
.	Syllable break ɹi.ækt
‿	Linking (absence of a break)

DIACRITICS   Diacritics may be placed above a symbol with a descender, e.g. ŋ̊

̥	Voiceless	n̥ d̥	̤	Breathy voiced	b̤ a̤	̪	Dental	t̪ d̪
̬	Voiced	s̬ t̬	̰	Creaky voiced	b̰ a̰	̺	Apical	t̺ d̺
ʰ	Aspirated	tʰ dʰ	̼	Linguolabial	t̼ d̼	̻	Laminal	t̻ d̻
̹	More rounded	ɔ̹	ʷ	Labialized	tʷ dʷ	̃	Nasalized	ẽ
̜	Less rounded	ɔ̜	ʲ	Palatalized	tʲ dʲ	ⁿ	Nasal release	dⁿ
̟	Advanced	u̟	ˠ	Velarized	tˠ dˠ	ˡ	Lateral release	dˡ
̠	Retracted	e̠	ˤ	Pharyngealized	tˤ dˤ	̚	No audible release	d̚
̈	Centralized	ë	̴	Velarized or pharyngealized	ɫ			
̽	Mid-centralized	e̽	̝	Raised	e̝ (ɹ̝ = voiced alveolar fricative)			
̩	Syllabic	n̩	̞	Lowered	e̞ (β̞ = voiced bilabial approximant)			
̯	Non-syllabic	e̯	̘	Advanced Tongue Root	e̘			
˞	Rhoticity	ɚ a˞	̙	Retracted Tongue Root	e̙			

TONES AND WORD ACCENTS

LEVEL			CONTOUR		
e̋ or	˥	Extra high	ě or	˩˥	Rising
é	˦	High	ê	˥˩	Falling
ē	˧	Mid	e᷄	˦˥	High rising
è	˨	Low	e᷅	˩˨	Low rising
ȅ	˩	Extra low	e᷈	˧˦˧	Rising-falling
↓	Downstep		↗	Global rise
↑	Upstep		↘	Global fall

Figure 1.4 The International Phonetic Alphabet IPA Chart, www.langsci.ucl.ac.uk/ipa/ipachart.html, available under a Creative Commons Attribution-Sharealike 3.0 Unported License. Copyright © 2005 International Phonetic Association.

TABLE 1.1 IPA symbols for the consonants of English

	Initial				Final	Medial
p	pat	pie	pen	pin	whip	upper
b	bat	buy	Ben	bin	bib	rubber
m	mat	my	men	minion	whim	summer
f	fat	fight	fen	fin	whiff	suffer
v	vat	vie	vendor	vintage	live	ever
θ		thigh		thin	with	Ethel
ð	that	thy	then		bathe	weather
t	tat	tie	ten	tin	wit	retool
d	data	dye	den	din	mid	redo
n	Nat	night		ninja	win	renew
s	sat	sigh	sensor	sin	miss	presser
z	zap		zen	zip	wiz	buzzer
l	lateral	lie	lentil	lip	will	filler
r	rat	rye	rent	rip	where	terror
ʃ	shack	shy	shell	ship	wish	pressure
ʒ				beige	measure	
tʃ	chat	chai	check	chip	witch	etcher
dʒ	jack	giant	gender	gin	edge	edger
k	cat	kite	Ken	kin	wick	wrecker
g	gap	guy		wig	mugger	
ŋ				wing	singer	
h	hat	high	hen	hip		ahead
w	whack	why	when	win		away
j	yak		yen	yip		

TABLE 1.2 Active articulators, passive articulators, and place of articulation

Active articulator	Passive articulator	Place of articulation
lower lip	upper lip	bilabial
	upper teeth	labiodental
tongue tip or blade	upper teeth	dental
	alveolar ridge	alveolar
	postalveolar region	retroflex (tip)
	postalveolar region	postalveolar (blade)
	hard palate	palatal (blade)
tongue body	hard palate	palatal
	soft palate	velar
	uvula	uvular
tongue root	pharyngeal wall	pharyngeal
larynx		laryngeal

Japanese has a bilabial fricative (IPA [ɸ] instead of [f]). This sound, as in the native Japanese pronunciation of *futon*, is made by blowing through pursed lips, the same motion as blowing out a candle.

The lower lip is rather limited in the places at which it can make a constriction. The tongue front is the most versatile of the active articulators, moving to at least four different places of articulation. The tongue tip moves forward to the upper teeth for the sounds at the beginning of *thin* and *then*. These **dental** fricatives are written [θ] (voiceless) and [ð] (voiced).

The English sounds [t], [d], [n], and [l] are made with the tongue tip at the alveolar ridge, the **alveolar** place of articulation. The fricatives [s] and [z] are also alveolar. For these fricatives the tongue forms a narrow groove under the alveolar ridge like a spout that shoots a stream of air against the teeth, producing a high-pitched hissing sound. Though the place of articulation for these fricatives is alveolar, the front teeth are necessary to create the proper high-pitched hiss, as all children discover when they lose their baby teeth.

The fricatives [ʃ] and [ʒ] (as in the middle of *pressure* and *measure*) are made further back, with the blade of the tongue making a constriction at the **postalveolar** place of articulation. (Interestingly, [ʒ] doesn't occur in initial position in English, except in obvious borrowings from French, such as *genre*.) The affricates in *church* and *judge* are also postalveolar. The IPA symbols for these sounds are [ʧ] and [ʤ]: two symbols are used for the combination of stop plus fricative, linked by a ligature. (In other transcription systems commonly used in linguistics books, [ʃ], [ʒ], [tʃ], and [dʒ] are written with hatchecks: [š], [ž], [č], [ǰ].) English doesn't have any postalveolar stops or nasals, though other languages do (for example, French *agneau* 'lamb', and Spanish *año* 'year,' both pronounced [aɲo], though with a stress difference).

Usually the blade of the tongue is used to make a postalveolar constriction. It is also possible, however, for the tip of the tongue to curl back to make a constriction in this area. If the tip of the tongue curls back, the sound is called **retroflex**. (The IPA symbols for these sounds have a little hook under the symbol, recalling the curling back of the tongue.) For some (but not all) American speakers, [r] is a retroflex approximant. Can you determine whether your own tongue tip curls back in a word like *road*? There are no other retroflex sounds in English, though other languages, notably Hindi and other languages of India, have a full set of retroflex stops, fricatives, and nasals. A telltale sign of an Indian accent in English is substituting retroflex stops for English alveolars.

The sound at the beginning of the English words *you* and *yacht* is **palatal** (a palatal glide, to be exact). The whole middle section of the tongue, including blade and body, is pushed straight up to narrow the space between the tongue and hard palate. The IPA symbol for a palatal glide is [j]. (Think Scandinavian *ja*.) English doesn't have any other palatal sounds, but they're not hard to make. Start with [j] (as in *you*), and then make it voiceless. The result is a voiceless palatal fricative, used for example in German words such as *ich* [iç], meaning 'I'.

Moving further back in the vocal tract, the next place of articulation is **velar**, in which the tongue body moves up to make constriction against the velum, high in the back of the mouth. The English sounds [k] and [g] are velar stops. In English, the sequence of letters *ng*, as at the end of *song* or *ring*, usually indicate a velar nasal. In the word *song*, you don't make a sequence of alveolar nasal followed by velar stop (*n-g*), but a single nasal sound at the same place as [k] or [g]. (Feel how little your tongue moves when you say the word *king*.) The IPA symbol for a velar nasal stop is [ŋ]. As with [ʒ], English uses [ŋ] only at the end of words (*song*) or in the middle (*singer*), never at the beginning, although with practice you can learn to pronounce words like Thai [ŋa:] 'tusk' or Australian names like *Ngaio*. The native German sound at the end of the name *Bach* is a voiceless velar fricative, [x]. To make this sound, begin with a [k], then loosen the constriction slightly, letting a little turbulent airflow pass through.

The tongue body can also make constrictions further back, at the **uvular** place of articulation. To make a uvular stop, begin with a [k] or [g], then move the tongue a few centimeters back. Uvular stops are common in many Native American languages, as well as in Arabic and Hebrew. The native Arabic pronunciation of the country name *Qatar* begins with a uvular stop. Constrictions can also be made deep in the throat, with the tongue root moving back toward the pharyngeal wall. These voiced and voiceless **pharyngeal** fricatives are also found in Arabic and Hebrew.

Finally, consonants can be made with the larynx as the only articulator. The sound [h] consists of the noise of air rushing through the open vocal folds, and may be considered a **laryngeal** fricative. It is also possible to close the vocal folds up tight, stopping the airflow at the larynx, a **glottal stop** (IPA [ʔ]). This is the sound in the middle of the English expression *uh-oh*. If you pronounce this slowly, you can feel the constriction in the larynx. In other languages, like Hawai'ian, the glottal stop is used as a regular consonant. In the word *Hawai'i* the apostrophe stands for a glottal stop. A glottal stop also stands in for certain /t/ sounds in some English words, though exactly which words are affected depends on the dialect: for many Americans, words like *button* and *mitten* have glottal stops; in parts of London *kitty* and *pretty* have glottal stops.

One English consonant remains to be discussed: the glide [w], as in *wear*. This sound combines a narrowing of the vocal tract at the velar place of articulation with rounding of the lips. It is thus a **double articulation**, a labiovelar glide. While double articulations at various places of articulation are not hard to make (given the independence of the active articulators), they can be hard for the ear to distinguish, so double articulations other than labiovelars are rare.

In summary, there are eleven common places of articulation – bilabial, labiodental, dental, alveolar, postalveolar, retroflex, palatal, velar, uvular, pharyngeal, and laryngeal – though no single language makes consonants using all of the places of articulation.

Vowels

Vowels are harder to describe than consonants. By definition, vowels have an open vocal tract, so the tongue doesn't actually touch the upper surface of the vocal tract at any particular place and the term *place of articulation* isn't really appropriate. Instead, different vowels are described in terms of the ways in which the tongue body and lips move. Linguists classify vowels by the height of the tongue body, whether it is bunched toward the front or back of the mouth, and whether the lips are rounded.

If describing vowel systems in general is a difficult task, describing the vowels of English is even more so. One reason is because there are a lot of them. The most common number of vowels for a language to have is five. Though English writers use just five letters to encode their vowels (relics of an older system), the English language uses more than a dozen different vowel sounds. Another reason is because the exact number of vowels and exact vowel quality differ from dialect to dialect, much more so than for the consonants. For example, the word *mate* as pronounced by a speaker from Perth sounds a lot (though not exactly) like the word *might* as pronounced by a speaker from Baltimore. The word *my* spoken by a native of Atlanta sounds similar to *mar* as pronounced in Boston, and *ma* as pronounced in Seattle. For most speakers on the East coast of the United States, the words *caught* and *cot* have two different vowel sounds; but for most speakers on the West coast, the two words are pronounced the same.

Table 1.3 gives the IPA symbols, with example words, for the vowels of "General American" (GA) English – that is, English as it is more or less spoken in the central United States ("more or less" since every dialect of English has particular regional characteristics, and the ideal speaker of pure "General American" doesn't exist). In England, the "standard" dialect to which BBC announcers and school teachers aspire is known as RP (for "Received Pronunciation"); it is usually this dialect, rather than American, which is closer to the many versions of English spoken around the world, such as Singaporean, South African, and Indian

TABLE 1.3 IPA symbols for the vowels of American English

i	bead	key	he
ɪ	bid	kit	
e	bade	kate	hey
ɛ	bed	ketchup	
æ	bad	cat	
u	booed	coot	who
ʊ	book	cook	
o	bode	coat	hoe
ɔ	baud	caught	haw
a	body	cot	ha
ʌ	bud	cut	
ɝ	bird	curt	her
ɚ			murder [mɝdɚ]
ə	about		rosa's [rozəz]
ɨ			roses [rozɨz]
aʊ	bowed	count	how
ɔɪ	boy	coy	ahoy
aɪ	bide	kite	high

English. (Other varieties, such as Australian and Scottish, have their own unique systems.) Some of the major pronunciation differences between GA and RP vowels are noted in this section; see the references listed at the end of this chapter, as well as Chapter 9, for more information on the many regional and international varieties of English.

Figure 1.5 charts the positions of (GA) English vowels relative to each other, based roughly on the position of the highest point of the tongue during that vowel. The vowel space is larger at the top than at the bottom, because there is more room for tongue movement closer to the palate. (The astute reader will notice some differences in exactly where the vowel symbols are placed in Figures 1.4 and 1.5, particularly for **low** and **central vowels**. This is because the IPA provides many more symbols than are needed in any one language. If a linguist is concerned primarily with a general description of the set of sounds that are needed to distinguish the words of a language (as we are here), he/she will usually choose the more familiar symbols from among those the IPA makes available.)

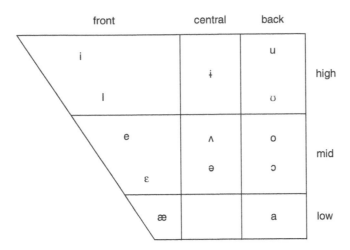

Figure 1.5 English vowels

The terms we use to classify different vowels refer to the highest point of the tongue during the vowel. The tongue body moves up for the **high vowels** [i, ɪ, ɨ, u, ʊ], down for the **low vowels** [æ, a], and stays in the middle for the **mid vowels** [e, ɛ, o, ɔ, ʌ, ə]. The tongue moves forward in the mouth for the **front vowels** [i, ɪ, e, ɛ, æ] and backward for the **back vowels** [u, ʊ, o, ɔ, a]. The vowels [ɨ, ʌ, ə] are central. Vowels also differ with respect to lip rounding. In General American English, the back vowels [u, ʊ, o, ɔ] are **round**, all other vowels are **unround**. In RP, the vowel in words like *body* is also round: the symbol for this low, back, round vowel is [ɒ]. In addition, English divides its vowels into two sets, **tense** and **lax**. The tense vowels [i, e, o, u] are longer, slightly higher, and produced with greater stiffening of the tongue root than their lax counterparts [ɪ, ɛ, ɔ, ʊ]. The tense/lax distinction doesn't really apply to low vowels. These descriptive terms can be combined to pick out a specific vowel: [ɪ] is high, front, lax, unround; [o] is mid, back, tense, round.

Distinct symbols are used for the set of vowels that occur only in short, unstressed syllables. (See the discussion of stress below.) The mid-central vowel [ə], called **schwa**, is heard in the first syllable of *about* and the second syllable of *Rosa's*. The high, central [ɨ] occurs in the second syllable of *roses*.

Suprasegmentals

Thus far, we have learned about individual sounds, but speaking involves stringing sounds together into larger units. Aspects of speech that influence stretches of sound larger than a single segment are called **suprasegmentals**. Suprasegmental aspects of speech include length, **tone**, intonation, syllable structure, and stress. Because suprasegmental aspects of speech involve the organization of sounds into larger units, the study of suprasegmentals straddles the domains of phonetics (the study of speech sounds as physical objects) and phonology (the study of how languages organize sounds into different patterns).

BOX 1.1 **TO "-ER" IN ENGLISH**

Special note should be made of the pronunciation of English vowels followed by [r]. The dialects of English can be divided into those that are "r-ful" (typified by GA) versus those that are "r-dropping" (typified by RP, but also including Australia, Boston, New York City, and some areas of the southeastern US). In r-ful dialects, [r] is pronounced following a vowel, so that *bear*, for example, is pronounced [ber] and *park* is [pʰark]. The tense/lax distinction is lost before [r], however: there is no contrast, in most r-ful dialects, between words like *Mary* and *merry*. In words like *fur*, *bird*, and *burr* the position of the tongue in the vowel is the same as for [r]: tongue dorsum backed and bunched, tongue tip raised. (That is, there's really no distinction between *burr* as in 'prickly seed' and *brrrr* as in 'I'm cold.') The symbol for this rhotic vowel is [ɝ] in stressed syllables and [ɚ] in unstressed, so that *murder*, for instance, is transcribed as [mɝdɚ]. In r-dropping dialects, postvocalic [r] is usually replaced by schwa or deleted, so that *bear* is [beə] and *park* is [pʰak]. (In RP, *park*, even without the [r], is distinct from both *pack* [pʰæk] and *pock* [pʰɒk]. The contrast is also maintained in Boston, where speakers use a distinctive fronted low vowel, but no [r], to "park the car in Harvard Yard.") For r-dropping dialects, the stressed vowel in words like *bird* and *fur* is transcribed [ɜ], a vowel intermediate between [ɛ] and [ʌ]. Unstressed *er* is simply [ə], so that *murder* is ['mɜdə] and *pander* and *panda* are homophonous as ['pʰændə]. Further examples of the pronunciation of central vowels in both r-ful and r-dropping dialects are shown in Table 1.4.

Finally, some vowels are **diphthongs**, which means that they combine two different positions in sequence. The diphthong [aɪ], as in General American *high*, moves from a low central position to high front. The diphthong [aʊ], as in General American *how*, moves from low central to high back. And [ɔɪ], as in *boy*, moves from mid back to high front. The tense vowels of English tend to be *diphthongized*, that is, the tongue changes position slightly over the course of the vowel. The vowel [e] is more exactly transcribed as [eɪ], and [o] as [oʊ] (or [əʊ] in RP). The change in position is not nearly as drastic as in the true diphthongs [aɪ] and [aʊ], however. More importantly, the "offglide" is distinctive in a true diphthong, but not in a vowel that is diphthongized. That is, changing [aɪ] to [a] or [aʊ] to [a] makes a different word: [raɪd] *ride* is not the same word as [rad]

rod; and [faʊnd] *found* is different from [fand] *fond*. On the other hand, pronouncing [eɪ] as [e] doesn't make a different word: it just makes you sound like you have a Spanish accent.

As mentioned above, in GA English, all the nonlow back vowels are round, and all the low vowels and front vowels are unround. Combining lip and tongue position in this way makes it easier for the ear to distinguish the different vowel sounds. Any language that has at least three vowels will have front vowels that are unround and back vowels that are round. Some languages (such as French, Dutch, and German) also have front round vowels, and others (such as Japanese and Korean) also have back unround vowels. In linguistics, when a sound is unusual or difficult to hear or to say, we say that that sound is **marked**. The easier, more common sound is **unmarked**. Front round vowels and voiceless sonorants, for example, are marked. Front unround vowels and voiced sonorants are unmarked. If a language uses the marked version of a sound, it also uses the unmarked version.

Introductory linguistics textbooks often simplify phonology by emphasizing the role of place and manner of articulation in making sounds, but you can see that there are many more choices involved. Speakers control the airstream mechanism, voicing, and nasality as well as the place and manner of articulation. Every sound is composed of smaller components that can be combined in different ways to make other sounds, and each of these components offers a (typically binary) opposition: voiced or voiceless, nasal or oral, open or closed, front or back, etc. Speakers of English are often biased by its alphabetic writing system; they automatically think of each sound as a letter – an autonomous atomic unit, equally related or unrelated to every other letter, so that [p] and [b] are no more closely or distantly related than say [g] and [s]. But sounds are built from lower-level vocal tract choices, and you change one sound into another by switching parameters for each choice (voiced to voiceless, stop to fricative, etc.). Think of "voiced," for example, not just as an adjective that describes a sound but as one parameter (a choice, a building block, a specific vocal tract configuration) that, in combination with other parameters, creates the sound. The phonetic symbol representing a given sound isn't the sound itself, but a "cover symbol" for the set of choices. This also means that the speech sounds of a language are related

BOX 1.1 (*cont.*)

to each other in important ways; some sets of sounds differ only by changing a single parameter, while others differ in the settings of several parameters. As we will discover in the section on phonology, it is these parameters (the **distinctive features**) of a sound or group of sounds, not the individual sounds or symbols themselves, that are important in describing sound patterns within a linguistic system.

TABLE 1.4 Pronunciation of central vowels in GA and RP

Symbol	Example	Spelling	Notes
ʌ	[mʌd] [rʌf]	mud rough	Used in stressed syllables
ə	[ˈpʰændə] [bəˈliv] [əˈbʌt] [ˈrozəz]	panda believe abut Rosa's	Used in unstressed syllables
ɨ	[ˈrozɨz] [rarɨd]	roses rotted	Used in suffixes
ɜ	[fɜ] [ˈbɜdən]	fur burden	In "r-dropping" dialects, including Boston and BBC English
ɝ	[ˈfɝ] [ˈbɝdən]	fur burden	In "r-ful" dialects, including General American; stressed syllables
ɚ	[ˈnɛvɚ] [ˈhɛlpɚ] [ˈsʌpɚ] [fɝˈðɚ]	never helper supper further	GA pronunciation, unstressed syllables

BOX 1.2 **SUMMARY OF VOCAL TRACT CHOICES**

The terms and symbols of phonetics describe the choices that a speaker must make in order to produce a linguistic sound:

1. How should I get the air moving? Generally, this will be pulmonic egressive: air forced out of the lungs.
2. Which active articulator should I use: lips, tongue tip, tongue body, tongue root, or larynx?
3. What kind of constriction should I make: stop, fricative, affricate, approximant, vowel?
4. Where should I make the constriction? For consonants, the choices are bilabial, labiodental, dental, alveolar, postalveolar, retroflex, palatal, velar, uvular, pharyngeal, and laryngeal; for vowels, the choices are high/mid/low, front/central/back, tense/lax, and round/unround.
5. Should the velum be open or closed?
6. What should I do with the larynx: voiced or voiceless, aspirated or unaspirated?

Length

Many factors influence how long it takes to articulate a given segment. Sometimes differences in vowel length are unintentional results of how different vowels are articulated. Low vowels, for which the mouth has to open wide, take longer to articulate than high vowels, for which little movement is necessary. In some languages, however, two segments may differ in length alone: the long segment and short counterpart are exactly the same, except that the former is (intentionally) held for a longer period of time, an extra "beat." These long segments may be written with a double symbol ([aa], [pp]) or with a colon after the usual symbol ([a:], [p:]). (Sometimes a horizontal bar, or macron, is used to indicate a long segment.) For example, Japanese makes length distinctions in both vowels and consonants. In Tokyo, you want to be careful to order [bi:.u] 'a beer' rather than [bi.u] 'a building,' and to ask directions to a certain [tori] 'street,' rather than a [to:.i] 'gate' or [to:.i:] 'bird.' We will reserve the term "long vowel" to refer to distinctions such as those in Japanese, where everything about the long/short vowel pair is the same, except for length.

Long consonants are known as **geminates**. English can create long consonants when two words come together – compare *bookcase* [bʊkkes] to *book ace* [bʊkes] or *top part* [tappa.t] to *top art* [tapa.t] – but we don't distinguish long and short consonants within words. When double consonants are written, for example in *supper* vs. *super*, they actually tell us about the quality of the vowel, not the length of the consonant.

> *You probably learned in elementary school about long and short vowels in English spelling (like "long a" as in* made *and "short a" as in* mad*), but this is more a distinction of vowel quality ([e] vs. [æ]) than of length. The long–short vowel terminology, while no longer linguistically accurate for English, is not completely random: 500 years ago, the difference between* made *and* mad *really was one of length, and the English vowel system was very similar to that of modern Japanese. Over the years, however, a series of sound changes affected the long and short vowels differently, pushing them out of alignment.*

Tone and intonation

The pitch of the voice carries a lot of information. It can tell you whether the speaker is a male or female, a large person or small, old or young. High pitch can tell you that a person is frightened; low pitch that he or she is angry. This sort of information isn't really linguistic, however, but physical or emotional. The terms tone and intonation refer to linguistic uses of pitch. Tone refers to the use of pitch to convey meaning at the word level; intonation refers to the use of pitch to convey meaning at the sentence or discourse level.

Intonation distinguishes different kinds of sentences or focuses attention on a particular word. For example, try reading the following sentences out loud (and dramatically):

"That's a cat?"
"Yup. That's a cat."
"A *cat*? I thought it was a mountain lion!"

The pitch of your voice moves in different directions on the word *cat*. On the first *cat*, pitch goes up, indicating a question. On the second, pitch falls, indicating a statement or confirmation. On the third *cat*, a more complicated fall–rise pattern indicates incredulity. (Typographically, we indicate these different "readings" with a question mark, period, and italics, respectively.) In each case, the sequence [kʰæt] refers to the same object, a feline. The pitch differences indicate only the role that the reference to the feline is playing in the current conversation: asking for information about the cat, providing it, or expressing disbelief regarding the information offered. All languages use intonation to some extent, though the patterns and meanings differ across languages.

In addition to intonation, most languages also use pitch to distinguish different words. In English, whether you say [kʰæt] with a rising pitch or falling pitch, the word still refers to a feline. In Thai, if you say [kʰaː] with rising pitch, it means 'leg'; but if you say it with falling pitch, it means 'value.' (There are actually five contrasting pitch patterns in Thai: high, low, mid, falling, and rising.) These words are as different as *cat* and *cut* to an English speaker. This use of pitch, to distinguish different words, is known as *tone*.

Although the idea of tones seems very strange to English speakers, the majority of the world's languages are tonal. The major European languages and their relatives are exceptional in *not* having tone.

Syllable structure

How many syllables are in the word *Appalachicola*? *Massachusetts*? *Antidisestablishmentarianism*? (six, four, and eleven, respectively.) English speakers have little trouble counting the number of syllables in a word, but linguists have a harder time defining what a syllable is.

One preliminary answer might be "a vowel and its surrounding consonants." Most of the syllables we encounter in English, in words like *pin, print*, or even *sprints*, fit this definition. However, it's perfectly possible to have a syllable without a vowel. We would all agree that *hidden* has two syllables, even if pronounced [hɪdn], with no vowel between the two consonants. Also, defining a syllable as "a vowel and the consonants around it" doesn't explain why some sequences of consonants are allowed and others are not. The sequence [prɪnt] is acceptable as a syllable in English, but the sequence [rpɪtn] is not acceptable as a single syllable in any language. Why is [prɪnt] a good syllable when [rpɪtn] is not?

The best answer (though not perfect) lies in the concept of sonority. **Sonority** can be defined as relative openness of the vocal tract, which corresponds directly to the relative loudness of a sound. The most sonorous sounds are the low vowels; the mouth is wide open, and the sound flows freely out. The least sonorous sounds are the voiceless stops; the mouth is completely shut, and no sound is made at all. Other sounds range between these two extremes.

The speech stream is organized into peaks and valleys of sonority. Languages generally do not choose long strings of consonants nor long strings of vowels. Rather, we alternate

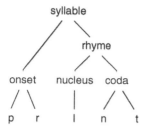

Figure 1.6 Syllable structure for the word *print*

sounds that are more sonorous and less sonorous: each stands out better against the background of the other. A syllable, then, may be defined as a way of organizing sounds around a peak of sonority.

Take the simple syllable *pin*. The vowel [ɪ] is the most sonorous sound in the sequence, flanked by less sonorous consonants. Thus there is a single sonority peak, and a single syllable. The syllable *print* also follows the principle of sonority. Sonority rises from [p] (voiceless stop) to [r] (rhotic) to [ɪ] (vowel), then falls from vowel to [n] (nasal) to [t] (stop). A single peak, a single syllable. Meanwhile, the sequence [rpɪtn] has three peaks; higher sonority [r], [ɪ], and [n] are interrupted by lowest sonority [p] and [t]. Thus (if it is pronounceable at all) it has three syllables, not one.

The most sonorous element of a syllable, the peak itself, is called the **nucleus**. Lower sonority sounds preceding the nucleus are called the **onset**; those following the nucleus are called the **coda**. The nucleus and coda together form the **rhyme**. A syllable structure tree diagram for the word *print* is shown in Figure 1.6. (In linguistics, such tree diagrams are often used to show how constituent parts of a larger unit are related, so you'll see more tree diagrams in other chapters!)

Since vowels are the most sonorous sounds, they usually constitute syllable nuclei, but that's not always the case. Sounds other than vowels may form sonority peaks, so that *hidden* and *prism* have one vowel but two syllables.

Sonority thus seems to capture most of our intuitions about syllable structure and explains a lot about possible syllables in the languages of the world. But sonority doesn't account for everything. There are some English words that clearly violate the principle of sonority – *sprints* and *sixths*, for example. Linguists aren't sure exactly how to deal with words like this. It may be that endings like plural [s] and ordinal [θ] are not really part of the syllable at all; rather they're tacked on in an "appendix" to the end of the word.

Stress

Linguistic stress is a prominence relation between syllables: certain syllables are longer, louder, higher-pitched, or more clearly articulated than those around them. Just as we can generally count the syllables in a word, we can generally pick out the syllable that's most prominent: *phoNOlogy, phoNEtics, SYNtax.*

There are at least three different levels of stress in English. Consider the word *Alabama.* The third syllable [bæ] is the most prominent, and bears the *main* or *primary stress* of the word, but the other three syllables do not receive equal stress. The first syllable has a full vowel quality [æ], though it is not quite as long or loud as the third, but the second and fourth syllables are short and weak, with the tongue not moving far from its central position. We say that the first syllable has *secondary stress*, while the second and fourth are completely unstressed.

Some languages do not use stress at all. In Japanese, for example, all the syllables in a word are sometimes pronounced with equal prominence. This gives quite a bit of trouble to English speakers. In 1996, for example, when the Winter Olympics were held in Japan, English commentators had a great deal of trouble deciding how to say the name of the host city: *NAgano? NaGAno? NagaNO?* In fact, the word is pronounced with all syllables equally stressed (or equally unstressed), a difficult task for an English speaker. Conversely, Japanese speakers often have a great deal of trouble with reducing the unstressed vowels of English, sounding overly careful to English ears.

Because stress is a prominence relation, stressed and unstressed syllables tend to alternate across the word: *ApalachiCOla*, for instance. In order for a syllable to be heard as prominent, it helps if it's surrounded by non-prominent syllables. In English, stress sometimes even moves around in order to accommodate an alternating pattern. In a word like *sixteen*, stress usually falls on the second syllable (*How old are you? SixTEEN.*). But put the word next to one that begins with a strongly stressed syllable, and stress may shift back in order to maintain an alternating pattern (*How long have you worked here? SIXteen YEARS.*) Linguists refer to a grouping of a stressed syllable and adjacent unstressed syllables as a **foot**. Choosing different kinds of feet (da-DUM vs. DA-dum) is important not only in poetry, but as part of defining a language's unfolding rhythm of speech.

Languages in which stress is completely predictable are called **fixed stress** systems. Fixed stress may be alternating, as in Pintupi, an Australian language where stress always falls on the first syllable and then on every other syllable after that: [KUra ululimpatjura] 'the first one (who is) our relation.' Other fixed stress systems may pick out just one syllable in the word as especially prominent. In Farsi, stress is always on the initial syllable, in Turkish always on the last syllable, in Polish always on the second-to-last syllable.

In other languages, stress is unpredictable: you just have to memorize which syllable gets stressed when you learn the word, in the same way you have to memorize whether it begins with [b] or [p]. This is called **lexical stress**. For example, Russian has a lexical stress system: if stress is placed on the first syllable, [duxi] means 'spirits'; stressed on the second syllable, it means 'perfume.'

The third type of system is **paradigmatic stress**, in which the stress patterns depend on what part of speech a word is – for example, a noun or a verb. The English system is mostly paradigmatic, with some unpredictable aspects. Generally, English verbs and adjectives follow one set of rules, nouns another. Thus English has pairs of words that differ only in stress, where one word is a noun and the other a verb: we reJECT the REject, reCORD the REcord, conVERT the CONvert, inSULT with an INsult, etc.

Acoustic phonetics

Thus far, we have talked about articulation, how speech sounds are made inside the mouth. But what happens inside the mouth is only part of the process. In order to understand how people use sound to communicate, we must also understand how the articulators turn air movements into sound, what happens to sound after it passes through the lips, how it travels through the air, and how it impacts on the ears and brain (and sometimes the microphones, recorders, and computers) of those who listen. These aspects of the linguistic study of sound fall under the heading of acoustic phonetics.

Sound waves

Speech sounds are caused by moving air. Articulation is all about getting air to move in ways that can be heard – vibrating, popping, or swishing. In this short introduction, we will focus on the patterns of vibration in voiced sounds, particularly vowels. But speech sounds are very complex, so it helps to start by thinking about something much simpler – a tuning fork.

Strike a tuning fork against a table or other hard object, and the tines of the fork will vibrate. Depending on the exact shape and size of the fork, the tines will vibrate at a particular rate, or **frequency**. A fork tuned to "orchestral A," for example, will vibrate at a frequency of 440 cycles per second (cps), where a *cycle* equals one back and forth motion of the end of the tine. ("Cycles per second" are often called "Hertz" – abbreviated Hz – after a famous physicist, Heinrich Hertz.)

Different objects have different inherent frequencies of vibration, which determine the pitch of the sound. A small handbell will vibrate faster and make a higher pitched sound than a huge churchbell, which will vibrate slower and make a lower pitched sound. Human beings can hear frequencies as low as about 20 Hz, and as high as about 20,000 Hz. Humans will not perceive vibrations faster or slower than that as sound, although dogs can hear frequencies up to 45,000 Hz and bats and dolphins over 100,000 Hz.

How does the vibration of the tuning fork make it to our ears as sound? As the ends of the tuning fork vibrate, they set the air particles next to them vibrating as well, following the same back and forth motion. These moving air particles alternately push and pull on the particles next to them, and those on the particles next to them, and so on, so that the pattern of vibration moves outward from the tuning fork like ripples in a pond. These moving patterns of vibration are called sound waves. When the sound waves reach our ears (or a microphone), they set the eardrum (or the membrane in the microphone) vibrating according to the same pattern. Inside the ear, the vibrations set off nerve impulses, which are interpreted by our brains as sound.

Simple and complex sounds

The motion of a tuning fork is very simple (back and forth, like a pendulum), and thus the sound wave it creates is also very simple. The sound such a simple vibration makes is a pure tone of a single frequency (like 440 Hz). But the vibrations of the vocal tract – and the sounds it makes – are more complicated.

The vocal tract is like a clarinet. The vocal folds are the reed, the source of the vibration. The column of air in the mouth is the column of air in the instrument, the filter of the vibration. And the speaker, of course, is the musician, changing the shape of the column of air to modulate the sound produced. Thinking about speech sounds in this way is called the **source-filter theory of speech production**.

This is how it works. As air passes out of the trachea and over the vocal folds, if the speaker holds them in the correct position, the folds begin to vibrate. They flap open and closed at a frequency between about 100 times per second (for a large adult male) and 300 times per second (for a child). But on top of this basic flapping motion, there are many different subripples in the moving vocal folds. Think of sheets flapping in the breeze on a laundry line; they don't flap stiffly up and down, but ripple in complicated patterns. Each of these little ripples contributes its own pattern of vibration to the sound, creating "overtones," or **harmonics**, in addition to the basic pitch of the speaker's voice. The basic rate of vibration, the **fundamental frequency**, determines the pitch, but the overtones create the different qualities of different sounds.

As the vocal folds vibrate, they start the air inside the vocal tract vibrating in the same complex way. The air in the vocal tract then filters the harmonic structure of the sound produced at the vocal folds. Certain ripples (that is, certain harmonics) are amplified, and other ripples (other harmonics) are damped out. *Which* harmonics are amplified depends on the shape of column(s) of air inside the vocal tract. Recall that different objects have different characteristic patterns of vibration, depending on their size and shape (handbells vs. churchbells, for instance). What is true of bells is also true of enclosed bodies of air. Differently shaped bodies of air will tend to vibrate at different frequencies. Harmonics that are "in tune" with the characteristic frequencies of a particular vocal tract shape will be amplified, those that are not in tune will be reduced. The speaker controls the filter by moving the tongue and lips to different positions, amplifying some harmonics and blocking out others. The most strongly amplified frequencies are called **formants**. Different vowel sounds have different formant structures.

So, depending on the shape of the tongue and lips, each vowel sound has a characteristic, complex pattern of vibration. The vibration moves out past the lips, and propagates into the world. The sound waves travel through the air at the rate of about 340 meters per second, until they impinge on a membrane tuned to receive them, such as the eardrum.

Hearing

The ear has three parts – the outer, middle, and inner ear, as shown in Figure 1.7. The outer ear consists of the visible shell of the ear (the **pinna**) and the ear canal leading down to the eardrum. The pinna helps to capture sounds better, and to locate sounds in space. The ear canal protects the eardrum, and also helps to amplify the sounds that are relevant for speech. Sound waves travel down the air in the ear canal until they reach the eardrum, which begins to vibrate.

Behind the eardrum, in the middle ear, are the three smallest bones in the body (the **ossicles**). The patterns of vibration are transferred from the eardrum through the bones of

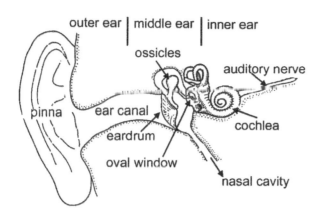

Figure 1.7 The hearing mechanism

the middle ear to the inner ear, the **cochlea**. This additional stage of transfer, through the middle ear, helps to amplify very soft sounds, and tone down very loud sounds. It is in the cochlea that hearing actually takes place. The cochlea looks like a curled-up snail shell, smaller than a marble. The cochlea is divided into upper and lower chambers, which are filled with fluid. Crucially, the membrane separating the two chambers, the cochlear membrane, is not uniform along its length, but is tapered. It is 3 millimeters thick and bony at one end and thin (just 1 millimeter) and flexible at the other. Embedded all along the membrane are tiny hair cells, the **cilia**, each attached to a nerve ending, and waving gently in the cochlear fluid.

As the eardrum vibrates, the bones of the middle ear vibrate, which in turn cause the membrane of the inner ear (the **oval window**) to vibrate, starting up waves of vibration in the fluid of the inner ear. The patterns of vibration in the cochlear fluid mirror the complex pattern of sound created in the vocal tract of the speaker – the fundamental frequency of the vibrating vocal folds as well as the harmonic characteristics of the different vowels.

Again recall that objects of different size and shape tend to vibrate at different frequencies. Because the cochlear membrane varies in shape along its length (thick at one end, thin at the other) different places along the membrane respond to different frequencies of vibration. The thick end vibrates in tune to low-pitched sounds, the thin end in tune to higher-pitched sounds, and parts of the membrane in between vibrate in tune to mid-range sounds. In response to a given pattern of vibration, cilia at different places along the cochlear membrane are activated, sending signals to the brain about the frequencies present in the incoming wave. The brain recombines the frequency information it perceives into the sounds of language.

Measuring speech

Until quite recently, the phonetician's ears were the only instruments available for the analysis of sound, and they are probably still the most finely tuned and reliable. Beginning in the 1900s, however, phoneticians began to discover ways to make sound visible. Early devices, such as oscilloscopes and sound spectrographs, used a microphone to transfer patterns of vibration in the air into patterns of variation in electrical current. These variations could then be displayed – on paper or a screen – or passed through banks of capacitors and resistors for further measurement and study.

In the first part of the twenty-first century, speech analysis is done by computer. Microphones still convert the vibration of the membrane into variations in electrical current. But then computers convert a continuously varying sound wave into a series of numbers; this is called an analog-to-digital (A-to-D) conversion. (Working in the opposite direction, getting a computer, digital video disk, or digital audio player to *make* sound, is D-to-A conversion.)

Once represented and stored in a digital format, sound files can be mathematically analyzed to separate out the different frequencies, and the results of the analysis displayed onscreen in various formats. Three common and useful displays are shown in Figure 1.8. All three show the utterance "A phoneme?" (These figures were created on a laptop computer, using software that was downloaded free from the internet.)

Figure 1.8A shows a **waveform**; the varying amplitude (corresponding to loudness) of the vibrations (on the y-axis) is plotted over time (on the x-axis). The duration of the utterance is one second. Above the waveform are the segments (roughly) corresponding to each part of the waveform. Note that the vowels [o] and [i] have the greatest amplitude, the obstruent [f] the least, and the nasals and unstressed [ə] have an intermediate amplitude. Figure 1.8A also shows a close-up view (magnified 12 times) of portions of the waveform. At this magnification, you can see the random noisiness of the fricative, and the complex, repeating pattern of vibration that is characteristic of each vowel. The patterns for [o] and [i] are different, and thus the vowel qualities are different. The waveform is a useful representation for seeing the overall structure of an utterance, identifying the different types of sounds (stop, vowel, nasal consonant), and measuring the durations of different aspects of the speech signal.

Because of all the communicative information carried by pitch changes, linguists often want to measure fundamental frequency over the course of an utterance. Figure 1.8B shows the result of such a computation, a **pitch track**. In this representation, the y-axis shows frequency, and time is on the x-axis. Notice that no frequency is calculated during the [f]. Since there is no vocal fold vibration during this segment, there is no frequency to measure. This pitch track shows that this speaker's voice has a baseline fundamental frequency of about 200 Hz, but that this frequency rises toward the end of the utterance, in a contour typical of a question.

Neither of these figures, however, has told us much about the quality of the vowel sounds. We can see from the waveforms that the vowel qualities in [o] and [i] are different, because the patterns look different, but the complex squiggles don't tell us much about the component overtones and thus about the vocal tract shape that made them. The computer can further analyze the sound wave to tease apart its component frequencies. The result of this analysis is a spectrogram, shown in Figure 1.8C.

As with a pitch track, the x-axis represents time, and the y-axis shows frequency. But instead of a single line graph, we see a complicated pattern of the many frequencies present in each sound. We want our analysis to tell us which frequencies are the loudest, because

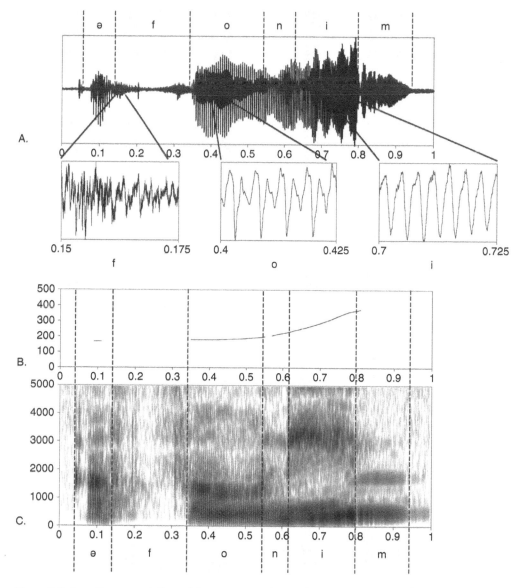

Figure 1.8 Acoustic representations of the utterance *A phoneme*? A. Waveform B. Pitch track. C. Spectrogram

once we know which frequencies have been amplified, we can use known formulas to figure out the (approximate) shape of the vocal tract that made them. This crucial third dimension, amplitude, is represented by the darkness of the lines. A dark bar at a certain frequency means that that frequency is strongly represented in the sound. Each vowel has a pattern of two or three most prominent frequencies, called **formants**, above the fundamental frequency of the speaker's vocal folds. For example, during the [o] vowel, we see a formant at about 1200 Hz. The [i] vowel has a different formant structure, with the second formant at about 3000 Hz.

Because the basic relationships between vocal tract shape and formant structure are known, we can infer the position of the tongue, which we can't see, from the formant structure on the spectrogram. Across speakers, the general relationships between speech sounds remain the same: for example, the second formant is always higher in [i] than in [o]. But because every person's vocal tract size and shape is unique, every person's formant structure is unique too. We recognize familiar voices, regardless of what they're saying, and in the hands of an expert, a spectrographic voice print is as unique as a fingerprint.

Phonology

What else could there be to say about the sounds of speech? Quite a lot. Language isn't just in the mouth or ears, but also in the brain. When we turn from analyzing the physical aspects of speech sounds to studying their cognitive organization, we move from phonetics to phonology. Phonology can never be completely divorced from phonetics, since sound patterns can never be completely separated from how they are produced and heard, and production and perception are always influenced by the overarching linguistic organization.

All human beings have basically the same structures in their vocal tracts and in their ears. So why are languages so different? To some extent, it is because they use different sounds from the repertoire of possible human vocal tract noises. Arabic uses pharyngeal and uvular fricatives, while English does not. French selects front round vowels (such as [y] and [œ]), English selects lax high vowels ([ɪ] and [ʊ]), and Spanish sticks to basic [i, e, a, o, u]. Thus, to some extent, learning to speak a new language is about learning to make new sounds.

But there's more to it than that. Languages differ not only in the sounds they use, but in how they organize those sounds into patterns. Consider, for example, the voiced obstruents of English and Spanish.

Phonemes and allophones

Both English and Spanish have the sounds [d] and [ð]. For example, English has *den* [dɛn] and *then* [ðɛn], while Spanish has [dama] 'lady' and [laðo] 'side.' Both sounds occur in both languages, but they differ in their *distributions* – that is, where the sounds appear – and in the information the difference between them conveys.

In General American English, there are several pairs of words that differ only in that one has [d] where the other has [ð]: *den* [dɛn] and *then* [ðɛn], *eider* [aɪdər] and *either* [aɪðər], *bade* [bed] and *bathe* [beð]. Pairs of words that differ in only a single sound in the same position within the word are called **minimal pairs**. (If you pronounce *either* as [iðər], then you have a near-minimal pair – two words that are almost exactly alike.) The existence of minimal pairs means that the difference between the two sounds is contrastive; change one sound into another and you've created a contrast in meaning (that is, you've made a different word). If two sounds are contrastive, their distribution is *unpredictable*. If I tell you

I'm thinking of an English word that rhymes with *when*, and starts with either [d] or [ð], you cannot predict which sound (or word) I have in mind. Look back at Tables 1.1 and 1.3, which give many examples of minimal and near-minimal pairs for different sounds in English.

Now compare this to the situation in Spanish:

[dama]	'lady'
[demonias]	'demons'
[dulse]	'sweet'
[disfɾas]	'disguise'
[laðo]	'side'
[universiðað]	'university'
[imbaliðo]	'invalid'
[grenaða]	'Grenada'
[siuðað]	'city'

Notice that [d] and [ð] have a different distribution in Spanish. There are no minimal pairs – no [ðama] contrasting with [dama], no [lado] contrasting with [laðo]. The difference between [d] and [ð] is not contrastive; the [d] versus [ð] difference is never used in Spanish to signal a difference in meaning. Instead, the two sounds have different distributions: only [d] is found in initial position, and only [ð] is found following a vowel. The distribution is *predictable*. If you know the context (the position in the word, or the surrounding sounds), you can predict whether [d] or [ð] will be used.

When the occurrence of two different sounds is predictable based on the context, we say that the two sounds are in **complementary distribution**. (Not "com*pli*mentary" in the sense of "nice," but "com*ple*mentary" in the mathematical sense that one half of a circle is the complement of the other half.) The sounds [d] and [ð] are in complementary distribution in Spanish. (The situation is slightly more complicated when contexts other than word-initial and postvocalic are considered, but the principle of complementary distribution holds. There is only [d] after [n], for instance, and only [ð] after [r].)

When two sounds in a language form minimal pairs (that is, if their distribution is unpredictable and contrastive), those two sounds represent different **phonemes**. When two sounds in a language are in complementary distribution (that is, their distribution is predictable and noncontrastive), the two sounds are **allophones** of the same phoneme. In English, [d] and [ð] represent different phonemes. In Spanish [d] and [ð] are allophones of the same phoneme.

Another way to say this is that a phoneme is a label for a group of sounds that are perceived by the speaker to be the "same" sound, and the allophones are the different ways of pronouncing that sound depending upon the context in which it is produced. To the Spanish speaker, if he/she pays any conscious attention at all, [ð] is just "a way of saying *d*." A speaker of the language knows when the [d] allophone is called for and when the [ð] allophone is appropriate. If you're learning Spanish as a second language, you may have been taught this distribution as a rule, something like "the sound [d] is pronounced as [ð] between vowels." There is no such rule relating [d] and [ð] in English. They are separate phonemes.

We may diagram the situation as follows:

English: /d/   /ð/   Spanish: /d/

[d]   [ð]   [d]   [ð]

word-initial   between vowels

Phonemes are indicated by slashes, while allophones are indicated by brackets. At the allophonic level, English and Spanish have the same sounds. At the phonemic level, English has a contrast where Spanish has none.

Differences in phonemic and allophonic distribution pose significant problems for speakers of one language who are learning to speak another. A native speaker of Spanish learning English will have trouble with the distinction between *den* and *then*. To him/her, [d] and [ð] count as the same sound, so he/she will tend to hear them that way, and to pronounce them according to the principles of his/her own language. A Spanish speaker may tend to say [dɛn] for *then* (using the word-initial allophone), and [æðe.] for *adder* (using the intervocalic allophone). These are not random errors, but a result of imposing the phonological organization of the first language onto the words of the second.

Discovering phonemes and allophones

In this section, we work through an example illustrating how to determine whether sounds belong to one or more phonemes. More practice examples can be found in the exercises at the end of the chapter.

An analysis must begin with some data. To start from scratch, a linguist would have to find a speaker or group of speakers of the language under investigation, ask for words and word meanings, and transcribe them. In the interests of time, we'll skip step one and

BOX 1.3 MINIMAL PAIRS IN SIGN LANGUAGE

One might wonder how it could be possible to study the phonology of sign language, since phonology is the study of sounds and the medium of sign language is non-auditory. However, linguists studying sign language have noted that there is internal structure in a sign much like the articulatory features proposed for phonemes in spoken languages. Each sign has three simultaneous components: a hand shape, movement, and a location. Indeed, there are minimal pairs with respect to these three components much like those in spoken language. For instance, the signs for *candy* and *apple* differ only in hand shape; both are placed at the chin and rotate the hand back and forth. *Candy* has a closed hand with the index finger pointing to the chin, while *apple* has a completely closed hand shape. *Ugly* and *summer* both have the same hand shapes and movement, but they are signed in a different location. *Train* and *chair* both have the same hand shape and location but a different movement. Notice that there is no semantic similarity between the pairs of words, just as *pat* and *pad* in English have no meaning correspondence. The signs are arbitrary in relation to the meaning (although there are some signs that have evolved from iconic signs). (See Sandler and Lillo-Martin 2006 for further discussion on phonological theories of sign language.)

TABLE 1.5 Some lexical items of Swahili

ŋgɔma	drum	watoto	children
bɔma	fort	ndoto	dream
ŋɔmbɛ	cattle	mboga	vegetable
ɔmba	pray	dʒogo	rooster
ɔna	see	ʃoka	axe
pɔɲa	cure	okota	pick up
ɲɔɲa	nurse	modʒa	one
ɔɲdʒa	taste	mtego	trap
ɔŋgeza	increase	kʰɔndo	sheep
ɲɔŋga	strangle	karɔŋgo	wash-out

assume that data have already been accurately collected. Further, in textbook exercises like this one, where available time and space is severely limited, the reader has to trust that the author has chosen the example words to be representative. In a real analysis, larger data sets would be required.

After the data have been collected, the second step in a phonemic analysis is to identify a set of sounds that are suspected to count as "the same." They might be chosen because they are similar, because they have turned out to be related to each other in a number of other languages, or because the linguist notices a limited distribution that he/she suspects is complementary. Here, we examine the distribution of [ɔ] and [o] in Swahili (the data are from Gleason 1955). In Table 1.5, Swahili words containing the two vowels are listed in two columns, words with [ɔ] on the left and words with [o] on the right. Some words contain both.

Having collected and organized our data set, we proceed to search for patterns. First, look for minimal pairs. If any can be found, the analysis is finished: the two sounds are contrastive and therefore must belong to different phonemes. Here, we find no minimal pairs: there is no [boma] to match the existing word [bɔma]; no [ʃoka] to match the word [ʃoka]. So we suspect that that the distribution of [o] and [ɔ] may be predictable by context. The next step, then, is to look closely at the environments in which each sound occurs. It can be helpful to list out the immediately preceding and following sounds in each case: this helps to focus on the part of the word most likely to be relevant. Looking at immediately adjacent sounds doesn't always work – sometimes sounds can affect each other from some distance away – but it's a good place to start. This is done in Table 1.6, where a blank indicates the occurrence of each sound. The symbol # indicates the edge of a word, so that #__ indicates a word-initial sound, and __# indicates a word-final sound.

TABLE 1.6 Environments for [o] and [ɔ]

[ɔ]	[o]
g___m	t___t
b___m	d___t
ŋ___m	b___g
#___m	dʒ___g
#___n	ʃ___k
p___ɲ	k___t
ɲ ___ɲ	m___d
#___ɲ	g___#
#___ŋ	d___#
r___ŋ	#___k
kʰ___n	t___#

Look at the lists in Table 1.6. Try to determine whether there's anything that all the environments in one list have in common, but that doesn't occur in the other list. Sometimes the pattern jumps out at you (as it probably does here); sometimes a little more thought and work is needed. There doesn't seem to be anything systematic about the preceding sound that could condition the choice of a different vowel in this data set. Both lists contain a variety of preceding nasals and voiced and voiceless consonants. Particularly, both [o] and [ɔ] can follow [g], and both can occur at the beginning of a word. So we can't predict which vowel will occur based on preceding sound.

On the other hand, there *is* a pattern to the sounds that follow the vowel. The vowel [ɔ] only occurs before [m, n, ɲ, or ŋ], and the vowel [o] never occurs before any of these consonants. This establishes that the two sounds are in complementary distribution. Because the two sounds are in complementary distribution, we conclude that they belong to the same phoneme.

To complete the analysis, we need to state the rule for which allophones occur where. It would be correct to say that [ɔ] occurs before [m, n, ɲ, ŋ], and [o] occurs before [t, d, k, g] and in word-final position, but to just give a list of sounds is missing something. Phonological distributions seldom, if ever, depend on random lists of sounds with nothing in common. Phonological distributions depend on *natural classes*: sets of sounds that have something in common. The sounds [m, n, ɲ, ŋ] have something in common: they are all nasal consonants. The complement set [t, d, k, g, #] doesn't have any property in common: we can call this the "elsewhere case." Thus, we can state our analysis as follows: [o] and [ɔ] are in complementary distribution and allophones of one phoneme in Swahili: [ɔ] occurs before nasal consonants, [o] occurs elsewhere. This is diagrammed in Figure 1.9:

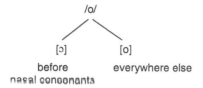

Figure 1.9 Distribution of [o] and [ɔ] in Swahili

The pattern can be restated as a generalization: the phoneme /o/ is pronounced [ɔ] before nasals.

Note that I've chosen to label the phoneme as /o/ rather than /ɔ/. To the extent that it's possible, a linguist will choose the less restricted variant (the elsewhere case) as the "basic form," and the more restricted variant as the "derived form." (Occurring in more environments doesn't necessarily mean occurring in more words. [o] and [ɔ] occur in an equal number of lexical items in this list of Swahili words.) It's simpler to state a generalization when the elsewhere case is chosen as the basic form. Statement *a* is simpler than statement *b*:

a. /o/ becomes [ɔ] before nasals.
b. /ɔ/ becomes [o] before non-nasal consonants or at the end of a word.

It's not always possible to definitively choose one environment as the elsewhere case, but all things being equal, the simpler analysis is always to be preferred. One should always try to make the analysis as simple and general as possible, consistent with the data.

BOX 1.4 ANOTHER LOOK AT PHONEMES AND ALLOPHONES

The example above shows a case where a distinction that is contrastive in English is not contrastive in another language. The reverse occurs too, of course. Consider the case of voiceless stops in Thai and English.

A voiceless stop ([p], [t], or [k]) may be produced with or without an extra puff of air, called *aspiration*. In English, you can feel the aspiration if you hold your fingertips an inch or so in front of your lips as you say *pop* or *pill*. But you won't feel any aspiration for a [p] that occurs after [s] as in *spot* or *spill*. In English, stops produced with an extra puff of air are aspirated, those without the extra puff are unaspirated. Speakers of both Thai and English produce a full set of aspirated voiceless stops [pʰ, tʰ, kʰ] and unaspirated voiceless stops [p, t, k]. Though the inventory of voiceless stops is the same, the languages use the inventory in different ways. Some Thai and English words using these sounds are shown below.

Thai:	Aspirated:		Unaspirated:	
	pʰàt	'to stir fry'	pàt	'to wipe'
	tʰun	'a fund'	tun	'to hoard'
	kʰâ:w	'step'	kâ:w	'rice'

English:	Aspirated:		Unaspirated:	
	pʰɪl	pill	spɪl	spill
	tʰɪl	till	stɪl	still
	kʰɪl	kill	skɪl	skill

In Thai, aspiration is contrastive. The difference between [p] and [pʰ] makes a difference in meaning, and thus minimal pairs with aspirated and unaspirated stops (such as [pʰàt] and [pàt]) are easy to find. [p] and [pʰ] are two different phonemes, as are [t] and [tʰ], and [k] and [kʰ].

There are, however, no minimal pairs for aspiration in English. Aspiration is never the *only* difference between two words. Instead, we can *predict* whether a stop in an English

BOX 1.4 (*cont.*)

word will be aspirated or unaspirated depending on its context. At the beginning of a word, a voiceless stop will be aspirated; after /s/, it will be unaspirated. In English, the single phoneme /p/ has two allophones: [p] and [pʰ].

The allophonic nature of aspiration in English is reflected in the **orthography**. English doesn't have two different written symbols for these two sounds (for [p]

and [pʰ], for example), whereas Thai does. An English speaker needs a lot of convincing to believe that the *p* sounds in *sport* and *port* are not phonetically identical. To him/her, they count as the same, because they are allophones of a single phoneme. The Thai speaker needs no such convincing. To him/her, [p] and [pʰ] are as different as [t] and [k].

Phonotactics

The first thing a phonologist working to describe a previously unknown language wants to figure out is its inventory of sounds: what sounds does the language use? But the second thing he/she wants to figure out is which sound differences the language uses to encode differences between words: what are the phonemes? Next, a phonologist tries to figure out the different allophones of each phoneme by identifying predictable patterns of complementary distribution. Answering questions about contrast and predictability of sounds in a language is the main work of phonology.

Languages do not allow random sequences of sounds; rather, the sound sequences a language allows are a systematic and predictable part of its structure. Languages have phonotactic constraints – restrictions on the types of sounds that are allowed to occur next to each other or in particular positions in the word. In English, for example, no word begins with the sequence [tl]. There are words like *train* and *plane*, but no *tlane*. This sequence is perfectly pronounceable and occurs in other languages (e.g. Navajo [tlee] 'night'). The sequence can occur in English if the two sounds are in different syllables, as in *At.lan.tic*. But English has a phonotactic constraint: *tl* ("t-l is illicit") at the beginning of a syllable – and therefore at the beginning of a word, as well. (The asterisk is used to indicate any sequence that is not possible in a given language.)

Another phonotactic constraint of English limits the sounds that are allowed to follow the diphthong [aʊ]. We have many words like *out, crowd, town, mouse, couch, south,* and *rouse.* But there are no words *aup, *auk, *aub, *awm, *aug, etc. If you make a list of all the [aʊ] words you can think of, you will discover that the only sounds allowed to follow [aʊ] are those made with the tongue tip and blade: [t], [d], [s], [z], [n], [θ], [ð], [tʃ], [dʒ] (and possibly [l] and [r], if you say *owl* and *hour* as one syllable). So one way of stating this English phonotactic constraint would be "The diphthong [aʊ] can only be followed by [t], [d], [s], [z], [n], [θ], [ð], [tʃ], [dʒ]." But we can do better. We want to capture the *generalization* that these sounds are not a random list, but all share some property. A better way to state this constraint is "The diphthong [aʊ] can only be followed by a consonant made with the tongue front." Phonological constraints seldom (if ever) target random collections of sounds. Rather, they almost always target groups of sounds that have one or more phonetic properties in common. Such groups are called **natural classes**.

One of the most common phonotactic constraints across languages is "Nasals must agree in place of articulation with a following stop." Think of English words that have a sequence of nasal + oral stop: *camp, hamper, bombard, paint, intelligent, wind, window*. Though there are some exceptions, the general pattern is for the bilabial stops [p] and [b] to be preceded by the bilabial nasal [m] and for the alveolar stops [t] and [d] to be preceded by the alveolar nasal [n]. What about words with [k] and [g]? We spell these words *nk* and *ng*, but if you listen carefully to your pronunciation of words like *think* and *linguistics*, you'll realize that these sequences are really [ŋk] and [ŋg] (the velar nasal [ŋ] preceding the velar stops [k] and [g]), and thus also follow the constraint. (Many words whose spelling ends in *ng*, like *sing* and *rang*, actually end in just the nasal [ŋ], with no [g] stop at all.)

There are many different phonetic dimensions that can define natural classes. Voicing is often important in phonotactic constraints. A common constraint is that sequences of obstruents must be either all voiced or all voiceless. In Russian, there are words like [vzbutʃki] 'scolding' and [fspleska] 'splash,' but not *[fzputʃgi]. In English, we have [sɪksθs], but not *[sɪksθz]. In native Japanese words (borrowings from Chinese or other languages are exempt), there can be only one voiced obstruent per word. So there are words like [saki] 'wine,' [kaze] 'wind,' and [zaseki] 'seat' (each with one or more voiceless obstruents), but there is no *[gaze] or *[guda].

Phonotactic constraints are often related to syllable structure. Many languages put constraints on the types of syllables they will allow. All languages allow syllables of the CV (Consonant–Vowel) type – that is, with an onset and a nucleus, but without a coda. This is the least marked and most common type of syllable. Some languages, like the West African language Senufo, allow only CV syllables. The preference for CV syllables results from two phonotactic constraints: "Syllables must have onsets" (a C before the V), and "Syllables must not have codas" (no C after the V).

Some languages have only one of these constraints. Hawai'ian, for example, does not allow codas, but does allow syllables that don't have onsets. Therefore, it allows syllables of the type V and CV, but never CVC. Hawai'an is also famous for having one of the smallest segmental inventories around – only five vowels [i, e, a, o, u] and eight consonants [p, k, ?, l, w, n, m, h]. That gives a grand total of 45 possible syllables (5 V and 40 CV combinations) to encode the thousands of words in the language. How do you use 45 syllables to make thousands of words? Hawai'ian words can be very, very long, with lots of repetition! The state fish, for example, is called the [hu.mu.hu.mu.nu.ku.nu.ku.a.pu.a.ʔa]. Note that every syllable is either CV or V, and that [ʔ] functions as a regular consonant.

Other languages allow CV and CVC but not VC. Every syllable in these languages must have an onset. Arabic and German are languages of this type. Words that are spelled with initial vowels in writing are actually pronounced with an initial glottal stop – for example, [ʔapfel] 'apple' in German, and [ʔal] 'the' in Arabic.

Many languages that allow syllables to have codas (CVC and VC) limit the sounds that can occur there. These restrictions are called **coda constraints**. In Thai, [p], [pʰ], and [b] may occur in onsets, but only [p] may appear in the coda. In Japanese, the only coda consonants allowed are nasals or the first half of geminates: [nip.pon] 'Japan,' [ʃim.bun] 'newspaper,' [gak.ko] 'school.' Constraints on onsets exist (e.g. no [ŋ] in onsets in English), but are much rarer. Finally, many languages allow at most one consonant in the coda and one in the onset. English is rather rare in allowing CCVCC, or even CCCVCCC words, like *shrink* or *sprints*. Russian words like [fspleska] (four consonants in a row) are rarer still.

> BOX 1.5 **PHONOTACTICS AND BORROWING**
>
> Phonotactic constraints often give rise to interesting forms when a more constrained language borrows a word from a less constrained language. Japan, for example, has borrowed the game of baseball from America, and many of the terms that go with it. But English baseball terms must be adapted to the syllable constraints of the Japanese language. A common strategy is to insert extra vowels to break up consonant clusters and turn codas into onsets. So *bat* becomes [bat.to], *strike* becomes [su.to.rai.ku], and *baseball* becomes [be.su.bu.ro]. Hawai'ian has the double challenge of a restricted inventory of sounds and limited syllable structure possibilities. The phrase *Merry Christmas* becomes [meli kalikimaki] in Hawai'ian. It looks unrecognizable, but you can easily work it out: change [r] into [l], [s] into [k], and add vowels as needed. Note that even English speakers don't pronounce the [t].
>
> Of course, English does the same with words it borrows from other languages. We pronounce *futon* as [futon] not [ɸuton], and the country of Qatar (pronounced, in Arabic, just like it's spelled [qatar]) as *cutter*. In those rare cases where we borrow a word from a language that allows even more syllable types than we do, the English strategy tends to be to drop the offending consonants rather than insert extra vowels. Greek, for example, allows words to begin with [pn] and [ps] as in [pneu] 'breath' and [psaike] 'spirit.' We preserve the Greek origin of words like *pneumonia* and *psychology* in the spelling, but not the pronunciation.

Alternation and allomorphs

Phonology is about contrast and predictability. We want to know what sounds in a language are contrastive phonemes, and we want to be able to predict the contexts in which the different allophones of a phoneme appear. Sometimes we do this by studying lists of words in order to discover different kinds of sound distributions. Sometimes we look at what happens to borrowed words. Another way is by studying **alternations**.

An alternation is seen when the same **morpheme** is pronounced different ways depending on the context. A morpheme is any entry in your mental dictionary; it can be a word or a part of a word, like a prefix (added to the beginning of a word) or a suffix (added to the end of a word). For example, in English, *cat* is a morpheme, and so is the plural suffix -*s*. As we put different morphemes together to create larger words, we create different contexts. Depending on the context, different forms of the morpheme, different **allomorphs**, are pronounced. The same phonotactic constraints that disallow certain sequences of sounds *within* morphemes also give rise to alternations when the combination of morphemes creates new environments that violate phonotactic constraints.

We saw that, within morphemes in English, nasals agree with the place of articulation of a following stop: remember *camp*, *wind*, and *think*. Because these nasals are within a single morpheme, we never see alternations in how they are pronounced. But some English prefixes that end with a nasal are pronounced differently when the prefix is added to words beginning with different sounds. Consider the negative prefix *in*-. Before a vowel or an alveolar, *in*- is pronounced [ɪn]: *inedible, inaudible, indelible, intolerable, insufferable*. But before the bilabials [m], [b], or [p], it becomes [ɪm]: *immovable, imbalance*, *impartial*. And before [k] or [g], it's pronounced [ɪŋ]. We don't change the spelling, because English doesn't have a separate letter for the velar nasal, but listen to your pronunciation of a word like *incorrect* and you'll realize the nasal is velar rather than alveolar. The phonotactic constraint "Nasals must agree in place of articulation with a following stop" applies not just within morphemes (like *camp* and *wind*) but also when morphemes are combined.

Natural classes help us to define the set of sounds that is targeted for alternation, the change itself, and the environments where the change takes place. This can be clearly seen in the case of the Spanish voiced stops and fricatives described above. We noted there that /d/ has two allophones in Spanish: [d] in initial position, and [ð] following a vowel. But the change is not limited to /d/ alone. It also affects /b/ and /g/. Whenever a voiced stop [b, d, g] follows a vowel, it changes to the corresponding voiced fricative [β, ð, ɣ].

[barselona]	'Barcelona'	[a βarselona]	'to Barcelona'
[bola]	'ball'	[la βola]	'the ball'
[data]	'date'	[la ðata]	'the date'
[gata]	'female cat'	[la ɣata]	'the female cat'

The set of sounds that undergoes change is a natural class: voiced stops. They all undergo the same change; they become voiced fricatives. And the environment in which the change occurs can be defined by a single phonetic parameter: after sounds that have an open vocal tract and continuous flow of air, like vowels, [s], and [r].

Types of phonological alternations

There are certain types of phonological processes that we find over and over again across languages. (See Chapter 8 for more examples of the following alternations in a diachronic (across time) perspective.)

Assimilation

The most common type of alternation is **assimilation**: two sounds that are different become more alike. Assimilation may be either *local*, when the two sounds are next to each other, or *long-distance*, where two sounds seem to affect each other even through other intervening segments.

Voicing assimilation is one very common alternation across languages. In English, the plural suffix agrees in voicing with a previous stop: *two cats* [kæts] and *two dogs* [dagz]. Another example is seen in Russian. The Russian word for 'from' is either [ot] or [od]: [od vzbútʃki] 'from a scolding,' [ot fspléska] 'from a splash.'

Local assimilation may also affect place of articulation. The English negative prefix *in-* is an example of a nasal assimilating in place of articulation to a following stop (*indecent* vs. *impossible*). Another example comes from Twi, a language of West Africa.

me-pɛ	'I like'	me-m-pɛ	'I do not like'
me-tɔ	'I buy'	me-n-tɔ	'I do not buy'
me-ka	'I say'	me-ŋ -ka	'I do not say'

The morpheme that means 'not' in Twi has three different allomorphs. It is always produced as a nasal consonant, but the nasal takes on the place of articulation of whatever consonant it's next to – bilabial next to bilabial, velar next to velar, etc.

The most extreme type of local assimilation is complete assimilation: two sounds that are next to each other become identical. Complete assimilation of adjacent vowels is found in many West African languages. In Yoruba, for example [ow**o**] 'money' plus [**e**po] 'oil' becomes [ow**ee**po] 'oil money.' In Igbo, [nwok**e**] 'man' plus [**a**] 'determiner' becomes [nwo**kaa**] 'that man.' The English prefix /ɪn/ can also undergo complete assimilation in certain words. Before most consonants, the nasal assimilates just to the place of articulation, as in *impartial*. But before [l] or [r], the assimilation of the nasal is total: *in + relevant* becomes *irrelevant*, *in + legible* becomes *illegible*.

Assimilation can also take place long-distance. Two segments that are not immediately adjacent may come to share some phonetic property. Vowel harmony is the prime example of long-distance assimilation. For example, in Turkish, the vowels in a word must be all front or all back, and the high vowels must be all round or all unround. The suffix meaning (roughly) 'of' therefore has different allomorphs, depending on the quality of the vowel in the preceding syllable: [ip-in] 'of the rope,' [pul-un] 'of the stamp.' In harmony systems, the vowels assimilate to each other, even though consonants intervene. Consonant harmonies also exist, though they are rarer.

Dissimilation

The opposite of assimilation is **dissimilation**. Two sounds that are similar become different. One impetus for dissimilation may be ease of articulation. Two sounds that are similar but not exactly the same seem to be particularly difficult to pronounce correctly right next to each other. (This principle forms the basis of many tongue twisters, such as the *sixth sheik's sixth sheep*.) One solution to the problem would be to make the similar sounds identical; another solution is to make them more different. An example of dissimilation is found in the history of Greek. In Ancient Greek, the word for *school* was [sxolio], with two adjacent voiceless fricatives. In Modern Greek, this has become [skolio], with a fricative–stop sequence instead. Dissimilation may also help hearers to realize that two segments are present, not just one. In Setswana (spoken in Botswana), voiced stops become voiceless after a (voiced) nasal consonant, perhaps to make the presence of the stop more obvious: [bona] 'see' becomes [mpona] 'see me.'

Insertion

Another common type of alternation is insertion (which phonologists call **epenthesis**). Insertion is usually related to syllable structure, as we saw above, when vowels are inserted to break up strings of consonants. This can happen in loan words (as in Japanese and Hawai'ian) or when morphemes come together. In English, when we want to add the plural suffix [z] to a word that already ends in [s] or [z], we insert a vowel [ɨ] to break up the two high-pitched fricatives: one dress [drɛs], two dresses [drɛsɨz].

Deletion

The opposite of insertion, of course, is **deletion**. Instead of breaking up a sequence of consonants with a vowel, a language may choose to delete one of the consonants (as in the loss of the initial [p] in *pneumonia*). *Grand* ends with [nd], *mother* starts with [m], but when the two words are put together, the medial [d] is usually deleted: [grænmʌðə.]. (The [n] may then assimilate to the [m], resulting in [græmmmʌðər].) Lardil (a language spoken in Australia) deletes final vowels from words of three or more syllables: [yalulu] 'flame' becomes [yalul].

Lenition and fortition

Another type of change is **lenition** – sounds become softer or weaker. Stops change to fricatives, fricatives change to approximants. The Spanish alternation [b, d, g] becomes [β, ð, ɣ] is an example of lenition. The opposite of lenition is **fortition**. Here, fricatives change into stops, as in Kikuyu (East Africa) "postnasal hardening": [ɣora] 'buy,' [ŋgoreetɛ] 'I have bought.'

Metathesis and reduplication

Other less common alternations include **metathesis** and **reduplication**. Metathesis means switching the order of sounds. For example, the English word *horse* used to be [hros], before the [ro] sequence was metathesized. Reduplication means copying. In English, we sometimes copy parts of words to convey a pejorative, diminutive sense: *teeny-tiny*, *itsy-bitsy*, or the more dismissive *syntax-schmintax*. But in other languages it's a regular part of the sound system. In Manam (Austronesian), [gara] means 'scrape' and [gara-gara-si] means 'scraping it.' You may also recall Hawai'ian [humuhumunukunukuapuaʔa] and Lardil [ʧumpuʧumpu].

Discovering alternations

The first step in doing an analysis of phonological alternation is to identify the different forms of the morpheme that need to be accounted for. The past-tense suffix in English has three forms: [t] as in *reached* [ritʃt], [d] as in *mowed* [moːd], and [ɨd] as in *rotted* [raɾɨd]. Table 1.7 gives a list of various words that take each suffix. The transcriptions show the pronunciation of the unsuffixed verb. (Transcription is broad, and noncontrastive details not relevant to the alternation are not included.)

As analysts, we want to discover if the alternation is conditioned by phonological environment. Therefore, the next step (as with an allophone analysis) is to list the environments where each allomorph occurs. In fact, the steps in doing a phoneme/allophone analysis and a morpheme alternation analysis are pretty much the same. The difference is one of focus. In a phoneme/allophone analysis, the linguist is looking at the distribution of sounds across the entire lexicon (though of course in a textbook example or exercise one can only look at a subset of representative words). In a morpheme alternation analysis, the linguist is looking at the variant forms of a specific word or affix. In both cases, however,

TABLE 1.7 Allomorphs of the English past-tense suffix

	[t]		[d]		[ɨd]
reached	[ritʃ]	mowed	[mo]	rotted	[rat]
ripped	[rɪp]	fibbed	[fɪb]	prodded	[prad]
laughed	[laf]	loved	[lʌv]	lifted	[lɪft]
camped	[kæmp]	rammed	[ræm]	boosted	[bust]
missed	[mɪs]	blazed	[blez]	carded	[kard]
reversed	[rivɝs]	blared	[bler]	handed	[hænd]
refreshed	[rifrɛʃ]	edged	[ɛdʒ]	created	[kriet]
picked	[pɪk]	begged	[bɛg]	crafted	[kræft]
inked	[ɪŋk]	banged	[bæŋ]	ranted	[rænt]
helped	[hɛlp]	canned	[kæn]	belted	[bɛlt]
milked	[mɪlk]	failed	[fel]	hated	[het]
hoped	[hop]	sued	[su]	asserted	[əsɝt]

the overall goal is the same: to discover which aspects of sound structure are contrastive and which are predictable according to the environment.

The environments for the variants of the English past-tense suffix are shown in Table 1.8. Since the alternating morpheme is a suffix, we can begin with the hypothesis that it is the final sound of the stem that conditions the change.

We can immediately note that the allomorphs are in complementary distribution: no sound occurs in more than one list. We can also note that each list forms a class that can be defined in phonetic terms: [ɨd] occurs following alveolar stops, [t] occurs following all other voiceless sounds, and [d] occurs following all other voiced sounds.

Further, we can see the activity of phonotactic constraints in motivating the alternation. The [ɨ] is inserted to break up a cluster of consonants ([td] or [dd]) that would otherwise be unpronounceable at the end of a word. The change from [d] to [t] after voiceless consonants brings the sequence into line with the constraint that requires obstruent clusters to agree in voicing. As was noted above, the phonotactic constraints rule out marked structures: the clusters that are "fixed up" are either hard to hear (like a second [d] in [hænddd], or hard to produce (like switching voicing twice in the middle of a consonant cluster like [lpd]).

To finish the analysis, we need to decide on the basic form of the morpheme, and state the generalizations that derive each of the variant forms. Here, we can be secure in choosing [d] as the elsewhere case, as the set of sounds that take [d] is the most diverse: vowels, sonorants, and voiced obstruents. (This set does in fact form the natural class of

TABLE 1.8 Environments for the English past-tense suffix

[t]	[d]	[ɨd]
tʃ __	o __	t __
p __	b __	d __
f __	v __	
s __	m __	
ʃ __	z __	
k __	r __	
p __	dʒ __	
	g __	
	ŋ __	
	n __	
	l __	
	u __	

voiced sounds, but that is more or less accidental: a suffix has to follow something, and if a sound isn't voiceless it has to be voiced.) We can take care of the problem of making sure that [t] and [d] get their own special form by applying the rule for the most specific case first. (This idea of taking the most specific case first, thus getting it out of the way so that succeeding statements could be made more generally, is originally due to the ancient Indian grammarian Pāṇini, and is still known as Pāṇini's Theorem.)

The overall generalization for forming the English past tense can be stated as:

a. The underlying form of the past-tense suffix is /d/
b. If the suffix is added to a word that ends with /t/ or /d/, a vowel is inserted to derive the surface form [ɨd], *otherwise*
c. If the suffix is added to a word that ends with a voiceless consonant, the surface form is [t], *otherwise*
d. The surface form is [d].

Phonological theory

The preceding sections have discussed some contrasts and alternations that are common in human languages. But phonologists want to know more than this. They want a generalization, not just a list. Phonologists don't want to know just "What is the inventory of sounds in Polish?" but "What is a possible inventory in any language?" They want to know not just "What alternations are common across languages?" but "What alternations are possible in any language?" They want to know not just "How are Russian and Ukrainian different?" but "How different can languages be?"

We have seen that languages choose different phonetic dimensions (different vocal tract gestures) to encode their contrasts. Voicing, aspiration, manner, and place of articulation can all be used contrastively. Similarly, we have seen these same dimensions used to define sets of sounds that are relevant for phonological alternations. Distinctive feature theory aims to encode all the phonetic dimensions that languages have available to encode contrasts and natural classes.

The linguist Roman Jakobson (1896–1982) proposed that each relevant dimension could be thought of as a plus or minus contrast. The speaker chooses whether a sound will be [+voice] (with vocal fold vibration) or [–voice] (without vocal fold vibration); [+nasal] (open velum) or [–nasal] (closed velum); [+sonorant] (a sonorant sound, without airstream obstruction) or [–sonorant] (an obstruent sound, with airstream obstruction); [–continuant] (a stop) or [+continuant] (not a stop), etc. Jakobson proposed both an acoustic and an articulatory definition for each of his features.

Every phoneme could be defined in terms of a set of distinctive features: [m], for example, would be [+labial, +nasal]. Features could also be used to define natural classes, and the changes that affect them. The class of voiced stops in Spanish would be [–sonorant, –continuant, +voice], and the change from stop to fricative would be [–continuant] becomes [+continuant].

By proposing a fixed, finite set of universal features, Jakobson attempted to define all the phonetic dimensions that could be phonologically relevant – that is, that could be used for contrasts and alternations. A possible human language would use these, and only these, features. Many of the features Jakobson proposed are still in use today; others have been replaced or refined.

Phonologists are also concerned with describing the relationship between phonemes (the **underlying representation**, or UR – the way words are stored in the brain) and allophones (the **surface representation**, or SR – the way words are actually pronounced). Noam Chomsky and Morris Halle in their influential 1968 book, *The Sound Pattern of English*, proposed that allophones are derived from phonemes by the application of **phonological rules**. These rules took the form

X → Y/A __ B

where X is the class of sounds affected, Y is the change, and A__B is the context, all written in terms of distinctive features. The rule above can be read "X becomes Y in the context of between A and B" or "AXB becomes AYB." Other special characters were used for word and morpheme boundaries: #___ means "word-initial position," and___# means "word-final position." Can you read the following two phonological rules, which describe alternations discussed above?

Rule 1:   [–continuant, –voice] → [+aspirated]/#___
Rule 2:   [–continuant, –sonorant, +voice] → [+continuant]/[+continuant]___

The first rule states that a voiceless stop becomes aspirated when it is produced at the beginning of a word. This describes word-initial aspiration of [p], [t], and [k] in English. The second rule states that a voiced stop becomes continuant (that is, a fricative) when it follows another nonstop sound. This describes how a voiced stop in Spanish [b, d, g] changes to voiced fricatives [β, ð, ɣ] whenever it is preceded by a vowel.

In a **derivation**, rules change the UR into the SR. Recall the discussion, above, of the pronunciation of the word *grandmother*. The basic, underlying, representation has a sequence of three consonants [ndm] in the middle. First, this sequence is simplified, by deletion of the [d]. Then, the [n] assimilates in place of articulation to the following [m], to which it is now adjacent. The result is that the medial consonants are in fact pronounced [mm]. A derivation shows this series of changes. Thus, the derivation of [græmmʌðər] looks like this:

Underlying representation:	grændmʌðər
Rule 1, deletion:	grænmʌðər
Rule 2, assimilation:	græmmʌðər
Surface representation:	græmmʌðər

Phonologists have proposed different ways of writing rules. For example, it might make more sense to think of assimilation as feature *sharing* rather than feature changing. One might write a rule of voicing assimilation by diagramming a single feature being shared from one consonant to another:

[–voice]

k æ t s

This way of writing rules is called **autosegmental representation**, because the features are treated as autonomous from the string of segments.

More recently, phonologists have questioned whether phonological rules are the best way to think of the relationship between underlying and surface representations. Rules can describe alternations, but they don't capture the fact that alternations tend to take place for a reason – to bring words into conformity with **phonotactic constraints**. Recent work in phonology has emphasized the importance of constraints in mediating between under-lying and surface representations. Such work proposes that all languages share the same set of constraints, but rank them differently. A given form may violate a lower-ranked constraint in order to meet a more important one. For instance, the pronunciation of /grændmʌðər/ as [græmmʌðər] indicates that English places a higher priority on the constraint that says "Don't have three consonants in a row" than on the constraint that says "every segment in the UR must appear in the SR."

CHAPTER SUMMARY

The goal of this chapter has been to describe the sounds of speech, from the point of view of a phonetician and of a phonologist. Phoneticians study the physical aspects of linguistic sounds: Movements of the structures of the vocal tract, place and manner of articulation, the propagation of sound waves through the air, hearing and **speech perception**, computer measurement of fundamental frequency and formant structure. Phonologists study the more abstract organization of sound patterns: syllable structure, phonotactic constraints, alternations, the relationship between underlying and surface representations.

We began this chapter by posing questions that phonologists and phoneticians ask, and have attempted to survey some of the preliminary answers that have been proposed. Phonologists and phoneticians have learned a lot about how speech sounds are made, how they are perceived, and how they are organized. But many questions remain.

- What new sounds and sound patterns remain to be discovered?
- How can we best (and most quickly) describe and preserve the sounds and sound patterns of the diverse languages that are dying out?
- As we gain more and more knowledge of how our mouths and ears work (from more and more sophisticated measuring devices), how can we incorporate this knowledge into our acoustic and articulatory models?
- As we gain more and more knowledge of how our brains work, how can we incorporate this knowledge into our phonological models?
- How do cognitive patterns and articulatory events influence and constrain each other?
- What is the right set of distinctive features? Are phonological features and articulatory gestures one and the same?
- Is the relationship between underlying and surface representation rule-based or constraint-based?
- How can we account for language change and language variation?
- How can we better understand how children acquire the phonology and phonetics of their native language?
- How can we better understand the process of learning a non-native language, and help those who are struggling to do so?

The studies that will answer these questions remain to be written.

Exercises

EXERCISES 1.1

Draw a mid-sagittal diagram of the vocal tract, using Figure 1.2 as a model. In your diagram:

- shade the larynx yellow
- shade the pharynx green
- shade the oral cavity red
- shade the nasal cavity blue

Then, label each of the active and passive articulators:

- trace the active articulators in red
- trace the passive articulators in blue

EXERCISE 1.2

Fill in the blanks to describe these consonants of English:

	Voicing	Nasality	Place of articulation	Manner of articulation	Sonorant/ obstruent
m	voiced	nasal	bilabial	stop	sonorant
s	voiceless	oral	alveolar	fricative	obstruent
g					
ʃ					
n					
d					
f					
ð					

EXERCISE 1.3

Fill in the blanks to describe the vowel symbols:

	Height	Front/back	Rounding	Tense/lax
ɪ	high	front	unround	lax
i				
ɛ				
o				
æ				
ɔ				
ʊ				

EXERCISE 1.4

Transcribe the following words in IPA:

transcribe	housetop	thoughtful	baseball
yellow	beans	annoyed	caught
computing	climb	joyous	code
movie	flimsy	than	spring break
phonology	books	choice	sunrise

EXERCISE 1.5

Write out the following passage (from Sapir 1933) in English orthography. Note that the symbol [ɾ] stands for an alveolar "tap," an allophone of American English t and d found in pretty ['prɪɾi] and later ['leɾər]. The symbol ['] precedes the stressed syllable.

ðə 'kansɛpt əv ðə 'fonim, ə 'fʌnkʃənəli sɪg'nɪfɪkənt 'junɪt ɪn ðə 'rɪdʒɪdli də'faɪnd 'parərn ɔr kʌnfɪgjə'reʃən əv saʊndz pə'kjulər tu ə 'læŋgwɪdʒ, æz dɪ'stɪnkt frəm ðæt əv ðə saʊnd ɔr fə'nɛrɪk 'ɛləmɛnt æz sʌtʃ, æn əb'dʒɛktɪvli də'faɪnəbəl 'ɛntɪɾi ɪn ði ar'tɪkjulerɪd ænd pɛr'sivd to'tælɪɾi əv spitʃ, ɪz bi'kʌmɪŋ mɔr ænd mɔr fə'mɪljər tu 'lɪŋgwists. ðə 'dɪfɪkəlti ðæt 'mɛni stɪl sim tə fil ɪn dɪs'tɪŋgɪʃɪŋ bə'twin ðə tu mʌst ə'vɛntʃuəli dɪsə'pir æz ðə rilə'zeʃən groz ðæt no 'ɛntɪɾi ɪn 'hjumən ɛk'spiriəns kæn bi 'ærəkwɪtli də'faɪndæz ðe mə'kænɪkəl sʌm̩ ɔr 'pradəkt əv ɪts 'fɪsɪkəl 'prapərtiz.

EXERCISE 1.6

Transcribe the following words, and draw a syllable tree for each. Explain how sonority is relevant in assigning sequences of consonants to the onset or coda.

arthritis
handbag
complained
linguist

EXERCISE 1.7

Make a list of American English words that contain the sequence [ju], such as beautiful and music. What natural class of consonants is prohibited from preceding [ju]?

EXERCISE 1.8

Consider the distribution of voiced and voiceless vowels in Japanese (data from Tsuchida 1996). Are [i] and [i̥] representatives of two distinct phonemes, or are they allophones of a single phoneme? What about [u] and [u̥]? Argue for your answer, either by citing (near-)minimal pairs from the data, or by describing the distributions of two sounds.

All voiced vowels:

kokoro	'heart'
sensei	'teacher'
kakko	'parenthesis'
suberu	'slip'
buka	'subordinate'
kidoo	'orbit'
omoʃiroi	'interesting'
banira	'vanilla'
jume	'dream'

Some voiceless vowels:

su̥peru	'spell'
ɸu̥ka	'incubation'
ki̥too	'prayer'
kosu̥to	'cost'

çiᶦtoo	'hit'
ʃuᶦto	'capital'
kiᶦppari	'clearly'
ɸuᶦkaɸuᶦka	'soft'
suᶦtasuᶦta	'quickly'
kokuᶦsai	'international'
suᶦʃimai	'sushi rice'

EXERCISE 1.9

Consider the distribution of [l] and [lʲ] (a palatalized version of [l], with a raised and fronted tongue body position) in Russian. Do they represent two different phonemes, or are they allophones of a single phoneme? Argue for your answer, either by citing (near-)minimal pairs from the data, or by describing the distributions of two sounds (data courtesy of Maria Gouskova).

Words with [l]:

lat	'agreement'
gala	'gala'
polka	'shelf'
mel	'chalk'
pol	'heat'

Words with [lʲ]:

milʲ	'of miles'
nebolʲ	'imaginary tale'
lʲat	'demon'
lʲot	'ice'
molʲ	'moth'
polʲka	'polka'

EXERCISE 1.10

Consider the distribution of [k] (voiceless velar stop) and [x] (voiceless velar fricative) in Florentine Italian (data from Villafana 2006). Do they represent two different phonemes, or allophones of the same phoneme? Argue for your answer, either by citing (near-)minimal pairs from the data, or by describing the distributions of two sounds.

laxasa	'the house'
poxo	'little'
bixa	'stack'
amixo	'friend'
fixi	'figs'
kwuoxo	'cook'
kwando	'when'
kapella	'chapel'
blalʲko	'white'
makkina	'machine'
kabina	'booth'

EXERCISE 1.11

Consider the following alternations that occur in English. Describe each as assimilation, dissimilation, lenition, fortition, epenthesis, or deletion. For each, list three more words that undergo the alternation.

a. Vowels are nasalized before a nasal consonant, in words such as *camper* [kæ̃mpər], *wrong* [rɔ̃ŋ], and *tone* [tõn].

b. In some dialects, [ð] and [θ] are pronounced [d] and [t], in words such as *then* [dɛn], *thin* [tɪn], and *mouth* [mɔt].

c. In many dialects, [r] is not pronounced when it follows a vowel, as in *car* [ka], *park* [pak], and *sure* [ʃuə].

d. Words with a sequence of nasal plus fricative are sometimes pronounced with a stop between nasal and fricative: *tense* [tɛnts], *something* [sʌmpθɪŋ], *sense* [sɛnts].

e. The prefix *con-*, meaning 'with,' has three different allomorphs: *conduct* [kəndʌkt], *complain* [kəmplen], *congress* [kaŋgrɛs].

SUGGESTIONS FOR FURTHER READING

Johnson, Keith 2003, *Acoustic and auditory phonetics*, 2nd edition, Oxford and Malden, MA: Blackwell. A very readable introduction to the physics of sound, speech perception, and computer speech processing.

Kachru, Braj, Kachru, Yamuna, and Nelson, Cecil (eds.) 2009, *The handbook of World Englishes*, Oxford and Malden, MA: Blackwell. Forty-two chapters by expert authors cover the history and variety of the international dialects of English.

Kenstowicz, Michael 1994, *Generative phonology*, Oxford and Malden, MA: Blackwell. A more advanced and thorough introduction to phonology, with extensive data sets.

Ladd, D. R. 2000, *Intonational phonology*, Cambridge University Press. Introduction to the study of intonation from a linguistic perspective.

Ladefoged, Peter, and Johnson, Keith 2010, *A course in phonetics*, 6th edition, Wadsworth Publishing. A practical guide to phonetics, emphasizing practice in articulation and transcription.

Ladefoged, Peter and Maddieson, Ian 1996, *The sounds of the world's languages*, Oxford and Malden, MA: Blackwell. A survey and detailed description of the articulation and acoustics of all the sounds in the IPA chart.

Spencer, Andrew 1996, *Phonology*, Oxford and Malden, MA: Blackwell. A very accessible introductory text.

Wolfram, Walt and Schilling-Estes, Natalie 2005. *American English: dialects and variation*, Oxford and Malden, MA Blackwell. As the title states, a survey of the varieties of English spoken in the United States.

Yip, Moira 2002, *Tone*, Cambridge University Press. A comprehensive overview of tonal phonology.

2 Words and their parts

KEY TERMS

- ablaut
- affix
- agreement
- aspect
- base
- case
- compound
- derivation
- feature
- gender
- infix
- inflection
- lexeme
- lexicon
- mood
- morpheme
- morphology
- number
- paradigm
- person
- prefix
- reduplication
- (ir)regular verb
- root
- stem
- suffix
- suppletion
- tense
- word
- zero derivation

CHAPTER PREVIEW

This chapter introduces the subject of morphology, the study of the internal structure of words and their meaningful parts. Morphological processes accomplish two basic purposes: (1) to create new words in a language and (2) to modify existing words. We may associate a word with a certain basic idea, image or event, but modifying the exact form of a word can also contribute important information, such as who is participating in an event, when or how it occurred, or something about the speaker's attitude toward it. The more complex the word, the more information of this sort it is likely to convey. By manipulating various parts of a word, we can shade, intensify, or even negate its basic meaning, or change its grammatical role within a sentence. Different languages, of course, have different ways of doing this.

GOALS

The goals of this chapter are to:

- **introduce key concepts in the study of complex word analysis**
- **provide a concise description of some of the varied morphological phenomena found among the world's languages**
- **illustrate methods used to derive and support linguistic generalizations about word structure in particular languages**
- **touch briefly on how knowledge of complex word forms comes to be acquired**

What is a word?

Imagine you were in an environment where everyone around you was speaking a language you'd never heard before, and you couldn't understand a single word of what they were saying. That typical phrase – "couldn't understand a single word" – underscores our intuition that words are the fundamental building blocks of language. The foremost task of any language learner, including young children acquiring their native language, is to figure out how to segment and analyze the wall of talking-noise around them into meaningful units – namely, words and their meaningful parts.

But what is a word, exactly? *Webster's Unabridged Dictionary* (1989) defines a *word* as the smallest independent unit of language, or one that can be separated from other such units in an utterance. In the following conversational exchange, (1b) demonstrates the independence of the word *tea*.

(1)   a. Which do you like better – coffee or *tea*?
     b. *Tea.*

Words can enter into grammatical constructions, such as phrases and sentences. For example, the word *tea* can be used in different positions in a sentence according to its grammatical role:

(2)   a. *Tea* is good for you.
     b. She doesn't drink *tea*.
     c. There are beneficial antioxidants in *tea*.

Tea is the subject of the sentence in (2a), the direct object in (2b), and the object of a preposition in (2c).

Our definition from *Webster's* continues: words are "usually separated by spaces in writing and distinguished phonologically, as by accent" (p. 1643). But this is only partially accurate. Although spaces are placed between words in the written form of many languages (like English), orthography (the written form of a language) cannot be a crucial component of wordhood. There are languages like Chinese which don't insert spaces between words in writing, but speakers of these languages still know what a word is in their language. Similarly, people who can't read and speakers of languages without writing systems know what words are in their languages, too.

On the other hand, phonology does play an important role across languages in identifying the boundaries between words. For example, consider the string /grinhaus/. (Recall from Chapter 1 that symbols between forward slashes represent how something is pronounced, using the phonemes of a language.) Phonological stress disambiguates the meaning of the utterances in (3a) and (3b), indicating that /grinhaus/ is a single (compound) word in (3a) but two distinct words in (3b):

(3)   a. They walked past a *GREENhouse*.
     b. They walked past a *green HOUSE*.

Phonology can help us identify words, but we need other information as well. Consider the following:

(4)   a. *Tea's* good for you.
        b. That shop sells *teas* from around the world.
        c. I asked him not to *tease* the cat.

Is *tea's* in (4a) one word or two? The sound form of *tea's* is phonetically identical to that of *teas* in (4b) and even *tease* in (4c); all are pronounced /tiz/. But your intuition is probably that the wordhood status of *tea's* is somehow grammatically different from that of *teas* or *tease*. There is an additional element in *tea's* which, although phonologically dependent on *tea* (as a contracted form of the word *is*), is nonetheless a distinct *grammatical* word.

Webster's also states that words are "typically thought of as representing an indivisible concept, action, or feeling, or as having a single referent." Clearly, the word *tease* in (4c) has a different referent than *teas* in (4b). But the word *teas* also means something a bit different than the simple word *tea* – something like 'more than one kind of tea.' This difference in meaning is conveyed by the ending *-s* (pronounced [z]) on the word *tea*. But this *-s* ending is not an independent word; rather, it must be attached directly to an independent word whose basic meaning it is modifying – in this case, to indicate *plural* meaning. We can conclude that even though *teas* is just one word, the *-s* ending is a distinct subpart that contributes some piece of additional information to the word's overall meaning.

It appears that we require a fairly complex definition of *word*, defining it in relation to meaning, grammar, and phonology. For now, let us more simply define a **word** (a surprisingly difficult term in linguistics) as an abstract sign that is the smallest grammatically independent unit of language.

All languages have words, but the particular sign a language uses to express a particular meaning is *arbitrary*. For example, there's nothing inherent in the sound form of the word *water* that actually carries the meaning of 'water.' French speakers refer to the very same stuff as *eau*, Japanese speakers call it *mizu*, and Italians *acqua*. The fingerspelled form of 'water' that was signed onto Helen Keller's outstretched palm as water flowed over the other enabled her to "break into" the system of words as abstract signs. Later, she would also learn how the meaning of 'water' was represented in another kind of abstract form – the system of raised dots known as Braille:

(5)

'water'

The human impulse to discover and create words, it seems, transcends even profound differences in physical capabilities.

The words of one's language make up its **lexicon**. One might think of the lexicon as a kind of mental dictionary where words are stored. Our knowledge of each word, like the lexical entries in a dictionary, includes several kinds of information. Consider what you know, for example, about the word *sleep*:

- how it is pronounced: /slip/
- what it means – informally, something like to repose or rest in the body's natural periodic unconscious state. Your knowledge of the meaning of *sleep* also includes the information that only animate objects – like babies, cats, and students (but not trees or ideas) – can get sleepy.
- the grammatical contexts in which the word can be used. *Sleep* is an intransitive verb (it doesn't take a direct object), as in the sentence *Sally sleeps late on weekends*. But it can also be a noun as in *John talks in his sleep*. It can be found in compound words such as *sleepwalking* and *sleep-deprived* and in idioms such as *let sleeping dogs lie*.
- that it is an **irregular** verb for past-tense marking in English, requiring that we memorize its past form *slept* /slɛpt/ instead of simply adding the regular past marker to produce *sleeped* /slipt/.

When you stop to consider for a moment all the (tens of thousands of) words that are in your lexicon and everything you already know about each of them, you can begin to appreciate the magnitude of the accomplishment of this impressive feat. Moreover, new items are continually being added, just as dictionaries are continually revised and updated (e.g. *beer goggles*, *DVD-player*). The meanings of the listed words might also change over time, or acquire (or lose) different shades of meaning (e.g. *dude*, *gay*).

However, the contemporary study of word formation is not as much about the study of existing, listed dictionary words as it is the study of *possible* words in one's language and the mental rules for constructing and understanding them. Not all of the words you can produce and interpret are listed in the lexicon, because the number of possible words is infinite. For example, a recent quick look through a single magazine turned up the following words:

(6)   outgeneraled
scrounginess
on-messagism
unanswerability
extraterritorialization
hyperparenting
transhumanists
balconied

In that same issue there were also many freely coined compound-word expressions, including the following:

(7)   thwack-time interval
poultry-litter composting
receipt-management strategy
cringe-making
floppy-haired
cultural studies semiotics junkies
snowy-headed
puzzled-chimp expression

It's possible that one of these newly created words will "stick" in your lexicon – perhaps popping up again someplace else as more people adopt it or maybe because you just like it. Most of these words, however, are destined to be immediately forgotten. But even though they are ephemeral, they demonstrate the human capacity to mentally represent the complex structure of words in one's language.

To further illustrate what you know about words, let's consider a word you're not likely to know (because I've made it up): *frimp*. If you heard it in the context of an English sentence such as *John likes to frimp on weekends*, then you would deduce that it's a verb that can be used intransitively (that is, without a direct object). And once you knew that, then even before learning its exact meaning (which would depend on the context and your knowledge that it's an "action"), you would already know how to construct several other word forms based on this verb. You'd know how to use its past form (*he frimped all day yesterday*) and progressive form (*he was in the kitchen frimping when I called*). You'd also know how to turn it into an adjective (*I wish he'd mend his frimping ways*). You would know to look up (or list) *frimp*, not *frimped* or *frimping*, as the "dictionary" form, because you'd assume that *frimp* is a **regular** verb. Since the *-ed* and *-ing* endings can attach to *all* regular verbs, the forms *frimped* and *frimping* don't really need to be listed in the lexical entry for *frimp*. You'd also know that John was a *frimper*. As you can see, you already know quite a lot about this hypothetical word!

Each language has its own rules and processes for creating new words, and these words are interpretable in their contexts even if they are never recorded in a dictionary. The forms of words may be simple or extremely complex; our knowledge of the mental rules and categories that enable us to produce and interpret them makes up the subject of morphology.

Morphology: the study of word structure

The branch of linguistics that is concerned with the relation between meaning and form, within words and between words, is known as **morphology**. Morphology literally means 'the study of form' – in particular, the forms of words. Although "form" in this context usually refers to the spoken sound or *phonological form* that is associated with a particular meaning, it doesn't necessarily have to – signed languages also have word forms. Instead of the articulators of the vocal tract, signed languages make use of the shape and movement of the hands. All languages, whether spoken or signed, have word forms.

Morphologists describe the constituent parts of words, what they mean, and how they may (and may not) be combined in the world's languages. The pairing of a meaning with a form applies to whole words, like *sleep*, as well as to parts of words like the 'past' meaning associated with the ending *-ed* as in *frimped*.

Morphology applies within words, as in the addition of a plural ending to *cat* /kæt/ to change its form to *cats* /kæts/ and its meaning to 'more than one cat.' It also applies across words, as when we alter the form of one word so that some part of it matches, or *agrees* with, some feature of another word, as shown in (8):

(8)   a. That cat sleep*s* all day.
      b. Those cat*s* sleep all day.

In the sentence in (8a), the word *cat* is a third-person singular (3SG) subject, which in most varieties of English requires that we add an *-s* to another word – the verb – when they occur together in a sentence. This verbal suffix "means" something like 'my subject is third person and singular.' In (8b), however, the word *cats* is plural, which in English doesn't require the verb to add any special agreeing form. (English is highly unusual among the world's languages in this regard!) In the examples above, notice that the words *that* and *those* also crossreference the singular vs. plural meaning distinction between *cat* and *cats*. This kind of morphological **agreement** between matching parts of words is widely observed among the world's languages.

Languages vary widely in their amount and functions of morphology (often as a result of historical development – see Chapter 8). For example, all languages need a way to signal grammatical roles such as subject and direct object (or, who did what to whom). English depends quite strictly on the order of words in a sentence to do this. The meaning of (9a) is very different from that of (9b):

(9)　a.　Brutus killed Caesar.
　　　b.　Caesar killed Brutus.

Latin, however, marks grammatical roles *morphologically*, and word order is consequently much freer; all the Latin sentences below mean 'Brutus killed Caesar':

(10)　*Latin* (Bauer 2003: 63)
　　　Brūtus Caesar*em* occīdit.
　　　Caesar*em* occīdit Brūtus.
　　　Occīdit Caesar*em* Brūtus.
　　　'Brutus killed Caesar.'

In Latin, the addition of *-em* to the noun *Caesar* indicates that Caesar is the direct object, or the one who got killed. (The subject, Brūtus, in this case is unmarked.) Here the morphological form of a noun, rather than its position in the sentence, signals its grammatical function. One of the most important functions of morphology is to distinguish the roles played by the various participants in an event; we could not interpret language without this information.

In the remainder of this chapter, we will examine some other functions of morphology, and also take a closer look at some key terms and concepts that linguists use to describe the processes of morphology.

Morphemes

We said earlier that *tea* and *teas* are both words with slightly different meanings, and that this difference is due to the *-s* ending on *teas*. But since *-s* is not itself a word, how can it have its own meaning? In fact, it is not words, but rather **morphemes**, that are the smallest units of language that combine both a form (the way they sound) and a meaning (what they mean). Words are made up of morphemes. Simple words consist of a single morpheme. Complex words consist of more than one morpheme. For example, *cat* is a simple word compared with *cats*, which contains two morphemes – the noun *cat* plus a plural marker -*s*. Similarly, in the word *unfriendly*, there are three morphemes: *un-*, *friend*, and -*ly*, each of which contributes some meaning to the overall word. Some words in morphologic-ally rich languages can contain so many morphemes that we need an entire complex sentence in English to translate them. Consider the following complex word from Turkish, which contains the lexical **root** *Avrupa* -'Europe' plus eleven additional morphemes (don't worry for now about the function of each morpheme as glossed below the word):

(11)   *Turkish* (Beard 1995: 56)
        Avrupalılaştırılamayacaklardansınız
        Avrupa-lı-laş-tır-ıl-a-ma-yacak-lar-dan-sın-ız
        Europe-an-ize-CAUSE-PASSIVE-POTENTIAL-NEG-FUT.PART-PL-ABL-2ND-PL
        'You (all) are among those who will not be able to be caused to become like Europeans.'

However, even in English, we can come up with a reasonably complex word that can more compactly express the approximate meaning of the latter part of the translation 'not able to be caused to become like Europeans':

(12)   You are among those who will be *unEuropeanizable*.
        The English word *unEuropeanizable* consists of the root *Europe* plus the morphemes *un-*, -*(i) an*, -*ize*, and -*able*. Each of these morphemes contributes to the overall meaning of the entire word.

> When a language has a morpheme with a grammatical meaning, we gloss it in small capital letters in the interlinear translation, in the same order in which the morphemes appear. So, in (11), tır means 'causative,' ıl means 'passive,' a means 'potential,' and so on. When a gloss appears with a dot within it, it means the morpheme includes both meanings, hence, acak means 'future participle' in Turkish. Example (11) has two morphemes glossed pl, for 'plural'; the first, lar, is the plural for the future participle, the second, ız, is the plural for second person.

In building words (and phrases and sentences), two basic kinds of morphemes are used. Morphemes with richer lexical "vocabulary" meaning (referring to things and qualities and actions in the world) are called lexical morphemes or **lexemes**. Lexemes typically belong to the "major" part-of-speech categories of nouns (N), verbs (V), or adjectives (A) (see Box 3.1 in Chapter 3); simple lexemes may serve as the root of more complex words. On the other hand, morphemes that contribute mainly grammatical information or indicate relationships between the lexemes are called **grammatical morphemes**. In the sentence in (13) below, the words *maniacal*, *little*, *dog*, *attempt*, *bite*, and *mailman* are all lexemes. The grammatical morphemes, which have been underlined, are *their*, -*al*, -*ed*, *to*, and *the*.

(13)   Their maniacal little dog attempted to bite the mailman.

Grammatical morphemes are the glue that holds the lexemes in a sentence together, shows their relations to each other, and also helps identify referents within a particular conversational context. In the sentence in (13), the pronoun *their* consists of grammatical features (third person, plural) that partially identify via agreement some previously mentioned referents (say, *John and Mary*), and simultaneously signals a possessor relation between them and the lexeme *dog*. Like the morpheme *the* (in the phrase *the mailman*), *their* also has definite reference, indicating that the speaker assumes the hearer knows who is being referred to. The past-tense marker *-ed* tells us that an event (the 'biting-attempt') has already happened. The morpheme *to* is a formal device (called an **infinitive** marker) for marking an untensed verb (*to bite*). Finally, although the word *maniacal* is a lexeme (because it is an adjective that refers to an attribute of the dog, just like *little*), it is a complex word derived by adding the morpheme *-al* to the root noun *maniac*. Thus, *-al* has the grammatical function of turning a noun into an adjective meaning 'having the qualities of' that noun.

Both lexemes and grammatical morphemes can be either **free** or **bound**. Bound morphemes must be attached either to a root or another morpheme, but free morphemes can stand alone. Most lexemes in English, such as *dog* and *bite*, are free morphemes. Suffixes, like *-ed* and *-al*, are bound. In many other languages, however, lexical roots are not free morphemes; they must be bound with other morphemes to yield a grammatical word. In Italian, for example, the root of the verb *lavor-* 'work' *must* be bound with grammatical morphemes such as tense and agreement markers:

(14) *Italian*
      Lavor-ano   a   casa.
      work-PRES.3PL   at   home
      'They work at home.'

A morpheme performing a particular grammatical function may be free in one language and bound in another. For example, the English infinitive marker *to* (as in the verb phrase *to win the election*) is a free morpheme. It can be separated from its verb by one or more intervening words (despite what prescriptive grammar books say!), as in *to very narrowly win the election*. In French, however, the verb *gagner* 'to win' consists of the root *gagn-* and the infinitive morpheme *-er*, which are tightly bound together in a single word and cannot be split up. Conversely, the regular past-tense marker *-ed* in English must be tightly bound to a verb, as in *attempt-ed*, *walk-ed*, or *call-ed*, but in Koranko (a West African language), the morpheme used to encode past tense is a free morpheme, an independent word:

(15) *Koranko* (Kastenholz 1987:109, cited in Julien 2002: 112)
      à   yá   kɔlɔmabolɔ   kári
      3SG   PAST   tree-branch   break
      'he/she broke a branch'

We can see that the past morpheme *yá* in Koranko is free because it can be separated from its verb *(kári* 'break') by an intervening direct object *(kɔlɔmabolɔ* 'tree branch').

The forms of morphemes

We observed earlier that morphemes combine both a form and a meaning. However, sometimes the exact form of a morpheme systematically varies under certain conditions,

---

BOX 2.1 **IDENTIFYING MORPHEMES**

Can you identify all the morphemes in the following English sentence?

The musicians reconsidered their director's unusual proposal.

Let's go word by word:

- *the*: a grammatical morpheme indicating that the referent of the following noun is definite (not just any musicians) and known to both the hearer and the speaker
- *musicians*: – the root lexeme *music*
  – the morpheme *-ian* indicates a person who works in some capacity connected to the meaning of the root
  – the plural marker *-s*, meaning 'more than one'
- *reconsidered*: – the root lexeme *consider*
  – the morpheme *re-*, meaning 'again'
  – the past-tense marker *-ed*
- *their*: – a grammatical morpheme indicating possession of the following noun by some plural third person
- *director's*: – the root lexeme *direct*
  – the morpheme *-or*, denoting someone who performs the action of the verb
  – the morpheme *-s*, indicating possession of something by the noun to which it is attached
- *unusual*: – the root lexeme *usual*
  – the morpheme *un-*, meaning 'not'
- *proposal*: – the root lexeme *propose*
  – the morpheme *-al*, turning the root verb into a noun

---

much like the way in which phonemes can be pronounced as different allophones depending upon the context in which they are produced, as observed in Chapter 1. And in fact, one of the most common factors influencing the form of a morpheme is phonology, or more precisely, some aspect of the local phonological environment. For example, in English orthography, regular nouns are marked for plural by adding *s* (or in some cases *es*) but the actual *sound* of the plural morpheme *s* varies between [s], [z], and [ɨz]. Consider the following pluralized English words:

(16)

	[z]		[s]		[ɨz]
peas	[pʰiːz]	puffs	[pʰʌfs]	peaches	[pʰitʃɨz]
charms	[tʃarmz]	charts	[tʃarts]	charges	[tʃardʒɨz]
mills	[mɪlz]	myths	[mɪθs]	misses	[mɪsɨz]
caves	[kʰevz]	cakes	[kʰeks]	cases	[kʰesɨz]
flags	[flægz]	flaps	[flæps]	flashes	[flæʃɨz]
plays	[pʰlez]	plates	[pʰlets]	phrases	[frezɨz]

The examples in (16) show that there are three possible forms of the plural suffix for regular nouns in English. These regular plural morpheme variants are in complementary distribution and are called **allomorphs**. In other words, the particular regular plural form is completely predictable depending on, or phonologically conditioned by, the final sound of the base. The [ɨz] form follows a class of fricatives called **sibilants** (/s, z, ʃ, ʒ, tʃ, dʒ/). The [-s] form follows all the other voiceless consonants (/p, f, θ, t, k/). The [-z] form follows all the voiced sounds (all vowels and all the voiced consonants). Each of these three plural forms makes it easier to hear the plural marking following different root word endings.

Although phonological factors are often responsible for allomorphic variation, allomorphy may also be conditioned by factors other than phonology. Many languages, for example, have different verb classes (called **conjugations**), which condition the form of affixes such as agreement markers. In Italian, the verbs *lavorare* 'to work,' *scrivere* 'to write,' and *dormire* 'to sleep' belong to three different conjugation classes (sometimes known as the *-are*, *-ere*, and *-ire* classes respectively, based on their infinitive ('to') forms, which are also allomorphs). The suffix *-o* attaches to a verb root in any class and means 'agreement with a first-person, singular subject' (1sg.), as shown below:

(17) *Italian*

lavor-*o*	scriv-*o*	dorm-*o*
work-1SG	write-1SG	sleep-1SG
'I work'	'I write'	'I sleep'

For some other agreement categories, however, such as 'second person, plural' (2pl.), verbs in these conjugation classes require different forms of the agreement marker:

lavor-*ate*	scriv-*ete*	dorm-*ite*
work-2PL	write-2PL	sleep-2PL
You (pl.) work'	'You (pl.) write'	'You (pl.) sleep'

This is an example of *morphologically* conditioned allomorphy, since conjugation classes are formal morphological categories.

Finally, semantic factors may also play a role in determining how morphemes can be realized. The English prefix *un-* (meaning 'not') can readily attach to adjectives in the first column in (18) but not the second (Katamba and Stonham 2006: 80). Why not?

(18)
unwell	*unill
unloved	*unhated
unhappy	*unsad
unwise	*unfoolish
unclean	*undirty

If we wanted to express the negated form of *ill*, *hated*, *sad*, *foolish*, and *dirty*, we'd simply have to use the free-morpheme variant *not* instead of *un-*. In a pair of words representing opposite poles of a semantic contrast (such as *happy* and *sad*), the positive value (*happy*) is usually the **unmarked** (or more neutral or normal) quality, from which the more **marked** negative value can be derived by adding the affix *un-*. Lexemes already containing the negative value (*sad*) often cannot take a negative affix (*unsad).

Some morphological operations of the world's languages

BOX 2.2 PRACTICE WITH CONDITIONED ALLOMORPHY

The Turkish data below exhibit allomorphy (see Chapter 1). Can you identify the allomorphs and determine what is conditioning them?

Turkish

adamlar	'men'	günler	'days'
anneler	'mothers'	ipler	'threads'
atlar	'horses'	jıllar	'years'
aylar	'months'	kalemler	'pencils'
bankalar	'banks'	kediler	'cats'
başlar	'heads'	kitaplar	'books'
camiler	'mosques'	kızlar	'girls'
çocuklar	'children'	masalar	'tables'
dersler	'lessons'	mevsimler	'seasons'
dişçiler	'dentists'	oteller	'hotels'
eller	'hands'	sonlar	'ends'
elmalar	'apples'	umutlar	'hopes'
gözler	'eyes'	üzümler	'grapes'

From the English translations, you can see that every Turkish word above has a plural meaning. Can you identify a likely plural morpheme for each word? (In a true acquisition situation, you would hear – and be able to contrast – each of these words in both plural and singular contexts, such as *elma* 'apple' vs. *elmalar* 'apples,' and *kedi* 'cat' vs. *kediler* 'cats.') In some cases, the plural form is *-lar* whereas in the others it's *-ler*. Is this difference predictable or is it random? In other words, if you were learning Turkish and came across a new singular noun that you hadn't heard before, would you know how to pluralize it?

First, it doesn't look as if the meaning of the word conditions the morpheme's form. For example, looking at body parts, animals, and buildings, we find *baş-lar* 'heads' but *el-ler* 'hands'; *at-lar* 'horses' but *kedi-ler* 'cats'; *banka-lar* 'banks' but *otel-ler* 'hotels,' and so on. Gender doesn't look promising either; *adam-lar* 'men' is male and *anne-ler* 'mothers' is female, but *kız-lar* 'girls' is also female. (In fact, Turkish does not distinguish grammatical gender.) The final sound of the lexical base might determine which form to use (as it does in English plurals), but compare, for example, *ip-ler* vs. *kitap-lar*, both of which end in /p/, or *gün-ler* vs. *son-lar*, both of which end in /n/. Bases ending in a vowel also contrast, as in *cami-ler* vs. *masa-lar*.

Now look at the last vowel in every root. Making a list of which ones co-occur with each plural form, we get the following distribution:

a, u, ı (= /ɨ/), o   *-lar*
e, i, ö, ü   *-ler*

The roots whose final vowels have the feature [+front] are followed by the plural suffix with a [+front] vowel (*-ler*), whereas roots with [–front] final vowels are followed by the plural suffix with a [–front] vowel (*-lar*). This process is called **vowel harmony**, and since it involves (phonological) feature matching, you might think of it as a kind of phonological "agreement." The plural forms *-lar* and *-ler* are allomorphs in complementary distribution, and the choice of one or the other allomorph is determined in this case by vowel harmony, a kind of phonological conditioning.

In this section we'll examine some of the morphological processes languages use to modify the form and meaning of lexemes:

- affixation: the addition of a discrete morpheme either before, after, inside of, or around a root or another affix
- reduplication: the copying of some part of a root
- ablaut and suppletion: the change or replacement of some part of a root
- suprasegmental change: a shift in tone or stress to signal a grammatical function

Affixation

The most common morphological process for modifying a root is by adding something to it – the process of affixation. Most of the world's languages use some kind of affixing to indicate grammatical information about a word or its relation to other words. An **affix** is a grammatical morpheme which (by definition) must be bound to a root or to another affix. Any form an affix attaches to, whether simple or complex, is called a **base** (or a **stem**). Affixes which attach to the right, or end, of a base are called **suffixes**. Affixes which attach to the left, or front, of a base are called **prefixes**. The complex English word *uninterpretability*, for example, consists of the root lexeme *interpret*, a prefix *un-* and the suffixes *-able*, and *-ity*.

(19) *English*
      un-interpret-able-ity →   uninterpretability

Some languages, such as Turkish, are primarily suffixing. This is shown in the Turkish example we observed earlier, repeated below as (20). In this word, there are eleven suffixes following the root *Avrupa-* 'Europe':

(20) *Turkish* (Beard 1995: 56)
      Avrupa-lı-laş-tıl-a-mı-yacak-lar-dan-sın-ız.
      Europe-an-ize-CAUSE-PASSIVE-POTENTIAL-NEG-FUT.PART-PL-ABL-2ND-PL
      'You (all) are among those who will not be able to be caused to become like Europeans.'

Other languages, like Chichewa (the national language of Malawi), are mostly prefixing; the example below shows six prefixes preceding the root *phwany* 'smash':

(21) *Chichewa* (Mchombo 1998: 503)
      Mkângo   s-ú-na-ká-ngo-wá-phwányá   maûngu.
      3lion   NEG-3SUBJ-PAST-go-just-6OBJ-smash   6pumpkins
      'The lion did not just go smash them, the pumpkins.'

The simplest and most common way to build word structure is to cumulatively add suffixes or prefixes to derive a more complex word, as in the English, Turkish, and Chichewa examples above. This kind of affixation is sometimes referred to as concatenative morphology, since discrete morphemes appear linked together (or concatenated) like beads on a string.

Other types of affixation

In addition to prefixes and suffixes, some languages make use of **infixes**, a kind of affix that is inserted inside a lexical root. Infixing is less common than suffixing or prefixing across the world's languages. An example of verb root infixing from Tagalog (the national language of the Philippines) is shown in (22):

(22) *Tagalog* (Himmelmann 2004)

tulong	'help'	t-*um*-ulong	'helped
bili	'buy'	b-*um*-ili	'bought'
hanap	'search'	h-*um*-anap	'searched'

Another unusual kind of affixation is **circumfixing**, in which a two-part or discontinuous morpheme surrounds a root. Many past participles in German are formed this way, as shown in (23):

(23) *German*

ge-kann-*t*	'known'
ge-läute-*t*	'rung'
ge-schüttel-*t*	'shaken'
ge-zeig-*t*	'shown'

Although infixing and circumfixing involve either splitting up the lexical root or splitting up the grammatical morpheme (and thus are not truly concatenative processes), there is still a one-to-one correspondence between a particular morpheme and a particular grammatical function. In Tagalog, the infix -*um*- indicates past tense. In German the past participle is formed by circumfixing the discontinuous morpheme *ge-t* around the verb.

An even more interesting kind of infixation is found in Semitic languages such as Arabic and Hebrew. In these languages certain sequences of vowels are interspersed throughout an abstract lexical root consisting only of consonants. For example, the root *ktb* in Arabic is associated with the meaning 'write' but it is a bound root; the sequence of sounds *ktb* is never uttered by itself but must be filled in with specific vowels in a specific pattern in order to derive an actual word. The particular choice and position of vowels determines the overall meaning of the word, as shown in (24):

(24) *Arabic*

katab	'to write'
kataba	'he wrote'
kutib	'has been written'

BOX 2.3 **ARABIC WORD FORMATION**

Try analyzing Arabic word formation using the lexical root *drs*, meaning 'study.' Based on the examples in (24), how do you say 'he studied,' 'has been studied,' 'be studying,' and 'school' in Arabic?

– The template for the past-tense form 'he studied' is *CaCaCa* → *darasa*.
– The template for the perfect passive form meaning 'has been studied' is *CuCiC* → *duris*.
– The template for the present progressive form 'be studying' is *aCCuC* → *adrus*.
– 'school' is made up of the prefix *ma-* (which means roughly 'a place') combined with the template *CCaCa* → *madrasa* 'a place for studying.'

---

aktub	'be writing'
kitaab	'book'
kutub	'books'
kaatib	'clerk'
maktaba	'library, bookstore'

In this kind of root-and-vowel-pattern morphology, certain grammatical categories like 'past tense' cannot be associated with an individual affix. Instead, they're associated with an entire pattern, or template, of vowels superimposed upon a lexical root consisting of only consonants. Thus, a past-marked verb in Arabic consists of a consonant-and-vowel template that looks like *CaCaCa* (where C represents a root consonant, e.g. *kataba*), and the present progressive form is the *aCCuC* template (e.g. *aktub*).

Reduplication

Suppose you were learning Tagalog and heard the future-tense forms for the verbs *tawag* 'call' and *takbo* 'run' shown in (25):

(25)   *Tagalog* (Schachter and Otanes 1972; Himmelmann 2004)

ROOT		FUTURE	
tawag	'call'	ta-tawag	'will call'
takbo	'run'	ta-takbo	'will run'

You might guess that the future-tense morpheme in Tagalog is the prefix *ta-* 'will.' This would be a good guess on the basis of such a limited sample of data. But suppose you then heard the future-tense forms of *bisita* 'visit' and *bili* 'buy':

bisita	'visit'	bi-bisita	'will visit'
bili	'buy'	bi-bili	'will buy'

Now you have at least two possible hypotheses: either there are two (or more) distinct morphemes (*ta-* and *bi-*) for expressing the future tense, or something else a little more interesting is going on. More data should help you decide:

pasok	'enter'	pa-pasok	'will enter'
alis	'leave'	a-alis	'will leave'
dalo	'attend'	da-dalo	'will attend'
lakad	'walk'	la-lakad	'will walk'
gawa	'make'	ga-gawa	'will make'
kain	'eat'	ka-kain	'will eat'
sunod	'obey'	su-sunod	'will obey'

For each of the future forms, the first syllable of the root is copied and prefixed to the root to form the future tense. Although it looks like a case of simple prefixation in some respects, there is no single pre-specified morpheme or even a set of morphemes that we could point to as having the meaning 'future.' Rather, the future tense is derived by a morphological process that copies a subset of the phonemes of each individual root. This copying process is called **reduplication**.

In reduplication, sometimes the entire word is copied, or sometimes just part of the word (as in the Tagalog examples above), and sometimes part of the root is copied along with some fixed or pre-specified morpheme. In the following example from Ilokano (another language spoken in the Philippines), reduplication is used to derive a verb with a "pre-tentative" meaning from an abstract noun:

(26) *Ilokano* (Rubino 2002)

singpet	'virtue'	agin-si-singpet	'pretend to be virtuous'
baknang	'wealth'	agim-ba-baknang	'pretend to be rich'

In the 'pretend' verbal forms there is a specific prefix *agiN-* that attaches to the first CV (consonant and vowel) copied from the root. The capital *N* in the prefix indicates that the last sound in the prefix is a nasal which assimilates to the place of articulation of the first (copied) consonant of the root. So in the case of *singpet* 'virtue,' the initial *si-* of the root is copied, which in turn determines (or conditions) the final nasal consonant of *agin-* (since /s/ and /n/ share the same place of articulation), to yield the 'pretend' verbal form *aginsisingpet* 'pretend to be virtuous.' Similarly, for *baknang*, the initial *ba-* of the root is copied and conditions the form of the prefix *agim-* (since /b/ and /m/ share the same place of articulation). The Ilokano pretentative construction offers another example of how phonological processes like nasal assimilation often condition the ultimate form of morphemes.

BOX 2.4 **ENGLISH PIG LATIN**

Try pronouncing the following phonetically transcribed utterance, which involves reduplication in which, for every derived word, part of an English root is copied and combined with some pre-specified material. Can you reconstruct the English roots and decipher the utterance?

Then see if you can analyze the derived words in terms of (partial) reduplication.

u-dej u-jej o-nej aʊ-hej u-tej ik-spej ɪg-pej ætin-lej?

If you learned the English-based word game Pig Latin as a child, the pattern in the words above should sound familiar. How might a linguist who knew English but didn't know Pig Latin analyze this

> ### BOX 2.4 (*cont.*)
>
> utterance? Observe that every word ends with a morpheme containing at least one consonant and the fixed sequence -*ej*, yielding the suffix -*C(C)ej*. The consonant in this suffix is different for every word, which should give us a clue that the consonant is what's being copied from the root. But the base to which the suffix is affixed in each of the first four words above doesn't even contain a consonant. In fact *every* word in the utterance begins with a vowel sound. That's a clue that the consonant copied from the root has been deleted from the initial position of the root in the derived word. Following up on our hypothesis, we get the following English roots (in phonetic transcription) and the corresponding derived Pig Latin words:
>
> | *English* | | *Pig Latin* | |
> |-----------|------------|-------------|------------|
> | du | 'do' | u-dej | 'do' |
> | ju | 'you' | u-jej | 'you' |
> | no | 'know' | o-nej | 'know' |
> | haʊ | 'how' | aʊ-hej | 'how' |
> | tu | 'to' | u-tej | 'to' |
> | spik | 'speak' | ik-spej | 'speak' |
> | pɪg | 'Pig' | ɪg-pej | 'Pig' |
> | lætiin | 'Latin' | ætiin-lej | 'Latin' |
>
> Language games of this sort occur in many different languages with different types of insertions of reduplication of words or parts of words. Try and find some "Pig-Latin" data in other languages and see if you can crack the code. Knowledge of syllables, codas, and other prosodic categories (see Chapter 1) may help you decipher the various languages.

Ablaut and suppletion

Another kind of morphological operation, called **ablaut**, signals a grammatical change by substituting one vowel for another in a lexical root. Consider past-tense marking in English verbs, which may be regular or irregular.

(27) *English*

Regular		Irregular	
ROOT	PAST	ROOT	PAST
call	called	fall	fell
glide	glided	slide	slid
like	liked	strike	struck
bake	baked	take	took
live	lived	give	gave
share	shared	swear	swore
confide	confided	ride	rode

The regular verbs are marked for past tense by simply concatenating the root with the grammatical morpheme -*ed*. But forming the past tense for irregular verbs is a nonconcatenative process; the past tense is not marked by adding a prefix or suffix but by a vowel change. Moreover, for these verbs there is no clearly identifiable, pre-specified morpheme that we can associate with the grammatical meaning 'past.' The particular vowel change will depend rather idiosyncratically on the particular (irregular) root lexeme, and must be memorized. In these cases, we can't say that the past-tense morpheme is just the changed vowel; rather, the whole word form (for example *rode*) resulting from the morphological process of ablaut is the past-tense form. In these verbs, the lexical meaning and the grammatical function 'past' are more synthetically fused than in regular past-tense marking.

More radically, sometimes grammatically related forms bear very little resemblance to each other. Consider the following pairs:

(28)   *English*

ROOT	PAST
catch	caught
buy	bought
think	thought
teach	taught
seek	sought

In these cases, all of the root after the initial consonant has been deleted. All the past-tense forms in (28) have the same rhyme (/-ɔt/) despite having very different lexeme roots. This is a case of partial **suppletion**, in which nearly the entire root appears to have been replaced by a completely different form, leaving only the original root onsets. The English pair *go–went* is a case of total suppletion – *went* shares nothing at all with *go*.

Tone and stress

Another nonconcatenative morphological process often used to signal a contrast in grammatical meaning is the use of tone. In Somali, one way in which some nouns can be pluralized is by shifting the high tone on the penultimate (next-to-last) syllable in the singular form onto the final syllable in the plural:

(29)   *Somali* (Lecarme 2002)

SINGULAR		PLURAL	
árday	'student'	ardáy	'students'
díbi	'bull'	dibí	'bulls'
mádax	'head'	madáx	'heads'
túug	'thief'	tuúg	'thieves'

Some languages use changes in syllable stress to indicate grammatical information. For example, some English nouns have been derived from verbs simply by shifting the stress from the second to the first syllable. Compare the nouns derived by stress shift (in the second column) with the nouns derived from the same verbs via affixation (in the third column).

(30)

VERB	NOUN	NOUN
convíct	cónvict	conviction
permít	pérmit	permission

progréss	prógress	progression
rebél	rébel	rebellion
recórd	récord	recording

In this section we have looked at some of the ways in which the world's languages build and modify the structure of words, including affixation, reduplication, internal root change, and shifts in tone and stress. What purposes do all these operations serve? We turn next to that question.

Two purposes of morphology: derivation and inflection

Morphological processes are traditionally classified into two broad types, each with a rather different function. Among the major lexical categories – nouns (N), verbs (V), and adjectives (A) – **derivational** morphology creates new lexemes from existing ones, often with a change in meaning. In example (30) above, we saw that it is possible to derive two different nouns from the verb *convict* via two different operations. The first noun, *cónvict*, was derived by stress shift and denotes a person who has been convicted. The second noun, *conviction*, was derived by affixation and denotes the outcome or result of being convicted. In this case, the morphological operations of stress shift and affixation were both used for derivational purposes, since two lexemes (nouns) were created from another lexeme (a verb).

Inflectional morphology, on the other hand, adds grammatical information to a lexeme, in accordance with the particular syntactic requirements of a language. Consider the following English sentence:

(31)   He plans to contact her in a few weeks.

The particular (suppletive) forms of the pronouns *he* and *her* are required by the syntactic roles they play in the sentence as subject and object, respectively; furthermore, the verb *plan* must be affixed with *-s* to agree with its third-person, singular (3sg.) subject, and the noun *week* must also be affixed with plural *-s* as required by the quantifier phrase *a few*. Thus, in this example, the morphological mechanisms of suppletion and affixation were both used for inflectional purposes – to convey grammatical information. Consider how ungrammatical the result would be if these particular syntactic requirements were not met; that is, if the wrong suppletive forms of the pronouns were used or if the required affixes were not added:

(32)   *Him plan to contact she in a few week.

Both derivation and inflection often co-occur within the same word, although in English there is typically only one inflectional operation per word. (There may be several derivational ones.) Consider the complex English word *dehumidifiers*. Creating this word requires three derivational operations and one inflectional operation, each subsequent step building on the base of the previous one:

(33)   humid   – an adjective, the lexical root
        humidify   – step 1: a transitive verb is derived by suffixing *-ify*, meaning to 'cause
                          something to become humid'

dehumidify	– step 2: a transitive verb is derived from the base *humidify* by prefixing *de-*, meaning 'to remove, reverse or perform the opposite action'
dehumidifier	– step 3: a noun is derived from the base *dehumidify* by adding the suffix *-er*, meaning 'something which performs the action of'
dehumidifiers	– step 4: the noun is made grammatically plural (inflected) by adding the regular plural suffix *-s* (in its allomorphic form [-z])

Typically, if a morphological operation causes a word-category change (such as from adjective to verb, as in *humid → humidify*), the process is considered derivational, since a new major-category lexeme has been created from an existing one. However, not all derivational operations cause a category change; for example, the prefix *de-* above attaches to a verb and derives another verb with a different meaning. Inflection, on the other hand, does not usually produce a category change. Adding a plural affix to a noun, for example, only grammatically augments that noun; it does not change its category. Similarly, adding an agreement marker to a verb results in the same verb, but one with an added formal feature. We will take a closer look at derivation in the next section, and at inflection in the following section.

Derivation

As mentioned above, derivation creates or *derives* new lexemes from existing ones. It allows new words to enter a language, even if sometimes only fleetingly in a particular conversation or magazine text or e-mail message. Derivation is also extremely useful for expressing phrases more compactly. It is much more efficient, for instance, to refer to someone working in the field of science, politics, or banking as a scient*ist*, politic*ian*, or bank*er* than to have to repeatedly use more cumbersome phrases such as "someone who works in the field of ..." Derivation is a kind of shorthand system that allows us to economize – by packing more information into shorter utterances.

Although all the morphological processes outlined above are employed among the world's languages to derive new words, in this section we will focus on two: affixation (the most common process), and another kind of morphological process especially relevant to derivation – **compounding**.

Derivational affixes

Derivational affixation is the most common way among the world's languages to derive one lexeme from another. As mentioned above, derivation often changes the lexical category of a word, or its meaning, or both. We can observe some examples of this in various languages below:

(34)   *Mandarin Chinese* (Li and Thompson 1981: 41–42)

gōngyè-*huà*	dòngwù-*xué*	kēxué-*jiā*
industry-V	animal-'ology'	science-ist
'industrialize'	'zoology'	'scientist'

German

Zerstör-*ung*   Einsam-*keit*   erb-*lich*
destroy-N   lonely-N   inherit-A
'destruction'   'loneliness'   'hereditary'

French

faibl-*esse*   chant-*eur*   rapide-*ment*
weak-N   sing-er   rapid-Adv
'weakness'   'singer'   'rapidly'

In each of the examples above, a suffix has been applied to a particular kind of lexeme to derive another. In many cases, there is a category change; for example, the suffix -*ung* in German applies to verbs to derive a noun indicating a result of the verb (*zerstör* -'destroy' → *Zerstörung* 'destruction'). (Nouns are conventionally capitalized in German orthography.) The French suffix -*esse* attaches to adjectives to derive nouns meaning something like 'the state or quality of being A' (*faible* 'weak' → *faiblesse* 'weakness'). The Chinese suffix -*jiā* derives a noun from another noun; here there is no category change but an agentive meaning is added — that of someone who practices in the field of the base noun (*kēxué* 'science' → *kēxuéjiā* 'scientist').

Let's turn now to English, a language that is quite rich in derivational morphology, with several different affixes sometimes sharing a similar function. Consider the following data:

(35)   sing-er   appli-cant
        violin-ist   prank-ster
        magic-ian   cook

In each word in (35), a noun has been derived that bears an obvious agentive relation to the root: a singer sings, a violinist plays the violin, a magician performs magic, an applicant applies for something, a prankster commits pranks, and a cook cooks. The agentive meaning in these examples is expressed by five different suffixes or, as in the case of *cook*, by nothing at all (the latter process is called **zero derivation**).

However, not all the affixes in (35) above can attach freely to any root. The suffix -*er*, for example, can only attach to verbs (*singer, smoker*), while the suffix -*ist* attaches only to nouns or adjectives (*violinist, cartoonist*), and -*ian* attaches only to nouns, especially those of Greek origin (*mathematician, politician*).

Because derivational affixes are selective in what they can modify, they generally apply in a particular order within a complex word. Consider again our earlier example of *dehumidifier*. Although the order of each step was spelled out in (33) above, we can more formally notate the derivational order by using various methods, such as a tree diagram as shown in (36a), bracketing (36b), or simple numbering (36c):

(36) a.

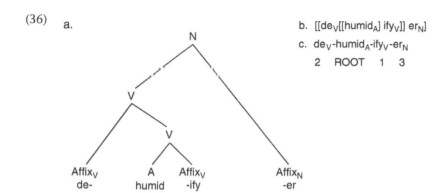

b. [[de$_V$[[humid$_A$] ify$_V$]] er$_N$]

c. de$_V$-humid$_A$-ify$_V$-er$_N$

2   ROOT   1   3

Some of the many derivational affixes of English are shown below.

(37)

Prefixes	Category selected	Category derived	Examples
de-	V	V	demagnetize, decompress
dis-	V	V	disentangle, dislocate
mis-	V	V	mismatch, mismanage
pre-	V	V	preview, predigest
re-	V	V	reappear, repossess
un-	A	A	unhappy, unproductive
un-	V	V	unwrap, unzip
Suffixes			
-able	V	A	bearable, washable
-al	V	N	approval, rebuttal
-ant	V	N	applicant, inhabitant
-ate	A	V	activate, validate
-en	A	V	redden, shorten
-er	A	A	singer, gambler
-ful	N	A	plentiful, beautiful
-ian	N	N	magician, musician
-ify	A/N	V	purify, beautify
-ion	V	N	detection, discussion
-ist	N/A	N	artist, activist
-ity	A	N	sensitivity, portability
-ive	V	A	oppressive, instructive
-ize	N	V	vaporize, magnetize
-ment	V	N	management, settlement
-ness	A	N	happiness, fullness
-y	N	A	watery, snowy

Some derivational affixes are very **productive**; that is, they can apply almost without exception to a certain kind of base. For example, the affix *-able* freely attaches to transitive verbs, deriving a new adjective with the meaning 'able to be V-ed' (as in *washable, faxable, analyzable*). On the other hand, some derivational affixes occur in only a small number of words and aren't productive, such as *-dom* (*kingdom, wisdom, boredom*) and *-th* (*warmth, truth, width*). Derivational affixes that are very productive at some point in the history of a language may become less so over time. The feminizing suffix *-ess* used to be more productive than it is today. Although there are still some words in common usage such as *actress*, *princess*, and *goddess*, the words in (38) were also once more widely used in English:

(38) authoress   janitress
      ambassadress   manageress
      editress   mayoress
      governess   poetess
      huntress   proprietoress

This decline in the productivity of *-ess* affixation has likely been fueled by social factors that favor terms that de-emphasize or are completely neutral with regard to sex, such as *flight attendant* (instead of *stewardess*) and *server* (instead of *waitress*).

Compounding

Compounding is the concatenation of two (or more) lexemes to form a single new lexeme. Because compounding always results in the creation of a new lexeme, it is a good example of a derivational process. In English and many other languages, compounding is highly productive and a primary source of new vocabulary. Some English examples are shown below:

(39) *English*
      greenhouse   soy sauce   man-made
      moonlight   coast guard   brown-eyed
      download   long shot   long-range

As shown above, English compounds are sometimes written as a single word, or as words separated by a space or a hyphen; however, they are all considered by linguists to be compounds. The characteristic pronunciation for English compounds is for the stress to fall on the first lexeme in a two-lexeme compound (although there are exceptions). Recall the difference in pronunciation between the compounded word *gréenhouse* (a place to grow plants) vs. the phrase *green hóuse* (a house that is green).

In some languages, such as English, German, and Dutch, compounding can be highly **recursive**, meaning that a derived compound can serve as the base for further compounding:

(40) toe + nail
      toenail + clipper
      toenail clipper + accident
      toenail clipper accident + insurance
      toenail clipper accident insurance + company
      toenail clipper accident insurance company + employee
      toenail clipper accident insurance company employee + benefits etc.

BOX 2.5 **COMPOUND WORD OR SYNTACTIC PHRASE?**

We might ask whether compounds like *toenail clipper accident insurance company* ... are really words rather than syntactic phrases. Everyone seems to agree that *toenail* is a word and *a toenail clipper* still seems pretty wordlike. Is there some definable point at which complex words lose their wordhood status and become syntactic phrases? If you recall the highly complex derived Turkish word shown earlier in example (11) that must be translated as an entire complex sentence in other languages, you'll understand why linguists have been debating this question for years! And yet, even the most complex form in (40) above is still more wordlike than phrasal. Recall that morphological derivation renders utterances more compact; now imagine the complexity of the sort of syntactic phrase we'd need to capture a similar meaning: 'the benefits of the employees of a company that sells insurance in case of accidents that involve the use of clippers that are used to clip the nails on one's toes.' (And even this horrid phrase contains 'shortcuts' – the derived words *employees*, *insurance*, and *clippers*.)

In each successive derivation in (40), it is the rightmost element that identifies what the compounded word is; in other words, a *toenail clipper* is a particular kind of clipper (as opposed to say, a hedge clipper or nose-hair clipper); a *toenail clipper accident* is an accident that somehow involves a toenail clipper, etc. This identifying element is called the **head**; its meaning and part-of-speech category determine that of the entire compound overall. English compounds are typically right-headed. Thus, *chocolate milk* is a kind of milk but *milk chocolate* is a kind of chocolate. Both compounds are nouns, because both *milk* and *chocolate* are nouns. The examples below demonstrate right-headedness in compounds involving various word categories in addition to the type of noun–noun compounding we have looked at so far.

(41) *Noun compounds*   *Adjective compounds*   *Verb compounds*
      N + N chocolate milk, toenail   N + A headstrong, skin-deep   N + V handpick, fingerspell
      A + N softball, shortcake   A + A bittersweet, aquamarine   A + V blacklist, soft-pedal
      V + N drawstring, driveway   V + A slaphappy, punch-drunk   V + V blowdry, shrinkwrap
      P + N instep, oversight   P + A underripe, overgrown   P + V undertake, oversleep

However, there are many compounds in English in which the overall category and meaning are not determined by the rightmost element. A few examples are given in (42):

(42) over$_P$ + weight$_N$ →   overweight$_A$
      make$_V$ + shift$_V$ →   makeshift$_A$
      lack$_V$ + luster$_N$ →   lackluster$_A$
      make$_V$ + believe$_V$ →   make-believe$_{A/N}$
      speak$_V$ + easy$_A$ →   speakeasy$_N$
      up$_{Adv}$ + keep$_V$ →   upkeep$_N$

Moreover, there is a quite productive class of compounding in English in which certain types of verb phrases (verbs plus adverbs, prepositions or verb particles) are compounded into nouns. In this case, the right-head generalization does not hold at all:

(43) kickback   screw-up   payoff   buyout
      sing-along   breakdown   pullover   sit-up
      breakthrough   giveaway   workout   getaway
      drawback   get-together   drive-in   heads-up

In these cases, the morphological process of zero derivation has applied in addition to compounding, turning verbal phrases (like *break dówn*) into compound nouns (*bréakdown*). Since neither lexeme in the compound determines its overall grammatical category or meaning, these compounds are generally considered unheaded.

BOX 2.6 **COMPOUNDING IN VARIOUS LANGUAGES**

Some examples of compounds in other languages are provided below. Can you identify whether they are right-headed or left-headed?

Hebrew	(Berman 1997: 323)
orex-din	tapúax-adama
conductor-law	apple-earth
'lawyer'	'potato'

Japanese	(Shibatani and Kageyama 1988: 454)
hai-zara	kosi-kakeru
ash-plate	waist-hang
'ashtray'	'to sit down'

Mandarin Chinese	(Li and Thompson 1981: 47–49)
fēi-jī	hé-mǎ
fly-machine	river-horse
'airplane'	'hippopotamus'

Jacaltec (a Mayan language)	(Spencer 1991: 349)
potx'-om txitam	'il-om 'anma
kill-er pig	watch-er people
'pig-killer'	'people-watcher'

To help determine the head of each compound, we can apply the simple 'is a' test employed above; for example, *chocolate milk* 'is a' kind of milk, not a kind of chocolate, and thus *milk* is the head and the compound is right-headed. Let's analyze a few of the above compounds.

In Hebrew, the compound *orex-din* 'lawyer' is a person who practices ('conducts') law, rather than a kind of law; therefore, we deduce that the word *orex* 'conductor' is the head of the compound and the compound is left-headed. Now look at the other Hebrew compound, *tapúax-adama* 'potato.' Is a potato a kind of apple or a kind of earth? Well, metaphorically, it's much closer to being a kind of apple than a kind of earth. (For those who know French, the resemblance to the French word for 'potato' will be obvious: *pomme de terre* 'earth apple.') Thus we conclude that *tapúax* 'apple' is the head and the compound is left-headed. From our very limited sample of data it appears that Hebrew compounds are left-headed.

Next let's turn to the Japanese compound *kosi-kakeru* 'to sit down.' The first word *kosi* 'waist' is a noun and the second *kakeru* 'hang' is a verb; the resulting compound is a verb. Which element is the head? Since sitting down is a kind of "hanging" of one's waist rather than a kind of waist and since the

---

BOX 2.6 (cont.)

resulting compound is a verb overall, it appears that *kakeru* 'hang' is the head and the compound is right-headed. The other Japanese compound *hai-zara* 'ashtray' is also clearly right-headed: an ashtray is a kind of plate, not a kind of ash. It appears that compounding in Japanese is right-headed (but of course we'd need more data to confirm this).

Similar analyses indicate that the compounds in Chinese above are right-headed, whereas those in Jacaltec are left-headed.

Inflection

We observed earlier that morphological **inflection** adds grammatical information to a lexeme, depending on the particular syntactic requirements of a language. The kind of information added indicates a property or a **feature** within a set of grammatical contrasts, such as singular vs. plural, first person vs. second, masculine vs. feminine, past vs. nonpast, and many others. By "syntactic requirements of a language," we mean contexts in which a particular language requires us to make such a contrastive distinction. For example, the presence of the quantifier *two* in the following English sentence creates a context in which the grammatical feature [+plural] must be realized on any noun that could fill in the blank in the following sentence:

(44)   Olivia bought *two*____online yesterday.

"Plural" is a feature associated with nouns in English (and many other languages), whether it's a simple noun, such as *book*, or a derivationally complex one, such as *dehumidifier*. It's also important to note that it is merely the grammatical information [+plural] that is required in this context by the rules of English syntax, rather than any particular morphological form. For example, we could still produce a grammatically well-formed sentence by filling in the blank with the irregularly pluralized nouns *mice* or *theses*. In other words, as long as the noun is plural, the syntax "doesn't care" which particular form is chosen. It's the job of the language-specific rules of morphology to determine how an abstract feature should be realized phonologically and to select the right form.

The following sections provide a mini-catalogue of some of the more common grammatical contrasts marked by inflectional morphology across the world's languages.

Person

Person is a grammatical feature that distinguishes entities referred to in an utterance. First person refers to the speaker (in English, *I/me*), and second person refers to the addressee (*you*). Third person is a default category that refers to everything else (for example, *she/her, he/him, it, the dog, John, the fact that it might rain today*). Person is often combined with **number** (see the next section) and thus we often speak of person–number combinations such as 'third person singular' (3sg.) or 'first person plural' (1pl.), etc.

When we speak of the inflectional categories of person (and/or number), we're usually referring to a grammatical agreement relation, most often subject–verb agreement. Languages which distinguish grammatical persons typically require that a verb agree with its subject's person feature, and occasionally with that of its object as well (such as Swahili). Subject–verb agreement helps to indicate which noun in a sentence is "doing" which verb. This is particularly valuable in languages with free word order, in which subjects can come before or after their verbs. English (which has relatively fixed word order) has only one inflectional agreement marker for its regular verbs (and only on present-tense verbs): 3sg. -s, as in *he/she/it runs*. Below is a partial **paradigm** (an orderly display of related forms, for example, as here, contrasting persons and numbers) for present-tense, subject–verb person/number agreement in Polish, a language with much richer verbal agreement contrasts, for the verb *kochać* 'to love.'

(45) *Polish present tense*

Person	Singular		Plural	
1	kocham	'I love'	kochamy	'we love'
2	kochasz	'you (sing.) love'	kochacie	'you (pl.) love'
3	kocha	'he, she loves'	kochajă	'they love'

This table shows that Polish speakers use a different inflectional form of the verb depending on the person/number features of the subject.

> **Inflection in American Sign Language (ASL)**
> *Verbal inflection in ASL morphology is interesting in that it displays some typologically rare patterns concerning morphology. There are three classes of verbs: "agreeing" verbs (which agree with the subject or object), "plain" verbs (which do not display any agreement), and locative verbs (which agree with the location). The sign begins in the location reserved for the subject and ends in the location reserved for the object. The speaker's body indicates first person, a location toward the listener indicates second person, and the third person is referred to by pointing toward some designated space away from both speaker and listener. These locations are considered by many ASL researchers to be inflections on the verb, and an overt pronoun can be used along with these inflections. What is interesting is that several different spaces can be used for referring to different people. There is no ambiguity when changing third person referents (consider how the pronoun* he *or* she *can change referents throughout a conversation) – one simply begins or ends the sign in a different space when changing third-person referents (Sandler and Lillo-Martin 2006).*

Number

Number is a grammatical property of nouns (and as we've already seen, often marked via agreement on verbs and other elements such as determiners and adjectives). The most fundamental contrast is between **singular** ('one') and **plural** ('more than one'), although many languages also mark a distinct **dual** form ('two'). Slovenian marks this three-way number contrast, as shown in (46). (The noun *mest* 'city' is in nominative case, to be discussed shortly.)

(46) *Slovenian*

mest*o*	(sing.)	'city'
mest*i*	(dual)	'two cities'
mest*a*	(plur.)	'cities'

Even in languages that have grammatical number distinctions there are some nouns that cannot be counted and therefore cannot be pluralized. For example, in English, abstract nouns such as *companionship*, *carelessness*, and *peace* have no plural form. Nouns that denote non-individuated material like *rice*, *lettuce*, or *toilet paper* are also typically not pluralizable (unless we mean something like 'kinds of' rice, lettuce, or toilet paper). This type of noun is called a **mass** or **noncount** noun. A noun that is a mass noun in one language may be countable in another. In English, for example, *furniture* is a mass noun (*furnitures), whereas in French, it is countable (*meuble, meubles*). In this situation, English must resort to using an additional word that can individuate parts of the mass, such as a *piece* of furniture, a *grain* of rice, a *head* of lettuce, or a *roll* of toilet paper.

In some languages which appear to lack regular grammatical number distinctions, such as Chinese, most nouns are individuated in this way. Consequently, Chinese has a highly developed system of **classifiers**, a kind of grammatical morpheme that affixes to quantifiers (like 'one,' 'some,' 'many,' 'three,' etc.) or demonstratives ('this' and 'that'):

(47) *Mandarin Chinese*

wŭ-ge rén	zhèi-běn shū	nèi-zhāng zhǐ
five-CL person	this-CL book	that-CL paper
'five people'	'this book'	'that sheet of paper'

There are dozens of classifiers in Mandarin Chinese. The choice of classifier depends on the particular noun and often must simply be memorized. Some patterns exist, such as the use of the classifier *-tiáo* for elongated objects, such as 'snake,' 'rope,' 'river,' 'tail,' and also for most four-legged mammals; however, there are several exceptions. For many native Chinese speakers today, however, the most frequently used classifier *-ge* has begun to take on a more general all-purpose character and is gradually replacing many of the more specialized ones (Li and Thompson, 1981: 112).

Gender

In many languages, nouns are sorted into different classes that other words – such as adjectives, determiners, pronouns, or verbs (or some combination of these) – must agree with. These noun classes are often referred to as **gender**, etymologically descended from Latin *genus* and French *genre*, meaning 'kind' or 'sort.' Gender agreement helps to indicate which adjectives, determiners, etc. are associated with a particular noun. In languages that mark grammatical gender, every noun is assigned to a class. You might be familiar with terms like "masculine" and "feminine" to describe these classes in some languages with a two-way distinction (like French and Spanish), or "masculine," "feminine," and "neuter" for some with a three-way distinction (like German and Russian).

Sometimes gender is indicated on the noun itself. In the Spanish examples in (48), the masculine noun *amigo* ('friend, masc.') ends in *-o* whereas its feminine counterpart *amiga* ('friend, fem.') ends in *-a*. Observe that the forms of the indefinite article *un/una* and the adjective *americano/a* agree with the gender of the noun:

(48) *Spanish*
      un   amigo   american*o*   (masc.)   'an American friend (male)'
      un*a* amig*a* american*a*   (fem.)   'an American friend (female)'

However, many nouns in Spanish are not so obviously marked. The gender of Spanish nouns that end either in consonants or vowels other than *-o* and *-a* must be learned:

(49) el balcón   (masc.)   'the balcony'   el coche   (masc.)   'the car'
      la razón   (fem.)   'the reason'   la noche   (fem.)   'the night'

Even worse, there are "misleading" nouns ending in *-a* that are masculine and some ending in *-o* that are feminine:

(50) el clima   (masc.)   'the climate'   la mano   (fem.)   'the hand'
      el día   (masc.)   'the day'   la foto   (fem.)   'the photo'

The way to determine a noun's gender is by observing the type of determiners, adjectives, etc. that agree with it. The gender of a noun is conclusively confirmed by agreement.

Languages which mark gender differ in terms of the types of words that must agree with the noun. In the Spanish examples above, the articles (such as *un/una* and *el/la*) and adjectives (such as *americano/a*) agree. In the following German examples, only the articles agree; the adjective *junge* does not change its form:

(51) *German*
      der junge Mann   (masc.)   'the young man'
      die junge Frau   (fem.)   'the young woman'
      das junge Mädchen   (neut.)   'the young girl'

In the Swahili sentence below, the subject noun *ki-kapu* 'basket,' which belongs to Swahili noun class 7, requires agreement on the adjective (*ki-kubwa* 'large'), quantifier (*ki-moja* 'one'), and verb (*ki-lianguka* 'fell') – all indicated by the 'noun class 7' prefix *ki-*:

(52) *Swahili*   (Corbett 1991: 117)
      ki-kapu   *ki*-kubwa   *ki*-moja   *ki*-lianguka
      7-basket   7-large   7-one   7-fell
      'one large basket fell'

Perhaps you're surprised at a language having a "noun class 7." Swahili (also called Kiswahili) belongs to the family of Bantu languages spoken throughout much of the southern half of Africa. Like most Bantu languages, it has a very elaborate gender system. There are between ten and twenty noun classes in Bantu languages (compared with the two to four found in most Indo-European languages), and Swahili has about fifteen (depending on how these are analyzed). Among the world's languages, the basis for assigning nouns to gender classes is often complex and, as you can see from the examples above, goes well beyond semantic-based concepts of "masculine" or "feminine" (see Box 2.7).

BOX 2.7   HOW DO NOUNS GET A GENDER?

Although gender in many languages at least partially correlates with sex-based distinctions, you can see from the examples in the text that morphological gender is also assigned in most cases independently of semantic "maleness" or "femaleness." (For linguists the word *gender* means 'kind' rather than 'sex.') So how is a noun assigned to a particular class? There are two main ways – either on the basis of its meaning or its form. Most systems are mixed; that is, some nouns are assigned on the basis of meaning and others according to their form.

In French, for example, nouns denoting male referents are masculine and those denoting females are feminine – a meaning-based distinction for gender class assignment. What about all the other nouns – the overwhelming majority? Two studies (Mel'čuk 1958; Tucker, Lambert, and Rigault 1977) found surprisingly accurate predictors of the gender of non-semantic-based nouns in French derivational morphology and phonology. For example, noun compounds derived from verb phrases in French are masculine, even if the final (object) noun in the compound is feminine, as in *porte-monnaie* = carries-money (fem.) = 'purse' (masc.). Similarly, 99.8% of nouns ending in *-tion* /sjɔ̃/ are feminine (e.g. *action* /aksjɔ̃/ 'action'); 97.2% of nouns ending in /o/ are masculine (e.g. *mot* /mo/ 'word'), as are 94.2% of nouns ending in /ʒ/ (e.g. *potage* /pɔtaʒ/ 'soup'), and so on. Children acquiring French are able to keep track of these regularities, and probably learn the exceptions in much the same way that children acquiring English learn the past-tense forms of irregular verbs. In fact, the French gender-assignment system is so heavily phonology-based that deaf children who learn to speak French do not acquire it, because they cannot hear the language (Tucker *et al.* 1977: 59, cited in Corbett 1991: 61).

In languages with highly complex noun class systems, such as Swahili, the gender system is also mixed, with nouns assigned to particular classes either on the basis of their meaning or their form. Some of the semantic features used to classify nouns in these languages are humanness, sex, animacy (with distinctions for some kinds of plants and animals), body parts, size, and shape, although there are exceptions in many classes. Membership in other classes is phonologically or morphologically determined. In Bantu languages, for instance, there are distinct classes for the plural referents of nouns of another given class. Recall the Swahili example above in (52) meaning 'one large basket fell.' If we were to change 'one' to a plural number, e.g. 'three,' the noun class of *ki-kapu* 'basket' would change from 'class 7' to 'class 8' *vi-kapu* 'baskets,' and all the agreement markers on the other sentential elements would change as well from *ki-* to *vi-*:

vi-kapu	*vi*-kubwa	*vi*-tatu	*vi*-lianguka	(Corbett 1991: 44)
8-baskets	8-large	8-three	8-fell	

'three large baskets fell'

Thus, the "meaning" of gender class 8 in Swahili is 'plural of class 7 nouns.'

What if a language (or more precisely, a speaker) can't decide which class to use? As we observed earlier with the Chinese classifier system, languages with complex noun class systems may often designate one class as a kind of general all-purpose default gender. This gender is typically overgeneralized by children and especially second-language learners; it gradually absorbs the nouns of smaller, more obscure classes, and may also serve as the primary class for new nouns that enter a language.

Case

We observed earlier that one of the most important functions of morphology is to distinguish the roles played by the various participants in an event. **Case** is a grammatical category that does this, by indicating a particular noun's relation to some other element in a clause or phrase. Typically, case marking indicates the relation of the noun to the verb (as its subject, direct object, or indirect object) or to another noun (as in a possessive or locational relation). Before we see how these relations are morphologically marked in different languages, let's briefly consider these relations as illustrated in the English sentence in (53).

(53)   John gave Mary his sister's old bicycle.

In this sentence, the verb *gave* is related to three nouns, the giver (*John*), the gift (*bicycle*), and the recipient (*Mary*). The giver *John* is the subject of *gave*, the gift *bicycle* is the direct object, and the recipient *Mary* is the indirect object. In addition, there are two possessive relations – one between John and his sister (marked with the possessive pronoun *his*), and another between his sister and the bicycle (marked with the possessive affix -*s* on *sister*). In languages that mark case distinctions, many of these relations would be indicated by inflectional morphology. Consider the same sentence in Slovenian, for example. (In (54), case forms are labeled as follows: **nominative** for subjects, **accusative** for direct objects, and **dative** for indirect objects.)

(54)   *Slovenian* (Dominik Rus, p.c.)

Janez	je	dal	Marij-i	sestr-in-o	star-o	kol-o.
John.NOM	is	given	Mary-DAT	sister-POSS-ACC	old-ACC	bicycle-ACC

'John gave Mary his sister's old bicycle.'

In Slovenian, nominative case is unmarked; the base form of the noun receives no affix. Other cases are marked: dative by the suffix -*i* and accusative by -*o*. Notice that adjectives such as *staro* 'old' and *sestrino* 'sister's' (which is considered a possessive adjective in Slovenian) also agree in case marking with the noun they are modifying.

In addition to indicating grammatical roles such as subject, object, and possession, many languages with extensive case-marking systems also use inflectional morphology to mark the kinds of locational relations for which English uses prepositions (like *to, from, at,* etc.). These locational suffixes are called **locative** case inflections. Here are some examples of this type of case suffixing in Lezghian, an indigenous language of the Caucasus spoken in southern Russia:

(55)   *Lezghian*   (Beard 1995: 261–262)

sev	'bear'	sev-rek	'under the bear'
sev-rev	'at the bear('s)'	sev-rek-di	'to under the bear'
sev-rev-di	'toward the bear'	sev-rek-aj	'out from under the bear'
sev-rev-aj	'away from the bear'	sev-re	'in the bear'
sev-rex^h	'behind the bear'	sev-rej-aj	'out of the bear'
sev-rex^h-aj	'out from behind the bear'	sev-rel-aj	'off of the bear'

The locative case affixes of Lezghian provide another illustration of one language using bound morphemes to perform the same function that free morphemes (e.g. prepositions) perform in another.

Tense

All animal communication systems can convey information about a current or imminent situation – a warning signal, for example, or a mating call. Humans are exceptional in that we can talk about events that occurred in the past, no matter how distant, or speculate about situations that may or may not happen far into the future. All human languages have ways for locating situations in time – for example, through the use of lexical expressions like *yesterday, the day after tomorrow, when the sun sets*, or *in the rainy season*. In addition, many languages also use a morphological category called **tense** to locate an event or state in relation to a point in time. In simple tenses, such as past, present, and future, that reference point is "now," at the moment of speaking. The past tense, for example, indicates that an event took place prior to the moment of speaking, as shown below for English and Japanese:

(56)   Last night I *went* to a karaoke bar.

(57)   *Japanese*
Yuube   karaoke   baa-ni   ikimasi-*ta*
last night   karaoke   bar-to   go-PAST
'Last night I went to a karaoke bar.'

The use of the past tense here indicates that the event of my going to a karaoke bar happened sometime prior to the moment of my telling about it; that time is more precisely specified by the adverbial phrase *last night*.

Whereas past tense marks an event as occurring prior to the moment of speech, the future tense situates an event sometime after the moment of speech. Note that while we often speak of a 'future tense' in English, it is not morphologically marked via inflection; rather we use various auxiliary forms or the simple present form:

(58)   He's leaving next week.
He's going to leave next week.
He will leave next week.
He leaves next week.

For this reason, English is claimed to morphologically distinguish only two tenses: past and nonpast. Other languages, such as Italian, do have morphological future tense:

(59)   *Italian*
Part-*ir*-à   la   settimana   prossima
leave-FUT-3SG   the   week   next
'He will leave next week.'

Not all languages morphologically mark tense. Dyirbal (an Australian language) and Burmese are claimed to lack tense (Comrie 1985). So is Chinese, as shown below:

(60)   *Mandarin Chinese*   (Li and Thompson 1981: 214)

zuótiān	yè-lǐ	wǒ	mèng-jiàn	wǒ	mǔqīn
yesterday	night-in	1sg	dream-perceive	1sg	mother

'Last night I dreamed about my mother.'

In (60), there is no past-tense marker on the verb *mèngjiàn* 'dream' (or anywhere else in the sentence). The past time of the event is simply lexically indicated by the expression *zuótiān* 'yesterday.' Although all languages are able to express semantic time reference lexically, this should not be confused with the formal grammatical category of tense.

Aspect

Whereas tense is concerned with locating an (entire) event in time relative to the moment of speaking, **aspect** is a grammatical category that encodes a different kind of temporal characteristic, such as whether an action is (or was) completed, ongoing, repeated (iterative), or habitual. For example, in English one can say:

(61)   a. John is painting the kitchen.
        b. John was painting the kitchen.
        c. John painted the kitchen.

The difference between (61a) and (61b) is a tense distinction (i.e. present vs. past), whereas the difference between (61b) and (61c) is an aspectual distinction. Both (61b) and (61c) are in the past tense; however, the form *was painting* in (61b), often called the **progressive** form in English, indicates that the action of painting was ongoing and it's quite possible that John never completed painting the kitchen. (Imagine if John was interrupted after he'd just begun painting.) The example in (61c), however, indicates that John did finish painting – that is, the painting of the kitchen was completed. This aspectual distinction is found in many languages; the "ongoing" meaning is sometimes referred to by linguists as the **imperfective** and the "completed" meaning is called the **perfective**. An example of how imperfective aspect is used in French and Spanish is shown below:

(62)   *French and Spanish*   (Comrie 1976: 3)

Jean	*lisait*	quand	j'entrai
Juan	*leía*	cuando	entré
John	read-*IMP*	when	(I) enter-PAST

'John was reading when I entered.'

The verb forms *lisait* and *leía* (French and Spanish, respectively) indicate that John was in the process of reading when he was interrupted by my entering, and we cannot assume that he finished whatever he was reading.

The following example from Chinese illustrates perfective aspect:

(63)   *Mandarin Chinese* (Li and Thompson 1981: 213)

wǒ	chī-*le*	fàn	zài	zǒu
I	eat-*PERF*	rice	then	go

'I'll go after I eat.'

In (63), the verb *chī* 'eat' bears the perfective marker *-le*, indicating that the action of going will occur after eating has been completed. (Note that in English we could also translate this sentence using a roughly equivalent morphological construction – the present perfect form: 'I'll go after I've eat*en*.')

Aspect should be distinguished from tense. In the Chinese sentence in (63), for example, the act of eating is marked as "complete" and yet is not in the past. In practice, however, these two categories are often highly interactive. Consider again sentence (61c) in English: *John painted the kitchen*. For events such as kitchen-painting, our English "past-tense" form also encodes perfective aspect. In other words, the entire painting event is situated prior to the moment of speaking (past tense), *and* the painting of the kitchen was completed (perfective aspect). Similarly, the nonpast (present) tense (for example, *is painting* in the sentence *John is painting the kitchen*) indicates that the event is situated in time at the moment of speaking (tense), and also indicates that the action is still ongoing (imperfective aspect).

Mood

Mood is a grammatical category that expresses **modality** – aspects of meaning having to do with possibilities that may not be actual, and that often reflect a speaker's belief, opinion, or attitude about the content of an utterance. Although often morphologically marked on verbs, mood really applies to entire clauses, to indicate whether the speaker thinks a proposition is true, or likely, or doubtful, or is something he/she wonders about, or hopes or wishes for. Mood may also be expressed by free morphemes, such as modal auxiliaries – words like *can*, *must*, or *should* in English, for example. Some common mood distinctions across languages are the **indicative**, used for making declarative assertions, the **interrogative**, used for asking questions, and the **imperative**, used for giving commands. We also find languages which use a special mood form known as the **subjunctive** to express desire, hope, or doubt, and the **conditional** to express what one would or should do. Examples illustrating indicative (64a), subjunctive (64b), imperative (64c), and conditional (64d) moods of the Italian verb *venire* 'to come' are given below:

(64)   *Italian*

     a. *Viene*   dalla   biblioteca.
        come.3SG.PRES.*IND*   from.the   library
        'He/she is coming from the library.'

     b. Spero   che   *venga*   presto   domani.
        hope.1SG.PRES.IND   that   come.3SG.PRES.*SUBJUNCT*   early   tomorrow
        'I hope that he/she comes early tomorrow.'

     c. *Vieni*   a   casa   presto.
        come.2SG(FAM.).*IMPER*   to   home   soon
        'Come home soon.'

     d. *Verrebbe*   voluntieri,   ma   non   serà   in   città.
        come.3SG.PRES.*COND*   gladly   but   not   be.3SG.FUT   in   town
        'He/she would gladly come, but he/she won't be in town.'

Another interesting modal function often expressed inflectionally in languages is **evidentiality**, in which the speaker indicates a degree of certainty or doubt about a proposition based on the kind of evidence available for it. Think for a moment about how important it is for humans to be able to evaluate the reliability of an information-source – our survival literally depends on it. For example, we're likely to believe what we've witnessed firsthand with our own eyes more than what we've heard from secondhand reports by others. In English, we convey our degree of confidence in the truth of an assertion by lexical means, as in phrases like *I know* ... or *I heard* ... or *I doubt* ... or by the use of adverbs such as *apparently*. However, other languages directly inflect these meanings on the verb. In Quechua, for example, there is a three-way evidentiality distinction, as shown below:

(65)   *Quechua*   (Sánchez 2003: 21)
a. kaya-n-*mi*   sanurya.
   be-3SG-*AFFIRM*   carrots
   'There ARE carrots.'
b. huk   hunaq-*shi*   pukla-shun.
   one   day-*REPORT*   play-1PL.INCHOAT
   'We will play one day (they say).'
c. Pay   rura-nqa-*tr*.
   he   do-3-SG.fut-*DUBITATIVE*
   '(I doubt) he will do it.'

In (65a) the verbal affix *-mi* indicates firsthand knowledge (affirmative), in (65b) the affix *-shi* relays information based on hearsay (reported), and in (65c) the affix *-tr* expresses doubt (dubitative). In Quechua these markers also serve to place focus on the word they are affixed to.

Grammatical mood may also express wonder, surprise, or disappointment with a result that is contrary to expectation. The following examples illustrate the "five modes" for verbs in Menomini, an Algonquian Native American language:

(66)   *Menomini*   (Hockett 1958, cited in Palmer 1986: 2)
         piw   'he comes/is coming/came'
         piwen   'he is said to be coming / it is said that he came'
         pi?   'is he coming? / did he come?'
         piasah   'so he is coming after all! (despite our expectation to the contrary)'
         piapah   'but he was going to come! (and now it turns out that he is not)'

The semantically varied and complex category of mood shades the meaning of a sentence, by conveying some opinion, attitude, or emotion about its content as perceived by the speaker. All languages have a way to express mood distinctions, and many do so morphologically.

Acquiring inflectional contrasts

If you have formally studied a language that has rich subject–verb agreement or grammatical gender distinctions, such as Spanish, Arabic, Swahili, or German, then you've probably memorized tables of neatly arranged verb forms or lists of vocabulary words in which information about the gender of nouns was provided. But what if you were a child acquiring Swahili or Spanish naturally? It's important to remember that in a child's natural acquisition environment, words do not come annotated with information such as *"coche* (masc.)" or *"noche* (fem.)." What the student in a language classroom learns via the memorizing of lists and paradigms, the preliterate child must acquire from subconscious attention to the contrasting distribution and co-occurrences of **morphophonological** distinctions in the language they hear. In languages with complex morphology, this is a remarkable feat.

Consider all the information that is artificially condensed in a morphology example or problem set (including the ones in this chapter), such as English glosses and translations. Children acquiring a language don't get this kind of help. Instead, they swim in a linguistic sea where the meaning of an utterance and distinctions such as case, number, person, gender, conjugation class, and so on, must be deduced in context and compared with minimally contrasting forms that have already been acquired. It is the gradual accumulation of such minimal contrasts that leads to the child's formulation and increasing refinement of grammatical categories.

The aggregate knowledge accumulated over countless hours of exposure to a language in context is quite literally "lost in translation" in the way data are carefully handpicked and presented in linguistics textbooks. For that reason, we encourage you to consider someday undertaking some real field work of your own; you've done it already – as a child!

BOX 2.8 INSTRUCTED VS. NATURALISTIC ACQUISITION OF MORPHOLOGICAL AGREEMENT: AN EXAMPLE

If you've studied French in a foreign-language classroom setting, you probably learned that adjectives must agree with the nouns they modify in gender and number. Let's focus for a moment on gender agreement. It's likely that you were provided with a list of adjectives and the following rule: "To form the feminine of an adjective, add *e* to the masculine form" (e.g. Barson 1981: 101). (In some cases there might be some other minor spelling change as well.) The list below is quite typical (data from Bauer 2003: 38–39):

ORTHOGRAPHY		PRONUNCIATION		
MASC.	FEM.	MASC.	FEM.	
mauvais	mauvais*e*	/movɛ/	/movɛz/	'bad'
heureux	heureus*e*	/œʁø/	/œʁøz/	'happy'
grand	grand*e*	/gʁã/	/gʁãd/	'big'
long	longu*e*	/lɔ̃/	/lɔ̃g/	'long'
chaud	chaud*e*	/ʃo/	/ʃod/	'hot'
vert	vert*e*	/vɛʁ/	/vɛʁt/	'green'
froid	froid*e*	/fʁwa/	/fʁwad/	'cold'
petit	petit*e*	/pəti/	/pətit/	'little'
blanc	blanch*e*	/blã/	/blãʃ/	'white'
faux	fauss*e*	/fo/	/fos/	'false'

Note that this rule is completely based on written orthography; it suggests that final feminine *e* is an inflectional affix. This way of "looking at it" might help a second language learner (who already knows

BOX 2.8 (*cont.*)

how to read) to learn the pattern. However, morphology is not based on orthography, but on morphemes which are sequences of *sounds*.

Now imagine a young child acquiring French who hasn't yet learned to read or spell. But children of preschool age already know and use correctly both the masculine and feminine forms of the adjectives listed above. So what "rule" does the preliterate child follow to acquire them? Let's look at how the words above are pronounced – the only kind of evidence available to the child.

The preliterate child cannot make use of a spelling rule that adds a letter (*e*). Note that the feminine form has an added consonant *sound* at the end of the word compared with its masculine counterpart. However, as Bauer (2003) points out, there is no way to predict from the masculine form which added consonant the feminine form will take. This is determined by each word. The only rule the child can establish on the basis of the phonological data is that the masculine adjective can be predictably derived by deleting the final consonant sound from the feminine adjective. This is the *opposite* order of derivation from the spelling-based orthographic rule presented in French language textbooks, and illustrates how different the mental representations of morphological rules can be between native vs. classroom-instructed language acquirers!

CHAPTER SUMMARY

A key part of knowing a language is the ability to construct and interpret the *words* of that language. The branch of linguistics that is concerned with the relation between form and meaning within words and between words is called *morphology*. The basic unit of language that combines both a form and a meaning is the *morpheme*. Simple words consist of just one morpheme, whereas complex words consist of more than one morpheme and may consist of many. There are different kinds of morphemes. Those bearing richer lexical meaning and belonging to the major lexical categories of nouns (N), verbs (V), and adjectives (A) are called *lexemes*, and may serve as the *root* for additional morphological operations. Those serving primarily to signal a grammatical function are called *grammatical morphemes*. The actual phonetic forms of morphemes can vary systematically depending on certain conditioning factors; these variant forms are known as *allomorphs*.

Languages make use of various morphological operations to modify the form and meaning of lexemes. The most common process is *affixation*, in which a morpheme is added to a base (either a root or another affix). Other processes include *reduplication* (the copying of all or part of a root), internal root changes such as *ablaut* and *suppletion* (involving the replacement of all or some part of a root's segments), suprasegmental change (in which a shift in word stress or tone is used to signal a morphological contrast), and *compounding* (in which two lexemes are combined to form a new lexeme). These morphological operations are used in the service of two major functions: *derivation* and *inflection*.

Derivational morphology creates new lexemes from existing ones, with a change in the word's lexical category or meaning, or both. *Inflectional* morphology adds grammatical information to a lexeme, as required by the particular grammatical rules of each language. Some common inflectional contrasts found among the world's languages are *person*, *number, gender, case, tense, aspect*, and *mood*.

Finally, we briefly considered how children manage to acquire some of these grammatical contrasts. Children appear to be able to keep track of distributional regularities found in the input – for example, correlations between gender distinctions and the phonological regularities of roots. The meanings of grammatical forms such as case and tense marking must be deduced from the use of these forms in informative and minimally contrastive language contexts.

Exercises

EXERCISE 2.1

Indonesian. Consider the Indonesian reciprocal forms below (from Sneddon 1996: 104):

ROOT		RECIPROCAL	
tolong	'help'	tolong-menolong	'help each other'
pukul	'hit'	pukul-memukul	'hit each other'
kunjung	'visit'	kunjung-meŋunjung	'visit each other'
peluk	'embrace'	peluk-memeluk	'embrace each other'
telpon	'telephone'	telpon-menelpon	'telephone each other'

a. Given these data, can you derive the rule for forming the reciprocal in Indonesian? Pay attention to any phonological changes that may occur.

b. Given this rule, how would you form the reciprocal form of the roots *tikam* 'stab,' *pinjam* 'borrow,' and *tawar* 'bargain'?

tikam	'stab'	_____	'stab each other'
pinjam	'borrow'	_____	'borrow from each other'
tawar	'bargain'	_____	'bargain with each other'

EXERCISE 2.2

Finnish. The Finnish data below (from Leney 1993) are given in both the nominative and the partitive case. Partitive is used for quantified nouns, such as *monta kilometri-ä* 'many kilometer-PART,' *kolme kuningas-ta* 'three king-PART' or *lasi viini-ä* 'a glass of wine-PART.' Study the data and answer the questions that follow.

BASE (NOM)		PARTITIVE
kilometri	'kilometer'	kilometriä
kuningas	'king'	kuningasta
viini	'wine'	viiniä
runo	'poem'	runoa
hautausmaa	'cemetery'	hautausmaata
leipä	'bread'	leipää
tytär	'daughter'	tytärtä
tyttö	'girl'	tyttöä
katu	'street'	katua
kyljys	'pork chop'	kyljystä

sana	'word'	sanaa
olut	'beer'	olutta
tee	'tea'	teetä
mies	'man'	miestä
tie	'road'	tietä
näytös	'act'	näytöstä
pullo	'bottle'	pulloa
kollega	'colleague'	kollegaa

a. The data exhibit allomorphy. Identify the allomorphs and describe how they're conditioned. (Hint: the umlaut ' ¨ ' diacritic indicates that a vowel has been fronted.)

b. Provide the correct partitive forms for the following Finnish words:

henkilö	'person'	_____
loma	'holiday'	_____
esitys	'performance'	_____
maa	'country'	_____

EXERCISE 2.3

Yoruba. Consider the following data from Yoruba, a language spoken in Nigeria (from Akinlabi, to appear). (Tone marks have been omitted for the sake of simplicity.)

gbona	'be warm'	gbigbona	'warmth, heat'
dara	'be good'	didara	'goodness'
won	'cost a lot'	wiwon	'costliness'
je	'eat'	jije	'(act of) eating'
ran	'sew'	riran	'(act of) sewing'
gbe	'take'		
mu	'drink'		

a. Please provide the likely forms for the meanings '(act of) taking' and '(act of) drinking.'

b. What morphological process from the chapter text is illustrated in these data, and what is its function? Describe how the forms on the right are derived from those on the left.

EXERCISE 2.4

Hebrew. Consider the following data (from Glinert 1989; Simon Mauck p.c.):

tarbut	'culture'	məturbat	'cultured'
koxav	'star'	məkuxav	'starry'
pilpel	'pepper'	məpupal	'witty'
petam	'cow'	məputam	'fat'

a. What are the category and meaning of the derived word forms on the right? How were they derived?

b. How would you derive similar forms from the following bases?

lamed	'knowledge'	_____	'educated'
tipeʃ	'fool'	_____	'foolish'
kavod	'honor'	_____	'honored'

EXERCISE 2.5

English. Analyze each of the following words into their constituent morphemes. Show the order in which each word was derived, justifying your analysis.

a. rehospitalization
b. incomprehensibility
c. unpreparedness
d. disenfranchisement

EXERCISE 2.6

English. Consider the following English data and answer the questions that follow.

A		B	
deep	deepen	low	*lowen
white	whiten	blue	*bluen
red	redden	green	*greenen
fat	fatten	obese	*obesen
wide	widen	narrow	*narrowen
dark	darken	dim	*dimmen
short	shorten	tall	*tallen
less	lessen	more	*moren
moist	moisten	dry	*dryen
cheap	cheapen	expensive	*expensiven
sad	sadden	happy	*happien
tough	toughen	strong	*strongen
fresh	freshen	stale	*stalen
straight	straighten	curved	*curveden
sweet	sweeten	sour	*souren
coarse	coarsen	fine	*finen
live	(en)liven	dull	*dullen

1. What meaning does the English suffix *-en* add to the words in the A column? What category does *-en* select, and what category results from its affixation?
2. As shown by the unacceptable words in the B column, *-en* cannot be freely attached, but rather is subject to some restrictions. Can you determine these restrictions? Are they phonological, morphological, or semantic? Please generate additional examples of your own to test your hypothesis. If you find any exceptions, please try to account for these as best as possible.

EXERCISE 2.7

Consider the brief discussion on p. 97 on how children acquire inflectional contrasts in context. Try to think of scenarios by which the child could do this. For example, children might acquire case distinctions by observing a noun spoken in different contexts in different roles in relation to an event, e.g. 'The girl-NOM was patting the dog-ACC' vs. 'The girl-NOM pulled the dog-GEN tail-ACC,' vs. 'The dog-NOM bit the girl-ACC.' Can you create some contexts for acquiring other inflections, such as tense, aspect, number, gender, and mood?

EXERCISE 2.8

Albanian. Consider the following data (from Camaj 1984) and answer the questions below:

sjellim	'we bring'
sillesh	'you (sing.) are brought'
posjell	'I am bringing'
sillem	'I am brought'
posillem	'I am being brought'

dotəsillem	'I will be brought'
sillemi	'we are brought'
dotəsjelləsh	'you (sing.) will bring'
letəsjelləsh	'you (sing.) should bring'
dotəsjell	'I will bring'
posjellim	'we are bringing'
dotəsjellim	'we will bring'
posillemi	'we are being brought'
dotəsillesh	'you (sing.) will be brought'
letəsjellim	'we should bring'

a. Give the likely Albanian forms for the following:

'should'   _____
progressive morpheme   _____
future morpheme   _____

b. What are the two stem forms for 'bring' found in these data and what is the difference in their meaning?
c. Give the likely Albanian forms for the following:

'I bring'   _____
'you are being brought'   _____
'we will be brought'   _____
'I should bring'   _____

EXERCISE 2.9

Spanish. Study the following data and answer the questions that follow:

breve	'brief'	la brevedad	'briefness, brevity'
corto	'short; bashful'	la cortedad	'shortness; shyness'
cruel	'cruel'	la crueldad	'cruelty'
enfermo	'ill, sick'	la enfermedad	'illness'
(el) hermano	'brother'	la hermandad	'brotherhood'
impropio	'improper'	la impropiedad	'impropriety'
leve	'light, trivial'	la levedad	'lightness'
liviano	'fickle'	la liviandad	'fickleness'
mal	'evil'	la maldad	'wickedness'
solo	'alone, solitary'	la soledad	'solitude'
vario	'various'	la variedad	'variety'
(la) viuda	'widow'	la viudedad	'widowhood'

a. Explain how the words on the right are derived from those on the left, accounting for any allomorphy. What is the general meaning of the derived form?
b. Why do you think all the derived words are feminine gender? (Hint: see Box 2.7.)
c. Provide the likely Spanish derived forms for the following:

ebrio	'drunk'	_____	'drunkenness'
igual	'equal'	_____	'equality'
vasto	'vast'	_____	'vastness'
(el) vecino	'neighbor'	_____	'neighborhood'

EXERCISE 2.10

Runyankore (data adapted from Morris and Kirwan 1972). Runyankore is an East African Bantu language spoken in Uganda. Like other Bantu languages, it has a complex noun class system. The structure of a typical Runyankore noun consists of an initial vowel (IV), a noun class prefix (NC), and the stem

For example:

o-mu-kazi

IV-NC-woman

'woman'

Consider the Runyankore nouns in the data set below and answer the following questions:

1. Group the nouns into classes. How many noun classes are represented in the data set? Please label each class. (You may use any labeling system, such as class 1, class 2, etc.)
2. Do any of your noun classes have an identifiable meaning or function? Can you find any examples in the data where the NC prefix appears to contribute some meaning to the stem?
3. What determines the initial vowel for each noun? Please describe its distribution.
4. Some of the noun class prefixes exhibit allomorphy. Please describe the distribution of the allomorphs.
5. Given the singular or plural form of the Runyankore words below, please supply the missing form.

'gift'	e-ki-conco	'gifts'	
'seed'	e-m-bibo	'seeds'	
'spear'	e-i-cumu	'spears'	
'child'	–	'children'	a-ba-ana
'weapon'	–	'weapons'	e-bi-kwato
'thief'	–	'thieves'	a-ba-shuma

6. Given that the Runyankore word for 'man' is *o-mu-shaija*, what do you think is a likely word for 'manhood'?
7. Given that the Runyankore word for 'cultivation' is *o-bu-hingi*, what do you think is a likely word for 'cultivator'?
8. Given that the Runyankore word for 'witchcraft' is *o-bu-cecezi*, what do you think is a likely word for 'witch, sorcerer'?

bean	e-ki-himba	goat	e-m-buzi
beans	e-bi-himba	goats	e-m-buzi
billy goat	e-m-paya	haste	o-bw-ira
billy goats	e-m-paya	house	e-n-ju
bird	e-n-yonyi	houses	e-n-ju
birds	e-n-yonyi	hunter	o-mu-hiigi
book	e-ki-tabo	hunters	a-ba-hiigi
books	e-bi-tabo	ignorance	o-bu-shema
boy	o-mw-ojo	king	o-mu-gabe
boys	a-b-oojo	kings	a-ba-gabe
branch	e-i-taagi	knife	e-Ø-misyo
branches	a-ma-taagi	knives	e-Ø-misyo
bull	e-Ø-numi	magic	o-bu-rogo
bulls	e-Ø-numi	man	o-mu-shaija
captivity	o-bu-nyagwa	men	a-ba-shaija
carpenter	o-mu-baizi	paper	e-m-papura
carpenters	a-ba-baizi	papers	e-m-papura
carpentry	o-bu-baizi	parent	o-mu-zaire
chair	e-n-tebe	parents	a-ba-zaire
chairs	e-n-tebe	person	o-mu-ntu
chicken	e-n-koko	people	a-ba-ntu

chickens	e-n-koko	road	e-n-guuto
chief	o-mw-ami	roads	e-n-guuto
chiefs	a-ba-ami	school	e-i-shomero
confidence	o-bw-esigye	schools	a-ma-shomero
cultivation	o-bu-hingi	sharpness	o-bw-ogi
day, sun	e-i-zooba	swamp	e-i-teme
days, suns	a-ma-zooba	swamps	a-ma-teme
distress	o-bu-saasi	table	e-Ø-meeza
doctor	o-mu-shaho	tables	e-Ø-meeza
doctors	a-ba-shaho	teacher	o-mw-egyesa
dog	e-m-bwa	teachers	a-b-eegyesa
dogs	e-m-bwa	thing	e-ki-ntu
egg	e-i-huri	things	e-bi-ntu
eggs	a-ma-huri	witchcraft	o-bu-cecezi
fear	o-bw-oba	word	e-ki-gambo
flower	e-ki-rabyo	words	e-bi-gambo
flowers	e-bi-rabyo	workman	o-mu-kozi
girl	o-mw-ishiki	workmen	a-ba-kozi
girls	a-ba-ishiki		

SUGGESTIONS FOR FURTHER READING

Bauer, L. 2003, *Introducing linguistic morphology*, 2nd edition, Washington, DC: Georgetown University Press. This book is a well-written introduction to morphology with a good balance between data and theoretical issues. The second edition includes new chapters on psycholinguistic approaches to morphology and morphological change over time within a language.

Katamba, F. and Stonham, J. 2006, *Morphology*, 2nd edition, New York: Palgrave Macmillan. This book offers the clearest, best-organized generative introduction to morphology, with lots of interesting data and exercises. The second edition includes a new chapter presenting an overview of optimality theory.

Pinker, S. 1994, "Words, words, words," *The language instinct* (chapter 5), New York: William Morrow. This chapter from Pinker's popular book on language is accessible, entertaining, and filled with many interesting facts, such as: the word *glamour* comes from the word *grammar*; English verbs have four inflectional forms (e.g. *quack, quacks, quacked, quacking*), whereas Turkish verbs have around two million; and the average English-speaking high school graduate probably knows around 60,000 words – about four times more than the number of words used by Shakespeare.

Spencer, A. 1991, *Morphological theory: an introduction to word structure in generative grammar*, Oxford and Malden, MA: Blackwell. At a more advanced level, this is one of the most comprehensive morphology textbooks available. It provides a good overview of various schools of thought and theoretical debates in the field. The exercises are also more challenging.

3 The structure of sentences

CHAPTER PREVIEW

In order to understand the subtleties of sentence structure, it is necessary to understand how phrases are built from the words they contain and how phrases are combined into larger phrases and sentences. It is also necessary to understand what can happen to phrases and sentences after they are built – namely, parts of them can be moved and deleted. Movement and deletion take place under particular restrictions, and speakers "know" these restrictions, apparently without being taught. All languages share these fundamental structural properties, but the principles that underlie them are broad enough to allow considerable differences among languages. The chapter includes a sampling of these differences.

GOALS

The goals of this chapter are to:

- **explain how to conduct an analysis of the sentence structure of English**
- **explain how the structure of sentences is represented in modern syntactic theory**
- **explain the concept "poverty of the stimulus"**
- **explain the notions "language organ" and "Universal Grammar"**

- present examples of subtle restrictions that limit the ways in which sentences can be constructed and interpreted
- present a few examples of differences in sentence structure in languages from around the world

Poverty of the stimulus

Human language is built on a foundation of grammatical principles. These principles interact to form a complex system that is wielded with ease by every speaker of every language. However, these speakers (including you) have probably never heard of these principles, precisely because they don't have to be taught. The grammatical principles we are talking about don't have much to do with the grammar you learned in school. In fact, what schoolchildren know about language goes beyond what they should be able to derive from what they hear, and very far beyond anything they are explicitly taught. The idea that people display a knowledge of grammar that is deeper than what they could get from the evidence around them is called the poverty-of-the-stimulus argument.

The amazing robot basketball player

To get a clearer idea of what **poverty of the stimulus** means, imagine this science fiction tale. Suppose somebody found an exquisitely anthropomorphic robot in a remote part of a desert. The scientists who examined the robot eventually figured out how to activate it. When they did, the robot behaved like a person, but seemed very puzzled about the world around it, as if it had never seen it before. The scientists decided to try an experiment, allowing the robot to watch several basketball games. (Please don't ask why they would do that!) The robot watched a dozen or so games very intently. These games were well played, with players seldom committing infractions, and then only unintentionally. However, the games were loosely officiated, with some violations called, but most not.

The robot then was suited up and was put in a game. Much to everyone's amazement, it proved to be an excellent basketball player who knew the game very well. At first, it seemed that the robot was simply a very careful observer. It was doing everything that it had seen the players do. But then a particularly observant scientist noticed something odd about the robot's game. Although it did most of the things it had seen the players do, it never broke any rules. For example, it never started to dribble again after it had stopped, and it never tried to run with the ball without dribbling. The scientist thought this was notable because, although the robot had rarely seen human players doing these things, it would be very advantageous to do them. Why did the robot conclude that "the double dribble" and "traveling" were not allowed, rather than assuming that the human players simply weren't taking advantage of some very useful strategies?

Perhaps, thought the scientist, the robot concluded that anything it hadn't seen was against the rules, but this turned out not to be true. The robot had never seen anyone dribble the ball behind his back, but on several occasions it did just that. How did it know this is allowed? Even more remarkably, on two occasions it leaped into the air and fell on its back while slapping the ball forward to keep it from going into the defensive half of the court after its team had brought it into the offensive end. This prevented a back-court violation, but how did the robot know? In the games it had watched there were never any back-court violations.

The scientist decided to interview the robot. She set up a monitor and showed a carefully selected video of a number of basketball plays – some showing violations of the rules and some showing unusual but legal plays – and asked the robot if what it saw was against the rules or not.

What happened next was remarkable. The robot accurately pointed out the plays that were allowed and the ones that were not, with almost no errors. In the case of rule violations, the scientist would ask the robot what rule was violated. But the robot could not tell her the rule, just that the play wasn't allowed. When the scientist asked, the robot affirmed that it had never seen anyone play basketball before the experiment. The scientist reluctantly came to a conclusion that was as unavoidable as it was improbable. *The robot had been preprogrammed with the rules of basketball without being aware of it!*

Applying the metaphor to the structure of sentences

It is just this sort of reasoning that has led many linguists to the conclusion that people are "preprogrammed" with principles of grammar. In the first few years of life, children undergo extensive cognitive development with respect to language, and we call the resulting cognitive language systems "grammars." A grammar, in this view, is biological – a **language organ** (Anderson and Lightfoot 2002). We don't know just how a grammar is *physically* represented in an individual's brain. But the systematic behavior that people display when they speak, and when they are asked whether or not certain structures are allowed, makes it possible for us to describe the grammar quite specifically. Just as the robot became intuitively aware of the rules of basketball as it watched some games, the grammar *emerge*s when children are exposed to particular languages, and its emergence is closely guided by genetically encoded principles. For example, English speakers have grammars that allow *Kim loves herself*, but not *People around Kim love herself*. English speakers can tell you that the first example is fine and the second isn't, but they can't tell you why. If they try to explain the rule, they are likely to get it wrong. They almost certainly were not taught anything about these examples in school.

The grammar: an English example

A grammar, in this sense, must contain certain elements. It must include a list of words and a set of rules for grouping the words into phrases. The rules that guide sentence structure will be the focus of the majority of the chapter. (On the rules that guide how words are put together, see Chapter 2.) The study of these rules, and of sentence structure in general, is referred to as syntax. In this section of the chapter, we will demonstrate how to carefully conduct a syntactic analysis of English. The goal of the analysis is to create a partial representation of the grammar (language organ) of an English speaker.

The lexicon and syntactic categories

The words of a language are stored in a **lexicon** – a mental dictionary in people's brains rather than in a book. Each word has a lexical entry which contains information on how to pronounce the word, what it means, and (most importantly for our purposes) its **syntactic category**. The syntactic category of a word gives information about where it can appear in a sentence – this is sometimes called its syntactic distribution. In (1), there is a sample lexical entry for the word *bee*.

(1) *Pronunciation:* [bi]
     Meaning: a buzzing, flying insect; has yellow and black stripes; makes honey, etc.
     Syntactic category: Noun

You probably have encountered syntactic categories before as they are sometimes referred to as "parts of speech" (noun, adjective, etc.). Perhaps you even learned definitions for them that had to do with their meaning ('a noun is a person, place or thing' or 'a verb is an action'). However, these meaning-based definitions are unreliable (Is *admiration* a person, place or thing? Is *contain* an action?). Syntactic categories will be defined henceforth according to where they can appear in a sentence or phrase.

A certain type of word can appear after prepositions (*on campus*), after articles (*the bee*) and after adjectives (*the small snail*). We will call these words nouns. Crucially, no other word has to follow the noun when it appears after a preposition, determiner or adjective (that is, there are no other words required after *campus*, *bee* and *snail*). Another type of word can follow modals (*will/must/may/should contain*) and can be negated by *not*, using sentences similar to *I will not cook the turkey*. We will call these words verbs.

In addition to their differing distributions within sentences, different syntactic categories also can take different kinds of endings. For example, English nouns can take a a plural suffix *-s* as in *bees* or *snails*. Verbs can take a past-tense suffix *-ed* as in *cooked*. These differences are morphological in nature (relating to the form of words; see Chapter 2), but they are also useful indicators of syntactic category.

Another type of syntactic category can appear between articles and nouns (*the massive clouds*), and we will call these words adjectives. Adjectives do not take a consistent ending, but some adjectives can end in the comparative suffix *-er* (*the smaller clouds*). The last major type of syntactic category has a distribution that is difficult to define, but they often end in *-ly* (*Frankly, I never liked Henry* and *The dog quickly ate the kibble*). We will call these words adverbs.

The distributional descriptions above are intended as guidelines – not all nouns, verbs, adjectives, and adverbs fulfill all the relevant criteria, but most do. Nouns, verbs, adjectives and adverbs are often called **lexical categories** – they are semantically contentful and contribute directly to the meaning of the sentence. This is in contrast to the **functional categories** – words in functional categories are semantically weak, and contribute more to the structure of sentences than to the meaning. Functional syntactic categories include **determiners** (members of this category include demonstratives like *this* and *those*, as well as articles like *the* and *a*) and prepositions (*at, from, into*). We will introduce more functional categories as we examine more and more complex sentences.

All in all, then, we've introduced six syntactic categories: nouns, verbs, adjectives, and adverbs (lexical categories), and determiners and prepositions (functional categories). Please see the table of grammatical categories for a summary of the information in this section (the table also contains information on two additional functional categories, inflection and complementizer, that will be introduced later on in the chapter).

BOX 3.1 DETERMINING THE SYNTACTIC CATEGORY OF A WORD

These days grammar isn't taught in grade school as explicitly as it was in the 1950s and 1960s. Determining the syntactic category of a word in your native language can be difficult because you acquired it without much explicit instruction and use it just fine without any terminology. Many students are daunted by the terms *adverb, noun, verb, gerund,* etc. The traditional definitions, such as "a noun is a person, place or thing," don't work well for words like *singing* or *love* which are abstract events or notions. In addition, figuring out which category a word belongs to is complicated by the existence of homonyms: words that sound and are spelled the same but have different meanings – and those meanings may be in more than one syntactic category. For example, *fax* can be a noun, as in (i), or it can be a verb as in (ii).

(i)   The fax arrived yesterday. [*fax* = a noun]
(ii) The administrator faxed the document yesterday. [*fax* = a verb]

To make things more confusing, nouns and adjectives can be derived from verbs:

(iii) The choir is singing the national anthem. [*singing* = a verb]
(iv) Their singing was beautiful. [*singing* = a noun]
(v)   *The Singing Neanderthals* is a book by Steven Mithen. [*singing* = an adjective]

How then is a student to know which category a word belongs to? The best way to determine the category of a word is to look at the kinds of morphemes it co-occurs with. In (i), for example, the word *fax* co-occurs with a determiner, the definite article *the.* As a noun, it could also co-occur with a possessive determiner, such as *his fax.* It can be modified by an adjective, as in *the long fax,* or even by an entire modifying phrase such as *the fax that is sitting on the desk.* In languages that have case marking (see Chapters 2 and 4), it is typically nouns that are marked for case, even if they have been derived from verbs. English words inflected with the *-ing* suffix are tricky, as they can be verbs, nouns, or adjectives, as shown in examples (iii), (iv), and (v). Nouns derived from verbs this way are called gerunds.

In (ii), the word *fax* is used as a verb. In English this process of turning nouns into verbs occurs frequently and easily. No special morphology is required other than applying the appropriate inflections that co-occur with verbs, such as tense and person/number agreement (e.g. *I fax-ed it, She fax-es documents often*), or by adding the infinitive marker (e.g. *to fax*). Verbs may appear with auxiliary verbs, such as forms of *have* or *be* (e.g. *We have faxed you the offer, He is faxing it over right now*), or modals (see Chapters 2 and 4) (e.g. *We should fax it right away*). Verbs are often modified by adverbs, and in fact, one way of distinguishing verbs from nouns is by comparing forms of modification; although adverbs can modify verbs, only adjectives modify nouns:

(vi) We *recently* faxed him the documents. [*recently* is an adverb modifying the verb *fax*]
       *We *recent* faxed him the documents. [*recent* is an adjective and cannot modify verbs]
(vii) Their *recent* fax surprised us. [*recent* is an adjective modifying the noun *fax*]
       *Their *recently* fax surprised us. [*recently* is an adverb and cannot modify nouns]

BOX 3.1 *(cont.)*

Examples of some of the most common syntactic categories are listed below. Notice that some words appear in more than one category. Make up a sentence using each of these words in its different syntactic categories.

Type	Syntactic category	Abbreviation	Examples
Lexical	Noun	N	puppy, park, happiness, dog, freedom, run, blue, hit, well, work, London, Mary, interest
Lexical	Verb	V	take, run, be, eat, think, clean, hit, have, work, interest
Lexical	Adjective	A	good, red, big, happy, blue, awkward, clean, interesting
Lexical	Adverb	Adv	happily, quickly, initially, awkwardly, well, very, really, often
Functional	Preposition	P	in, at, on, between, to, over, by
Functional	Determiner	D	this, the, a/an
Functional	Inflection	I	can, PRES, PAST
Functional	Complementizer	C	that, whether, if

The rules: a starting point

Now that we have a better understanding of the set of words which make up sentences, we can start to investigate the structure of the sentences themselves. A fundamental property of the grammar of every language is that it is **compositional**: sentences are made of clauses and phrases, which in turn are made up of smaller clauses and phrases or words. We can use rules to capture how different types of words combine to make phrases, which in turn combine to make sentences. A phrase structure rule is a **descriptive** tool, a way to express a pattern in how words and phrases and clauses are combined by native speakers of a language. It is not a **prescriptive** device (what a speaker *should* do); grammars – and phrase structure rules – seek to represent what native speakers do, not tell them how to do it. (See Box 3.2 for more on descriptivism and prescriptivism.)

Consider the following sentence:

(2)   The adorable puppy licked a cranky cat.

One of the goals of an analysis of sentence structure is to figure out the set of rules that can describe all the possible sentences of a language. Since (2) is a possible sentence of English,

---

BOX 3.2 **PRESCRIPTIVE RULES**

Grammaticality as a concept is different from the idea of "proper" or "correct" English that you may have been taught in school. For example, you may have been told that infinitives (*to go, to laugh, to dance*) should not be "split" – no words should come between *to* and the verb. In conversation and in written English, though, this "rule" is broken all the time without anyone even noticing (consider the classic science fiction quote: *to boldly go where no one has gone before*). Did you notice the split infinitive in the main text of this section of the chapter? The odds are, probably not.

Sentences with split infinitives are naturally acceptable to English speakers and thus considered grammatical. Rules like "don't split infinitives" are simply a different type of rule than grammatical rules. Such rules are often called prescriptive rules and are most generously viewed as rules to help people write clearly. Prescriptive rules should not be mistaken for the largely unconscious rules of phrase structure that we will investigate. Bear in mind that you had to be told at some point not to split infinitives, and perhaps you check your writing to this day to make sure you abide by that rule. However, nobody told you that sentences must start with noun phrases (as we will see below), and you never have to check your writing or your speech to make sure that you did not break this rule.

---

we need to have a rule for it. If we simply list in a row all the syntactic categories that are found in (2), the rule will look like the following:

(3)   *Sentence rule: version 1*
Sentence → Determiner Adjective Noun Verb Determiner Adjective Noun

This can be read as a "A sentence contains a determiner, an adjective, a noun, a verb, a determiner, an adjective and a noun, in that order." Obviously, not all sentences contain all of these categories, though, so we need to revise our rule.

One way we can begin to refine the rule in (3) is by noticing that some of the words in (2) seem more related than others. The words *the* and *adorable* group most naturally with *puppy*, and the words *a* and *cranky* group most naturally with *cat*. Let's call each of these groups (*the adorable puppy* and *the cranky cat*) noun phrases (NPs). Now we can write a new version of the sentence rule.

(4)   *Sentence rule: version 2*
Sentence → NP Verb NP

We can also write a rule describing the contents of an NP itself. For the NPs in (2), that's a determiner (*a/the*) an adjective (*adorable/cranky*) and a noun (*puppy/cat*). Both determiners and adjectives are optional members of noun phrases in general (consider this modified version of (2): *Puppies licked cats*). We will express this by putting parentheses around them in the rule.

(5)   NP → (Determiner) (Adjective) Noun

This can be read "a noun phrase contains an optional determiner, an optional adjective and an obligatory noun, in that order." Since the noun is the obligatory element, we name the whole phrase after it. In syntactic terminology, the noun is the **head** of the noun phrase.

Note that the NP rule in (5) allows noun phrases to contain just a noun (since the noun is the only obligatory element), a determiner and a noun, an adjective and a noun, or all three categories at once. All of these different kinds of NPs are possible (*puppies*, *the puppies*, *brown puppies*, *the brown puppies*), which is evidence that our rule is on the right track.

The technical term for a "natural grouping of words" like an NP is a **constituent**. There are various tests to determine whether a particular string of words is a constituent. We will focus on the replacement test. If a group of words can be replaced by a single word, then that group of words is a constituent. For example, we can replace *the adorable puppy* with *it*, resulting in the sentence *It licked a cranky cat*. Since this sentence is an acceptable sentence of English, we have confirmed that *the adorable puppy* is a constituent, specifically, an NP.

Consider now the following sentence:

(6)   The adorable puppy licked a cranky cat, and so did the ugly pug.

What did the ugly pug do? It licked a cranky cat, just like the adorable puppy. The word *so* seems to be replacing the string of words *licked a cranky cat*. This means that *licked a cranky cat* must be a constituent. We'll call this constituent a verb phrase (VP). This is because the verb is obligatory and the NP following it is optional, depending on the verb in the sentence (consider *The adorable puppy ran*).

(7)   VP → Verb (NP)

We can now revise our sentence rule even further:

(8)   *Sentence rule: version 3*
Sentence → NP VP

Version 3 still accounts for our original sentence (2) : *the adorable puppy* is the first NP, and then there is a VP that contains *licked* (a verb) and *a cranky cat* (an NP). However, it is a significant improvement over versions 1 and 2. This is because it can describe many more sentences than (2) and many more sentences than versions 1 or 2 – it is a more general rule. It can describe sentences that have an NP after the VP and sentences that don't (since NP is optional in the VP rule). It accounts for sentences that have determiners before all the nouns or sentences that don't (since determiners are optional in the NP rule). And so forth. It is a goal of sentence structure analyses to create the most general rules possible while staying true to the facts. Many, many sentences of English conform to the rule in (8), as you can investigate for yourself.

So far, we have the following sentence structure rules for the grammar of English. Note that we have started to use abbreviations to represent the rules more perspicuously (D = determiner, A = adjective, N = noun, V = verb).

(9)   Sentence → NP VP
NP → (D) (A) N
VP → V (NP)

These rules are known as **phrase structure rules**, since they describe the structure of phrases and sentences in a language.

Most of the sentences that we investigate in this part of the chapter are acceptable sentences of English, sentences that any native speaker would recognize as valid strings of words of the language. The linguistic term for this is grammaticality; (10) is a **grammatical** sentence of English.

(10)   The dog ate the kibble.

In contrast, the string of words *Ate the dog the kibble* is not an acceptable sentence of English, and it is accordingly called **ungrammatical** by linguists. Ungrammatical sentences are conventionally notated with an initial asterisk, as in (11).

(11)   *Ate the dog the kibble

We have been focused on ensuring that our phrase structure rules can account for grammatical sentences like (2). ((2) is in fact generated by the rules; make sure you can see how.) However, we also need to ensure that the phrase structure rules do not predict ungrammatical sentences like (11).

Thankfully, the phrase structure rules in (9) do not predict a sentence like (11). The sentence rule states that a sentence must begin with an NP, but *ate* is a verb, and verbs do not occur in NPs according to the NP rule. This is a sign that the phrase structure rules are properly formulated. However, the phrase structure rules in (9) *do* predict some ungrammatical sentences – for example, *The puppy arrived the cat*. This indicates that our account of the grammar still needs further revision. We will not address this particular problem, but for the study of sentence structure, it is important to keep in mind that ungrammatical sentences can be as important as grammatical ones.

Syntactic trees

There is another, more graphical way to represent the information that phrase structure rules convey, and it is used widely by syntacticians today. Syntacticians very often draw **syntactic trees** to represent the structure of a sentence. In a syntactic tree, the members of a constituent are connected by lines that are conventionally called branches. These figures are called trees because, as they become more detailed, they begin to look like upside-down trees. Consider Figure 3.1, which is the syntactic tree for the NP *a fuzzy kitten*. Each of the members of the constituent NP (the determiner *a*, the adjective *fuzzy*, and the noun *kitten*) are connected to the NP via branches. Note that the category and phrase labels

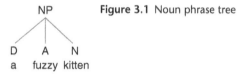

Figure 3.1 Noun phrase tree

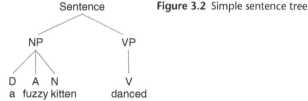

Figure 3.2 Simple sentence tree

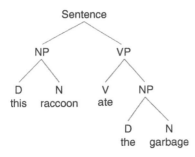

Figure 3.3 More complex sentence tree

at both ends of a branch on a tree are called nodes – D is a node, A is a node, N is a node and NP is a node. In a sense, we can "read" the NP phrase structure rule off the tree by starting at the NP node and working downwards.

Consider the more complicated sentence *A fuzzy kitten danced*. This sentence can be generated by following the phrase structure rules in (9); it consists of an NP (*a fuzzy kitten*) followed by a VP (which contains just the V *danced*). The syntactic tree for this sentence is in Figure 3.2.

From the top of the tree, the Sentence node branches into NP and VP, in keeping with the Sentence rule that states that a Sentence contains an NP and a VP. The NP node branches into D, A, and N as per the NP rule (and as we saw in Figure 3.1). The VP node has just a single branch below it leading down to its lone member, the verb *danced*. Again, we could "read" the phrase structure rules off the tree by starting at the sentence node and working downwards. Syntactic trees represent the same information as phrase structural rules, just in a different way, similar to how pie charts and bar graphs can represent the same statistics through different visual organization.

Consider one last example sentence: *This raccoon ate the garbage*. Note again that this sentence is generated by following our phrase structure rules; it consists of an NP (the determiner *this* and the noun *raccoon*) and a VP (which contains the verb *ate* and the NP *the garbage*). The syntactic tree for this sentence is Figure 3.3; work through it to see how it follows the phrase structure rules.

Syntactic trees do have one advantage over phrase structure rules. They make visually obvious the hierarchical structure of sentences – how words are put together to make constituents, and how constituents are embedded inside one another to make larger and larger phrases, which in turn make sentences. In Figure 3.3, the D *the* and the N *garbage* form an NP. The resulting NP combined with the V *ate* forms a VP. This VP in turn combined with an NP (*this raccoon*) makes a sentence. This is the heart of sentence structure – precisely generating the complicated structure of sentences and phrases, a structure which you may not have even been aware of until you read this chapter.

Prepositional phrases

Let's continue our investigation of English phrase structure. So far, our phrase structure rules in (9) mention the syntactic categories noun, verb, adjective, and determiner. We will now discuss the syntax of prepositions (*in, at, through, behind*). Consider the sentence *The student put the puppy on the chair.* We have a preposition *on* that seems to form a natural group with *the chair.* We can thus hypothesize that *on the chair* is a constituent. We can test the hypothesis using the replacement test for constituency.

(12)   The student put the puppy there.

Since *on the chair* can be replaced with a single word (*there*) as in (12), it is a constituent.

We will call the new constituent a prepositional phrase, abbreviated PP. We know that it contains the preposition *on* and also *the chair. The chair* is recognizable to us – it's a constituent that we've seen before, specifically, a determiner and a noun and therefore an NP. The phrase structure rule for the internal structure of prepositional phrases is as follows:

(13)   PP → P NP

In other words, a prepositional phrase contains a preposition and a noun phrase, in that order. Figure 3.4 shows the tree for the PP *on the chair* according to our new phrase structure rule in (13). Note that any kind of NP can follow a preposition: just a noun (*on campus*), a determiner and a noun (*on the chair*), an adjective and a noun (*for small children*), and a determiner, and adjective and a noun (*on the large table*).

Now that we've determined the internal structure of the PP, we can ask about where it appears in a sentence. Consider again our starting sentence: *The student put the puppy on the chair.* The PP comes last in the sentence, but we need more data to determine its exact position in the structure. Specifically, it is not clear whether the PP is part of the VP constituent, i.e. connected to VP via a branch (let's call this option 1) or whether it is connected to S with a branch and separate from the VP constituent (let's call this option 2). See Figure 3.5 for a tree showing option 1 (PP as under the VP) and Figure 3.6 for a tree

```
     PP                    Figure 3.4 Prepositional phrase tree
    /  \
   P    NP
   on   /  \
       D    N
       the  chair
```

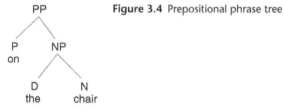

Figure 3.5 Option 1: PP under VP

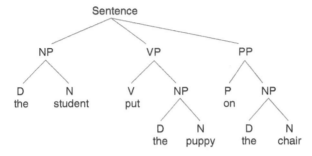

Figure 3.6 Option 2: PP under Sentence

showing option 2 (PP as under the S). We now have two competing analyses of how PPs fit into sentences. How can we decide between these two options?

In fact, we can use the replacement test. In option 1, the PP is part of the VP constituent. In option 2, it is not. Therefore, option 1 predicts that when we replace a VP with a single word, we can also replace the PP since it is part of the VP. Option 2 does not make this prediction. Consider (14).

(14)   The student put the puppy on the chair, and so did the teacher.

In (14), it is understood that the teacher also put the puppy on the chair. Therefore, the PP *on the chair* is part of the constituent replaced by *so*, and it must be part of the VP constituent. It follows that option 1 must be the right way to represent the prepositional phrase in the hierarchical structure of (12). The tree in Figure 3.5, where the PP is underneath the VP node, is the correct structure for the sentence *The student put the puppy on the chair*.

In this section, we have not only investigated the syntax of a new syntactic category (prepositions), but we have also seen how syntactic argumentation works. We had two competing hypotheses for the structure of prepositional phrases within a sentence, and we distinguished them using a diagnostic for constituency.

Adjectives and determiners

The next syntactic category that we will deal with is adjectives (*yellow, big, round, French,* etc.). It seems reasonable to assume that, like the other lexical categories, adjectives form a phrase unto themselves: adjective phrases (APs).

(15)   AP → A

This is particularly true given that adjectives can appear with associated words like *very* and *quite* as in *very yellow* or *quite round*. These words seem to go together with the adjective, that is, form a part of the Adjective Phrase. Exercise 3.4 asks you to determine the syntactic category of *very* and *quite*, and to revise the phrase structure rule for APs in (15) to include them. For now, let's just modify the NP rule to reflect the fact that adjectives are their own phrases, that is, APs.

(16)   NP → (D) (AP) N

Figure 3.7 shows the tree for the NP *a small possum* using the new/revised phrase structure rules in (15) and (16).

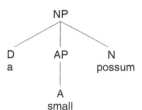

Figure 3.7 Adjective phrase tree

What should we do about determiners? How do they fit into the rules we just sketched? Since the mid 1980s, most linguists have assumed that there are **Determiner Phrases** (DPs) (for reasons we don't have space to go into here) and that they consist of a determiner followed by an NP.

(17)   DP → D NP

This requires us to revise our NP rule, namely, to remove the determiner from it. The revised NP rule is in (18).

(18)   NP → (AP) N

Consider the tree for *the mouse* in Figure 3.8.

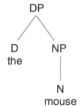

Figure 3.8 Determiner Phrase tree

The rule in (17) applies first, yielding the determiner *the* and an NP. Then the rule in (18) applies, adding a branch under the NP leading to the N *mouse*. To take a more complicated example, consider the tree in Figure 3.9 for the NP *the small mouse*. The rule in (17) again applies first, yielding the D *the* and an NP. We know that an NP can contain an AP and an N from the rule in (18). The N here is *mouse*, and the AP contains the A *small* (following the rule in (15)).

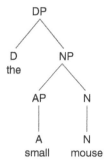

Figure 3.9 Determiner Phrase tree with adjective

Adding DPs to the grammar in this way is a more radical step than it may seem. DP is now the "topmost level" of most of the constituents that we previously called NPs. *The adorable puppy* and *a cranky cat* from (2), for example, are DPs under this new rule system – there is just no other way to have a determiner otherwise. Keeping this in mind, our final list of phrase structure rules is below.

(19)   Sentence → DP VP
VP → V (DP) (PP)
PP → P DP
DP → D NP
NP → (AP) N
AP → A

The discussion in this section of the chapter has been intended to give you a sense of the methodology of syntax, as if English were a totally unstudied language. We have examined its words and its sentences, and discovered its main constituents and how the constituents are ordered. We have developed a set of phrase structure rules to capture the generalizations about constituency and ordering that we have found.

However, syntacticians have of course been working on English (and many other languages) for many years now. The next section gives you a taste of the current approach to phrase structure: projection.

The grammar: modern theory

In this section, the basics of modern syntactic theory are laid out. The discussion is fairly high-level, but it connects back to the discussion in the previous section. The section introduces a new way of building syntactic trees (from the bottom up) as well as several new terms for specific positions in syntactic trees (**specifier** and **complement**). Finally, our stock of functional categories will be enriched with two new categories (**inflection** and **complementizer**).

Projection

We have informally discussed syntactic trees as if they follow phrase structure rules from the "top down." However, current research on grammar assumes that syntactic trees are constructed "bottom-up" through a series of specific structure-building operations. To build phrases and sentences from a bottom-up perspective, we start with the syntactic categories themselves – determiners, nouns, adjectives, etc. The categories then project phrases of the same category (for example, a noun projects an NP; Figure 3.10). This is one of the basic operations in modern phrase structure. From a **projection** perspective, you can think of a syntactic category as a kind of seed and its projection as a stalk that it sends out. Projection does have certain advantages over a top-down approach – primarily, it makes the grammar simpler, and one of the overall goals of linguistics is to have our analyses be as simple and elegant as possible.

Let's start with the simple sentence *Those children want a puppy* and see how a projection approach works. The grammar starts by selecting the nouns *children* and *puppy* from the lexicon and letting them project NPs, as in Figure 3.10.

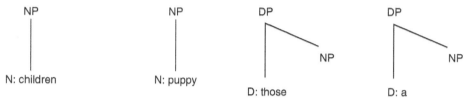

Figure 3.10 Projection of two simple NPs

Figure 3.11 Projection of DP from determiners *those* and *a*

Similarly, the determiners *those* and *a* project DPs, as in Figure 3.11. Each of these determiners not only projects a phrasal node of its own category (a DP), but also branches out to another node called its **complement**, the phrase it needs to be complete. The complement of a determiner is an NP.

A similar case is the projection from the verb *want*, which is shown in Figure 3.12. *Want* is a transitive verb that requires a direct object to come after it, so it projects a VP but also branches out to another node for the direct object, its complement. *Want* takes a DP direct object, so its complement is a DP.

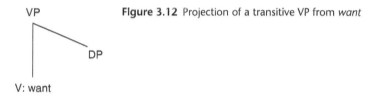

Figure 3.12 Projection of a transitive VP from *want*

Merger

Once the complement nodes of the determiners and the verb are projected, these categories must be combined with a phrase of the type they need. To do that, the grammar must have a mechanism that combines phrases. This is done by **merging** one phrase with another. **Merger** is the second main type of structure-building operation.

Each of the determiners in our example – *those* and *a* – projects a DP, and each of these DPs needs an NP as its complement. The grammar has already projected the two NPs, in Figure 3.10, and the two DPs, in Figure 3.11. All it has to do is merge the two NPs into the two DPs, and the DPs will be complete. The way this works is illustrated in Figure 3.13.

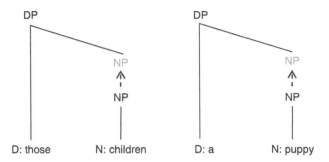

Figure 3.13 NP *children* merges with the Complement NP node in DP *those* to create DP *those children*. NP *puppy* merges with the complement NP node projected from D *a* to create DP *a puppy*

Notice that at the beginning of a merger, there are two NP nodes, but only one NP afterwards. In a merger, the two nodes blend together to form one merged node. Recall that in Figure 3.12, the verb phrase whose head is *want* needed a DP complement, which can now be merged into the VP as illustrated in Figure 3.14.

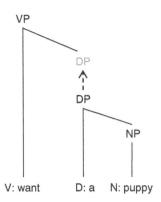

Figure 3.14 DP *a puppy* merges with complement DP node projected from V *want* to create VP *want a puppy*

We now have the first phrase in Figure 3.13 (*those children*) and the phrase in Figure 3.14 (*want a puppy*) which the grammar has created by merger. A new functional category is needed to put them together. Previously, we used the Sentence node to put together these two phrases (recall the rule: Sentence → DP VP). However, "Sentence" is not a syntactic category of English like noun, determiner, or verb, and previous linguistic research has argued that, to be maximally simple, the grammar should only use syntactic categories.

In fact, there is a functional category available to replace the Sentence node. This category, called **inflection**, is responsible for the tense of the sentence (among other duties). Consider the data below.

(20)   a. *The puppy jump
     b. The puppy jumps
     c. The puppy jumped

(20a) is ungrammatical, but (20b) and (20c) are grammatical. The difference between (20a) and (20b,c) is inflection, or more specifically, tense. There is a present-tense suffix *-s* on *run* in (20b) and a past-tense suffix *-ed* in (20c). Inflection is thus what makes a sentence a sentence – what connects phrases into one proposition – so it is a valid replacement for the sentence node. Therefore, we will assume there is an **Inflection Phrase** (IP) projected from present and past tense, as well as from modals like *can* or *may* (try adding *can* to (20a) – it has much the same ameliorating effect as adding a tense suffix), as in Figure 3.15.

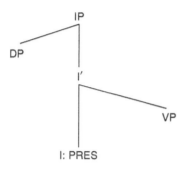

Figure 3.15 Projection of IP from PRES

The role of inflection in the structure of sentences is somewhat different from the role of the phrases we have projected so far. Inflection phrases provide the central "scaffolding" for a sentence, a structure to which the more meaningful lexical category phrases will be attached. In the sentence we have been working with (*Those children want a puppy*), the head of the inflection is not a word you can hear, but the abstract element PRES (present tense; sometimes present tense is realized as *-s* and sometimes it is purely abstract).

Even for a functional category, inflection is special. Like verbs and prepositions, it projects a complement branch; to be complete it has to have a verb phrase attached. But inflection phrases are also unusual because they also project a **specifier position**. A specifier requires an extra level of structure with a particular configuration. There is an intermediate node between the lowest category (I) and the IP. In modern linguistic theory this intermediate node is called I′, pronounced "I-bar." The complement verb phrase branches from I′ and the specifier branches in the opposite direction from the higher IP. This upper piece of structure is called a "specifier" for a reason that was explainable in earlier versions of syntactic theory, but now is simply a conventional technical term. The specifier of an inflection phrase is the subject of the sentence, here a determiner phrase. Inflection phrases typically have determiner phrases as their specifiers, although other phrases are possible.

The structure resulting from joining DP and VP with IP is shown in Figure 3.16. Notice that at first the DP and VP complements projected from IP have no content. To give them content, the DP containing *those children* is merged with the DP in the specifier position of IP (this is our first example of specifier merger) and the VP containing *want a puppy* is merged with the VP. The Inflection Phrase combines and relates the content of the DP and the VP. The result is shown in Figure 3.16.

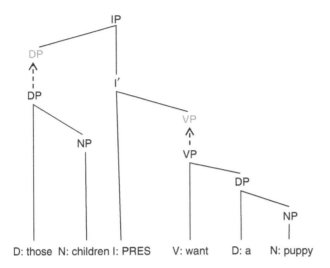

Figure 3.16 Merger of DP and VP into the specifier and complementizer positions of IP

The generation of the sentence by the grammar is almost complete. There has to be a mechanism to get the present tense (PRES) attached to the verb. In this sentence, PRES is not audible so you can't hear whether it attached or not. But if our sentence had been *My child wants a puppy*, we could have seen the present-tense marker in the suffix *-s*. The mechanism that combines verbs and their tense turned out to be surprisingly complicated for syntactic theory, so we'll just state here that there is a way to get tense inflections where they belong.

Our grammar must have one more functional category, the **complementizer**. The complementizers are bolded in (21).

(21)   a. I heard **that** those children want a puppy
       b. He wondered **if** it would rain

Complementizers allow sentences to be embedded in other sentences. For example, in a sentence like (21a), the sentence *those children want a puppy* is embedded in a higher sentence as the complement of the verb *heard*. **Complementizer Phrases** (CPs) also are necessary to understand the structure of questions and relative clauses (e.g. *The man who came in was angry*), as well as indirect quotations (e.g. *He said that those children want a puppy*). Complementizers take inflection phrases as complements. The projection of a CP looks like Figure 3.17.

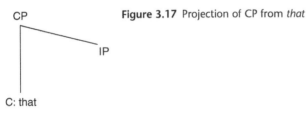

Figure 3.17 Projection of CP from *that*

In a sentence like *I heard that those children want a puppy* – following merger of the IP *those children want a puppy* – the CP would look like Figure 3.18.

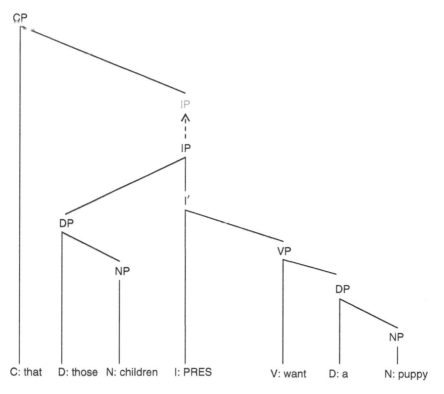

Figure 3.18 IP *those children want a puppy* merges with CP headed by Complementizer *that* to create CP *(I heard) that those children want a puppy*

BOX 3.3 DETERMINER PHRASE AND POSSESSION

We have introduced several categories that we have called **functional**. The functional nature of Inflection Phrases is easy to see, since they serve as the "scaffold structure" for sentences, holding the inflection and the positions for the subject Determiner Phrase and the main Verb Phrase. Similarly Complementizer Phrases have the function of providing the structure for embedded clauses. But what about Determiner Phrases? From the examples we have shown, determiner seems just like a lexical category, projecting a phrase and a complement branch from a head with some semantic content.

One clearly functional duty of Determiner Phrases is to provide the scaffolding for possessive constructions, like *The cowboy's hat*. This possessive construction is a DP projected from an unusual determiner, the possessive morpheme spelled *'s*. The possessive determiner projects an NP complement, as usual, and this time it also projects a specifier (like inflection phrases do). The projection looks like this:

BOX 3.3 **(cont.)**

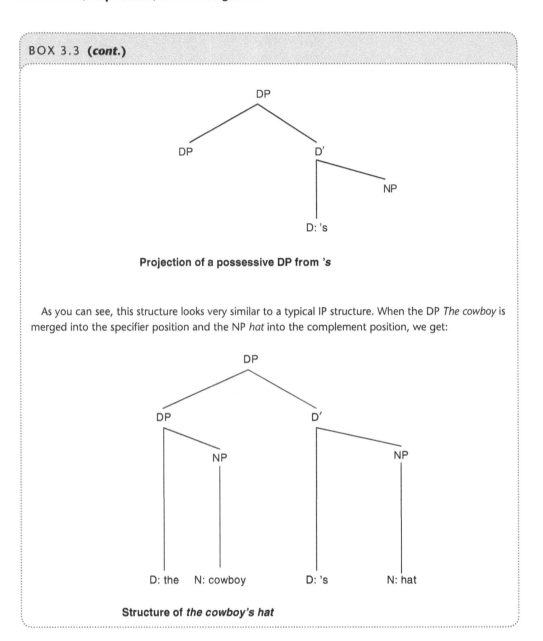

Projection of a possessive DP from 's

As you can see, this structure looks very similar to a typical IP structure. When the DP *The cowboy* is merged into the specifier position and the NP *hat* into the complement position, we get:

Structure of *the cowboy's hat*

Adjunction

There are two methods for building phrases that we have seen thus far: projection and merger. We have seen how words project a phrase of their same category, and how merger joins phrases by placing one phrase into the complement or specifier of another phrase. It is also possible to merge phrases that are not complements or specifiers. This is called **adjunction** and it adds modifiers to phrases. Heads, complements, and specifiers make up the core meaning of a phrase, while modifiers add extra description. Modifiers that we have encountered thus far include adjectives (*small, yellow, adorable*) and adverbs (*honestly,* *slowly, tirelessly*). Since adjoined phrases are different from heads, complements, and specifiers, adjunction creates a site for merger by extending the phrasal node of the host phrase.

Figures 3.19–3.21 illustrate adjunction from a bottom-up point of view. Suppose we want to add an adjective to the subject of our example sentence so that it reads. *Those little children want a puppy.* We would adjoin the adjective phrase *little* to the noun phrase *children.* First, the grammar would project a new adjective phrase (AP) from the adjective *little,* as in Figure 3.19.

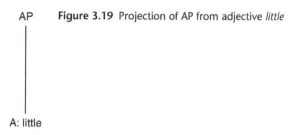

AP **Figure 3.19** Projection of AP from adjective *little*

A: little

The grammar then would create the "roof-shaped" structure circled in Figure 3.20 that extends the NP *children.*

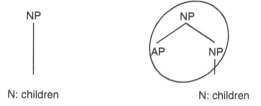

Figure 3.20 Extension of the NP *children* to accommodate the adjunction of AP

The new AP would be merged into this new structure. This is shown in Figure 3.21.

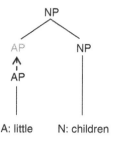

Figure 3.21 AP *little* merges with the adjunction structure to create *little children*

Now suppose we add an adverb to our sentence so that it reads: *Those little children want a puppy badly.* The adverb *badly* would project an adverb phrase (AdvP), which the grammar would then merge with the verb phrase *want a puppy,* using the same mechanism. Figures 3.22 and 3.23 show the merger of the adverb phrase *badly* with the VP *want a puppy.*

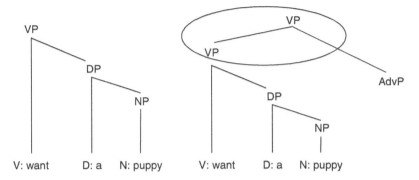

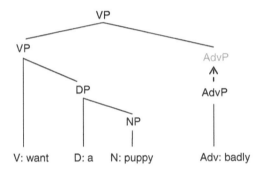

Figure 3.22 Extension of the VP *want a puppy* to accommodate the adjunction of AdvP (Adverb Phrase).

Building the rest of the structure for *Those little children want a puppy badly* would proceed in the following way. First the NP in Figure 3.21 would be merged with the complement branch of the DP headed by *those*, as in Figure 3.13, to create the DP *those little children*. The resulting DP and the VP in Figure 3.23, *want a puppy badly*, would be merged into IP as before to create the whole sentence (IP).

Figure 3.23 AdvP *badly* merges with the adjunction structure to create *want a puppy badly*

In this section, we have run through several examples of how to build trees from the bottom up, using projection, merger, and adjunction. You have seen in brief the syntactic concepts and categories that are common in current syntactic work, including complements, specifiers, inflection and Inflection Phrases, and complementizers and Complementizer Phrases.

Grammars are finite; language is not

Although capable of complex processes, human beings' brains are finite. There are a limited number of cells in the human brain, and therefore a limited (though large) number of connections between those cells. Since grammars are part of people's brains, grammars must be finite, too. But an individual human being has the capacity to understand and produce an infinite number of sentences. People say and hear completely new, or novel, sentences all the time. Take any sentence from the last chapter. Although you had never heard it, read it, or said it before in just that form, you were able to understand what it means. How can a finite grammar have an infinite capacity for producing and understanding sentences?

Regardless of where we were raised and whether we grew up in some English-speaking community or in Tokyo or Ulan Bator, speakers of every language have **recursive devices** – means by which the same grammatical processes can apply more than once – in their grammars that make it possible for them to produce sentences of indefinite length.

Multiple adjunction

One such recursive device is the rule for adjoining adjectives. We can insert adjectives repeatedly with no principled limit by repeated **adjunction**. You can easily imagine someone saying, *She fell in love with this intelligent guy*. This is accomplished by adjoining the adjective *intelligent* to the noun phrase *guy*. But it would be possible to go a lot beyond that; you could say, *She fell in love with this intelligent, handsome, considerate, romantic, thoughtful, adorable guy* simply by adjoining more adjectives. The grammar would not prevent you from going on and on, because the rule for adjoining adjectives is recursive.

Embedding

A more complex recursive device allows any sentence to be placed in the larger frame of another sentence. Start with what you think is the longest sentence you can imagine; you can make it longer simply by putting *He said that. . .* in front of it. If your original sentence was *The woman in New York wore a black dress*, it would be lengthened to *He said that the woman in New York wore a black dress*. You could lengthen that sentence by using the same structure again. Even if you have already added *He said that*, you could add something similar: *She said that he said that the woman in New York wore a black dress*. You could keep reframing your developing sentence indefinitely: *Bill knew that Jill thought that Tom said that. . .* You might get tired, but your grammar would never limit the length of your sentence.

Another kind of embedding involves the use of relative clauses. Maybe you remember the children's song, "The House that Jack Built":

> This is the house that Jack built.
> This is the cheese that lay in the house that Jack built.
> This is the mouse that nibbled the cheese that lay in the house that Jack built.

If you had the patience and lived long enough, you could string relative clauses together indefinitely: *This is the cow that kicked the dog that chased the cat that killed the rat that caught the mouse that nibbled the cheese that lay in the house that Jack built.*

Coordination

Another recursive device found in all languages is **coordination**. Coordination links two (or more) sentences (or phrases, or words) together on equal terms, using coordinating conjunctions like *and*, *but*, and *or*: *You can try or you can give up*. Sentences can be coordinated indefinitely as well: *Rick went to a movie, and Ellen went to the store, and Stuart worked, but Mike slept and Sue read a book. . .*

The significance of recursion

Because grammars have recursive devices which permit expressions to be indefinitely long, the various recursive devices can be combined to produce an infinite variety of sentences: *This is the house that Sue knew that Jack built and this is the mouse that Bill saw eating the savory, delicious, yellow, gourmet cheese...* Since recursion is an integral part of the grammar, it follows that no one can learn a language by memorizing all the sentences of that language. There must be some other explanation for how human beings are able to learn them.

Restrictions on the grammar

Thus far in the chapter, we have shown how sentence structure is projected from syntactic categories, and how it is represented in syntactic trees. Besides building sentence structure, though, the grammar can also move phrases and clauses around, copying them from their original position, and merging them somewhere else. In the question *What would the puppy like?*, the word *what* is understood to be the direct object of *like*. Direct objects of verbs follow the verb in English (*The puppy likes bacon*), but *what* appears at the front of the sentence. Linguists have hypothesized, therefore, that *what* is projected and merged to the right of *like*, but then moves to a higher position in the sentence (note that the modal *would* also comes before the subject of the sentence, unlike in a statement where it would come after the subject). The starting state of the sentence *What would the puppy like?* is shown to the left of the arrow in (22), and the endpoint to the right of the arrow

(22)   The puppy would like what → What would the puppy like

These questions are often referred to as **wh-questions** because they involve movement of **wh-words** like *what, when, where, who, which*, etc. The grammar can also delete portions of the structure. In the sentence *The puppy likes tuna and the cat does, too*, we understand that the cat also likes tuna, but the verb phrase *likes tuna* has been deleted from the second clause and replaced by *does, too*. Movement of a syntactic constituent is theorized to take two steps – copying the constituent to a new position in the sentence and deleting the original constituent – because grammar behaves as if something (a "trace") is left behind after a constituent has been moved. For example, in (22) the role of *what* as direct object of the verb *like* is "recoverable" from its original position as the complement of *like*. Deletion and movement are both restricted in quite subtle ways. English speakers "know" the restrictions on deletion and movement in a way analogous to the fictitious robot who "knew" rules of basketball that it had never been taught. The combination of watching basketball and the robot's internal programming made it possible for it to play the game by the rules. In the same way, English speakers' experience with English in childhood, combined with the linguistic genotype that they have inherited, makes it possible for them to show knowledge of the language, including its untaught principles.

> ### BOX 3.4 REPRESENTING PHRASE STRUCTURE WITH BRACKETS
>
> So far, we have represented phrasal structure using tree diagrams, which are graphically useful for showing the hierarchical relationships between words and phrases, but take up a lot of space. Linguists often use a linear format, called a labeled bracketing, to represent sentences:
>
> [IP[DP those children][VP want [DP a puppy]]]
>
> In this format, brackets surround everything underneath a node, and the bracket is labeled with the same label that a node in a tree would have. The entire sentence, within the outermost brackets, is an IP. Within the IP there is a DP (*those children*) followed by a VP (*want a puppy*). The verb phrase consists of *want*, which we have chosen not to label explicitly, and another DP (*a puppy*). When they use this format, linguists leave out much of the internal structure of each of the constituent phrases, unless it is relevant to a particular analysis.

You can do without *that*, but not always

Let us take one example. In English, complementizers like *that* are optional, unlike equivalent words in Dutch, French, Spanish, Italian, and other languages, where complementizers are required. So a child raised in an English-speaking home might hear the sentences of (23a–c) pronounced with or without the complementizer *that*. These experiences would show them that *that* is optional so they will learn a complementizer-deletion rule like (23d).

(23)   a. Peter said [CP that/0 [IP Kay left]].
       b. Kay doesn't believe [CP that/0 Ray is smart].
       c. It was obvious [CP that/0 [IP Kay left]].
       d. That → 0

So far, we can see that children learn different things about their native languages, depending on the input they are exposed to. However, children also know things about their language that they could never have learned in this way. In fact, *that* is not always optional; it is required in the contexts of (24), where the asterisk next to the zero means that deletion of *that* renders the sentence ungrammatical.

(24)   a. Peter said yesterday in Chicago [that/*0 Kay had left].
       b. Fay believes, but [IP Kay doesn't [VP [V e [CP that/*0 Ray is smart]]]].
       c. [that/*0 Kay left] was obvious to all of us.

Something in the English grammar – and therefore in the English speaker's brain – requires the complementizer *that* in these kinds of sentences. But no adult or child ever says *Kay left was obvious to all of us*, so no one can point out to a child that this is an ungrammatical sentence in English. This is called negative evidence, information about what does *not* occur in a language. Children hear sentences like (24) only with complementizers, but they can't possibly learn from what they hear that the complementizer is *not* optional in just the contexts in (24). Children acquiring English "know" that the cases in (24) are impossible, but since they don't have evidence to learn this from, this knowledge must be coming from somewhere else. A straightforward answer is that the mental organ for language – which many linguists call **Universal Grammar** or UG – must be playing some role. This conclusion matches the scientist's conclusion that the robot must have been programmed with basketball rules, because it hadn't seen enough evidence to learn them by watching basketball games.

The facts that we are presenting may seem too commonplace to require explanation. "Of course you can't say 'Kay left was obvious to all of us'," you might think, "Anybody can see that." But in Isaac Newton's time, everybody knew that apples fall down, and nobody thought it was anything that needed to be explained. Newton advanced the field of physics and made a place for himself in history by asking "Why?" Linguists are doing the same thing when they ask questions about *that*-deletion. The results we get are surprising in the same way that the discovery of gravity was, though they are not yet as widely known.

The problem of *that* complementizer deletion is that *that* can be deleted in English in some contexts, but not in others. To see why, let's consider (23a) in detail. Figure 3.24 shows the tree structure of the verb phrase of (23a). (We're assuming that the abstract inflection PAST has already become part of the verb *leave* giving the past-tense form *left*. The same thing has happened with *said*.) If you look carefully at Figure 3.24, you will see that [CP (*that*) [IP *Kay left*]] is the complement of the verb phrase, and also directly adjacent to the head of that verb phrase, *said*. The same is true of the other examples in (23), where *that* deletion is possible.

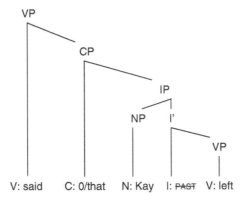

Figure 3.24 *That Kay left* as part of the complement of *said* and adjacent to *said*

In (24a), on the other hand, the CP [CP (*that*) [IP *Kay had left*]] is still the complement of *say*, but it is not adjacent to *say*; it is adjacent to *Chicago* (and *Chicago* is not the head of the verb phrase and the CP containing *Kay had left* is not the complement of *Chicago*). In (24b) the CP containing *Ray is smart* is the complement of the elided but understood verb *believe*, which is not overt (the *e* means empty), and in (24c), the clause is the complement of nothing (it's the subject of the sentence).

By juxtaposing sentences in (23) and (24), linguists can deduce that the following principle is part of Universal Grammar.

(25)   If a language allows *that* complementizers to be deleted at all, they can be deleted only if they are adjacent to an overt head and they are in that head's complement.

With this principle, we solve this particular poverty-of-stimulus problem. Children learning English learn that the *that* complementizer can be deleted because they hear some kinds of sentences in which *that* may appear, but doesn't have to. In other types of sentences, like the ones in (24), they always hear *that*, never examples of its deletion. But the conditions under which *that* cannot be deleted depend on some very subtle properties of grammar, involving notions like a clause being a complement of some audible word, and nothing like this is ever part of children's experience. Since children are sensitive to it anyway, we conclude that they "know" this principle already.

Heavy Determiner Phrase movement

There are a number of other instances in which some principle about adjacency to a complement is operative, including **"heavy" DP movement**. This applies when the grammar moves to the right a long, complicated DP from a position where it would occur if it were shorter. For example, while it would be natural to say *I saw the bird on a twig*, if you wanted to describe that bird more fully, you might switch things around – *I saw on a twig the most amazing, multicolored, long-feathered bird* – moving the long DP complement of *saw* all the way to the right end of the sentence. Under the approach we are presenting, that means copying and moving the "heavy" DP and then deleting the copied element. In the examples below, the DPs are in brackets, the original position of the DP is noted by struck-through text; note also that the sentence resulting from moving the DP is written in italics.

(26)   I gave [~~the small box of books that Sasha packed up yesterday~~] to Chris [the small box of books that Sasha packed up yesterday]
I gave to Chris the small box of books that Sasha packed up yesterday.

In (26) the "heavy" DP *the small box of books that Sasha packed up yesterday* is the complement of *gave*, and it can be moved to the end of the sentence. However, consider (27).

(27)   *[[~~the small box of books that Sasha packed up yesterday~~] has arrived] [the small box of books that Sasha packed up yesterday].
**has arrived the small box of books that Sasha packed up yesterday*

In (27), we see that the same heavy DP can't be moved when it is first in the sentence – that is, when it is not adjacent to an overt word. This shows us that we can expand the principle in (25) so that it applies to more than just complementizers. The expanded version is in (28) (recall that movement involves copying a phrase to a new position and then deleting the original).

(28)   An element, if it is deletable, can be deleted if it is adjacent to an overt head, and it is in that head's complement.

In (27), the DP (the clause struck through) is not the complement of anything, so it cannot possibly conform to the principle in (28). Actually executing the movement results in an ungrammatical sentence. Note that our principle has become more general, covering more data (both complementizer deletion and heavy DP movement) while retaining accuracy. An efficient increase in descriptive adequacy (and explanatory power) like this is called **parsimony**, a positive result for a grammatical theory.

The problem illustrated by the example in (27) thus is another poverty-of-stimulus problem to be solved by our UG principle about phrasal deletion. We postulate that children can learn from their environment that complementizers may be omitted and that heavy DPs may be moved. This much has to be learned, because it is not true of all languages. However, children learning English do not *learn* the restrictions. They can't learn that complementizers cannot be omitted in (24), or that *the small box of books that Sasha packed yesterday* cannot be moved in (27) because they are unlearnable. There is no relevant evidence of these restrictions in what children hear. Postulating that children already "know" the simple UG condition (28) – which comes from their genes, not their experience – permits us to say that children learn a few simple things from their experience and, once they learn these things, they have a surprisingly complex capacity that enables them to omit complementizers and move heavy DPs appropriately. And much more, as we shall see.

> **Other restrictions on movement and deletion**
> *Not all movements and deletions are subject to the restrictions we have described here. Wh-movement under some circumstances, for example, is subject to restrictions we do not have the space to illustrate.*

The Binding Theory

Another major type of restriction on the grammar is found in the distribution of pronouns: *he*, *her*, *it*, etc. Linguists have long been intrigued by the constraints on where pronouns, reflexive pronouns (*herself*, *itself*, etc.), and full noun phrases can appear. These constraints are about how these elements can be interpreted, depending on where they appear in a structure, rather than being about movement or deletion.

Consider the facts in (29). The pronouns *she* and *her* may refer to Kim in (29a, b) but not in (29c, d).

(29)   a. Kim_i loves $her_{i,j}$ mother.
　　　　b. Kim_i expected $she_{i,j}$ would win.
　　　　c. Kim_i expected her_j to win.
　　　　d. Kim_i loves her_j.

> **Use of subscripts to indicate coreference**
> *We express coreference by using the subscripted indices i and j; elements referring to the same person or referent will have the same subscripted index. In (29a, b), Kim may refer to the same person (and have the same index i) as her and she, but her and she may also refer to some other (female) person, indicated by the index j. In contrast, in (29c, d) her must refer to somebody else than (and has a different index from) Kim.*

Consider also the facts in (30). Sentences (30a, b) may be statements about one person named Kim (so the same index is possible). However, (30c–e) may only be interpreted as statements about two people of the same name (distinct indices). We know this independently of context or of any aspect of the speech situation; we seem to know this simply from the way the words are arranged – from the form of the expression itself.

(30) a. Kim_i's father says $Kim_{i,j}$ is happy.
b. Kim_i's father loves $Kim_{i,j}$'s mother.
c. Kim_i loves Kim_j's mother.
d. Kim_i says Kim_j is happy.
e. Kim_i says Kim_j's mother is happy.

How does the form of the expression convey all this information? Why, for example, may *her* refer to Kim in (29a) but the two *Kims* in (30c) may not refer to the same person? Why may *she* refer to Kim in (29b) but not *her* in (29c)? Here is another area where children acquire a system which goes far beyond the input they receive.

Again we have elaborate subconscious knowledge, which is not acquired through instruction of any kind; you were probably not aware of these distinctions until you read the last paragraph. A child may hear (29a) in a context where *her* clearly refers to Kim or in a context where *her* refers to another woman unnamed in this expression, perhaps the queen of England. On the other hand, sentence (29d) is heard only in a context where *her* refers to another woman – in fact to any woman other than Kim. Children come to know this without being supplied with evidence or being told that *her* cannot refer to Kim. If there is no learning here, then that would explain why we do not observe children making errors in the reference of names and pronouns (except in a very specific domain, which we will not discuss); they show no signs of learning by trial-and-error. But how can we say that there is no learning? Is there an alternative?

The well-known linguist Noam Chomsky proposed the **Binding Theory** as a solution to these poverty-of-stimulus problems (Chomsky 1981). The Binding Theory permitted a dramatic simplification of these facts, if we assume that it is a component of Universal Grammar. The Binding Theory is stated, somewhat roughly, in (31). Like all components of UG, it is available to humans in *advance* of experience, actually enabling us to *interpret* our experience. The Binding Theory divides nominals (a cover term for nouns and pronouns) into three types: **anaphors** like *himself, themselves* (also known as reflexive pronouns), **pronouns** like *she, her, their*, and **names** (everything else).

(31) Binding Theory

Principle A:	Anaphors are coindexed with the subject of their Domain.
Principle B:	Pronouns are not coindexed with the subject of their Domain.
Principle C:	Names are not coindexed with the subject of *any* clause located to their left in the sentence in which the name appears.

Each nominal has a Domain, which is roughly its clause. The Binding Theory determines whether each nominal is coindexed with the subject of its clause or a clause to its left, or not. If the nominal *is* coindexed with the subject of its own or another clause to the left, it is said to be bound. That is how the Binding Theory gets its name.

(32)   a. [IP *[DP **Kim's mother**]* washed herself].
      b. [IP *[DP **Kim's mother**]* washed her].
      c. [IP [DP Kim's mother] said that [IP *[DP **the doctor**]* washed her]].
      d. [IP Kim said that [IP *[DP **the doctor**]* washed her]].
      e. [IP **Kim** said that [IP *[DP **the doctor**]* washed Kim]].

Let's see how these three simple principles predict the facts of English nominals. For each sentence, you should check to see what each nominal can and cannot refer to. Next, we have to first determine which of the three principles in (31) applies, and then check whether the theory matches your judgments.

In (32a), who can *herself* refer to? *Herself* is an anaphor, so it should obey Principle A, meaning it is coindexed with (and refers to) the subject of its own clause – its inflection phrase (IP). The boldface, italicized determiner phrase in (32a) is the subject of this clause, so *herself* must be coindexed with *Kim's mother*. It can't refer to just *Kim* because *Kim* is only *part* of the subject. So the only possible interpretation of *herself* in (32a) is that it refers to *Kim's mother*.

In (32b), *her* may refer to *Kim* or to some other female person not mentioned in the sentence. *Her* is a pronoun, so Principle B applies. Principle B says that *her* cannot refer to the subject of its own clause. If *her* referred to *Kim's mother*, the subject of its clause, it would be *bound* within its Domain, like *herself* is in (32a). But the rule for pronouns is the opposite of the rule for anaphors; it is forbidden for pronouns to be bound within their Domains. So *her* cannot refer to *Kim's mother*. Principle B states only that the pronoun *her* in (32b) cannot refer to its own subject. So *Her* can refer to *Kim* in (32b), because *Kim* is only part of the subject, or it may refer to any female person that makes sense in context, even if she is not mentioned in the sentence.

(32c) introduces an additional complexity, an embedded clause. *The doctor* is the subject of the clause in which the pronoun *her* is located, so according to Principle B *the doctor* cannot bind *her*; they can't refer to the same person. Although *Kim's mother* is the subject of an IP, it doesn't matter, since the Domain for *her* is only the lower IP. Whatever relationships we find beyond the pronoun's IP don't matter. In fact, *her* could refer to *Kim's mother*, to *Kim*, or to some other female person. The Binding Theory doesn't tell us what *her* can refer to – just that it can't refer to the subject of its own clause – *her* is free to refer to anyone else. Similarly, in (32d), *her* may be coindexed with *Kim*, but doesn't have to be, because *Kim* is outside of the Domain of the pronoun *her*.

The considerations in (32e) are different. *Kim* is a name, so Principle C of the Binding Theory applies. Principle C is the only one that doesn't refer to a Domain. It says that names must not be bound by *any* subject to their left in a sentence, period. The DP *the doctor* is a leftward subject, so it cannot refer to *Kim*. But the other *Kim* is excluded as well. It's not in the same clause as the lower *Kim*, but it is still a leftward subject. As a result, (32e) necessarily refers to two Kims; the lower *Kim* must be a different person than the higher *Kim*.

BOX 3.5 **EXCEPTIONS THAT PROVE THE RULE**

Occasionally, you might encounter examples like the one in the Bo Nanas cartoon that clearly violate the Binding Theory. The last clause in what Bo says contains a violation of Principle B, that a pronoun cannot refer to the subject of its own clause. The last clause in the cartoon has the structure in (i).

(i) [CP [IP I didn't [VP like me very much]]]

The pronoun *me* refers to Bo Nanas, who is also the referent of *I. I* is the subject of the clause containing *me*. The Binding Theory says that the anaphor *myself* is required here (and that *me* here cannot refer to the subject of its clause). But this exception actually *proves* the rule. Bo Nanas has sent himself a gift of leftover Halloween candy to make himself feel special. He wants it to seem that the package has been sent by someone else. His comment on the shabbiness of the gift is in the context of the pretense that the "I" who sent the gift is someone other than the "me" who received it. In that sense, Bo Nanas the sender is not the same person as Bo Nanas the receiver, and the cartoonist, John Kovaleski, exploits the Binding Theory to make that point. If there were no Principle B, the use of *me* would not be nearly so effective.

© 2004, John Kovaleski. Reprinted with permission

Notice also that (i) is the complement of the verb *thought. That,* which could have appeared adjacent to *thought,* has been deleted, as permitted by the principle in (25). The use of *myself* in the *if*-clause in the cartoon is an example of the adverbial use of an anaphor, which we don't cover in this chapter, although it turns out to conform to the Binding Theory.

The Binding Theory cannot be learned from the language that young children hear. It is part of UG, part of what children bring to their initial experience with language. As part of UG, children already "know" the three categories of nominals and the restrictions on their coreference. Children need only learn from language experience which words in their language fit into these categories – which words are anaphors, which are pronouns, and which are names. This they can do from positive evidence in the sentences that they hear. Once a child has learned that *themselves* is an anaphor, *her* is a pronoun, and so on, all the appropriate indexing relations follow, with no further learning required. The result is a simple system that covers an infinite number of possibilities.

BOX 3.6 **NOAM CHOMSKY**

Noam Chomsky is the leading scholar in the study of the structure of sentences. He is responsible not only for the Binding Theory, but for developing the argument from the poverty of stimulus, the concept of Universal Grammar, and the entire approach to syntactic analysis that is central to this chapter. The appearance of his monograph *Syntactic Structures* in 1957 revolutionized the study of syntax. The ideas presented there formed part of a more extensive work, *The Logical Structure of Linguistic Theory*, published in 1975 but widely circulated over the previous twenty years. His current work, represented by *The Minimalist Program* (1995) and related work over the past ten years, focuses on deriving the fewest and simplest principles that can explain the unlearnable aspects of linguistic grammars.

Chomsky is currently Institute Professor in the Department of Linguistics and Philosophy at the Massachusetts Institute of Technology. He has lectured at many universities in the United States and in other countries, and is the recipient of numerous honorary degrees and awards. He has written and lectured widely on linguistics, philosophy, intellectual history, contemporary issues, international affairs, and US foreign policy. Some of his most recent books are *A New Generation Draws the Line*; *New Horizons in the Study of Language and Mind*; *Rogue States*; *9–11: Was there an Alternative?*; *Understanding Power*; *On Nature and Language*; *Pirates and Emperors, Old and New*; *Chomsky on Democracy and Education*; *Middle East Illusions*; and *Hegemony or Survival*.

Summary

We have examined several areas of people's grammars and seen that we can account for complex arrays of distinctions between structures that people readily recognize as grammatical or ungrammatical. This ability comes from simple information at the level of UG that interacts with simple, grammar-specific information that is readily learnable from a child's linguistic experience. The picture we have painted of children learning the grammars of languages is a more nuanced version of the fantasy about the basketball-playing robot. The robot didn't know anything about basketball until it experienced people playing the game. But once it had the opportunity to watch and play the game, it turned out to have knowledge of basketball that went beyond anything it could have learned from its experience. In other words, its knowledge of basketball was a poverty-of-stimulus problem. Just as the scientist concluded that there must have been some preprogramming in the robot's case, linguists who pursue the line of research we have shown you also conclude that children are born prepared in specific ways to learn languages. They are born with a biological language organ – Universal Grammar.

Differences in syntax across languages

So far, we have focused on Universal Grammar and some of the principles that seem to be an intrinsic part of the language organ. On the other hand, within those principles, there is room for plenty of interesting differences in syntax from one language to another. We are now going to turn to some of those differences. Some of them touch on aspects of syntax that we have presented. For example, we have seen that complements appear to the right of their heads in English. In the sentence *The small dog chewed the bone*, the DP *the bone* is the complement of the verb *chewed*, and it is to the right of *chewed*. However, complements do not always appear to the right of their heads in all languages. We also briefly discussed wh-movement in English, where the wh-word *what* moves to the front in a sentence like *What would the puppy like?*. However, not all languages have movable wh-phrases.

Finally, we will present another syntactic phenomenon that we haven't yet mentioned, but that turns up in different ways. This is the feature of some languages that places nouns in various categories, with syntactic consequences. We call these **genders**, because that is what they are called in European languages that categorize nouns as feminine, masculine, and sometimes neuter. But languages elsewhere in the world categorize their nouns into many more genders than just two or three. We'll look at the ten or more genders in Swahili (also called Kiswahili) and the scores of genders in Thai.

Head–complement order in Hindi

In English, we have seen that the complements of verbs and of prepositions are attached to the right of the verb or preposition (the complements are underlined: *I like <u>tuna</u>, on <u>the chair</u>*). In Hindi, verb phrases have complements branching to the left, as in (33a). There are no *pre*positional phrases in Hindi; instead Hindi has *post*positions with complements to the left, like verb phrases, as in (33b).

(33) a. [_{VP} wah   pillaa   caahnaa]
               that   puppy   want

      b. [[_{PP} ghar   mɛ̃ɛ̃]
                house   in

Children learning Hindi get evidence from the language around them that the head–complement relationship is left-branching. However, although word order varies across languages, the complements of verbs and pre- or postpositional phrases behave like complements in any language.

Immobile wh-words in Thai

The treatment of question words in many languages is a lot less complicated than it is in English. In English and in many other European languages, question words are moved to the front of their sentences. In other languages the words that would be translated as wh-words in English simply remain in their original positions. This is true of Thai, where questions are asked as in (34) (examples from Haas and Subhanka 1945: 58–59; an honorific is a word that conveys respect for the addressee – they are required in certain languages).

(34) a. satăaniiródfay   jùu   **thîinăj**   khràb
         station-railroad   be-located   where   (honorific)
         'Where is the railroad station?'

      b. khun   jàag   cà?   sýy   **ʔàraj**
         you   want   will   buy   what
         'What do you want to buy?'

      c. ródfay   cà?   ɔ̀ɔg   **mýaray**
         train   will   leave   when
         'When will the train leave?'

Thai children hear these question words in the same location in which they are understood. Although UG gives them the principles they would need for movement, these principles are not needed for elements like *thîinăj, ʔàraj,* and *mýaray,* since they don't move.

Gender in languages

Many languages have genders associated with all their nouns. English refers to gender only in third-person pronouns, and then gender is "natural" gender, with *he* and *him* referring to people and animals that are sexually male, *she* and *her* referring to females and *it* for everything else (except for the outmoded practice of referring to ships and maybe automobiles as *she*). In a language like German, though, every noun has a masculine, feminine, or neuter gender. Sometimes the genders are just the ones you would expect, so *Frau* 'woman' is feminine and *Mann* 'man' is masculine. Usually, though, the assignment of gender is quite arbitrary. For example, of the common eating utensils, *Messer* 'knife' is neuter, *Gabel* 'fork' is feminine, and *Löffel* 'spoon' is masculine. When these words are put into phrases, determiners and adjectives have to have endings that match the gender of the nouns, so that you get the distinctions in (35).

(35) a. [$_{DP}$ ein   klein*es*   Messer]
              a   small   knife

      b. [$_{DP}$ eine   klein*e*   Gabel]
              a   small   fork

      b. [$_{DP}$ ein   klein*er*   Löffel]
              a   small   spoon

These gender assignments have to be learned by anyone learning German. Generally you can't guess what gender a noun belongs to. There is nothing particularly feminine about a fork, for instance, or masculine about a spoon.

The task of learning genders in Swahili, a Bantu language widely spoken in East Africa, is much more daunting. Swahili has some ten genders, which are usually called noun classes. Bantu experts count the genders in different ways, so the number of genders is given as anywhere from seven to eighteen. Like the genders in German and other European languages, Swahili genders (noun classes) have meanings, but the assignment of nouns to genders is sometimes arbitrary, like the German words for knife, fork, and spoon. For example, the *m/mi* class (so called because of the prefixes on singular and plural nouns, respectively) is sometimes called the "tree" class, because many of the nouns in it refer to trees and plants, but there are words for tools and other things that have this gender, as well.

Swahili genders have a pervasive effect in the syntax of sentences. Not only do adjectives have to have matching prefixes (not suffixes, as in German), but the nouns themselves and the verbs they agree with also have to have the right prefixes. Some of how this works is illustrated in (36) (examples adapted from *Languages of the World 7: African Language Families*, and Katamba 2003).

(36) a. M-tu   m-moja   m-refu   a-li-anguka
         M-person   m-one   m-tall   m-PAST-fall
         'One tall person fell.'

      b. Ki-kapu   ki-dogo   ki-mifika
         Ki-basket   ki-little ki-arrived
         'The little basket arrived.'

In (36a), *mtu* is Swahili for 'person' and the root *-tu* belongs, naturally enough, to the "person" (*m/wa*) gender. The words for 'one' and 'tall' modifying *mtu* share the "person" gender prefix. So does the verb root *-anguka* 'fall,' even though the prefix is pronounced *a-*. *Kikapu* 'basket' has the "inanimate object" (*ki/vi*) gender. As (36b) shows, its modifier 'little' and the verb in its clause 'arrived' all share the appropriate gender prefix. In the case of transitive verbs, the verb agrees with both its subject and its complement.

(37) Wa-toto   wa-na-ki-soma   ki-tabu
      Wa-child   wa-pres-ki-read   ki-book
      'The children are reading the book.'

In (37), the root -*toto* 'child,' also in the *m/wa* gender, has the plural prefix for its gender, as does the verb. But the verb also agrees with its object -*tabu* from the *ki/vi* gender. Similar agreement patterns exist for the remaining eight or so genders. In these examples, the meaning of the noun matches the meaning of the gender, but this is not always the case. The *ki/vi* "inanimate object" gender also includes a few words for people and animals and some body parts.

In Thai, nouns are categorized in a gender-like way, but in Thai, there are literally scores of genders. Thai is not a language with prefixes or suffixes, so the genders show up in a very different way. Thai does not indicate whether an object is plural, so whether you are talking about one or many things is inferred from the context. If you want to specify a specific number of things, it is necessary to use a *classifier* along with the number. Consider the Thai examples in (38).

(38) a. phǒm   rúucàg   khruu
         I   know   teacher.
         'I know a teacher.'
         'I know teachers.'

      b. phǒm   rúucàg   khruu   khon   sɔ̌ɔŋ
         I   know   teacher   Clf.   two
         'I know two teachers.'

In (38a), only the context would determine whether I know a teacher or a number of teachers. In (38b), I specify that I know two teachers, and the classifier used for people has to be used. If I wanted to say that I see two clouds, I would use a different classifier, as in (39).

(39) phǒm   hěn   mêeg   kɔ̌ɔn   sɔ̌ɔŋ
      I   see   cloud   Clf.   two
      'I see two clouds.'

The classifier *kɔ̌ɔn* means things that are perceived as lumps, including stones and lumps of sugar, as well as clouds. Thai classifiers (genders) often refer to physical properties. For example, the classifier *baj* represents the gender for fruits and *phy̌yn* is the gender including pieces of cloth in a form than can be used, like towels and curtains. But like most gender systems, there is considerable unpredictability about what nouns are in what gender. The gender represented by *baj* includes not only fruits, but also eggs and containers. Another gender, calling for the classifier *khan*, covers umbrellas, forks and spoons, streetcars and automobiles (Haas and Subhanka 1945).

Languages have a tendency to group nouns in categories that sometimes have a relationship to the meanings of the nouns that are included, but are often entirely arbitrary.

These categories are called genders in European languages, and we have used the term for the categories in Swahili and Thai to emphasize what they have in common. Gender has an effect on the syntax of the languages that have gender, but these effects are quite different from one type of language to another.

CHAPTER SUMMARY

Perhaps the most startling thing about the structure of sentences is not about structure at all, but the fact that much of grammatical structure does not have to be learned. People "know" a lot about what is or isn't a possible grammatical structure without having been taught, or even having had the right kind of experience to have learned it. Instead, there appears to be a language organ that encompasses a person's language ability, with its own intrinsic properties. These properties determine much of what the ultimate structure of someone's grammar will be, independently of their experience. This line of reasoning is called the poverty-of-the-stimulus argument.

One principle of the structure of sentences is **compositionality**; the fact that sentences are composed of clauses and phrases, which in turn are made up of smaller clauses and phrases or words. Rules of phrase structure can capture the generalizations about what types of phrases can appear where in sentences, and what kinds of phrases and words can appear within other phrases. The same task is achieved in modern syntactic theory by projection of simple phrases from words from the mental lexicon. Some phrases have complement and/or specifier branches which merge with phrases that have been projected from other words. A special kind of merger is called adjunction, which allows modifiers (such as adjectives) to be included in phrases. Once phrases are constructed by projection and merger, they can be further modified by movement and deletion.

Grammars are finite but are capable of producing an infinite number of sentences. This is achieved by recursion, which allows the same grammatical processes to apply repeatedly, with no principled limitation on how often they may apply. This means that there is no longest sentence in any language, and consequently no limit to the number of sentences it has. Three recursive devices that all languages have are multiple adjunction, embedding, and coordination.

From birth, children seem to "know" structural principles restricting the movement and deletion of phrases. Without being taught, they also "know" the principles of the Binding Theory, which limits the possibilities of coreference between nominal expressions.

This chapter has emphasized what is in common across languages, but there are remarkable differences among languages as well. The word order between heads and complements can vary and not all languages have movable wh-phrases. Grammatical gender is far more varied and important to the syntax of many languages than it is in English.

Exercises

Identifying syntactic categories

EXERCISE 3.1

Identify the syntactic category or categories of each of the following words. Then justify your choice using the distributional definitions provided above. NB: many of the definitions are multi-part. A word need only fulfill one of the parts to count as a member of a syntactic category.

1. hamster
2. recently
3. large
4. love
5. illuminate
6. printer
7. cool
8. yesterday

The predictions of phrase structure rules

EXERCISE 3.2

Consider the following phrase structure rules (repeated here from (9) on p. 112):

Sentence → NP VP
NP → (D) (A) N
VP → V (NP)

Can these phrase structure rules generate each of the sentences below? Say precisely why or why not.

1. Gray mice eat cheese.
2. That book is excellent.
3. The fish swallowed the bait.
4. The student bought shoes at the mall.

Drawing trees

EXERCISE 3.3

Assuming that all the phrase structure rules from (19) hold, draw syntactic trees for the following sentences:

1. The dog left.
2. A rabbit went into the small hole.
3. The student watched a long movie.
4. The dancers ate the healthy food.
5. The student left a thick textbook in the classroom.
6. Some people run. (*some* is a determiner)
7. The bus drove by the tourists.
8. The little brown bird pecked the bagel.

Adjective Phrases

EXERCISE 3.4

Consider the following data:

a. The small hamster squeaked.
b. The <u>very</u> small hamster squeaked
c. That building is large.
d. That building is <u>quite</u> large.
e. The student created a bizarre painting.
f. The student created a <u>most</u> bizarre painting.

1. Do the underlined words meet any of the distributional criteria for lexical categories? If so, identify their category. If not, propose a new lexical category for them.
2. Revise the phrase structure rule for APs in (15) (p. 116) to account for the data above.
3. Draw the syntactic tree for sentences (b) and (f).

Modifying the VP rule

EXERCISE 3.5

Now consider the following data:

a. The rabbit is very cute.
b. The teacher considers the student quite intelligent.
c. The food looked good to the hungry diners.
d. The sushi is amazing.
e. The student found the book boring.
f. The goldfish looks very tasty to the kitten.
   1. These sentences cannot be generated by the phrase structure rules in (19). Say precisely why.
   2. Revise the phrase structure rule for VPs in (19) to account for the data above.
   3. Draw the syntactic tree for sentences (c) and (e).

Drawing syntactic trees using projection

EXERCISE 3.6

This series of steps will take you through the steps necessary to draw the tree for the sentence: *The snow melted* using a projection approach. Show all your steps.

a. Project a determiner phrase from the determiner *the*. Don't forget the complement.
b. Project a noun phrase from the noun *snow*.
c. Project a verb phrase from the verb *melt*. (Note: *melt* does not take a complement).
d. Merge the NP projected in b into the DP projected in a.
e. Project an Inflection Phrase from the inflection *ed*. Be sure you include all the required structure.
f. Merge the DP resulting from d into the IP projected in e.
g. Merge the VP projected in c into IP projected in e.

EXERCISE 3.7

Follow these steps to construct the tree structure for: *Those young people will drink the lattes.* Show all your steps.

a. Project a DP from *those.*
b. Project an NP from *people.*
c. Project an adjective phrase from *young.*
d. Merge the AP projected in c to the NP projected in b by adjunction. (Note: Show just the result of the merger, not the process.)
e. Merge the NP created in d into the DP projected in a.
f. Project a VP from *drink.* Don't forget the complement.
g. Project an NP from *lattes.*
h. Project a DP from *the.*
i. Merge the NP projected in g into the DP projected in g.
j. Merge the DP projected in i into the VP projected in f.
k. Project an IP from *will.*
l. Merge the DP created in e into the specifier position of the IP projected in j.
m. Merge the VP created in j into the complement position of the IP projected in o.

EXERCISE 3.8

Follow these steps to create the tree structure for: *The gnome believes that the snow melted.* Show all your steps.

a. Project a determiner phrase from the determiner *the.*
b. Project a noun phrase from the noun *snow.*
c. Project a VP from *believe.* (Note: Don't forget the complement, here CP.)
d. Merge the NP projected in b into the DP projected in a.
e. Project a complementizer phrase from *that.* (Note: This CP will not need a specifier branch, but will, as always, need a complement IP.)
f. Merge the tree you created in Exercise 3.6 into the complementizer position of the CP projected in c.
e. Merge the CP created in f into the VP projected in c.
f. Project an IP from PRES.
g. Merge the DP projected resulting from d into the IP projected in f.
h. Merge the VP created in e into the IP projected in f.

Recursion

EXERCISE 3.9

List each of the recursive devices in each of the following sentences in the order in which they appear. The first one is done for you.

a. I think that you should take a long hard look at this and do it soon. Embedding: *that you should take a long hard look at this and do it soon.* Multiple adjunction: *long hard*

   Coordination: . . . *and do it soon*
b. The fat yellow cat ate John's juicy oversized hamburger.
c. I know that you think that I don't know much about chemistry.
d. Kim would like to buy the car that your uncle who lives in the townhouse has for sale.

e. I would rather go but you would rather stay.

f. That wise old woman who lives in the village that holds a market every week knows that dishonest people think they can cheat her but she won't let them.

Restrictions on movement

EXERCISE 3.10

Consider the tree you constructed in Exercise 3.8. An acceptable variant of this sentence is *The gnome believes the snow melted*. Explain how this variant can be permissibly derived from the structure you built in Exercise 3.8.

EXERCISE 3.11

Consider the following examples:

a. I punished the three young rapscallions severely.

b. I punished severely the three young rapscallions.

c. The three young rapscallions took their punishment bravely.

d. *Took their punishment bravely the three young rapscallions.

We can derive b from a by heavy DP shift of *the three young rapscallions*. Explain why we cannot derive d from c by the same movement.

Binding Theory

EXERCISE 3.12

Consider the following sentence:
[$_{IP}$ [$_{NP}$ Jane's sister] [$_{VP}$ reminded her [$_{CP}$ that [$_{IP}$ the new graduate had promised to improve herself]]]].

a. Of *Jane, Jane's sister, her,* and *the new graduate,* which one is *herself* required to refer to, according to the Binding Theory?

b. Explain what principle of the Binding Theory predicts this coreference.

c. Of *Jane* and *Jane's sister,* the Binding Theory permits *her* to refer to one, but not the other. Which one is *her* allowed to refer to?

d. Explain how a principle of the Binding Theory predicts this result.

e. According to the Binding Theory, *the new graduate* can refer to one of *Jane* or *Jane's sister,* but not the other. Which one is it?

f. Explain how a principle of the Binding Theory allows one coreference, but not the other.

Word order in "Hindlish"

EXERCISE 3.13

"Hindlish" is a made-up language consisting of English words and Hindi word order. Translate the following from English to Hindlish. The first one is done for you. (Notes: (i) Hindlish has no determiners meaning *the* or *a/an.* (ii) The whole verb phrase, including its complement, is last in Hindlish.)

a. English: The children in the house want a puppy.
Hindlish: House in children puppy want.

b. English: I read a book in the garden.
Hindlish:
c. English: The men at work build cars in a factory.
Hindlish:

Word order in Amharic

EXERCISE 3.14

Consider the following data from Amharic, a Semitic language spoken in Ethiopia. *Almaz* is a female proper name (some data from Appleyard 1995).

a. Almaz bet   ayyäčč
Almaz house saw = 'Almaz saw a house'
b. Almaz doro   wät' bällačč
Almaz chicken stew ate = 'Almaz ate chicken stew'
c. t'äräp'p'eza sïr
table   under = 'under a table'
d. ya   säw man näw
that man who is = 'Who is that man?'
e. ïssu mïn yastämïrallu
he   what teach = 'What does he teach?'

1. What direction do complements branch in Amharic?
2. Do wh-words move in Amharic?

Gender in "Enghili"

EXERCISE 3.15

"Enghili" is a made-up language that has genders that work like gender in Swahili, but has English words. Also, tense in Enghili works the way it does in Swahili, as a morpheme that comes somewhere before the verb root. Translate the following Enghili sentences into English. The first one is done for you. The morpheme for the present tense in Enghili is *pre* and the morpheme for the past tense is *pa*. As in Hindlish, there are no determiners meaning *the* or *a/an*. They will have to be supplied where English needs them. Also in Enghili, noun modifiers follow their nouns. The following is a list of Enghili nouns and genders that you will need:

Noun	Gender prefixes (singular/plural)
child	m/wa
book	ki/vi
car	ki/vi
tree	m/mi

a. Enghili: mchild mprekiread kibook.
English: The child reads a book.
b. Enghili: kicar kipamstrike mtree.
English:

c. Enghili: wagirl wapamkiss mbaby.
    English:
d. Enghili: Mitree mitwo mipafall.
    English:

"Thailish" gender

EXERCISE 3.16

"Thailish" is yet another made-up language with English words. Thailish has genders that work as in Thai, and lacks endings for singular/plural or tense, as Thai does. Like Hindlish and Enghili, there are no words for *the* or *a/an*. The nouns you will need are assigned to their gender classifiers in the table below. Translate the following English sentences into Thailish. The first one is done for you.

Gender classifiers

Person	Stick	Globe
child	pencil	apple
girl	bat	ball
student		
man		
king		

a. English: The children ate two apples.
    Thailish: child eat apple two globe.
b. English: Three girls chased two balls.
    Thailish:
c. English: One bat touched two balls.
    Thailish:
d. English: The players used one bat.
    Thailish:
e. English: Each student has five pencils. (Hint: *Each* works like a number in Thailish.)
    Thailish:
f. English: The men bowed to the king.
    Thailish:

SUGGESTIONS FOR FURTHER READING

Baker, Mark C. 2001, *The atoms of language: the mind's hidden rules of grammar*, New York: Basic Books. Another book for nonspecialists about Universal Grammar, but focusing on the differences among languages, with examples. *The atoms of language* is somewhat more challenging than Pinker's *The language instinct*.

Carnie, Andrew 2007, *Syntax: a generative introduction*, Blackwell. A standard university-level textbook in syntax which delves deeper into many of the topics explored in this chapter including phrase structure, Binding Theory, and movement.

Pinker, Steven 1994, *The language instinct*, New York: HarperCollins. An engagingly written and prize-winning book for nonspecialists explaining the concept of Universal Grammar, which Pinker calls the language instinct.

Radford, Andrew 2004, *Minimalist syntax: exploring the structure of English*, Cambridge University Press. Clearly written, but detailed and technical, presentation of the modern theory of syntax described in this chapter.

4   Meaning

KEY TERMS

- anaphora
- compositionality
- context of use
- implicature
- indexicality
- intensionality
- lexical semantics
- modifier
- pragmatics
- predicate
- presupposition
- proposition
- quantifier
- reference
- semantic meaning
- semantics
- speaker's meaning
- speech act
- subject
- thematic role

CHAPTER PREVIEW

There are two main fields within linguistics that study meaning. **Semantics** focuses on the literal meanings of words, phrases, and sentences; it is concerned with how grammatical processes build complex meanings out of simpler ones. **Pragmatics** focuses on the use of language in particular situations; it aims to explain how factors outside language contribute to both literal meaning and nonliteral meanings which speakers communicate using language. Most linguists who study meaning combine the study of semantics and pragmatics. While a semanticist is technically someone who studies semantics, in fact most semanticists investigate both semantics and pragmatics. In this chapter, we will first discuss semantics, and then pragmatics. To conclude the chapter, we will examine some foundational philosophical issues which are relevant to thinking about meaning and will discuss some of the different theoretical perspectives on meaning which are popular within linguistics today.

GOALS

The goals of this chapter are to:

- **explain the difference between speaker's meaning and semantic meaning**
- **introduce the complexity of lexical semantics and the basics of one way of thinking about lexical meaning**
- **illustrate the role of the major grammatical constituents in semantic meaning: subjects and other arguments, predicates, modifiers, and quantifiers**

- describe the nature of intensional meaning and the basics of three intensional phenomena: modality, tense, and aspect
- introduce four key pragmatic concepts: indexicality, presupposition, speech acts, and implicature
- illustrate how speaker's meaning is dependent on the context of use
- allow students to apply key concepts to novel data
- discuss the strengths and weaknesses of psychological and referential theories of meaning

Speaker's meaning and semantic meaning

Everyone knows that language can be used to express meaning, but it is not easy to define meaning. One problem is that there are several dimensions of meaning. Imagine that I ask you, "Can you give me an apple?" while looking at a bowl of apples on the table beside you. What I literally asked is whether you have the ability to give me an apple; this is the **semantic meaning** of what I said. Sometimes people will make an annoying joke by responding only to the semantic meaning of such a question; they'll just answer, "Yes, I can." But what I almost certainly want is for you to give me one of the apples next to you, and I expect you to know that this is what I want. This **speaker's meaning** is what I intend to communicate, and it goes beyond the literal, semantic meaning of what I said.

Linguists study both semantic meaning and speaker's meaning. Let's look at semantic meaning first. To understand semantic meaning, we have to bring together three main components: the context in which a sentence is used, the meanings of the words in the sentence, and its morphological and syntactic structure. For example, suppose you say to me:

(1)   My dog chased a cat under the house.

Because (1) contains the pronoun *my*, part of its meaning depends on the fact that you uttered it. Since you uttered it, *my* refers to you. So to some extent the semantic meaning of a sentence depends on the **context of use** – the situation in which the sentence was uttered, by a particular speaker, to a particular addressee, at a particular time, and so forth. The semantic meaning of (1) also depends on the meanings of the individual words *dog*, *chased*, *a*, *cat*, etc.; therefore, semantic meaning depends on the **lexicon** of English. In addition, the morphological and syntactic structure of sentence (1) is crucial to its meaning. If the words were rearranged to make the sentence *A cat under the house chased my dog*, it would mean something different. So semantic meaning depends on the grammatical structure of the sentence.

Now let's think about the speaker's meaning of (1). Suppose that you know I've lost my cat and you say (1) to me. In that case, it would be likely that your speaker's meaning is to inform me that my cat may be hiding under the house, and to suggest that I go there to look for it. To understand where this meaning comes from, we need to bring together two components. First, the semantic meaning is certainly part of the picture; there is some kind of connection between your saying that your dog chased a cat under the house and your suggesting that I look for my lost cat under the house. But in order for me to understand your speaker's meaning, I have to assume that we both know my cat is missing, that you know I want to find it, and that you want to see that my cat is safely back home. These are additional aspects of the context of use which help to determine your speaker's meaning.

We can visualize the two kinds of meaning as follows:

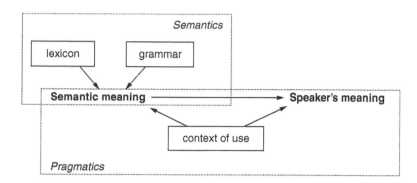

Semantics focuses on the link between the lexicon and the grammar and semantic meaning. **Pragmatics** focuses on the connection between context of use and both semantic and speaker's meaning.

Semantics

At first glance, the study of literal meaning may seem like a very dry subject. (When we say that somebody is "literal-minded," it is not usually a compliment.) But this first impression is largely because we assume that all languages are like our own in how they express meaning. Semantics gets interesting when we realize how little we know about the ways in which meaning gets expressed in various languages. Consider the following example from the Australian language Warlpiri (discussion is based on Bittner and Hale 1995):

(2) Maliki-rli   ka-Ø-ju   wiri-ngki   wajilipi-nyi.
    dog-ERG   PRES-3s-1s   big-ERG   chase-nonpast
    'A/the big dog is chasing me.'

The word-by-word gloss of this example shows the following. The first word is a noun meaning 'dog,' and it has a particular case suffix (ergative case), which marks it as associated with the subject of a transitive verb. The second word is an auxiliary indicating present tense, as well as the facts that a third person (not the speaker or addressee) is the subject of the clause and the first person (the speaker) is its object. The third word is a noun meaning 'big,' marked with the same ergative case as 'dog.' The fourth word is a verb meaning 'chase,' and its suffix indicates that the sentence is not about the past.

There are many puzzles in the semantics of Warlpiri. For example, the word meaning 'big' is a noun. English speakers might expect adjectives and nouns to be different, with 'big' being an adjective and 'dog' a noun. The fact that 'big' is a noun in Warlpiri raises a number of questions about the meanings of words – such as, what kinds of concepts can be expressed by nouns, by adjectives, by verbs, and so forth? The Warlpiri example also shows us that the semantic side of the process of putting words together into phrases and complete sentences is not necessarily simple. 'Big dog' is intuitively a single concept in this sentence, and it is expressed by the combination of the words for 'dog' and 'big.' But these two words are not adjacent to one another, as they would have to be in English and many other languages. Rather, their relation is encoded by the fact that they both have ergative suffixes.

Yet another interesting feature of this Warlpiri sentence is that it can mean either 'a big dog is chasing me' or 'the big dog is chasing me.' Warlpiri lacks the category of determiner, and so the distinction between 'a' and 'the' is not expressed by a word. Instead, Warlpiri speakers can make one meaning or the other more likely by various means, such as the order of words (the order given in (2) is just one of many possible in this language). In fact, many languages are like Warlpiri in not having words to make the distinction between 'a' and 'the' (technically known as **definiteness**), and this might be quite surprising from the point of view of English. A semantic concept that might be quite fundamental to one language might be much less important in another. Studying the semantics of different languages shows us the great variety of ways in which languages can accomplish the task of talking about the world. Identifying what is common to the semantics of all languages helps us understand what is unique about language and human nature.

> **Definiteness:** *A definite noun phrase picks out a particular thing (or things) which the speaker presents as known to the addressee, while an indefinite noun phrase introduces a new thing (or things). In English, noun phrases introduced by* the *are definite, while those introduced by* a *are indefinite. There are other kinds of definite and indefinite noun phrases in English as well. For example,* both *is definite, as can be seen by the fact that it means almost the same thing as* the two.

Fundamental semantic concepts and compositionality

The most fundamental semantic concepts describe how words, phrases, and sentences relate to each other and to the world.

Synonymy. Two words, phrases, or sentences are **synonyms** if they have the same semantic meaning. *I saw more than two and fewer than five dogs* is synonymous with *I saw three or four dogs*.

Antonymy. Two words are **antonyms** if they are opposed in semantic meaning. *Tall* and *short* are antonyms.

Hyponymy. A word is a **hyponym** of another if its semantic meaning is more specific than the other's. *Dog* is a hyponym of *animal*.

Hypernymy. A word is a **hypernym** of another if its semantic meaning is more general than the other's. *Animal* is a hypernym of *dog*.

Ambiguity. A word, phrase, or sentence is **ambiguous** if it has multiple semantic meanings. *Bank* is ambiguous (river bank vs. financial institution).

Entailment. A sentence entails another if the truth of the first guarantees the truth of the second. *I like all animals* entails *I like pigs*.

Tautology. A sentence is a tautology if it must be true. *If something is a big animal, it's an animal* is a tautology.

Contradicts. A sentence contradicts another if they can't both be true. *I like pigs* contradicts *I hate all animals*.

Contradiction. A sentence is a contradiction if it cannot be true. *That is a big animal, and it's not an animal* is a contradiction. (Intuitively, a contradiction is a sentence that contradicts itself.)

These concepts allow us to talk about meaning. With them we can say things like "The Warlpiri sentence (2) is ambiguous; it can mean *a* big dog or *the* big dog is chasing me."

You learned in previous chapters that grammar (morphology and syntax) generate novel words, phrases, and sentences – in fact, an infinite number of them. This gives us an infinite number of words, phrases, and sentences that can have meaning. In order to explain how an infinite number of pieces of language can be meaningful, and how we, as language users, can figure out the meanings of new ones every day, semanticists apply the **Principle of Compositionality**.

> **The Principle of Compositionality:** The semantic meaning of any unit of language is determined by the semantic meanings of its parts along with the way they are put together.

According to the Principle of Compositionality, the meaning of a sentence like *Mary liked you* is determined by (a) the meanings of the individual morphemes that make it up (*Mary*, *like*, *you*, "past") and (b) the morphological and syntactic structures of the sentence. The Principle of Compositionality doesn't just apply to sentences. It also implies that the meaning of the verb phrase *liked you* is determined by the meanings of its parts and the grammatical structure of the verb phrase, and that the meaning of the word *liked* is determined by the meanings of the two morphemes that make it up (*like* and *-ed*). The subfield of semantics known as **compositional semantics** (or **formal semantics**) is especially concerned with how the Principle of Compositionality applies, and consequently formal semanticists study the variety of grammatical patterns which occur in individual languages and across the languages of the world. Formal semantics developed in linguistics during the early 1970s under the influence of philosophers, especially Richard Montague (Montague 1974).

BOX 4.1 **IDIOMS**

There are some phrases which are exceptions to compositionality. An **idiom** is a phrase whose meaning is not what you'd expect given the meanings of the words making it up. In other words, idioms are not compositional: *keep an eye on X*, *get a handle on X*, and *kick the bucket* do not get their meaning exclusively from the meanings of their parts and the way they are put together. Idioms often get their meanings from metaphorical interpretations, often lost in the mists of history, but the case of *get a handle on X* is fairly clear; one might put a handle on a physical object to make it easier to carry, and to understand something is, metaphorically, to be able to carry it around in one's mind. Once one already knows what this idiom means, the choice of handle makes sense, but it can be very difficult to understand an idiom the first time one hears it. We typically need help to understand a new idiom, and once we do understand it, we remember its meaning as a complete pattern, or chunk. What are some other idioms in English or in another language which you are familiar with? How do you know what they mean?

Lexical semantics

While the principle of compositionality tells us that meanings are combined with other meanings to produce new meanings, it can only take us so far. Ultimately, the smallest pieces of language, morphemes and words, must have meanings in and of themselves, not derived in a compositional way. Lexical semantics is the study of these basic building blocks of meaning. In some cases, the meaning of a word is exceedingly simple. The meaning of an ordinary name, for example, is nothing other than the individual it refers to. We say that *Confucius* **refers** to a particular famous Chinese philosopher.

Lexical semantics is usually not so simple. The word *squirrel* seems at first as easy to describe as *Confucius*, but it is actually ambiguous. It can describe animals of a certain kind (*that squirrel bit me*), their meat (*I ate squirrel once*), or the species as a whole (*the squirrel is a rodent*). A word which has multiple related meanings in this way is **polysemous**, and in fact most words are polysemous to some extent; just glance at a dictionary. (Polysemy is a kind of ambiguity.)

> *Confucius is actually polysemous. Describe the multiple related meanings that this word has, and discuss whether they represent a pattern of polysemy common to other names. Can you think of any word which is truly unambiguous?*

Lexical semantics is often concerned with polysemy, in particular when a group of words displays the same pattern of related meanings. The ability of a word to refer to a thing as organism or food is common to words for organisms which can serve as food, though it is quite unnatural when we have a dedicated term for the food. Thus, elk can be cooked as elk and rice can be cooked as rice, but calf is cooked as veal, not as calf. (We say that *veal* blocks this use of *calf*.) The ability of a single word to refer to a specific object and to the species or kind of which that object is a member is typical in English; for example, we can use *book* to describe an individual object (*I lost your book*) or the kind of thing (*the book was an important invention*).

In describing the lexical semantics of a word, we can typically distinguish two kinds of meaning. On the one hand, there is usually a primitive, descriptive component. For example, at the core of the meanings of *squirrel* is its reference to certain animals and not others. There is not much linguists can say about this aspect of meaning, except to point it out in each case. The main interest in studying this first component of lexical meaning is that it allows us to observe which basic, unanalyzable concepts are important to speakers of particular languages.

On the other hand, in contrast to the primitive, descriptive component, we often have other, more systematic components of lexical meaning. The fact that the polysemy of *squirrel* is part of a larger pattern shows that there are systematic components of meaning at work. When linguists study lexical semantics, they are mainly interested in systematic lexical meaning of various kinds. Each category of morpheme and word raises different issues for lexical semantics. In the sections below, we'll discuss the lexical semantics of verbs (thematic roles), logical words (truth conditions), adjectives (scales), adverbs (events), quantifiers (relations between quantities), modals (possible worlds), and tense and aspect morphemes (times and events).

Subjects, predicates, and arguments

The meaning of a simple sentence is determined from the meanings of its parts. Most sentences are composed of a **subject** and a **predicate**. In simple English sentences, the subject is the first noun phrase (or DP) under the IP node in a sentence, and the predicate is the verb phrase of the sentence. According to the Principle of Compositionality, the meaning of such a sentence is determined in terms of the meaning of its subject and the meaning of its predicate. As pointed out above, names refer to particular things in the world, and other simple noun phrases are similar:

Elvis Presley, the President of France, she, I, that dog

The predicate typically contains a verb, adjective, noun, or prepositional phrase:

ran down the street (verb phrase)
is happy (is + adjective phrase)
is under the table (is + prepositional phrase)
is a butterfly (is + noun phrase)

A simple predicate describes a set of things in the world. For example, the predicate *is happy* describes some things (those which are happy) and not others. A predicate may describe different things depending on the context of use; for example, *is happy* may describe one set of people if used on one day, and a different set of people if used the next day. When someone understands the meaning of a predicate, they know what kinds of things it can describe, and what kinds of things it can't. For example, I know that *is happy* describes baby Benjamin right now (he's smiling) but it didn't describe him five minutes ago (he was crying).

The meaning of a sentence is called a proposition. A **proposition** is a complete thought, a statement which can be true or false. The proposition is true if the predicate accurately describes the referent of the subject. For example, sentence (3) expresses the thought (that is, proposition) that a certain person – the king of Rock and Roll, as they called him – ran down the street:

(3)   Elvis Presley ran down the street.

Semanticists usually describe propositions in terms of truth conditions. The **truth conditions** of (3) are as follows: (3) is true if Elvis Presley ran down the street, and it's false if he didn't. This seems obvious, of course, because it simply recapitulates something which you already know because you understand English. However, the truth conditions are important because they encapsulate what you learn about the world if I say (3) to you and you believe me. Truth conditions don't have to sound so tautological. If you and I know Elvis as Aaron and the street in question as Speedway, in the direction south, the truth conditions could just as well be stated as "Aaron ran south on Speedway." Truth conditions are, in essence, a summary of the information carried by a sentence. Another way to see the point of truth conditions is to consider the meaning of a simple signal, like the turn signal on a car. Turning on the left blinker "means" that the driver will turn left, and her signal was "true" (we might rather say "accurate" in this situation) if she does in fact turn left. In this respect, the truth conditions offer a good way of conceiving of meaning. The idea that the meaning of a sentence should be thought of in terms of its truth conditions goes back to the Polish logician Alfred Tarski (Tarski 1944).

Often a predicate contains, in addition to a verb, preposition, or adjective, one or more **arguments**. Arguments are elements which are needed in order to complete the meaning of a predicate; they bring the predicate closer to expressing a complete proposition. For example, the verb *hit* in sentence (4) has two arguments, the direct object, *the ball*, and the subject, *Mary*.

(4)   Mary hit the ball.

According to the Principle of Compositionality, the meaning of the predicate *hit the ball* is based on the meanings of *hit* and *the ball*. *The ball* refers to a particular thing (whichever ball is relevant in the context of use). The meaning of *hit* is made more complete by combining with *the ball*. Once it combines with *the ball*, we have a predicate which describes a set of things. This predicate must be put together with a subject in order to express a complete proposition.

Thematic roles

We have just seen how the meaning of a simple sentence is determined from the meanings of its parts. Another common way of thinking about this process uses the concept of a **thematic role** (Gruber 1965, Fillmore 1968, Jackendoff 1987). Thematic roles are often used to talk about the lexical semantics of words which describe actions, like verbs. In particular, thematic roles describe the roles which the subject and other arguments have in the action described by a verb. (More precisely, a thematic role is a part of a word's meaning which indicates the role that some entity plays in the action or relation which that word describes.) Some commonly used thematic roles are *agent*, *patient*, *theme*, *location*, *source*, and *goal*. For example, in (4), part of the meaning of the verb *hit* is associated with the roles <agent, patient>. When *hit* is used in a sentence like (4), the thematic role of "agent" is assigned to *Mary*, the subject, indicating that Mary was the "doer" of the action of hitting, while the thematic role of "patient" is assigned to *the ball*, indicating that the ball was acted on as part of the action of hitting. Here are some other thematic roles:

Agent: the individual which performs an action; the doer of the action
Patient: something which is acted upon as part of an action
Theme: something which moves, literally or metaphorically, as part of an action
Source: the location/individual from which movement occurs
Goal: the location/individual to which movement occurs
Location: the location at which something happens

Experiencer: someone who experiences something
Instrument: something an agent uses to make something happen
Cause: something that causes something to happen
Stimulus: something that causes an experience

The set of thematic roles associated with a particular word is called a **thematic grid**. Here are some examples of verbs with their thematic grids (enclosed in angled brackets):

(5)   Allen sent the book to Mary.
       send: <agent, theme, goal>

(6)   The corn ripened.
       ripen: <theme>

(7)   The sun ripened the corn.
       ripen: <cause, theme>

Notice that the verb *ripen* has two different thematic grids in (6) and (7), demonstrating an important point about thematic roles. *Ripen* has the role "theme" in (6) and (7) because we metaphorically view the change from unripe to ripe described by this verb as a kind of movement, but in (7) *the sun* is the cause of that movement. Many verbs have more than one thematic grid, and verbs can be classified according to which thematic grids they have as part of their definitions. For example, other verbs are like *ripen* in having both the <theme> grid and the <cause, theme> grid (e.g. *break, redden*). Linguists are interested in studying which verbs are associated with which thematic grids – both within a single language like English and across languages – because these patterns can tell us more about how these meanings of words are represented in our minds. For example, the pattern illustrated with *ripen* in (6)–(7) shows that our minds can make use of a "piece" of meaning that can be expressed as CAUSE. Historically, speakers of English employed a CAUSE+V process to change the verb *ripen*, as in (6), into a new version, *ripen* in (7), with a meaning which can be represented as CAUSE+*ripen*<theme>. Some languages, such as Japanese, have a morpheme meaning CAUSE, but in English this piece of meaning can be added without changing the pronunciation of the word. Words which, like *ripen*, have multiple related meanings are polysemous, and processes like CAUSE+V can help to explain how they become polysemous.

Thematic roles illustrate the connection between lexical semantics and syntax, because the meaning of a word often influences how it fits into the grammatical structure of the sentence; for example, the fact that *ripen* can have two different patterns of thematic roles explains why it can be used grammatically either with or without an object. Another example is the Warlpiri sentence discussed above. The fact that 'big' is expressed as a noun – as are other meanings, like 'how many' and 'in the middle,' which don't seem "noun-like" to English speakers – implies that the grammar of this language will be very different from that of English. The Warlpiri example shows why lexical semanticists study the meanings of words in multiple languages, both to find out how word meanings are similar across languages and to determine how they may differ.

Similar meanings can be expressed very differently in different languages. In the English sentence *I like pasta*, the subject *I* refers to the person who likes something, and the object *pasta* refers to the thing I like. The English verb *like* has the thematic grid <experiencer, stimulus>. In many languages, the person who likes something appears in the sentence as an indirect object, as in the Italian sentence (8).

(8) Mi   piace   la pasta.
     to-me   pleases   the pasta
     'Pasta is pleasing to me.'

Italian doesn't express the liking of things in the same way as English does. There is no verb equivalent to *likes* in Italian; *piacere* comes closest, but it expresses the relationship between "liker" and "liked thing" quite differently. The Italian verb has a thematic grid <stimulus, experiencer>. In this way it is similar to the English verb *please*, as in *Pasta pleases me*. *Piacere* and *please* are not equivalent, however; the experiencer is expressed as an indirect object with the Italian verb and a direct object with the English one.

English and Italian express the concept of "love" differently as well. In English, the verb *love* is often used in a way similar to *like*; we can say *I love pasta* as well as *I love my wife*. The Italian verb for 'love' (*amare*) has the same thematic grid as the English verb *love*, <experiencer, stimulus>, and the "lover" is the subject in both languages:

(9) Amo   mia   moglie.
     I-love   my   wife.

However, the meaning of *amare* is narrower and more serious than its English counterpart. To say *Amo la pasta* in Italian would be quite strange, indicating a serious emotional attachment to pasta. There is no simple correspondence between *like* and *love* and the corresponding verbs in Italian. They are similar in some ways and different in others, and this is the typical situation when one compares the meanings of words across different languages. Languages may divide up the space of meanings, the range of thoughts we want to express, in different ways.

BOX 4.2 **SEMANTICS IN THE LAW**

Semantic issues can be important in real life. Solan (2002) discusses an interesting example of how semantics can play a role in the interpretation of legal statutes. He writes: "Raymond Moskal, who lived in Pennsylvania, would buy used automobiles, set back the odometers, send the inaccurate mileage readings to Virginia along with other required information, and receive new titles from Virginia with the incorrect mileage. He would then sell the cars for inflated prices to unsuspecting customers. He was prosecuted and convicted for violating a statute that prohibits the interstate transportation of 'falsely made' securities." In short, Moskal got real titles that contained false information.

The law in question was the following (it is made clear elsewhere that car titles count as "securities"):

Whoever, with unlawful or fraudulent intent, transports in interstate or foreign commerce any falsely made, forged, altered, or counterfeited securities or tax stamps, knowing the same to have

BOX 4.2 (*cont.*)

been falsely made, forged, altered, or counterfeited... Shall be fined under this title or imprisoned not more than ten years, or both.

(18 USC § 2314 (2001))

The US Supreme Court agreed that Moskal could be punished under this law, but Justice Scalia dissented for two reasons based on the meaning of the phrase *falsely made*. One reason had to do with the historical meaning of the phrase *falsely made* in legal documents and the other had to do with its ordinary meaning. Justice Scalia showed that in the 100 years up to 1939, when the statute was written, legal documents had used *falsely made* to mean 'forged' or 'counterfeit.' Thus, it seems that the meaning of this crucial phrase had changed, at least within the world of law, between the time the law was written and the time it was applied to Moskal. Scalia's other argument was that the phrase *falsely made*, in its ordinary meaning, includes only things that are counterfeit, not real documents that are made to contain false information.

After looking at the usage of the phrase in a database of contemporary English, Solan concluded that Scalia's ordinary meaning argument is wrong. He shows that *falsely made* typically means 'made to include false information,' as in "[W]hen falsely made, this accusation [child abuse] can be enormously destructive." In other words, a *falsely made accusation* means that that accusation contained false information, and Solan assumes by analogy that a *falsely made car title* would be a car title containing false information.

- Assuming Solan's description of the situation is accurate, do you agree with Justice Scalia or the majority?
- How convincing do you find Scalia's historical argument?
- Do you think that Solan is correct that *falsely made* means the same thing when applied to an accusation and when applied to a document? Is a falsely made car title a counterfeit car title or a car title containing false information?
- What do you think of Solan's strategy of looking at things like a database of newspaper columns to determine the ordinary meaning of a controversial phrase?

Logical words

So far, we have focused on how the meaning of a simple sentence is composed of the meanings of its parts, but the principle of compositionality also applies to more complex sentences made by combining simpler sentences. Sentences may be modified and connected using such words as *not*, *and*, and *or*. The meanings of these words are traditionally explained in terms of the truth conditional conception of meaning. For example, the word *not* reverses the truth conditions of a sentence, so that sentence (10a) is true if, and only if, (10b) is false, and vice versa.

(10)   a. The President of France is under the table.
        b. The President of France is not under the table.

Similarly, a sentence which is made by joining two sentences with *and* is true if, and only if, the two component sentences are true. A sentence which is made by joining two sentences with *or* is true if, and only if, at least one of the component sentences is true.

(11)   a. Elvis Presley ran down the street and Mary hit the ball.
       b. Elvis Presley ran down the street or Mary hit the ball.

This view of the meanings of *not, and*, and *or* is drawn historically from the field of logic, part of philosophy. The traditional goal of logic is to explain what patterns of reasoning are valid, and the words *not, and*, and *or* are among the words which are especially important for this enterprise.

In many sentences, the meanings of these logical words seem to be more than is specified by simple truth conditions. For example, sentence (12) seems to say that Elvis made the peanut butter sandwich *before* going to the pool:

(12)   Elvis Presley made a peanut butter sandwich and sat down by the pool.

One might doubt, therefore, whether truth conditions give an adequate description of the meanings of these logical words. Those who think that truth conditions are adequate argue that the 'before' meaning in (12) belongs to speaker's meaning, not semantic meaning, and should be explained as part of pragmatics, not semantics.

Modifiers

We have discussed how the meanings of a verb, its arguments, and its subject are combined through thematic roles. Other elements besides these can contribute to the meaning of a sentence, however. For example, the italicized items in (13) are not arguments:

(13)   a. Shelby walked *quickly*.
       b. Shelby barked *in the park*.
       c. Mary ate the *old* bagel.
       d. The bagel [*which Mary ate*] was old.

The adverb in (13a), the prepositional phrase in (13b), the adjective in (13c), and the relative clause in (13d) are not arguments, but rather *modifiers* of the phrase heads they are associated with. Modifiers add meaning to a phrase, but are not needed to complete the meaning of that phrase. For example, the phrase *the bagel* is complete on its own. (It refers to a particular bagel.) Yet, while we don't need an adjective to make a complete meaning, an adjective can certainly add useful extra information. The modifying adjective *old* provides some useful extra information in (13c); it lets us know that the bagel we're talking about is old.

Adjectives

We have already seen that adjectives and nouns may function as predicates; that is, they describe sets of things. When an adjective modifies a noun, the resulting adjective–noun combination is itself a predicate. In the simplest cases it simply describes those things which are described by both the adjective and noun individually, for example *a living fish* and *a colorless liquid*. The phrase *a living fish* describes those things which are both living and a fish. Such adjectives are called intersective. Not all adjectives are intersective. For example, the adjective *former* in *a former student* doesn't describe someone who is both former and a student. Relative clauses are also intersective. In (13d), the phrase *the bagel which Mary ate* describes those things which are bagels and which were eaten by Mary.

Adjectives may take arguments, just like verbs. (This is true whether they modify a noun or serve as the main predicate of a sentence.) For example, in the phrase *proud of Mary*, the noun phrase *Mary* serves as an argument of *proud*. Some adjectives can take arguments which specify how the thing they describe relates to a scale. A **scale** is an ordered set of values for some property. For example, the adjective *old* relates to a scale of ages, and this scale might be expressed in years: <0 years, 1 year, 2 years, ...>. (It could also be specified in days, months, or other appropriate units of time.) The adjective *old* may take an argument like *ten years* which specifies a value on this scale. So if I say *John is a ten-year-old child*, I describe John in terms of how his age falls on this scale: he is one of the children whose age measures "ten years" on the scale of ages.

Adjectives differ in the type of scale they are associated with. Consider, for example, *tall* and *full*. Both adjectives involve scales, *tall* a scale of height and *full* a scale of volume. But there is a difference between the two: we understand what it is for a glass to be *completely full*, while *completely tall makes no sense. Lexical semanticists have explained this difference in terms of properties of the respective scales. The scale for *full* is closed (there's a point beyond which something cannot get more full), while the scale for *tall* is open (there's no conceptual limit to how tall something can be). This distinction between closed and open scales is crucial to the lexical semantics of adjectives.

Many adjectives display the property of **vagueness**. A word is vague if it has a single, general meaning, which becomes more specific in a particular context of use. Adjectives which, like *old*, relate to a scale are vague when they do not mention a particular value on the scale. For instance, the sentence *John is old* doesn't say how old he is; it says that his age is greater than some unspecified level that has to be inferred from the context of use, and exactly how old that is can vary depending on what we're talking about. *John is old* might indicate that his age is more than forty years in one situation (if we're talking about a professional sports team) or that he's over ninety in another (if we're talking about a retirement community). Other adjectives are vague in ways that don't relate to a scale. For example, the adjective *good* can describe something as morally good (*a good deed*), as tasty (*a good pie*), as appropriate for a given use (*a good dress for the dance*), and so forth. These differences in meaning don't seem to relate to one another in terms of a scale of goodness (though there may be scales of goodness relevant within each one separately). It is often difficult to distinguish vagueness from polysemy. As mentioned above, polysemous words have multiple different, but related, meanings; vagueness, in contrast, describes a single general meaning which becomes more specific in a particular context of use. Since it involves more than one meaning, polysemy is a kind of ambiguity, but vagueness is not.

Adverbs and adverbials

Just as adjectives modify nouns, adverbs modify other kinds of words and phrases, including verbs and sentences. Many adverbs can modify verbs and sentences because they describe events. The idea of describing the meanings of sentences using the notion of event was introduced by the philosopher Donald Davidson (Davidson 1967). An event is an occurrence, something that happens, an action. For example, (14a) can be paraphrased as "an event of John walking occurred, and this event took place yesterday," and *yesterday* contributes the description of this event as having taken place yesterday. (14b) does not contain an adverb, but it does contain a prepositional phrase, *in the garden*, that functions very much like an adverb. A phrase which functions like an adverb is an adverbial. Sentence (14b) can be paraphrased in a way that makes clear that the adverbial describes an event as "an event of Shelby barking occurred, and this event took place in the garden."

(14)   a. John walked yesterday.
       b. Shelby barked in the garden.

The kind of adverb/adverbial illustrated in (14) is similar to an intersective adjective. Just as *an old car* describes things which are both old and a car, (14a) says that an event occurred which is both a "yesterday" event and a "John walking" event. Many semanticists believe that adverbs and adverbials of this type show us that the ability to refer to events is a fundamental aspect of how human language expresses meaning.

Some adverbials are not intersective descriptors of events:

(15)   a. Surprisingly, Jane ate the whole pie.
       b. Mary intentionally crashed the car.

In (15a), *surprisingly* says something about the speaker's attitude toward what happened. In (15b), *intentionally* says something about Mary's state of mind as she crashed the car. In other words, the meaning of *intentionally* is closely connected to the subject of the sentence. There is a wide variety of types of adverbials in human language, and it remains an open question how best to understand them all.

> **Events and thematic roles**
> *The concept of event also can clarify the meanings of thematic roles. For example, Susan is the agent in* Susan threw the ball *because she is responsible for the event taking place. Without her, there would be no throwing. The ball is the patient of the sentence, and this is due to its role in the event as well. The ball is the patient because it is acted upon, and moves, as part of this event. As an exercise, consider how the notion of event can clarify other thematic roles, such as goal, location, and instrument.*

Quantification

We have seen that noun phrases can refer to individuals and that they also can function as predicates. Certain noun phrases, called **quantifiers** – like *nobody, everyone, some dogs, three or four stones, much of the water on earth, most Dutch people, many young animals* – can function syntactically as arguments (subjects, objects, and so forth) but they do not refer to particular objects or individuals. This is obvious in the case of *nobody*, but it applies to the others as well. When you talk about *some dogs*, you're not talking about any particular group of dogs you could walk over to and touch (for that meaning, you would use *those dogs* or *the dogs*). Rather, quantifiers are used to create sentences which say something about the quantities (numbers or amounts) of things. For example, the following sentence says that the number of mammals with fur is greater than the number of mammals without fur.

(16)   Most mammals have fur.

To understand how the meaning of a sentence with a quantifier is built up composition-ally, we can think of the sentence as divided into three parts. Quantifiers are typically noun phrases which contain a determiner. The determiner is "Part 1," and the rest of the noun phrase, called the **restrictor**, is "Part 2." Together, the determiner and restrictor form the quantifier. "Part 3," called the **scope**, is the remainder of the sentence:

Most	mammals	have fur.
Part 1	Part 2	Part 3
determiner	restrictor	scope

The restrictor and scope are predicates, describing sets of things. Part 1, the determiner, indicates a relationship between the things described by the restrictor and those described by the scope, and the relationship always has to do with quantities. For example, in (16) *most* says that the number of things which are described by both the restrictor and the scope is greater than the number of things described by the restrictor but not the scope.

The term "scope" is not used solely in connection with quantification; it refers generally to the part of a sentence over which some word or phrase has a semantic effect. The examples in (17) show that scope is relevant to the meaning of phrases with adjectives:

(17)   a. old fake [gun]
         b. fake [old gun]

The scope of *fake* is indicated by brackets, and the difference in meaning between (17a) and (17b) is due to the fact that the scope of *fake* is *gun* in the first example and *old gun* in the second. Therefore, in (17a) we are talking about an old thing which is designed to look like a gun, but which is not actually a gun. In (17b) we are talking about a thing which is designed to look like an old gun but isn't an old gun; it might be a gun, but if so it isn't an old one.

Not all quantifiers are noun phrases. For example, adverbial quantifiers like *always* can quantify over times, as in the following:

(18)   John is always ready to help.

Sentence (18) means something like "At all (relevant) times, John is ready to help." Quantifying over times is not the only function of quantifiers of this type (contrary to what most people think at first). Examples like the following show this (Geach 1962):

(19)   If a farmer owns a donkey, he always beats it.

This sentence does not mean that farmers who own donkeys are beating their donkeys *all the time*. Rather, it means that every farmer beats all of the donkeys he owns. In this example, *always* quantifies over farmers and donkeys, not times. Quantifiers are a complex topic and the subject of much research by linguists.

BOX 4.3 SCOPE AMBIGUITY

If a sentence contains more than one scope-bearing element, sometimes there will be a **scope ambiguity**, depending on which of the two is interpreted as inside the scope of the other. Consider the two meanings of the following sentence:

I showed one bagel to every student.

The first meaning involves just one bagel: I showed this same bagel to student 1, student 2, and so on. The second meaning involves at least as many bagels as students: I showed bagel 1 to student 1, bagel 2 to student 2, and so on. In order to understand the meaning of this sentence, we have to identify the restrictor and the scope for each quantifier. Because there are two quantifiers, there are two possible ways of dividing the sentence up depending on which quantifier we assume is more important. If we assume *one bagel* is more important, we get the following diagram, where the other quantifier, *every student*, becomes part of *one bagel's* scope:

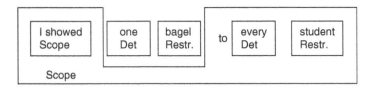

We say that *one bagel* has wide scope and *every student* has narrow scope. This diagram represents the idea that *one bagel* comes "first" in the interpretation (or has "priority"), while *every student* comes second, and it corresponds to a meaning like this: "You can find one bagel of which the following is true: I showed it to every student." It is common within syntax and semantics to indicate the scope of quantifiers using phrase structure trees. This can't be done based on the surface structure, but it can be if all of the quantifiers are moved to the beginning of the sentence:

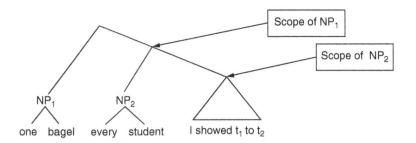

(For simplicity, a lot of detail has been left out of this tree, including all the labels for the nodes and the internal structure of "I showed t_1 to t_2.") A phrase structure tree indicating the scopes of all the quantifiers and other aspects of meaning is known as the sentence's **Logical Form** (or **LF**).

Scope ambiguity can be a source of humor, as in the following evaluation of a candidate not worthy of promotion: "I can assure you that no person would be better for the job." And this line from Jane Wagner's play *The Search for Signs of Intelligent Life in the Universe*: "All my life I've always wanted to *be* somebody. But I see now I should have been more specific." (Both examples are from linguist Beatrice Santorini, www.ling.upenn.edu/-beatrice/humor/contents.html.)

Intensionality

Semanticists divide the semantic meanings of words and phrases into two main subtypes: **extensional** and **intensional** meaning. So far we have focused on extensional meanings, which are simpler. Extensional meanings have to do only with how things *actually* are *at a given point in time*. They have to do with the here-and-now. Consider the following two noun phrases:

(20)   a. The President of France
      b. François Hollande

At the time I'm writing this the President of France is François Hollande, so at this point in time (20a) and (20b) refer to the same person. They have the same extensional meaning.

   Intensional meaning has to do with how things *could be at other times* or *in hypothetical circumstances*. For example, at other times, in the past and in the future, (20a) and (20b) will not refer to the same person. Their intensional meanings therefore differ. Following the philosopher Gottlob Frege (Frege 1892), the term **reference** is often used for extensional meaning, while **sense** is used for intensional meaning. In this section, we'll look at a variety of intensional meanings.

BOX 4.4 **SENSE AND REFERENCE**

In some cases, reference is all that's important to the sentence's meaning, while in other sentences sense is crucial. This difference can be detected through a substitution test. Consider the fill-in-the-blank sentence in (i). One can fill the underlined position with *The President of France* or *François Hollande*, and at the time I'm writing this, it won't make a difference to whether the sentence is true or not. That is, since (ii) is true at the time I'm writing this, so is (iii), and vice versa.

(i) _____is meeting with the American President today.
(ii) The President of France is meeting with the American President today.
(iii) François Hollande is meeting with the American President today.

Because *The President of France* can be substituted for *François Hollande* – and vice versa – without changing whether the sentence is true or false, we classify these sentences as extensional.
   Another fill-in-the-blank sentence, (iv), fails the substitution test:

(iv) One day,_____will be a woman.
(v) One day, the President of France will be a woman.
(vi) One day, François Hollande will be a woman.

Though (v) is true (let us assume), (vi) is not. This failure of substitution tells us that the intensional meaning of the subject is relevant to this sentence. Specifically, it is the future tense indicated by *will* which makes these sentences intensional, because the future tense makes the sentence depend on what will occur in the future, not merely the here-and-now.

Modality

Modality refers to aspects of meaning which cause sentences to be about the nonactual – that is, about alternative possibilities for how things could be. For example, (21) says that

John is kind to animals in actuality, but (22) does not. (22) is about the mere possibility that John is kind to animals. It says that this possibility is (morally) better than the alternative, not being kind to animals.

(21)   John is kind to animals.

(22)   John should be kind to animals.

Modality can be expressed through a variety of grammatical categories: modal auxiliary verbs (for example, *should, must, can, would*), nouns (*possibility, necessity, probability, requirement*), adjectives (*possible, necessary, probable*), as well as other means. Here are some examples of modal sentences:

(23)   a. I must have left my keys in the car.
        b. If I had dropped my keys on my way to the car, they would be on the steps or on the street.
        c. It is a requirement of this university that everyone study Armenian.
        d. Since the keys aren't on the street, it is probable that they are in the car.

Each of these sentences is about alternative possibilities for how things could be. For example, (23b) asks us to consider the possibility that I dropped my keys on the way to the car.

Semanticists often make the meanings of modal words explicit in terms of the notion of **possible world**. Possible worlds help explain the semantics of modals because they provide a straightforward way of talking about alternative possibilities for how things could be. For every different way things could be, we assume a possible world like that. In terms of the concept of possible worlds, (23b) tells us to consider possible worlds in which I dropped my keys on the way to the car. In those worlds, according to the sentence, the keys are on the steps or the street. Likewise, (23c) says that only possible worlds in which everyone studies Armenian are acceptable as far as the university's rules go. Many semanticists believe that possible worlds are needed to understand modality, and since every language can express modality, this suggests that the ability to imagine alternative ways that the world could be – alternative possible worlds – is an essential part of the human capacity to use language. If this is so, it raises even deeper questions: was the ability to conceive of alternative possible worlds a precondition of developing language, a result of developing language, or something which co-evolved with language?

Modals can be categorized in various ways. **Epistemic** modals involve reference to facts that we know. For example, *must* in (23a) is epistemic; it implicitly means '*given what I know*, I must have left my keys in the car.' It is easier to see the fact that (23a) is epistemic by contrasting it with (24), a sign in a hotel parking garage:

(24)   Guests should leave their keys in the car.

(24) is not about what we know; rather, it is about procedures or rules, and could be paraphrased as '*given the rules of the hotel*, guests should leave their keys in the car.' Modals which are about rules, right and wrong, obligations, and so forth are known as **deontic** modals. (23a, b, and d) are epistemic, while (23c) is deontic.

Tense and aspect

Tense and aspect are semantic categories having to do with time. Tense and aspect may lead to a sentence being about the past or future, not only the present, and so they have intensional meaning. Tense refers to features of language which locate the situation or event being described in time. English has a past tense, illustrated in (25), and a present tense, illustrated in (26):

(25)   Mary knew Armenian.

(26)   Mary knows Armenian.

Traditional grammar teachers say that English also has a future tense, indicated by *will*, but many semanticists doubt this. *Will* is grammatically very like a modal auxiliary verb, along with *must, can,* and the like; in addition, the so-called present tense can be used to describe the future:

(27)   Mary starts her new job tomorrow.

These semanticists would say that *will* is actually a modal word, not a tense word.

Whether or not English has a future tense, there are quite a few languages (like Japanese, for example) which have only two tenses, past and nonpast. There are also languages (like Chinese) with no grammatical tense at all. Of course, these languages allow one to say everything that needs to be said about where an event takes place in time. They have the ability to say that an event took place in the past, is taking place in the present, or will take place in the future. For example, they may use an adverb (like *yesterday*) or adverbial (*in the past*) to make clear that an event took place in the past. In some cases, common sense alone would be enough to determine that an event was past; if one is talking about the actions of Confucius, for example, most people would know they are past. In such a situation, the use of an explicit past tense, as in English, is not necessary.

Aspect refers to features of language which describe how events unfold in time, like the English progressive (the *be+VERB-ing* verb form in (28a)) and perfect (the *have+VERB-en* form in (28b)):

(28)   a. Noah is drawing a picture of a train.
         b. Ben has fallen asleep.

(28a) describes the event of Noah's drawing a picture of a train as ongoing at the present time and leaves open whether he'll ever complete the picture, while (28b) describes the event of Ben falling asleep as past and completed.

Across languages, aspectual meanings differ in both subtle and dramatic ways. For example, in English it is impossible to use a past adverb like *yesterday* with sentences in the present tense plus perfect aspect, but in many languages (like the Italian in (29b)) these kinds of combinations are acceptable:

(29)   a. *Mary has left yesterday
         b. Maria   è   partita   ieri.
            Maria   is   left   yesterday.

More dramatically, Mandarin Chinese has a number of aspectual words which express meanings similar to, but more precise than, the English perfect. For example, *le* in (30a) indicates that he has become old, and *guo* in (31a) indicates that he has had the experience of eating pigs' feet. Though both cases can be translated with the perfect in English, reversing *le* and *guo* in these examples (as in (30b) and (31b)) would lead to very different for meanings: (30b) means 'he's been old before' (but isn't now), and (31b) would mean 'he ate pigs' feet.'

(30)   Ta   lao   le.
       He   old   ASPECT
       'He has gotten old.'

    b. Ta   lao   guo.
       He   old   ASPECT
       'He has been old before.'

(31)   a. Ta   chi   guo   zhujiao.
       He   eat   ASPECT   pig-feet
       'He has eaten pigs' feet.'

    b. Ta   chi   le   zhujiao.
       He   eat   ASPECT   pig-feet
       'He ate pigs' feet.'

Aspectual class differs from aspect in that it is not about grammatical forms but a classification of complete sentences with regard to how the situations they describe unfold in time. The notion of aspectual class goes back to Aristotle and has been extensively studied in semantics. Some important aspectual classes are given in (32):

(32)   a. *States: situations which don't inherently involve change*
    Examples: Bob is tall. Maria is cute. Frank knows how to drive a car.

Statives are sentences which describe states, while nonstative sentences can be called eventive. Eventives can be further classified as achievements, activities, and accomplishments.

b. *Achievements: changes which we conceive of as instantaneous*
Examples: Bob arrived. (Bob's position changes from "not-here" to "here.")
Maria was born at noon.
c. *Activities (or processes): change over time, with no particular end point.*
Examples: Bob ran around in circles. (Bob's position changes constantly.)
Maria cried.
d. *Accomplishments: change with a particular end point.*
Examples: Bob ran one mile. (The end point is when Bob completes the mile- long course.)
Maria built a tower.

The concept of aspectual class is important in many ways. The aspectual class of a sentence helps determine what modifiers it can occur with. Thus, activities can occur with *for (time)* adverbials, but not with *in (time)* adverbials, as in (33a). States cannot be in the progressive, as seen in (33b). And finally, *when* clauses are interpreted differently based on whether they combine with state or non-state sentences, (33c–d).

(33) a. Maria cried for/*in an hour.
      b. *Bob is being tall.
      c. When John came home from the war, Bob was tall.
      d. When John came home from the war, Maria cried.

(33c) means that Bob was already tall when John arrived home, while (33d) means that Maria cried just after he arrived. Notice that sentences can be somewhat flexible about the aspectual class they are in. Thus, (33b) makes sense if we think of Bob as a young child pretending to be tall. In that case, *be tall* doesn't mean literally to be tall, but rather something like 'act tall.'

BOX 4.5 **HABITUAL ASPECT IN AFRICAN AMERICAN ENGLISH**

Knowledge of aspect and aspectual verbal class can be an important factor in analyzing the grammar of nonstandard dialects. African American English has a verbal aspect – *be VERBing*, as in *He be workin'* – that expresses habituality. Habituality is not distinguished in the standard English verbal system and AAE *be VERBing* is different from the progressive tense in standard English, which has a similar construction. For example, *The printer be printing 100 pages per minute* means that the printer has the capacity to print 100 pages per minute, not that the printer is at that particular moment printing 100 pages per minute (Green 2002).

We can test this knowledge not only by asking native speakers of the dialect their intuition about the meaning of the sentence but also by analyzing restrictions on aspectual classes in the two dialects. In standard English, statives – verbs like *to know*, or predicates such as *to be tall* – cannot occur in the progressive tense. *She is knowing the answer* is senseless, and *She is being tall* only makes sense metaphorically, as 'acting tall.' However, in AAE, a stative can occur in the *be-VERBing* aspect; *Mary be knowing the answer* is a perfectly grammatical sentence, meaning that Mary generally or habitually knows the answer. Knowing the aspectual distinctions made by different dialects helps linguists identify subtle distinctions in meaning that might otherwise be thought of just as morphological variation.

Semantics summary

The two main branches of semantics are lexical semantics and compositional semantics. Lexical semantics seeks to explain how words mean, while compositional semantics focuses on the process of building up more complex meanings from simpler ones. In this section, we have looked at some of the linguistic categories that can be studied from a semantic perspective, including names, modifiers, predicates and arguments, quantifiers, and intensional elements like modals, tense, and aspect. We have also encountered some theoretical ideas used to explain meaning, such as thematic roles, possible worlds, and events. The goal of semantics is to give a precise theory, using ideas like these, which allows us to understand the lexical and compositional semantics of any human language. Languages are complex and diverse, however, so achieving this goal is a long way off.

Pragmatics 1: meaning and context

Recall the definitions of semantics and pragmatics at the beginning of this chapter. Pragmatics concerns both the relationship between context of use and sentence meaning, and the relationships among sentence meaning, context of use, and speaker's meaning. In this section we will focus on how the context of use contributes to semantic meaning.

Indexicality, context-dependency, and anaphora

Indexicals are words whose semantic meanings depend in a direct way on the context of use. Some simple examples are *I*, *you*, *here*, and *now*. The pronoun *I* refers to the person who says it (except in cases like direct quotes, where it refers to the person being quoted); the word *here* refers to the place where it is spoken, and so forth. Indexicality is similar to the phenomenon of vagueness, discussed earlier. Recall that adjectives like *old* can be vague, in that what counts as old depends on what is being talked about. "What is being talked about" is an aspect of context of use. Another term, **deixis**, is also used for cases in which meaning depends on context of use, and the terms *deixis* and *indexicality* are often used interchangeably.

The "classic" indexicals (like *I*, *you*, *here*, and *now*) are strictly tied to the context of use; their reference depends solely on the context of use. Other words are more flexible. They sometimes get their meaning from the context of use, but not always. An example is *she*. I could say *She is cute* in a situation in which we are both looking at a baby girl. In that case, *she* would refer to this girl by virtue of the context of use. However, the reference of *she* can be determined in other ways. In (34a), *she* can get its meaning from the previous sentence, and in (34b) it can get its meaning within the sentence itself, from *no girl in this class*:

(34) a. Do you see that baby girl over there? She is cute.
      b. No girl in this class doubts that she is cute.

When a word or phrase picks up its meaning from some other piece of language nearby, the relationship between the two is called **anaphora**. A word which gets its meaning in this way is an **anaphor**, and the piece of language which gives the anaphor its meaning is its **antecedent**. In (34a), the antecedent of *she* is *that baby girl over there*.

Both indexicality and anaphora demonstrate the fact that the meaning of a word or phrase often depends crucially on the context of use. More importantly, in different languages certain features of the context are relevant to indexicality and anaphora, while others are not. In English the participants in the conversation, the place and time at which a word is uttered, what is being talked about, and those people and things that have been explicitly mentioned are pragmatically important features of the situation in which language is used. (And there are many others.) Investigating the range of deictic expressions in a given language can help us determine what aspects of the situation comprise the context which speakers use to construct meaning. Languages may differ in which aspects of context are important to them; for example, some languages, such as Korean, explicitly encode the level of formality of the conversation. While level of formality is important to English speakers, it is not grammatically relevant in the same way as it is in Korean.

> ### BOX 4.6 **DISCOURSE ANAPHORA**
>
> There are several kinds of anaphora. Some types of anaphora are semantic in nature, while others are purely pragmatic. The relationship between the quantifier *no girl in this class* and *she* in (34b) is an example of purely semantic anaphora; the semantic nature of this anaphora is clear because the antecedent of *she* doesn't in any sense refer to a particular girl. Therefore, we can't say that the context of use tells us what *she* refers to. Rather, you might say that the meaning of *she* is derived from the (quantificational) meaning of its antecedent. Example (34a) illustrates a kind of pragmatic anaphora called discourse anaphora. Discourse anaphora occurs when the anaphor and antecedent are in different sentences. It only works with certain antecedents. While the antecedents in (i)–(iii) allow discourse anaphora, (iv)–(v) do not:
>
> (i) This baby girl was born on January 1. She is cute.
> (ii) Maria was born on January 1. She is cute.
> (iii) A baby girl lives next door to me. She is cute.
> (iv) No baby girl lives next door to me. ??She is cute.
> (v) Each baby girl was born with hair. ??She was cute.
>
> The first three sentences are acceptable because the antecedents in these cases provide a reference for the anaphor *she*. In contrast, *no baby girl* and *each baby girl* (in (iv) and (v)) don't provide a reference for *she*, since they are quantifiers, and this is why anaphora doesn't work in these examples.

Presupposition

The sentence *John stopped crying at noon* only makes sense if it is assumed that John was crying just before noon. If I say this to you, and you know that John had not been crying at all, you would feel that what I say is out of place or that you'd been misled. We say that the sentence *John stopped crying at noon* **presupposes** that John was crying just before noon. Many words, phrases, and structures create presuppositions. Here are some examples of sentences followed by their presuppositions (in parentheses):

(35)   a. Each of the boys in the room is nice. (There are some boys in the room.)
       b. That pig is fat. (That is a pig.)
       c. John is crying again. (John has cried before.)
       d. It is Bob who stole the chocolate. (Somebody stole the chocolate.)

Presuppositions are not just anything which a speaker happens to take for granted. Presupposition occurs when a speaker's choice of words shows that he or she is taking something for granted. For example, part of the meaning of the word *again* is that someone who uses it indicates that he/she is taking for granted that whatever is being talked about happened before. For this reason, we say that (35c) presupposes that John has cried before. (The speaker of (35c) might take other things for granted, such as the fact that you should comfort people who are crying, but you can't determine this just by looking at (35c) itself. Therefore, we wouldn't say that (35c) presupposes, in the linguist's sense, that one should comfort crying people.)

Presuppositions are often understood in terms of the notion of **common ground**, as discussed by the philosopher Robert Stalnaker (Stalnaker 1974, 1978). The common ground is the set of propositions which the participants in a conversation mutually assume. (They don't have to actually believe these propositions, but they at least act as if they do.) In any normal conversation, many things are implicitly in the common ground – that the sun comes up every morning, that the speaker and the hearer are alive, that things fall down when you release them in the air, and so forth. Other propositions may get into the common ground because they are explicitly stated. For example, if I say to you "I'm hungry" (and you think I'm being sincere), henceforth the proposition that I'm hungry will be part of the common ground; that is, we will both assume it to be true (until something changes – for example, I eat something). The common ground is a major part of the context of use, and helps us make explicit the role of presupposition in the use of sentences like *John stopped crying at noon*: The sentence is only appropriate if the common ground already contains the information that John was crying just before noon or if that information can be added without arousing controversy.

In television shows about lawyers and detectives, presupposition is often turned to the benefit of a crafty investigator. Suppose a detective suspects X of committing a murder in New Jersey, but has no clear evidence that X has traveled there. The detective might casually ask, "How was your trip to New Jersey?" This sentence presupposes that the suspect has been there, and so an answer to the question will provide the crucial evidence that X has recently been to New Jersey. (If X is smart, he will respond without answering, perhaps saying "What trip to New Jersey?")

> *Presuppositions are a powerful persuasive strategy. Identify several presuppositions in newspaper editorials, political speeches, and advertising. Compare them to presuppositions found by your classmates.*

Pragmatics 2: meaning and the intention to communicate

Indexicality and presupposition are aspects of pragmatics which mostly have to do with the relationship between context of use and semantic meaning. In this section, we'll investigate the other major subdomain of pragmatics, the relationships among semantic meaning, context of use, and speaker's meaning.

The Gricean view of meaning

Semantics views meaning from the compositional perspective: the meaning of a sentence is built up from the meanings of its parts. The smallest parts get their meanings from the lexicon, and then these meanings get put together according to rules which pay attention to the grammatical structure of the sentence. However, not all aspects of meaning can be explained by this compositional "bottom-up" approach, and a complementary "top-down" view of meaning has focused on the intentions of language users. More precisely, when A says something to B, A intends for B to be affected in a certain way. If A says "It's raining," for example, A may intend for B to believe that it's raining (and perhaps to open an umbrella or come inside). This perspective helps us understand many aspects of speaker's meaning.

Implicature

The idea that meaning is based in the intentions of speakers is most clearly revealed in H. P. Grice's theory of conversational **implicature** (Grice 1957, 1975). Very often, when someone says something, he or she doesn't mean exactly what the words literally mean. That is, the (speaker's) meaning differs from the (semantic) meaning. For example, the semantic meaning of "There's a bear sneaking up behind you!" doesn't involve the concept of warning; it just reports a fact. However, it's quite likely that a warning is part of what the speaker means. This "extra meaning" which goes beyond what the words literally say is an implicature of the sentence. Grice explained how speaker's meaning can be determined in such cases by positing a **Cooperative Principle** that all speakers and hearers assume when speaking to each other:

> Cooperative Principle: speaker's meaning can be calculated on the basis of semantic meaning and the assumption that speakers are behaving rationally and cooperatively.

Grice broke this general principle into four conversational **maxims** to explain what rationality and cooperativeness are:

> The maxim of Quality: make your contribution one that is true rather than false.

> The maxim of Quantity: provide the information that is required for the purposes of the conversation, but no more.

> The maxim of Relevance: make your contributions relevant.

> The maxim of Manner: be clear and orderly in your talk.

These maxims are not rules to be followed in the sense that traffic laws are. Rather, they are *assumptions* which we use to try to make sense of what people say. That is, we assume that people follow the four maxims when they talk, and this helps us figure out what they mean. Consider (36), for example:

(36)   There are three students in the class: Mary, Bob, and Jill.
       A: Which students passed the exam?
       B: Mary and Bob.

In this conversation, in addition to concluding that Mary and Bob passed the exam, A is likely to infer that Jill didn't. However, B never said that Jill didn't pass the exam, so why would A infer this? By assuming that B is following the four maxims, A can figure that B gave as much true information as was required and relevant (maxims of Quality, Quantity, and Relevance). Since it would be relevant to say that Jill passed if she actually had passed, A can infer that B didn't include Jill in the list of people who passed because B doesn't think that Jill passed (so long as other assumptions hold, such as that B knows Jill is in the class). Moreover, B knows that A would figure this way, and so said "Mary and Bob" with the understanding that A would conclude that Jill didn't pass. In this way, the idea that Jill didn't pass becomes part of the speaker's meaning of B's utterance. That is, B uses the Cooperative Principle and maxims to implicate that Jill didn't pass.

Another example of implicature was hinted at earlier in example (12):

(12)   Elvis Presley made a peanut butter sandwich and sat down beside the pool.

This sentence seems to mean that Elvis made the peanut butter sandwich before going to the pool. This 'before' meaning is not part of the semantic meaning of *and* (as given by truth conditions); it is an implicature. According to Grice's maxim of Manner, we should present information in an orderly way, and in most cases that includes mentioning events in the order in which they occurred. Therefore, a hearer can conclude that the speaker means to say that Elvis made the sandwich before sitting down by the pool.

Because the Gricean maxims are not rigid rules, like rules of law, but are flexible assumptions about how speakers behave, they can be broken, or **flouted**, to implicate further meanings. Flouting a maxim occurs when a speaker uses language in a way which appears, in an obvious way, to violate a maxim. For example, if you ask me whether I think your new shirt is attractive, and I say "It was probably inexpensive," my reply seems to violate the maxim of relevance – I didn't answer your question. However, because you assume that, despite appearances, I am conforming to relevance, you try to figure out how what I said *could be* relevant. Since my utterance avoided answering your question by mentioning a reason why you might have bought an unattractive shirt, you will infer that I don't like the shirt. This inference can become an implicature of the sentence, that is, part of my speaker's meaning.

BOX 4.7 **CULTURE-SPECIFIC IMPLICATURE**

Cultural assumptions can be crucial in determining speaker's meaning. For example, if two Chinese people are looking at the dessert display in a French restaurant, and one says to the other, "That tart is not too sweet," she almost certainly intends this comment as praise of the tart. She might intend to implicate that her dinner partner should order a tart, as opposed to the éclair or mousse. This speaker's meaning arises, in part, from the fact that it is common knowledge among Chinese people that most of them find western desserts too sweet. Among some other groups, the same comment ("That tart is not too sweet") could be interpreted as a criticism, rather than a compliment. Notice that the cultural specificity of the speaker's meaning in this example is not a fact about the Chinese language. The implicature could arise whether the two people are speaking Chinese or French or English. What's crucial is the common assumption that people like them don't enjoy sweet desserts.

Speech acts

Another important figure in the development of pragmatics is John Austin (Austin 1962). He pointed out that when people use language, they are performing a kind of action. He called these actions **speech acts**. It's easy to see the "act" nature of language when a minister says, "I now pronounce you husband and wife" in a wedding ceremony. By virtue of this sentence being said by an appropriate person, the engaged couple becomes a married couple. Most speech acts are not so "official," but they all rely on the speaker using an utterance to signal his/her intention to accomplish some action and the hearer inferring that action from the utterance. When people make bets and threats and promises, offer congratulations and apologies, or issue orders or challenges, they are using language to accomplish actions. Consider the contrast between (37a) and (37b):

(37)   a. I promise to visit tomorrow.
        b. She promised to visit tomorrow.

(37a) performs the act of promising: if you say it, you've promised something. If you don't visit the next day, the person you said it to can complain that you broke your promise. Example (37b) simply reports a promise by somebody else; you haven't promised anything yourself.

Sentences which perform actions, like (37a), are known as **performatives**, while other sentences, (37b), are called **constatives**. A good test of whether a sentence is a performative is whether you can insert the word *hereby* before the verb: "I hereby promise/challenge/bet..." make sense, but "I hereby walk/see/like..." do not. As Austin pointed out, however, even constatives perform actions of some sort; (37b) performs the action of *reporting* her promise. Thus, the distinction between performatives and constatives may not be as important as the idea that all sentences can be used to perform actions of various sorts.

In trying to understand the various types of acts that sentences may perform, Austin proposed three "levels" of speech act:

Locutionary acts: grammar-internal actions like articulating a certain sound, using a certain morpheme, referring to a particular person. (These are the "acts" which fall under phonetics, phonology, morphology, syntax, and semantics. They are usually not of much interest to people studying pragmatics.)

Illocutionary acts: actions of communication like asserting a fact, asking a question, requesting an action, making a promise, or giving a warning.

Perlocutionary acts: actions which go beyond communication, like annoying, frightening, or tricking someone by what you tell them.

For example, suppose speaker A says to hearer B:

(38)   There's a bear sneaking up behind you!

At the locutionary level, A utters the word *there* and refers to the addressee with the word *you* (among many other locutionary acts). At the illocutionary level, A asserts a fact (that there's a bear sneaking up behind B) and warns B that he or she is in danger. At the perlocutionary level, A frightens B and causes B to run away. Linguists often speak of the illocutionary *force* of a sentence. The illocutionary force is the type of communicative intention that the speaker has. For example, (38) has the illocutionary force of warning, while (37a) has the force of promising and (37b) has the force of reporting or asserting. The context in which the sentence is uttered is crucial in interpreting the illocutionary force of a speech act; if a loan shark to whom you owe money says "I promise to visit tomorrow," the speech act intended may be a threat (disguised as a promise).

Pragmatics summary

Pragmatics is fundamentally about how the context of use contributes to meaning, both semantic meaning and speaker's meaning. The core topics of pragmatics are indexicality, presupposition, implicature, and speech acts, but in reality there is no limit to the ways in which context can influence meaning. Situations can even develop which allow words to mean things they never meant before. For example, several families are having dinner together, and two of the teenagers are secretly dating. They each separately make an excuse to leave the dinner to their parents, expressing a wish to go work on their chemistry assignment, and they have an enjoyable time together. After this, they start to say things like "Don't you need to work on your chemistry homework?" to indicate a desire to sneak off together – a new pragmatic meaning for sentences of that kind.

Philosophical issues

Linguists who study meaning spend most of their time on the kinds of topics described above. However, underlying these linguistic topics are important philosophical issues concerning the nature of meaning. There are two fundamental perspectives on the very basic question, what is meaning? According to the *psychological* view, meanings are concepts, ideas, or some other sort of mental entity. According to the *referential* view, meanings are aspects of the world (or possible worlds) that can be described or referred to with language.

The psychological view

According to the psychological view of meaning, when we study semantics we are studying something that exists in the mind or brain of language users (e.g. Jackendoff 1990, Lakoff 1987, Talmy 2000, Wierzbicka 1996). We might say, for example, that the meaning of a simple word like *apple* is the concept which language users associate with the word. In other words, that which lets us think about apples is what is symbolized by the word *apple*. When we speak to others, fundamentally what we are trying to do is evoke in their minds the same concepts as we have active in our own mind (or very similar concepts, at least).

Many linguists working in the field of lexical semantics take a psychological view. In the sections on thematic roles and lexical semantics, we noted that lexical semanticists aim to explain things like why polysemous words have the meanings they do and why different languages have both similarities and differences in what their words mean. One of the main strengths of the psychological view is that it allows us to address such questions. For example, in English we have lots of words for different kinds of cars but fewer words for different kinds of igloos. This is presumably because users of English have had more exposure to, and a better understanding of, cars than igloos. Therefore, they would have developed a richer group of car-related concepts than igloo-related ones. This in turn would allow the development of more car-words than igloo-words. More sophisticated applications of this perspective frequently have to do with language change and polysemy. A well-studied example of this is the English word *over* (e.g. Tyler and Evans 2003). The basic meaning of *over* ('above in space') is connected to various other meanings (e.g. 'the other side of,' as in *The house is over the river*, or 'finished,' as in *The movie is over*). A psychologically based theory of meaning would aim to explain these other meanings in terms of the ways in which the concept has been extended over time from its basic meaning. For example, if you're going to go to the other side of a river, you are likely to be above the river at some point. This might lead to a new meaning for *over* which is similar to 'the other side of.'

A psychological theory of semantics may, but need not, adopt the Sapir–Whorf hypothesis. The **Sapir–Whorf hypothesis**, named after Edward Sapir and Benjamin Lee Whorf, states that what we can think is affected by the language we speak. For example, a language spoken by a community that lives in the desert may have few words for kinds of fish. According to the Sapir–Whorf hypothesis, this would keep the members of this community from seeing and understanding differences among fish which are obvious to speakers of other languages (who live near water). That is, their thinking about fish is constrained by their language; their thinking about fish can be no richer than the language they have for talking about them.

A very important thing to keep in mind as you consider the Sapir–Whorf hypothesis is that languages are living entities which change to meet their users' changing needs. A language may have no word for a certain kind of animal because its speakers have rarely seen one, but if that animal becomes common where the speakers live, they can introduce a word. They might change the meaning of a word they already have, create a word using the language's morphological system, or borrow a word from another language that already has one. A dictionary will show you many examples of these processes. For example, the word *computer* originally meant 'one who does computations,' and then was used to refer to the newly invented machine. An example of borrowing is *tomato*, from a Nahuatl word, to refer to the vegetable when it was "discovered" in the New World.

Several problems with the psychological perspective have been pointed out. Perhaps the most important problems arise from the fact that what one's words mean can depend more on the way other people use those words than on one's own concepts. Hilary Putnam gives a famous hypothetical example (Putnam 1975): Putnam has heard of two kinds of trees, beeches and elms, but doesn't know anything about either except that they are deciduous trees which grow on the east coast of North America. Nothing in Putnam's mind distinguishes the meaning of *beech* from the meaning of *elm*. Nevertheless, Putnam means beech when he uses the word *beech* and means elm when he uses the word *elm*. This should be clear if you imagine Putnam walking up to you, pointing at a tree, and asking "Is that a beech?" If the tree is in fact a beech, the answer is "yes," but if it's an elm the answer is "no." Since the mental concepts that Putnam associates with *beech* and *elm* are just alike, this difference in meaning can't be due to what's in his mind. Putnam's use of the word *beech* means beech because that's what the word means in English. That is, the meaning is determined, at least in large part, by the larger linguistic community and the environment in which this community resides.

The referential view

The other major perspective on the nature of meaning is that meanings are features of the world. For example, the meaning of a name like *Aristotle* is just the person it refers to in the world. This way of thinking is followed by most compositional semanticists as well as some lexical semanticists, and it solves Putnam's problem: *beech* describes one set of things in the world, *elm* describes another, and the English-speaking community at large determines which is which.

The referential view is neutral on whether the world, as described by language, is objective and independent of our thinking about it. On the one hand, it might be that the category of beeches is "real" in a deep metaphysical sense. In that case, those who follow the referential view could simply say that the word *beech* names the things which really are beeches. On the other hand, it might be that the category of beeches is only an artifact of the way our minds work or of our culture; the things we call beeches may only form a group because we see them that way. Still, the community of language users can employ the word *beech* to describe the members of this group.

There are problems for the referential view as well (Frege 1892). In some cases, two words may refer to the same things in the world, and yet they seem to differ in meaning. For example, *water* and H_2O refer to the same thing, but do they really have the same meaning? Perhaps not. Suppose I don't know that H_2O is water. I might think that H_2O *is poisonous* is a true sentence and that *water is not poisonous* is also true. But if *water* and H_2O have the same meaning, the two sentences should contradict one another. How can I think the very same thing is poisonous and not? Philosophers and linguists agree that this is a difficult problem.

CHAPTER SUMMARY

Semantic meaning is the literal meaning of a word, phrase, or sentence; speaker's meaning is what a language user intends to communicate by his or her words. Semantic meaning is derived in accordance with the Principle of Compositionality through the interplay of lexical meaning, grammatical structure, and the context of use. Speaker's meaning is in turn derived from the interaction between semantic meaning and the context of use. Semantics, the study of semantic meaning, focuses on the contribution which particular words or features of grammar make to meaning, and in this vein semanticists study such things as individual parts of speech, predicates, arguments, quantifiers, and so forth. Pragmatics aims to explain the ways in which context of use contributes to semantic meaning, and the ways in which speakers use language, in specific contexts, to convey the particular speaker's meanings they want to convey.

Exercises

EXERCISE 4.1

Which of the basic semantic relations and proportios outlined in the text (synonymy, entailment, etc.) are exemplified by the following?

a. Nobody likes enchiladas.
Mary likes enchiladas.
b. Nobody is at the party and Al is enjoying the party more than anyone else.
c. memory (as in "I have a good memory," "I have beautiful memories of my trip to Amalfi," and "I need to buy some more memory for my computer")
d. Either it's raining in Delhi now, or it isn't.
e. top (as in "You'll find it on top of the refrigerator" and "When I was a boy, I enjoyed playing with a top")
f. Nobody likes enchiladas.
Mary doesn't like enchiladas.
g. I love beans.
I don't hate beans.

EXERCISE 4.2

Classify the following adjectives according to whether they are intersective or not and whether they are vague or not: *tall, previous, red, ideological, mere, ugly, even* (as in *even number*).

EXERCISE 4.3

Explain the meanings of the following sentences, focusing on the role of quantifiers. Identify the restrictor and the scope, and say what set-relationship holds between them if the sentence is true.

a. Every dog has a tail.
b. Three or four people like Mary.
c. Nobody around here speaks French.

EXERCISE 4.4

In Box 4.3, we saw how to arrive at one meaning of *I showed one bagel to every student* by putting *every student* inside the scope of *one bagel*. We would derive the other meaning by doing it the other way around, putting *one bagel* inside the scope of *every student*. Draw a "box diagram" and a Logical Form tree similar to those presented in the text which represent this second meaning.

EXERCISE 4.5

Here are some more sentences with scope ambiguities. For each, describe the two meanings and indicate which two words or phrases create the ambiguity:

a. I don't like every student.
b. Two unicorns seem to be in the garden.
c. During your visit to Rome, you must visit one fountain.

EXERCISE 4.6

Draw box diagrams and Logical Form trees for each meaning of the sentences in Exercise 4.5.

EXERCISE 4.7

Give examples in which the following adverbs quantify over times, and examples where they quantify over ordinary objects (the example in the text used donkeys): *usually, often, never.*

EXERCISE 4.8

Which of the following words have modal meaning? Which have aspectual meaning?
   finish, probably, impossible, beginning, certainty

EXERCISE 4.9

Categorize the modality in the following sentences as epistemic, deontic, or "other."

a. Dogs may not enter the subway.
b. If you love animals, you ought to be a vegetarian.
c. Birds can fly.
d. You can probably find a book about raccoons in the library.

EXERCISE 4.10

The English present tense has some unusual properties:

a. Maria is tall.
b. Maria cries.
c. *Maria cries right now.

Sentence (a) is unremarkable, but sentence (b) does not simply describe an event which is taking place at the present moment. Example (c) is quite strange. Describe the restrictions on the English present tense in terms of the aspectual classes of sentences. (You will need to come up with more examples than (a)–(c) to see the picture clearly.)

EXERCISE 4.11

Describe the meaning of each of the following words in a way that makes clear how it can be indexical: *nearby, return, tomorrow, above, local, ahead.*

EXERCISE 4.12

What do the following sentences presuppose? Sentences may have one or more presuppositions.

a. John continued smoking.
b. Each of the Russian students in the class surmised that the answer was hard to figure out.
c. It's surprising that Mary likes to eat meat.
d. Everyone's paper is worth reading.
e. Why is it that most students enjoy studying semantics?
f. Why can't students in the music school do a minor?
g. Sue's students want more chocolate in class.
h. Who put the "Linguists do it in trees" bumper sticker on the wall?
i. Hey, who ate the last donut?

EXERCISE 4.13

Describe contexts in which each of the following sentences would create an implicature by flouting and explain which maxim is being flouted in each case.

a. Your answer to the question was adequate.
b. It's a wonderful party, but I have to get up early tomorrow.
c. I'll die if you don't give me another bite of that delicious cake.

EXERCISE 4.14

Examine a letter to the editor in a newspaper or a piece of junk mail, and circle at least five indexicals. Then identify an implicature of the writer. What Gricean maxim (or maxims) gives rise to this implicature? Why does the writer use implicature in this case, rather than explicitly saying what he or she means?

EXERCISE 4.15

It is difficult to test whether the Sapir–Whorf hypothesis is correct because differences in language typically correlate with differences in experience. For example, people who speak a language with few words for different kinds of fish probably live in a place where they see few fish. If the way they think about fish is different from the way a seafaring people think about them, this could be due to their lack of experience with fish, rather than the lack of words in their language. Discuss what kinds of studies or experiments one could do to test the Sapir–Whorf hypothesis.

SUGGESTIONS FOR FURTHER READING

Green, G. 1996, *Pragmatics and natural language understanding*, 2nd edition, Mahwah, NJ: Lawrence Erlbaum. This short, engagingly written book discusses a remarkably wide range of issues in pragmatics. It emphasizes a single, coherent perspective on the nature of pragmatics: pragmatics is a component of cognitive science which aims to understand the crucial role which the intentions and plans of speakers have in creating meaning.

Levinson, S. 1983, *Pragmatics*, Cambridge University Press. This is the classic pragmatics textbook, laying out in detail how pragmatic theory had developed up until the time it was written. It thoroughly discusses all of the main areas of pragmatics, including indexicality, presupposition, speech acts, and implicature, and also explores the connections between pragmatics and the study of discourse.

Martin, R. 1987, *The meaning of language*, Cambridge, MA: MIT Press. This book gives an accessible introduction to the philosophical issues relevant to the study of meaning, including many not touched on in this chapter. It also briefly develops some standard ideas about compositional semantics.

Portner, P. 2004, *What is meaning? An introduction to formal semantics*, Oxford and Malden, MA: Blackwell. This book gives a introduction to contemporary formal semantics without requiring any logical or mathematical machinery. It discusses philosophical issues and the meanings of a wide variety of words and grammatical constructions, including referential noun phrases, predicates, modifiers, quantifiers, tense, aspect, and modality.

5 Discourse

KEY TERMS

- act structure
- adjacency pair
- back channels
- coherence
- cohesion
- cohesive ties
- discourse
- Discourse
- discourse markers
- exchange structure
- fragmentation
- genre
- idea structure
- information state
- integration
- narrative
- participation framework
- recipient design
- referent
- register
- repair
- schema
- speech act
- speech event
- speech situation
- tone units
- transcription
- turn at talk
- turn continuers
- turn transition place
- utterance

CHAPTER PREVIEW

Discourse is the use of language above and beyond the sentence: how people use language in texts and contexts. Discourse analysts focus on peoples' actual utterances and try to figure out what processes make those utterances appear the way they do. Through discourse, people

- **represent the world**
- **convey communicative intentions**
- **organize thoughts into communicative actions**
- **arrange information so it is accessible to others**
- **engage in actions and interactions with one another**
- **convey their identities and relationships**

This chapter provides an overview of central concepts and methods through in-depth discussion and analyses of spoken discourse and written discourse. Models of function and coherence in spoken discourse are also presented.

GOALS

The goals of this chapter are to:

- **define discourse and demonstrate how to analyze spoken and written discourse**
- **explain the relationship between structure and function in discourse**

- demonstrate how repair in discourse works
- describe the effects of recipient design
- explicate the relationship between text and context
- describe the planes of discourse and their relationships

Language use above and beyond the sentence

Almost everything that we do in our everyday lives depends on language. In fact, it is hard to even imagine what our world would be like without language. So much of what keeps people and societies together depends crucially on language. We need language to make and enforce laws; get and distribute valued resources; create and maintain personal and public relationships; teach children our ways of "being," "thinking," and "doing"; engage in scholarly inquiry; preserve our past and plan our future. Language allows us to make friends (and enemies), joke and argue with each other, celebrate happy occasions and mourn sad ones.

But what is there about language that lets us engage in so wide a range of activities? Certainly sounds, morphemes, lexical items, and sentences are part of the story. Sounds produce acoustic signals that combine to convey propositions that are systematically arranged into grammatical strings. But what happens then? A sound, morpheme, word, sentence, or proposition almost never occurs on its own. They are put together in discourse.

In this chapter, we learn about **discourse analysis**, the branch of linguistics that focuses on *language use above and beyond the sentence*. The terms "above" and "beyond" may sound like we're embarking on an interstellar expedition of some kind, but they capture different features of the "discourse" mission. For most of its long scholarly tradition, linguistics perceived the sentence as the limit of the language system. Linguists focused mainly on the forms of language (sounds, morphemes, word, and sentences); how language was *used in context* was not explored. Speakers, hearers, and situations were outside the realm of analysis. It is by examining units larger than sentences, then, that discourse analysts go "above" the sentence. And it is by examining aspects of the world in which language is used that discourse analysts go "beyond" the sentence. At the same time, it is important to remember that real people, using language in the real world (and in the rush of real time) are analyzing discourse as well – drawing inferences about meaning from features of the discourse.

Because of its broad reach into the psychological, social, and cultural worlds, discourse analysis draws from many different disciplines and from a variety of traditions within linguistics. The construction of discourse involves several simultaneous processes. Some are the linguistic processes of arranging sentences and conveying meanings. Beyond these linguistic processes are cognitive processes that underlie the organization of thoughts into verbal form. The organization of information is influenced by discourse processes that draw on interactional roles (who is speaking? who is listening?) as well as more stable social relationships among people (for example, one's role in a family or one's socioeconomic status). Still other discourse processes draw upon implicit cultural models – displayed by our elders and our peers – of what we should do, how we should act, and what kinds of people we should be.

A discourse differs from a random sequence of sentences because it has **coherence** – it conveys meaning that is greater than the sum of its parts. It is not unusual to think of something as having its own identity beyond the identities of the smaller parts within that entity. For example, culture is more than what we do: it is a way of thinking about the world and a way of locating ourselves in that world that guides the way we act. Likewise, society is more than the sum total of the individuals who live in it. Cultures and societies are not simply the coincidental result of human instincts, individual drives and personalities. So, too, discourse is more than the addition of separate sentences to each other. Rather, there are structured relationships among the parts that result in something new and different.

Discourse is a unit of language above and beyond a mere accumulation of sounds, morphemes, words, clauses, and sentences. It is easy to think of a *written discourse* this way. A novel, short story, essay or poem has an identity that develops through patterned relationships among sentences, among ideas or characters, through repetition or variation of rhythm and rhyme. In the same way, when we construct and co-construct *spoken discourse* by talking to each other, underlying processes of speaking, thinking, acting, and interacting come together to produce an overall sense of "what is going on."

BOX 5.1 **FORMAL VERSUS FUNCTIONAL APPROACHES TO ANALYZING LANGUAGE**

The analysis of linguistic performance – and the social and cultural inferences it allows – raises important questions about the relation of language to other human systems. Does language form a separate system of rules, different in kind and function from other rules of human thought and behavior? If not, then to what other systems could it be related? Is language related to cognition? Is it embedded within social norms and cultural prisms? The degree to which knowledge of language is part of a more inclusive body of knowledge through which we live our daily lives is an ongoing topic of discussion in the field of linguistics. The linguistic anthropologist Dell Hymes (1974: 79) suggests that the structural (i.e. formalist) and functional approaches to analyzing language differ in a number of ways.

Structural approach	Functional approach
Focuses on structure of language (a code) as a grammar.	Focuses on structure of speech (as acts, events) as ways of speaking.
Analyzes language structure before any (optional) analysis of language use. Assumes that language use derives from language structure.	Analyzes language use before analysis of language structure. Assumes that language structure and use are integrated; organization of language use reveals additional structural features.
Assumes that the most important function of language is referential, i.e. the use of language to describe the world through propositions.	Assumes that language has a range of functions, including referential, stylistic, and social functions.

BOX 5.1 (*cont.*)

Structural approach	Functional approach
Studies the elements and structures of language separately from contexts of use; ignores the culture (ways of acting, thinking, and being) of those using the language.	Studies the elements and structures of language within their contexts of use; attends to the culture (ways of acting, thinking, and being) of those using the language.
Assumes that language structure is independent of social functions and uses. Any language can (potentially) serve any social, cultural, or stylistic purpose.	Assumes that languages, varieties, and styles can be adapted to different situations, functions, and uses, and gain different social values for their users.
Assumes that language is a single code within a homogeneous community: each speaker replicates a uniform structure.	Assumes that language comprises a repertoire of speech styles within a diverse community: each speaker adds to an organized matrix of diversity.
Assumes the uniformity of speakers, hearers, actions, events, and communities across world languages.	Seeks to investigate the diversity of speakers, hearers, actions, events, and communities within world languages.

Most linguists who analyze discourse adopt, at least partially, a functional approach to language. This is not surprising: observing and analyzing what people *do* with language leads naturally to an interest in the "work" that language can do – the functions it enables people to perform.

Data: language use in everyday life

Analysis of discourse is always analysis of *language use*. This means that linguists studying discourse usually do not ask native speakers of a language for their intuitions about grammaticality or engage in thought experiments about meaning. Rather, discourse analysts examine actual samples of people interacting with each other (by either speaking or writing) in everyday situations. They believe that the structure of discourse can be discovered not from peoples' intuitions about what they *might, could*, or *would* say, but primarily from analyses of what people *do* say. Discourse analysis focuses on the patterns in which sentences (and other units such as acts and turns) appear in the texts that are constructed as people interact with one another in social contexts.

Like other linguists, discourse analysts believe that the form of language is governed by abstract linguistic rules that are part of speakers' competence. But added to linguistic rules are principles that guide performance, the *use* of language. Knowledge about discourse is part of what Hymes (1974) has called **communicative competence** – our tacit cultural knowledge about how to use language in different speech situations, how to interact with different people engaged together in different speech events, and how to use language to perform different acts.

We can see how our knowledge about language intersects with our knowledge about social and cultural life by taking a look at the discourse examples below, drawn from a collection of routine speech events:

(1) Gail: Hello?
     Debby: Oh hi, you're home already!

We can infer a great deal about what is going on in this brief exchange from features of the interchange. Gail and Debby seem to be talking on the phone; *hello* with rising intonation (represented by the ?) is typical of the way Americans answer the phone. Notice that Debby doesn't ask for Gail (for example, *Hi, is Gail there?*), nor does she identify herself (*Hi, this is Debby*). What Debby doesn't say, then, allows us to infer that Debby and Gail know each other pretty well; Debby recognizes Gail's voice and seems to assume that Gail will recognize hers. We can also infer (from the exclamation *oh*) that Gail's presence is surprising to Debby. And the statement *you're home already*, shows that Debby knows something about Gail's intended schedule.

Snippets of discourse from our daily lives show us how much we – as "after-the-fact" analysts and as real-time language users – can infer about "what is going on" from routine uses of language. Likewise, gathering examples of routine speech acts (such as requests, compliments, apologies) and speech events (such as face-to-face greetings or telephone openings) can reveal both their similarities and their differences. However, although collecting examples of discourse from our own everyday lives is valuable, it has several limitations. First, when we hear an interesting bit of discourse and then jot it down, we usually cannot capture stretches of discourse that are longer than a few sentences or turns at talk. (A turn at talk is the period of time in which someone is granted and/or takes the opportunity to speak.) Second, it is difficult to reconstruct the nuances of speech, particularly when several people are interacting with each other. These nuances are especially helpful when we try to figure out how it is that interlocutors (people talking to one another) interpret what is going on; crucial information can reside in a pause, a sigh, a downward intonation, a simple *oh* or *well*, or the arrangement of words in a sentence (for example, *I want the cake* versus *The cake is what I want*). It is impossible to recall all of the speech that appears throughout the course of a speech event (the type of interaction that participants assume is going on) or the speech situation (the type of occasion or encounter). And because our memories are fallible, we usually fill in details based on our prior knowledge of what typically happens.

The ethnography of communication

Dell Hymes (a linguistic anthropologist) developed a subfield of linguistics and anthropology called "ethnography of communication." He persuaded linguists and anthropologists to analyze the social, cultural, and linguistic properties of three units embedded in one another:

Speech act: *an action performed by one person through speech. It can be labeled by a noun that names the act. The speaker intends to perform the act and that intention is recognized by the recipient. Examples: a greeting, a request, a boast, a compliment.*

> **Speech event**: *an interaction between two or more people in which more than one speech act occurs. Examples: greetings, request, and compliance.*
> **Speech situation**: *a social occasion with more than one speech event. During the occasion, speech contributes to what happens, but it is not necessarily all that happens. Examples: a classroom, a party.*

Discourse analysts correct for the limitations of relying only upon what they hear in their everyday lives in several ways. The way that they do so depends partially upon the topic they are studying and partially upon their interest in generalizing their findings. For example, discourse analysts who are interested in how groups of people use discourse to communicate at work often do fieldwork in a workplace. There they observe activities (e.g. meetings, chats at the water cooler) and interview people who perform different tasks (e.g. managers, secretaries). They can then propose generalizations about that workplace and perhaps about other workplaces with similar characteristics.

Other discourse analysts may be interested in a particular aspect of discourse: how do people apologize to one another? When, where, and why do people use the word *like* (as in *I'm like, "Oh no!"* or *It was like a crazy thing, like weird*)? Then they may rely upon tape-recorded speech from a wide variety of settings and occasions, paying less attention to obtaining a sample that represents a subset of people and their activities in a particular social setting, and more attention to getting enough examples of the discourse phenomena in which they are interested. Still other discourse analysts might be interested not in the discourse of a particular setting, or one aspect of discourse, but in *every* aspect of only *one* discourse. They might delve into all the details of several minutes of a single conversation, aiming to understand how it is that two people use many different facets of language to construct a discourse that makes sense to them at that time.

Regardless of their type of inquiry, most discourse analysts rely upon audio or video-recordings of interactions between people in which speech is the main medium of communication. Once speech has been recorded, analysts have to then produce a **transcript** – a written version of what was said that captures numerous aspects of language use, ranging from features of speech (such as intonation, volume, and nonfluencies) to aspects of interaction (such as overlaps between turns at talk) and, if possible, aspects of nonvocal behavior (such as gaze and gesture). Transcriptions of spoken discourse look quite different than other scripts with which we might be familiar. For example, unlike most scripts for dramatic productions, linguists' transcripts try to indicate features of speech production and interaction, often using notations like those in Box 5.2 on transcription conventions.

> **Analysis tip**
> *I always keep a tablet of paper nearby to jot down observations, questions, and ideas about what I am transcribing. Those who transcribe right on the computer can keep two files open at the same time, or just insert comments (in a different font or type size) alongside the material in the transcription file.*

Transcribing spoken discourse is challenging and often frustrating, not to mention time-consuming: some linguists spend close to ten hours transcribing just one hour of speech. But fortunately, what results is a transcript that they can analyze from different angles years after the original speech. The process of transcribing is also very instructive! By listening – again and again – and trying to fine tune one's written record of what is said, linguists often end up doing preliminary analyses.

BOX 5.2 **TRANSCRIPTION CONVENTIONS (ADAPTED FROM SCHIFFRIN 1987; TANNEN 1989)**

Transcribing a conversation is an invaluable analytic tool. It freezes moments in time and allows the discourse analyst to focus on particular aspects of the conversation. But it is important to remember that transcribing speech is, unavoidably, a selective and interpretive representation of a subset of what goes on in a conversation. For example, Elinor Ochs (1979) found that the traditional convention of ordering turns at talk one under the other misrepresented the collaborative nature of caregiver–child interactions; putting adult and child utterances in separate side-by-side columns allows the viewer to see their very different roles – e.g. how caregivers accommodate to the limitations of young children's developing linguistic and communicative competence.

When you transcribe, you make lots of choices, depending on what questions you are asking about the data. For example, how do you want to "chunk" the stream of talk into lines of transcript? By speaker? By speaker and "T-units" (an independent clause and its dependencies) or smaller intonation units? How do you want to represent pronunciation of words (giving, givin', [gɪvɪn])? How carefully do you want to time pauses? Which prosodic features (like amplitude and pitch) do you want to capture?

Discourse analysts use a variety of symbols to represent aspects of speech, including the following:

.	sentence-final falling intonation
'	clause-final intonation ("more to come")
!	exclamatory intonation
?	final rise, as in a yes/no question
...	pause of 1/2 second or more
'	primary stress
CAPS	emphatic stress
[	overlapping speech.
]	no perceptible inter-turn pause
:	elongated vowel sound
-	glottal stop: sound abruptly cut off
" "	dialogue, quoted words
( )	"parenthetical" intonation: lower amplitude and pitch plus flattened intonation contour
hhh	laughter (h = one second)
=	at right of line indicates segment to be continued after another's turn; at left of line indicates continuation of prior segment after another's turn
/?/	inaudible utterance
{ }	transcriber comment on what is said

You can see many of these symbols in the excerpts of discourse throughout this chapter.

Spoken and written discourse: a first look

We create discourse by speaking or writing. These two processes rely upon language, of course, but they do so in strikingly different ways. And not surprisingly, their products achieve coherence through very different means. We can see this briefly by comparing the following excerpts from a story that Gina *tells* her friend Sue (in 2a) and *writes* (in 2b). In both excerpts, Gina introduces a story about how her love for magnolia blossoms got her into trouble when she tried to smell a blossom that then snapped off in her hand.

(2) a. Gina: Have you ever smelled a magnolia blossom?
         Sue: Mmhmm.
         Gina: Absolutely gorgeous.
         Sue: Yeah, they're great.

     b. On one particular morning this summer, there was a certain fragrance that
         I recognized to be a glorious magnolia.

In both versions, Gina describes the scent of a particular flower, a magnolia blossom. In the spoken version (2a), Gina involves Sue in her description; they both use short tone units to take short turns at talk. (Tone units are segments of speech production that are bounded by changes in timing, intonation, and pitch.) Gina first asks Sue if she has ever *smelled* such a blossom (a sensory experience referred to by a verb). After Sue acknowledges that she has (*Mmhmm*), Gina presents her own assessment of their scent (*Absolutely gorgeous*). Because Sue agrees (*Yeah*), and then adds her own description (*they're great*), both women have become jointly involved in the remembered pleasure of magnolia blossoms.

In Gina's written version (2b), the intensity of the magnolia scent is not unpacked, piece by piece, across turns and short units. Rather, the *fragrance* is integrated into a complex sentence in which a great deal of other information is packed. Gina introduces the flower by recalling the process through which she encountered it. The fragrance appears at a specific time (*On one particular morning this summer*). The existence (*there was*) of *a certain fragrance* (referred to as a static thing by a noun) allows Gina to recognize the presence of a *glorious magnolia*. Although some of the same basic material is presented in both segments, Gina phrases and organizes the information differently.

In the following sections, we will learn more about the properties of spoken and written discourse and how to analyze both of these ways of creating discourse. We compare two transcripts to describe several different aspects of spoken discourse and explain some basic concepts and tools of analysis. We then broaden our understanding of discourse processes and structures by briefly comparing spoken discourse with samples of written discourse.

Spoken discourse

In spoken discourse, different kinds of processes – and different configurations of language – work rapidly together to produce coherence. When we speak to each other, we try to achieve several goals, sometimes all at the same time. For example, we verbalize thoughts, introduce new information, repair errors in what we say, take turns at talk, think of others, and perform acts. We achieve these goals by using and connecting a range of different units – speech acts, idea units, turns at talk, as well as sentences. Speakers anticipate what their recipients need (e.g. how much information do they need?) and want (e.g. how polite do they expect me to be?). Speakers design what they say in relation to "educated" guesses about their hearers. These guesses are based on both past experience and the current interaction.

To exemplify these points we will discuss two segments of spoken discourse from the same speech situation – a sociolinguistic research interview – in which one speaker seeks information from another about a specific topic of interest. Together the two segments will illustrate a variety of processes and structures, including question/answer sequences, lengthy repairs of unclear meanings, exchanges of short turns at talk, and maintenance of a long turn at talk in which a story is told. Also illustrated is how people jointly ease new information into a discourse and collaboratively develop topics of talk.

We begin with an excerpt from an interview that took place while Anne (a linguistics student) was driving Ceil (a local resident of Philadelphia) around the city in order to learn more about its neighborhoods. The exchange begins as Ceil and Anne enter a part of Philadelphia with an Italian market. Both Ceil and Anne like shopping at the market and Ceil describes how she and her cousin used to use public transportation (*the trolley car*) to go to the market.

(3)   (a) Ceil: This is Washington Avenue.
        (b)   Now here's a great section.
        (c)   Over at Ninth Street.
        (d) Anne: Right.
        (e)   That's- that's the Ita[lian market, huh?
        (f) Ceil: [Yeh, Italian market.
        (g)   And I wish we had one up, where [we lived at.
        (h) Anne: [Yeh.
        (i)   Oh, I do, [too.
        (j) Ceil: [Oh:, I'd love to have one up there because-
        (k)   oh, I enjoy its-
        (l)   I love to come down there.
        (m) Anne: Yeh.
        (n)   It's fun. It's fun. No kidding.
        (o) Ceil: It really is.
        (p)   I mean, like uh-
        (q)   We used to come down on the trolley cars.=
        (r) Anne: Yeh.
        (s) Ceil: =And bring the-
        (t)   like we only had- like Ann and I, we- my cousin, Ann?=
        (u) Anne: Mmhmm.
        (v) Ceil: =We-like she had Jesse and I had my Kenny.=
        (w) Anne: Mmhmm

(x) Ceil: =And we used to bring them two down on the trolley car.
(y)   And bags of uh,   [groceries. Carry all the bags, right?
(z) Anne: Is that [so?
(aa) Anne: A lot of women from Port Richmond still um, go down that way.

Read the excerpt closely several times, not just to understand the content, but also to get a feeling for the rhythm of the interaction (e.g. who speaks when) and to "hear it" in your own head. You will then be more ready for the "guided readings" that a discourse analysis can provide.

Sequential and distributional analyses

Two kinds of "readings" typically are combined in discourse analyses. One "reading" focuses on the *sequence* of what happens: who says what and when? What is its significance at that particular point in the discourse; how is it related to what came before and what will come after? The other "reading" focuses on the *distribution* of specific features or qualities of language in the discourse; what forms, or ways of speaking, occur where? Do some features of language occur together more than others? If so, what could account for this co-occurrence?

Imagine that you're interested in learning about classroom discourse. You hear a student answer a teacher's question by prefacing it with *well* and you're curious about the use of *well* in the classroom. How do you start your analysis? A sequential analysis focuses on the details of the specific question/answer speech event – its setting, the participants, the informational content of the question and its answer, and so on. What you would learn about *well* would be its specific contribution to the meanings that are emerging at that moment in the classroom. A distributional analysis would start by finding all the uses of *well* in the classroom and then identifying their different contexts of use, including (but not limited to) question/answer speech events. What you would learn about *well* would be its relationship with other features of the discourse, e.g. its use with different participants, contents of questions and answers, and so on. The two analyses together enrich our understanding of individual moments in a particular interaction and of more general discourse features and processes.

Repair and recipient design

As we noted above, Anne and Ceil are driving around Philadelphia. In (a) to (c), Ceil identifies (and praises) the section of the city that they have just entered. Anne labels the section (e), Ceil agrees with the label (f) and assesses it again. As Anne is agreeing *Oh, I do, too* (i), Ceil begins to explain why she likes the market in *Oh:, I'd love to have one up there because-* (j). Ceil and Anne continue to praise the market (in (k) through (o)), and then, as indicated by the **discourse markers** *I mean* and *like*, Ceil begins to explain her fondness for the market through an example. (Discourse markers are small words and phrases that indicate how what someone is *about to say* (often at the beginning of a spoken utterance) fits into what *has already been said* and into what they are *about to say next*.)

BOX 5.3 **REPAIR SEQUENCES**

Repair sequences are routines in discourse which allow interlocutors to negotiate the face-threatening situation which arises when one speaker makes a mistake. Repair sequences have two components, initiation and repair, each of which can be handled by the speaker who made the mistake (self) or another participant (other). Initiation identifies the trouble source and repair fixes it. Each repair sequence communicates a different message. For example, the speaker who made the mistake can "self-initiate/self-repair," like Nan in the example below, sending the face-saving message "I know I made a mistake but I caught it and I can fix it."

Nan: She was givin me a:ll the people that were go:ne this yea:r I mean this quarter y'know
Jan: Yeah

If the speaker doesn't recognize the trouble source, the other can initiate a repair but allow the speaker to make the actual repair (and prove his competence):

Ken: Is Al here today?
Dan: Yeah. (2.0)
Roger: He IS? hh eh heh
Dan: Well he was.

Notice that Roger waits 2 seconds before initiating the repair and then points Dan toward the trouble source (*He IS?*).
     What is the message sent by Al's other-initiated other-repair (below)?

Ken: He likes that waitress over there.
Al: You mean waiter, don't you? That's a man.

(o) Ceil: It really is.
(p)   I mean, like uh-
(q)   We used to come down on the trolley cars.

Notice, however, what happens as Ceil begins to refer to those who used to accompany her to the market. Ceil self-initiates a repair by interrupting her own utterance in (s) *And bring the* – marking something about that utterance as a trouble source. The article *the* usually precedes a noun whose referent (the thing being spoken about) is definite (that is, relatively familiar or identifiable to the listener). Ceil is about to refer to some referent as if Anne knows who she's talking about, but apparently realizes that Anne won't know who she's talking about without more information. Her next several utterances provide the necessary information. In (t) Ceil begins to clarify who they used to bring (*like we only had-*) and then realizes that she must back up even further to explain who *we* refers to (*like Ann and I, we- my cousin, Ann?*). In (v), she begins to return to her story but detours again to further identify the initial referents: *We- like she had Jesse and I had my Kenny*. In (x), when Ceil completes her self-repair (and the utterance started in (q)) – *and we used to bring them two down on the trolley car* – the repetition of *the trolley cars* (q) and *bring* (s) from the repair self-initiation helps us (and Anne) infer that *them two* (x) – which refers to Jesse and Kenny in the previous sentence – also supplies the missing referent in the interrupted noun phrase *the-* in (q).

Both the wealth of detail provided in the repair, and the cohesive ties between its self-initiation and self-completion, show **recipient design** – the process whereby a speaker takes the listener into account when presenting information. The information that Ceil added about Ann (*my cousin, Ann?*), for example, showed that she had gauged Anne's lack of familiarity with members of her extended family. Likewise, Ceil's repetition of *trolley car* from the repair self-initiation to its self-completion attended to Anne's need to place the referent back into the description that had been interrupted.

What else can we notice about spoken discourse from the transcript in (3)? What about the ways in which each person contributes to the discourse? If we look at the sheer amount of talk from each person, it looks like Ceil was the main speaker. And although Ceil and Anne both took **turns at talk**, what they said in those turns was quite different. Anne asked Ceil a question (*That's- that's the Italian market, huh?* (e)) that drew upon Ceil's knowledge of the city. Anne also agreed with points that Ceil had made: *Yeh* (h) and *Oh, I do, too* (i). And while Ceil was adding information to help Anne recognize the referent, Anne used **back channels** to signal Ceil that it is okay for her to continue talking. (Back channels are brief utterances like *mmhmm* that speakers use to signal they are paying attention, but don't want to talk just yet.)

Comparing transcripts

Although close analysis of a single transcript can help us learn about discourse, gathering together different transcripts and comparing them is also essential. The tools that people use when they are talking to one another are often the same at some level (e.g. turn-taking recurs in almost all discourse) but different at other levels (e.g. the ways that turns are exchanged may differ). Capturing what is the same, and identifying what is different, is an important part of discourse analysis. We all engage in many different kinds of discourse throughout our daily lives and don't improvise or construct new rules each and every time we speak. Rather, much of our communicative competence consists of general principles about how to speak and ways of modifying those principles to specific circumstances. If we want to build up generalizations about discourse, then, a good way to do it is to gather together examples of discourse that are the same in some ways (e.g. all from sociolinguistic interviews) but different in other ways (e.g. from different people). Likewise, it is useful to compare the discourse of different kinds of speech situations and speech events in order to see how the social features of those situations and events are related to the way we use language.

The transcript in (4) below is also from a sociolinguistic interview, but the speech events and speech acts that occur are quite different. In (4), Jack, his wife Freda, and their nephew Rob have been talking with me about different facets of life in Philadelphia, the city whose speech I have been studying. Jack has been boasting about his childhood friendship with Joey Gottlieb, who became a well-known comedian known as Joey Bishop. The section below begins when Freda mentions that Jack and Joey shared their Bar Mitzvah (a rite of passage for Jewish boys when they turn thirteen).

(4)   (a) Freda: They were Bar Mitzvahed together. Him and uh.. Joey.

(b) Debby:]Really?

(c) Jack: We went to school together.

(d)   We were in the same hh room together.

(e)   We used to hooky together!

(f)   He played the piano, I played the violin in the assembly.

(g)   hhhwe used to jazz it up.

(h) Debby: Did you go to Southern?

(i) Jack: Southern High. Yeh.

(j) Debby: Southern High, yeh.

(k) Jack: Y' know that teacher that came over to me, over at uh . . .

(l)   She used to be- take care of all the entertaining, =

(m) Freda: Yes I do.

(n) Rob: Lamberton?

(o) Jack: =]and musical things, y' know.

(p)   She used to raise holy hell with both of [us!

(q) Freda: [Oh I bet she's had a lot of kids at-

(r)   that passed through her, [that. . . became-. . . became all =

(s) Jack: [Oh::! But she remembered me! =

(t) Freda: = all kinds of things! hhhh[hhhhhhhhhhhhhhhhhI guess your mother knew of:=

(u) Jack: =[She used to say to me, to Joey Bishop=

(v) Freda: =]all these. . ...

(w) Jack: = ["Don't you play the piano, when he plays elegies!"=

(x) Freda: dif[ferent- that became. . .   ]different things!=

(y) Jack: =One day-   [He and I:

(z) Freda: =]Different things like [jail: birds, and eh comedians! And. . .

(aa) Jack:]One day he and I were [supposed to play elegies,

(bb) Freda: [How m- long has your mother been teaching?

(cc) Debby: Well she hasn't been teaching that long.=

(dd) Freda: Oh. [Cause:-   [That's very h- very=

(ee) Debby: = [But she keeps in touch with some of [them.

(ff) Freda: = interesting to look back!

(gg) Jack: Y'know one day, she- we- I was supposed to play elegy on the violin.

(hh)   D' you remember then?

(ii) Freda:]Oh, yes!   [Oh, that's the=

(jj) Jack:]All kids would [play that.=

(kk) Freda: = first! [My! My!

(ll) Jack: [So he was supposed to accompany me.

(mm)		On the piano.
(nn)		So she had to teach him the chords.
(oo)		He only hit certain chords while I'm playin' elegy.
(pp)		So, everything is set fine,
(qq)		I get up,
(rr)		and I start to play elegy,
(ss)		and he's givin' me the chords.
(tt)		And in a chord, he goes DAA da da da daa, da DAAA!
(uu)		Well the whole: audience broke up!
(vv)		Because they don't wanna hear that elegy y' know!
(ww)		And we:...=
(xx)	Freda:	]That-hhhhhhhhhh
(yy)	Jack:	= y' know then I knew, he had the-
(zz)		I realized he did have dry wit. =
(aaa)		He knew how to get the- he knew the whole audience'd laugh
(bbb)		so he must've had something to him
(ccc)		Even this teacher, this one that- she laughed.
(ddd)	Freda:	Even the teachers, huh?
(eee)	Jack:	She couldn't help it!

The interchange among Jack, Freda, Rob, and me (Debby) changes shape during the course of talk. From lines (a) to (ll), for example, several people are active speakers, sometimes speaking at the same time. Jack and Freda overlap, for example, in lines (p) to (s) after Jack has mentioned his high school teacher, in (k) and (l). Then two different conversations develop: Freda asks me about my mother (who used to be a teacher) while Jack continues to talk about his own high school teacher (in lines (t) to (aa)). Jack eventually dominates the floor when he tells a story in lines (gg) to (eee).

Adjacency pairs

The conversations in (4) and (3) are both initiated by interviewers' questions. Semantically, questions are incomplete propositions; they are missing the "who," "what," when," "where," "why," or "how" of a proposition, or their polarity (positive or negative) is unknown (did something happen or not? is a description accurate?). The propositional incompleteness of questions is part of their discourse function. They perform speech acts (requests for information or action) that have interactional consequences; questions open up a "slot" in which whatever is heard next will be assessed as an answer ("completing" the question). This kind of relationship between two utterances in discourse is called an **adjacency pair** – a two-part sequence in which the first part sets up a strong expectation that a particular second part will be provided. This expectation is so strong that the first part constrains the interpretation of the second part. For example, even a silence after a question will be interpreted as a kind of answer – if only a reluctance or inability to provide an answer.

The two parts of an adjacency pair help people organize their conversations because they set up expectations for what will happen next. These expectations help both speakers and hearers. If I thank you for doing me a favor, for example, that gives you clues about what I'm thinking and what you should do next, making it easier for you to know what to say. I also simplify my own job since I know what to listen for. Indeed, a missing "second part" of an adjacency pair can be disconcerting; we typically listen for closure of the adjacency pair (e.g. why didn't he say *You're welcome?*), even those that come much later than the first part.

Participation frameworks

We saw in example (3) how Ceil made a lengthy self-repair so that Anne would know who she was talking about. Jack also introduces a new referent into his discourse, but he uses a question to do so, in (k):

(k) Jack: Y' know that teacher that came over to me, over at uh . . .
(l)   She used to be- take care of all the entertaining, =
(m) Freda: Yes I do.
(n) Rob: Lamberton?
(o) Jack: =]and musical things, y' know.

The information that Jack provides about the teacher is enough for Freda to recognize the "teacher" referent (*Yes I do* (m)). Because Jack's description does not include the teacher's name, Rob interprets it as a self-initiation of a repair sequence and offers an **other-repair** – a repair of a problematic item in another speaker's utterance. Rob provides the name of Jack's referent (*Lamberton?* (n)). Rob and Freda speak at the same time and overlap with Jack's continuing description of the teacher (l-o). Jack's description of the teacher in (l) could have ended where Freda and Rob started talking, and they anticipated this **turn-transition place** – a place often marked by syntactic closure, intonational boundary, and/or propositional completion where another may begin a turn at talk.

Rob and Freda's differing responses in (m) and (n) show that listeners may react to different aspects of what another person has said. The ways that people interacting with one another take responsibility for speaking, listening, and acting are part of the participation framework. Sometimes participation frameworks change when people adopt different roles and/or split off into separate interactions, perhaps to pursue divergent topics or establish a different relationship. For example, when Freda brings up my mother (who had been a teacher) in (t), (v), and (x), and then asks *How m- long has your mother been teaching?* (bb), she invites me to take a different, more active role in the conversation.

Freda's attempt to create a new participation framework overlaps with Jack's continuing talk about his music teacher, in (u) and (w). Jack opens a new participant framework when he tells a story (from lines (aa) to (ccc)) in which he holds the floor pretty much on his own. But he had to signal the shift to this turn-taking and storytelling status in (y), (aa), and (gg) with the repetition of the phrase *one day*.

Once Jack gains the floor in (gg), he tells a narrative, a recounting of an experience in which past events are told in the order in which they occurred. Jack's narrative is about a recital in which he and Joey were supposed to play an elegy, a formal (often mournful) musical composition. Joey, however, jazzes it up by playing a cartoon jingle ("Shave and a haircut, two bits!") instead of the expected chords.

Narratives

Narratives contrast with other genres and speech events in a number of ways. Narratives organize information differently than other genres, such as descriptions, explanations, and lists. For example, narratives present events in temporal order of occurrence, but lists need not, as we can see in Jack's list of habitual activities with Joey ((c) through (g)). Narratives have a different participation framework; storytellers tend to hold the floor alone. And finally, the content of a fully formed oral narrative of personal experience (in American English) has a relatively fixed structure, consisting of the following parts (usually in this order):

- **Abstract:** a summary of the experience or its point
- **Orientation:** background description (who, where, when, why, how)
- **Complicating action:** "what happened," a series of temporally ordered events (often called "narrative" clauses) that have beginning and end points
- **Evaluation:** syntactic, prosodic, textual alterations of the narrative norm that highlight important parts of the story and/or help convey why the story is being told (i.e. the point of the story)
- **Coda**: closure that brings the "past" of the narrative to the "present" of the interaction in which it was told

Whereas it is relatively easy to identify the abstract, complicating action, and coda in Jack's narrative, it may be more difficult to identify the orientation and evaluation. Many orientations describe the background scene – who is present, where, and when. Jack had already introduced his friend Joey and the teacher prior to the narrative, but Jack does spend a fair amount of time, in lines (ll) to (oo), familiarizing his listeners with what typically happens in a recital. This is crucial for the point of the story; if the audience doesn't have a **schema** (a set of structured expectations of what is supposed to happen), then they can't recognize a deviation from expectation. Yet the break in expectation is what underlies the humor in Jack's story and is crucial for its point.

But what actually is the point of the story? Here we need to turn to the evaluation. One way in which people telling stories often indicate evaluation is by using the historical present tense – the use of the present tense to convey past events. The historical present is buried within the language of the narrative clauses, as in *So, everything is set fine* (pp) through *and in a chord, he goes DAA da da da da, da DAAA!* (tt). Also highlighting the humor of the story is Jack's singing of the tune; breaking into melody is clearly noticeable through its contrast with the rest of the story. And clearly the humor of Joey's musical prank works; the audience laughs (*Well the whole: audience broke up!* (uu)), as does the teacher in *Even this teacher, this one that-she laughed* (ccc).

Summary: spoken discourse

In this section, we have illustrated how different configurations of language work together to produce coherence in spoken discourse. We have highlighted some of the ways that speakers try to achieve several goals, sometimes simultaneously.

- introducing new information in relation to the anticipated needs of their hearers
- linking information through cohesive ties
- repairing errors
- initiating adjacency pairs with actions that have sequential consequences for listeners' next actions

Together, interlocutors distribute turns at talk and develop different frameworks in which to interact. Discourse consists of a variety of different units (for example, clauses, sentences, turns, and speech acts) that tie together different strands of talk. As we will see in the next section, not all of these processes appear in written discourse. Those that do, work somewhat differently because of the complex differences between spoken and written discourse.

BOX 5.4 **REGISTERS**

Language variation according to the situation in which it is used is called register variation, and varieties of a language that are typical of a particular situation of use are called **registers**. Each situation makes its own communicative demands – informational, social, referential, expressive – and people use the features of their language which meet the communicative demands of the situation. The set of language features – phonological, lexical, syntactic, and pragmatic – which is normally used to meet the demands of a particular communicative situation is the register of that situation.

Sociolinguist Dell Hymes proposed the acronym SPEAKING as a mnemonic (or memory aid) for remembering the components of most speech situations. Think of the SPEAKING mnemonic as a grid; each element is a variable, a range of possible values which may describe the situation. Filling in the value of each variable in the SPEAKING grid goes a long way toward describing a given communicative situation.

Setting	Physical location and social significance
Participants	Respective social status, local roles in interaction
Ends	Purpose of the event, respective goals of the participants
Act sequences	Speech acts that are functionally or conventionally appropriate to the situation
Key	Tone or mood (e.g. serious, ironic)
Instrumentalities	Mode of communication (e.g. spoken, written, via telephone)
Norms	Expectations of behavior and their interpretation
Genres	Type of event (e.g. conversation, lecture, sermon)

To show how the SPEAKING grid helps describe a speech situation – and how the situation demands particular uses of language – imagine a cooking class:

- The *setting* is a kitchen being used as a classroom, so tables have been arranged to allow students to see and practice the techniques the teacher is demonstrating. The shared physical setting allows use

BOX 5.4 *(cont.)*

of definite articles ("Put *the* butter in *the* saucepan") and deictic pronouns ("Now add *this* to *that*"), as well as first- and second-person pronouns and temporal references ("Now *I* want *you* to stir briskly *for two minutes*"). Food and cooking vocabulary are also frequent.

- The *participants* are the chef/teacher and the students/clients. Their physical placement in the kitchen reflects their respective roles, as does their use of language. For example, many of the teacher's verbs are imperatives, while the students use the auxiliary *do* frequently to ask questions (e.g. "How *do* I...?" and "*Does* this look right?").
- The *ends* of the speech event are several. Teacher and students have a shared goal of transferring knowledge about cooking, but have different relations to that goal. The students' goal is to learn new cooking techniques and recipes – and probably to enjoy the process, as well. The teacher shares these goals but mainly as a means toward the broader goal of keeping clients satisfied and generating new business.
- The cooking class includes a number of routinized *act sequences*. At the beginning of the class, the teacher greets the students, then introduces the topic of that day's class. The teacher then demonstrates and explains cooking techniques, offering definitions of technical terms and verbal explanations of physical actions (like chopping, slicing, etc.). The students attempt to imitate the teacher's actions, ask questions, seek clarification, and request confirmation that they are performing the actions correctly. These acts are sequenced in conventionalized routines; for example, the teacher gives a directive ("Stir briskly for two minutes"), a student asks for clarification ("Like this?"), and the teacher offers confirmation ("Yes, good") or further instruction ("A little slower").
- The *key* of the class varies, from serious (instructions and warnings) to entertaining (anecdotes about fallen soufflés and burned sauces). Instructions are characterized by (present-tense) imperative verbs and reference to objects in the classroom ("Take the pan of onions off the flame"), while anecdotes are characterized by past-tense verbs and third-person reference to nonpresent people and objects ("The customer began fanning his mouth and drank three glasses of water").
- The main *instrumentality* of the class is spoken discourse, but students may refer to written recipes or take notes. Recipes share some of the features of the teacher's instructions (directive verbs, definite articles) but do not include the teacher's definitions and explanations. Students use abbreviations and delete articles to save time and space in their notes ("Add 1 Tsp sug to sauce").
- The *norms* of interaction include, for example, recognition that suggestions from the teacher ("You might want to turn down the flame") are usually directives, and that requests by students for clarification ("Am I doing this right?") are often requests for the teacher's approval ("Yes, good job").
- The *genre* of the event is "class." This helps teacher and students to recognize the range of language use that is conventionally appropriate to the situation.

All of the linguistic and discourse features mentioned above co-occur frequently in cooking classes and therefore are part of the register of a cooking class.

Following the work of Douglas Biber, linguists have identified the sets of linguistic features that tend to co-occur across many speech (and writing) situations. The main communicative functions that those sets of features serve include interpersonal involvement, presentation of information, narration, description, and persuasion. With our varying emphases on these basic communicative tools, we mark and construct each speech situation.

Written discourse

Learning to speak seems to occur without much effort; it is woven seamlessly into our early childhood socialization. But learning to write is often a formal and explicit process that includes instruction in graphic conventions (printing letters as well as connecting them together in **script**), technology (how to use a keyboard and manage computer files), punctuation (e.g. when to use commas, semi-colons, and colons) and rules of "correct" grammar (e.g. "No prepositions at the ends of sentences"). Why can't we just write the way we speak? One reason is that written texts have longevity, a "shelf life"; they can be read and reread and examined more closely than transitory speech. Sometimes written texts also become part of a cultural canon; they serve as official bearers of wisdom, insight, and institutional knowledge that can be passed down over time and generation. And this means that ideologies about what language *should* be – the standard variety with the power of social institutions behind it (see Chapter 11) – often have a strong impact on the way we write.

Of course, not all written discourse is held up to such high standards. In addition to literature, chapters in academic textbooks, legal briefs, and minutes of corporate meetings, we find comic books, self-help manuals, grocery lists, and diaries. Clearly, the latter genres of written discourse are not subject to the same standards of correctness as the former. Yet, despite the wide-ranging differences among written genres, they all differ from spoken discourse in several crucial ways.

Fragmentation and integration

One major difference is that speaking is faster than writing. This difference has an impact on the final product. When speaking, we can move more rapidly from one idea or thought to another, resulting in what Chafe (1982) calls **fragmentation**, the segmentation of information into small, syntactically simple chunks of language that present roughly one idea at a time. When writing, we have time to mold a group of ideas into a complex whole in which various types and levels of information are integrated into sentences. **Integration** is thus the arrangement of information into long, syntactically complex chunks of language that present more than one idea at a time.

We can see the difference between fragmentation and integration by looking at the introduction of new referents into discourse – people, places, or things that have not yet been mentioned. Recall, for example, Ceil's introduction of the boys accompanying her and Ann on the trolley car in (3): *like we only had- like Ann and I, we-my cousin, Ann? We- like she had Jesse and I had my Kenny*; and *we used to bring them two down on the trolley car*. However, if Ceil were writing a memory book about the Italian market, she might use a complex sentence such as the following: *Before our other children were born, my cousin Ann and I used to take our two boys, Jesse and Kenny, on the trolley car to the Italian market*. Notice that the referring expression itself (*our two boys, Jesse and Kenny*) would be buried within a complex of other information about time, activity, and other referents, and followed by a description of where they were going and how they got there – all in one sentence! The crucial information about the referent, then, would be integrated with other information in one complex syntactic unit, rather than fragmented into different tone units (segments of speech production that are bounded by changes in timing, intonation, and pitch) and turns at talk.

Writing to be read

Another crucial difference between spoken and written discourse is the role of the recipient. In spoken genres, the recipient is a co-participant in the evolving discourse in two ways: (a) the recipient provides feedback through back channels or by asking for clarification; (b) the recipient gets a chance to become a speaker. These differences boil down to differences in participation framework. In spoken discourse, participants are more likely to face similar opportunities (and challenges) as they alternate between the roles of "speaker" and "listener." How participants manage these shifts can have profound impacts on the overall flow of discourse. Recall, for example, how Jack had to maneuver around the alternate conversations that developed between Freda and Debby before he could begin his story. Even then, he could pursue his story only after he had secured Freda's attention by bringing up a recently shared experience.

Producers and recipients of written discourse interact in very different participation frameworks than those engaged in spoken discourse. Writers have to anticipate the informational needs of their intended recipients, as well as what will maintain readers' interest, without the benefit of immediate feedback. Writers try to be clear and to create involvement with their material and with their intended readers. Here they can draw upon structures that are easy for readers to process (like short and simple sentences), as well as dramatic devices (like metaphor and visual imagery) to make it exciting and engrossing. And just as speakers orient what they say to their listeners' needs and interests, so too writers try to anticipate a particular type of reader.

Depending on how writers construct their "ideal" readers, they use different aspects of language to maintain readers' interest and to make the text relevant to their readers' needs and goals. This means that writers – like speakers – also design their discourse for their projected recipients. A good way to see this is to compare different written genres with one another. Like the comparison of spoken genres that occur during different speech events and speech situations, scholars sometimes call this a comparison between registers, ways of using language that reflect different facets of its context (e.g. participants, goals, and setting).

The written texts in (5a) and (5b) share some general register features, but they also differ in various ways. (5a) is from a newspaper column in which young adults seek advice about their personal relationships. (5b) is from the back of a bottle of hair conditioner.

(5)   a. Tell Me About It ® By Carolyn Hax

Washington Post, Sunday, January 2, 2005; page M01

Dear Carolyn: I have finally met a guy I really like. We have been seeing each other on and off for a couple of months. Should I ask where this relationship is going or just see where it takes us? I have been raised to believe the guy should bring up stuff like that. I'm worried that if I say I would like to be exclusive I might scare him off.

C: I was raised that way, too, but then reconditioned to believe that if honesty kills your relationship, then it was already dying of natural causes. "Where is this going?" still lays it on him. Asking to be exclusive is honest, and also such a compliment that it would be a shame to withhold it out of fear that he might not agree.

b. HEADRESS VOLUMIZING LEAVE-IN CONDITIONER is blended with Panthenol, Vegetable Ceramides and Kerotin Amino Acids to add incredible body and lustre to any hair type. As hairdressing, the concentrated formula instantly releases tangles and increases combability to control styles. When used as a styling tool with thermal appliances, HEADRESS protects hair from heat and dryness while adding fullness and shine. Time released Antioxidants, UVA and UVB Protectors guard against harsh environmental elements so hair continuously shines with radiant health.

[A section explaining the technology of Headress has been left out]

DIRECTIONS: Apply a small amount to palm of hand. Rub hands together and distribute evenly through hair. Comb through and blow dry, or dry naturally. Style as desired.

[Three sections left out: guarantee, contact information, list of 34 ingredients, information about manufacturer]

Let's look first at the content of these texts and how they are constructed: what is being conveyed and how? Both texts are about a problem and a solution. The problem in each is how to manage something – commitment in a relationship, unruly hair – whose solution may require the reader to be assertive, either verbally (*Should I ask ...*) or physically (*to control styles*). Each solution requires a transformation of some sort from an initial state. Asking about commitment requires being *reconditioned* from the way *one was raised*. So too, *gaining body and lustre* in one's hair is the result of a *conditioner*.

Both texts rely upon the integration of more than one idea in each sentence to present their respective problems and solutions. For example, the last sentence of C's advice (5a) integrates two pieces of information about *asking to be exclusive*: it is honest; it is a compliment. The last sentence in the *HEADRESS* description (5b) also integrates two solutions – *time released Antioxidants* and *UVA and UVB Protectors* – to *guard against* the problem of *harsh environmental elements*.

These sentences don't just present solutions to problems; they also positively evaluate those solutions. The *Dear Carolyn* text calls the solution (*asking to be exclusive*) *such a compliment that it would be a shame to withhold it*; the alternative (not asking to be exclusive) is negatively evaluated (*a shame*). In the *HEADRESS* text, the product's ingredients provide protection *so hair continuously shines with radiant health*, evoking glowing, positive images, reminiscent of the sun. So although neither text comes right out and says "this is the right solution for you!," this message is clearly implied through the texts.

These problem/solution texts also construct and reflect their participation frameworks – the roles and identities of the writer and the reader. The topic of each text is likely to be relevant to a limited set of readers – young women – simply because the problems concern a boyfriend (5a) and hair (5b). Despite this broad similarity, the two texts set up different relationships and identities. Although we don't know anything about the identity of the person asking for advice in (5a), the identity of the person *giving* advice appears several times, encouraging reader involvement with the writer as a real person. In contrast, in the *HEADRESS* text the only information about the source of the text is the name of a company and how to contact it.

The language of the two texts also creates different types of involvement between writer and reader, which in turn help to construct their respective social identities. *Dear Carolyn* uses casual terms like *a guy* and *stuff like that*, typical of a young adult chatting with a friend on the phone. The *HEADRESS* description is filled with referring expressions that are not part of our everyday vocabulary – e.g. *thermal appliance* instead of 'hairdryer' – or that we may not even know (*Panthenol? Vegetable Ceramides?*). This unfamiliarity lends the text an air of scientific legitimacy. Whereas the advice column resembles a chat between friends, the *HEADRESS* text mimics a consultation with an expert professional.

Differences in what is being conveyed (and how), and identities (and relationship) of writer and reader, come together in the way each text proposes a solution to the problem. In the advice column, C's response establishes camaraderie (*I was raised that way, too*). In *HEADRESS*, on the other hand, the *DIRECTIONS* are a list of imperative sentences: there are no subject pronouns, just verbs (*apply, rub, distribute, comb*) that instruct and command, conveying a sense of routine procedure, not personal concern.

Dividing discourse by how it is created – by writing or speaking – overlooks the many different genres and registers within each type. But there are still some overall differences. Spoken discourse is more fragmented and written discourse is more integrated. Although people are certainly judged by the way they speak, the longevity of many written texts subjects them to further and more intense scrutiny and to higher standards. All language users, however, orient their discourse to whoever will hear (or read) what they say (or write). Whereas speakers have the chance to continuously adjust what they say – sometimes with the help of their listeners – writers have the luxury of more time. Yet both end up honing their messages, shaping and reshaping them to structure information in ways that set up nuanced and complex relationships with their recipients.

Language functions

All approaches to discourse analysis address the functions of language, the structures of texts, and the relationship between text and context. A main function of language is *referential*: we use language to convey information about entities (e.g. people, objects), as well as their attributes, actions, and relationships. But language also has *social* and *expressive* functions that allow us to do things – like thanking, boasting, insulting, and apologizing – that convey to others how we feel about them and other things. We also use language to persuade others of our convictions and urge them toward action by crafting texts that demonstrate the logic and appeal of those convictions.

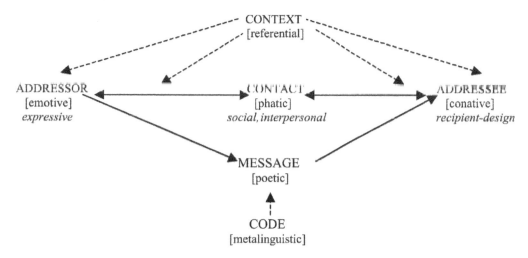

Figure 5.1 Speech situation and functions. Each facet of the situation is in upper case; the language function is in brackets. Terms that have been used interchangeably with Jakobson's terms are in italics.

Figure 5.1 (adapted and modified from Jakobson 1960) presents six functions of language – six jobs that people accomplish by using language. Jakobson's model of language functions represents the speech situation as a multidimensional set of relationships, a bit like a multifaceted diamond.

When we view the speech situation from different angles, we see different facets, different connections between the components of the speech situation, the features of language used, and the communicative function performed by that language. Each language function is related to a different facet of the speech situation. The arrows in Figure 5.1 indicate the relationship between speech situation and function, and suggest how different aspects of the speech situation – and different functions – are related to one another. The unbroken arrows indicate paths by which ADDRESSOR and ADDRESSEE are connected – back and forth through CONTACT or unidirectionally through a MESSAGE. The arrows in dashes indicate that CONTEXT pervades the way ADDRESSOR and ADDRESSEE speak, as well as the circumstances of their CONTACT. The dotted arrow from CODE to MESSAGE highlights the contribution of language to the MESSAGE.

- Referential function: sentences focusing on aspects of the speech situation mainly serve a referential function. For example, a sentence like *The coffee is hot* relates a proposition about some aspect of the participants' shared context to their respective roles in the interaction and the circumstances of their contact (some reason for remarking on the temperature of the coffee). However, CONTEXT influences the ADDRESSOR'S and ADDRESSEE'S identities and the kind of CONTACT between them. For example, if your close friend works part time in a coffee shop, when you go in to buy coffee, the context of your contact will (at least partially) include a waiter/customer relationship.
- Phatic function: sentences focusing on the relationship (CONTACT) between participants mainly serve a phatic function. For example, *Hi! Good to see you!* provides little information

about the surrounding context, but as a first part of a greeting sequence, it initiates an interaction and a renegotiation of the status of the participants' relationship.

- Poetic function: sentences that focus on the MESSAGE itself serve mainly a poetic function. For example, Carl Sandburg's line, *The fog comes in on little cat feet*, manipulates the CODE to convey the silent approach of the fog through metaphor.
- Emotive function: sentences that express the impact of some facet of the external world (context) or internal world (feelings, sensations) on the ADDRESSOR mainly serve the emotive function. For example, *I am hungry* states an internal condition of the ADDRESSOR. But because it may be interpreted as a request that the ADDRESSEE make dinner it may also have a conative function.
- Conative function: sentences that focus on the relation of the ADDRESSEE to the context or the interaction mainly serve the conative function. For example, *Are you hungry?* can be interpreted as either a request for information from the addressee or as an invitation to join the addressor for dinner.
- Metalinguistic function: sentences focusing on the relation between code and situation serve mainly a metalinguistic function. For example, asking *Did you just say "Don" or "Dawn" was coming?* focuses on the pronunciation and reference of some prior word.

Sentences typically serve more than one function at a time. Although a sentence may have a *primary* function, it is likely to be *multifunctional*. Suppose, for example, someone says *What time is it?* The sentence's primary function is conative: it is a question that requests something of the addressee. But it may also have a phatic function if it opens contact. And it certainly has an emotive function (it conveys a need of the addressor) and a referential function (it makes reference to the world outside language).

Planes of discourse

Jakobson's model of language functions stresses the context "beyond the sentence," but it ignores the *text* – the unit of language "above the sentence." What we say or write never occurs in a vacuum: it is always surrounded by other information in other utterances. The accumulation of information through successive chunks of language complicates the view of multifunctionality presented in Jakobson's model. Since functions pile up with each successive sentence, how do we manage to sort out which functions we should pay attention to and which we may safely ignore? How are sentences with multiple functions strung together to create coherent texts?

To answer this question, we must shift our attention from the "sentence" to the **utterance**, a contextualized sentence. Whereas a sentence is a string of words put together by the grammatical rules of a language, an utterance is the realization of a sentence in a textual and social context – including both the utterances which surround it and the situation in which it is uttered. An utterance is the intersection of many planes of context, and as we speak and listen, we rely on these intersecting planes of context to convey and interpret the meaning of each utterance. An utterance thus expresses far more meaning than the sentence it contains.

The examples in (6) can help disentangle the difference between sentence and utterance.

(6) a.   Discourse analysis is fun.
     b.   Discourse analysis is fun.

     c. Bob: I really like my linguistics courses.
         Sue: Oh I do too! Discourse analysis is fun.

Although the sentences are the same, the three occurrences of *Discourse analysis is fun* in (6) are three different utterances, because they are produced in different contexts. Although (6a) and (6b) appear in the same *social* context (as examples presented in a textbook), there is a difference in their *textual* contexts: (6a) is the first appearance of the sentence, and (6b) is the second appearance (a repetition) of the sentence. (6a) and (6b) both differ from (6c), as well. Although (6c) is an illustration in a textbook, it is also part of an interaction between two interlocutors, so it has a different social context than (6a) and (6b).

Focusing on utterances allows us to see how several planes of context are related to, and expressed through, the language used in an utterance. Like the facets of a diamond, an utterance simultaneously has meaning as:

- a reflection of a social relationship (who are you? who am I?)
- part of a social exchange (who will talk now?)
- a speech act (what are you *doing* through your words?)
- shared knowledge (what can I assume you already know?)
- a proposition (what are you saying about the world?)

Each utterance is simultaneously part of – and has meaning in – a **participation framework**, an **exchange structure**, an **act structure**, an **information state**, and an **idea structure**. Each utterance is connected to other utterances and to the context on each of these planes of discourse; part of each utterance's meaning *is* these connections. Speakers indicate which aspects of meaning of a prior utterance they are emphasizing by the construction and focus of their own "next" utterances in a discourse.

Participation framework

The **participation framework** is the way that people organize and maintain an interaction by adopting and adapting roles, identities, and ways of acting and interacting. Included are all aspects of the relationship between a speaker and hearer that become relevant whenever they are interacting with one another, either in the "real time" of spoken discourse or the "displaced time" of written texts. We continuously align with others through what we say. For example, we frequently depend upon what is being said (and how it is being said) to assess the status of our relationship with another speaker: is he trying to convince me to take his point of view? Does she seem distant? Have I hurt her feelings? Why does he now seem skeptical about our plan to go out tonight? What we say and how we say it are thus critical to the formation, management, and negotiation of our interpersonal relationships.

Exchange structure

The **exchange structure** concerns the way people take turns in talk: how do we know when to start talking? Do we ever overlap, and if so, where, when, how and why? What does such overlap mean to the person already talking? How is exchange in multiparty talk managed? Because participation in spoken discourse typically requires alternating between the roles of speaker and hearer, the exchange structure is connected to the participation framework. Thus we might find that turn-taking would differ along with participation framework. During a job interview, for example, we might wait for a potential employer to finish his/her question before we start the answer. When gossiping or joking around with an old friend, however, we might end up talking at the same time, viewing our overlapping turns as welcome signs of enthusiasm and solidarity.

Act structures

Act structures are ordered sequences of actions performed through speech. For example, the first parts of adjacency pairs like questions, greetings, and compliments constrain the interpretation of the following utterance (and the role of its speaker). An accusation presents the accused with the act choices of confession, denial, or counter-accusation. An accepted bet will eventually recast one participant as the winner and the other as the loser (and maybe debtor). Speech acts have still other consequences for participants and their relationship. Almost all speech acts – commands, questions, requests, hints, compliments, warnings, promises, denials – allow people to exert different degrees of responsibility and control that create feelings of distance or solidarity, power or equality between speaker and hearer.

Information state

The **information state** is the distribution of knowledge among people interacting with one another. Speakers take into account their listeners' informational needs as they construct their utterances: what common knowledge can the speaker assume? How does he/she present brand new information?

Often we can see changes in the information state by looking at the nuts and bolts of repairs, like Ceil's repairs in example (3) that filled in information that Anne didn't have. But we can also find speakers accommodating to their hearers' knowledge by looking at the choice of words, and their arrangement, in sentences that don't undergo repair. For example, speakers in conversation mix together old information (which they believe their addressees know or can figure out) with new information (which they believe their addressees don't know and can't figure out). The utterances in (7a–c) all introduce new referents into a conversation:

(7) a. *there*'s a school in my mother's neighborhood like that
     b. *they* have those big three-story houses on Chestnut Street
     c. *y*'know that guy down the street? who's remodeling his house?

Syntactic subjects – the italicized forms at the beginning of the sentences in (7) – rarely introduce new referents to a conversation. The minimal information conveyed by simple and uninformative initial clauses (like *there is*, *they have*, and *y'know*) puts the focus on the new information at the end of the sentence.

Idea structure

Idea structure concerns the organization of information within a sentence and the organization of propositions in a text: how bits of information are linked together within, and across, sentences. Different genres typically have different idea structures. Recall the problem-solution organization of the advice column and hair conditioner label. Recall also Jack's narrative in example (4). Once Jack got started on his story, each clause presented an event in the order in which it was presumed to have occurred. A narrative has an idea structure with a linear organization based on temporal progression. The email entries below show two other genres – a list (8) and an explanation (9).

BOX 5.5 **COHESION AND COHESIVE TIES**

Repetition is one of six language devices that help to join information together as a text by providing cohesive ties (Halliday and Hasan 1976) among different sentences. Other cohesive devices are reference (e.g. through pronouns), substitution (using paraphrases), ellipsis (deleting material that is easily recoverable from the sentence or text), conjunction (words like *and* or *but* that connect sentences), and lexical relations (e.g. words whose meanings are semantically related, e.g. *fruit* and *pear*). The following short excerpt from a recipe illustrates the different kinds of cohesive ties.

Apple₁ pudding₅.

First₂ you₃ peel and chop *the fruit₁*   *Then₂*   ₃ {sprinkle *it₁*   with sugar and₃ toss with the raisins}₄.
                lexical relation   conjunction ellipsis   reference   ellipsis

[text left out] Bake *the mixture₄* for one hour. *You₃* may serve *the pudding₅* with vanilla ice cream.
               substitution   repetition   repetition

Italicized words and phrases sharing the same subscript number are connected by a cohesive tie (labeled underneath each tie). So, for example, *Apple* is tied to *the fruit* by the cohesive device of lexical relation, and *First* and *Then* are tied by conjunction. The first reference to the reader (*you*) is tied to the elided subject pronouns of the following verb phrases and repeated *you* in the last sentence, and *the mixture* is a substitution for the product of those two verb phrases, indicated by curly brackets { }. Finally, the repetition of *pudding*, in the title and the last sentence, bookends the whole text.

Out of 36 words in the excerpt (counting the elided subject pronouns), more than half are linked in cohesive ties which help the reader understand the meaning of not just each sentence, but the entire text.

(8)   Okay, here's the grocery list. Don't forget the fruit – we need apples, pears, if they're ripe
enough, bananas. And we also need some milk and eggs. And if you can find something
good for dessert, like some chocolate chip cookies or small pastries, that would be great!

(9)   I don't really think we should go out tonight. For one thing, it's supposed to snow. And I'm
really tired. I just finished work and would rather just watch a movie on TV or something.
So is that okay with you?

The idea structure of the list in (8) reflects semantic relationships among the items to be
bought at the food store. Fruit is a superordinate set that includes apples, pears, and
bananas. Milk and eggs are items that both require refrigeration in the dairy section of
stores. And dessert includes cookies and pastries. The idea structure of the explanation in (9),
however, is based on the relationship between a conclusion (not to go out) and the events
(or states) that justify that conclusion (weather, physical state, time, alternative activity).

Linking together planes of discourse

Although we have been discussing each plane of discourse separately, we need to remember that every utterance is simultaneously part of – and has meaning on – different planes
of discourse. We can get a clearer picture of these relationships by taking a look at the
discourse in (10), an excerpt from an interaction between a librarian and a patron at the
reference desk of a public library.

(10)   (a) Patron: There used to be a monthly report that comes from S-Securities
Exchange Commission...
(b)   on insiders' transactions,
(c) Librarian: Uh huh
(d) Patron: and many years ago you used to carry it,
(e)   and I haven't seen it in a long time.

Part of the librarian's job is to help patrons find material in the library. After opening this
speech situation (e.g. with eye contact or *excuse me*), patrons typically use the speech act
"request" to get help. Although the patron doesn't say anything like "Can you give me..." or
"Do you have...," her utterance still performs the speech act of a request. We know this (as do
librarians and library patrons) because the participation framework (the identities and roles
of librarians and patrons) helps us recognize that an utterance that sounds as if it is asserting
the existence of a report (*There used to be a monthly report* (a)) is also performing a request.

Notice that the utterance about the existence of the monthly report appears as a long
and complex sentence spread over four lines in the transcript ((a), (b), (d), and (e)). These
lines reflect different tone units, segments of speech production that are bounded by
changes in timing, intonation, and pitch. Because the sentence is spread out over multiple
tone units, it ends up bypassing turn-transition places (locations at which the listener
is given the option of taking a turn) and allows the patron to complete the speech act
(a request) that is pivotal to the speech event and speech situation.

The division of the patron's long sentence into four tone units also reflects the information state and the recipient design of the utterance for the librarian. The patron pauses
after providing two pieces of information about the item she's looking for: its frequency

(*a monthly report*) and source (*that comes from S-Securities Exchange Commission*). This pause is an opportunity for the librarian to display her recognition of the requested item and to comply with the request. When that doesn't happen, the patron continues her description of the report, in (b), (d), and (e), pausing after each new piece of potential identifying information to give the librarian another chance to respond. The pauses at the turn-transition places after (a), (b), (d), and (e) make it easier for the librarian to complete the adjacency pair and respond to the patron's request at the earliest possible point. The act structure, the participation structure, the exchange structure, the information state, and the idea structure thus reinforce each other to make the production and the interpretation of the request (and its response) clear and efficient.

CHAPTER SUMMARY

Discourse is made up of patterned arrangements of smaller units, such as propositions, speech acts, and conversational turns. But discourse becomes more than the sum of its smaller parts. It becomes a coherent unit through both "bottom-up" and "top-down" processes. We construct coherence bottom-up in real time by building upon our own, and each others', prior utterances and their various facets of meaning. At the same time, however, our sense of the larger activity in which we are participating – the speech event, speech situation, and genre that we perceive ourselves to be constructing – provides an overall top-down frame for organizing those smaller units of the discourse. For example, turns at talk are negotiated as participants speak, but participants also are aware of larger expectations about how to share the "floor" that are imposed by the speech event (e.g. a discussion) in a speech situation (e.g. a classroom). Thus the very same turn-taking pattern may take on very different meanings depending on whether it is taking place in a classroom, in a courtroom, or during a first date.

The bottom-up and top-down organizations of discourse work in synchrony. The overall frame helps us figure out how to interpret what is being said and done. It also helps us figure out where to place the smaller units in relation to one another. Yet choices that we make about the smaller units – should I take a turn now? should I issue a direct order or make a more subtle hint? – can also alter the general definition of what is "going on" in a situation. The combination and coordination of all the different facets of discourse – the structures that they create and the frames that they reflect – are what gives discourse its coherence, our overall sense of what is going on.

The multifaceted nature of discourse also arises because we try to achieve several goals when we speak to each other, often all at the same time. We verbalize thoughts, introduce new information, repair errors in what we say, take turns at talk, think of others, perform acts, display identities and relationships. We are continuously anticipating what our recipients need (e.g. how much information do they need?) and want (e.g. how polite do they expect me to be?). We achieve these multiple goals when we are speaking by using a range of different units, including sentences, tone units, utterances, and speech acts, whose functional links to one another help tie together different planes of discourse.

Discourse analyses – peering into the small details of moment-by-moment talk – can be very detailed. And such details are in keeping with the assumption that knowledge and meaning are developed, and displayed, through social actions and recurrent practices, both of which depend upon language. Yet for some scholars the scope of discourse stretches beyond language and its immediate context of use to include what Gee (1999: 17) has called "Discourse" (with a capital D): "socially accepted associations among ways of using language, of thinking, valuing, acting and interacting, in the 'right' places and at the 'right' times with the 'right' objects." This conception of Discourse reaches way above the sentence and even further beyond the contexts of speech act, speech event, and speech situations. It makes explicit that our communicative competence – our knowledge of how to use language in everyday life – is an integral part of our culture.

Exercises

EXERCISE 5.1

What inferences would you draw from the two conversational excerpts below? What is the social relationship? The setting? And what features of "what is said" (e.g. what specific words and phrases?) allow you to make these inferences?

(i) Debby: Manela, sorry to bother you, but are the payroll forms ready?
     Manela: Oh sure. Here they are.

(ii) Mr. Kay: Okay, let's get started. First we'll go over the problems from last night.

EXERCISE 5.2

Differences in the ways we use language to act and interact often arise through differences in their "context." Collect ten to fifteen examples of phone openings, and ten to fifteen examples of face-to-face greetings. What differences *between* them can you identify in who talks when, and the use of words (e.g. *hello, hi*) and questions. What about differences *within* each context? Does the way you (or your interlocutors) talk seem to be related to how well you know each other, or when you've spoken to them last?

EXERCISE 5.3

Try to change the discourse markers you use in your everyday conversations. For example, answer each question that someone asks you with *well*. Completely stop using *like* or *y'know*. Add *and* to every sentence or utterance. Keep a log of your own ability to make these changes. What changes were the hardest to make? What do the changes tell you about these discourse markers?

EXERCISE 5.4

Identify question/answer adjacency pairs in the transcribed excerpts in this chapter. Analyze those adjacency pairs, as well as questions that you hear in classes and conversations, to answer the following:
– Are all utterances that end with a rising intonation questions?
– Are questions always performed through interrogative sentences?

– Does there seem to be one person who asks questions and others who answer? If so, does that division seem to be related to the participants' roles in the conversation? How?

EXERCISE 5.5

Reread Jack's story in example (4) in this chapter and answer the following questions:

a. What is Jack doing while Freda is talking to me?
b. What thread of the prior talk does he pursue?
c. Where and how does the turn-taking become competitive?
d. How and when does Jack finally get a turn at talk in which he is the only speaker?

– Where does the abstract appear? Does Jack try out or self-repair different abstracts? Why might he do so?
– Where is the orientation? What background information is presented?
– What occurs during the complicating action?
– Is the story brought back to the present?
– What aspects of language evaluate "what happened"?
– What is the point of the story?

EXERCISE 5.6

Write Jack's spoken narrative from (4) in one of the following written genres: an entry in a private journal or diary; a personal letter to a friend; a posting on your blog; support for a thesis in an essay that young boys are mischievous. What changes did you make? Which were easy to decide upon? Which did you struggle with?

EXERCISE 5.7

If you use instant messaging to communicate with friends or family, how do you manage your back channels? How do you take turns? Are adjacency pairs completed? Consider your answer in terms of the difference between spoken and written discourse.

EXERCISE 5.8

Requests are one of the most studied of all speech acts. The philosopher John Searle suggested that the following rules underlie the production and interpretation of requests:

Type of rule

Propositional content	Future act A of H
Preparatory	(a) H is able to do A. S believes H is able to do A.
	(b) It is not obvious to both S and H that H will do A in the normal course of events of his own accord.
Sincerity	S wants H to do A.
Essential	Counts as an attempt to get H to do A.

There are many ways to make a request. Whereas some seem direct and might be subcategorized as orders (e.g. *Come over now!*), others are very indirect and might be subcategorized as hints (e.g. *I'm really lonely and I'm wondering if you're doing anything now*). Jot down and compare the requests you hear people making, including some written requests. You'll be surprised at how much variety you find!

EXERCISE 5.9

Fill in the empty cells of the SPEAKING grid below, following from the information given in each column. Then explain the phonological, lexical, syntactic, and pragmatic features which you think would characterize each speech event. The topic of all three speech events is: income taxes.

Setting	Senate	Bar	Dinner at home
Participants	Elected officials	Drinking buddies	Parents and children
Ends	To enact new laws		
Act sequences	Statement + response		
Key	Serious		
Instrumentalities	Prepared speech		
Norms	Roberts' rules of order		
Genre	Debate		
Characteristic			
Features			

Now choose a speech event which you are familiar with and analyze it using the SPEAKING grid. Then identify features that are characteristic of the language used in that speech event.

EXERCISE 5.10

Identify the features of the "recipe register" in the excerpt below. Then describe the situation in which a recipe is used and explain how the register features meet the communicative demands of that situation.

Fettucine al limone
4 oz. butter (1 stick)
1½ cups heavy cream
zest and juice of 2 lemons
salt, freshly ground pepper, and nutmeg
1lb. fettucine
grated Parmigiano-Reggiano

Melt butter in a heavy saucepan. Add cream and stir to incorporate. When sauce is heated, add lemon juice, zest, salt, pepper, and nutmeg to taste. Toss with piping hot fettucine and Parmigiano-Reggiano and serve immediately. Serves 6.

EXERCISE 5.11

Take any stretch of the transcripts in examples (3) or (4) in the chapter and identify the primary and secondary functions served by each utterance, using Jakobson's model of discourse functions. Explain why and how you think each sentence serves those functions. Then take one of the two texts in example (6) in the chapter and perform the same functional analysis. Finally, compare your functional analyses of the spoken and written texts. Which functions are emphasized? Are functions performed in the same way in the two texts?

SUGGESTIONS FOR FURTHER READING

Chafe, Wallace 1994, *Discourse, consciousness and time*, Chicago University Press. A thought-provoking interdisciplinary exploration of the relationship between language and consciousness. The relationship between our "flow" of thoughts and our speech patterns tells us much about spoken and written discourse; time, memory, and experience; information structure in sentence and discourse.

Edwards, Jane A. 2001, "The transcription of discourse," in D. Schiffrin, D. Tannen, and H. Hamilton (eds.) 2001, *Handbook of discourse analysis*, Oxford: Blackwell. A comprehensive discussion of transcription choices depending on the nature of the interaction, the theoretical framework, and the research question.

Gee, James Paul 1999, *An introduction to discourse analysis*, London: Routledge. An integrated and highly accessible presentation of theories about discourse and research tools, that together relate the methods and results of discourse analyses to issues in language learning and teaching, psychology, anthropology, communication, and education.

Jaworski, Adam and Coupland, Nikolas (eds.) 1999, *The discourse reader*, London: Routledge. A collection of classic articles that present both foundational articles, as well as contemporary exemplars of perspectives, in the areas of meaning and context; methods and resources for studying discourse; sequence and structure; negotiating social relationships; identity and subjectivity; power, ideology and control. Excellent companion for *Handbook of discourse analysis* (below).

Johnstone, Barbara 2002, *Discourse analysis*, Malden, MA: Blackwell. Presents a set of techniques for systematically studying what is "meant" in discourse. Chapters cover the relationship between discourse (both spoken and written) and various aspects of language structure, as well as facets of context, such as participants and prior discourse. Discussion questions and ideas for small research projects are interspersed throughout the volume.

Schiffrin, Deborah 1987, *Discourse markers*, Cambridge University Press. Illuminates the wide-ranging roles of small words (such as *well, but, now*) and phrases (such as *y'know, I mean*) that pervade everyday spoken discourse. Analyses are supported by in-depth analyses of these "markers" in conversations, narratives, and arguments.

Schiffrin, Deborah 1994, *Approaches to discourse*, Oxford: Blackwell. Compares six approaches to discourse analysis whose disciplinary origins include anthropology, linguistics, philosophy, and sociology. Comparisons are presented through overviews of each perspective, in-depth analyses (of discourse segments, question/answer pairs, information structure, speech acts, and references) and comparison among theoretical constructs.

Schiffrin, D., Tannen, D., and Hamilton, H. (eds.) 2001, *Handbook of discourse analysis*, Oxford: Blackwell. An invaluable collection of forty-one specially commissioned articles from experts in the field; articles cover a wide range of topics, issues, and perspectives. Sections cover the relationship of discourse analysis to linguistics; the linking of theory to practice; political, social, and institutional discourse; culture, community, and genre; discourse across disciplines. An excellent complement to *The discourse reader* (above).

6 Child language acquisition

CHAPTER PREVIEW

How children acquire language has long intrigued scholars and nonscholars alike. Parents of young children are often amazed at how quickly their babies move from cooing and babbling to forceful one- and two-word demands. Linguists and psychologists, in turn, have been interested in understanding the stages and mechanisms by which all children become competent users of language (or, in most of the world, languages) by age three or four. Indeed, children from all backgrounds, and under diverse learning conditions, tend to pass through similar phases in learning their mother tongues. Researchers are interested in exploring these processes to gain a better understanding of how children accomplish this remarkable feat, but also because the nature of these processes holds important implications for larger debates in the field of linguistics. Understanding the mechanisms of how children acquire their language(s) can shed important light on the nature of language, as well as on the nature of human learning.

This chapter will first explore how researchers gather data on child language acquisition. We will review three approaches to child language acquisition research: parental diaries, observational studies, and experimental studies. After briefly discussing the advantages and disadvantages of these research approaches, we'll turn to some of the actual data. Specifically, we will look at the major milestones of language development in phonology, semantics, morphology, and syntax. We'll also examine the extent to which these processes differ depending on the cultural context and the language being acquired. Lastly, after reviewing some of the major research findings, we will consider how researchers explain these data, outlining the major theoretical positions in the hotly debated field of child language acquisition.

GOALS

The goals of this chapter are to:

- **introduce the main research methods for investigating child language acquisition**
- **describe the milestones of child language development**
- **provide an overview of crosslinguistic and crosscultural aspects of child language acquisition**
- **analyze the major theories employed to explain child language acquisition**

Gathering data on language acquisition

How can we best study how children learn to use language? Because our research subjects are so young, traditional means of data collection are often inadequate. We cannot, for instance, ask a one-year-old to define what she means when she says "ba-ba" or to judge the grammaticality of a sentence. Children's language comprehension skills generally outpace their production abilities, so relying on children's verbal output alone provides only a partial picture of the acquisition process. Furthermore, recent research suggests that language learning begins even *before* birth: for instance, infants show a preference for the sounds of their mother's native language just days after being born, thus indicating that some kind of language learning has taken place *in utero*, long before subjects can serve as research participants in most studies.

In collecting and analyzing child language, researchers often strive for naturalness and **representativeness** in their data. Natural data are similar to the language children use in everyday life with familiar conversational partners (like the child's parents) in familiar contexts (like the home) doing routine activities (like playing). Representativeness refers to two goals: first, the language data collected from a particular child should be representative of the language used by that child every day. Thus, if a bilingual child normally speaks mostly Spanish with his mother, a sample of English conversation between the mother and child would not be representative of their everyday interactional patterns. Second, the children studied should be representative of the general population under investigation – for example, Spanish–English bilingual four-year-olds. Below, three approaches to collecting child language data are briefly described and critiqued in terms of naturalness and representativeness.

Parental diaries

Some of the earliest studies of child language acquisition are found in parents' detailed descriptions of their children's language development, generally referred to as **parental diaries**. While early attempts date as far back as the eighteenth century, most parental diaries, such as those of Charles Darwin, come from the late nineteenth and first half of the twentieth century. The most famous of these is Werner Leopold's four-volume account of his daughter Hildegard's simultaneous acquisition of German and English. Leopold was a German–English bilingual of German ancestry; his wife was an American with German roots, but English was her dominant language. Leopold kept meticulous notes beginning at Hildegard's eighth week of life, with most of the data focusing on her first two years. He also theorized extensively in his diaries and described his working hypotheses on her language development. (See Box 6.1 for examples.)

Leopold's diaries provide rich details and important insights into the process of language learning in general as well as bilingual language acquisition in particular; however, they suffer from many of the shortcomings of all parental diary studies. An inherent problem in this type of research is the fact that a diary consists of *one* observer who is taking notes on just *one* child, raising the question of whether Hildegard is representative of all children. Furthermore, the only linguistic forms described in great detail are the utterances that Hildegard directed at Leopold or which she used around Leopold, providing a potentially limited and unrepresentative sample. There are probably errors and omissions in

---

BOX 6.1 **LEOPOLD'S DIARIES**

The following excerpts from Leopold's diary demonstrate a parental diary's anecdotal style and how the parent may also be able to record the child's confidence level and type of utterances said in the second language.

February 18, 1934.

The progress in German is now more considerable. She utters her requests often spontaneously in German, although often with the plea *You help me to say it*. Several times she has found her own formulation, without imitation of a fixed model .... The correlative statements *Ich liebe dich* and *Ich dich auch* have become a sort of family game at the lunch table. Hildegard gives the second statement often in the form *Ich liebe dich auch*. The addition of the verb shows the influence of English *I like you too*, which cannot be said without the verb. For the same reason this version is more successful with her than '*Ich hab dich lieb*', which would be the more natural expression for monolingual children.

March 3, 1934.

English: *When you take my overshoes off, my shoes come off with*. This might be German influence. *Where is that kit?* When I did not understand, she explained: *kitty*. It was an incorrect back-formation on the model of *doggie-dog*, etc. ... The imperfections of her English are slight and exceptional. She speaks much and with perfect fluency; nearly everything is correct. The majority of the mistakes which remain concern strong verbs, as in popular speech. Weak past-tense forms like *writed* intrude frequently.

(Leopold 1949b: 52).

transcription, compounded by the fact that there were no audiotapes of the data. Perhaps more importantly, there is a natural tendency for the parent (or any observer) to selectively focus on out-of-the-ordinary (and more interesting) samples rather than on routine and everyday utterances. Thus, while Leopold's diary remains a classic in the field, it provides just one particular vantage point on the language acquisition process, a vantage point which is privileged in terms of the data's naturalness (as Hildegard spoke freely in the company of her own father), but limited in terms of its representativeness.

Observational studies

Starting in the early 1960s, researchers began to audio record and transcribe the everyday speech of children in order to understand how they learned to comprehend and produce basic English sentence structures. Some of the earliest and best known of these **observational studies** are those of Roger Brown, who directed a research project at Harvard University which studied the language of three children (from three families, none related to Brown) in great detail. Brown's classic book, *A First Language: The Early Stages* (1973), documents the development of Adam, Sarah, and Eve's language. The book presents some of the first explanations of the development of grammatical and morphological systems over time.

> *The following excerpt demonstrates how Brown looked at child language systematically across the three children. Some errors he finds occur often, as in past-tense formation, while other types never occur, as in the application of the progressive aspect:*
>
> *The children created such errors as* comed *and* drinked, *and* doos *(do + -s for third-person subject) and* stand ups *and* mans *(plural) and* sheeps *(plural) and* mines *(possessive) . . . the progressive in our data alone is not overgeneralized . . . Why should no errors occur with the progressive inflection when they do occur with all other inflections?*
> *. . . The subclassification of verbs which governs the progressive is a principled one whereas the subclassifications governing the applicability of the regular past, third plural, and possessive inflections are all unprincipled. . . . The verbs* want, like, need, know, see *and* hear, *which may not ordinarily take the progressive inflection in American English can be semantically distinguished from the many verbs that may take the progressive inflection; the former are all involunatary states.*
> (Brown 1973: 324–325)
>
> *By looking at the gaps in errors by children Brown was able to uncover children's cabability for easily grasping the patterns of the English language.*

Many other observational studies have since been conducted. In these studies, researchers typically audiotape (and more recently also videotape) a small number of children (one at a time) interacting in natural contexts regularly over an extended period. These recordings are then transcribed and analyzed. This approach allows researchers to examine, for instance, how questions or past-tense formulations develop over time among different children, identifying both general patterns and individual differences.

Other observational studies of child language, more anthropological in nature, have focused on language socialization practices. These studies attempt to uncover how children

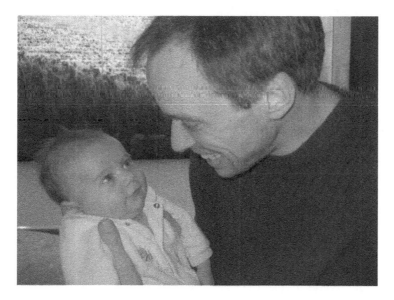

Figure 6.1 In some cultures, even very young infants are treated as valid conversational partners

are socialized into culturally appropriate language behavior and how linguistic competence develops, with an emphasis on how these patterns of interaction and parents' ideologies about language vary crossculturally. For instance, in some families, children are viewed as conversational partners from birth, with cries, grunts, and early babbling sounds treated as meaningful communication attempts (see Figure 6.1). This is far from universal, however; in much of the world, infants' early sounds are not assigned any particular meaning or communicative intent.

Observational studies have tended to be **longitudinal** – that is, they have followed the same participants over several months or perhaps as long as several years. **Cross-sectional** observational studies, although less common, have also been conducted. These studies record the language behavior of participants from at least two different groups; for instance, a group of two-year-old Korean-American children and a similar group of two-year-old Mexican-American children might be compared in a cross-sectional study.

Because of the time-intensive nature of collecting, transcribing, and analyzing hours of language data in such close detail, often these observational studies include only small numbers of child participants. Thus, while observational studies such as these get high marks for providing relatively natural data as well as data which are representative of the child's normal speech, it is not always clear to what extent the few participants are representative of the wider population under study. One way researchers have attempted to overcome this drawback has been to share their transcripts. The primary channel for doing so is the Child Language Data Exchange System (CHILDES; see http://childes.psy.cmu.edu/). CHILDES has allowed researchers not only to examine acquisition patterns and processes across larger numbers of children, but also to investigate how patterns differ across children from different language groups. (See Box 6.2 for an example of a transcript from the CHILDES database.)

BOX 6.2 **CHILDES DATABASE**

This transcript is a conversation between a child, Ethan, age 2;2, and his mother from the Providence database available through the CHILDES database. The *xx* denote unintelligble speech and the words in parentheses note a potential alternate prounction if the speech was unclear. There are many different databases available, some of which are longitudinal studies of several children, while others vary with respect to age group, language, tasks, and type of conversation. Most transcripts are tagged so that they are searchable for particular words or phrases and/or grammatical constructions. The types of tags vary between different databases depending on the researcher's particular area of study.

  (Source: CHILDES database, Providence: eth33.cha. Full conversation available http://childes.psy.cmu.edu/data/Eng-USA/)

*CHI:	watermelon.
*MOT:	watermelon?
*MOT:	it's not watermelon.
*CHI:	it's berry.
*MOT:	it's berry.
*MOT:	Mister Berry.
*CHI:	it's watermelon berry.
*CHI:	watermelon belly [?] xx.
*MOT:	watermelon belly.
*MOT:	watermelon belly?
*MOT:	berry.
*CHI:	xx.
*CHI:	watermelon belly.
*MOT:	yeah [: yes], watermelon belly.

Experimental studies

Experimental studies constitute a third approach to collecting child language data. A wide range of methodological approaches falls under this rubric, including those which are more naturalistic in design and those which involve more tightly controlled tests. In general, experimental studies tend to have narrowly defined research questions (for example, at what age can infants recognize their own name or the sound of their mother's voice?) and to use more controlled (and sometimes considered artificial) methods of collecting data, such as the HASP described below. Experimental language data tend to be elicited through carefully designed techniques rather than observed and described as they naturally unfold. Lastly, experimental studies tend to collect less data overall from each participant, but to have a greater number of participants. This means that although the data might be less naturalistic, they have a higher chance of accurately representing the population under study.

   One of the most widely used experimental procedures to investigate when and how infants begin to make sense of the language around them is the **high-amplitude sucking paradigm** (**HASP**). This procedure relies on infants' reactions to stimuli – in particular, the fact that they will suck at a higher rate when presented with novel stimuli. Using a pacifier attached to a machine which records the rate and strength of the infant's sucking, researchers can measure, for instance, whether the infant perceives a difference between two similar sounds or two words, such as *lice* and *rice*. In order to test this, the infant is given a pacifier and then presented with, for instance, the word *lice*. At first, the rate of sucking increases, but as *lice* is presented repeatedly, the infant becomes "bored" with the sound and the rate begins to decline. At this point, *rice* is presented; if the rate of sucking increases again, researchers interpret this as evidence that the child has detected the new sound and thus can discriminate between *lice* and *rice*. If the rate of sucking remains the same, one can assume the child does not distinguish between the two stimuli. This technique can be used with infants who are only a few days old, as all babies are born with a sucking reflex.

In addition to techniques aimed at measuring auditory discrimination, there are also a number of methods for assessing the production and comprehension of children's syntax. For example, in elicited production, a game (for example, with a puppet) or a picture is used to lead children to produce particular sentences. (The "wug" test discussed below is an example of elicited production.) Another commonly used technique is the truth-value judgment task. Here, the child is presented with a story (typically acted out with puppets or shown with pictures) and then asked to render a yes/no judgment about whether a statement accurately describes what happened in the story. Such techniques have been important in revealing much of what we know about children's early language abilities, the topic of the following section.

The data: milestones in child language development

All normally developing children, acquiring any of the world's spoken or signed languages, follow a similar path of language development and reach the major milestones in the same order. However, there is significant variability in the age at which these milestones are reached.

The first sounds

The techniques described above have yielded much of what we know about infant language ability in the early months, and in particular what we know about the development of **speech perception** during the first year of life. Speech perception – which includes, for instance, the ability to segment the speech stream into meaningful units, to recognize one's own name in the speech stream, or to distinguish between similar sounding vowels (e.g. /ee/ and /oo/) – is a critical skill that infants develop early in life. These early language skills also involve visual information; for instance, infants as young as two months have been shown to be able to match vowel sounds they hear with the appropriate lip, mouth, and face movements. These early speech perception skills related to the sound structure of language may help infants to **bootstrap** into more complex language competencies; bootstrapping refers to the possibility that skills in one area of language might help the child to develop competencies in other language areas. For instance, infants' ability to recognize their own names in the speech stream (which appears around the fifth month) may provide them with a means to recognize novel, adjacent words. (See Box 6.3.)

Early research in speech perception demonstrated that during their first few months of life, infants are able to discriminate between similar sounds (for example, between /b/ and /p/) both in their native language(s) as well as in other languages. Over time, however, infants become more attuned to their native language(s) and less able to make sound distinctions

BOX 6.3 **HOW FAMILIAR NAMES HELP BABIES BEGIN TO SEGMENT SPEECH**

How do infants learn to segment the speech stream and to recognize individual words? Bortfeld *et al.* (2005) provided evidence that infants can exploit familiar words, such as their own names, to segment adjacent unfamiliar words from a fluent stream of speech. In other words, infants' names appear to serve as an "anchor" in the speech stream, helping them to disambiguate the words which come just after their name.

Using the "headturn preference procedure," the experimenters first familiarized 24 six-month-old infants with two six-sentence passages. In one passage, each of the sentences contained the baby's own name followed by a novel word (e.g. "Emma's feet"). Here, *feet* is the familiar-name target. In the other passage, each of the six sentences contained a different name (i.e. not the baby's own) followed by another novel word (e.g. "Autumn's cup"). Here, *cup* is the alternate-name target. Infants were paired so that the alternate-name passage for one infant was the familiar-name passage for another, and vice versa. The researchers then sought to determine whether infants had formed a preference for the familiar-name target relative to the alternate-name target (and nonfamiliarized control words) by testing them on each in isolation. Stimuli were presented through loudspeakers located on each side of a testing booth; the dependent variable was how long infants oriented to the side on which the word was being played. Bortfeld and her colleagues found that the infants listened significantly longer to the familiar-name target than to the alternate-name target, while there was no difference in how long the infants attended to the alternate-name targets and the nonfamiliarized controls.

A second experiment produced similar results, indicating that six-month-old infants likewise displayed a preference for words linked with another familiar name, this time the moniker for their mother (Mommy or Mama), over words linked with an unfamiliar name (Lolly or Lola). Based on these results, the researchers concluded that familiar names provide a useful means for infants to break into a fluent stream of speech and segment out previously unfamiliar words that follow those names.

in other languages. Janet Werker and her colleagues, for instance, working with Hindi- and English-speaking adults and English-learning infants, illustrated that while English-learning infants (six to eight months old) and Hindi-speaking adults could distinguish between the Hindi sounds of /da/ and /Da/, English-speaking adults could not. Her work demonstrated that English-learning infants seem to lose this skill quite quickly, with the sharpest decline in perceptual ability occurring around the end of the first year of life. This line of research underscores the fact that infants are born with the capacity to learn any language in the world, but the capacity to hear like a native fades very early on.

The first sound made by all infants is crying. All infants can do this immediately from birth; although crying may signal distress, discomfort, boredom, or other emotions in the first month of life, it is not an intentional attempt to communicate. From about the second to fifth month, infants engage in **cooing**. Coos are generally vowel-like sounds that are often interpreted as signs of pleasure and playfulness.

All infants begin to **babble** anywhere between four and six months and generally continue to do so until they reach around one year of age. Babbling is characterized by vowel or consonant–vowel sounds such as *ouw-ouw* or *ma-ma*. At this age, infants' tongues tend to be relatively large compared to the size of their mouths, and as a result, these sounds will often be palatals, such as [y] or [ñ]. Labial sounds such as [b] and [m] are also common. Babbling begins to conform to the sound patterns of the adults' language between six and ten months of age, with adult native speakers showing the ability to discriminate the babbles of Chinese, Arabic, English, or French infants.

Babbling is seemingly innate and unconscious, but also interactive and social. All infants, including those who are born deaf, go through a period of oral babbling. Deaf infants' oral babbling tends to consist of a smaller total number of sounds, with certain consonants (e.g. nasals and fricatives) predominating. Their babbling is random, generally not interactive, and tapers off sooner than that of hearing infants. However, deaf infants who are learning a signed language, such as American Sign Language (ASL), also go through a period of "gestural babbling," which corresponds to signed language and greatly differs from the much more random gesturing of hearing babies without this exposure. Although there is no meaning (such as a demand for food) associated with this babbling for hearing or for deaf infants, it can be a source of interactive play. In some cultures, infants are encouraged to continue to babble by caregivers' smiles or touches, or by their own babbling in return. Infants will often stop babbling in order to listen to their interlocutor (sometimes engaging in give-and-take exchanges known as **proto-conversations**), and around the fifth month, some infants are able to immediately imitate simple sound sequences presented to them.

The first words

Sometime around their first birthdays, children begin to assign specific meanings to the sounds they produce. These first words mark the beginning of what is known as the **holophrastic stage**. Holophrastic means 'characterized by one-word sentences'; infants tend to use single words to communicate a variety of complex functions. For instance, the word *mama* might be a bid for mother's attention, a descriptive comment upon seeing mother walk past, or a request for something which mother typically provides, such as food. Through contextual cues, parents often claim to understand the meaning of these holophrases (engaging in what is sometimes called "rich interpretation"), although this is difficult to verify empirically. While parents are often very proud of a child who is an early talker, there is little evidence that the timing of the first words corresponds to later intelligence or age of achievement of other developmental milestones. (Indeed, Albert Einstein reportedly did not start talking until age three or four!) Further, there is no evidence that learning two languages results in language delay. (See Box 6.4.)

Children's words at this stage tend to be concrete objects which are grounded in and central to everyday experiences and interactions (such as *light, tree, water*), rather than abstract concepts (*peace, happiness*). These first words tend to be **content words** (*bear* or *bed*) rather than **function words** (*the, and, on*). For children learning English, most first words are nouns. This seems to be related to the fact that sentences in English typically end with nouns, where they are salient, or more noticeable, to learners. This is not the case for children learning all languages, however. For instance, as discussed below, Korean-learning infants' first words are often verbs; in the Korean language, verbs are sentence-final and sentences may consist of only a verb.

> ## BOX 6.4 BILINGUALISM AND THE LANGUAGE DELAY MYTH
>
> It is widely believed that learning more than one language causes a delay in language acquisition overall. In order to test this assumption, Pearson *et al.* (1997) compared two groups of children ranging from eight months to two and a half years. One group consisted of children acquiring English only, while the other were acquiring English and Spanish simultaneously. Parents were asked to complete questionnaires regarding the words their children could produce. The findings revealed that bilingual children acquired the two languages at the same rate and timetable as the monolingual children. In addition, when the bilingual children's Spanish and English words were added together in one list, the size of their vocabulary list was similar to the size of the monolingual children's vocabulary. This division of the total vocabulary list between two languages would appear to be a "delay" in the acquistion of the vocabulary of one language by bilingual children. However, by the time children reach the age of four or five, the time it takes all children to become fully fluent in even one language, the bilingual children have vocabularies equal to that of their monolingual peers (or twice that of their monolingual peers if one adds the vocabularies of both languages).

While working to master the vocabulary around them, children often engage in both semantic **overextension** and **underextension**. For instance, a child may overextend the meaning of the word *water* to include not just drinking water, but also juice, milk, and soda. Underextension, which seems to be less common, refers to the reverse phenomenon: a child, for example, might use *baby* only to refer to an infant sibling and not to the other babies he/she encounters.

Around age two, children enter the **two-word stage**, characterized by use of phrases which are not more than two words. For English-learning infants, this typically means combining a subject and verb (e.g. *baby cry*, *mama sleep*) or a verb and modifier (e.g. *eat now*, *go out*). The ordering of these two-word phrases is not fixed, however, and there tends to be limited systematic use of grammatical morphology (for example, the possessive is formed as *Lucia bed* rather than *Lucia's bed*).

As in many other stages of their linguistic development, children's capacity for comprehending words outpaces their production ability. For instance, around the age of one, children can typically *understand* about seventy different words, but only productively *use* about six. There is about a four- to six-month delay between when children can comprehend a given number of words and when they can produce that many words themselves. Sometime around the end of the second year, children's productive vocabulary begins to develop rapidly; this is sometimes known as the **vocabulary spurt**. During this period, children begin to add about two hundred words a month to their vocabularies!

At approximately two and half years of age, children begin to produce phrases of three or more words, entering the **multi-word stage** (e.g. *Graham go out*, *Daddy cook dinner*, *Esperanza food all gone*). Children's language at this stage has been described as **telegraphic speech** because, like the economical language used in telegraphs, it is seemingly direct and makes only limited use of morphological and syntactic markers.

First sentences: morphological and syntactic development

Many diary, observational, and experimental studies have documented and explored how children become competent users of their language's system of morphology and syntax. From this research, we know that for all languages, both signed and spoken, this process seems to involve the formation of internal "rules"; in other words, children's increasingly regular use of grammatical forms (even non-adultlike or "incorrect" usages such as *broked* or *foots*) may reflect children's developing grammatical rule systems.

We also know that children seem to begin to acquire this grammatical competence at a very young age and, as in vocabulary development, comprehension skills outpace production. For instance, children who are only seventeen months of age, and typically still producing only one- or two-word utterances, tend to look longer at video clips that correctly correspond to the grammar of the oral commentary. For instance, children who hear "The bear sat on the bird" and are shown two pictures (one of a bear sitting on a bird and another of a bird sitting on a bear) will look longer at the picture where the bear is sitting on the bird. This research demonstrates that even at very young ages children are tuned into the semantic significance of their language's grammatical structures.

Research has also demonstrated that morphological and syntactic development is predictable. In other words, all children follow similar patterns and pass through the same developmental sequences as their competence develops. Although there is some variation depending on the language being acquired, many patterns and processes are constant across different language and cultural groups. Below we focus on these patterns for children acquiring English; in the following section, we'll highlight some of the crosslinguistic and crosscultural differences that have been documented.

The development of inflectional and derivational morphology in children's productive language becomes apparent once the child enters the multiple-word stage and continues through age five. The development of inflectional morphology was the focus of early and intensive investigation. Brown's investigation of Adam, Sarah, and Eve, discussed above, made important advances in this area. (See Box 6.5.)

Through analysis of Adam, Sarah, and Eve's spontaneous speech, Brown mapped out when different grammatical morphemes consistently appeared in their speech and how this corresponded to other aspects of their language, in particular to **mean length of utterance (MLU)**. MLU is a widely used measurement of the complexity of children's language and is calculated from the average number of *morphemes* (not words) per utterance. Brown illustrated that: (1) the order of acquisition was similar across the three unacquainted children (with present progressive, plural, and past irregular verb forms appearing first); (2) the age at which children acquired competence in using these forms varied widely (compare, for instance, Eve and Adam at age two years and three months in Box 6.5); and (3) the MLU stage served as a good index of the level of development for grammatical morphology (and indeed was much more predictive of grammatical development than age). More recent research has stressed the importance of vocabulary as a predictor of grammatical development.

Another early study which sheds light on when children acquire inflectional morphology was Jean Berko's famous "wug" study. Rather than recording and analyzing

BOX 6.5 ACQUISITION OF GRAMMATICAL MORPHEMES BY ADAM, SARAH, AND EVE BY MLU STAGE (I–V) AND AGE (YEAR; MONTH)

This table presents the stages of acquisition of grammatical forms by three children. Their ages at each stage are presented in italicized parentheses. The first number in the parentheses represents the year and the second the month. Thus *2;3* signifies that the child is two years and three months old.

Adam		Sarah		Eve	
I	*(2;3)*	I	*(2;3)*	I	*(1;6)*
II	*(2;6)* Present progressive Plural	II	*(2;10)* Plural Present progressive Past irregular Possessive	II	*(1;9)* Present progressive

III	*(2;11)*
	Uncontractible
	  copula
	Past irregular
		III	*(3;1)*
			Uncontractible
			  copula
			Articles
				III	*(1;11)*
					Plural
					Possessive
					Past regular

IV	*(3;2)* Articles Third person irregular Possessive	IV	*(3;8)* Third person regular	IV	*(2;2)*

V	*(3;6)*
	Third person regular
	
	Past regular
	Uncontractable
	  auxiliary
	Contractable
	  copula
	Contractable
	  auxiliary
		V	*(4;0)*
			Past regular
			Uncontractible
			  auxiliary
			Contractable
			  copula
			Third person
			  irregular
			Contractible
			  auxiliary
				V	*(2;3)*
					Uncontractible
					  copula
					Past irregular
					Articles
					Third person
					  regular
					Third person
					  irregular
					Uncontractible
					  auxiliary
					Contractible
					  copula
					Contractible
					  auxiliary

Note: Table adapted from Brown (1973).
Stages (I–V) correspond to mean length of utterance (MLU): stage I, MLU = 1.75; stage II, MLU = 2.25; stage III, MLU = 2.75; stage IV, MLU = 3.50; stage V, MLU = 4. Acquisition of a grammatical form was defined as three successive samples in which the morpheme appears at least 90 percent of the time in obligatory contexts.

To calculate the MLU, count the first 100 utterances of a transcribed sample of a child's language. Next, count the number of morphemes in each utterance and then add up the number of morphemes in all of the 100 utterances. Finally, divide this total by 100 to get the mean length of utterance. If you don't have 100 utterances, count the number of utterances you have and divide the total number of morphemes by the number of utterances (adapted from Brown 1973). Count catenatives (e.g. *wanna, doncha*) as one morpheme. Also, don't count fillers (*um, oh*) or sounds (*aack*, etc.).

Figure 6.2 The Wug test

This is a wug.

Now there is another one.
There are two of them.
There are two –.

children's spontaneous speech as Brown did, Berko asked young children of different ages to form the plural of unknown, nonsense creatures, such as "wugs." (See Figure 6.2.) The experimenter pointed to an item and said, "This is a wug." She then showed a picture with the same two animals and said, "Now here is another one. There are two of them. There are two____?" Berko found that even preschool children were able to form the plural correctly, demonstrating that they had learned the rule for forming plurals and could apply this rule correctly in novel contexts, and were not just repeating forms which they had previously heard.

In developing these rules, children pass through predictable stages. For instance, children **overgeneralize** in the early phases of acquisition, meaning that they apply the regular rules of grammar to irregular nouns and verbs. Overgeneralization leads to forms that we sometimes hear in the speech of young children such as *goed, eated, foots,* and *fishes*. This process is often described as consisting of three phases:

- *Phase 1:* The child uses the correct past tense of *go*, for instance, but does not relate this past-tense *went* to present-tense *go*. Rather, *went* is treated as a separate lexical item.
- *Phase 2:* The child constructs a rule for forming the past tense and begins to overgeneralize this rule to irregular forms such as *go* (resulting in forms such as *goed*).

- *Phase 3:* The child learns that there are (many) exceptions to this rule and acquires the ability to apply this rule selectively.

Note that from the observer's or parents' perspectives, this development is "U-shaped" – that is, children can appear to be decreasing rather than increasing in their accuracy of past-tense use as they enter phase 2. However, this apparent "back-sliding" is an important sign of linguistic development.

We see similar patterns, known as "developmental sequences," in other areas of grammar, such as the formation of English negatives and interrogatives. As outlined in Box 6.6, children move through identifiable stages, although these stages are more continuous and overlapping than discrete. Note that from the parents' perspective, children's development is also not always straightforward. For instance, a child is likely to produce inverted yes/no questions (*Did William eat cake?*), while still using normal declarative word order for wh-questions (*How Miranda go out?*). (See Chapter 13 for related developmental patterns in second language acquisition.)

BOX 6.6 DEVELOPMENT OF ENGLISH NEGATIVES AND QUESTIONS (ADAPTED FROM AKMAJIAN *ET AL.* 1995)

Stage	Negatives	Yes/no questions	wh-questions
One-word stage	Use of single word *No* *Allgone*	Use of single word with rising intonation *Sleeping?*	Use of single word with rising intonation *Cookie?*
Early multi-word stage	Single negative word occurs at start of sentence only *No sleeping* *No go outside* *Allgone Cheerios*	No use of auxiliaries; no inversion of word order; rising intonation *Drink water?* *Go outside?*	Limited use of *where* and *what* at start of sentence only *Where doggie?* *What box?* *Where mommy sleeping?*
Mid multi-word stage	Negative word appears between subject and predicate; use of (unanalyzed) *can't* and *don't* *Baby no sleep* *Mommy can't go out.* *She don't eat that.*	Auxiliaries in negative sentences; rising intonation; no inversion of word order *She can't eat?* *See baby?* *Daddy cook dinner?*	Greater use of other wh-words; still no inversion of word order *Why baby sleeping?* *Who talking?*
Late multi-word stage	Greater range of auxiliaries used; auxiliaries in positive and negative sentences *I didn't eat it.* *She doesn't watch TV.* *Mommy can't go out.*	Auxiliaries used in positive sentences; inversion of auxiliary appears. *Did you eat cake?* *Can't she play now?* *Will mommy eat cake?*	Additional wh-words used; still no inversion of word order *How she go out?* *What he eats?* *Where he can go?*

These data highlight the extent to which negation and interrogative development are interrelated and also dependent upon development of the necessary vocabulary. For instance, both questions and negatives are dependent upon acquisition of the verb auxiliary system (including, for instance, *do, does, did, is, am, have, has*) and modals (for example, *can, could, may, might*). These data also demonstrate the rule-governed nature of children's language production: the "mistakes" in the examples here are generally not the result of children repeating the language that surrounds them; rather, they reflect the developing rule system of children's language. Lastly, while there has been a general tendency for researchers to focus on explaining the "mistakes" that children make, it is worth stressing that, given the many opportunities for incorrect or unconventional language use, grammatical errors are in fact quite uncommon, perhaps reflecting children's highly conservative (and risk-averse) approach to learning and generalization.

Crosslinguistic and crosscultural aspects of language acquisition

As we've seen, all children pass through the major milestones of language development in the same order regardless of the language they are learning. However, language systems differ in dramatic ways; for example, Mandarin uses lexical tone, Quechua marks evidentiality (see Chapter 2, p. 96), while English does neither. Variation like this suggests that speakers of different languages use the same basic mental mechanisms (for instance, working memory or perceptual processing) but may use them differently depending on the language being spoken.

Because so much of the research on language acquisition has been conducted among English-speaking children, it is difficult at times to distinguish between English-specific processes and universal processes – that is, those that are common to all languages. In recent decades, however, there has been a major push to explore first language acquisition from a crosslinguistic perspective. Overall, this research has shown that, while there are many patterns that hold true across all languages, there are also some important and intriguing differences. We highlight some of the findings in terms of lexical and grammatical development here.

Lexical and grammatical development

Comparative and crosslinguistic research on word comprehension and production has been conducted in more than a dozen languages, including such diverse languages as Afrikaans, Croatian, Sign Language of the Netherlands, and Swedish. This research, which relies on standardized parental report instruments, has reached two conclusions which seem to hold universally: (1) onset times appear very similar across languages for both word comprehension (eight to ten months) and word production (eleven to thirteen months); and (2) wide individual variation exists *within* each language concerning the pace and size of vocabulary growth (for example, at two years, children's productive vocabularies range from 1 to 500 items).

Another line of research on word production concerns the emergence of nouns and verbs. While it was long believed that nouns were the first words to appear in children's speech, researchers examining Korean recently have argued that this is not universally the case. Gopnik and Choi (1995) presented data demonstrating that verbs are among the first items acquired by Korean children, a fact probably related to their salient sentence-final position in Korean. They further suggest that this difference holds implications for cognitive development; for example, Korean children tend to perform better on tasks which are related to verbs (tool-usage tests), while English-speaking children perform better on noun-related tasks (object categorization tests).

Other crosslinguistic research has focused on the development of grammatical competence. Across the world, young children seem to use their developing grammatical competence to attempt to convey similar intents, including, for instance, possession, location, and volition. Nevertheless, there are important differences in the linguistic forms that young children use to convey these meanings. These differences reflect the nature of the language being acquired by the young child. For instance, Turkish children appear to have mastered the entire system of case morphology at age two, reflecting the high degree of regularity and phonological saliency of the Turkish inflectional system. Similarly, young Italian children use relative clauses to a much greater degree than young English-speaking children, possibly reflecting the frequency of this form for common pragmatic functions in Italian.

These structural differences across languages influence the nature of the developmental sequence for each language. For instance, recall the developmental sequence for the formation of English wh-questions discussed in Box 6.6. Because English wh-questions require inversion of word order *and* use of an auxiliary verb, even children in the multi-word stage still produce utterances such as *Where she sleep?* Children who are learning languages which do not require auxiliaries for question formation, such as Italian or Spanish, sound much more "adultlike" in the use of their questions from a young age. Spanish-speaking children, for instance, correctly form the same question – *¿Dónde durmió?* (literally "where sleep?") – from a younger age.

Cultural differences

In addition to these important crosslinguistic differences, there are also significant cross-cultural differences. Children are born into distinct communicative systems around the world. These systems potentially stress different aspects of child-rearing and hold different ideologies concerning language use and what it means to be a "good" child, often resulting in different interactional patterns with and around the infant. Elinor Ochs, for instance, describes how Samoan caregiving patterns differ dramatically from those of most US households. Most notably, young Samoan children are not believed to have individual personalities or control over their behavior; thus, in sharp contrast to common parenting practices in the US, very young children are not expected to initiate talk and their early vocalizations are not interpreted as meaningful attempts to communicate.

Such differences in language socialization practices are apparent at a young age: for instance, in Central American homes, infants' interactions are mostly with multiple social partners, whereas in European-American homes, infants' interactions are mostly with one adult person at a time. In the United States, European-American mothers tend to actively participate in verbal exchanges with their children and place greater attention on

BOX 6.7 **ANALYZING CROSSCULTURAL DIFFERENCES IN CHILDREN'S NARRATIVES**

In addition to investigating crosslinguistic differences in the acquisition of grammar, researchers have also examined crosscultural differences in other aspects of language, such as narratives. As might be expected, the organization, presentation, and content of typical stories vary from one culture to the next. Children learn these culture-specific conventions for narratives through interaction with their parents.

In one study to compare Spanish-speaking mothers from Central America and English-speaking mothers of European-American descent, Gigliana Melzi (2000) sought to determine if there were differences in how the two groups of mothers supported or scaffolded their children's narrative skills. To this end, the researcher visited the mothers and their preschool children in their homes and asked the children to talk about four past events the children had experienced. The exchanges between the mothers and their children were compared on a range of measures.

Melzi concluded that there were significant differences between the two groups of mothers and the ways in which they supported their children's contributions to conversations about past experiences. Thus, while Central American mothers served as active listeners, giving their children more control over the storytelling process and showing less concern for the overall organization of the story, European-American mothers took a more active role in helping the children organize the narrative and include relevant information. As for the reason for this difference, Melzi speculates that it may be due to the socialization goals of the two groups. As she explains, Latino parents typically "place greater emphasis on interpersonal relations and appropriate social demeanor, whereas European-American parents place greater emphasis on autonomy and the development of cognitive skills" (2000: 173).

task-specific goals (like organizing a narrative chronologically) than on social conversational goals (like including all those present in the conversation). (See Box 6.7.) In contrast, in the highly social environments of Latino homes, mothers' roles might be to support children's conversations with others. For example, researchers have reported that Mexican-American family members explicitly instructed preverbal infants to participate in social conversations through the use of *dile* ('tell him/her'). Through these early interactions, children learn to participate in multiparty conversations from a very young age.

This line of research suggests that communication patterns such as these influence children's language and literacy interactions in the classroom as well as their school performance more generally. Shirley Brice Heath, for example, demonstrated how cultural patterns of communication in different communities in the US South prepared children differently for language and literacy tasks at school.

Bilingualism

The final difference in language acquisition to be discussed in this section concerns not *which* languages are being learned, but rather the *number* of languages acquired by a child. In the United States, monolingualism and monolingual child-rearing remains the norm. In many other parts of the world, however, bilingual and multilingual child-rearing are standard. Indeed, it is estimated that roughly half of the world grows up speaking more than one language, a fact which provides the kernel of truth for the joke in Box 6.8.

BOX 6.8 **A NOT-SO FUNNY JOKE...**

Question: What do you call someone who speaks three languages?
Answer: A trilingual.
Question: What to you call someone who speaks two languages?
Answer: A bilingual.
Question: What do you call someone who speaks just one language?
Answer: An American!

Because monolingualism is so prevalent in the United States, there has long been a tendency within the country (but also elsewhere) to view it as the norm or standard, and in some instances, even as desirable. In fact, up until the 1960s, most psychological research tended to support the notion that bilingualism resulted in lower intelligence and diminished cognitive abilities.

This paradigm shifted dramatically with Peal and Lambert's (1962) research among French–English bilinguals in Montreal, Canada. Unlike previous research on bilingualism, these researchers took important steps to ensure that the groups were comparable; so, as an example, the monolinguals and bilinguals tested by Peal and Lambert came from similar social and economic backgrounds. This research, which was subsequently supported by many other investigations, demonstrated that bilinguals outperformed monolinguals on 15 of the 18 variables measuring intelligence. The bilinguals seemed to demonstrate greater **metalinguistic awareness** (knowledge and awareness about language as a system) and mental flexibility, as well as the ability to think more abstractly.

Yet despite the demonstrated benefits of bilingualism, it remains a controversial topic in many contexts. For instance, bilingual education has been a hotly contested political issue in the US (even though decades of research show it to be effective); bilingual parents receive conflicting advice and are often told by teachers and speech pathologists that they should use only one language (typically the language of the school) with their children.

One worrisome aspect of bilingual language acquisition for some parents and teachers is the fact that all bilingual children go through a period of **code-mixing**, that is, they move back and forth between their two languages, seemingly without discrimination. (Code-mixing is generally distinguished from **code-switching**, which consists of *intentional* use of more than one language for symbolic, strategic, or communicative purposes by bilinguals.)

Code-mixing, however, is a normal phase of bilingual language development. It seems to be universal among bilingual children and is apparent even at the babbling stage. Some have argued that code-mixing reflects children's developing grammar and lexical system and the lack of differentiation between the two languages (see the "unitary system hypothesis" below). Code-mixing might also be the result of a child's limited vocabulary (that is, the child may only know the names of some items in one language). More recently, child language researchers have explained code-mixing as early code-switching, demonstrating

BOX 6.9 **CODE-MIXING OR CODE-SWITCHING?**

Lanza (1992) studied two children from Norwegian-American families living in Oslo, Norway, to observe their bilingual language use and code-mixing. Each had an American mother and a Norwegian father with whom the child was to exclusively speak English and Norwegian, respectively, following what is sometimes known as the one-language-one-parent rule. Lanza found that children knew when to use Norwegian and when to use English, and also mixed (or switched between) the two languages in the appropriate situation – that is, the child used English with the mother, Norwegian with the father, and mixed the two when the family was together such as at meal times. This showed that the children were aware of socio-contextual cues for language choice and use.

In reality, the one-language-one-parent rule is not always strictly followed. Lanza found that one family in particular was more lax about the policy and would switch back and forth between the two languages. This tendency to be more lax had implications for the child's language development. In particular, the child tended to prefer Norwegian overall and would speak more Norwegian than English with his mother with whom he was supposed to speak English. This finding could imply that the child was a less than balanced bilingual, but Lanza noted that the child could also have been responding to the parent's code-mixing (or switching). In general, both children tended to mix the two languages with the parent who was less strict about the one-language-one-parent rule. Whether or not the children's mixing was a response to the parent's code-switching or represents less balanced bilingualism is unclear. However, it is clear that bilingual input seems to foster code-mixing, and children are aware of the contexts in which it is appropriate to code-mix (or switch).

that even very young children have the social or strategic competence to move between two languages depending on the conversational context. (See Box 6.9 for Lanza's study on Norwegian and English code-mixing.)

Young children's code-mixes have generated substantial research by sociolinguists and psycholinguists. Psycholinguists in particular have examined early code-mixing with an eye to understanding the nature and organization of the two languages in the brain. Does a bilingual child begin with just one grammar and lexical system that later becomes differentiated as the child learns to distinguish between the two languages? Or does a bilingual child have two grammatical and lexical systems from the outset? The former position is known as the **unitary system hypothesis**, while the latter is referred to as the **separate systems hypothesis**. The primary evidence supporting the unitary system hypothesis is that all young children seem to go through a period of mixing their two languages, particularly at the lexical level. Supporters of the separate systems hypothesis, in turn, point to the fact that even very young children can differentiate between their languages prior to entering into the two-word phase and are often sensitive to their interlocutors' language competences.

As suggested here, research on bilingualism is controversial and complicated. The results of studies are sometimes conflicting, in part because the bilingual population is very diverse. Bilingual child-rearing takes many varied shapes and forms, and bilingualism can be achieved through different routes. For instance, in some homes, parents adhere to the one-person-one-language rule (with, for instance, the mother only speaking Japanese

BOX 6.10 **THE MAGNET-LIKE PULL TOWARDS ENGLISH**

Maintaining a heritage language can be difficult even for the largest of minority languages such as Spanish, which 12 percent of the US population speaks. Rumbaut, Massey, and Bean (2006) examined demographic data from Southern California's large Latino population. Their findings suggest that Mexican immigrants arriving in Southern California today can expect only one in twenty of their great-grandchildren to speak fluent Spanish. As they explain, "Even in the nations' largest Spanish-speaking enclave, within a border region that historically belonged to Mexico, Spanish appears to be well on the way to a natural death by the third generation of US residence."

While Spanish maintenance among the descendants of Mexican and Central American immigrants was slightly higher than among other groups, they still followed the usual pattern of switching to English as the years passed. For instance, among Mexican Americans with two US-born parents (and three or more foreign-born grandparents), only 17 percent spoke fluent Spanish. Among those with only one or two foreign-born grandparents, Spanish fluency was only 7 percent. And only 5 percent of Mexican Americans with US-born parents and US-born grandparents spoke Spanish fluently. As Rumbaut *et al.* observe, their findings illustrate clearly that English is not threatened: "What is endangered instead is the survival of non-English languages that immigrants bring with them to the United States" (2006: 458–459). This study demonstrates that if parents want to maintain their heritage language, they must work very hard to fight against the monolingual trend which favors the larger society's dominant language.

to the child and the father German), also known as Grammont's Principle; in others, both parents engage in extended code-switching and move freely between one language and another; and in still others, children use one language at home and another in their school or community. The amount of exposure to and interaction in each language directly contributes to competency levels. For instance, researchers studied young Spanish–English incipient bilingual children (aged eight months to two and a half years) and found a strong correlation between the amount of interactive exposure and the size of the active vocabulary in each language. While some active lexicon seems to develop with only 20 percent exposure time to the language, much more is needed for a child to become close to equally proficient in both languages.

Research has also demonstrated that children are sensitive to the status of their language in the wider societal context. For instance, many parents in the US who speak a language other than English in the home struggle to promote bilingualism among their children. They often find that once children begin formal schooling, English becomes children's preferred or dominant language. (See Box 6.10 for how this tendency affects minority languages such as Spanish in the US.)

These different language-learning experiences and contexts impact on children's language competencies in important ways. Most children are stronger in one language, and nearly all children tend to associate each language with particular contexts, skills, and activities. As a result, there are in fact relatively few **balanced bilinguals**, or individuals who have identical and native competence in all areas of both languages. This is hardly surprising when we consider that bilinguals tend to use each of their languages for different functions, for example, at home versus at work. The notion that the only "true" bilingual is a perfectly balanced bilingual is misleading. Research points to the fact that bilinguals are not "two monolinguals" in one person, but, rather, individuals whose competencies reflect their particular learning experiences and patterns of language use.

Explaining the data

Now that we have covered some of the central findings concerning language acquisition, we turn to some of the different theories that try to explain *how* children acquire language. In order to be credible or viable, these theories must account for the central facts of child language development discussed above, including:

a. the rapid rate of development;
b. the systematic regularities concerning which items are early or late acquired, as well as the routine errors children make in this process; and
c. how language learning can be accounted for given children's varied environments.

Each of the explanations presented here is embedded in different schools of thought or paradigms within the fields of linguistics and psychology. Below we outline the major tenets of each of these paradigms and describe how each attempts to account for the processes described above.

Behaviorism

One of the early explanations of language acquisition was rooted in behaviorism, a theory that held that language is essentially a habit, a behavior like any other, which is mastered through general learning principles. These principles include imitation, **reinforcement**, and punishment. For instance, a child might imitate a parent's use of the word *duck*. The parent, upon hearing the child's word, might provide positive reinforcement, such as "Yes, it's a duck!" and a smile, or, alternatively, might look away if the child's utterance is not comprehended. In this way, the child's more target-like utterances are rewarded (and thus tend to be repeated) while the non-target-like utterances are "punished" (and thus generally disappear over time). As parents' expectations for their child's language change as the child grows, they alter their reinforcement strategies. Thus, while *da* might be an acceptable rendering of *duck* for a two-year-old (and thus would be reinforced), the use of *da* by a four-year-old might not be deemed appropriate and thus would not be reinforced. Through these general learning mechanisms, the child's utterances are shaped to fit the standards of his/her particular speech community. As B. F. Skinner, a psychologist and one of the main proponents of behaviorism, explained, "a child acquires verbal behavior when relatively unpatterned vocalizations, selectively reinforced, gradually assume forms which produce appropriate consequences in a given verbal community" (1959: 31).

As can be seen from this very simple example, behaviorists tend to focus on observable behaviors rather than internal or innate processes. Accordingly, they assume that children are essentially "interested bystanders," bringing no special abilities or innate mechanisms to bear on the language acquisition process. While this approach has a certain common-sense appeal, behaviorism is no longer the dominant research paradigm in the study of child language. Its downfall began with Noam Chomsky's scathing review of Skinner's book, *Verbal Behavior*. This review heralded the beginning of the "cognitive revolution" and a more innatist approach to language acquisition, to which we turn next.

Nativism

In contrast to behaviorists, nativists hold that language is not the result of general learning mechanisms, but rather is an innate capacity. This special capacity is limited to humans and differs in important ways from any type of animal communication. Nativists rest their argument on several observations. First, nativists point out that all children, barring severe cognitive or physical limitations, acquire language easily and rapidly. Whereas most adults typically struggle for decades to master the complexities of a second or foreign language, nativists note that children reach near mastery of their native tongue in just a few short years, without instruction or any apparent effort. Furthermore, nativists point out that much of the data discussed above shows that all children, regardless of the language they are learning or the quantity or quality of input they receive from their caregivers, acquire their mother tongue at the same rate and by progressing through the same developmental stages. If, as the behaviorists argued, language acquisition was critically dependent on parental reinforcement strategies, why then do we see such striking uniformity?

Secondly, nativists have argued that the adult speech that young children hear is a poor model – filled, for instance, with incomplete sentences, false starts, and slips of the tongue. Nevertheless, children take this fragmentary and "degenerate" input and are able to construct a complex grammar – far more complex than they could have ever learned from reinforcement or general learning mechanisms. (See Box 6.11 for an extension of this argument in an unusual context.) The point that input alone is inadequate to support children's language learning has been referred to as the **poverty-of-the-stimulus** argument.

Thirdly, nativists contend that children rarely receive specific feedback, sometimes referred to as negative evidence, on the grammaticality of their utterances, as adults typically focus on the *content* of a child's utterance rather than its linguistic accuracy. Furthermore, on those rare occasions when adults do provide feedback or explicit language instruction to their children, the children are by and large oblivious to it.

Finally, nativists assert that children create or generate a rule-based system. If children were truly relying upon imitation and reinforcement to learn their native tongue, why then, would they produce such utterances as *He goed to the store* and *We saw mouses today*? Presumably, such sentences never would have been uttered by an adult. Nativists argue that these overregularization errors are evidence that the child is in the process of creating language, testing hypotheses about language, and, in general, acquiring the *rules* of the language.

In short, nativists argue that the only possible explanation for the *uniformity* of the language acquisition process, the *complexity* of the linguistic knowledge children possess

BOX 6.11 **NICARAGUAN SIGN LANGUAGE**

Pidgins, simplified languages that have no native speakers but are used in contexts of (limited) inter-group contact such as trade, have been studied by linguists for decades. In particular, linguists have been interested in how pidgins develop into **creoles** – that is, full-blown, grammatically complex languages that are the mother tongues of their speakers. Linguists have argued that children of pidgin-speaking parents can take the fragmentary input they hear, elaborate upon it, and create a language – a creole – with a complex grammar and a rich vocabulary. Typically, this process of creolization takes many years; however, in the mid 1980s linguists witnessed the very quick emergence of Nicaraguan Sign Language (NSL) among young deaf children in Nicaragua.

Prior to 1970, there was no formal education system in Nicaragua for the deaf. Deaf children were sequestered at home and had little contact with others, as deafness was highly stigmatized. These children, whose parents were often illiterate in Spanish and did not know any sign language, developed "home signs" – simple, idiosyncratic systems for communicating with their hearing relatives. In the late 1970s, however, schools for the deaf were finally established and, for the first time, deaf children met and befriended other deaf children. They were not taught sign language at the school, though: the official policy was to teach them to lipread and fingerspell Spanish words. The children, however, developed their own system of communication – a kind of pidgin sign language that incorporated elements of the home signs and contained a rudimentary grammar of rules for stringing those signs together. The children did not learn the grammar from their teachers, as the teachers did not know any sign languages; nor had they learned it from their nonsigning parents or from books.

Sign language experts visited Nicaragua in the 1980s to study the children. They found that the older signers were actually *less fluent* (used less complex signs, signed more slowly or hesitantly) than the younger signers – those children who had entered the school at a later date and learned more recently. For instance, older children signed for manner and path of motion events simultaneously while younger, more fluent children signed manner and path sequentially. Thus, as the younger children learned the language in the 1980s and 1990s, this type of segmented and sequenced construction very quickly became the preferred way of communicating motion events. In other words, in an unusually short period of time, NSL had developed into a full and complex system, complete with the meaning-packed combinatorial systems that are the hallmark of language.

at such young ages despite the *scarcity* of the feedback they receive, and the *generative* nature of language itself – is that language must be innate. More specifically, language is claimed to be a species-specific or uniquely human cognitive capacity which is the result of an innate **language acquisition device** (sometimes referred to as "the LAD"). Although the location and content of the LAD remains a topic of debate (neurologists have identified multiple areas of the brain responsible for the perception, comprehension, and production of language), the LAD is supposedly what allows children to attend to language and develop an appropriate grammar quickly, without effort, and with no specialized input.

There is, however, according to some researchers, a time limit, also known as a **critical** or **sensitive period**, for this process to take place, and evidence suggests that after this period has ended (typically around puberty), complete acquisition of a first or second language becomes difficult, if not impossible. Nativists often point to feral children such as Genie as evidence of such a critical period. Genie was raised from a very young age in a state of linguistic (as well as emotional and physical) deprivation and never gained age-appropriate competence in her first language.

The nativist approach to language learning has been a major force within the field of linguistics (and beyond). However, in recent years it has come under increasing attack and criticism from several directions on both theoretical and empirical grounds. One line of attack has come from proponents of connectionism; another, more empirical attack comes from proponents of social interactionism.

Connectionism

Nativists argue that the linguistic input children receive is not rich enough to support the extraction of complex linguistic generalizations; therefore, children must by necessity be endowed with an innate knowledge of linguistic rules that guide the language acquisition process. Connectionists challenge this argument. Specifically, they contend that general learning mechanisms – such as sensitivity to distributional patterns in the input – are sufficient for at least some aspects of language acquisition, including syntax.

This approach, also variously known as the "information processing approach" or a **parallel distributed processing (PDP)** approach, generally holds that processing is carried out by nodes (roughly analogous to neurons) that are connected to other nodes in a network by pathways that vary in their strength. While the exact architecture of these networks is beyond the scope of this chapter, the key characteristic of these networks is that they do not contain knowledge of symbolic rules. Rather, they have the ability to make associations based on regularities they detect in the input.

For example, whereas nativists have argued that children's overgeneralization of the regular past-tense ending (such as *Lucas goed* or *Isaac holded the baby ducks*) is evidence that children have knowledge of an abstract rule which they apply (initially, a bit overzealously) to verbs, connectionists argue that it is not necessary to assume that children's linguistic knowledge is based on any innate rules. Rather, they argue that children can learn the regularities of the language through an inductive process based on exposure to many examples.

To support these claims, connectionists have created computer models (also called neural networks). These models are typically fed linguistic input (for example, a certain number of verbs and their past tenses) and then asked to produce output for a novel form (e.g. generate the past tense of WALK or SING). Rumelhart and McClelland (1986), for example, reported that their neural network learned to produce the correct past tense for both regular (e.g. WALK) and irregular (e.g. SING) verbs. These networks contained no *a priori* knowledge of linguistic rules, but rather exhibited rule-like behavior after having been exposed to many examples.

Connectionist models have been criticized for, among other things, only addressing a small aspect of language acquisition (typically syntax) and for task veridicality (i.e. the conditions in which networks are fed input differ from those in which children are exposed to language). However, the increasing sophistication of connectionist models will, if nothing else, motivate linguists to reconsider the nativist approach to language acquisition.

Social interactionism

In contrast to the nativists (who emphasize the importance of innate linguistic knowledge) and the connectionists (who stress the role of general learning mechanisms), social inter-actionists point to the importance of child–caregiver interactions in the language acquisition process. Although social interactionists generally do not deny the existence of some type of LAD, they tend to minimize its importance and instead stress the role of the **LASS (language acquisition support system)** in explaining child language acquisition.

Social interactionists have focused on the characteristics of the language used within these interactions, and, in particular, on **child-directed speech** (**CDS**, also known as *motherese* or *baby talk*). Caregivers, when interacting with children, tend to use a special form of speech – including short, simple sentences with higher pitch and exaggerated intonation, as well as sentences focused on the objects and events in the child's immediate environment. Caregiver speech may also include increased use of diminutives (e.g. *doggie* or *kittie*), as well as repetition and imitation. In addition, caregivers of young children may also use recasts – more target-like reformulations of the child's original ungrammatical utterance – to help the child master more complex language forms. This type of speech, while varying in shape and form and not used in all speech communities in the same way, is believed to help attract the child's attention to problematic forms and to actively involve him/her in the conversation.

For social interactionists, important parts of the LASS are the daily contacts and emotional bonds a child has with his/her caregivers while being played with, fed, and bathed. Even before they are capable of producing speech, children can interact with their care-givers in these interactions (for example, through eye gaze and smiles). Through these interactions and ritualized patterns of language use (such as *peekaboo* and *Where's baby?*), children gradually learn about turn-taking and become aware of the communicative nature of language. Children begin to recognize the language patterns that are produced within these interactions and are eventually able to produce them on their own. As children become more adept at communicating these patterns, their caregivers in turn are prompted to use more complex language forms, facilitating more mature and sophisticated interactions. In this way, the caregiver supports, or scaffolds, the child's emerging linguistic system. Of course, the nature of this parental support and the types of scaffolding provided to children vary across cultures (see Box 6.7).

Researchers working within the social interactionist paradigm have sought to determine the relationship between these interactions and children's language development. They argue that **child-directed speech** seems to be especially geared to facilitate language learning (see Box 6.12). Social interactionists tend to disagree with nativists about the nature of children's input and specifically take issue with the poverty-of-stimulus argument. In particular, they point to the fact that while parents do not "teach grammar" in any formal way, children receive many types of feedback about the effectiveness of their language every time they speak, and this effectiveness is related to the grammatical correctness of their utterances. Furthermore, while nativists have tended to focus on the acquisition of syntax and morphology, researchers who have focused on other areas, such as vocabulary development, have documented the frequency of the language input that children receive (in terms of words per hour) and shown a clear relationship between the language which children hear and the language which they produce.

However, as with the other approaches discussed so far in this chapter, social interactionism has also had its fair share of criticism, including an inadequate focus on how children learn the structure of the language. Nevertheless, this approach, with its emphasis on the social aspect of language learning, may have important contributions to make to a more complete theory of first language acquisition.

What's at stake in the child language debate?

As noted at the outset of this chapter, what is at stake in the study of child language acquisition is not only our grasp of how children acquire language, but also our understanding of the human mind and how it works. Within psychology (and many other fields), there has been a very long-standing debate concerning the relative importance of *nature* and *nurture* in human development, with the naturists stressing the importance of biological and genetic programming and the nurturists pointing to the role of the environment. In terms of language acquisition theory, the nativists, of course, sit on the "nature" side. The behaviorists belong on the far end of the "nurture" side of this debate. While there is growing agreement that both *nature* and *nurture* are critical, scientists disagree on the relative importance of each.

In addition to informing the debate on nature vs. nurture, the study of language acquisition raises many important and interesting questions about the specifics of brain organization and function. Is there a region of the brain which is dedicated to the task of acquiring language? If so, this would support a modular view of the human mind. Can other species learn language? If so, this would undermine many claims that the human mind is unique. Other questions, such as whether there is a critical period for language acquisition, how large a role input and feedback play in the language acquisition process,

BOX 6.12 **PET TALK VS. BABY TALK**

Speech addressed to babies and to animals is commonly perceived as special and similar; there may be higher pitch, exaggerated intonation, and "special" words (e.g. *baby-waby, putty tat*). The first research to actually test this perception, in 2002, compared speech addressed to animals and to infants. In this study, the researchers compared the speech of twelve mothers (all native speakers of Australian English) to their six-month-old infants and to their pets (cats or dogs) while engaged in a conversation using a toy sheep, a shoe, and a toy shark as props. The mothers' speech was measured along three dimensions: (1) pitch, (2) affect (the amount of positive emotion in the voice), and (3) vowel hyperarticulation (overemphasizing the vowel by lengthening it). The researchers found that the mothers used a higher pitch and more affect while speaking to infants and pets than to adults. In addition, they found that the mothers used significantly more vowel hyperarticulation with their infants than with either their pets or other adults. Burnham *et al.* concluded that the greater use of vowel hyperarticulation could be interpreted as didactic: the mothers were sensitive to their infants' linguistic potential and thus altered their language to reflect this. As the researchers explained, "speakers are sensitive to their audience, both in regard to acoustic preferences and emotional needs, and in terms of potential linguistic ability."

(Burnham *et al.* 2002: 1435)

and crosscultural differences in language acquisition, all have implications for our understanding of the human mind.

Finally, the study of child language acquisition is related to our understanding of language as a system. How we understand and explain child language acquisition is interwoven with researchers' conceptions of language. For instance, researchers who view language as a system of abstract rules for generating an infinite number of sentences find evidence that children are developing rule-systems. In turn, researchers who conceptualize language as a broader communicative system which varies culturally tend to focus, for instance, on children's mastery of pragmatic competence appropriate to their speech community. In this way, the study of child language acquisition is intimately connected with different approaches to the study of language more generally.

CHAPTER SUMMARY

There are many methods for studying how children acquire languages – including diary studies, experiments, and observational methods. All of these have helped researchers gain a better understanding of the stages that children pass through on their way to mastering their native language. Many of these stages – such as the one-word and two-word stages – appear to be universal; however, there are important crosslinguistic and crosscultural variations that need to be taken into account in any theory of first language acquisition. Although to date no complete theory has successfully dealt with all aspects of language acquisition, the theories of nativism, behaviorism, connectionism, and social interactionism each have important insights to contribute to our understanding of children's language development.

The study of first language acquisition is a dynamic field with many unanswered and exciting questions awaiting further research. Which theory (or which combination of theories) best accounts for children's development of language? How much crosslinguistic and crosscultural variation exists in language acquisition? How can arriving at more complete answers to these questions inform our understanding of the human mind? Although these questions are far from being answered, future research will bring us closer to solving the puzzle.

Exercises

EXERCISE 6.1

Examine the following conversation between a father and his two-year-old son, Trevor, while they are playing with blocks. What is the MLU of the child's utterances? (Refer to Box 6.5 for details on how to compute this.) According to Brown, at what stage of development is this child?

Father:	whatcha doing munch?
Child:	hi.
Father:	whatcha doing?
Child:	let's play dis.
Child:	let's play dis together.
Father:	play this together?
Child:	let's play together.
Father:	okay.
Child:	ride you up.

Child:	airplane.
Child:	ooom. (onomatopoeia)
Child:	land in duh water.
Father:	gonna land on the water?
Child:	yeah
Father:	like the ones out there?
Child:	yep.
Father:	oh, here comes one right now.
Father:	o:h.
Father:	here he comes.
Father:	what's he doing?
Child:	um he's flying away.
Child:	babye airplane.

(Source: CHILDES database, Demetras1:tre01.cha.
Full conversation available http://childes.psy.cmu.edu/data/Eng-USA/)

EXERCISE 6.2

Using both the conversation below (between a mother and her 2;2 son, Jimmy) and the conversation provided in Exercise 1, what do you notice about the parents' responding strategies to their children? How would you describe their interactional strategies or styles? What significance might this have for language acquisition?

Child:	cheese lada (family-specific form)
Mother:	cheese lada (family-specific form)
Mother:	and what else?
Child:	an wice.
Mother:	rice!
Child:	I get [//] I (w)ann(a) get cheese &la
Mother:	he knows you want a cheese enchilada. . .
Mother:	what is this?
Mother:	is that a bolt?
Child:	uh huh.
Mother:	yeah.
Child:	dis can . . .
Mother:	well try it.
Mother:	there!
Mother:	what color is that wrench?
Child:	xxx.
Child:	&o orange.
Mother:	orange.
Mother:	yeah.
Mother:	is that your favorite color?
Child:	I like black chelly beans.
Mother:	you like black jelly beans?
Mother:	that's what Uncle Ace likes, isn't it?

(Source: CHILDES database)

EXERCISE 6.3

In the table below, look at the children's uses of words and their referents, that is, the objects which those words are used to refer to. What features or characteristics of the objects or events do the children appear to be relying on in their uses of these words?

Word		Referents
(a)	chair	chair, sofa, bench, window seat, car seat, bed
(b)	computer	laptop computer, desk where computer usually sits (even if computer is not there)
(c)	leaf	leaf or leaves, grass, moss, green carpet, green towel, spinach, lettuce, avocado

EXERCISE 6.4

The following are examples of children's pronunciations of common English nouns. How do they differ from the standard adult pronunciation? Are there any sounds or sound sequences that seem to be particularly difficult? What patterns are evident in the children's pronunciations?

Word	Pronunciation	Word	Pronunciation
bottle	[baba]	key	[ti]
butterfly	[bʌfai]	duck	[gʌk]
tub	[bʌb]	water	[wawa]
baby	[bibi]	stop	[tɔp]
tree	[ti]	blanket	[bæki]
candy	[kæki]	doggie	[gɔgi]
banana	[nænə]	this	[dɪs]

SUGGESTIONS FOR FURTHER READING

Brown, R. 1973, *A first language: the early stages*, Cambridge, MA: Harvard University Press. This classic work on first language acquisition documents the language development of the three young children Adam, Eve, and Sarah in close detail.

Hart, B. and Risley, T. R. 1995, *Meaningful differences in the everyday experience of young American children*, Baltimore, MD: Paul H. Brookes. This book, authored by two prominent behaviorists, analyzes family language use patterns in forty-two homes over a two-year period. They report that there were many differences in the quantity and quality of talk which young children heard in different homes and that these differences were closely linked to significant differences in children's rate of vocabulary development and IQ test scores.

King, K. and Mackey, A. 2007, *The bilingual edge: why, how and when to teach your child a second language*. New York: HarperCollins. This popular-audience book reviews current research on bilingualism, second language teaching, and bilingual child-rearing.

Lust, B. C. and Foley, C. (eds.) 2003, *First language acquisition: the essential readings*, Cambridge, MA: MIT Press. This is a collection of twenty-nine classic papers, mostly dating from the late 1950s to the 1980s.

Pinker, S. 1999, *Words and rules: the ingredients of language*, New York: Basic Books. This engaging book examines the acquisition and use of regular and irregular verbs in great detail, arguing that the nativist approach is more powerful than connectionist models in fitting and explaining the data.

Plunkett, K. (ed.) 1998, *Language acquisition and connectionism*, Hove, UK: Psychology Press. This collection of papers from a special issue of *Language and Cognitive Processes* provides a good overview of language acquisition from a connectionist perspective.

Slobin, D. I. (ed.) 1985–1997, *The crosslinguistic study of language acquisition*, vols. 1–5, Hillsdale, NJ: Lawrence Erlbaum. This five-volume set presents studies of language acquisition among children from all over the world.

Schieffelin, B. B. 1990, *The give and take of everyday life: language socialization of Kaluli children*, New York: Cambridge University Press. This anthropologically and ethnographically oriented book describes and analyzes language socialization and language learning processes among Kaluli children in Papua New Guinea.

7 Language and the brain

CHAPTER PREVIEW

Language is rooted in the biology of the brain. Therefore understanding the biology of language is critical to understanding language itself. The vast majority of research on the biological bases of language has focused on brain anatomy, mainly attempting to identify which parts of the brain underlie which language functions, such as lexical or grammatical abilities. However, the biology of language can also be investigated at many other levels, from cells to molecules to genes. Moreover, the study of all these aspects of biology must be complemented by and integrated with **psycholinguistic** studies of how language is actually used as we speak and understand; with investigations of language acquisition; and with the theoretical linguistic examination of the architecture of language. Taken together, these provide an insight into the ultimate goal of understanding the **biocognitive** or **neurocognitive** bases of language. This in turn should eventually shed light on higher-level aspects of language use, such as discourse, historical change, dialect variation, and reading and writing, as well as important applications like language teaching and computer models of language.

This chapter is organized as follows:

- The first section summarizes the biology of the brain, from anatomical structures down through neurons to molecules and genes.
- Next we introduce four broad questions in the study of the biology of language: (1) What are the biological substrates of language learning, knowledge, and processing? That is, which anatomical structures, molecules, genes, and so on underlie language? (2) What are the biotemporal dynamics of language processing? That is, what does the movie of the biological substrates of language during real-time language processing actually look like? (3) Do different language functions depend on distinct biological substrates? In other words, are language functions separable? (4) Are the biological substrates of language dedicated exclusively to language (domain-specific), or do they also underlie nonlanguage functions (domain-general)?
- Once we know the questions, we can discuss methods for seeking their answers. The third section explains the importance of converging evidence, and describes the primary methods that are used to study the biology of language: the lesion method; hemodynamic neuroimaging, with a focus on functional Magnetic Resonance Imaging (fMRI); Event-Related Potentials (ERPs); magnetoencephalography (MEG); direct brain recording and stimulation; and Transcranial Magnetic Stimulation (TMS).
- The fourth section covers a wide range of evidence on the biology of language, and discusses theoretical explanations that have been proposed to account for this evidence.
- Finally, we conclude with a summary of the chapter, and a brief look at the wide-open future of the study of the biology of language.

GOALS

The goals of this chapter are to:

- provide a summary of the biology of the brain
- introduce the main questions in the study of the biology of language
- explain the primary methods used to investigate the biology of language
- present an overview of the evidence on the biology of language, and the theoretical explanations that have been proposed to account for this evidence

The biology of the brain

Before asking questions about the biological bases of language in the brain, we must first understand the biology of the brain. So let's take a brief tour of brain anatomy, and of the cellular and molecular substrates of brain function.

The cerebrum

The largest part of the brain, and the most important for cognition, is the **cerebrum** (Figure 7.1). The cerebrum is composed of two **hemispheres**, which are more or less mirror images of each other. Each hemisphere can be broken down into four lobes: the frontal lobe, temporal lobe, parietal lobe, and occipital lobe (Figure 7.1). Additionally, each

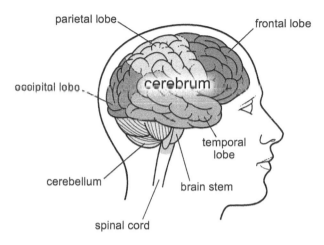

Figure 7.1 The brain. Each hemisphere of the cerebrum is composed of four lobes. Below the cerebrum at the back of the head is the cerebellum, which also contains two hemispheres

hemisphere contains multiple smaller **anatomical structures** known as **gyri** (singular: **gyrus**) and **sulci** (singular: **sulcus**). The gyri are the ridges and plateaus on the convoluted surface of the brain, and the sulci are the valleys and canyons that lie between them (Figure 7.2). There is sufficient consistency across different human brains in the topography of these structures to allow the structures to be given specific names, such as the *inferior frontal gyrus*, or the *superior temporal sulcus*. Although these terms may seem strange at first, they are important to remember because they provide us with a clear way to refer to the structures, in much the same way that geographical terms allow one to refer unambiguously to different regions on the earth's surface. However, it is important to emphasize that human brains are not all exactly the same, and in fact there are substantial **individual differences** with respect to the precise location and shape of each gyrus and sulcus.

Many of the names of the gyri and sulci contain terms like "superior" and "inferior" that are used to refer to different directions in the brain. That is, just as we use convenient terms like north, south, east, and west to refer to different geographical directions, so there are terms to indicate the different anatomical directions in the brain. **Superior** means up, **inferior** means down, **anterior** means in front of, and **posterior** means behind. Thus the superior temporal gyrus is above the middle temporal gyrus, which in turn is above the inferior temporal gyrus (Figure 7.2). Additionally, **lateral** means toward the outside of the brain on either side (i.e. toward either side of the head), whereas **medial** means toward the middle of the head, from each side – that is, toward the place where the two hemispheres meet. Finally, one can use the term **ventral** to refer to the bottom of the brain, and **dorsal** to refer to the top of the brain.

The cerebral cortex and its neurons

Each cerebral hemisphere is covered all the way around (both laterally and medially) with **cortex**. The term comes from the Latin word for 'bark,' since it is essentially the bark – the

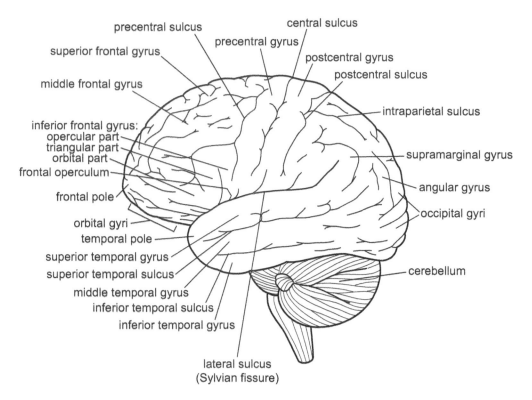

Figure 7.2 A lateral view of anatomical structures in the left hemispheres of the cerebrum and the cerebellum. The same structures are found on the right side

outermost portion – of the brain. Cerebral cortex contains nerve cells, or **neurons**. The brain contains tens or even hundreds of billions of neurons, which are highly interconnected. Cognitive as well as lower-level brain function emerges from the **biochemical** and **electrochemical** activation and interaction of multiple neurons.

A prototypical neuron is shown in Figure 7.3. Electrochemical nerve impulses originate in the dendrites and cell body, and are conducted along the axon to the axon terminals. The myelin insulation around the axon improves the transmission speed of the nerve impulses. When an impulse arrives at an axon terminal, it results in the release of molecules called **neurotransmitters**, which cross the **synapse** between the axon terminal of the originating neuron and the dendrites and cell body of another neuron. The neurotransmitters then bind to receptor molecules on the receiving neurons, which may cause that neuron in turn to generate its own nerve impulse.

Because the dendrites and cell bodies tend to be grayish in actual brains, the cerebral cortex and other tissue that contains them is called gray matter. In contrast, the myelin-covered axons that connect the various gray matter structures are white, because myelin is made of fat. Therefore the tissue in the brain that contains bundles of axons is called white matter.

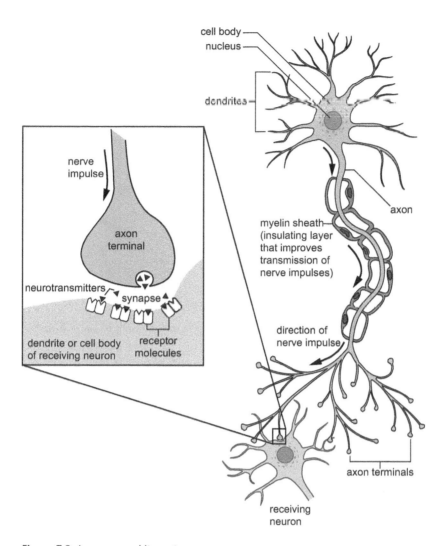

Figure 7.3 A neuron and its parts

Cytoarchitectonics: the distribution of neurons in the cortex

There are many types of neurons in the cerebral cortex, and different regions of cortex differ in the types of neurons they contain, as well as in the neurons' distribution across cortical layers. This allows us to differentiate brain regions with respect to these differences in their cellular makeup – that is, with respect to their **cytoarchitectonics**. The simplest distinction is that between **neocortex** – which contains six neuronal layers, and is found in almost all of the cerebrum except for certain medial temporal lobe regions – and evolutionarily older forms of cortex, which contain fewer neuronal layers, and are found in these medial temporal regions.

Finer-grained cytoarchitectonic distinctions between cortical regions, including within neocortex, can also be made. Moreover, particular cytoarchitectonic regions are found in

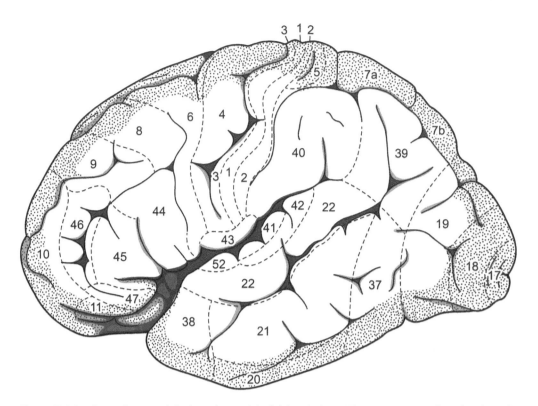

Figure 7.4 Brodmann's areas of the lateral part of the left hemisphere. The same areas are found in the right hemisphere. Not shown are the Brodmann's areas of the medial part of the cerebrum

more or less the same location in the cerebrum in different people. Thanks to this consistency, these regions can serve as anatomical landmarks. Although different ways of mapping cytoarchitectonic regions have been developed, by far the most widely used cytoarchitectonic mapping system today is that developed by Korbinian Brodmann in the early 1900s (Brodmann 1909) (Figure 7.4). Each **Brodmann's area** (also referred to simply as **BA**) has a different cytoarchitectonic makeup (i.e. each contains somewhat different neuron types or distributions of neurons), and each has a different anatomical location in the cerebrum. Note, however, that since most of the methods used in the study of the biology of language (see below) provide only structural anatomical information, with no cytoarchitectonic information at all, claims regarding the cytoarchitectonic basis of language (e.g. "grammar can be localized to BA 44") must be taken only as approximations.

The cerebellum, subcortical structures, and networks in the brain

Most studies of the brain basis of higher cognitive functions, including language, have focused on cortical regions of the cerebrum, especially lateral neocortical regions, as shown in Figures 7.2 and 7.4. However, it has become increasingly clear that other brain structures also play roles in language. The **cerebellum**, which lies below the cerebrum at the back of

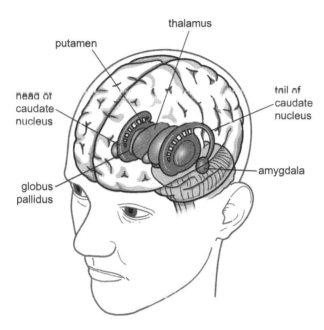

Figure 7.5 A whole-head view of some subcortical structures, including the basal ganglia. In each hemisphere, the basal ganglia consist of several substructures, of which the caudate nucleus, putamen, and globus pallidus are indicated here

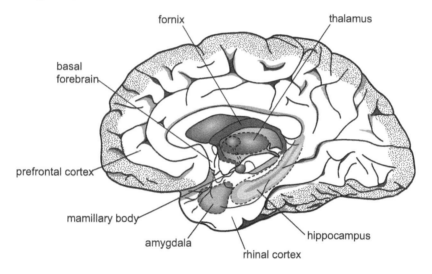

Figure 7.6 A medial view of the cerebrum, including the hippocampus and various structures to which it is closely connected

the head (see Figure 7.1), used to be thought of as a structure important only for movement. However, accumulating evidence also implicates the cerebellum in language, memory, emotion, and other cognitive domains. There are also a number of **subcortical structures** deep inside the cerebrum itself (Figures 7.5 and 7.6). Whereas these gray matter structures, which include the **basal ganglia** and the **hippocampus**, were previously thought to be mainly involved in domains such as movement and memory, recent evidence, as we will see below, suggests they are also important for language.

Finally, it is important to keep in mind that no part of the brain acts on its own. Rather, the brain is made up of *networks* of structures that work together to solve problems. It is therefore important to identify the entire network, or *system*, that accomplishes a given set of functions, as well as how each of its parts contributes to those functions.

Questions about the biology of language

There are many questions that we might ask about the biology of language. Here we focus on four broad issues, all of which have been and continue to be major areas of research: biological substrates, biotemporal dynamics, separability, and domain specificity.

Biological substrates: what are the biological bases of language?

What anatomical structures, cytoarchitectonic regions, brain networks, neuron types, neurotransmitters, hormones, genes, and other biological substrates does language depend on, and what specific functional roles in language does each one play? The biological underpinnings of language are interesting in their own right, but they are also likely to shed light on the processing and representation of language. For example, the existence of distinct biological correlates for different aspects of language, such as lexical and syntactic processing, clearly has implications for the structure of language. Moreover, because evidence suggests that important language and nonlanguage functions depend on common neurocognitive substrates, which work similarly across these different domains, our vast *independent* knowledge of the brain and its role in other cognitive functions is likely to lead to novel predictions about *language* – predictions that would be far less likely to be entertained in the isolated study of language alone.

Although the biological substrates of language can be investigated at many levels, the **functional neuroanatomy** of language has been by far the most intensively examined. The goal here is to *map*, or **localize**, particular language functions to particular brain regions. The most common approach is to map language and other cognitive functions to anatomical structures such as specific gyri or sulci in one or the other hemisphere (or **bilaterally**, i.e. on both sides). Although the vast majority of studies of the brain bases of language have focused on neuroanatomy, one can also examine other biological substrates of language, including the types of neurons, neurotransmitters, and receptors involved in language. Each type has a particular regional distribution in the brain. For example, the neurotransmitter dopamine is especially prevalent in frontal cortex, the basal ganglia, and certain other structures. Therefore one can also *localize* the types of neurons, neurotransmitters, and receptors that underlie language. **Hormones** also have a strong influence on brain functioning, again with particular effects in particular brain regions. For example, estrogen plays a key role in learning in the hippocampus. Importantly, because much is known about the biology of the cells and molecules in the brain, and their roles in nonlanguage functions in animals as well as humans, one can make novel predictions about their potential roles in language – including their **pharmacological** (drug) effects, which are especially important for the remediation of language disorders.

Finally, interest in the genetics of language has increased dramatically in recent years. Different alleles (versions) of the same gene vary in their functionality (e.g. different alleles for a receptor gene may differ in their ability to bind a given neurotransmitter), often resulting in subtle differences well within the normal range. The field of **behavioral genetics** takes advantage of such variation to examine the genetic basis of differences in linguistic (and other cognitive) functions between individuals or groups. Twin studies test whether language abilities are more highly correlated for identical twins, who share 100 percent of their genetic material, than for fraternal twins, who share, on average, only 50 percent of their genetic material. Such a pattern would suggest that genetic factors do indeed affect these abilities. Similarly, in adoption studies one examines the relative strength of correlations between adopted children and their biological relatives on the one hand, and between these children and their adoptive relatives on the other. Linkage studies and association studies use a variety of techniques to identify the actual regions of chromosomes, or even the genes themselves, that are associated with a particular language function or dysfunction. It is even possible to reveal exactly *how* genes and their mutations lead to particular behaviors. For example, some genes are known to code for specific neurotransmitter receptors, which in turn can be shown to underlie language or other cognitive domains.

Biotemporal dynamics: what does the movie of brain activity during language use look like?

It's one thing to tie language functions to particular brain structures, or even to specific cells, molecules, or genes. But we also want to know how these biological substrates are used as one is actually producing or comprehending language. The **spatiotemporal dynamics** of language processing takes into account not only the anatomy of language, but also its real-time temporal interplay, i.e. which structures are activated when, and in what order. Thus to know the spatiotemporal dynamics of language processing is essentially to know the movie of brain activity through time. For example, studies have begun to reveal the storyboard of brain activity as one names pictures, processes syntax, or produces English past-tense forms (see Figure 7.11). More generally, the **biotemporal dynamics** of language refers to the real-time biology of language processing, reflecting the real-time interplay not only of the brain structures underlying language, but also of the cellular, molecular, and even genetic bases of this domain.

Separability: do different language functions depend on different biological substrates?

A major question in the study of language is whether different language functions depend on distinct or common biocognitive substrates. This question tends to divide researchers into contrasting camps of "splitters" and "lumpers." The splitters argue that different aspects of language depend on distinct biocognitive correlates. Over the years, various researchers have suggested a wide range of language splits, including grammar vs. lexicon, morphology vs. syntax, syntactic knowledge vs. syntactic processing, and lexical acquisition vs. lexical knowledge. According to the splitters, these various linguistic domains or functions are **separable**. That is, each one depends largely on its own biocognitive substrates, which can operate for the most part independently of the substrates of other language functions. In contrast, lumpers deny separability, and instead suggest that different aspects of language share common neurocognitive correlates.

Of course many intermediate positions can be taken between the far-lumpers and the far-splitters. For example, one view admits the existence of distinct biocognitive substrates, but argues that these interact to such an extent that they are functionally inseparable with respect to their role in many language functions (McClelland and Patterson 2002). Another view claims that there exists a major split between stored lexicalized knowledge and the grammatical composition of complex structures, and that this split holds over several linguistic domains, including syntax and morphology (Ullman 2001).

Domain specificity: are the biological substrates of language dedicated exclusively to language?

Are the biological substrates that underlie language dedicated exclusively to this cognitive capacity – that is are they **domain-specific**? Or are they domain-general in that they *also* underlie other, nonlanguage, functions? This issue is related to but distinct from the issue of separability. In the case of separability, we are asking whether two or more aspects of *language*, such as lexical and grammatical abilities, rely on the same or different substrates. In contrast, here we are asking whether language depends on substrates that also underlie *nonlanguage* functions, such as attention, memory, or movement.

Just as with separability, here too we find lumpers and splitters, as well as those in between. The far-splitters argue that language, or specific language functions, depend on substrates that are dedicated solely to these functions (Fodor 1983; Grodzinsky 2000; van der Lely 2005). The far-lumpers argue instead that there is nothing special at all about language, and that all aspects of language depend on domain-general systems or mechanisms (Elman *et al.* 1996; McClelland *et al.* 1986; Seidenberg 1997). In between we find a number of positions, such as the suggestion that lexicalized knowledge and grammatical composition depend on distinct brain systems that each underlie a particular type of memory (Ullman 2001).

Finally, it is important to keep in mind that the question of domain-specificity is distinct from that of another issue, that of **species-specificity**. In the case of domain-specificity, we are asking whether language depends on neurocognitive substrates that also underlie other functions *in humans*. In the case of species-specificity, we are asking whether language, or particular language abilities, depends on substrates that also exist in *other* animals, even if they underlie somewhat different functions. For example, it has been argued that recursion is uniquely human (but possibly dependent on domain-general mechanisms in humans), whereas other aspects of language, such as learning concepts, may rely on substrates that are also found in other species (Hauser *et al.* 2002). Note that demonstrating that a nonhuman species can carry out a particular human function (e.g. recursion) does *not* mean that this species is using the same biocognitive substrates as humans to perform the function, since many tasks can be carried out by more than one mechanism or system in the brain.

BOX 7.1 **DISSOCIATIONS**

The *separability* of two functions is generally examined by testing for **dissociations** between the biocognitive correlates (e.g. brain activity) of these functions. In a "single dissociation," one of the functions being tested is more strongly associated with a particular biocognitive correlate than is the other. For example, greater neural activity in a specific brain region may be found for grammatical than for lexical processing, or damage to this region may result in greater grammatical than lexical impairments. However, single dissociations do not necessarily suggest that the two functions actually depend on different substrates. Rather, one function or task might simply be more difficult. For example, if lexical processing simply requires fewer brain resources than grammatical processing, or if the lexical task is easier than the task probing grammar, one might find less activation and fewer impairments for the lexical than the grammatical task, even if the two depend on the same neural correlates.

Double dissociations largely avoid this problem. In a double dissociation, one function is associated with one biocognitive substrate, while another function is associated with another substrate. For example, one region might be more active during grammatical than lexical processing, while another region shows greater activation for lexical than for grammatical processing. Similarly, damage to one brain structure may cause greater grammatical impairments, while damage to another structure causes greater lexical deficits. In these cases it is difficult to argue that one or the other function or task is too easy, since each yielded greater activation and impairments than the other. Thus double dissociations suggest separability. *However*, exactly *which* functions are separable might not be clear. Thus if the tasks probing lexicon and grammar differ not just in their dependence on lexicon and grammar, but *also* in other ways (e.g. in semantics and phonology), then these factors rather than lexicon and grammar may actually explain the double dissociation. Therefore careful experimental design controlling for all potential confounding factors is critical.

What if one does *not* find any dissociations? On the one hand, a lack of dissociations might be taken to suggest a lack of separability. Indeed, such a conclusion is often drawn. However, in science the lack of a difference (a "null result") cannot easily be taken to imply that there is in fact no difference. Rather, one might be using the wrong tasks, the wrong methods, not analyzing the data appropriately, and so on. For example, the method might not be sensitive enough to detect the different brain regions involved, or the tasks might not actually properly test lexical or grammatical abilities.

Methods in the study of the biology of language

How can we answer the questions laid out above? Although the options were more restricted ten or twenty years ago, today a wide range of methods are available. However, none is perfect, and each method has a different set of strengths and weaknesses. Researchers try to choose the most appropriate techniques for answering a given question. For example, some methods are better at localizing functions in the brain, while others are better at revealing the time courses of these processes. Researchers try to obtain **converging evidence** from more than one method – ideally from a whole range of methods – since findings from multiple methods that all point to the same conclusion are more convincing than findings from any single approach.

Here we will briefly examine some methods that are currently widely used in the study of brain and language, as well as some that have thus far been employed primarily in other areas of cognitive neuroscience, but promise to become increasingly relevant in the study of language. Note that this is not an exhaustive list; other approaches include near-infrared spectroscopy (NIRS) and a wide range of techniques for identifying the molecular substrates of cognition.

Biological methods must be complemented by behavioral and computational approaches. A wide range of psycholinguistic measurements can shed light on some of the questions above. For example, reaction times of spoken or manual responses, or the locations and timing of eye movements during reading, can elucidate questions of temporal dynamics and separability. Similarly, evidence from theoretical linguistics (e.g. acceptability judgments) can shed light on issues of separability as well as representation. Computational modeling of the neural and cognitive bases of language can demonstrate the plausibility of hypothesized mechanisms at various levels of investigation (e.g. from molecular mechanisms on up), and can lead to important new predictions. Ideally, researchers obtain and evaluate all of these types of data, together with the sorts of neural evidence described below, producing a multifaceted perspective, and the widest possible array of potential converging evidence.

The lesion method

If a person suffers from brain damage, and then loses the ability to do certain things, one might reasonably infer that the lost functions depended on the damaged structures. For example, if lesions to particular temporal lobe structures consistently lead to impairments of lexical processing, one may infer that these structures are necessary for lexical processing. The identification of such structure–function correspondences underlies the basic logic of the lesion method.

Until recently, the lesion method was the only approach that was widely used in the study of the brain bases of language. Although it may seem somewhat crude, it can be used to test for separability, domain-specificity, and localization, and it has led to important advances in our understanding of language. The lesion approach is still commonly employed today, not just to infer normal brain function, but also to understand the consequences of a variety of neural insults. It is used, first of all, with patients who have **acute** damage, such as stroke victims, head trauma patients, or in cases where specific portions of the brain have been surgically removed to remove tumors or other diseased tissue (e.g. the famous patient H.M.). In addition, the method is used to study progressive neurological dysfunction, such as in **Alzheimer's disease**, **Parkinson's disease**, **Huntington's disease**, and other adult-onset **neurodegenerative diseases**. In some of these disorders the degeneration in early stages of the disease is quite limited to specific brain structures (e.g. the basal ganglia in Hungtington's disease), allowing for relatively clear structure–function inferences.

However, there are also a number of problems with the lesion method. Clearly, scientists cannot go around lesioning their subjects. One must test those patients who happen to have suffered from one or another type of brain injury. But such "accidental experiments" are not ideal. One cannot choose the location or size of the lesion, which may involve multiple brain structures, complicating structure–function inferences: how do you know which brain structure does what when many structures are damaged? Timing is also an issue. If one waits too long after the onset of an acute brain lesion, other structures may take over some of the functions that the damaged structure used to perform. Such **compensation** confuses the original relationship between the damaged brain structures and the impaired functions. On the other hand, if one tests a patient too quickly after a stroke or head injury, the loss of function can be much greater than is attributable to the damaged regions, because nearby regions are often temporarily affected by factors such as tissue swelling and decreased blood flow. In practice, researchers tend to err on the side of longer periods of time, usually waiting months or even a year or more after acute brain damage before testing a patient.

Although the lesion method is often applied to the study of adult-onset brain damage, the logic also holds for children. However, with child-onset lesions, as well as in developmental brain disorders such as **Specific Language Impairment (SLI)**, **dyslexia**, **autism**, or **Williams syndrome**, one must be particularly careful since children's brains are still developing, and are highly **plastic**. In many cases, this neural plasticity will enable children to compensate for brain damage or dysfunction – usually much more successfully than adults. Any differences between these children and typically developing children may therefore reflect compensatory mechanisms as well as, or perhaps instead of, any dysfunction caused by their abnormally developing brains.

> H.M., who died in 2008, was a patient suffering from anterograde amnesia as a result of a 1953 surgery to address his epilepsy. In this surgery most of his medial temporal lobe structures were removed in both hemispheres.

Hemodynamic neuroimaging

Recent technological advances now allow us to actually image brain activity – in children and adults, with or without brain or behavioral impairments. Because one can test normal individuals, it is possible to avoid problems such as compensation that are intrinsic to the lesion method. The general experimental approach is to take images of brain activity while subjects perform tasks that engage cognitive processes of interest. Typically one compares brain activation between two or more conditions that are designed to differ *only* with respect to the specific functions of interest. For example, studies have examined differences in brain activity during the processing of nouns and verbs, regular and irregular inflected forms, or sentences with varying degrees of syntactic complexity. Such studies can reveal

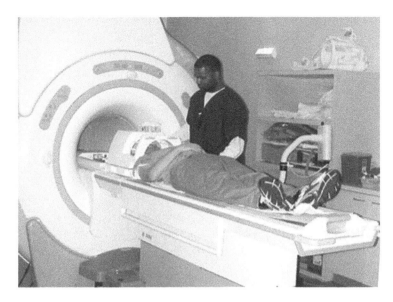

Figure 7.7 A person being prepared for an MRI scan. He will slide into the open hole (the "bore"), around which the MR magnet is situated. The subject's head is enclosed in a "head coil," which transmits the radio waves that knock the hydrogen atoms out of alignment within the magnetic field. The head coil also receives the signal back from the hydrogen atoms as they return to a stable alignment

structure–function correlations (for localization) or single and double dissociations (for separability and domain-specificity). Importantly, **neuroimaging** reveals which structures are *involved* in a particular function, whereas lesion studies reveal which structures are *necessary*.

Perhaps the best-known imaging methods are those that map changes in blood flow in the brain – that is, brain **hemodynamics**. These techniques take advantage of the fact that when neurons increase their firing rate, certain changes in the blood stream occur, such as increases in blood flow and changes in the oxygen level in the blood. fMRI (functional Magnetic Resonance Image) is by far the most widely used hemodynamic neuroimaging method today. Subjects are placed in a scanner with an extremely powerful magnetic field (Figure 7.7) – typically more than ten thousand times stronger than the earth's magnetic field. Because atoms such as hydrogen (which is very common in the brain – in water, fat, proteins, etc.) are sensitive to magnetic forces, they line up in the magnetic field, just as a compass needle aligns with a magnet placed nearby. The scanner then uses radio waves to knock the atoms out of alignment, and records the characteristic signals they release as they come back into alignment in the field. These signals are then picked up by a receiver in the scanner, which uses them to reconstruct an image of the brain.

In addition to fMRI, hemodynamic imaging techniques include SPECT (Single Photon Emission Computed Tomography) and PET (Positron Emission Tomography). Functional imaging with SPECT is now rare, and PET is no longer used as widely as it was in the 1990s for this purpose – though both *techniques are still very useful for identifying the neurotransmitters and other molecules that underlie language and other cognitive processes. Both SPECT and PET image radioactive tracers in the blood, and so have potential health risks. Thus both methods are relatively **invasive**, and therefore are not ideal. Moreover, their accuracy in localizing activation to particular brain regions is limited by their **spatial resolution**, which is not as good as that of the newer technique of fMRI.*

In a *structural* magnetic resonance (MR) image, the anatomical structures of the brain are reconstructed, taking advantage of the fact that hydrogen atoms in different molecules (e.g. fat, proteins, water) give off different signals (see the image of the brain itself in Figure 7.10 below). In the *functional* MR images that constitute fMRI, one takes advantage of changes in oxygenation levels in the blood. Somewhat counter-intuitively, when neurons increase their firing rate (and thus increase their need for oxygen and glucose for energy), one generally observes an *increase* in oxygenated hemoglobin as compared to deoxygenated hemoglobin, as the blood brings in more oxygen than the neurons actually use. fMRI detects the resulting change in the ratio between oxygenated and deoxygenated hemoglobin, which is known as the blood oxygenation level dependent (BOLD) effect. Because brain regions with different amounts of neural activity will have different ratios, fMRI can indirectly image regional differences in neural activity between task conditions.

fMRI provides superb spatial resolution, allowing one to distinguish areas of activation even a few millimeters apart. Moreover, because structural images of brain anatomy can be acquired in the same scanning session as the functional images of fMRI, it is easy to align and overlay the functional (activation) images from a given subject onto his or her own structural (anatomical) images. This allows one to localize brain activity to precise structures in each subject. Also, unlike PET, fMRI does not involve radiation, so a given subject can be scanned multiple times with no known adverse effects. This is especially important for examining the slow changes in brain activity that accompany development, learning, or therapeutic intervention for disorders. In these cases, subjects can be brought back to the lab for multiple scanning sessions over the course of days, weeks, months, or even years.

However, as with every method, fMRI has its limitations. First, the very strong magnetic fields of the MRI scanner can be quite dangerous in some circumstances (e.g. if you have shrapnel in your body). Second, the hemodynamic changes that take place in response to neural activity are too slow (on the order of seconds) to allow the detection of real-time processing, so one can't use fMRI to measure the spatiotemporal dynamics of language – that is, the movie of language use. It is therefore important to test a given linguistic process not only with fMRI, but also with techniques such as ERPs or MEG (see below) that can measure brain activity every millisecond or even faster – that is, with techniques that have very high **temporal resolution**.

Event-related potentials

Event-related potentials (ERPs) are scalp-recorded electrical potentials of the brain activity that takes place after subjects are presented with a stimulus "event," such as a word,

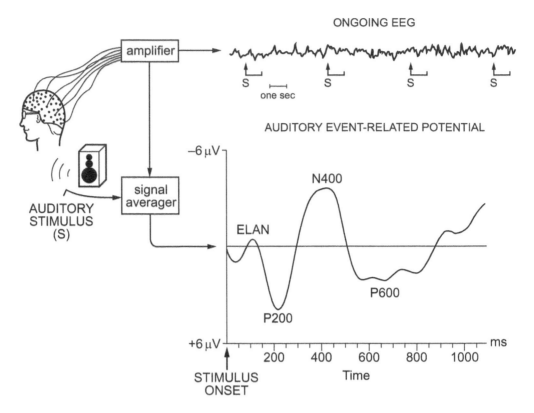

Figure 7.8 The process of measuring event-related potentials (ERPs) (adapted from Hillyard and Kutas 1983)

picture, or sound (Figure 7.8). The electrical potentials are recorded at the scalp from electrodes that are bound to ERP caps, allowing for the easy application and consistent placement of electrodes on the head. Each stimulus – such as the auditory stimulus in Figure 7.8 – is time-locked to the ongoing **EEG (Electroencephalogram)**. After being amplified, these time-locked signals are averaged to eliminate the part of the signal that is not specific to the stimulus, resulting in the ERP waveform.

Higher cognitive processes relevant to language comprehension, such as those underlying lexical access or syntactic processing, are reflected in characteristic changes in the ERP signal between about 100 and 1000 milliseconds after presentation of the stimulus event (e.g. after seeing or hearing a word). Characteristic peaks (i.e. "bumps" or "dips") in the ERP wave that are consistently found in particular experimental conditions are referred to as **ERP components**. These include the so-called ELAN, P200, N400, and P600 components labeled in Figure 7.8 (shown here for only a single electrode). Different ERP components can be identified and distinguished by various factors, including their peak latency (the time between the stimulus onset and the peak of the component), their peak amplitude (the height of the peak), their scalp distribution (which electrodes the component is strongest at and extends to), and their polarity (whether they have positive or negative voltage peaks; in ERP diagrams, such as that shown in Figure 7.8, negative is traditionally shown as up rather than down!).

As with hemodynamic neuroimaging like fMRI, in an ERP experiment subjects perform tasks that probe particular cognitive functions, and one typically compares the ERP signals between contrasting experimental conditions. Unlike hemodynamic imaging techniques, however, ERPs reflect actual electrophysiological neuronal activity, not changes in blood flow that are only indirectly related to brain activity. Electrophysiological changes in neurons take place on the order of milliseconds. They can be measured at the scalp without delay and with virtually unlimited temporal resolution, with up to 20,000 or more measurements per second. Therefore one can actually record brain activity in real time during ongoing language processing. This is a major reason why ERPs have been widely used to complement traditional psycholinguistic techniques in the study of language processing.

Unfortunately, ERPs' advantage in temporal resolution is accompanied by a strong disadvantage in spatial resolution. It turns out to be quite difficult, though not impossible, to identify the actual brain structures that generate scalp-recorded potentials. Not only is the electrical potential warped as it passes through the skull, but in addition, there is the "inverse problem": an infinite number of different combinations of sources within the brain can generate identical patterns at the scalp. Although the inverse problem can be somewhat overcome by using information from structural and functional MRI to limit the possible sources of signal in the brain (e.g. by assuming that only areas activated by fMRI in the same task are likely to generate the ERP signal), some uncertainty remains, and therefore one cannot localize the ERP signal with a high degree of reliability.

ERPs also have other limitations. The electrical activity of a single neuron firing is much too small to measure outside the brain. ERPs are generally detectable only when hundreds or even thousands of neurons with a similar geometrical orientation are active at the same time. It turns out that only certain types of neurons tend to have these properties, and therefore it is mainly these neurons that are captured by ERPs. Finally, speaking out loud is quite problematic in ERP studies because of the electrical noise produced both by muscles and by motor neurons, so almost all ERP language studies are limited to language perception (reading or listening).

Magnetoencephalography

Magnetoencephalography (MEG) can be thought of as providing the magnetic equivalent to ERPs. All electrical currents have a magnetic field around them. Although the magnetic fields around currents in the brain are very weak, extremely sensitive detectors called SQUIDs (Superconducting QUantum Interference Devices) can pick up changes in these fields – as long as the testing room is heavily shielded against magnetic interference from computers, power lines, passing trains, and the like. A large number of SQUIDs can be packed in a helmet, which is simply lowered on the subject's head. The subject then performs language or other cognitive tasks, and the researcher compares the magnetic fields between experimental conditions.

Like ERPs, MEG can measure electrophysiological brain activity at very high temporal resolutions, for example, every millisecond. However, MEG allows one to localize the source of brain activity with a somewhat higher degree of reliability than with ERPs; even though the inverse problem remains, the magnetic field is warped far less by the skull than are electrical potentials. By overlaying this localized activity on anatomical images obtained with MRI, one can see which brain structures are likely to be producing the activity. So, MEG is reasonably good at providing us with our goal of a real-time movie of the brain. Nevertheless, like ERPs, it only captures a subset of the brain regions and neurons in the brain – although generally a different set of neurons than ERP, making the two technologies somewhat complementary.

Direct brain recording and stimulation

ERPs and MEG measure electrical and magnetic fields outside the skull and scalp, giving only partial and approximate evidence of neuronal activity within the brain itself. However, in very special circumstances one can measure brain activity directly. Patients with severe epilepsy can sometimes be cured by surgical removal of the epileptic tissue (the source of epileptic seizures). The surgeon needs to find out exactly where the tissue is. To do this, he/she typically removes the scalp, skull, and brain coverings over the portion of the brain where the epileptic tissue is thought to lie. Then a grid of electrodes is implanted on the surface of the cortex. Very fine probes can also be inserted deep into the brain, closer to the suspected epileptic tissue. These depth probes are studded with electrodes that can pick up and distinguish signals from a few hundred cells. (Some recently developed probes can even distinguish the firing of single cells!) Then the brain is covered up again, with the electrode wires passed carefully through the bandaged scalp, and extending to computers that record brain activity. The patient can lie comfortably in bed during recording, which can last several days or more. Signals from epileptic seizures during this time are used to localize their source (much like localizing an earthquake epicenter from several listening stations), allowing its subsequent surgical removal while leaving other tissue intact.

While the electrodes are implanted, the surgeon can also perform experiments that identify the particular brain areas that underlie language, motor, and other critical functions in the patient, so that these areas can be avoided during surgery. In these experiments, the patient is given various tasks probing these functions. While the patient performs a task, one can not only *record* activity from the various electrodes, but also *stimulate* the brain tissue between any pair of electrodes (by passing a small current between them). Typically this stimulation results in a temporary lesion, impairing the functions that depend on that particular tissue. However, stimulation can also actually trigger behaviors, such as involuntary speech. In either case, by stimulating different electrodes on the grid or in the depth probes, and seeing which ones impair or trigger a particular function, the researcher can map the function in the brain.

In addition to helping the patient directly, these experiments can tell us more generally how language and other cognitive functions are organized in the brain. Because the detectors are placed directly on or in the brain, this technique allows for excellent localization, even to the cellular level, as well as sub-millisecond temporal resolution. Additionally, the technique is unique in allowing for both localized recording *and* direct stimulation.

However, the method also has certain drawbacks. First, one must be cautious in generalizing the results to normal brains, since the epilepsy reflects neural abnormalities and may have led to various forms of compensation. Additionally, direct brain recording and stimulation studies can only localize functions near the electrodes that are in place in each patient, leaving most of the brain's activity unmeasured. Thus it is important to complement and cross-validate direct brain recording and stimulation with global mapping techniques such as fMRI.

Transcranial Magnetic Stimulation

If you've ever wanted to use a remote control to modify the behavior of your family and friends, Transcranial Magnetic Stimulation (TMS) may interest you. This method allows researchers to stimulate the brain without the need to perform surgery. The technique takes advantage of the fact that the skull allows magnetic fields to pass through relatively freely (see MEG, above). It works by using a powerful electric current in a coil of wire to generate a magnetic field that rapidly rises and falls in strength, which in turn induces electrical stimulation of the brain. By directing these magnetic fields to specific locations in the brain, the researcher can stimulate regions selectively.

As with direct brain stimulation, this may result in turning behaviors either on or off. For example, TMS directed at your motor cortex can cause you to twitch your thumb. Moreover, because TMS can also inhibit behaviors, it offers the unprecedented ability to produce temporary "lesions" – i.e. neuronal dysfunction – in otherwise healthy subjects. The disrupted function produced by TMS can be limited to relatively small areas of the brain (roughly 1.0 to 1.5 square centimeters), restricting the number of different structures that are likely to be affected. Moreover, because the disruption is temporary (generally lasting only about 100 milliseconds), subjects can be tested both before and after stimulation, and compensation for the disrupted function is very unlikely to occur.

However, there are limitations to what can be achieved with TMS. Not all structures in the brain are equally accessible, and stimulation is largely limited to cortical regions that are relatively near the surface of the brain, close to the skull. The short duration of the effects of TMS, while advantageous with respect to compensation and the subjects' well-being, is also somewhat limiting, as measurements of the disrupted functions need to be carefully synchronized with the application of the magnetic field. Nevertheless, TMS offers a relatively noninvasive method by which to assess structure–function correspondences, and to test for questions of localization, separability, and domain-specificity.

Finally, by *repeatedly* applying TMS pulses (rTMS), effects of much longer duration can be achieved. These longer-term effects are useful not only for minimizing the problem of synchronization, but also for the therapeutic intervention of brain and behavioral disorders. However, rTMS is also more dangerous than single-pulse TMS, and has caused epileptic seizures in a small number of subjects. These dangers can be mitigated by the strict adherence to standard safety measures, but the use of rTMS nevertheless requires more care than the use of TMS.

Evidence and explanations

Using the methods described in the previous section, together with various other techniques for identifying the biological, psychological, and representational bases of language, researchers have made substantial progress in answering the questions discussed above. Here we will go over some of the biological evidence that addresses these questions, and various theoretical explanations that have been proposed to account for this evidence. We will restrict our discussion to native (first) language, and will concentrate primarily on data from adults. So as you read the rest of this section, keep in mind that we are talking about what *your* brain is probably doing as you use your native language – although it is important to keep in mind that individuals can and do differ.

In the following text we cover evidence and explanations related to the biocognition of the mental lexicon, **conceptual-semantics**, phonology, syntax, and morphology. The biology of other aspects of language, such as **prosody** and compositional semantics, is less well studied, and is not addressed in much detail here. All anatomical structures referred to below can be found in the brain figures presented earlier in the chapter (Figures 7.1, 7.2, 7.4, 7.5, and 7.6). Relevant lateral regions are also directly indicated in Figure 7.9 (see shaded area).

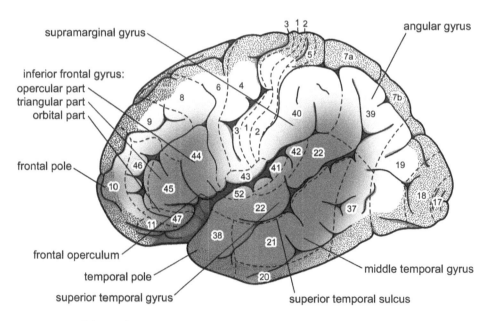

Figure 7.9 Left hemisphere regions implicated in language, as discussed in this section. These regions include classical Wernicke's and Broca's areas. Wernicke's area is generally taken to correspond to the posterior portion of the superior temporal gyrus (posterior BA 22). Broca's area usually refers to BA 44 and BA 45, or in structural terms, the opercular part and the triangular part of the inferior frontal gyrus

The lexicon, conceptual-semantics, and phonology

We can ask all kinds of questions about the biology of words, and of their sounds and meanings. What parts of the brain, and what neurotransmitters and hormones, help us understand, learn, store, and retrieve words? Do different biological substrates underlie the sound patterns that form words (and perhaps phonology more generally) on the one hand, and word meanings (and perhaps conceptual-semantics more generally) on the other? Do different types of words, such as nouns or verbs, or words with different meanings, depend on different neural substrates? Do genes play a role in vocabulary acquisition and the use of words? And are the biological underpinnings of words only for words, or do they also underlie other things you do, such as memorizing facts? And can the answers to any of these questions help us understand other problems, such as how children acquire words, how the lexicon is structured, how computers might learn words, how words change over the centuries, or what therapeutic approaches can help brain-damaged patients, or children with developmental disorders, who have lexical impairments? Here we discuss research that begins to answer some of these questions.

The significance of the temporal lobes: full of words, sound, and meaning

The use of lexical knowledge depends heavily on the temporal lobes, mainly but not only in the left hemisphere. Focal brain damage from acute lesions (e.g. due to strokes) has long pointed to this important role of temporal cortex. Patients whose damage is relatively restricted to the temporal lobes from degenerative disease, including Alzheimer's disease and **semantic dementia**, also have severe lexical deficits. Numerous PET and fMRI studies have found activation in temporal-lobe regions during tasks that involve word forms or meanings, or even word-specific grammatical knowledge such as argument structure. Temporal-lobe activation is observed in lexical tasks both in receptive language (listening or reading) and in expressive language (speaking), such as when subjects name pictures of objects. In ERP studies, manipulations of lexical factors affect the "N400" component, which has been tied to temporal-lobe structures. For example, larger N400s are generated by lower-frequency words (those we've heard or seen less often, such as *newt* as compared to *frog*) and words that are more concrete (e.g. *raccoon* as compared to *country*). Similarly, direct brain recordings and MEG have shown that lexical processing depends on neural activity in various temporal lobe regions (Halgren *et al.* 2002; Nobre *et al.* 1994). A more recent study reported that directly stimulating temporal-lobe areas impairs the naming of objects or actions (Corina *et al.* 2005). Moreover, the repetitive stimulation (rTMS) of **Wernicke's area** can actually speed up performance in a picture-naming task (Mottaghy *et al.* 1999).

Different lexically related functions depend on different structures within the temporal lobes. The use of phonological word forms (the strings of phonemes that constitute the sound patterns of words), and perhaps phonological and/or phonetic processing more generally, relies heavily on mid-to-posterior superior temporal cortex (i.e. mid-to-posterior BA 22; see Figure 7.9). This region has been implicated in both hemispheres.

Although it is commonly assumed that the left hemisphere is **dominant** for all aspects of phonological processing, a number of studies have shown that hemispheric dominance varies with the task being performed. Some evidence suggests that while the left hemisphere is dominant for phonological processing in speech production, during auditory comprehension both left and right superior temporal regions are involved – although the two sides seem to play somewhat different roles. For example, the left side might detect rapid acoustic changes such as those found in formants of phonemes, whereas the right may be more important for detecting slow changes, like those that occur in prosody (Hickok and Poeppel 2004).

The use of conceptual-semantic knowledge, and possibly of nonphonological lexical information stored in **lexical entries**, seems to be supported by cortical areas largely distinct from the superior temporal region that underlies word forms and phonology. These conceptual/lexical areas include temporal cortex in front of and below the word-form/phonology region, with a somewhat greater role on the left than the right side. In hemodynamic neuroimaging studies, this cortical area is activated bilaterally, but especially on the left, by processing real words, whereas the region for word forms and phonology is engaged by pseudo-words like *blick*, whose phonological word forms are not accompanied by any meanings.

Words, sound, and meaning: the temporal lobes do not act alone

The temporal lobes are not the only brain structures that play a role in lexically related knowledge and processing. Evidence suggests that word forms and phonology depend not just on mid-to-posterior superior temporal cortex, but also on nearby cortex in the supramarginal gyrus (BA 40), as well as an area near the boundary of BA 6 and BA 44 that seems to play a role in phonological working memory (holding and rehearsing information actively in mind, such as one might do with a phone number after looking it up and before dialing it).

The right hemisphere of the cerebellum (which is closely connected to the left rather than the right hemisphere of the cerebrum) seems to underlie searching for lexical knowledge. In contrast, retrieving or selecting this knowledge instead depends on the basal ganglia and portions of the inferior frontal gyrus – i.e. **Broca's area** and BA 47. Evidence for these functional roles comes not only from neuroimaging studies, but also from lesion studies. For example, individuals with acute lesions to inferior frontal regions and patients with Parkinson's disease (who have both frontal and basal ganglia degeneration) generally have word-finding trouble, but have less difficulty in recognizing words. Moreover, children with Specific Language Impairment, in which Broca's area is abnormal, have trouble recalling words but are largely spared in their lexical knowledge (Ullman and Pierpont 2005). Interestingly, within the inferior frontal region, BA 44 may play a role in selecting competing lexical alternatives, while the more anterior/ventral area (BA 45/47) underlies their retrieval (Thompson-Schill *et al.* 1997). BA 45/47 may in fact be involved more broadly in retrieving and maintaining lexical and semantic representations as part of working memory. Finally, a much more anterior frontal region, the frontal pole (in BA 10), may verify or monitor retrieved items.

What's the difference between a giraffe and a screwdriver?

Right now, as you are reading the words "giraffe" and "screwdriver," specific parts of your brain are lighting up – and in fact different areas are being activated by these two words. Evidence suggests that understanding words from different conceptual categories depends on different networks of brain structures. Specifically, word meanings depend on cortex adjacent to those areas that underlie the sensory or motor functions that are linked to these meanings. These same cortical regions are also activated by *non*linguistic tasks, such as object recognition or even mental imagery, related to the same concepts. For example, words denoting items with strong visual attributes such as form or color involve temporal-occipital areas involved in these attributes near visual cortex. In fact, specific subregions of these areas, and even individual neurons, may be partly specialized for different types of categories in which visual form is important, such as animals (e.g. giraffes), faces, and houses. Similarly, a posterior lateral temporal region near an area implicated in motion perception are activated by naming tools (such as screwdrivers), actions or verbs, as well as simply perceiving or remembering these items. In fact, patients with damage to this region, or subjects with direct brain stimulation in this region, have particular trouble naming these types of items. Interestingly, within this posterior temporal region, an area around the superior temporal sulcus may play a role for items with biological motion, such as animals or humans, whereas an area just below it in middle temporal cortex may be more important for items with nonbiological motion, such as tools. Finally, naming tools (e.g. screwdrivers again!) and actions activates frontal motor regions that are also involved in actual movement, as well as in the mental imagery of movement.

Different brain regions underlie nouns and verbs – or do they?

A neuroanatomical difference appears to exist between nouns and verbs. Whereas verbs are strongly linked to left frontal cortex, nouns depend more on left temporal regions. For example, patients with frontal lesions often have more difficulty producing verbs, whereas the opposite holds for left temporal damage. The reasons for this dichotomy are not yet clear, and may involve one or more factors, including lexical, conceptual-semantic, and grammatical differences between nouns and verbs. The *lexical–grammatical* hypothesis argues that lexical knowledge in the brain is organized anatomically according to grammatical word category, such as noun and verb. Other explanations have taken a different tack. *Semantic* hypotheses suggest that the dissociations actually reflect differences in the conceptual-semantics of nouns and verbs rather than the word category distinction itself. For example, the dissociation may reflect the fact that verbs tend to represent actions (which are associated with frontal motor regions; see above), whereas nouns often represent visualizable objects (which are associated with temporal-occipital regions; see above). Alternatively, *morphosyntactic* hypotheses suggest that verbs and nouns differentially depend on **morphosyntactic** processes that involve frontal lobe structures. It remains to be seen which of these perspectives (alone or in combination) will best explain the data, or whether a new explanation will be necessary.

Naming pictures: the movie

The spatiotemporal dynamics of lexical processing have been best studied in word production. Evidence from many different methods has been brought together to understand this process, including data from lesion studies, SPECT, PET, fMRI, ERPs, MEG, direct brain recording and stimulation, TMS, and behavioral (psycholinguistic) response time analysis. Whereas no one method on its own could have provided so complete a picture, the various methods have been synergistically combined to create a movie of the spatiotemporal dynamics of word production – albeit with some scenes either out of focus or still missing completely.

Although researchers have studied the spatiotemporal dynamics of a number of different experimental tasks of word production, here we focus on picture naming. In this task, subjects are asked to simply name out loud the object shown in each picture. Even such an apparently simple task requires the coordinated activity of multiple brain structures over time. Moreover, these various subprocesses take place very quickly: on average, it takes only about 600 milliseconds to actually start saying the name of a picture, so each subprocess must take place within that timeframe.

The initial stage of word production seems to involve the selection of the concept that will be expressed. This process depends on occipital and ventral temporal regions and is typically completed within about 175 milliseconds after the picture is presented. Once the concept has been selected, an appropriate lexical entry for the concept seems to be retrieved from memory. The lexical entry specifies the word's grammatical category (e.g. noun), as well as other syntactic information, such as grammatical gender (for example, feminine or masculine in languages like French). This process depends on a central region of the left middle temporal gyrus, and takes place roughly between 175 and 250 milliseconds. At this point, the phonological word form is retrieved, providing the information necessary to pronounce the word. This process depends largely on Wernicke's area, and takes place roughly between 250 and 330 milliseconds after the picture was shown.

At the next stage, evidence suggests that the word's phonological information is relayed to Broca's area, where the sounds in the word – even across different morphemes – are brought together with each other and with information about the word's stress pattern and syllable structure. This seems to take place from about 330 to 455 milliseconds. For example, producing the bisyllabic plural form *horses* seems to involve the selection and combination of the stem *horse* and the plural affix -*s*. Once this step is complete, phonetic encoding turns the abstract phonological information into the proper sequence of muscle movements necessary to articulate the word. This final process, which takes about another 145 milliseconds (i.e. ending at about 600 milliseconds after the picture was shown), also depends on Broca's area, with additional possible contributions from frontal motor regions and the cerebellum.

The data described above are presented largely from the perspective of an explanatory model proposed by Willem Levelt and his colleagues at the Max Planck Institute for Psycholinguistics. Although other models of word production have also been proposed, all seem to be more or less in agreement on the basic stages laid out above. They differ either in some of their specifics, or with respect to the larger issue of **serial** versus

interactive processes. Whereas Levelt's model describes serial stages (i.e. a sequence of steps), other models, such as that proposed by Gary Dell, suggest more interactivity between the subprocesses. According to Dell, activation in the different stages overlaps in time, and feedback is possible between them.

Learning words depends on medial temporal lobe structures

Evidence suggests that word learning depends on medial temporal lobe structures, including the hippocampus. Neuroimaging studies show activation increases in these regions while people are learning words (Breitenstein *et al.* 2005). Patients with **anterograde amnesia**, which is associated with damage to the hippocampus and other medial temporal lobe structures, are impaired in learning new word forms or meanings. For example, the well-studied amnesic patient H.M., most of whose medial temporal lobe structures were surgically removed from both hemispheres, has profound deficits in learning new word forms and conceptual knowledge. Thus he does not appear to have any knowledge of words like *nerd, granola,* or *bikini* that came into the English language after his surgery in 1953 (Postle and Corkin 1998).

Acetylcholine and estrogen modulate aspects of the lexicon and conceptual-semantics

The neurotransmitter **acetylcholine**, which plays an important role in hippocampal function, seems to be implicated in aspects of word learning. For example, the drug scopolamine, which blocks acetylcholine, impairs one's ability to memorize word forms, while leaving working memory and the processing of previously learned lexical-semantic knowledge relatively intact. Patients with Alzheimer's disease, which involves a severe loss of acetylcholine activity in the hippocampus, are particularly impaired in learning new word forms and meanings; and giving these patients cholinesterase inhibitors, which increase the amount of acetylcholine in synapses, improves these learning abilities.

Aspects of the acquisition and processing of lexical and conceptual-semantic knowledge are also modulated by estrogen. In postmenopausal women, estrogen therapy improves the ability to remember word forms and to generate lists of words in a category. Neuroimaging studies have linked such improvements at least in part to medial temporal lobe structures. Giving estrogen to men can also help them at these tasks (Miles *et al.* 1998). Even prior to menopause, women are better at these tasks when they are at high estrogen levels in their menstrual cycle than at low levels. Finally, it is interesting to note that these estrogen effects may be at least partly explained via the action of acetylcholine (Shughrue *et al.* 2000).

Do your lexical abilities depend on your genes?

Obviously the words you use are not specified by your genes, but have to be learned. However, the biocognitive substrates of word learning, as well as of word use, do seem to be affected by genetic factors. Twin studies of children suggest that aspects of lexical acquisition, as measured by the size of children's spoken vocabulary, are strongly influenced by genetic factors. As with many genetic effects, the influence of genetics on vocabulary becomes stronger as the child gets older. In adoption studies, both receptive vocabulary and verbal fluency have been shown to be strongly influenced by genetics. However, it is important to point out that in all of these studies, children's surrounding environment plays an important role too – it's not just in the genes. Moreover, it is not yet clear to what extent these genetic influences might be specific to lexical abilities. Data from developmental disorders also suggest some degree of lexical heritability. Thus Specific Language Impairment, which has an important genetic basis, is typically accompanied by impairments in lexical retrieval, though lexical knowledge in children with the disorder is generally relatively spared. Overall, the evidence suggests that genetic (as well as environmental) factors have an important influence on lexical acquisition and processing.

Separability

We have seen above that there is substantial separability among different types of lexically related functions. Evidence suggests the existence of different temporal-lobe regions for word forms versus lexical-conceptual and abstract lexical knowledge; distinct brain structures, including inferior frontal, basal ganglia and cerebellar, for lexical retrieval, selection, and search; separate cortical regions for words from different conceptual categories, based on the categories' sensory and motor attributes; frontal regions for verbs versus temporal regions for nouns (or some sort of analogous conceptual or grammatical distinction); and medial temporal structures for the acquisition of lexical knowledge versus neocortical regions for the storage or processing of that knowledge after it has been learned. So, even when we restrict our focus to the lexicon, there appears to be substantial separability among different linguistic functions. However, this separability does *not* imply that any of the brain structures that underlie the various lexical functions are associated with *only* these functions; that is, separability does not imply domain-specificity.

Are the biological substrates of lexical abilities domain-specific?

It is difficult in principle to demonstrate domain-specificity. For example, one might show double dissociations between lexical processing and attention, between lexical processing and motor function, between lexical processing and … the list goes on. How can we test every possible function, with every possible task? Not surprisingly, there is little if any good evidence that the biocognitive substrates of lexical abilities are dedicated to language. In contrast, there is increasing evidence for biocognitive associations between lexical and nonlinguistic conceptual-semantic functions, suggesting that these functions depend on common biocognitive substrates. For example, we have seen that the same neural substrates are activated by words from a given conceptual category and by nonlinguistic tasks that tap the same concepts. Other evidence not reviewed above also supports a common basis for lexical and conceptual-semantic functions. For example, data suggest that the biocognitive substrates of lexical acquisition – such as the hippocampus, acetylcholine, and estrogen – also underlie learning information about concepts, facts, events, and the like. For example, H.M. and other amnesics are typically impaired at remembering not only new words, but also new facts (e.g. that the Soviet Union does not exist any more) and personally experienced events (e.g. that he met you five minutes ago). These and other findings have led to

---

BOX 7.2 **A BIOCOGNITIVE PERSPECTIVE ON LEXICON AND GRAMMAR: THE DECLARATIVE/PROCEDURAL THEORY**

The basic premise of the Declarative/Procedural Theory is that language depends on two well-studied brain memory systems that have been implicated in nonlanguage functions in animals and humans (Ullman 2001, 2004). The declarative memory system underlies the learning, representation, and use of knowledge about facts and events, such as the fact that chairs are for sitting on, or that you had ravioli for dinner last night. The knowledge learned in this system is at least partly, but not completely, **explicit** – that is, available to conscious awareness. The hippocampus and other medial temporal structures learn new memories, which eventually depend largely on neocortical regions, particularly in the temporal lobes. Declarative memory function can be enhanced by estrogen, perhaps via the modulation of the neurotransmitter acetylcholine.

The **procedural memory** system underlies the **implicit** (nonconscious) learning of new, and the control of long-established, motor and cognitive "skills" and "habits," especially those involving sequences and rules – for example, riding a bicycle, fly-fishing, or learning probabilistic rules. The system is composed of a network of interconnected brain structures rooted in frontal/basal-ganglia circuits, including BA 44 in Broca's area. The neurotransmitter dopamine plays a particularly important role in aspects of procedural learning. For example, patients with Parkinson's disease, who suffer from a loss of dopamine-producing cells in the basal ganglia, have trouble with procedural learning.

According to the Declarative/Procedural Theory, each of the two memory systems plays analogous roles in its nonlinguistic and linguistic functions. The distinction between declarative and procedural memory largely parallels the distinction between lexicalized knowledge and rule-based grammatical composition. Declarative memory underlies all idiosyncratic word-specific knowledge, including the sounds and meanings of words, and whether a word takes a morphologically irregular form. The procedural memory system supports the implicit acquisition of grammar rules, and the rule-governed sequential and hierarchical computation of complex linguistic structures. This system plays computationally analogous roles across grammatical subdomains, including syntax and morphology (e.g. in the composition of English regular past tenses, *walk* + *-ed*). In the main text we discuss different sources of evidence that support these various predictions.

However, complex structures can also be learned and processed in declarative memory; for example, they can be stored as chunks (e.g. *walked*). The extent to which such structures will depend on one or the other memory system likely depends on many factors, including which of the two systems is more available for learning and processing. For example, individuals or groups with better declarative memory or worse procedural memory should depend more on declarative and less on procedural memory. Indeed, evidence suggests that women, who show declarative memory advantages as compared to men (possibly due to their higher levels of estrogen), rely more on declarative memory than do men when processing complex structures (Ullman *et al.* 2008). And children and adults with Specific Language Impairment, *FOXP2* mutations, or autism, all of whom appear to have procedural memory deficits (Ullman and Pierpont 2005; Walenski *et al.* 2006), seem to depend more on declarative memory for complex forms than do typically developing individuals.

---

the proposal that lexical memory depends on **declarative memory**, a brain system that underlies the learning and use of knowledge about facts and events (see Box 7.2).

Syntax

The biocognition of syntax is still less well understood than that of the lexicon, conceptual-semantics, or phonology. This is perhaps not surprising, given the particular

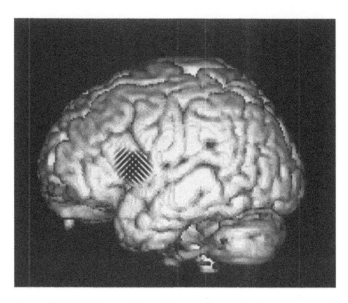

Figure 7.10 A left lateral view of the cerebrum showing greater activation for the production of sentences as compared to word lists (see text). The two overlapping (crosshatched) areas of activation, which encompass BA 44 and the frontal operculum, reflect two experiments that used the same stimuli on two different sets of subjects. (Figure adapted from Indefrey et al. 2004)

complexity of syntax. Nevertheless, the evidence thus far has begun to shed light on a variety of questions, including the functional neuroanatomy of syntax, the spatiotemporal dynamics of syntactic processing, and the biocognitive separability and domain-specificity of this linguistic function.

Broca's region is important for syntax

First of all, an area called **Broca's region** clearly plays an important role in syntactic processing. Broca's region is taken to encompass not only Broca's area itself (BA 44 and BA 45), but also down to include BA 47 and back to include the frontal operculum. Numerous neuroimaging studies have found activation within this region during receptive language tasks engaging syntactic processing. For example, in an early PET study of English sentences, syntactically complex sentences ("center-embedded" sentences like *The juice that the child spilled stained the rug*) yielded more activation in BA 44 than less complex sentences ("right-branching" sentences like *The child spilled the juice that stained the rug*) (Stromswold *et al.* 1996). Broca's region is also implicated in expressive language. In a neuroimaging investigation of German, subjects showed more activation in BA 44 and the frontal operculum when they produced sentences than phrases, which in turn yielded more activation than simple word lists (Indefrey *et al.* 2004). That is, activation increased with syntactic complexity (Figure 7.10).

Studies of adult-onset brain damage also suggest a role for Broca's region in syntax. Acute adult-onset lesions of Broca's area and surrounding cortex is associated with

agrammatism – that is, syntactically and morphologically simplified speech. Patients with agrammatic **aphasia** (e.g. patients with **Broca's aphasia**) have difficulty with bound and unbound morphemes – i.e. affixes (bound morphemes) and function words (unbound morphemes), which are often dropped or substituted by these patients. Agrammatics seem to have an especially difficult time with linguistic structures and morphemes that depend on categories which are higher in the hierarchy (such as IP), as compared to those that are lower (such as NP). Interestingly, damage that is *restricted* to Broca's area itself generally only produces transient aphasia. The lesion must be somewhat larger for persistent agrammatism, underscoring the importance of nearby cortical regions in syntax.

The syntactic impairments of agrammatic patients are not limited to expressive language. These patients also often have substantial difficulty in receptive language, particularly in using syntactic structure to understand sentences. According to one view, they have specific syntactic deficits in relating elements in a sentence (Grodzinsky 2000). This hypothesis depends on assumptions made by certain linguistic theories that posit that the computation of a sentence involves moving words or phrases from one position in a sentence to another. This is thought to leave a hidden marker (e.g. a "trace") in the element's original position. For example, in the passive sentence *The cow is chased* <trace> *by the horse*, the <trace> shows the position from where *the cow* was moved. Agrammatic patients, in particular those with damage to Broca's area, are posited to have lost the ability to relate moved elements to their original positions (i.e. to the traces).

Evidence from developmental disorders also implicates Broca's area in syntax. Children with Specific Language Impairment, who have particular abnormalities in Broca's area, have a wide range of syntactic impairments in both speech and comprehension. Like agrammatic patients, these children seem to have particular trouble with morphemes that depend on higher functional categories. Additionally, Broca's area abnormalities have been observed in children with autism, which is associated with syntactic difficulties both in production and comprehension (Walenski *et al.* 2006).

It is important to point out that not all of Broca's region underlies the same syntactic functions. Rather, different subregions seem to have different roles. Although the evidence to date does not allow one to draw unambiguous conclusions about the precise functions of the particular parts of Broca's region, certain patterns are beginning to emerge. For example, according to one view, the frontal operculum and perhaps nearby cortex in inferior BA 44 contributes to local **structure building**, whereas more anterior and superior portions of BA 44 support long-distance dependencies and syntactic working memory, and BA 45/47 underlies aspects of semantic processing at the sentence level (Friederici 2002; Opitz and Friederici 2007).

But it's not only Broca's region: a role for temporal cortex and the basal ganglia

Syntax does not depend only on Broca's region. A wide range of neuroimaging studies of sentence processing have implicated both anterior and posterior portions of the temporal lobe, especially in the left hemisphere. An anterior region seems to include anterior portions of the superior temporal gyrus (BA 22), superior temporal sulcus, and middle temporal gyrus (BA 21), and extends forward to the temporal pole (in BA 38). It has been suggested that this anterior temporal region underlies access to information about the grammatical category of words, which feeds into online structure-building processes in Broca's area. Such a role is consistent with independent evidence implicating this region in lexical processes (see above). The posterior temporal region, which has been posited to support auditory working memory (Dronkers *et al.* 2004) or syntactic integration (Friederici 2004), appears to include posterior portions of the superior temporal gyrus (BA 22), superior temporal sulcus, and middle temporal gyrus, and may extend back to the angular gyrus (BA 39).

Evidence also suggests that the basal ganglia play a role in syntax. Patients with Parkinson's disease (who suffer from basal ganglia degeneration) show syntactic impairments in both production and comprehension. Likewise, patients with Huntington's disease show syntactic impairments in their speech. Specific Language Impairment – which, as we have seen, is tied to important syntactic impairments – is associated with abnormalities not only of Broca's area, but also of the basal ganglia, especially the caudate nucleus. Neuroimaging studies have reported basal ganglia activation for syntactic violations and for processing rapidly as opposed to slowly presented sentences. So what do the basal ganglia do for syntax? That's not yet clear, though it has been suggested that basal ganglia structures may underlie sequencing in syntax, learning rule-governed syntactic (and other grammatical) patterns, and syntactic integration (Friederici 2004; Lieberman 2002; Ullman 2004).

Understanding sentences: the movie

The spatiotemporal dynamics of syntax have mainly been studied in sentence comprehension. As in word production, our understanding of the spatiotemporal dynamics of sentence comprehension derives from many different sources of evidence, including studies of brain-damaged patients, hemodynamic neuroimaging, ERPs, MEG, and psycholinguistic studies. However, because syntactic processing is extremely complex, a clear understanding of it has yet to emerge, and different researchers have interpreted the data in somewhat different ways. Here we present the data on auditory sentence comprehension (i.e. listening to sentences) in light of the most comprehensive neurocognitive interpretation (i.e. model) proposed thus far, developed by Angela Friederici and her colleagues at the Max Planck Institute for Human Cognitive and Brain Sciences. Following this, we briefly discuss other possible interpretations of the data.

When you hear each word in a sentence (e.g. in the sentence *The dog barked at the hedgehog*), your brain first performs phonological processing in order to identify the word form, at which point syntactic processing begins. At about 150 to 200 milliseconds after the word begins, its grammatical category (e.g. noun for *dog*) may be accessed in the anterior superior temporal cortex. This allows the word to be incorporated into the syntactic structure, which takes place around the same time period in the region of the frontal operculum and inferior BA 44. This structure building also requires maintaining the structural representation in working memory, which depends on superior and anterior portions of BA 44. Aspects of these various processes are reflected in the "ELAN" (Early Left Anterior Negativity), ERP component.

At this point, the lexical entry can be accessed, allowing for subsequent morphosyntactic and semantic integration. Both of these processes seem to take place about 300 to 500 milliseconds after word onset. Morphosyntactic integration (e.g., for agreement), which involves the area of BA 44, perhaps extending to BA 45, is reflected in the "LAN" (Left Anterior Negativity) ERP component. Semantic integration, on the other hand, relies on temporal lobe regions and BA 45/47, and is reflected in the N400 ERP component (see above).

In the final stage of processing the word within the ongoing sentence, any ambiguities or errors are sorted out in order to arrive at a final syntactic structure and semantic interpretation. For example, the sentence *While Mary was walking the dog chased the car* is prone to misinterpretation, as *the dog* is likely to be initially interpreted as the direct object of *walking*. However, this interpretation causes the next word (*chased*) to be difficult to integrate into the sentence. Revision and repair processes are therefore called upon to find a solution, which in this case involves recognizing that *walking* does not need a direct object, so that *the dog* is actually serving as the *subject* of *chased*. (These sentences are often called "garden-path" sentences, as the reader is initially led "down the garden path" in reading and interpreting them.) Thus the initial interpretation of the sentence, *While Mary was walking the dog* <clause boundary> *chased . . .* is corrected to: *While Mary was walking* <clause boundary> *the dog chased . . .* These revision/repair processes are reflected in the "P600" ERP component in response to the word that brings attention to the problem (e.g. *chased*). The neural bases of this process are still not well understood, though they may depend partly on the basal ganglia.

It is important to emphasize that this series of steps is only one interpretation of the data. Although Friederici's model is perhaps the best-specified neurocognitive perspective, other interpretations have also been proposed. As in word production, models of sentence comprehension tend to assume either serial processing – i.e. a relatively strict sequence of distinct steps of syntactic and semantic subprocesses – or interactive processing, in which these subprocesses are heavily interdependent and tend to occur at the same time. The model proposed by Friederici emphasizes serial subprocesses, but also acknowledges that some of these interact, in particular in the last phase during syntactic revision and repair.

Do your genes play a role in syntax?

Twin studies suggest that the development of syntax, and morphosyntax in particular, is at least partly influenced by genetic factors – apparently more so than the development of vocabulary. Evidence for a genetic influence on syntax is found in studies of both language production and language comprehension. However, as with vocabulary, it remains unclear to what extent these factors may be specific to syntax. Data from hereditary developmental disorders also support a role for genetics in syntax. Thus as we have seen above, Specific Language Impairment is strongly associated with a variety of syntactic (as well as other) impairments.

Perhaps the best-studied gene responsible for developmental language disorders is the *FOXP2* gene. Mutations of this gene were originally found in about half the members of a large family (the "KE family") who have a hereditary developmental disorder. The affected members of this family suffer from speech and language deficits, including of syntax and morphology, although they clearly also have nonlinguistic impairments, such as of motor sequencing. Both human and animal (rodent and monkey) studies have shown that the gene is expressed (i.e. turned on) at high levels in the basal ganglia (especially in the caudate nucleus), particularly in the developing embryo. These structures have been found to be abnormal in affected members of the KE family. However, much remains unknown about the gene and its relation to linguistic and nonlinguistic functions. Further research is likely to shed light on this question, as well as other aspects of the genetics of language.

Is there separability within syntax, or between syntax and other linguistic domains?

As we have seen above, different syntactic processes seem to depend on different brain structures. There also appears to be some degree of neurocognitive separability between syntactic and *other* linguistic processing, such as lexical/semantic and phonological processing – although, given the fact that these functions are *also* required in syntactic processing (as we have seen), they are likely to be engaged in syntactic processing studies as well. Therefore clear neurocognitive dissociations between syntax and these other domains are not expected. For example, BA 45/47 and anterior temporal cortex are critical in lexical and semantic processing, but they also play roles in sentence processing, albeit roles that seem to reflect their core lexical and semantic functions.

Are the biocognitive substrates of syntax domain-specific?

As we have seen above, it is very difficult to demonstrate domain-specificity. Indeed, there is little if any strong biocognitive data supporting the domain-specificity of syntax. Even perhaps the best evidence, from a group of children with Specific Language Impairment who appear to have only syntactic deficits (van der Lely 2005) is problematic, largely because these children have been tested only on a restricted range of nonlinguistic tasks. In contrast, accumulating evidence suggests strong biocognitive associations between syntactic and certain nonlinguistic functions. For example, BA 44 and the basal ganglia underlie not just syntax, but also a range of nonlinguistic functions, including motor and music processing (see Box 7.3 below). Indeed, it has been proposed that these brain structures' computational roles in syntax reflect their linguistic *and* nonlinguistic roles in the procedural memory system, which may be specialized for sequences and rules across multiple cognitive domains (Box 7.2). Evidence supporting this view comes from a variety of sources (Ullman 2004). For example, Specific Language Impairment is associated not only with syntactic deficits, but also with impairments of complex sequential movements and learning problems in procedural memory. Similarly, patients with Parkinson's disease, Huntington's disease, or agrammatic aphasia have motor impairments as well as problems with sequence learning.

BOX 7.3 **MUSIC AND LANGUAGE**

Both music and language contain hierarchically organized sequences of basic elements that unfold over time. Music can be broken down into sequences of notes and chords (i.e. three or more notes played simultaneously), whereas language consists of sequences of units such as phonemes, morphemes, and words. In both language and music, lower-level units are arranged in a rule-governed hierarchical configuration to form higher-order structures, such as morphologically complex words, phrases, and sentences in language, and motifs, phrases, and movements in music.

Converging evidence from multiple methods suggests that receptive sentence processing and music perception depend on very similar anatomical substrates. As we have seen, aspects of syntactic processing depend on cortex in and around BA 44, which is activated by syntactic violations. Similarly, both fMRI and MEG studies have reported activation of BA 44 in response to unexpected chords in musical sequences. In language, activation of this region is largely lateralized to the left, while in music it tends to be bilateral, with a slight lateralization to the right hemisphere. Temporal lobe regions have also been implicated in both language and music perception. Both the anterior and posterior portions of superior temporal cortex that underlie syntactic processing have also been shown to be active when people encounter an unexpected chord or change in instrument. Finally, studies have found similar ERP patterns to syntactic violations of language and to harmonic deviations in musical sequences, though again, those for language are more left lateralized than those for music.

Morphology

In the previous section we have seen that a number of different brain structures support syntax, including morphosyntax. Here we focus on the distinction between regular and irregular morphophonology, which has been intensively studied over the past two decades – especially in inflectional morphology, but also in derivational morphology.

Where are rats and mice in the brain? The neuroanatomy of regular and irregular forms

Patients with temporal lobe damage have greater difficulty producing, recognizing, and reading irregular than regular inflected forms (e.g. *dug*, *kept*, or *mice* versus *walked*, *played*, or *rats*). This pattern has been found for English inflectional morphology in patients with acute lesions, Alzheimer's disease, or semantic dementia, as well as for Italian in Alzheimer's patients. In contrast, damage to frontal and/or basal ganglia structures – in Parkinson's disease, Huntington's disease, and patients with acute lesions – has often (but not always) been shown to affect regulars more than irregulars.

ERP studies of receptive language in English, German, and Italian have found that whereas the inappropriate presence or absence of irregular inflection (e.g. Yesterday I *dig* a hole) often elicits N400s (which depend on temporal lobe structures; see above), inappropriate regular affixation (e.g. Yesterday I *walk* over there) generally leads to LANs (which are linked to left frontal structures). ERP and MEG studies of expressive language have found that whereas producing English irregular past-tense forms elicits temporal lobe activity, producing regular past-tense forms yields activation in frontal regions.

In hemodynamic neuroimaging studies, irregulars have elicited particular activation in a broad range of structures, including the left middle temporal gyrus, other temporal and parietal regions, and the cerebellum. In contrast, a number of studies have reported that regular morphological forms elicit activation in Broca's region and the basal ganglia. For example, a PET study of Finnish, a morphologically very rich and productive language, reported greater activation in Broca's area while subjects listened to regular inflected nouns than to **monomorphemic** forms (like *cat* in English) (Laine *et al.* 1999). Similarly, an fMRI study of English inflectional *and* derivational morphology found that the visual presentation of regular inflected forms (*-ed* or *-ing* suffixed) and regular derivational forms (with productive affixes, such as *-ness* and *-less)* elicited greater activation in Broca's area and in the caudate nucleus of the left basal ganglia than irregular derivational forms (with relatively unproductive affixes, such as *-ity* and *-ation*) or monomorphemic words (Vannest *et al.* 2005).

Thus the evidence suggests that, in both expressive and receptive language, irregulars and regulars depend on largely different brain structures, with the former relying heavily on temporal lobe regions, while the latter rely strongly on frontal cortex, especially Broca's region, as well as the basal ganglia structures.

Producing rats and mice: the movie

At least one ERP and two MEG studies have examined the time course of English past-tense production (Dhond *et al.* 2003; Lavric *et al.* 2001; Rhee *et al.* 1999). These three studies yielded largely similar patterns. In all three, the production of *irregular* past tenses (e.g. *dug*) yielded left temporal-lobe activation between 250 and 340 milliseconds after presentation of the stem (e.g. *dig*, which is used to prompt the subject). This is similar to the pattern of activation found between 250 and 330 milliseconds in portions of left temporal cortex for the retrieval of word forms in picture naming tasks. *Regulars* (e.g. *walked*) also showed consistency across the three studies, eliciting activation in frontal cortex – specifically localized to Broca's area in one study – between 310 and 470 milliseconds after stem presentation in all three studies. Again, this pattern is similar to that found in picture naming, in which Broca's area has been found to underlie the combination of sound patterns, including morphemes, between 330 and 455 milliseconds.

The separability and computation of regular and irregular morphology

Substantial evidence thus suggests dissociations between regular and irregular morphological forms. Two very different theoretical perspectives have offered explanations for this pattern. According to "dual-system" hypotheses, the differences in the brain structures underlying irregulars and regulars reflect the difference between lexical processes (for irregulars, which are posited to be stored in the lexicon) and rule-governed compositional processes that also underlie syntax (for regulars) (e.g. see Box 7.2 and Pinker and Ullman 2002). In contrast, "single-mechanism" hypotheses deny morphological composition, arguing instead that regulars and irregulars both depend on the same computational mechanisms – i.e. statistical learning mechanisms that can be modeled by connectionist (i.e. "neural network") simulations. For example, according to one single-mechanism

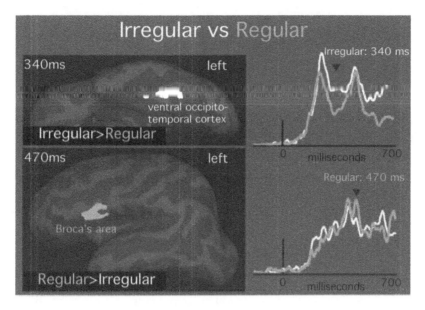

Figure 7.11 An MEG study of past-tense production. Displayed here are two areas that showed significant differences in activation between regulars and irregulars at particular points in time after the presentation of the prompt (see text; figure adapted from Dhond *et al.* 2003)

model, regulars and irregulars both depend on closely interconnected networks that underlie phonological and semantic processing (McClelland and Patterson 2002).

The two views can be empirically distinguished. Whereas dual-system hypotheses predict double dissociations between regulars and irregulars, single-mechanism models do not, once other differences between the word types (e.g. phonological complexity, real-world frequency) are controlled for. Although the evidence has not unambiguously distinguished between these two competing views, accumulating evidence such as the double dissociations discussed in the text above seems to favor a dual-system perspective.

Are the biological substrates of regular and irregular morphology dedicated to these functions?

Evidence suggests that irregulars depend on biocognitive substrates that underlie not just lexical memory, but also conceptual-semantics, and declarative memory more generally. For example, patients with Alzheimer's disease are impaired not only at producing irregulars, but also at finding words and factual knowledge, and at learning this knowledge. Likewise, regulars seem to depend on substrates that underlie both syntax and procedural memory. Thus patients with frontal or basal ganglia damage, such as those with Parkinson's disease, show impairments across regulars, syntax, motor function, and procedural memory. In one study of Parkinson's disease, the patients with greater difficulty at sequential movements also had greater difficulty producing regular (but not irregular) past-tense forms (Ullman *et al.* 1997). These and other data suggest that irregular and regular morphological forms are supported by domain-general brain memory systems (see Box 7.2). However, as with many of the other questions discussed in this chapter, the jury is still out, and the issue remains to be resolved by future research.

CHAPTER SUMMARY

At the beginning of this chapter, we situated the study of the biology of language in a broader scientific context. We emphasized that one must consider every aspect of the biology of language, which must moreover be examined together with the processing and representation of language. First, we took a tour of the biology of the brain, from neuroanatomy down to neurons, hormones, neurotransmitters, and genes. Second, we discussed several major questions that have been asked about the biology of language. Third, we examined the primary methods that are currently used to investigate the biological bases of language. We emphasized the importance of using multiple complementary methods in order to obtain converging evidence. Fourth, we reviewed existing evidence on the neurobiology of language, and discussed explanations that have been proposed to account for this evidence. We examined in some detail evidence and explanations regarding the mental lexicon, conceptual-semantics, phonology, syntax, and morphology. We showed how many of the questions asked earlier in the chapter are beginning to be answered. Thus researchers have now acquired reasonable evidence as to which language functions seem to rely on which brain structures, and are even starting to understand which molecules and genes they may depend on.

The study of the biology of language is just beginning. In fact, most of the evidence presented in this chapter was reported within the past fifteen years. The recent emergence of many of the techniques described above, as well as others that will soon appear, is likely to lead to an ever-larger explosion of research on the biological bases of language. Moreover, as attention increasingly turns from neuroanatomy down to the cellular, molecular, and genetic levels, and as the study of all the biological bases of language is increasingly integrated with the investigation of the processing and representation of language, our understanding of the biocognition of language, and of its implications for a whole host of larger issues, will grow dramatically. The future is wide open and exciting.

Exercises

EXERCISE 7.1

What is a neuron?

The inferior frontal gyrus is made up of three parts. Name them.

Which gyri and which Brodmann's areas are generally taken to correspond to Broca's area?

EXERCISE 7.2

Explain why a double dissociation is more convincing than a single dissociation.

Why is it difficult to demonstrate domain-specificity?

Which methods are most appropriate for localizing functions to particular brain structures? Explain your answer.

EXERCISE 7.3

Which methods are best for revealing the spatiotemporal course of language processing? Explain your answer.

EXERCISE 7.4

What are the advantages and disadvantages of direct cortical recording as compared to ERPs?

EXERCISE 7.5

List the anatomical structures, hormones, and neurotransmitters that have been implicated in the acquisition, representation, or processing of lexical knowledge, and briefly explain the apparent functional role(s) of each.

EXERCISE 7.6

What explanations have been given for the noun/verb dissociations that have been observed?

EXERCISE 7.7

What evidence presented in this chapter suggests common biological substrates between lexical memory and declarative memory?

EXERCISE 7.8

List the lexical, conceptual-semantic, phonological, syntactic, or morphological functions that have been tied to BA 44.

List the lexical, conceptual-semantic, phonological, syntactic, or morphological functions that have been tied to BA 45.

EXERCISE 7.9

What are the different stages involved in auditory sentence processing, according to the model proposed by Friederici and her colleagues? Provide the approximate timing and anatomical structures for each stage.

EXERCISE 7.10

List the evidence described in the morphology section of this chapter that you think is problematic for either a dual-system or single-mechanism view, and explain why.

SUGGESTIONS FOR FURTHER READING

Gaskell, M. G. (ed.) 2007, *The Oxford handbook of psycholinguistics*. Oxford University Press. This is a nice overview of psycholinguistic theory and research.

Gazzaniga, Michael S. (ed.) 2004, *The cognitive neurosciences*, Cambridge, MA: MIT Press. The chapters in the language section of this book discuss in some depth a number of the topics addressed in the present chapter.

Hickok, G. and Poeppel, D. 2004, "Special issue: Towards a new functional anatomy of language," *Cognition* **92**(1–2). This special issue is dedicated to current evidence and theories on the brain bases of language.

Stemmer, B. and Whitaker, H. A. 2008. *Handbook of the neuroscience of language*. Oxford: Elsevier. This book contains numerous short chapters on a wide range of topics in the study of brain and language.

8 Language change

CHAPTER PREVIEW

Most subfields of linguistics – like most of the chapters in this book – take a synchronic perspective toward language, trying to describe and explain language as a system at a given point in time (usually, the present). This is a useful simplification that has enabled much of the progress made by modern linguistics, but in reality languages are constantly, incrementally changing. As the chapters on both child and second language acquisition also show, looking at language as a changing, developing system offers valuable insights into its structure and use. Studying language diachronically (over time) also helps us to better understand prehistorical cultures.

   This chapter discusses the causes, processes, and mechanisms of language change, which are the concerns of historical linguistics. First, we'll discuss the causes of language change and describe the four main kinds of language change. Then we'll discuss in more detail some of the mechanisms of language change. Finally, we will see how linguists use knowledge of these processes to reconstruct languages that are no longer spoken, from evidence in the languages descended from them.

GOALS

The goals of this chapter are to:

- **explain how and why languages change over time:**
  - **how sound changes happen**
  - **how changes in morphology and syntax happen**
  - **how the meanings of words change**
- **show how linguists reconstruct languages no longer spoken**
- **relate language change over time to dialect and register variation and child language acquisition**

Languages change

Evidence from earlier speech, similarities between related languages, and differences between dialects show that languages change over time. For example, in the fourteenth century, when Chaucer was writing *The Canterbury Tales*, the English words *see*, *tooth*, *make*, and *open* were pronounced as [se:] [to:θ] [ma:kɛn] [ɔ:pɛn]. The Latin word *caru* /kaɹu/ 'dear' is now pronounced /kaɹo/ *caro* in Spanish and /ʃeɹ/ *cher* in French. More contemporarily, the distinction between the vowel sounds in words like *pin/pen* and *tin/ten* has been lost in the South Midland and Southern dialect areas in the United States; in these areas the vowels [ɪ] and [ɛ] have merged before nasals into [ɪ]. Historical linguistics – sometimes also called **diachronic linguistics** – seeks to explain how languages change over time.

All languages adapt to meet the changing contexts and needs of their speech communities. Often languages change as a result of contact with other languages (and their cultures), so language change reflects the social, political, and military history of a speech community. By studying changes in its language, we can better understand the history of a culture. For example, the French-speaking Normans occupied England for three hundred years following the Norman Conquest (1066 CE); this had a profound impact on the English language, evident in words borrowed from French for many concepts in the domains of government, the military, and the law. *Government, nation, parliament, society, royal, law, court, attorney, judge, crime, jury* all derived from French, to list just a few. Three hundred years of French political dominance caused changes in English phonology, morphology, and syntax as well.

Language change is regular and systematic. Sound changes since Middle English have affected whole classes of sounds, not just *see, tooth, make,* and *open.* This regularity allows historical linguists to "read back" through the history of a language and reconstruct earlier forms. Knowing the range of forms that languages have used throughout their respective histories allows us to better understand the structural, systematic options and constraints that are universal to all human languages.

Causes of language change

Languages change because they are used by human beings, not machines. Human beings share common physiological and cognitive characteristics, but members of a speech community differ slightly in their knowledge and use of their shared language. Speakers of different regions, social classes, and generations use language differently (dialect variation), and all speakers use language differently in different situations (register variation). As children acquire their native language, they are exposed to this synchronic variation within their language. For example, speakers of any generation use more and less formal language depending on the situation. Parents (and other adults) tend to use more informal language to children. Children may acquire some informal features of the language in preference to their formal alternatives, and incremental changes in the language (tending toward greater informality) accumulate over generations. (This may help explain why each generation seems to feel that following generations are ruder and less eloquent, and are corrupting the language!) When a later generation acquires an innovation in the language introduced by a previous generation, the language changes.

Language change, though inevitable, is not steady; a language may experience little change for many generations and then undergo dramatic changes in the course of just a few lifetimes. Physiological, cognitive, and social forces motivate change, and most language change can be attributed to articulatory simplification, regularization, and contact between languages.

Articulatory simplification

Many changes in the phonology of a language are motivated by the physiological goal of enhancing ease of articulation. If a sequence of sounds in a language is difficult to pronounce, or is unnecessarily complex, it is likely to be simplified. For example, with the loss of the phoneme /ə/ in many positions (an earlier sound change), many consonant clusters arose in Russian. These clusters were in many cases simplified by assimilation:

Proto-Slavic:	/nožəka/	/səd^{j}ælat^{j}i/	/podəp^{j}isat^{j}i/
	'small foot'	'to do'	'to sign'
	↓	↓	↓
Russian:	/noška/	/z^{j}d^{j}élat^j/	/pat^{j}p^{j}isát^j/

(An arrow means 'changed into,' 'became.') This assimilation was regressive; the first member of the consonant cluster became more like the second sound. In this case, the first sounds became (de)voiced and palatalized (the diacritic ^{j} indicates palatalization) and more like the second sounds, making these words easier to pronounce.

Regularization

Languages are flexible, open, adapting systems, but they also exhibit many mechanisms for maintaining their integrity and regularity, in order to enable their speakers to continue to communicate (relatively) efficiently throughout all those changes. This cognitive motivation is known to anyone who has ever tried to learn a second language; a regular pattern is easier to learn than a pattern with lots of exceptions. Children acquiring their native languages prefer regular patterns too, and over time languages tend to erase irregularities. (There are other forces which periodically introduce new irregularities into any language, so this is an ongoing process.) For example, speakers of a language will often extend a pattern from one set of forms to an exceptional form. The past tense of the verb *fell* (as in *to fell a tree*) is *felled*; the past tense of *shell* is *shelled*. The past tense of *swell* used to be *swal*, but now uses the regular past-tense marker *-ed* as to become *swelled*: *His chest swelled with pride.* The vowel change survives in the older past participle and adjectival form *swollen*: *a swollen ankle.*

Language contact

Languages often change as a result of contact with speakers of another language, an important social force. Sometimes the speakers of one language conquer the speakers of another and impose the conquering language on the conquered for a time, as in the case of the Norman Conquest of England. Members of the conquered speech community are motivated to use the language of their conquerors to gain access to social resources (power, wealth, education, etc.) which are controlled by the conquerors. Over time, the conqueror's words supplement or replace the corresponding words in the conquered language. For example, English speakers acquired new words for cuisine from their French-speaking conquerors. In Old English, the words for animals and for their meat were the same. But Normans ate *porc* and *mouton*, so English gained this semantic distinction, too: Middle English farmers raised *pigs* and *sheep*, but ate *pork* and *mutton*.

Borrowing can also result from economic and cultural contact between languages, as when one speech community adopts (or adapts) the name for a new invention or concept from another language. For example, when the sport of baseball was adopted by the Japanese, its name was borrowed and adapted to Japanese phonology and syllable structure as *besuboru*. Such **loan words** adapt the original word to the phonological constraints of the borrowing language. Much of the spread of English as an international lingua franca (common language) has been through the domains of science and technology, where it has been easier for speakers of other languages to adopt the English names of new concepts and inventions (for example, *television*, *computer*, *dot com*) than to coin their own.

Kinds of language change

All facets of a language change over time, including a speech community's norms for appropriately using the language, but historical linguists focus on four types of language change: phonological change, morphological change, syntactic change, and semantic change. Because the subsystems of language are interdependent, a change in one subsystem can initiate a chain reaction of changes in other subsystems.

BOX 8.1 ORIGINS OF LANGUAGE

The origins of human language are shrouded in the mists of prehistory. From reconstructions of protolanguages we know that human beings were speaking long before recorded history, but we don't know just when language first developed. However, as summarized in an article in the *New York Times* ("Early Voices: The Leap to Language" by Nicholas Wade, July 15, 2003), recent research from the fields of animal communication, archaeology, and genetics provides a few clues.

– Although no other animal has anything like the complexity of human language, many species do communicate. Birds have elaborate mating calls. Bees signal direction and distance to food sources. Primates have a variety of alarm calls for different predators. Chimpanzees and apes can even learn several hundred signed words, but they lack the ability to combine them with anything like the syntactic complexity of human languages. (Chimpanzees can learn to order their symbols to get what they want – for example, signing 'give me orange' – but they often change the order of signs and there is no evidence of grammatical categories like tense, number, agreement, or articles in primate signing.) However, some researchers believe that the neural systems for producing and perceiving sounds that exist in other species were the evolutionary precursors for human language. Even Noam Chomsky recently argued that animals' brains have many of the components of language, but that somehow – perhaps by mutation – only human brains linked these components all together.

– Dr. Derek Bickerton of the University of Hawai'i claims that language may have followed the same path by which some new languages develop even today. He argues that humans may have developed a simple protolanguage – words without syntax – thousands of years before developing the hierarchical, recursive syntax of modern human language. This protolanguage may have looked like pidgins, simplified contact languages composed of individual words and simple phrases which are developed between speech communities which have no language in common. When a new generation of children acquires a pidgin as their native language, it becomes a creole – a full-fledged language with morphology and syntax.

Bickerton believes that the need to communicate decontextualized information may have been the motivating force behind the development of language. The selective advantage for individuals – and groups – who could communicate more complex information would have been tremendous – great enough to account for the apparently rapid spread of language. Food gatherers who could share information about the location of food sources would have been very popular, as would hunters who could plan and supervise more successful hunts. Groups of early humans who had developed language would also have had a distinct and often lethal advantage in conflicts with groups who had not developed language, facilitating the spread of language.

– In Africa, archaeologists have found skeletons of early humans dating back to 100,000 years ago, buried with the same crude stone tools as were used by Neanderthals and their predecessors. But around 50,000 years ago, the archaeological record shows important changes in the way early humans lived – more sophisticated tools, art, and even evidence of long-distance trade. Some archaeologists believe that these artifacts reflect a genetic change affecting the way early humans used their brains – a change which might also have included the development of language. Modern humans, homo sapiens, appear to have developed first in Africa and then spread across the world. If language first appeared and spread among a small population of homo sapiens in Africa, the competitive advantage of language would help to explain the spread of homo sapiens to the rest of the world – and perhaps the disappearance of their Neanderthal competitors.

– Studies of a British family known as KE may even have identified a gene responsible for language. Of 29 members of the KE family across three generations, 14 have a language disorder which makes it difficult for them to pronounce words, speak grammatically, and even write. Geneticists at the University of Oxford discovered a specific gene, called FOXP2, which is different in members of the KE family. FOXP2 switches on other genes in particular areas of the brain during fetal development.

BOX 8.1 (*cont.*)

The language disorder of the KE family is extremely rare because any change in the FOXP2 gene's protein sequence is almost always fatal. Dr. Svante Paabo and colleagues at the Max Planck Institute for Evolutionary Anthropology in Leipzig, Germany, found that there have been just two changes in the FOXP2 protein sequence since six million years ago, when the hominid species broke off from other primates. The second change in FOXP2 seems to have taken place about 100,000 years ago, before modern humans spread out from Africa. These genetic changes swept through the human population, suggesting that they conferred some large selective advantage – like the ability to produce and interpret complex words and sentences very rapidly. If the KE family's language disorder represents the pre-change human genome, FOXP2 may be the genetic key to language. By mapping the other genes that FOXP2 switches on in fetal development and then tracing the areas of the brain that these genes control, researchers may be able to identify the neural basis of language.

Phonological change

Phonological change refers to any change in the sound system of a language – particularly its phonemes and their distribution. In fact, all elements of a language's sound system – syllable structure, tones, and stress patterns – change over time, but historical linguists tend to focus on changes in segmental phonology.

Most sound changes start out as small but regular variations in a phoneme's surface articulation which are motivated, or conditioned, by its immediate phonetic context. For example, in many dialects of Spanish [n] has changed to [ŋ] word finally. Words such as *son* 'they are' and *bien* 'well, very,' which used to be pronounced [son] and [bjen], are now pronounced [soŋ] and [bjeŋ] in these dialects. This is, however, merely a phonetic/allophonic change, since the new sound [ŋ] does not contrast with [n]; there are no pairs of words which differ only in using the [n] or [ŋ] sound.

Many phonological changes start out as phonetic changes – limited allophonic rules (often simplifying articulation or improving the salience of a phoneme); but over successive generations of speakers some of these allophones become contrastive phonemes in their own right, changing the phonemic inventory of the language and resulting in phonological change. (And often, sound changes spark subsequent changes in the phonology, morphology, and even syntax of the language.) For example, in early Old English (449–700 CE) the phonemes /f θ s/ were pronounced [f θ s] (that is, unvoiced) everywhere. About 700 CE, Old English speakers were voicing these fricatives whenever they occurred between voiced sounds (assimilating the unvoiced phonemes /f θ s/ to the surrounding voiced phonemes). This allophonic change produced the new allophones [v ð z], which generations of (later) Old English speakers understood as their respective underlying unvoiced phonemes /f θ s/. So, in Table 8.1, *five* was pronounced [fi:f] and *fifth* was pronounced [fi:fta] because the /f/ phonemes were not surrounded by voiced sounds. But the Old English Word for *sea monster*, which had been pronounced [fi:fɛl] before 700 CE, was later pronounced [fi:vɛl], because the second /f/ phoneme was articulated between,

TABLE 8.1 Old English fricatives after 700 CE

fi:f	[fi:f]	'five'	fi:fel	[fi:vɛl]	'sea monster'
fi:fta	[fi:ftɑ]	'fifth'			
bæth	[bæθ]	'bath'	bathu	[baðʊ]	'baths'
so:na	[so:nɑ]	'immediately'	ma:se	[ma:zɛ]	'titmouse'
hu:s	[hu:s]	'house'			

and assimilated to, its surrounding voiced sounds (in this case, vowels). Likewise, the /θ/ and /s/ phonemes in *baths* and *titmouse* became voiced ([baðʊ] and [ma:zɛ]) as they assimilated to their surrounding vowels. The phonology of later Old English speakers included an allophonic rule that their predecessors' phonology did not have, and generations of speakers after 700 CE grew up regularly (and unconsciously) voicing the underlying unvoiced phonemes /f θ s/ whenever they were surrounded by voiced elements.

These voiced allophones became independent phonemes in Middle English (1100–1500) and early Modern English. How do we know this? In Old English the voiced fricatives [v ð z] had appeared only as allophones of the phonemes /f θ s/ when pronounced between two voiced sounds, but they started appearing in new environments in which the allophonic "fricative voicing rule" did not apply (that is, not just between voiced sounds).

Words were borrowed from French and Scandinavian which had [v ð z] at the beginning, such as *very, vanity, voice, zenith, zone* (from French) and *they, them, their* (from Old Norse). In addition, the initial [θ] in unstressed words, such as *the, this*, became voiced [ð] through lenition. And finally, the final *-e* [ə], as in *give, lose,* and *bathe*, was no longer pronounced (although it survived in written spelling as the "silent *e*") but the voicing on the final fricatives remained.

As a result of these sound changes and borrowings, the voiced fricatives of Old English were no longer simply allophones of voiceless fricatives in a voiced environment but rather occurred in overlapping environments and the voiced and voiceless fricatives became contrastive (that is, could be used to indicate a difference in meaning). Generations of Middle English speakers no longer "heard" the voiced fricatives [v ð z] as allophones of the phonemes /f θ s/, but as new, contrastive phonemes in their own right. The inventory of English phonemes and their relations had changed. The addition of new phonemes to the phonemic inventory of a language is one example of phonological change.

Morphological change

Morphological change refers to any change in the morphophonemic system (the morphemes and their phonemic representation) of a language. One of the most dramatic changes in the English language involved how nouns were morphologically marked to indicate certain kinds of information. Old English, like Modern Russian, allowed relatively free word order. The subject of a sentence could appear before or after the verb (and before

BOX 8.2 **MORE ON PHONEMIC CHANGE: UMLAUTING**

For another example of phonemic change, consider a sound change in pre-Old English known as umlaut. In umlauting, a back vowel was fronted when followed by the front vowel /i/ or the front semivowel /y/ in the following syllable. Thus, the back vowels [ʊ u: o:] changed to the front vowels [ö ü: ö:]. The Old English words and their pre-Old English sources in the table below illustrate some of these changes. (The pre-Old English sources are marked with an asterisk to indicate that these are reconstructed, not attested, forms.)

Umlaut in Pre-Old English and Old English

Pre-Old English I:	Pre-Old English II	Old English	
*sunyo:	*sünyo:	sönn	'sin'
*mu:si	*mü:si	mü:s	'mice'
*bo:ki	*bö:ki	bö:c	'book (dative)'
*go:si	*gö:si	gö:s	'geese'

This sound change created the front allophones [ö ü: ö:], sounds that did not exist earlier, from the phonemes /ʊ u: o:/, respectively. This was a mere phonetic or allophonic change, but later in Old English it became phonemic. Through an unrelated change, the following unaccented front vowel /i/ and the semivowel /y/ – which had conditioned the umlaut change – were lost, but the umlauted vowels remained. New generations heard the umlauted vowels of their elders, but no longer recognized that they were related to the back vowel phonemes. The speech community's model of their phonemic resources of contrastive sounds for building words had changed. The umlauted vowels [ü: ö:] now contrasted with other vowels, e.g. /mu:s/ 'mouse' /mü:s/ 'mice' and /go:s/ 'goose' /gö:s/ 'geese,' and became independent phonemes /ü: ö:/. Later, by Middle English, /ü: ö:/ changed to /i: e:/ and merged with the existing phonemes /i: e:/ occurring in /wi:f/ 'wife' and /be:tɛ/ 'beet.' Once the umlaut became phonemic, it produced allomorphic alternations attested in pairs such as /mu:s/ 'mouse' /mi:s/ 'mice' and /go:s/ 'goose' /ge:s/ 'geese.' With all these changes, you can begin to see why you would be unable to understand a speaker of Old English!

or after the direct object), for example. To indicate the role of a particular noun in a sentence – its relation to the verb and other nouns – every noun was marked with a case ending. Old English nouns were inflected with endings denoting a variety of cases: nominative, accusative, genitive, dative, and instrumental singular and plural. For example, /gɹʊnd/ 'ground' was inflected as follows:

	Singular	Plural	
Nominative and accusative	/gɹʊnd/	/gɹʊndɑs/	'ground/grounds'
Genitive	/gɹʊndɛs/	/gɹʊndɑ/	'of ground / of grounds'
Dative and instrumental	/gɹʊndɛ/	/gɹʊndʊm/	'to, with ground / to, with grounds'

Case distinction began to be lost in Middle English, when the Old English unstressed genitive plural /-ɑ/, dative singular /-ɛ/, and dative/instrumental plural /-ʊm/ endings collapsed into the single ending /-ɛ/. The final /-ɛ/ subsequently reduced to /-ə/ and then was completely lost in early Modern English. Because of these sound changes, by the time of Modern English (*c.* 1700) the system of case inflection was almost entirely lost. Singular and plural are still morphologically marked today, but there is no morphological clue to a noun's case (whether it is the subject or object of the verb in a sentence, recipient of the object, etc.). The one case which is still marked is the genitive (possessive) 's ending.

Syntactic change

Syntactic change refers to change in the grammatical system of a language. Once case was no longer marked by inflectional affixes, speakers of Middle English had to find some other way of indicating the role each noun played in a sentence in relation to the verb and to other nouns. Old English, because it had a rich case-marking system, had allowed relatively free word order. Simple sentences usually put the subject first, followed by the verb and then the object (SVO), but in a number of circumstances the verb came first (VSO) or the object came before the verb (SOV). As the case-marking system was lost, word order in Middle English became increasingly fixed as SVO, so speakers could indicate the grammatical relations of nouns in clauses.

Semantic change

Semantic change is mainly concerned with changes in the meanings of words. These changes are usually incremental and can be traced historically. Where documents exist from earlier times, linguists can infer the meaning of a word from its use in context. For example, the meanings of the Modern English words *nice* and *silly* are the results of odysseys of semantic change. In Latin the combination of *ne* 'not' plus the verb *sci:-re* 'to know' resulted in *nescius*, meaning 'ignorant.' It survived as *nice*, meaning 'lazy, simple,' in Old French. It was then borrowed into Middle English as *nice*, where it meant 'foolish, simple, fastidious, delicious.' In Modern English its meanings are solely positive ('enjoyable,' 'polite'). The form for *silly* in Old English was *sælig* [sæliɣ] and meant 'blessed, fortunate.' In Middle English it changed to *seli* [sɛli] or *sili* [sɪli] with the meaning of 'pitiable, innocent.' In Modern English, *silly* means 'stupid,' 'frivolous,' 'dazed.'

The meanings of words can change in a variety of ways. As the experience and understanding of the world of a speech community change, the words for things (and differences and relations between things) may change as well. New words may be coined for new objects and concepts (like *television* and *x-rays*), but often speech communities adapt the meanings of existing words. In **broadening**, the range of meaning of a word increases. For example, in Middle English *bird* meant 'young bird'; along with a change in pronunciation, in Modern English its meaning broadened to the entire genus, *bird*. **Metonymy** is a particular kind of broadening, in which a word referring to a characteristic or concept associated with a semantic domain is used to represent the entire domain. For example, *silver* extended from referring to the metal to mean also 'items of tableware or other household goods that are made of silver, coated with silver plate, or made of silver colored metal.' Although its use is waning, nowadays *silver* can refer to dining utensils made from any metal. The range of meaning of a word can decrease and become less general, by the process of **narrowing**. So, for example, Old English *hund* 'dog' narrowed to Modern English *hound* to refer to 'a particular breed of dog.'

The evaluative dimension of a word's meaning can also change, acquiring new negative or positive associations. In **pejoration**, the meaning of a word acquires a negative value. Consider the current meaning of *mistress*, which was originally a borrowing from Old French *maistresse* 'a woman who rules.' Semantic changes are sometimes revealing of social attitudes; notice that *master* (from Old French *maistre* 'a man who rules') has none of the sexual meaning of *mistress*. Of course, the meaning of a word can also take a turn for the better. In **amelioration**, the meaning of a word acquires a more positive value. For example, Modern English *pretty* came from Old English *prætig* 'deceitful, tricky.'

Words change meaning because people use language creatively. Sometimes a change in meaning is motivated by **metaphor**, the perception of similarity between two things or situations. For example English *grave* 'sad, serious' originally meant 'heavy' (from Latin *gravis*). In Sanskrit, *guru* 'heavy' metaphorically acquired a second meaning, 'weighty, important, a person worthy of honor.' (Only the second meaning was then borrowed into English and has come to mean knowledgeable person.) Similarly, in **ellipsis**, a word takes the meaning of a whole phrase, e.g. *a daily paper* becomes *a daily*, *a painting by Picasso* becomes *a Picasso*, and *a private soldier* becomes *a private*. As is seen in the phrases *a daily* and *a private*, in which the adjectives *daily* and *private* have become nouns, ellipsis may lead to a change in the grammatical category of words. English *bus* is another example of such change: it is a shortened form of the Latin *omnibus* 'for everybody,' in which a Latin case ending (dative/ablative pl. *-bus*) has been lexicalized as a noun.

Grammaticalization refers to a semantic change in which a lexical morpheme is transformed into a grammatical morpheme. An obvious example is the English lexical morpheme *will*, which earlier meant 'want.' Evidence of its original meaning is seen in phrases such a *have the will* [desire], *good will* [wishes, desires], *if you will* [want to]. Its German cognate *will* '(he/she) wants' still occurs with the same meaning. But with the loss of its sense of 'want' English *will* was grammaticalized as a 'future' marker, and since grammaticalized forms often show phonetic erosion or reduction, it shows contractions such as *I'll*, *she'll*, *the man'll be there*. The inflectional suffixes in many languages were often independent words that have been grammaticalized. The Old Hungarian lative case marker *-bele*, as in *vilagbele* 'into the world' and its reduced form *-ba*, which occurs in Modern Hungarian *vilagba*, was originally a lexical morpheme *bele* 'guts, core.' The French derivational suffix *-ment*, in *doucement* 'gently,' 'softly,' smoothly,' was originally a noun in Latin, as in *dulce mente* 'with a sweet mind.' The English preposition *from* has its origin in the Old English *fram* 'strong, good,' literally 'forward.' This is how grammatical morphemes often originate and free nouns become adverbs, affixes, and prepositions.

When suffixes, parts of compounds, or phrases become independent words, the process is called lexicalization. They have to be learned separately as independent words. Examples of this can be seen in the lexicalization of the Latin dative/ablative plural suffix *-bus* as the noun *bus* from the shortened *omnibus*. Other examples of lexicalization in English are *ism* (communism), *teen* (teen-ager), *daily* (daily newspaper), *drive-in* (drive-in theater).

TABLE 8.2 Latin /k/ in French

(a) Latin /k/ French /k/			(b) Latin /k/ French /s/			(c) Latin /k/ French /ʃ/		
cor	coeur	'heart'	centum	cent	'hundred'	cantāre	chanter	'sing'
clārus	clair	'clear'	cervus	cerf	'hart'	carbō	charbon	'coal'
quandō	quand	'when'	cinis	cendre	'ashes'	causa	chose	'thing'

We have seen that a sound change can lead to morphological and syntactic changes; a sound change can result in semantic change as well. When unstressed vowels in English were lost, the Old English [é:are] 'ear' and [é:ar] 'grain of a plant with the husk on it,' became phonetically alike, and since the referents have some resemblance, speakers of Modern English assume that an *ear* of grain is metaphorically related to the *ear* of an animal.

Mechanisms of language change

There are three main mechanisms creating language change: **sound change**, **borrowing**, and **analogical creation**.

Sound change

Sound change is a change in the way members of a speech community pronounce particular sounds; it takes place constantly but slowly. Sound changes result in phonological changes (changes to the phonology of the language). Tracing sound changes helps linguists to determine relatedness among languages and reconstruct languages no longer spoken, and to distinguish loan words such as *dentist* and *pedestrian* from native words such as *tooth* and *foot*.

Conditioned sound change

Most sound changes are dependent on, or conditioned by, phonetic environment. Phonetically conditioned changes are exactly like the allophonic rules found (synchronically) in all languages. As we saw earlier, the voicing of fricatives in Old English was conditioned by the assimilation of the unvoiced fricative when surrounded by voiced sounds. Another example of a conditioned sound change is what happened to the phoneme /k/ as Latin evolved into French. As shown in Table 8.2 (which presents Latin and French spellings), Latin /k/ changed to /s/ before /e/, /ʃ/ before /a/, and remained unchanged before /o/ or before another consonant.

Unconditioned sound change

Not all sound changes are conditioned by a specific phonetic environment. Sometimes the changes are much more extensive, involving several related sounds. As an example of an

TABLE 8.3 The Great Vowel Shift in English

Middle English (Chaucer)		Early Modern (Shakespeare)		Modern English	
name	**[aː]**	name	**[æ']**	name	**[eː]**
bete	**[eː]**	beet	**[iː]**	beet	**[iː]**
foal	**[ɔː]**	foal	**[oː]**	foal	**[oː]**
fol	**[oː]**	fool	**[uː]**	fool	**[uː]**
bite	**[iː]**	bite	**[əi]**	bite	**[aɪ]**
foul	**[uː]**	foul	**[əu]**	foul	**[aʊ]**

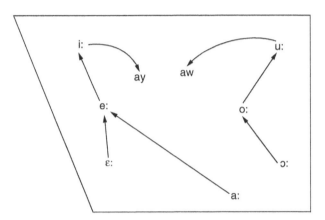

Figure 8.1 The Great Vowel Shift in English

unconditioned sound change, consider the series of changes known as the **Great Vowel Shift** in which the long vowels of Middle English were unconditionally but systematically raised in Early Modern English. The following examples are taken from Middle English (Chaucer 1340–1400), Early Modern English (Shakespeare 1564–1616), and Modern English.

As Table 8.3 and Figure 8.1 show, the low-central vowel /aː/ and the low front vowel /æ/ raised and then merged to /eː/, and the mid-front vowel /eː/ raised to /iː/. The low back vowel /ɔː/ raised to /oː/, and Middle English /oː/ shifted up to /uː/. Since Middle English /iː/ and /uː/ were already high, they changed into the diphthongs /ay/ and /aw/, respectively. What caused this wholesale shift in the English vowel system is still debated, but it may have been motivated by a need for greater ease of articulation and discrimination among the vowels. Every language tends to maximize the discriminability of its sounds, in order to minimize ambiguities of meaning. English before the Great Vowel Shift had a relatively large number of vowels, which seems to have led to "overcrowding" of the available phonological "space." Such overcrowding creates ambiguities of meaning

("Did he mean a 'foal' or a 'fool'?") and generations of speakers of English incrementally shifted their pronunciation to make their meanings clearer. Of course, shifting one vowel to another articulatory position in a limited phonological space can create a new phonetic conflict ("Did he mean a 'fool' or a 'foul'?") and eventually a whole set of related sounds shifted.

Chain shifts

A sound change may initiate a set of changes known as **chain shifts**. The Great Vowel Shift is an example of a **push chain** of sound changes. The earlier long vowel /a:/ of Chaucer's time changed to /æ:/ in Shakespeare's time (/na:mə/ → /næ:m/ 'name'). In conjunction with the loss of the final schwa, this change in vowel quality created ambiguities between minimal pairs, as two words which had previously been distinguished by their vowels were now pronounced with the same vowel. (Imagine the confusion if Modern English words like *pat* and *sat* and *bat* were pronounced the same way as *pet* and *set* and *bet*.) These ambiguities pushed the original /æ:/ to /e:/ (/bæ:tə/ → /be:t/ 'beat' – which subsequently changed to /bi:t/ in later years). This created a new set of ambiguities, which then pushed the original /e:/ to /i:/ (/be:tə/ → /bi:t/ 'beet'), creating yet another set of ambiguities, which then pushed the original /i:/ to /əi/ (/bi:tə/ → /bəit/ 'bite'). This last step actually created a new phoneme in the phonological system – the diphthong /ay/. Similarly the rounded vowel /o:/ changed to /o:/ (/fɔ:l/ → /fo:l/ 'foal') and pushed the original /o:/ to /u:/ (/fo:l/ → /fu:l/ 'fool'), which then pushed the original /u:/ to /əu/ (/fu:l/ → /fəul/ 'foul').

In a **pull chain**, a change in one sound may create a gap in the phonemic pattern, in the space from which the sound shifted. This can motivate a subsequent sound change by "pulling" another sound in the phonemic pattern to fill the gap. But this pulling may create another gap, only to be filled by another pulling. The process may continue until a stable distribution of phonemes throughout the phonological space is achieved. For example, as Latin evolved into Spanish, Latin intervocalic voiced /d/ and /g/ were lost: Latin *cadēre* → Spanish *caer* 'to fall,' Latin *rēgīna* → Spanish *reina* 'queen.' The loss of intervocalic /d/ and /g/ created a gap in the Spanish consonant system which was filled by voicing the Latin intervocalic stops /t k/: Latin *vita* → Spanish *vida* 'life,' Latin *amīca* → Spanish *amiga* 'female friend.' But this, in turn, created a gap where the intervocalic voiceless stops /t k/ had been, which then was filled by reducing the Latin intervocalic geminates /tt kk/ to single voiceless stops /t k/: Latin *gutta* → Spanish *gota* 'drop,' Latin *bucca* [bukka] 'puffed out cheek' → Spanish *boca* [boka] 'mouth.' (If this sounds a bit circular, remember that languages don't "know where they're going" and changes like these occur over generations, so speakers of a language typically are not aware of language change.)

Once sound changes occur in a language, the prior (changed) sounds no longer exist. However, they often leave clues that allow us to determine their **relative chronology**, the order in which those sound changes occurred. For example, in Middle English, the voiceless palatal fricative [ç] was pronounced before /t/ in such words as *night* [niçt], *light* [liçt], and *right* [riçt]. As the modern pronunciation of these words shows, two changes

TABLE 8.4 Merger (Old English /ɛ a ʊ/ → Middle English /ɛ/)

Old English	Middle English	Modern English	
/lɑmɑ/	/la:mɛ/	/leym/	'lame'
/grʊnd-ɛ/	/gru:nd-ɛ/	/graʊnd-/	'ground'
/mɛdʊ/	/mɛ:dɛ/	/miyd/	'mead, liquor'

occurred: [ç] was deleted before /t/, and the preceding short vowel /i/ was lengthened to /i:/. This **compensatory lengthening** must have taken place before the Great Vowel Shift. How can we tell? Remember that as a result of the Great Vowel Shift, the high vowel /i:/ was pushed into a new address in the vowel space – the diphthong /ay/. The vowels in *night*, *light*, and *right* must have been /i:/ when the Great Vowel Shift began, to have been changed into the diphthong /ay/, so the lengthening change from /i/ to /i:/ must have preceded the Great Vowel Shift. Notice that we find in language change the same kind of rule-ordering that is found in synchronic phonological theory, a further reminder of the close connection between the synchronic structure of language and the diachronic processes of language change.

Mergers and splits

In the process of language change, existing phonemes may drift close together and produce a **merger**, or a single phoneme may **split** into two phonemes. A sound may also change into another (new) sound without any merger or split.

We have seen an example of merger and its consequences earlier: unstressed Old English /ɛ a ʊ/ merged into Middle English /ɛ/ (which then changed to /ə/, and later was lost in Early Modern English), as shown in Table 8.4. After this phonological change, the phonemes /ɛ a ʊ/ ceased to contrast word finally, causing inflectional and syntactic changes – the simplification of the Old English case-marking system and the fixing of word order – described earlier.

Splits are always conditioned. Often a merger and a split occur together. By about 600 BCE, Latin /s/ split into /r/ between vowels and /s/ elsewhere. Thus, the earlier intervocalic /s/ of *genesis* 'of the type' became /r/ in *generis*. However, the intervocalic /r/ resulting from this split merged with the pre-existing /r/ in words like *mīror* 'wonder,' which always had an intervocalic /r/. This change, known as **Latin rhotacism**, caused a *phonological change* by affecting the distribution of the phonemes /s/ and /r/, and also a *morphological change* by creating some allomorphic alternation, such as *flōs* 'flower' (nominative singular) vs. *flōr-is* 'flower' (genitive singular) and *es-t* 'be present' vs. *er-it* 'be future.'

Processes of sound change

The sounds of a language can change in a variety of ways, most commonly by **assimilation**, **dissimilation**, **deletion**, **epenthesis**, **compensatory lengthening**, **metathesis**, **haplology**, and **contamination**. (Chapter 1 also discusses some of these

BOX 8.3 **A BRIEF HISTORY OF ENGLISH**

Many of our examples of language change have been drawn from the development of English, so a brief history of the language may be useful. Modern English is a rich example of the role of language contact in language change; in broad strokes, it was shaped by a series of invasions over the course of 1,000 years. The language was originally brought to Britain by Germanic tribes (the Angles, Saxons, and Jutes), influenced by invading Norsemen, and finally transformed by the occupation of French-speaking Normans.

Pre-English. Around 400 BCE, the Celtic-speaking peoples, who were descended from the original Indo-Europeans and had spread throughout Europe, migrated to the British Isles. The Celtic language survives in Modern Irish and Scots Gaelic and Welsh, but the Celtic contribution to what became English was overrun by a series of invasions. The first of these invasions was led by Julius Caesar in 43 BCE. The Romans colonized and ruled the southern half of "Britannia" for 400 years, but very little Latin influence on the Celtic languages carried over to English.

Old English: c. 600–1100 CE. The Romans withdrew from Britain as their empire collapsed in the early fifth century. They were soon replaced by Germanic-speaking invaders – the Jutes, the Angles, the Saxons, and later the Frisians. The invading tribes settled in different parts of the island, and by 600 CE, spoke dialects – of what we call "Old English" – which were distinct from the Germanic languages spoken on the continent. The Anglo-Saxons overwhelmed the Celts linguistically as well as militarily; Old English contained just a few Celtic words, but the most frequently used words in English today – words like *the*, *is*, and *you* – are of Anglo-Saxon origin. Gradually, the country became known as *Engla-land* – the land of the Angles – and their language was called *Englisc*.

Old English was influenced by Latin in the seventh century when St. Augustine and a group of monks converted Britain to Christianity. Dozens of Latinate words survive from this period – including *angel* and *devil*, *disciple*, *martyr*, and *shrine*. Christian churches and monasteries produced many written texts – excellent evidence of what Old English was like.

Between 800 and 1050, invasions by the Vikings had a profound impact on Old English. In 878 King Alfred of Wessex beat the Vikings in battle and forced a treaty by which the Vikings withdrew to the north and the Old English-speaking Saxons ruled the south. Alfred created a sense of national identity among the various groups of Saxons in the south by appealing to their shared language and mandating that English, not Latin, would be the language of education.

The Saxons and the Vikings lived alongside each other for generations (despite occasional wars), and their continued contact played a significant role in greatly simplifying the structure of Old English. Old English and Old Norse speakers shared many Germanic root words but their grammatical and inflectional systems differed. Over generations of contact, Old English lost many of its inflectional markings and borrowed dozens of words of Norse origin, like *hit*, *skin*, *want*, and *wrong*, and even pronouns like *them*, *they*, and *their*. Many of these borrowed words were added alongside Old English synonyms – for example, *rear* (English) and *raise* (Norse).

Middle English: c. 1100–1500. In 1066, William of Normandy won the Battle of Hastings, and French became the language of government, religion, and education in England for nearly 300 years. Bilingualism gradually became common among those who dealt with both upper (French-speaking) and lower (English-speaking) classes. By 1300, thousands of French words had been borrowed into English, especially in the domains of power: *nation*, *nobility*, *crown*, and *parliament* – not to mention *government* and *religion*. The language contact led to a further simplification of the English phonological system: Old English diphthongs were simplified into long vowels; word-initial consonant clusters like *kn-* in knight were simplified (though many kept their earlier spelling); and short unstressed vowels merged into the schwa sound. These phonological changes led to the loss of most remaining case and gender morphemic distinctions, which in turn caused English to become a much more fixed word-order grammatical system.

In the thirteenth century, the English kings lost Normandy – and their ties to the French – and English once again became a symbol of national identity. In 1362 English became the language of the law courts — with many words borrowed from French: e.g. *judge*, *court*, *attorney*, *crime*, and *sue*. Chaucer wrote *The Canterbury Tales* in Middle English around 1380. The London dialect's status as the 'standard' was codified in

1474 when William Caxton brought the printing press to England and based his spellings on London pronunciations. The Great Vowel Shift (*c.* 1450–1650) marks the transition from Middle to Modern English. The spellings of many English words persist from before the shift and reflect the Middle English pronunciation.

Modern English: c. 1500–present. The language settled into its relatively fixed Subject–Verb–Object word order, but continued its acquisitive ways, adding thousands of borrowed words to its lexicon.

Shakespeare, writing in the late 1500s and drawing from continental sources for his plots, also imported many foreign words. The King James Bible, first published in 1611, set a long-standing model for written English. During the eighteenth-century classical period of English literature, writers not only borrowed hundreds of Latin and Greek words, they even coined new words using Latin and Greek morphemes. The British Empire imported words from all around the world. The scientific, industrial, and communication revolutions of the nineteenth and twentieth centuries inspired new technical vocabularies, and English spread – particularly as a scientific lingua franca – throughout the world. At the same time, immigrants to English-speaking countries continue to make contributions to the lexical richness of the language. Throughout its history, English has been a heavy borrower of words from other languages. While its most frequently used words are overwhelmingly "native" (that is, of Anglo-Saxon origin), some 60 percent of the 20,000 words in common use are borrowed.

phonological processes because allophonic alternations in the synchronic structure of a language are the mechanisms of many processes of language change.) Some of these changes are part of the ongoing evolution of each language toward greater ease of articulation, while others are motivated by influences from other languages or changes in the needs of the speech community. These forces of change interact to ensure that a language is never stable and is always changing.

In **assimilation** a sound changes in the direction of a nearby sound, often for ease of articulation. The most common kind of assimilation is regressive assimilation, in which the first member of a consonant cluster changes in the direction of the second sound. For example:

Latin:	octō	noctem	factum	ruptum	septem
	'eight'	'night'	'done'	'broken'	'seven'
	↓	↓	↓	↓	↓
Italian:	otto	notte	fatto	rotto	sette

In progressive assimilation, the second consonant is altered:

Sanskrit:	putra 'son'	mitra 'friend'	šukra 'Venus'
	↓	↓	↓
Prakrit:	putta	mitta	sukka

Assimilation can be total, as the above examples show, or it can be partial: Sanskrit *šakuntalā* 'Shakuntala, a woman's name' changed into Prakrit *saundalā*, and Sanskrit *kintu* 'but' became Prakrit *kindu*. The change from /nt/ to /nd/ shows partial progressive assimilation, because /t/ took only the feature of voicing from the preceding /n/ (and not its manner of articulation).

The opposite of assimilation is **dissimilation**, in which similar sounds become less similar. For example, Latin *peregrínus* 'foreigner, stranger' became Italian *pellegrino* and French *pèlerin* 'foreigner, pilgrim, traveler.' (In Spanish, however, the original sequence remains unchanged: *peregrino*.) Similar dissimilation occurred when Sanskrit *daridra* became Bhojpuri *daliddar* 'poor.' Sanskrit *sammāna* became Bhojpuri *sanmān* 'honor,' a dissimilation in which *mm* became *nm*.

Unstressed vowels often get deleted from the interior of a word. This kind of loss or **deletion** is called **syncope**. For example, Vulgar Latin *pópulu* 'people' became French *peuple* and Spanish *pueblo*; Vulgar Latin *fābulare* became Spanish *hablar* 'to speak.' (Vulgar, or spoken, Latin was the link between Classical Latin and the modern Romance languages.) Similarly, Proto-Slavic *otədalə* → Russian *oddal* 'gave back,' and Proto-Slavic *bʲəratʲi* → Russian *bʲratʲ* 'to take.' Vowels don't just disappear from words over night, of course. Vowel deletion is usually preceded by vowel reduction; a vowel in some words (often in unstressed syllables) becomes shorter, more lax, and more central before disappearing from those words entirely. Each successive generation hears (and produces) a shorter and less differentiated vowel, until finally the vowel is no longer part of those words.

Consonants can also be deleted over time. For example, when some complex consonant clusters were produced by the loss of Proto-Slavic /ə/ in Russian, they were simplified by deletion of one of the consonants:

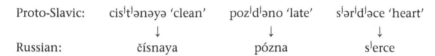

Proto-Slavic: cisʲtʲənəyə 'clean'   pozʲdʲəno 'late'   sʲərʲdʲəce 'heart'
                      ↓   ↓   ↓
Russian: čísnaya   pózna   sʲerce

Apocope, another kind of deletion, refers to the loss of a sound, usually a vowel, at the end of a word:

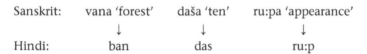

Sanskrit: vana 'forest'   daša 'ten'   ru:pa 'appearance'
                   ↓   ↓   ↓
Hindi: ban   das   ru:p

As another example, Old English *asce, oxa, sunu* became Modern English *ash, ox, son*, respectively. Some speakers of English show consonantal apocopation in *chile* for *child* and *ole* for *old*.

When a sound is inserted into a word, it is called **epenthesis**. The insertion of a sound at the beginning of a word is known as **prosthesis**. Latin words beginning with *s* plus a stop consonant show a prosthetic *e* in Spanish: Latin *scuta* 'shield,' *scola* 'school,' *stabula* 'stable' became Spanish *escudo, escuela, estable*, respectively. When a vowel is inserted between two consonants, it is called an **anaptyxis** or **svarabhakti** vowel:

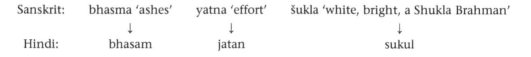

Sanskrit: bhasma 'ashes'   yatna 'effort'   šukla 'white, bright, a Shukla Brahman'
                   ↓   ↓   ↓
Hindi: bhasam   jatan   sukul

Excrescence is a kind of epenthesis in which, for ease of articulation, a consonant is inserted between other consonants: Old English *thȳmel, scamol, slumere, æmetig, thunor, spinel* became Modern English *thimble, shambles, slumber, empty, thunder, spindle*. In these examples, the loss of the Old English unstressed vowels after the nasals created a hard-to-pronounce consonant cluster, within which the excrescent stop /b/, /p/, or /d/ was inserted.

The weakening or loss of consonants is sometimes accompanied by **compensatory** lengthening of a preceding vowel. As we saw before, after the Middle English [ç] was lost before /t/ in *night* [niçt], *light* [liçt], and *right* [riçt], the preceding vowel /i/ was lengthened and subsequently changed to the diphthong /ay/ in Modern English. Another example of such lengthening is:

Sanskrit:	sapta 'seven'	tapta 'hot'	putra 'son'
	↓	↓	↓
Prakrit:	satta	tatta	putta
	↓	↓	↓
Hindi:	sāt	tāt	pūt

After the Prakrit assimilation, the geminated consonants were simplified and the preceding vowel /a/ or /u/ was lengthened in Hindi.

Sometimes the positions of sounds are transposed, a process called **metathesis**. For example, Old English *hros, brid, thridda, beorht, thurh, wyrhta* became Modern English *horse, bird, third, bright, through, Wright*. Spanish shows sporadic metathesis in which Latin /r...l/ was changed to /l...r/; for example, Latin *parabola* became Spanish *palabra* 'word.'

In **haplology**, a repeated sequence of sounds is reduced to a single occurrence. Thus, the expected form for the Latin feminine agent-noun 'nurse' ought to be *nūtrītrīx* (*nūtrī* 'nourish' plus the feminine agent *trīx*), but the actual form is *nūtrīx*. Similarly, Latin *stīpipendium* 'wage-payment' actually appears as *stīpendium*. Ancient Greek *amphi-phoréos* 'both-side-carrier' appears as *amphoréōs* 'amphora.'

Borrowing

One of the most important sources of language change is contact between speakers of different languages. The adoption of elements from another language or dialect is linguistic **borrowing**. The borrowed elements are usually lexical items, known as **loan words**, but morphological and syntactic patterns can also be borrowed. The language from which elements are borrowed is called the **donor**, and the borrowing language is called the **recipient** language. For example, the words *pundit*, *yoga*, and *guru* have been borrowed by the recipient language, English, from the donor language, Hindi.

An element may be borrowed from another language because of its **prestige** or because it fills a need or gap in the borrowing language. When an element is borrowed from a language which is culturally or politically dominant, the motive is **prestige**. Often the prestige factor leads to extensive borrowing from the dominant, or **super-stratum**, language into the **substratum** language. For example, Hindi could do perfectly well with the native words *subah kā kʰānā*, *dopahar kā kʰānā*, and *rāt kā kʰānā* (*subah* 'morning,' *dopahar* 'noon,' *rāt* 'night,' *kā* 'possessive postposition,' *kʰānā* 'meal'). But for reasons of prestige, *breakfast*, *lunch*, and *dinner* have been borrowed by many speakers of Hindi from English. The **need-filling** motive is obvious when the recipient language borrows new objects and concepts along with their names. Thus, Hindi acquired the words *radio*, *train*, *railway*, and *coffee* along with the objects they represent. Similarly, English acquired the words *pundit*, *yoga*, and *guru* along with the concepts they represent.

When speakers adapt material already present in their language for the objects and concepts belonging to the donor language, the process is called **loan shift** or **loan translation**. Typically, a loan translation is created by literally translating elements from the donor language into compound words in the borrowing language. For example, the English *almighty*, *handbook*, and *Monday* are loan translations of Latin *omnipotens* (*omni-* 'all' + *potēns* 'powerful'), *manuālis liber* (*manuālis-* 'hand' + *liber* 'book'), and *diēs lunae* (*diēs-* 'day' + *lunae* 'moon'). Other examples of loan translation are the English words *librarian*, *clerk*, *pilot*, *journalist* imported into Indonesian as *juru pustaka* 'expert book,' *juru tulis* 'expert write,' *juru terbeang* 'expert fly,' *juru berita* 'expert news.'

Lexical borrowing frequently leads to further changes in the recipient language. Often borrowed items are changed to conform to native linguistic rules, a process known as **adaptation** in which foreign sounds occurring in loan words are replaced by their nearest phonetic equivalents in the borrowing language. For example, in Japanese the dental stop /t/ has three variants: [ts] before [u], [tʃ] before [i y], and [t] before [e a o]. Thus, the English loan words beginning with an alveolar /t/, as in *touring*, *team*, *tube*, and *tank* have been adapted in Japanese (along with the addition of a final vowel required by Japanese syllable structure) as *tsuriñgu*, *tʃiimu*, *tʃyuubu*, and *tañku*, respectively. (In these examples *ñ* symbolizes a syllabic nasal.) Similarly, English *violin* has been adapted in Japanese as *baioriñ*, with the substitution of /b/ and /r/ for the English /v/ and /l/. For another example, consider the English words *bandana* and *thug*, borrowed from the Hindi *bā:dʰana* 'to tie,' and *tʰag* 'a swindler.' The Hindi voiced aspirated dental stop [dʰ] and the voiceless aspirated retroflex stop [tʰ] have been replaced by the closest English sounds, [d] and [tʰ], respectively. (Notice also that the Hindi nasal vowel [ã:] in *bā:dʰana* has been split into a vowel plus nasal consonant [æ:n] in the English word.) An aspirated retroflex was spelled as *th* and then mispronounced as a dental fricative to produce Modern English *thug*.

Recall the discussion on page 293 that loan words may cause phonological change by introducing patterns which were not previously permitted in the borrowing language. As we saw before, earlier English did not have the phonemes /v ð z/. The allophones /v ð z/ occurred only as intervocalic variants of the phonemes /f θ s/. However, loan words from French and Scandivanian, which had these variants in initial position as well, caused [v ð z] to contrast frequently with [f θ s] at the beginning of words and thus become separate English phonemes in their own right. Likewise, the phoneme /ʒ/ entered English only through French loan words such as *rouge*, *garage*, *collage*, *mirage*, but does not occur initially in English words.

Borrowing can also lead to morphological change in the recipient language. Many nouns have been imported into English from Latin and Greek with their plural as well as their singular forms. This has enriched English inflectional morphology by providing new ways to form plurals. Some of these nouns are Latin *datum/data*, *vertebra/vertebrae*, *nucleus/nuclei*, *index/indices*, *matrix/matrices*, *analysis/analyses*, and Greek *criterion/criteria* and *stigma/stigmata*. (Some speakers of English form the plural of these nouns by adding *-s*, while *data* is often treated as a singular, as in *The data is being collected*.) The importation of Romance words such as *opaque/opacity*, *electric/electricity*, and *eccentric/eccentricity* introduced into English a Latin stress rule and the Romance morphophonemic rule /k/ → /s/ in certain environments.

Borrowing can also lead to syntactic change in the borrowing language. Loan shift from English has affected the syntactic representation of interrogative and relative pronouns in a variety of Yiddish spoken in the United States (Hockett 1958: 411). Unlike English *who*, which represents both interrogative and relative pronouns, Yiddish has two forms, interrogative *ver* 'who' and relative *vos* 'who.' By analogy with the English usage of *who*, some Yiddish speakers in the United States use the single form *ver* for both. Thus, they have the expected *ver iz do?* for 'who is here?' but *der mentš ver iz do* (instead of the expected *der mentš vos iz do*) for 'the man who is here.'

Borrowing increases the vocabulary of the recipient language, but it can also lead to other semantic changes, as well. In English the old word for 'animal' was *deer* (Old English *dēor*), like German *Tier* 'animal.' When the Latin *animal* was borrowed into English, the meaning of *deer* was restricted to a particular animal that was hunted. Similarly, when Hindi borrowed the Sanskrit word *stana* 'breast,' the old Hindi word for 'breast,' *tʰan*, was restricted to 'animal (nonhuman) breast.' When the Savoyard dialect of French borrowed *père* 'father' and *mère* 'mother' from Standard French, the original Savoyard words for 'father' and 'mother,' *pâre* and *mâre*, became restricted to male and female cattle (Anttila 1972: 143).

Etymology

Kelley Ross, a philosophy professor in California with an interest in historical linguistics, relates an interesting etymology for adobe *on his website (*www.friesian.com/egypt.htm*):*

"Adobe" is the Spanish word for mud brick ... [which] seems to have been borrowed from the Arabic word الطوب *ʾaṭṭûb 'the mud brick' ... But 'aṭṭûb, is not ultimately from Arabic; it was borrowed from Coptic, which has the word* Τωβ *tôb 'mud brick'* ✎ ⌐ *ḏbı, which is in turn from the Middle Egyptian word for mud brick, with a phonogram for* db *and an ideographic determinative for 'brick.'*

Thus, we use the same word for the same objects that the Egyptians commanded the Israelites to make for the palaces of Pharaoh.

Analogy

Speakers of a language tend to prefer regular patterns over patterns with many exceptions. Regular patterns are more easily acquired by children (and exceptions are more easily forgotten). Borrowing and other processes of language change may introduce irregularities into the language. The processes of analogy help to reassert regularity in the patterns of the language. Analogy involves the modification or creation of linguistic forms by (over) generalization of an existing pattern. Children overgeneralize frequently in acquiring their native language; for example, by analogy with the way past tense is morphologically indicated on most verbs (add -ed, so the past tense of *walk* is *walked*), children acquiring English pass through a stage in which they say *goed* and *bringed*.

Sometimes a word is reshaped on the basis of frequent association with some other word belonging to the same semantic field. This process is called contamination. For example, the historically expected *femelle* [fēməl] or [fiməl] has been altered to *female* [fímel] because of its habitual paring with *male*. Similar influence can be seen in Vulgar Latin *gravis* → *grevis* 'heavy' by association with *levis* 'light,' *sinister* → *sinexter* 'left' after *dexter* 'right,' and *reddere* → *rendere* 'give up,' after *prendere* 'seize.'

Hypercorrection is another kind of analogical change, in which a changed form is mistakenly assumed to be more correct than a correct form, which it replaces. For example, some Americans say *Marthy* for *Martha*, or *Ameriky* for *America*. If they are taught that the final vowel /-i/ in these words is "incorrect," sometimes they go too far and say *Cincinnata* for *Cincinnati*, or *Missoura* for *Missouri*, substituting a final /-ə/ for a correct /-i/. Here the hypercorrected forms are the incorrect *Cincinnata* and *Missoura* (Hall 1964: 362).

Sometimes new forms are created or existing forms receive a new interpretation through **folk etymology** or **reanalysis**, when speakers of a language misconstrue the morphological constituents of a word. Thus, *hamburger* (whose true etymology is 'the city of Hamburg' + *er* 'someone from') has been reanalyzed as *ham+burger* 'burger made with ham.' It is quite irrelevant that ham is not used in *hamburger*. Subsequently, by the analogy of this folk etymology, new forms such as *cheeseburger, chiliburger*, and plain *burger* have been created.

Another form of reanalysis that can lead to the formation of a new word is the process of **back formation**. For example, English *pea* is a back formation from the Old English singular *pise*. The Old English plural was *pisan*. Old English singular *pise*, later pronounced as /pi:z/, was analogically reinterpreted as a plural – /pi: + z/. This led to the back formation of singular *pea*, with Old English singular *pise* reanalyzed as a new plural form, *peas*.

When the structural analysis of an older form is analogically replaced by an analysis which makes "more sense" to a speaker, we speak of **metanalysis** or **recutting**. For example, the modern English *adder* (a kind of snake) comes from the Old English *nœddre*. The change came about when the Old English article–noun sequence *a + nœddre* was reanalyzed in Middle English as *an + œddre*. No such metanalysis occurred in German, where the cognate is *Natter* 'adder, viper.'

> **Folk etymology: from America to Italy and back**
> *Christopher Columbus brought back many new plant varieties from the "New World," including the tomato. At first, Europeans thought tomatoes were poisonous, but by the 1700s, tomatoes were being fried and eaten like eggplants. In Italy, tomatoes were even given the eggplant's old nickname,* pomo di moro, *or 'fruit of the Moors.' (In the Middle Ages, Moorish and Turkish traders were often given lexical credit for new products; New World corn is still called* granturco, *or 'Turkish grain,' by many Italian farmers.)* Pomo di moro *was subsequently contracted to* pomodoro (pomo d'oro), *which English-speaking historians have erroneously translated as 'apples of gold.'*

BOX 8.4 **PIDGINS AND CREOLES: RAPID LANGUAGE CHANGE?**

Pidgin languages develop when people who do not share a language have to deal with each other for limited purposes, like trade. They develop a way of speaking that takes most of its vocabulary from one language (in the best-known cases, a European language), and combines words in short groups with flexible word order. The following excerpt from Hawai'ian Pidgin English, spoken in the early twentieth century, is fairly typical (Bickerton 1981:13):

Olsem	hyuman	laif	olsem.	gud	rodu	get,	enguru	get,	mauntin	get –	no?
All same	human	life	all same	good	road	get,	angle	get,	mountain	get	no

'Human life's just like that. There's good roads, there's sharp corners, there's mountains – right?'

If the use of a pidgin expands beyond minimal contact situations and acquires native speakers, it becomes a creole. (The language that is now called Hawai'ian Pidgin is actually a creole.) Creoles are at first glance like pidgins, but on closer inspection they turn out to have the kind of grammatical structure you might find in any language. Tok Pisin (despite its name) is a creole and one of the official languages of Papua New Guinea. Below is a request for someone to write an grammar of Tok Pisin for the online encyclopedia Wikipedia:

Sapos	yu	save	grama	bilong	Tok	Pisin	plis	halivim
Suppose	you	know	grammar	belong	Tok	Pisin	please	help

raitim	buk i	skulim	Tok	Pisin,	long	*Wikibooks*
write	book	school	Tok	Pisin	along	Wikibooks.

'If you know Tok Pisin grammar, please help write a book for teaching Tok Pisin on Wikibooks.'

Unlike the Hawai'ian Pidgin English example, the Tok Pisin sentence has considerable structure, and much of it is not like English, although English originally supplied most of its vocabulary. For example, the morpheme *i* is a marker of the beginning of a predicate, and must be used after a subject in the third person. The suffix *-im* on the verb stems *haliv-* and *rait-* marks them as transitive verbs. The sentence also contains a structured *if*-clause, more complex syntax than you would expect in a pidgin.

According to the standard view, creoles develop their richer morphology and syntax at a much more rapid pace than is normally observed in language change. Creoles are thought to develop within only one generation, as children exposed to a pidgin language which was previously spoken only by adults acquire it as their native language. One hypothesis about why this should be so is the "bioprogram hypothesis," that this happens because children bring the resources of Universal Grammar to bear on learning the language (Bickerton 1984, 1990). Previous generations of adults, having developed the pidgin in adulthood, did not have the full access to UG that children do, hence the pidgin remains relatively unstructured. The idea that creoles develop rapidly or undergo change differently from change in other languages has recently been challenged by several scholars, including DeGraff (1999) and Thomason (2001: 157–189).

Linguistic reconstruction and language families

All languages are constantly changing, and over the course of a thousand years these changes can have a dramatic cumulative effect. If we could bring together a Roman who spoke Latin (0 CE), a descendant of his who spoke Old French (1000 CE), and another descendant who spoke Modern French, no one of them could understand the other two. For example, for the eighth month of the year the Roman would have said [augustum], the speaker of Old French [aúst], and the modern French speaker [u] (Hall 1964: 277). So long as a speech community forms a tight-knit group, language changes tend to spread to all the speakers of the language. But often the community is broken up into two or more subcommunities (for example, by migration or geopolitical separation), and then changes which begin in one subcommunity tend to remain within that subcommunity and, as a result, the languages of these different subcommunities diverge. If the **divergence** becomes so great that the subcommunities no longer understand each other, then we say that each subcommunity has become an independent speech community with its own language. Whenever two or more languages develop in this way from a single language, we say that they are genetically related or **sister languages** and any group of such related languages constitutes a **language family**, descended from a common parent or **protolanguage**.

Students of French, Spanish, and Italian often recognize similarities between these languages; words in the three languages for the same referent often sound similar, and the three languages share many similar rules for inflecting verbs and constructing sentences. This is not surprising. French, Spanish, and Italian all developed from regional dialects of the Latin spoken by soldiers and administrators of the Roman Empire. Students of Modern German and English often notice similar words in the two languages, which developed from dialects of an earlier Proto-Germanic language. Reaching farther back into linguistic prehistory (for which no written records exist), Latin and Proto-Germanic are both descended from an even earlier protolanguage, Proto-Indo-European. So is Sanskrit, which is the protolanguage of many modern languages of the Indian subcontinent.

Figure 8.2 provides a simplified look at the group of languages which evolved from Proto-Indo-European (PIE). It is simplified in that languages which are no longer spoken and have no "living" descendants are not included. It also simplifies the relations between some languages – for example, suggesting that Slavic languages all split from Proto-Slavic at the same time and are all equally related. Languages evolve over generations, not as abruptly and discretely as a family tree suggests. It is also important to remember that the Indo-European language family is just one of dozens of language families around the world.

How do we know that languages like Latin, German, and Sanskrit, so geographically distant and seemingly different from each other, are in fact historically related to each other? In order to study linguistic prehistory, linguists make use of two interrelated techniques: the **comparative method** and **internal reconstruction**.

The comparative method

Because the processes of language change are systematic, historical linguists can "read back" through the evidence of those changes to reconstruct earlier versions of the language. Much of this evidence lies in the existence of cognates – that is, phonetically similar words with the same referent – in two or more languages. The comparative method infers a

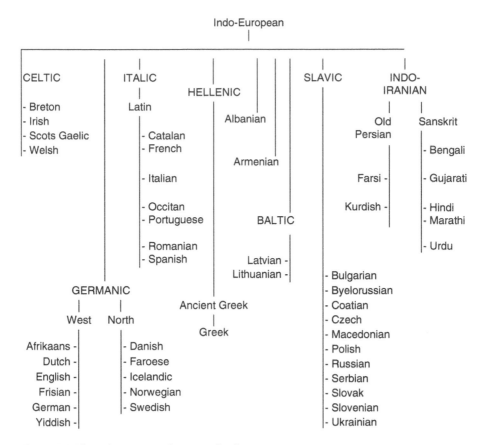

Figure 8.2 The Indo-European language family

common parent or protolanguage from a comparison of the cognate forms found in sister languages, and from analysis of the changes that have occurred in various sister languages.

The principal steps involved in the comparative method are assembling cognates, establishing sets of correspondences, and reconstructing the forms of the protolanguage. The sounds of the protolanguage are reconstructed first. Then, with a reconstructed phonology, the vocabulary and grammar of the protolanguage can be reconstructed (at least partially) as well.

Assembling cognates and establishing sound correspondences

Cognates are words in two or more languages which refer to the same referent with similar sequences of sounds. Since the sequence of sounds that denotes a particular meaning is arbitrary, when we find words from different languages which have systematic phonetic correspondences, we infer that they came from a common parent language. Cognates usually belong to the basic vocabulary (body parts, kinship terms, numerals, household items, and articles and pronouns) inherited from the protolanguage.

The eighteen sets of cognates in Table 8.5 are drawn from the Indo-European languages Greek, Latin, Sanskrit, and Germanic. These sets of cognates are organized into six sets of

TABLE 8.5 Sets of cognates from Greek, Latin, Sanskrit, and Germanic and their sound correspondences

	Greek	Latin	Sanskrit	Germanic		Distribution
1a	**pa**té:r	**pa**ter	**pi**tá:	**fadar**	'father'	word-initial
1b	ane**p**siós 'cousin'	ne**po**:s 'grandson'	ná**pa**:t 'descendant'	ne**fa** (OE) 'nephew'		word-medial
1c	s**p**ecio	s**p**aš	s**p**eho:n	'see, spy'		after *s*
1d	hu**p**ér	su**p**er	u**p**ári	u**b**ar (OHG)	'over'	between voiced sounds[†]
2a	**t**reîs	**t**re:s	**t**ráyas	Θrija	'three'	word-initial
2b	phrá:**te**r	fra:**t**er	bhrá:**ta**:	broΘar	'clansman/ brother'	word-medial
2c	és**ti**	es**t**	ás**ti**	is**t**	'is'	after *s*
2d	pa**té**:r	pa**t**er	pi**t**á:	fa**d**ar	'father'	between voiced sounds[†]
3a	(he)**k**atón	**c**entum	šatá	**h**unda	'100'	word-initial
3b	dé:**k**a	de**c**em	dá**š**a	tai**h**un	'10'	word-medial
3c	s**k**ótos		**ch**a:yá:	s**k**adus	'darkness/ shadow'	after *s*
3d	he**k**urá	so**cr**us	švašrú:s	swi**g**ur (OHG)	'mother-in-law'	between voiced sounds[†]
4a	**b**eltíon 'better'	(de:)**b**ilis 'weak'	**b**áli:ya:n 'stronger'	**p**al (LG) 'firm'		word-initial
4b	du**b**us (Lithuanian)			dlu**p**s	'deep'	word-medial
5a	**d**é:ka	**d**ecem	**d**áša	taihun	'10'	word-initial
5b	é**d**omai 'I shall eat'	e**d**o: 'I eat'	á**d**mi 'I eat'	e**t**an (OE) 'eat'		word-medial
6a	**g**énos 'kin'	**g**enus 'tribe'	**j**ánas 'race'	**k**uni 'race'		word-initial
6b	a**g**rós 'field'	a**g**er 'fields'	á**j**ras 'plain'	æ**c**er (OE) 'field'		word-medial

(Unless otherwise labeled, the Germanic cognates are from Gothic. OE = Old English, OHG = Old High German, LG = Low German, G = German.)

[†] not preceded by the accent attested in Greek and Sanskrit

corresponding sounds – sounds which differ slightly but systematically across the sister languages, leaving traces of sound changes that occurred in one sister language but not in the others. The six sets of sound correspondences in Table 8.5 occur frequently in cognate sets from Greek, Latin, Sanskrit, and Germanic, so we assume that the words they represent, so similar in sound and meaning, must have sprung from a common source. (The corresponding sounds in each cognate set are printed in boldface letters; the right-hand column indicates the phonetic environment of the corresponding sounds in those cognates.)

Reconstructing the protosounds

In order to reconstruct the protosounds of the common (parent) language, the sets of sound correspondences given in Table 8.5 are treated like phones in phonemic analysis. Sounds occurring in contrastive distribution are assumed to have developed from different protosounds. Sound correspondence sets 1a–b, 2a–b, 3a–b, 4a–b, 5a–b, and 6a–b are contrastive, since they occur word-initially (and in many cases word-medially) under similar phonetic conditions. Hence, we infer that the sounds in these sets must come from different phonemes in the protolanguage. We infer that sounds occurring in noncontrastive sets developed from a single protosound (just as noncontrastive sounds in a single language are considered allophones of a single underlying phoneme). For example, the **p, b**, and **f** sounds in cognate sets 1a–d do not contrast: in cognate set 1c **p** occurs after an *s* in all four languages; in cognate set 1d **p** (**b** in Germanic) occurs between voiced sounds when not preceded by an accent attested in Greek and Sanskrit; and in cognate sets 1a and 1b, **p** (**f** in Germanic) occurs elsewhere (word-initially and word-medially).

The differences among the languages in cognate sets 1a–d (word-initial and word-medial **f** and intervocalic **b** in Germanic, where the other languages have **p**) are systematic and predictable if we posit that these sounds have their source in a single Proto-Indo-European phoneme ****p** which underwent sound changes in German but not in Greek, Latin, and Sanskrit. (Protosounds are marked by an asterisk*, which means "reconstructed, not directly documented.") As in phonological analysis within a single language, this hypothesis follows the **criterion of plurality**, since the majority of the languages (Greek, Latin, and Sanskrit) have the sound **p**. Under this analysis, Proto-Indo-European ****p** remained unchanged in German after an unvoiced s, changed to a voiced **b** between voiced sounds when not preceded by an accent, and changed to **f** elsewhere. This is a simpler theory than, for example, trying to explain how all these different languages somehow derived the phoneme **p** from Germanic **p, b**, and **f**. It is also more phonetically plausible.

The sounds **t, d**, and θ in cognate sets 2a–d have the same predictable distribution as **p** in cognate sets 1a–d. By the same reasoning as for **p**, we reconstruct a Proto-Indo-European ****t** for these sets, and infer that in Germanic it remained unchanged after an *s*, changed to **d** between voiced sounds not preceded by the accent attested in Greek and Sanskrit, and changed to θ elsewhere.

For cognate sets 3a–d, in which the sounds are also in complementary distribution and follow the same pattern as **p** and **t**, we reconstruct a Proto-Indo-European ****k**, and infer a similar sound change in Germanic in which the proto ****k** remained unchanged after an *s*, changed to **g** between voiced sounds, and changed to **h** elsewhere. Our hypothesis of sound change in German gains support from its generalizability; it provides a common account of the natural class of voiceless stops. (We must also posit that in Sanskrit *k changed to palatal š and the combination *sk produced *ch* initially and *cch* medially, so the analysis is not complete, but it covers a lot of data with good descriptive accuracy and **phonetic plausibility**.)

Using this kind of reasoning, for cognate sets 4, 5, and 6 we reconstruct Proto-Indo-European *b, *d, and *g, respectively, and assume that these sounds became voiceless **p, t, k** in Germanic and that the proto *g became palatal **j** in Sanskrit.

This analysis leads to the reconstruction of the following phonemes in Proto-Indo-European: *p, *t, *k, *b, *d, *g. With enough cognate sets, it would be possible to reconstruct the remaining sounds of the protolanguage, and from this foundation to reconstruct its grammatical and lexical morphemes, inflectional and derivational systems, and the rest of its grammatical structure.

Early historical linguists

The analytic process we've just summarized encapsulates some of the major findings of historical linguists from the late 1700s through the 1800s. By observing systematic sound correspondences like these among a variety of modern languages, historical linguists reconstructed their common protolanguage, and deduced the genetic relations between those modern languages, as well as many of the changes that had occurred in them.

In 1786, Sir William Jones delivered a paper describing similarities between Sanskrit, Latin, and Greek. He argued that these similarities were too systematic to be attributable to chance and concluded that they had developed from a common source. Jones's work sparked many advances in historical linguistics over the next several decades. In 1814 Rasmus Rask formalized the techniques of the comparative method – assembling cognates and deducing rules to account for systematic sound changes to reconstruct protolanguages. Other linguists extended the Indo-European family tree to include Persian and the Germanic languages.

In 1822 Jacob Grimm (a linguist as well as a collector of German folktales) described the systematic shift from the PIE consonants to the Germanic consonants, which subsequently became known as **Grimm's Law**. For example, according to Grimm's Law, PIE voiceless stops [p t k] became Germanic voiceless fricatives [f θ h] and PIE voiced stops [b d g] became Germanic voiceless stops [p t k], accounting for the sets of sound correspondences in Table 8.5. Grimm's Law explained a number of other Germanic consonant shifts as well, making the case for the genetic relation of the Germanic languages to the Romance languages. There were exceptions to Grimm's Law, but they were systematically related to specific phonetic environments, allowing historical linguists accounting for these exceptions to discover even more about Proto-Indo-European and subsequent changes in its daughter languages.

As you can see from our reconstruction of PIE voiced and voiceless stops, the comparative method is highly successful in showing what the protosounds were like, some aspects of the prehistory of the phonologies of each of the cognate languages, and ways in which they differ from each other. However, reconstructed sounds are less precise phonetically than the cognate sounds on which they are based. Not surprisingly, the comparative method leads to a reconstructed model of the protolanguage which is regular and variation-free, whereas in reality languages have substantial irregularity and variation.

Internal reconstruction

Unlike comparative reconstruction, which relies on the comparison of forms across related languages, **internal reconstruction** relies on analysis of forms within a single language. Some morphophonemic changes in the history of a language leave noticeable traces in its current forms, so that by analyzing these traces we can reconstruct earlier forms of some morphemes and the changes which led to their current forms. Comparative and internal evidence are often compared for corroboration or refinement of a posited reconstruction of a protolanguage.

Earlier we saw that sound change tends to cause morphological change by creating allomorphs. For example, Old High German had pairs of alternating allomorphs: *lamb ~ lemb*, *kalb ~ kelb*, and *blat ~ blet*, as follows:

Nominative singular	Nominative plural	
lamb	lembir	'lamb'
kalb	kelbir	'calf'
blat	bletir	'leaf'

We can infer that the /a/ ~ /e/ alternation in these allomorphs springs from a single phoneme /a/, which became /e/ before /-ir/. This is phonetically plausible because the fronting of a back vowel before a suffix containing a front vowel is a common phonetic change (assimilation). Using just the facts of Old High German, we can deduce that earlier forms of the language had only one nominative morpheme for each of these words (*lamb*, *kalb*, and *blat*), until a sound change (assimilation) led to the development of new allomorphs.

Historical linguistics and culture

In addition to helping us better understand the structure of language, its range of variation over time, and the processes by which it can change, historical linguistics also sheds light on the cultural contexts of speakers of earlier languages. Historical linguists are like archaeologists, piecing together linguistic artifacts in order to better understand earlier civilizations through the interpretation of their reconstructed languages. For example, in Indo-European languages we find related words with the meaning 'dog' (Greek *kúōn*, Latin *canis*, Sanskrit *švan*, Old English *hund*), but no related words for 'cat' (Greek *aiélouros*, Latin *fēlēs*, Sanskrit *mārjār*, Old English *catt*). This tells us that speakers of Proto-Indo-European were familiar with dogs (because its daughter languages have cognates for 'dog' stemming from a common PIE word) but not cats (because the daughter languages independently coined or borrowed new words for 'cat'). Evidence of this kind can be used to determine the original homeland of the speakers, their culture, and the nature of their activities and beliefs.

Languages change over time to meet the changing situations and needs of their speakers. Consequently, the historical record of a language's changes sheds light on the cultural and material development of its speech community. For example, since early Germanic writing was done on wood, bone, and stone, the original meaning of Old English *wrītan (write)* was 'scratch.' (In New High German, the cognate of *write* is *reissen*, which still means 'tear, scratch,' and in Dutch it is *rijten* 'to tear.') When the Latin word *scrībere* 'to write' was borrowed into Old English, the semantics of *write* was extended to include 'scribe, write.' The borrowed word *scribe* was phonetically adapted as *shrive* in Old English and eventually became more restricted to a technical religious meaning of 'to hear confession and give absolution.' Thus *shrive*, as a loan word, and *write* with its extended meaning, not only illustrate the impact of borrowing on the meaning and use of a form, but trace the history and relations of concepts in the language.

CHAPTER SUMMARY

All languages change over time, adapting to meet the changing contexts and needs of their speech communities. The kinds and the mechanisms of language change described in this chapter are operating all the time in all languages (although the pace of change varies). Languages are flexible systems that continually seek a balance between simplification and elaboration, incorporating new influences while preserving orderliness. Language change is motivated by "external" forces, such as contact with other languages and cultures (and the borrowing of words), and by "internal" forces, such as articulatory simplification and regularization, part of a language's ongoing evolution to maintain a stable sound and meaning system. Synchronic (dialect and register) variation provides the fuel for diachronic change, through the language acquisition of successive generations of children.

All facets of a language change over time – its phonology, morphology, syntax, and semantics, as well as the speech community's norms for appropriately using the language. Synchronic allophonic processes – such as assimilation and dissimilation, deletion and insertion, lengthening and reordering of sounds – result in diachronic changes in a language's phonological system. Phonemes merge and split, sometimes creating chains of phoneme shifts. Morphological changes often involve simplification or elaboration of the language's system of case marking, while syntactic changes often involve changes in the word order of sentences. The meanings of words can broaden or narrow, or take on new evaluative associations. Words for new referents can be coined fresh, or borrowed from other languages.

Language change provides strong evidence that the various components of language are crucially interdependent: phonological changes can lead to morphological and syntactic changes, lexical changes like borrowing can lead to phonological changes. The traces left by changes in languages allow historical linguists to assemble cognates in two or more languages, establish sets of form correspondences, and reconstruct the forms of the parent language. From this evidence they can determine historical relations between languages within a language family and reconstruct earlier protolanguages, which provide insights into the cultures and relations of prehistorical peoples.

Exercises

EXERCISE 8.1

Proto-Indo-European – Old Persian. Write rules for the changes affecting the evolution of Proto-Indo-European labial and dental stop consonants and vowels in Old Persian. (You may want to review the sections on conditioned and unconditioned sound change.) Are the changes in Old Persian phonemic or merely allophonic? Notice the item in 8 is from Avestan, a sister of Old Persian; however, in this case don't let it affect your rules.

	Proto-Indo-European	Old Persian	
1.	pəte:r	pita:	'father'
2.	apo	apa	'away'
3.	pro	fra	'before'
4.	bʰra:te:r	bra:ta:	'brother'
5.	ubʰo:	uba:	'both'
6.	tar	tar	'cross over'
7.	eti	ati	'beyond'
8.	triti:yo	θritiya (Avestan)	'third'
9.	dwiti:yo	dviti:ya	'second'
10.	ped	pad	'foot'
11.	dʰwor	duvar	'door'
12.	dʰe:	da:	'put'

EXERCISE 8.2

Sanskrit – Pali. Write rules for the changes affecting the evolution of Sanskrit consonant clusters in Pali. (You may want to review the discussion of assimilation in the section on the processes of sound change.) [t ɖ] = retroflex stops, [s] = alveolar sibilant, [ṣ] = retroflex sibilant, [ʃ] = palatal sibilant, [ɽ] = retroflex flap, [ɳ] = retroflex nasal)

Part 1. What rule is indicated by the following examples?

	Sanskrit	Pali	
1.	bʰukta	bʰutta	'enjoyed'
2.	kʰaɖga	kʰagga	'sword'
3.	yukta	yutta	'united'

Part II: What modifications to this rule need to be made for aspirated stops?

4.	dugdʰa	duddʰa	'milk'
5.	sadbʰa:va	sabbʰa:va	'good feeling'
6.	labdʰa	laddʰa	'obtained'

Part III: Now consider the assimilation of liquids and stops. How should the rule be modified?

7.	alpa	appa	'few'
8.	valkala	vakkala	'tree-bark'
9.	kalpa	kappa	'an eon'
10.	pʰa:lguna	pʰagguɳa	name of a month

11.	čakra	čakka	'wheel'
12.	ma:rga	magga	'path'
13.	čitra	čitta	'picture'
14.	artʰa	attʰa	'meaning'
15.	bʰadra	bʰadda	'a good person'

Part IV: What rule(s) describe(s) the assimilation of stops and nasals?

16.	nagna	nagga	'naked'
17.	agni	aggi	'fire'
18.	vigʰna	viggʰa	'disturbance'
19.	sapatni:	savatti	'co-wife'
20.	yugma	yugga	'twin'

Part V: What rule(s) govern(s) the assimilation of nasals with liquids and other nasals?

21.	dʰarma	dʰamma	'law'
22.	kaṇa	kaṇṇa	'ear'
23.	gulma	gumma	'a bush'
24.	janma	jamma	'birth'
25.	nimna	ninna	'deep'
26.	puṇya	puṇṇa	'virtuous act'
27.	saumya	somma	'placid'

Part VI: Write down the rules that account for all these assimilatory changes.

EXERCISE 8.3

Hindi. What is the phonemic status of the sibilants [s ʃ ṣ] in Hindi given in (A) and how is this status affected by the words borrowed from Sanskrit given in (B)?

(A)	1.	satya	'truth'
	2.	ma:s	'month'
	3.	masa:	'mosquito'
	4.	naṣṭ	'ruined'
	5.	past	'exhausted'
	6.	duṣṭ	'wicked'
	7.	paʃčim	'west'
	8.	niʃčay	'certain'
	9.	taskar	'thief'
	10.	spaṣṭ	'clear'

(B)	11.	ʃãtru	'enemy'
	12.	na:ʃ	'ruin'
	13.	do:ṣ	'fault'
	14.	pa:ṣ a:ṇ	'stone'
	15.	ʃuṣ ka	'dry'
	16.	paʃu	'animal'
	17.	ṣo:ḍ aʃi:	'16th day of mourning'
	18.	uṣa:	'dawn'

EXERCISE 8.4

Hindi. What is the distribution of the retroflex consonants [ɖ] and [ɽ] in the following data from Hindi in (A) and how is this distribution affected by the words borrowed into Hindi from Sanskrit, English, and Portuguese in (B)?

(A)
1.	ɖo:ra:	'thread'
2.	anɖa:	'egg'
3.	laɖɖu:	'a kind of sweet'
4.	ɖa:l	'branch'
5.	kaɽa:	'hard'
6.	pe:ɽ	'tree'
7.	a:ɽ	'screen'
8.	ta:ɽ	'palm tree'

(B)
9.	niɖar	'fearless'
10.	ro:ɖ	'road'
11.	so:ɖa:	'soda'
12.	pa:uɖar	'powder'
13.	pago:ɖa:	'pagoda'
14.	pɛɖ	'pad'

EXERCISE 8.5

English. The following examples show that some voiceless fricatives of earlier English have become voiced in Modern English. Determine the phonological condition under which the voicing occurs. Also state the morphological changes which the voicing of the fricatives creates in Modern English (see the sections on phonological and morphological change, especially the parts relating to allomorphs). In Old English *th* represents a voiceless fricative.

	Old English	Modern English
1.	gift	gift
2.	geifan	give
3.	li:f	life
4.	lifian	live
5.	bæth	bath
6.	bathian	bathe
7.	soth	sooth
8.	so:thian	soothe
9.	græs	grass
10.	grasian	graze
11.	glæs	glass
12.	glassen (Middle English)	glaze

EXERCISE 8.6

English. The following is a sample text of Middle English, from Chaucer's *The Tale of Melibee* (c. 1380). For each sentence, describe how the morphology, syntax, semantics, and lexical items differ from present-day English. The present-day English equivalents are given in the parentheses. (For more examples from Middle English see Algeo 1972: 159.)

1. Sume (some) he iaf (gave) up, and sume (some) ne (not) iaf (gave) he noht (not).
2. Thre (three) of his olde (old) foes han (have) it espyed (noticed).
3. Wepyng (weeping) is no thing (by no means) defended (forbidden) to hym (him) that soroweful (sorrowful) is.
4. My lord, I you biseche (beseech) as hertely (heartily) as I dar (dare) and kan (can), ne (not) haste (hasten) yow (you) nat (not) to (too) faste (fast).
5. But seyeth (tell) and conseileth (counsel) me as you liketh (pleases you).
6. His wif (wife) and eek (also) his doghter (daughter) hath (has) he left inwith (within) his hous (house).

EXERCISE 8.7

In the following, identify the kind of semantic change involved (broadening, narrowing, metonymy, etc.).

1. Latin *virtu:s* 'manliness' in Italian as a loan word *vertù* 'ability, skill'
2. Middle English *dogge* 'a particular breed of dog,' in Modern English *dog*
3. English *pigeon* in Melanesian Pidgin as *pisin* 'bird'
4. In Old English *mete* 'food' in Modern English *meat* 'edible flesh'
5. Latin *orbus* 'deprived (of anything); orphan' in Italian occurs as *órbo* 'deprived of eyesight, blind'
6. Latin *e:li:mina:re* 'to put out over the threshold, i.e. to throw out of the house' in English as a loan word *eliminate* 'to get rid of, to do away with'
7. Latin *insulta:re* 'to leap upon, to jump,' in English as a loan word *insult* 'to say or do something rude that offends somebody else'
8. Old English *knáfa* [*knáva*] 'boy' in Modern English as *knave* 'rogue, scoundrel'
9. Middle English *fonned* (past participle of *fonnen* 'to act as a fool') in Modern English as *fond* 'feeling affection for somebody or something'
10. The changed meaning of the words *pen* and *sword* in the saying "The *pen* is mightier than the *sword*"

EXERCISE 8.8

Reconstruct the vowels for the protolanguage and write rules for the sound changes. Ignore the accent and parenthetical items.

	Sanskrit	Greek	
1.	sádas	édos	'seat'
2.	asti	ésti	'is'
3.	jánas	génos	'race, people'
4.	pátis	pósis	'husband'
5.	dáma	dómis	'house'
6.	ávi	ó(w)is	'sheep'
7.	ájras	agrós	'field'
8.	ápa	ápo	'away, from'
9.	ánti	anti	'opposite, near'
10.	má:s	mé:n	'month'
11.	sa:mi	e:mi-	'half'
12.	má:	mé:	'not (prohibitive)'
13.	á:šu	o:kús	'swift'
14.	pa:t	pó:s	'foot'
15.	dá:nam	dô:ron	'gift'
16.	sva:dú-	a:dús	'sweet'
17.	má:ta:	má:te:r	'mother'

18.	bhrá:ta:	phrá:te:r	'brother, tribesman'
19.	é:dh(as)	aíth(o:)	'fuel, burn'
20.	éti	eĩsi	'he goes'
21.	véda	oĩda	'I know'
22.	šoṣa-	aûos	'drying up, dry'
23.	bódh(a:mi)	peúth(omai)	'I observe, find out'
24.	roká	leukós	'brightness'

EXERCISE 8.9

Greek. By means of internal reconstruction, reconstruct the shapes of the nominative forms in an earlier stage of Greek and indicate the changes that have taken place.

	'serf'	'grace'	'hope'	'bird'	'old man'
Nominative	θé:s	χápis	elpîs	óri:s	ɣéro:n
Genitive	θe:tos	χápitos	elpîðos	óri:θos	ɣéro:ntos
Dative	θe:ti	χápiti	elpîði	óri:θi	ɣ éro:nti

SUGGESTIONS FOR FURTHER READING

Aitchison, Jean 2001, *Language change: progress or decay?* 3rd edition, Cambridge University Press. An engaging overview of all major topics, with emphasis on the sociolinguistic perspective.

Bryson, Bill 1991, *The Mother Tongue: English and how it got that way*, New York: Perennial. An irreverent and anecdotal lay account by a renowned anglophile.

McMahon, April 1994, *Understanding language change*, Cambridge University Press. A more advanced and detailed book, which includes reviews of recent research.

Pyles, Thomas and Algeo, John 2004, *Origins and development of the English language*, 5th edition, New York: Heinle. This comprehensive account of the history of English is also useful as a reference text.

9 Dialect variation

KEY TERMS
- accent
- African American English (AAE)
- age-graded features
- apparent-time data
- auxiliary be
- copula be
- creole
- dense networks
- dialect
- double modals
- group-exclusive
- group-preferential
- inherent variability
- jargon
- lexical variation
- morphosyntactic variation
- multiplex networks
- nonstandard
- phonological variation
- pragmatic variation
- real-time data
- r-lessness
- slang
- sociolinguistics
- social networks
- sociolinguistic interview
- standard
- transition zones
- vernacular

CHAPTER PREVIEW

One of the central facts about human language that strikes us right away is its immense variability. There are anywhere from 5,000 to 8,000 languages in the world today, and all of those with more than a handful of speakers contain at least some subvarieties. In addition, languages exhibit variation over time, as any modern speaker of English who has ever tried to read Shakespeare, or even watch an old Hollywood movie, can tell you. In this chapter, our focus is on variation within languages, or dialect variation. We will explore the different types of dialect variation: regional, social class, ethnic, gender, and stylistic. We will look at patterns of variation on a number of different levels of language, including words and their meanings (**lexical variation**), pronunciations (**phonological variation**), sentence structures (syntactic variation or **morphosyntactic variation**), and even conventions for language use (**pragmatic variation** or discourse variation). We will also take a look at the intricate bond between dialect variation at any given moment in time and language variation over time, or language change. Finally, we consider the fate of dialect variation in an era of increasing globalization and find some surprising conclusions. Most of our examples of dialect variation are from English; however, nearly all languages are rich with variation. Before we begin, we must take a close look at some common beliefs about the nature of dialect variation which, upon closer inspection of actual data on dialect variation, turn out to be mistaken.

GOALS

The goals of this chapter are to:

- show that dialects that differ from the standard or socially most prestigious variety of a language are not linguistically inferior
- describe how languages show systematic patterns of variation based on linguistic and social factors
- exemplify how languages vary on all levels of organization – lexical, phonological, morphosyntactic, and pragmatic/discoursal
- demonstrate how individual speakers vary their ways of using language based on linguistic factors, situational factors such as formality, and social-psychological factors such as conversational purpose and the type of image speakers wish to project
- explain the relation between dialect variation and language change

The nature of dialect variation

Languages, dialects, and standards

Many people equate the term "language," as in "the English language" or "the French language," with the standard language – that is, that version of the language held to be correct in pedagogical grammar books and usage guides and used in education, the workplace, and the government. Because the standard is associated with education and sophistication, other varieties of the language are often considered to be lesser versions of the language – perhaps not as fully formed, or maybe "sloppy" in comparison with the standard. However, to the linguist, a language isn't just the standard version of the language but rather the sum of all the varieties that comprise it. Further, sociolinguistics (the study of language in its social context) has demonstrated that all varieties of language – including those quite far removed from "standard" or socially prestigious varieties – are equally complex, regularly patterned, and capable of serving as vehicles for the expression of any message their speakers might wish to communicate. Hence, the term dialect carries no negative connotations but is simply a neutral label to refer to any variety of a language, including the standard variety. Throughout this chapter, we use the term dialect in this neutral sense. In addition, in order to distinguish dialects that do not happen to be socially favored from more favored varieties, we will sometimes use the term nonstandard dialect or vernacular dialect. Again, no negative connotations are implied, and nonstandard should not be equated with substandard.

It is also important to note that dialects are not the same thing as **slang** or **jargon**. The term dialect is used to refer to an entire language variety, with features on all levels of language patterning (for example, phonology, grammar, and the lexicon). The term slang, on the other hand, is used chiefly to talk about lexical items. In addition, slang words typically carry some sort of non-neutral social meaning and usually have non-slang synonyms that are more neutral in tone. (Compare, for example, *wack* vs. *strange* or *kick the bucket* vs. *die*.) Further, slang words are usually considered to be short-lived, though, in reality, some "slang" terms have been around for generations. (For example, the terms *dough* for 'money' and *flunk* for 'fail' have been around since at least the early twentieth century.) Jargon also pertains to the lexical level of language and refers to terms associated with a particular sphere of activity – for example, computer jargon or legal jargon. A further point is that dialect is not the same thing as accent, since accent refers only to the phonological level of language, and dialects, again, are characterized by features on all linguistic levels.

A final issue that arises as we think about "language," "dialect," and related terms is how to determine whether a particular language variety should be classified as a dialect of another, larger language or whether it should "count" as a language in its own right. At first glance, it might seem that we could apply some relatively straightforward criteria: if two varieties are very similar linguistically and are mutually intelligible (that is, if the speakers of one variety can understand the speakers of the other and vice versa), then it seems that they should count as dialects of a single language. Conversely, varieties that are linguistically quite distinct and are not mutually intelligible should probably be classified as separate languages. In reality though, labeling varieties as "languages" or "dialects" is usually a bit more complicated, and what "counts" as a dialect vs. a language has as much – probably more – to do with cultural and political issues than with linguistic ones. Thus, for example, the different varieties of Chinese (e.g. Cantonese, Mandarin) are linguistically quite different from one another and are not mutually intelligible (at least in spoken form), and yet speakers of these varieties typically consider themselves to be speakers of a single language, Chinese. On the other hand, Swedish and Norwegian, which are considered two separate languages, are linguistically very similar, and many of their speakers can easily understand one another.

In addition, linguistic classifications and relations between language varieties can change, so that varieties once considered to be part of a single, larger language may come to be thought of as separate languages and may even become more linguistically different from one another as a result. For example, the Serbo-Croatian language, spoken in much of the area comprising the former Yugoslavia, is now considered by its speakers to be at least three different languages, Serbian, Croatian, and Bosnian, with Serbian being the official language of Serbia, Croatian the official language of Croatia, and all three the official languages of Bosnia-Herzegovina. The three languages are also becoming somewhat more different from one another, especially on the lexical and phonological levels, and language planners are attempting to introduce additional distinctions as well.

Again, the important point for linguists, and for linguistic study, is not whether we choose to call a variety a "language" or a "dialect," or whether we choose to uphold a particular variety as a "standard," but that all language varieties, no matter what their label or their political or social standing, are equally linguistically well formed and operate according to precise patterns or rules.

The regular patterning of dialects

So what exactly do we mean when we say that dialects are regularly patterned? It probably seems obvious that the standard variety or standard dialect has patterns. After all, grammar rules such as "Adverbs derived from adjectives usually take -*ly* endings," as in *She took a slow walk* vs. *She walked slowly*, are essentially explicit statements of patterns. However, not all rules for how we form words, put words into sentences, or pronounce things are written down. Rather, they are part of our unconscious knowledge of the regular patterning of our language. For example, all native English speakers know that adjectives usually come before nouns in phrases like *the red house* or *the blue book*. Yet this rule for adjective placement does not appear in any pedagogical grammar books for native speakers, and no native speaker ever had to consciously learn it. In other languages, there are different patterns; for example, in Spanish we find phrases like *la casa roja* (literally 'the house red') for 'the red house' and *el libro azul* (literally, 'the book blue') for 'the blue book.' And while this pattern is very different from the English one, it is nonetheless equally systematic. The same holds true for the patterns we find in nonstandard dialects of English and other languages.

For example, a feature found in a number of historically isolated dialects of American English, such as Appalachian English, is the use of an *a*-prefix (pronounced [ə]) on certain -*ing* words, as in *He went a-huntin'*. This feature, called *a*-prefixing, does not appear in any pedagogical grammar books and its usage is not taught in school. However, it does have regular patterns – where it can and cannot appear – even if people aren't consciously aware of them. Another example of a feature whose usage is governed by unconscious rules is reduction or deletion of *r* in certain word positions, as in [fiə] for *fear* and [fa:m] for *farm*. This feature is often referred to as **r-lessness** and is found in certain regional and social dialects in the US and in standard British English.

Why are standards held in such esteem?

If nonstandard dialects are just as regularly patterned as those that are considered standard, then why are some varieties more highly socially valued than others? Frankly, it's mostly a matter of fashion. As an example, let's consider the case of *r*-lessness. This feature is one of the most noticeable characteristics of standard British English (Received Pronunciation, or RP), often considered to be one of the most prestigious varieties of English in the world. Interestingly, though, proper Brits didn't always use *r*-less pronunciations. In fact, it wasn't until the eighteenth century that *r*-lessness began to spread through England, outward from the center of British cultural and political life in the southeast, eventually ousting *r*-pronunciation as part of the prestige norm. On the other side of the Atlantic, *r* had exactly the opposite history. Prior to World War II, *r*-lessness was considered to be a prestigious feature of American speech. Since that time, it has fallen out of social favor, and Americans who speak with *r*-less accents, such as New Yorkers and some Southerners, are now considered to be less "correct" than those who typically pronounce *r*'s.

Exercise 9.1 at the end of the chapter provides data on a-*prefixing in Appalachian English and takes you through the steps necessary to discover the rules governing its patterning. You should be able to use your unconscious knowledge of the regular patterning of language variation to discover these rules even if you are not a native speaker of Appalachian English or are not very familiar with the dialect. If you are not a native speaker of English, you may have more difficulty with this exercise, but you may be surprised to find that you know more about unconscious rules for variation in English than you think you do. An exercise enabling you to discover the patterning of r-lessness in the New England region of the US can be found on the companion website to this text.*

The shifting fate of *r* in different varieties of English over time, as well as the fact that *r*-lessness is valued in standard British English but devalued in standard American, tells us that there is nothing inherently "better" or "worse" about pronouncing your *r*'s or not. Instead, it all depends on who speaks in what way: if the elite members of a society, or other people who are widely admired, speak a certain way, then that way of talking is what gains social favor, and other equally serviceable types of speech get relegated to "substandard" status. Unfortunately, the seemingly whimsical turns of linguistic fashion often have grave consequences, and people who speak nonstandard varieties are often subject to discrimination on the basis of dialect, in the classroom, workplace, courtroom, and elsewhere.

Why dialects?

Given the potential negative consequences of speaking a nonstandard dialect, why do we continue to hear so much speech that differs from what we would consider to be standard? Some people feel that the answer lies in lack of exposure to the standard variety, perhaps through lack of education. Others are less kind and suggest that people speak nonstandard dialects because they are too "lazy" or "unintelligent" to learn to speak the standard. We have already seen that speaking *any* dialect requires following its often subtle rules, so laziness or lack of intelligence really cannot be the answer. Furthermore, many people with plenty of education speak nonstandard dialects, at least sometimes, and we can even hear political leaders speak with regional accents in their public speeches.

In truth, people use nonstandard dialects for important social reasons. For many, a nonstandard dialect is associated with home and their local neighborhood, and to abandon the dialect is practically equivalent to turning their back on their loved ones. For others, speaking nonstandardly carries connotations of coolness or toughness, so that people might even *add* nonstandard features to their speech, particularly in their teenage years, when it is especially important to "fit in" or "be cool." And many people use relatively standard varieties in certain settings but switch into more vernacular dialects in other situations, or switch within a single setting to achieve a certain effect. Again, we might think of a politician who uses a regional accent to give a "down home" feel to their words, to convey the message "I'm one of you."

We can even think of occasions when *not* speaking a particular nonstandard variety might be socially disastrous. For example, suppose a White teenage girl who was very popular in her high school in the San Fernando Valley area of California suddenly stopped using the language features associated with her regional, age, and social group – that is, the features of so-called "Valley Girl" talk (such as the use of *like* and *all* to introduce quotes, as in "I was *like*, 'What is she doing?'" or "She was *all*, 'Give me a break!'") – and instead began talking more like her upper-middle-class parents. We can imagine that her popularity might decline as rapidly as her use of the linguistic features that characterize her particular "in" group.

Inherent variability

All languages and language varieties, no matter how seemingly uniform, are inherently variable. For example, speakers of *r*-less dialects do not drop their *r*'s categorically (that is, every *r* all the time). This would be tantamount to saying that *r*-less dialects don't have *r* in their phonology, but they clearly do. Rather, their pronunciation of *r* is variable; they drop it sometimes. This variability is not random or haphazard; it patterns in regular ways, according to linguistic and social factors. The regular patterns that characterize languages and language varieties are very often variable rather than categorical. As with categorical rules, variable rules also display regular patterns based on linguistic factors. For example, some varieties of Spanish, such as Castilian Spanish, are characterized by the pronunciation of many /s/ sounds as [θ], as in the pronunciation of *hace frío* 'it's cold' as [haθe fɹio]. However, not all /s/ sounds are pronounced this way in these dialects, but only those spelled with *c* or *z*. Thus, a word like *vaso* 'glass' is pronounced as [vaso] rather than [vaθo]. We can see variability even in single words like *gracias* 'thank you,' pronounced [graθias]; the first /s/ sound, spelled with a *c*, is pronounced as [θ], but the second, spelled with an *s*, is pronounced as [s] (or sometimes [h] or [ø], in some Spanish varieties).

Linguistic variability also patterns regularly according to social factors such as social class and gender. In many communities, speakers in lower-social-class groups (as measured by income, occupation, and education) use nonstandard features more frequently than people in higher-class groups. In addition, though there are a number of exceptions, women often use standard speech features more frequently than men. The inherent variability of dialects extends to the individual level: everyone's use of dialect features fluctuates based on situational factors, such as the formality of the situation or who they're talking to, as well as social-psychological factors, such as whether they want to accommodate to or disassociate from the people they're with, or what type of image they wish to project.

One of the pioneering researchers in the patterned nature of dialect variability is William Labov. In the 1960s, Labov conducted a sociolinguistic study of the Lower East Side of New York City (Labov 1966). He conducted informal **sociolinguistic interviews** with hundreds of residents of different social-class groups who were native speakers of English and who grew up in the local area. He then examined how frequently a subset of these people used several features that are characteristic of the New York City dialect. In addition, he constructed his interview so that it would elicit speech of differing levels of formality, so he was able to examine differing usage levels in different styles as well. His analysis revealed quite regular patterns according to social class and style, as you can see in Figures 9.1 and 9.2. The first graph shows the patterning of a prestigious feature, *r*-pronunciation

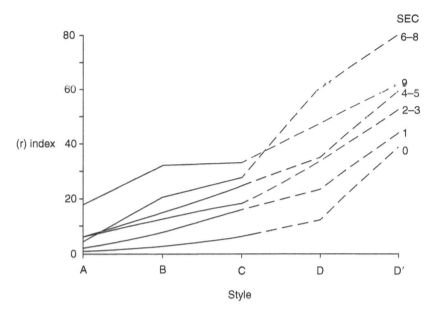

Figure 9.1 The regular patterning of a prestigious dialect feature according to social class and speech style: *r* in New York City English (adapted from William Labov 1972, *Sociolinguistic Patterns*, p. 114. Reprinted by permission of the University of Pennsylvania Press)

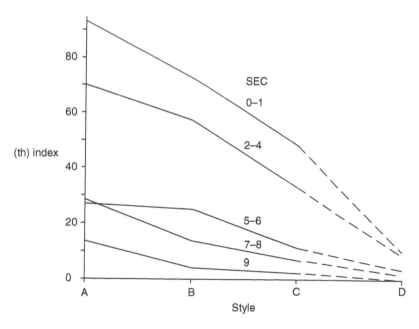

Figure 9.2 The regular patterning of a stigmatized dialect feature by social class and speech style: [t] for [θ] (e.g. *wit* for 'with') in New York City English (adapted from William Labov 1972, *Sociolinguistic Patterns*, p. 113. Reprinted by permission of the University of Pennsylvania Press)

(vs. the stigmatized *r*-lessness); the second graph shows the patterning of a stigmatized feature: the pronunciation of [θ] as [t], as in [wɪt] 'with' or [tɪŋ] 'thing.' The styles range from very informal (style A: casual speech) to very formal (style D, lists of isolated words). Minimal pairs (style D′) are considered to be even more formal (and self-conscious), since they involve interviewees' reading pairs of words, like *source/sauce* or *guard/god*, that differ by a single sound in standard American English but might sound the same in *r*-less New York City speech.

Figure 9.1 indicates that, in general, speakers in lower socioeconomic classes (SEC) use prestigious features less frequently, while those in progressively higher classes show progressively higher usage levels. At the same time, all class groups use the prestigious features more frequently as speakers move from the less self-conscious speech styles on the lefthand side of the graph to the more self-conscious styles on the right. The only exception to the regular patterns is the "crossover pattern" shown by the lower-middle class (SEC 6–8), who use the prestigious pronunciation more frequently than even speakers in the highest social class group (SEC 9) in the two most formal styles, word list style (D) and minimal pair style (D′). Labov refers to this crossover pattern as "hypercorrection" and attributes it to the status-consciousness and desire for upward mobility that he believes often characterizes groups in the middle of the socioeconomic hierarchy. Figure 9.2 indicates that speakers in lower socioeconomic classes use stigmatized features more frequently than those in higher classes and that speakers in all class groups use stigmatized features less and less as they move from casual, unselfconscious speech to situations in which they are more conscious of whether or not they are speaking "correctly."

BOX 9.1 **QUANTITATIVE SOCIOLINGUISTIC METHODS**

In order to identify how patterns of language variation correlate with linguistic and social factors, sociolinguists often conduct sociolinguistic surveys of communities of interest. They conduct sociolinguistic interviews with individuals from different social and age groups and then identify linguistic features with variable patterning. These features, called variables, must have at least two different ways in which they can be produced with no change in the meaning of the word or phrase in which they occur. One example of a variable is *r* vs. *r*-lessness in a word like *farm*, which can be pronounced as [farm] or [fa:m] with no change in meaning. Each different production of a variable is called a variant. For each variable selected, researchers note all instances where the variant of interest (e.g. *r*-lessness) could have occurred in the data. For example, *r* can only be realized as [ø] (that is, not pronounced) when it occurs after a vowel, as in *farm* or *fear*, but *not* when it occurs at the beginning of a word or after a consonant, as in *ring* or *bring*. For each of the cases (called tokens) where the variant could occur, researchers note how the token was produced (e.g. whether the *r* was pronounced or not), the linguistic environment of the token (e.g. whether the *r* was in a stressed syllable, as in *fear*, or unstressed syllable, as in *mother*), and the social characteristics of the speaker who uttered the token (e.g. African American middle-class female). Results are totaled for each speaker and then pooled for each social group within the community, yielding information such as percentage of *r*-lessness in each age, social class, gender, and ethnic group. Exercise 9.4 at the end of the chapter lets you try the quantitative sociolinguistic method yourself, using the variable pronunciation (*ing* or *in*) of the *-ing* ending on words like *swimming* and *walking*.

Levels of dialect variation

At first glance, it might seem fairly simple to divide languages into dialects. For example, it seems fairly clear that British English, American English, and Australian English are all separate dialects of English and that there are some broad differences between the varieties of Spanish spoken in Spain vs. those spoken in the Americas. But what about the various varieties of English spoken in the US or the many varieties of Spanish in the Americas? How many dialects of a given language are there, and how exactly do we draw our dividing lines? The answers to these questions are complicated by several factors. First, there is the issue of how finely we want to divide our dialects. For example, do we want to talk simply about Southern American English vs. Northern varieties, or do we want to talk about regional subvarieties within the south, such as those spoken in the Delmarva Peninsula, Virginia Piedmont, northeastern North Carolina, and Charleston, South Carolina? Similarly, are we interested simply in differences between, say, Mexican Spanish and Puerto Rican Spanish, or are we interested in more fine-grained differences between the different varieties of Spanish spoken in Mexico, or of Mexican Spanish as spoken in Mexico vs. various locations in the US? Second, patterns of regional variation intersect with patterns of variation based on social factors like social class and gender, and some socially based dialects may transcend region. For example, African American English (AAE) seems to be quite uniform across many regions of the US, even though there is some regional variation within this coherent language variety, as well as a great deal of variation according to social class and speech situation. In addition, as we have noted above, dialects differ from one another on all levels of language patterning, and dividing lines between varieties can look rather different depending on which types of feature we focus on.

Lexical variation

Perhaps the most noticeable differences between dialects are the different lexical items used in different varieties. For example, a *lift* in British English is called an *elevator* in American English, a *lorry* is called a *truck*, and a *jumper* is called a *sweater*. Similarly, speakers of Spanish varieties in the Americas use the lexical items *carro* 'car,' *jugo* 'juice,' and *computadora* 'computer,' while speakers of Spanish in Spain use *coche*, *zumo*, and *ordenador*, respectively. And such lexical variation is found not only across different countries or continents that share the same language but also within continents or countries. For example, in the US what a carbonated nonalcoholic beverage is called (e.g. *soda*, *pop*, *coke*, *cola*) varies across regions. And in some Spanish-speaking parts of the Caribbean, speakers say *guagua* for 'bus,' whereas *autobús* or *bus* are used elsewhere in Latin America. In addition to different terms being used to refer to the same items, we sometimes also find that a single term can be used to refer to different things in different dialects. For example, in northern Germany, where varieties of Low German are spoken, the word *Mücke* means 'mosquito,' while in parts of Austria, *Mücke* means 'gnat' or 'housefly.' Similarly, in parts of the Mid-Atlantic and southern US, the term *mosquito hawk* is used to refer to the dragonfly, while in other parts of the country (and even a few places in Virginia, in the Mid-Atlantic), *mosquito hawk* refers to the crane fly, a large mosquito-like insect that eats mosquitos. An example from Spanish is *tortilla*, which in Latin America refers to a flour or corn wrap but in Spain is an omelet with egg and onion.

Finally, lexical variation within a language may result when different groups of speakers have different things to talk about, often as a result of migration to different locales. Thus, for example, it was only when English speakers began settling in North America that they encountered such animals as *chipmunks, raccoons, catbirds,* and *rattlesnakes,* and so borrowed the terms from native American languages in the case of the first two, and made up the terms by compounding existing lexical items in the second two instances. Similarly, Australian English and New Zealand English are rich with borrowed and invented lexical items for local flora, fauna, geographic features, place names, and social and cultural concepts. For example in Australian English, we speak of animals such as *kangaroos* and *dingos,* as well as bodies of water called *billabongs,* while New Zealand English is increasingly rich in words borrowed from the indigenous Maori language, for example *kia ora* 'hello/goodbye,' *Pakeha* 'non-Maori New Zealander,' and *kohanga reo* 'language nest,' or total immersion Maori language program for young children, a term that is reflective of continuing efforts to revitalize the indigenous language of New Zealand (e.g. Melchers and Shaw 2003: 107–113).

As many of us know from personal experience, meaning differences between dialects can be more than quaint curiosities, since they are often a source of confusion or embarrass-ment. For example, a speaker of Australian English who asks for a *trolley* in an American grocery store is apt to be met with blank stares rather than directed to what she is requesting (*a shopping cart*), while a resident of North or South Carolina who travels to Britain and innocently begins talking about how much he enjoys *shagging* (a type of dancing in his dialect region), might be considered very impolite indeed, since he has just used a British slang term for sexual intercourse. To make matters worse, relationships between words and meanings are often most complicated when we're referring to the most commonplace items, for example basic articles of clothing. To touch briefly on the potential confusion: the men's undergarment known as an *undershirt* in the US is a *vest* in England and a *singlet* in Australia and New Zealand (while a *vest* in the US is a *waistcoat* in England); men's *(under)pants* may be called simply *pants* in England (as well as Australia and New Zealand) but referred to as *shorts* in the US, while women's *panties* (US) are called *knickers* in England and *pants* in Australia and New Zealand (Bauer 2002: 43).

Dialect lexical differences can also be important markers of identity, including regional, social, ethnic, and national identity. For example, it is mostly New Yorkers or other residents of the northeastern US who know what the term *shlep* means (a borrowing from Yiddish, meaning to carry or lug), while residents of Pittsburgh, Pennsylvania, pride themselves on their unique vocabulary items like *gumband* for *rubberband.* And on a larger scale, national or official language policies often prescribe the non-use of lexical items borrowed from other languages and encourage the innovation of native-like terms for innovative items and concepts. For example, the French Language Academy has recommended against such English borrowings as *software* and *email* in favor of French-derived *logiciel* and *courriel,* while in New Zealand, the little-known Maori word *rangapu,* with the original meaning of 'group' or 'company,' has been revitalized with the modern meaning 'partnership,' and the term *rei irirangi,* literally 'spirit voice,' has been coined to mean 'radio.'

Phonological variation

Dialects differ from one another not only in terms of lexical items but also in terms of their pronunciation systems, or phonology. For example, in most dialects of Spanish in the Americas, the letters *c* and *z* are pronounced as [s] – so *gracias* 'thank you' is pronounced [grasias] – while in most dialects of Spanish in Spain, *c* and *z* are pronounced as [θ], as in [graθias] for *gracias*. In addition, in some varieties of Spanish in both Spain and the Americas (e.g. in Andalusian Spanish and Canary Islands Spanish, and in much of Central America and the Caribbean), syllable-final /s/ is often pronounced as [h], as in [grasiah], and it may even be deleted in a subset of these varieties, as in [grasia]. In Germany, there are a number of systematic pronunciation differences between Low German, spoken in the north of Germany, and Middle and Upper German, spoken in the more southern areas. For example, the sounds /s/, /f/, and /x/ in Middle and Upper German in words like *das* [das] 'the,' *Schiff* [ʃɪf] 'ship,' and *machen* [maxən] 'make,' are pronounced as [t], [p], and [k], respectively, in Low German, so that the phrase *das Schiff klar machen* 'to clear the ship' (i.e. to make the ship ready for departure) is pronounced as 'dat Schipp klar maken' (p.c. Barbara Soukup and Andrea Kleene, University of Vienna, 2014).

Pronunciation differences also serve to dintinguish dialects of English both across and within countries. As we noted above, one of the most noticeable differences between American English and British English is the pronunuciation or non-pronunciation of *r* in postvocalic word position. At the same time, though, there are pockets of *r*-lessness in the US (for example in the Boston area and parts of the American South) and areas of *r*-pronunciation in the British Isles (for example, Scotland). Similarly, whereas Australian English and New Zealand English are primarily *r*-less varieties, there is a heavily Scottish-influenced area in New Zealand's South Island in which *r* may be pronounced, sometimes as something of a "burr" reminiscent of Scots English. As British English spread beyond England's earliest overseas colonies in North America, New Zealand, and Australia to South Asia and Africa, so too did England's *r*-less pronunciations. One notable exception is Indian English, most of whose speakers pronounce their *r*'s, sometimes as a retroflex (i.e. with the tongue curled back) as is typical of American English. However, Indian English is most noted for its retroflex alveolars (i.e. /ʈ/, /ɖ/, /ʂ/, /ʐ/, /ɭ/ and prosodic features such as syllable timing (in which each syllable is of equal duration) and a relatively wide pitch range.

Vowel pronunciations are also of crucial importance in differentiating dialects, both large and small. One of the most noticeable differences between British and American English is the pronunciation of what to Americans is an /ae/ vowel in words like *path*, *grass*, and *laugh* as an [a:] in standard British English. This feature is very salient to Americans, who often use it in imitations of British English. However, they often use it wrongly, because they presume that /ae/ is categorically pronounced as [a:] in British English, when in reality some words have [ae] and others have [a:]. Nor is the patterning very neatly predictable, and so it is practically impossible for an American without linguistic training or accent coaching to give an accurate imitation. Even in the same phonological environments there are lexically based differences. For example, British [pa:θ], [gra:s], and [la:f] exist side by side with [mæθs] *maths*, [mæs] *mass*, and [gæf] *gaffe*.

Despite sometimes subtle patterns of pronunciation difference, American English and British English are generally fairly easy to differentiate, at least for native speakers of

English. However, differences in vowel pronunciations also serve to distinguish quite similar varieties. For example, to the untrained ear, Australian English and New Zealand English may sound practically alike; however, once one becomes familiar with just a couple of vowel differences, differentiating between the two dialects becomes much easier (as well as a fun way to amaze one's nonlinguist friends). The chief way to tell a speaker of New Zealand English from an Australian is in the pronunciation of the /ɪ/ vowel, as in a phrase like *fish and chips*. In Australian English, we will either hear something fairly close to standard British *fish and chips* or a bit of a raised /ɪ/, as in something close to *feesh and cheeps*. In contrast, New Zealanders are known for backing the /ɪ/ vowel into schwa territory, producing something like *fush and chups* (and often being mocked for it by Aussies). New Zealanders are also known for pronouncing /ɛ/ quite close to /ɪ/, as in something like *driss* for *dress*, though Australians will approximate this pronunciation. And because the two dialects are quite closely related, they also share many pronunciation features, for example the merger of the diphthongs in words like *near* and *square* ([ɪ-ə] and [e-ə]) so that words pairs like *hear/there* and *beer/bear* are turned into rhymes.

Pronunciation differences also serve to make even more fine-grained distinctions, for example, among different dialects in the US. A map of the major regional dialects of the US based on pronunciation differences is given in Figure 9.3. This map was compiled by Labov and his research associates at the University of Pennsylvania, based on telephone surveys

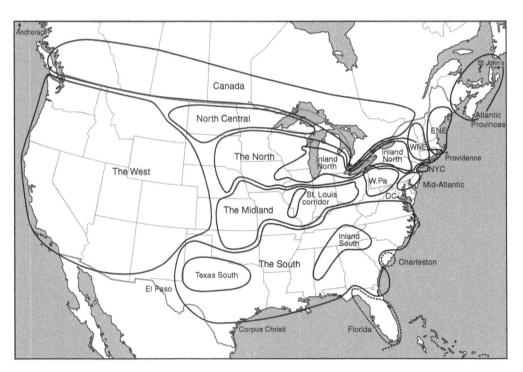

Figure 9.3 Dialect areas of the United States, based on telephone survey data (adapted from William Labov, Sharon Ash, and Charles Boberg 2006, *Atlas of North American English*, Berlin: Mouton de Gruyter, map 11.15. Reprinted by permission)

with speakers from all over the country. The focus was on urban areas (i.e. cities with populations above 50,000), since dialect changes tend to be more advanced in cities than in rural areas.

The dialect divisions on this map are based on speakers' pronunciations of several key vowel sounds, as well as relations among different vowel pronunciations. For example, the Inland North dialect is characterized by such features as the raising of /æ/ to [ɛ], so that a word like *bag* sounds something like *beg*, and the fronting of /ɑ/ toward /a/, so that a word like *Chicago* sounds like [šəkago] (or even something like [šəkægo]). The South is characterized by the frequent pronunciation of the /ay/ diphthong as a long monophthong, as in [ta:m] for *time*, as well as the fronting of /u/ and /o/ in words like *boot* and *boat*. Much of the rest of the US is characterized by the merger of /ɑ/ and /ɔ/, yielding pronunciations like [kɑt] for both *caught* and *cot*, with some exceptions such as the Mid-Atlantic, where /ɔ/ is raised toward /o/. In the Midland, the merger is still in progress, with different cities (and even different word pairs) showing different patterns.

> *You can find more information on Labov's telephone survey project (TELSUR) by going to www.ling. upenn.edu/phono_atlas/. You can also hear samples highlighting the phonological differences of various regional dialects of US English by going to the home page of the* Dictionary of American Regional English *at http://dare.wisc.edu/, navigating to the "Audio Samples" page, and downloading the audio clip (in.mp3 format) by clicking on the link at the top of the page. Samples of a wide variety of dialects of English throughout the world can be found on the website of the International Dialects of English Archive at http://web.ku.edu/~idea/.*

BOX 9.2 **THE NORTHERN CITIES VOWEL SHIFT**

For several decades, there has been an ongoing change in the pronunciations of a number of vowels in a large area of the northern US encompassing western New England; upstate New York; the extreme northern portions of Ohio, Indiana, and Illinois; and spreading into Michigan and Wisconsin. The change is especially concentrated in larger metropolitan areas and is known as the Northern Cities Vowel Shift. The term "shift" is used because the changing vowel pronunciations are tied to one another in what linguists call a chain shift. A chain shift occurs when a change in how one vowel is produced causes the organization of the vowel inventory of a language or dialect to become unbalanced, with too much "crowding" of one area of the vowel space and/or too much "empty space" in another. This imbalance is corrected by subsequent movement of other vowels in order to even out the vowel distribution once again. For example, the vowel pronunciation changes in the northern cities were triggered by the pronunciation of /æ/ as a higher, fronter vowel, as in [bɛg] for *bag*. This change left space in the low front area of vowel space. The low back vowel /ɑ/, as in *Chicago* [šəkago], is moving close to this space, while the mid back vowel /ɔ/ is moving down into /ɑ/ territory, resulting in the pronunciation of a word like *caught* /kɔt/ as [kɑt]. A diagram of this shift is given below. Note that in this diagram 'e' stands for /ɛ/, 'oh' stands for /ɔ/, and 'o' stands for /ɑ/. (To hear some of the pronunciations associated with the Northern Cities Vowel Shift, go to the companion website.)

BOX 9.2 (*cont.*)

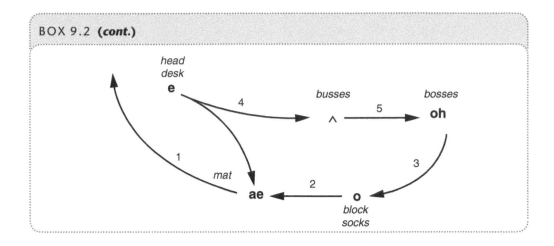

Morphosyntactic variation

Dialects can also be differentiated from one another in terms of morphosyntactic variation, how words are put together into sentences. For example, speakers of American English tend to use the form *gotten* as the past participle of *get*, as in *She has gotten used to it*, whereas British speakers tend to use *got*, as in *She has got used to it*. In addition, there are other differences involving *have* and *got*, as for example in American English *Do you have a match*? vs. British *Have you got a match*? There are also regional distinctions in morpho-syntax within the US and Britain. For example, in Scotland and the Northeast of England, speakers can use constructions such as *might could*, or *may can* (so-called **double modals**), in sentences such as *I might could do it*, which means something like 'I believe I could do it but am not quite sure.' This feature is also found in Southern varieties of American English, most likely reflecting the fact that many of the early English-speaking residents of the Southern US were of Scots or Scots-Irish origin. (The Scots-Irish were descendants of Scots who emigrated to Ulster, Northern Ireland, at the beginning of the seventeenth century.)

Australian English and New Zealand English share many grammatical features with standard British English but do have some distinguishing morphosyntactic features. For example, both varieties make extremely productive use of the noun suffixes *-ie* and *-o* as well as clipping, and forms that combine both morphological processes are common, for example *barbie* 'barbecue,' *Aussie* 'Australian,' *rellie* 'relative,' and *sammie* 'sandwich.' Simi-larly, the grammars of South Asian and African Englishes look a lot like those of British English, especially in written form and among more educated speakers, though we do see some differentiating traits, for example, the use of the progressive with stative verbs in Indian English (e.g. *I am knowing*), and the use of non-normative subject–verb agreement, or no agreement, in South African Englishes (e.g. *Does you go to school?*, *He like to read* [Bowerman 2004: 956]).

Morphosyntactic dialect differences also abound in other languages as well. For example, Montreal French differs from Parisian or "standard" French in that its speakers sometimes use *avoir* with verbs of movement that take *être* in compound tenses in standard French, as in *Hier, j'**ai** passé les voir* 'Yesterday I dropped by to see them,' rather than standard French *Hier, je **suis** passé les voir* (Sankoff and Thibault 1980). In addition, in vernacular dialects of French in both France and Canada, speakers often do not use *que* 'that' in sentences such as *Je veux (que) tu sortes* 'I want you to leave' (literally, 'I want (that) you leave'). There are also some morphosyntactic differences between varieties of Spanish spoken in Spain and those spoken in Latin America. For example, speakers of Spanish in Spain use the second-person plural pronoun *vosotros*, with its own set of endings on accompanying verbs, while those in Latin America use *Ustedes*, with its own verb endings; so a speaker of Castilian Spanish says *vosotros habláis* 'you (pl.) talk' while a speaker of Latin American Spanish says *Ustedes hablan*. Further, in much of Latin America (e.g. in Argentina and parts of Central America), the second-person singular pronoun *tú* is not used at all, with the older form *vos* (and different verbal endings) being used instead, as in *vos hablás* 'you talk' rather than *tú hablas*.

Pragmatic variation

Finally, dialects can differ, not only in terms of lexical items, pronunciations, and morphosyntax, but also in conventions of language use at a broader level – for example, in terms of how direct or indirect one is expected to be in conversation, or whether one should allow pauses between conversational turns, as well as how long those pauses should be. Thus, for example, speakers of Southern varieties of American English often engage in "small talk" before getting down to the business of a conversation, while Northerners tend to get more quickly "to the point." In addition, different cultural groups in the US may have quite different conventions for turn-taking in conversation. For example, speakers of Native American vernacular dialects of English in the Southwest tend to allow relatively long pauses between turns, while Jewish Americans in New York City not only tend to not pause between turns, but often even overlap each others' turns as a way of showing conversational involvement (Tannen [1984] 2005). Problems can arise when people who are used to different conventions for language use interact with one another; one person's normal conversational style, based on the conventions of his/her region or social group, might be misinterpreted as rude or excessively hesitant by someone who is used to quite different conventions. As with differences in pronunciation, sentence structure, and lexical items, it is important to recognize that pragmatic differences among dialects are just that – differences, and not deficiencies of some sort.

Shared features among dialects

We have seen that dialects can differ from one another on all levels of language variation; dividing lines between dialects can look quite different depending on what level we focus on. A further difficulty in dividing languages into dialects is that features are often shared across dialects. For example, *r*-lessness is found in some regional dialects in New England and the southeastern US, as well as in standard British English and many world Englishes derived from British English. Similarly, *a*-prefixing, as in *a-huntin' and a-fishin'*, can be found not only in Appalachian English but also in other historically isolated areas of the US such as some islands on the southeastern coast.

Features may be shared across social or ethnic dialects as well. For example, African American English (AAE) is considered to be one of the most distinctive dialects of American English. However, speakers of vernacular varieties of AAE share many features with speakers of Southern White vernacular dialects, including the pronunciation of /θ/ as [f], as in *birfday* for *birthday*, and the use of sentences with no *be* verb when *be* functions as a linking verb (**copula *be***), as in *They a nice group of people*, or helping verb (**auxiliary *be***), as in *They gonna come over*. It turns out that each dialect is unique, not because each is composed solely of its own unique features, but because each dialect combines language features in a unique way. In other words, features are often shared among dialects, but no two dialects are composed of exactly the same *set* of features.

In addition, dialects are often differentiated from one another not so much by presence or absence of certain features but by different usage levels for shared features, or different patterns of usage. For example, *r*-lessness can be found in vernacular varieties of AAE and in Southern White vernacular dialects; however, it is used to a much greater extent in vernacular AAE. In addition, whereas speakers of both vernacular AAE and vernacular Southern White dialects use sentences without the *are* form of copula and auxiliary *be* (e.g. *They nice, They gonna visit us*), only speakers of vernacular varieties of AAE show widespread use of sentences without the *is* form of the copula or auxiliary, as in *He nice* or *She gonna come visit us*. Although the construction of sentences without a copula is considered nonstandard in English, such constructions are perfectly standard in a number of languages, such as Russian. In addition, as with other language features we have been discussing, nonuse of copula and auxiliary *be* is variable rather than categorical, and this variability patterns according to regular rules. For example, nonuse of copula or auxiliary *be* in vernacular AAE tends to be more common before *gonna* and -*ing* verbs (as in *He gonna come over, She running*) than before noun phrases (e.g. *He a nice guy*).

Although many dialect features are shared across different dialects, there are some features that do seem to be unique to particular varieties. For example, the lexical item *gumband* 'rubberband' seems to be exclusive to Pittsburgh speech. In addition, despite its many shared features with Southern White varieties, AAE does have a few unique features, for example the use of *done* for resultatives or the future/conditional perfect, as in *She be done had her baby* for *She will have had her baby* (Rickford 1999: 6). Features that are unique to a particular language variety are called **group-exclusive** features, while those that may be prevalent in a certain variety but found to a lesser extent in others are **group-preferential**.

Further, although dialect maps such as the one in Figure 9.3 above may suggest that there are sharp dividing lines between regional dialects, in reality there are usually somewhat fuzzy **transition zones** between dialects, where we might find a mixture of features from dialects on either side of the zone, or perhaps features intermediate between the features of one dialect and those of a neighboring one. For example, speakers in the northeastern US have traditionally used the word *pail* to refer to a container often used to carry water or other liquids, while those in the South have traditionally used the word *bucket*. In between the two areas (e.g. in the Mid-Atlantic region), there is a good deal of variability, with some speakers using the word *pail* and others using *bucket*.

Finally, as noted above, regional variation intersects with several other types of variation, including variation by socioeconomic class, gender, and ethnicity. In the next section, we examine social-group-based variation of various types, as well as individually based variation, or stylistic variation.

Types of dialect variation

Social class and social network

Although early studies of dialect variation tended to focus on regional variation, researchers have long recognized that people within a given region may differ in the patterns of language they use depending on the social-class group to which they belong. (Class membership is traditionally determined by such measures as occupation, education level, and income.) Social-class-based language differences may have far graver social implications than regional variation. Varieties associated with lower social classes may be highly stigmatized and their speakers subject to scorn and social sanction (and even discriminated against in educational or employment opportunities), while dialects associated chiefly with region may be thought of simply as "interesting" or "unusual," or perhaps even "quaint" and "charming."

Beginning in the latter half of the twentieth century, sociolinguists began turning their focus to social-class-based variation. For example, in his pioneering study of variation in New York City English, Labov (1966) demonstrated that a number of dialect features showed regular patterns according to speakers' social class. As discussed above and shown in Figures 9.1 and 9.2 above, speakers in lower-class groups showed lower levels for standard or prestige features such as *r*-pronunciation in words like *fear* or *farm* and higher levels for vernacular or stigmatized features such as *r*-lessness or the pronunciation of [θ] as *t*, as in *wit* for 'with.' Conversely, speakers in higher social-class groups used standard or prestige features more frequently and nonstandard features less frequently.

Similar patterns of variation according to social class have also been found in other cities in the English-speaking world – for example in Detroit, Michigan (Shuy, Wolfram, and Riley 1967; Wolfram 1969); Norwich, England (Trudgill 1974); and Glasgow, Scotland (Macaulay 1976). In Norwich, Trudgill found a regular correlation between back vs. front pronunciations of the vowel in words like *path*, *grass*, and *after* and social class, with the working class producing more front variants (i.e. the American-sounding pronunciation) than the middle class, who produced more of the RP back variant, [ɑː]. Macaulay also found that Glasgow speakers belonging to lower-social-class groups produced more nonstandard variants than those in higher social classes for several pronunciation features, including the pronunciation of /au/ in words like *house* as more of an [u] (as in something like *hoos* for *house*) and the pronunciation of /t/ in certain word positions as a glottal stop, as in [bʌʔr] for *butter* and [gɛʔ] for *get*. In addition, regular correlations between socioeconomic status and usage levels for vernacular vs. standard features have been found in other languages – in the French of Montreal (Sankoff and Cedergren 1971, Sankoff and Vincent 1977) and the Spanish of Panama City (Cedergren 1973).

In studying social-class-based variation, it is important to realize that determining social-class membership or even identifying the relevant class divisions that characterize a given society may be quite difficult, especially since we may find quite different patterns of class division in different societies. Research on language variation in the Arabic-speaking world has shown that education seems to be the most important measure of socioeconomic status in Arabic-speaking communities (Al-Wer 1997), even though researchers in the western world often use occupation as a primary measure of status. Further, in the Arabic-speaking world, we cannot simply speak of nonstandard vs. standard language features, with "standard" being roughly equivalent to "prestigious." In the Arabic-speaking world, the true prestige variety, Classical Arabic, is not widely spoken; instead, higher-class speakers tend to use more modern varieties that are coming to serve as standards of communication across large regional areas or in large urban centers (Al-Wer 1997, Haeri 1997).

In addition, it is not always the case that everyone in a particular society orients toward a single common standard language. For example, in the mid 1980s, sociolinguist John Rickford (1986) found that the village of Cane Walk, Guyana, was sharply divided between two social-class groups rather than into a range of groups as in New York City. The two groups were the Estate Class, who worked on the sugar estates as unskilled laborers, and the Non-estate Class, who worked as foremen, drivers, and skilled tradesmen. Each group oriented to quite different language norms, with the Estate Class showing little inclination to conform to the standard English norms preferred by the Non-estate Class.

In addition to different patterns of language variation, different social-class groups also seem to play different roles in language change. We might be tempted to assume that language change begins in upper-class groups and gradually spreads into lower-class groups, since speakers of lower social standing might wish to emulate the speech patterns (and other behaviors) of those with more prestige. And indeed, some changes do spread this way – notably changes involving the adoption of a prestige feature of which speakers are quite consciously aware, like *r*-pronunciation in New York City. However, research has shown that many language changes operate below the level of conscious awareness, and these changes have their origins in *lower* social-class groups, especially those in the lower middle of the continuum (e.g. upper working class, lower middle class). Labov and others have suggested that these lower-middle groups may be so linguistically innovative because they are the most upwardly mobile of all class groups, hence very open to change.

Other researchers have suggested that it is not people's membership in a particular social group *per se* that correlates most closely with their readiness or reluctance to adopt language change but rather people's patterns of contact, or **social networks**. For example, in a groundbreaking sociolinguistic study of Belfast, Northern Ireland, Lesley Milroy and James Milroy showed that patterns of variation and change correlate quite well with whether or not speakers belonged to **dense** and **multiplex** social networks (e.g. J. Milroy and L. Milroy 1978, L. Milroy 1987). Dense social networks are those in which "everyone knows everyone else," and multiplex networks are those in which people interact with one another in more than one capacity, for example as a neighbor, workmate, and friend. In particular, Milroy and Milroy found that people who belonged to dense, multiplex networks tended to maintain local, vernacular speech features and to resist linguistic innovations from outside the local area. Conversely, those with loose social ties were much more open to language change. Milroy and Milroy's findings regarding the relationship between localized patterns of interaction and language change may help illuminate the large-scale patterns of language variation and change that are often found across social-class groups, since (in western society at least) people in the lower-middle classes typically have looser social network ties than those in the highest- and lowest-class groups. In addition, as we will see in the next section, studies of localized patterns of contact show us that general tendencies of particular social groups (e.g. class groups and gender groups) toward linguistic innovativeness vs. conservativeness do not always hold, and sometimes members of a particular social group such as a gender group may show quite different patterns of language variation and change in different local situations.

Gender-based patterns of variation

Sociolinguistic research on gender-based patterns of language variation has revealed a few fairly widespread patterns. For example, studies from all over the English-speaking world have found that, for stable language features – that is, features not currently undergoing change – women tend to be more standard than men. This has been found in a number of different standard Englishes around the world. For example, in all varieties of English, the pronunciation of the -ing ending on words like *swimming* or *running* as *ing* [ɪŋ] has long been considered to be standard, while the pronunciation of this ending as *in* [ɪn] (as in *swimmin'* for *swimming*) is considered to be nonstandard. Numerous studies dating back as far as the late 1950s have shown that girls and women tend to use higher levels of the -ing pronunciation than boys and men, whether in the New England area of the US (Fischer 1958); Norwich, England (Trudgill 1974); or Sydney, Australia (Horvath 1985).

At the same time, when it comes to language change, girls and women have often been found to adopt new features more quickly than boys and men – not only in English-speaking countries such as the US, Canada, and Scotland, but also in a range of other places such as Latin America, Spain, Hong Kong, and Taiwan. For example, in an early study of the systematic vowel changes affecting many cities in the inland northern US, Ralph Fasold (1968) found that women in one such city, Detroit, Michigan, were leading the change from [ɔ] to [ɑ] in words like *caught* [kɑt] and *bought* [bɑt], as well as the pronunciation of /æ/ in words like *bag* and *mad* as more of an [ɛ], as in [bɛg] for *bag*. The same female lead was still being observed decades later among teenagers in a Detroit-area high school in the early 1980s (Eckert 1988, 1989, 2000). In a very different speech community, Cairo, Egypt, Haeri (1994) found that women are far ahead of men in the ongoing rise in the palatalization of dental stops (as in [mamtyi] or [mamʧi] for /mamti/ 'my mother'), despite the fact that such palatalization is neither a feature of Classical Arabic nor a feature of what would be considered the "standard" variety of Egyptian Arabic.

At first glance it might be tempting to offer a universal explanation for patterns of gender-based variation – perhaps an explanation rooted in the biological differences in men and women, or the different cultural expectations for men and women in many of the world's societies. However, universal explanations end up falling short, since there are actually a number of exceptions to the widespread patterns, and patterns of variation according to speaker gender can be quite different in different communities, and even in different segments of the population within a single community. For example, in his large-scale study of New York City English, Labov found that there was more difference between women's and men's speech in the lower-middle-class groups than in other social classes. In addition, he found different patterns of gender-based variation in different speech styles: in careful speech, women used higher levels of standard features than men, as we might expect. In casual styles, however, women actually used more informal speech than men.

Even in much smaller populations, different subgroups may show different patterns of female–male language use. For example, in her in-depth sociolinguistic study of "jocks" and "burnouts" in a Detroit-area high school, Penelope Eckert found that all girls did not use language in the same way, nor did all boys share the same language variety. Different groups of girls and boys used language features differently. The jocks were those who oriented toward school and school-related activities, and planned to go on to college and to leave the Detroit area, while the burnouts were those oriented toward local urban institutions and activities rather than school and who planned to remain in the Detroit area after graduation. For certain language changes, for example the change from [ɔ] to [ɑ] in words like [kɑt] *caught*, girls in both groups led boys in their usage levels for the innovative pronunciations. However, for other, newer changes, for example the change from [ɛ] to [ə] in words like [bət] *bet*, burnout girls led burnout boys, but jock girls lagged behind jock boys.

It turns out that we need localized explanations to account for the sometimes highly localized patterning of gender-based language differences. In the case of the jocks and burnouts, both burnout girls and boys had more contact with people from urban Detroit, where the newest language changes were concentrated. Jocks, especially jock girls, had more limited contacts and a more suburban orientation and so were less quick to adopt the language features most associated with urban speech. In addition, there were different expectations for appropriate behavior for jock girls vs. burnout girls, with jock girls expected to be more "proper" and to speak more standardly than burnout girls.

Ethnicity-based variation

Another social characteristic that can have a big impact on the type of dialect we speak is ethnicity. It is important to noted that ethnicity-based patterns of variation have nothing to do with biology: just as a child of French descent who is raised in Japan by Japanese-speaking caregivers will speak Japanese rather than French, so too a child of African American descent raised in a White family in a primarily White neighborhood will speak a White rather than African American variety as his/her native dialect. Conversely, a White child raised by speakers of African American English (AAE) and surrounded by

AAE-speaking friends will speak AAE rather than a White dialect. Hence, similar to gender-based patterns of variation, ethnicity-based language differences are due to cultural rather than biological factors, some of which include early exposure to particular ethnic varieties, later patterns of contact with speakers of similar and different varieties, and societal expectations regarding "appropriate" ways of speaking for particular social groups.

The ethnic variety that has been most thoroughly studied is the variety spoken by many African Americans in the US, often referred to by sociolinguists as **African American English** (**AAE**). You may also hear the terms **Ebonics** or Black English. In addition, some researchers on African American culture and language use the term Hip-Hop Language or Hip-Hop Nation Language (HHNL). Although the language associated with hip-hop culture is widespread among young African Americans, it is not exactly equivalent to AAE, since HHNL is used by people of a range of ethnicities in the US and throughout the world (Alim 2004). In addition, AAE has a much longer history than hip-hop, which has been around only for several decades.

Like all other language varieties, AAE has distinguishing features and patterns of usage on all levels of language organization: phonological, morphosyntactic, and pragmatic. Much of the early development of this language variety took place in the American South, and so it shares many features with Southern White varieties. However, these shared features may be used to a greater or lesser extent in AAE than in White varieties, or they may pattern in different ways. For example, AAE and Southern White dialects share phonological features like *r*-lessness and the pronunciation of the /ay/ diphthong as a monophthong, as in [na:n] *nine* and [ɹa:d] *ride*. However, *r*-lessness is found to a greater extent in AAE than Southern White varieties. In addition, /ay/ monophthongization in Southern White varieties occurs before both voiced and voiceless consonants, as in [ɹa:d] *ride* and [ra:t] *right*; in AAE, however, [a:] for /ay/ occurs almost solely before voiced sounds, so that speakers of AAE will say [ɹa:d] for *ride* but [ɹaɪt] for *right*.

Some of the distinguishing morphosyntactic features of AAE, especially its more vernacular varieties, include constructions such as *He nice* or *They running* (discussed earlier), use of uninflected *be* in sentences indicating habitual or ongoing action, as in *He be late for school* (meaning 'He is usually/always late for school'), and use of the same verb form for all subject persons and numbers with regular present-tense verbs, as in *I go, you go, he go, we go, you all go, they go*. In vernacular versions of AAE, possession may occasionally be indicated by juxtaposition of the possessor with the possessed item (e.g. *John book*), though often an *-s* ending is used as well (e.g. *John's book*); and plurals may variably be indicated by an *-s* ending or by context alone (e.g. *three cats, three cat*). Again, although some of the morphosyntactic features of vernacular AAE are shared with Southern White vernaculars, they are often used differently. For example, as discussed above, both Southern Whites and Blacks may show nonuse of copula and auxiliary *be* in sentences with plural subjects (e.g. *They nice, They gonna come over*). However, it is mostly speakers of vernacular AAE who show nonuse of copula and auxiliary *be* in sentences with singular subjects, as in *She nice* or *He gonna fix dinner*.

Perhaps more than any other nonstandard language variety, AAE has long been embroiled in controversy. Some of the controversy is confined to academic circles.

For example, sociolinguists have long debated whether AAE has its origins in the early dialects of British English brought to the American colonies, or if it originated as a creole. A **creole** is a language arising from contact between different languages, often in situations of unequal power. It is composed of features from the different contact languages as well as features that seem to arise specifically in contact situations – for example, the loss of inflectional endings. In the case of AAE, the languages in contact would have been mainly various West African languages and the dialects of English spoken in the American South, where the largest populations of slaves existed. The debate over the origins of AAE still continues today. Some scholars point to shared features of AAE and White varieties (including British varieties) in support of the English origins of AAE. Others point to similarities between AAE and a number of the world's creoles in support of the creole origins of the variety. Creole-like features of AAE include nonuse of copula *be* (e.g. *He nice*), use of a single verb form for all subjects (e.g. *I go*, *she go*), and reduction of word-final consonant clusters (e.g. *las' night* for 'last night,' *Wes' End* for 'West End'). In recent years, some scholars have suggested that a compromise view may actually be the most correct, since sociohistorical and recent linguistic evidence suggests that different African American varieties in the US may have had different histories, with some being more strongly influenced early in their history by surrounding British vernacular varieties than others, and most being characterized by at least some features common in language contact situations.

> To practice identifying the phonological and morphosyntactic features of AAE, try the exercise on "Listening for ethnicity-based dialect features" on the companion website.

Other controversies surrounding AAE go beyond scholarly circles and can have a profound impact on people's lives. In particular, AAE has long been disparaged in educational and other institutional settings, and its speakers are often still discriminated against – ostensibly on the basis of language, though in many cases really on the basis of race. For example, schoolteachers often do not recognize the systematicity and well-formedness of dialects, such as AAE, that are considered to be nonstandard, and children who speak these varieties are often regarded as less intelligent and even language-impaired. Similarly, adult speakers of vernacular varieties of AAE may be less likely to get jobs for which they are qualified than speakers of more standard language varieties. In addition, although housing discrimination on the basis of race or ethnicity in the US is illegal, such discrimination does occur. For example, John Baugh, a sociolinguist who can speak in several different dialects, including AAE and standard English, designed an experiment in which he made phone calls inquiring about housing vacancies using vernacular AAE, Hispanic English, and standard (i.e. White) English. (Baugh's inquiries in the three different dialects can be heard on the companion website.) Sadly, Baugh found that he got more negative responses when he used vernacular AAE or Hispanic English than when he spoke in standard English. Although sociolinguists have been working for decades and continue to work to convey their scientific knowledge about the regular patterning of dialects to the general public, such incidents illustrate that we still have quite a long way to go in eliminating dialect discrimination, as well as the racial prejudices that often underlie discrimination on the basis of language or language variety.

> Go to the companion website to hear samples of age-based variation in a small, rural population of African Americans in Hyde County, on the coast of North Carolina, and samples of African American English, Lumbee Indian English, and White English in another rural North Carolina community, Robeson County, located in the southeastern portion of the state.

Sociolinguists are also working to gain a better understanding of variation within African American English, as well as the patterns that characterize other ethnicity-based language varieties in the US and throughout the world, including, for example, Chicano English and Native American varieties of English in the US; British Creole English in the UK; and Maori English in New Zealand.

Dialect and style

We have seen that people who speak a single language can speak quite differently from one another depending on where they're from and which social groups they belong to. In addition, every individual speaker can speak in a range of different styles, based on a variety of factors. For example, people in New York City show regular patterns of stylistic variation ranging from casual speech to the formal style they adopt when asked to read lists of words containing sounds they might be self-conscious about (e.g. the /ɹ/ sound in words like *source* or *guard*). In addition, people may vary their speech quite a bit depending on who they're addressing or conversing with. For example, sociolinguist Allan Bell (1984) studied the speech of several radio announcers in New Zealand and found that the same announcers used more standard British English when reading the news for a national station but used more features of New Zealand English when reading the news (often from the same script) for a local community station. Similarly, Nikolas Coupland (1980) studied the speech of an assistant in a travel agency during the course of her work day and found that she spoke more and less standardly depending on who she was speaking with – co-workers, clients, or fellow agents at other travel agencies. Among other features, both researchers investigated the pronunciation of /t/ between vowels (e.g. *butter*, *latter*) as the RP voiceless variant [t] vs. the voiced or flapped variant that characterizes American English but is considered nonstandard or casual in the UK and other British English-influenced countries. In both cases, pronunciation variation correlated with audience: in Bell's case, the radio announcers used more of the nonstandard variant when broadcasting to local audiences, while the travel assistant in Coupland's study used more of the voiced/flapped variant when talking with friends than with clients or travel agents with whom she had strictly a work relationship.

In addition to these contextual factors, people may adjust their speech styles according to social-psychological factors like whether they wish to conform with or disassociate from their co-conversationalists or what type of image they wish to project. For example, during a conversation with a difficult client, the travel assistant that Coupland studied shifted from fairly standard to more vernacular speech in order to indicate that she wished to be helpful and friendly rather than aloof and professional. While some style shifts can be quite short-lived, other patterns of stylistic variation can come to characterize a person or a group in general, so we can speak of a person's individual style or group styles like the jock and burnout styles studied by Eckert, or the Valley Girl style once associated with young women and teens in the San Fernando Valley area of California and subsequently spreading widely throughout the US.

> **Working to end dialect discrimination and misinformation: Walt Wolfram's dialect awareness programs**
>
> *One linguist who has played a prominent role in increasing awareness of the regularly patterned nature of dialect variation among educators and the general public is Walt Wolfram, Distinguished Professor of English Linguistics at North Carolina State University. Wolfram has worked for many years, at NCSU and several other US universities, as well as the Center for Applied Linguistics in Washington, DC (www.cal.org), to develop and implement dialect awareness programs for nonlinguists, including a series of documentary videos on varieties of English in North Carolina as well as curricula on language variation for elementary and middle-school children. (To learn more about Wolfram and his colleagues' various dialect awareness programs and materials, visit the website of the North Carolina Language at Life Project at North Carolina State University at www.ncsu.edu/linguistics/ncllp/index.php.)*

Age-based variation and language change

In addition to variation across geographic and social space, languages also show variation over time, or language change. Language change is intimately connected to variation at any given moment in time, since changes do not take place suddenly but rather have their roots in a period of variation. For example, people in upper-class British society did not decide one day in the eighteenth century to stop pronouncing their *r's* after vowels. Rather, the change from *r*-pronunciation to *r*-lessness was gradual and in fact never fully spread to all areas of the British Isles, and we still find lots of *r*-ful speech in the areas farthest removed from London, including Ireland, Scotland, and southwest England.

One of the most important findings of sociolinguistics is that, in addition to studying language changes after they have happened, we can actually observe language change in progress, by looking at patterns of variation in a cross-section of speakers of different ages in a given community at a single moment in time. Labov (1963) was one of the first researchers to make the connection between age-based variation and change, in a groundbreaking study of dialect variation in Martha's Vineyard, an island off the coast of Massachusetts. Labov focused mostly on the pronunciation of the /ay/ and /aw/ diphthongs in words like *sight* and *south*, respectively. He observed that different social groups on the island showed a greater or lesser tendency to use a raised, central pronunciation of these vowels, as in [əɪ] and [əʊ] instead of [aɪ] and [aʊ], respectively. In addition, Labov found that younger speakers tended to use these centralized pronunciations more frequently than older speakers, even though the centralized pronunciations are actually historically older than the [aɪ] and [aʊ] variants. Through comparing his findings with older records of speech in the Martha's Vineyard area, Labov was able to determine that a change from [aɪ] and [aʊ] back to the traditional [əɪ] and [əʊ] pronunciations was underway in the island community. In addition, he found that the newer "retro" pronunciations were concentrated among rural fishermen and others who strongly valued the traditional island way of life. He inferred that the innovative pronunciations carried connotations of islander identity and that speakers were using higher levels for these features as a sort of resistance to the growing influx of outsiders whose presence was beginning to be felt on Martha's Vineyard in the early 1960s.

Researchers in subsequent decades and in a multitude of communities throughout the world have continued to find similar patterns of age-based variation that are strongly indicative of language change in progress. Of course, any conclusions based on the patterning of variation at a given moment in time (so called **apparent-time data**) should always be checked against **real-time data** – that is, data from earlier studies of the same community or follow-up studies that test whether apparent changes have actually been sustained over time. In addition, investigators need to be careful that the different usage patterns they find in different generations of speakers are not temporary changes that speakers will "grow out of" as they advance in age, called **age-graded features**. This is particularly important if teenagers and younger speakers are included in the study, since teenagers often adopt very different speech patterns from adults (for example, the heavy use of slang) but conform more closely to adult language norms as they get older and begin to enter the workforce. Bearing in mind these cautions, the apparent-time method has proven to be a very instructive way of studying language change, including not only *what* changes have taken place and are currently underway but also *how* language changes progress through communities across different age groups, social groups, and styles.

The fate of dialect variation

So what types of changes actually *are* taking place in the various language varieties we find in the US and throughout the world? And is it the case that increasing intercommunication and the increasing influence of the mass media are leveling out dialect differences, and that dialect (and perhaps even language) diversity is destined to doom? Surprisingly, research indicates that while indeed some highly localized varieties in small communities are dying out, larger regional varieties are actually becoming more different from one another in some areas and being created anew in others. In the US, for example, there is increasing differentiation in the vowel pronunciations of northern and southern regions. In recent decades, regional and social varieties have arisen in the western US, which has long been more linguistically uniform than the eastern portion of the country. In England, some older, localized dialect features are giving way, not to long-accepted features of standard British English but to newer features and even formerly "nonstandard" features. For example, some formerly "lower-class" pronunciations have spread widely in south-eastern England, where we may now commonly hear such pronunciations as *fing* ([fɪŋ]) for *thing*, *bruvvuh* ([brəvə]) for *brother*, and *bo'l* ([baʔl]) for *bottle*. In addition, a new supra-local dialect seems to be arising in northeastern England as well (e.g. Watt and Milroy 1999, Watt 2002).

Although English may be becoming a global language, as the popularity of English grows, so too do the number of varieties of English spoken throughout the world. We have seen a number of examples of linguistic differences that separate the long-established major dialects of English: British English, American English (which encompasses US English and Canadian English), Australian English, and New Zealand English. There are also a host of varieties of English spoken by people as a second language in countries such as China, Japan, Saudi Arabia, and Zimbabwe. And, as with all dialects, the different world Englishes that become established are fully fledged language varieties with regular patterning on all levels of language variation. It seems likely, then, that despite the increasing reach of globalization and mass communication, dialect variation will persist and perhaps even strengthen. For, just as Labov found for Martha's Vineyard over half a century ago, dialects continue to serve as important symbols of local identity, and people everywhere seem determined to assert their unique identity, especially when outside forces threaten to undermine it.

BOX 9.3 **SMITH ISLAND ENGLISH: A RARE CASE OF DIALECT DEATH BY CONCENTRATION**

The dialect of Smith Island in Maryland's Chesapeake Bay is interesting, not only because it is very distinct from surrounding dialects and from standard American English, but because it is rapidly dying out – and in a very unusual way. Due to the increasing difficulty of making a living via small-scale maritime occupations, the island is rapidly losing population, as residents are forced to seek jobs on the mainland. In addition, the island is losing land mass and may in fact be sinking into the Chesapeake Bay. Some estimates suggest that Smith Island may be habitable for only 50 to 100 more years. Like many of the world's formerly remote locations, islanders are coming into ever-increasing contact with mainlanders. For example, in recent decades cable television and the internet have come to the island, and a daily school boat service to the mainland high school was implemented. (There is no high school on the island. Before the advent of the daily school boat service, island teens who wanted to attend high school had to board with mainland families, coming home only on weekends.) These changes might lead one to think that the unusual dialect would be on the decline.

Interestingly, though, Smith Island English actually seems to be becoming more rather than less distinctive from surrounding varieties, even as it loses speakers – a phenomenon sociolinguists call "dialect concentration." Dialect concentration contrasts with the more usual way in which languages and dialects die – called "dissipation." Dissipation refers to the replacement of distinguishing features with more widespread ones. Researchers have found that a number of distinguishing

BOX 9.3 *(cont.)*

phonological and morphosyntactic features are on the rise in Smith Island English. The phonological features undergoing concentration include the pronunciation of the /ay/ diphthong in words like *right* and *time* as more of an [əɪ] (similar to the Martha's Vineyard /ay/ sound), and the pronunciation of the /aw/ diphthong in words like *south* or *down* as more of an [ɛɪ] (pronounced more toward the front of the mouth), so that *down* sounds almost like *Dane*. Morphosyntactic features on the rise include the use of *it* to indicate existence where standard English would use *there*, as in *It was three men outside* for 'There were three men outside,' and the use of *weren't* for all forms of past *be* in negative contexts, as in *It weren't me* or *I weren't there* (in addition to standard *You weren't there, They weren't home*).

Several factors seem to account for the unusual way in which the island variety is moving toward death. Perhaps the most important is islanders' strong sense of community identity and personal distinctiveness from outsiders. Especially for those who choose to remain on the island despite the increasing difficulties, preserving and even heightening their unique dialect seems to be one way in which islanders can fight the tides, both socioeconomic and literal, that threaten to bring an end to their cherished way of life.

To hear how the Smith Island dialect has intensified over the past several generations, go to the companion website and listen to excerpts from interviews with old, middle-aged, and younger speakers. To compare this intensification with dialect dissipation, go to the companion website and listen to three speakers of different generations from Ocracoke Island, located in the Outer Banks chain of islands off the coast of North Carolina. In contrast to Smith Island, Ocracoke has experienced rapid population growth over the past several decades, as tourists and new residents flock to the island in ever-increasing numbers.

CHAPTER SUMMARY

In this chapter, we have explored the nature of dialect variation, or variation within a single language. We have seen that dialect variation is not random or haphazard but is regularly patterned according to both linguistic factors and social factors (for example, region, social class, social network, ethnicity, age). Dialects show regular patterns of variation on all levels of language, from the pronunciation of individual sounds to patterns for conducting entire conversations. In addition, individual speakers display stylistic variation according to such factors as the formality of the speech situation, who they're talking to, and what sort of image they wish to project. Dialect variation is intricately tied to language change, since changes do not take place suddenly but rather begin in variability between old and new features. It is even possible to see language change in progress, by looking at the speech of different age groups of speakers in a single community at a single moment in time. Finally, we have seen that, despite increasing intercommunication among the world's people and the increasing spread of English as a world language, dialect diversity is alive and well, and there are indications that dialect differences may be intensifying in some places even if they are dying out in others. Despite the fact that nonstandard or vernacular dialects are often wrongly disparaged as "improper" or "uneducated" speech, all dialects are bona fide forms of communication, and dialect differentiation is an important, often essential, component of cultural and personal distinctiveness.

Exercises

EXERCISE 9.1

A-prefixing in Appalachian English (adapted from Wolfram and Schilling-Estes 2006). Look at the sentence pairs in list A and decide which sentence in each pair sounds better with an *a*-prefix. For example, in the first sentence pair, does it sound better to say, *A-building is hard work* or *He was a-building a house*? For each sentence pair, just choose one sentence that sounds better with the *a*-.

   List A. Sentence pairs for a-prefixing

(1) a. Building is hard work.
     b. She was building a house.
(2) a. He likes hunting.
     b. He went hunting.
(3) a. The child was charming the adults.
     b. The child was very charming.
(4) a. He kept shocking the children.
     b. The store was shocking.
(5) a. They thought fishing was easy.
     b. They were fishing this morning.
(6) a. The fishing is still good here.
     b. They go fishing less now.

Examine each of the sentence pairs in terms of the choices for the *a*-prefix and answer the following questions.

- Do you think there is some pattern that guided your choice of an answer? You can tell if there is a definite pattern by checking with other people who did the same exercise on their own.
- Do you think that the pattern might be related to parts of speech? To answer this, see if there are any parts of speech where you *cannot* use the *a*-prefix. Look at *-ing* forms that function as verbs and compare those with *-ing* forms that operate as nouns or adjectives. For example, look at the use of *charming* as a verb and adjective in sentence 3.

The first step in figuring out the pattern for the *a*-prefix is related to the part of speech of the *-ing* word. Now let's look at another difference related to prepositions such as *from* and *by*. Based on the sentence pairs in list B, say whether or not the *a*-form can be used after a preposition. Use the same technique you used for list A. Select the sentence that sounds better for each sentence pair and say whether it is the sentence with or without the preposition.

List B. A further detail for a-*patterning*

(1) a. They make money by building houses.
    b. They make money building houses.
(2) a. People can't make enough money fishing.
    b. People can't make enough money from fishing.
(3) a. People destroy the beauty of the island through littering.
    b. People destroy the beauty of the island littering.

We now have another detail for figuring out the pattern for *a*-prefix use related to prepositions. But there is still another part to the pattern for *a*-prefix use. This time, however, it is related to pronunciation. For the following *-ing* words, try to figure out what it is about the pronunciation that makes one sentence sound better than the other. To help you figure out the pronunciation trait that is critical for this pattern, the stressed or accented syllable of each *-ing* word is marked with the symbol ′. Follow the same procedure that you did in choosing the sentence in each sentence pair that sounds better.

List C. Figuring out a pronunciation pattern for the a-*prefix*

(1) a. She was discóvering a trail.
    b. She was fóllowing a trail.
(2) a. She was repéating the chant.
    b. She was hóllering the chant.
(3) a. They were fíguring the change.
    b. They were forgétting the change.
(4) a. The teacher was remínding me to do my homework.
    b. The teacher was rámbling on about my homework.
(5) a. The were décorating the room.
    b. They were demánding more time off.

Say exactly how the pattern for using the *a*-prefix works. Be sure to include the three different details from your examination of the examples in Lists A, B, and C.

In list D, say which of the sentences may take an *a*-prefix. Use your understanding of the rule to explain why the *-ing* form may or may not take the *a*-prefix.

List D. Applying the a-*prefix rule*

(1) She kept handing me more work.
(2) The team was remémbering the game.
(3) The team won by playing great defense.
(4) The team was playing real hard.
(5) The coach was charming.

EXERCISE 9.2

Attitudes toward dialects (and their speakers). Think of three varieties of English or your native language and list some of the positive and negative values associated with people who speak each of the three varieties. Have you held certain beliefs about people's characteristics based on their dialects? What can you say about these beliefs after learning about the regular patterning of nonstandard as well as standard language varieties? If possible, think of a person (whether a public figure or someone you know personally) who doesn't seem to fit the stereotypes associated with the dialect they speak.

EXERCISE 9.3

Dialects in movies and television. Choose three characters in a movie or television show with identifiable dialects of English or another language and describe these characters and their dialects. Why do you think the show's creators chose to have the characters use those dialects? What associations/stereotypes do the dialects call forth?

EXERCISE 9.4

Investigating social and stylistic variation: -in *vs.* -ing. Record a conversation or informal interview with two native English speakers who differ according to one of the social characteristics discussed in this chapter, perhaps gender, social class, or ethnicity. You should conduct each conversation separately, and each should last at least half an hour. It is also very important that you obtain informed consent from each speaker to record them: do not attempt to conduct secret recordings without the permission of the participants!

Once you have made your recordings, listen to each recording and note carefully each word ending in *-ing* and whether the *-ing* was pronounced as *in* or *ing*. If there are any words where you feel like the *ing* would never be pronounced as *in* (e.g. *ring*), note these down but exclude them from your final calculations. Add up how many *in* pronunciations out of total *ing* words you had for each speaker and calculate a percentage figure as well. Do the two speakers show different usage levels for this dialect feature? If so, why do you think this is? Did either of the two speakers seem to have different usage levels at different moments in the conversation/interview? If so, why do you think this might be?

EXERCISE 9.5

Gender and language variation. Researchers have found different patterns for gender-based language differences based on social class and speech style: for example, in some communities, there is more differentiation between women's and men's speech in the lower-middle/upper-working class than in other social classes; in addition, in some communities, women use more standard forms than men in formal settings but more vernacular speech than men in casual settings. Patterns of gender-based variation can also vary from conversation to conversation, depending on who is talking to whom. Reflect on your own language usages with people of different genders. Do you talk differently when talking with a same-gender friend vs. a friend of a different gender? What about a single-gender vs. mixed-gender group? Do the differences depend solely on gender or also other factors (e.g. age, familiarity)? Does sexual orientation make a difference? Provide examples of the linguistic differences you notice, whether pragmatic, lexical, phonological, or morphosyntactic.

EXERCISE 9.6

Language variation and language change. Researchers have found evidence that inserting *of* into so-called "inverted degree constructions," as in *It's not that big (of) a deal* or *It's not that bad (of) a problem,* may be a change in progress in American English. In addition, they have found evidence that the insertion of *of* is not random but may be affected by certain linguistic and social factors (Nylund and Seals 2010, forthcoming). Research is still ongoing, however, and conclusions are tentative.

To help researchers determine whether inverted degree constructions with *of* are indeed on the rise, as well as possible conditioning factors on the variable use of *of*, administer the following short survey to a selected population of English speakers of different age groups. In choosing your sample of people to survey, you will want to carefully consider what factors you want to control for vs. what factors you want to test as possible conditioning factors for *of* insertion – for example, native vs. non-native speaker status, regionality, gender, ethnicity. Bear in mind that the more factors you include, the more people you will have to survey to obtain meaningful results. You will also want to ensure that your sample is as balanced as possible – for example, by surveying the same number of people of each age group, each gender group, etc. In addition, you will need to decide how to administer the survey – on paper, orally, or perhaps online. The introduction to the survey may be adapted to suit your particular needs.

When you have collected all your survey results, compile them in order to determine whether reported use of *of* in inverted degree constructions indeed correlates with age and therefore may be a change in progress. What other social factors correlate with reported *of* usage, if any? Are there any correlations with linguistic factors? Present your results in the form of a short written report accompanied by tables and graphs, where appropriate.

SURVEY

Researchers in the Georgetown University Linguistics Department are conducting a survey of the use of particular types of sentences in English, all of which involve matters of degree (big/small, good/bad, etc.). You can help us out by taking a few minutes to give us your responses to the following survey. All information you provide will be used solely for our research purposes and cannot be used to identify you in any way.

Please indicate whether you would say each of the following:

	Yes	Sometimes	No
1) It's not that big of a deal.	___	___	___
2) It's not that big of a loss.	___	___	___
3) It's not that good a book.	___	___	___
4) It's not that small a loss.	___	___	___
5) It's not that helpful of a book.	___	___	___
6) It's not that bad of a book.	___	___	___
7) It's not that minimal a loss.	___	___	___
8) It's not that useful a tool.	___	___	___
9) It's not that boring a book.	___	___	___
10) It's not that wonderful of a deal.	___	___	___
11) It's not that awful of a book.	___	___	___
12) It's not that terrible a deal.	___	___	___
13) It's not that interesting of a book.	___	___	___

Age: _____
Gender: _____
Ethnicity: _____
Where did you grow up? _____
What is your native language? _____
[Add other blanks as appropriate]

SUGGESTIONS FOR FURTHER READING

Chambers, J. K. 2009, *Sociolinguistic theory: linguistic variation and its social significance*, revised edition, Oxford and Malden, MA: Blackwell. This book is a substantive introduction to language variation study, covering the patterning of variation according to a full range of linguistic and social features, illustrated with clear, succinct examples from some of the most important sociolinguistic studies that have been undertaken. Also included are insightful discussions of assumptions and theories underlying variation analysis, as well as the relationship of variation analysis/sociolinguistics to theoretical or formal linguistics.

Crystal, David 2003, *English as a global language*, 2nd edition, Cambridge University Press. This book offers an accessible discussion of the spread of English throughout the world, including such topics as why English is spreading so widely, changes affecting different varieties of English around the world, and the fate of English as a global language.

Rickford, John R. 1999, *African American Vernacular English*, Oxford and Malden, MA: Blackwell. This book provides a detailed look at the most thoroughly studied of all language varieties, African American English. Included are sections on the current patterning and historical development of AAE, as well as educational implications of this important dialect variety.

Wolfram, Walt, and Schilling-Estes, Natalie 2006, *American English: dialects and variation*, 2nd edition, Oxford and Malden, MA: Blackwell. This book offers an in-depth look at the nature of dialect variation in general, as well as patterns of variation in American English in particular.

10 Language and culture

CHAPTER PREVIEW

Language and culture are closely intertwined in complex ways; indeed, many anthropological linguists argue that they are inseparable. The meaning of utterances comes not only from the words spoken but also from culturally agreed-upon conventions for how those words are used and interpreted, as well as from how they have been used in the past within a given culture. This chapter illustrates the relationship between language and culture by examining representative scenarios of conversational interactions between speakers who grew up in different countries speaking different languages, and between Americans of different ethnic and regional backgrounds. An opening scenario of an interaction between an American student and his German counterparts illustrates culturally influenced aspects of language that can cause miscommunication or mutual misjudgment of intentions and abilities. Next, we introduce the concept of **framing** and explore how differences in framing can exacerbate discrimination and social inequality. This is illustrated with reference to John Gumperz's studies of interethnic communication. We move then to discussion of politeness strategies and the conversational styles that result from their systematic use of features like overlap, **rate of speech**, and **indirectness**. We then consider the ritual nature of conversation. Differences in conversational rituals are illustrated with examples from language and gender. The concept "complementary schismogenesis" accounts for why things often get worse rather than better when people with different styles talk to each other. Finally, we consider the extent to which language shapes thinking and provides a way to order and see coherence in the world, and we suggest that language and culture are better thought of as a single entity: languaculture.

GOALS

The goals of this chapter are to:

- explore and explain the relationship between language and culture
- identify the role played by language in crosscultural encounters
- show how crosscultural encounters provide insight into how language works to create meaning
- identify the specific linguistic elements that speakers use to convey meaning in conversation and how they can vary from one culture to another
- become familiar with key terms and concepts in anthropological linguistic analyses of linguistic relativity

Culturally influenced aspects of language

An American university student arrives in Germany to begin a study-abroad program. With his deep knowledge of current events and international affairs, he is well prepared for and enthusiastic about the adventure before him. But as he begins to interact with German university students, things start to go wrong. Almost immediately after learning that he is American, many German students launch into vitriolic attacks on American foreign policy or passionate arguments about religion. There is no way that our American student is going to talk about religion with someone he doesn't know. And he is so offended by the attacks on his country and by the belligerent tone used to present them that he usually clams up. If he does try to respond to the accusations, the German students typically try to cut him off or shout him down. The American student comes away from these conversations shaken, increasingly convinced that German students are opinion-ated, arrogant, and rude. For their part, the German students are frustrated that their attempts to begin a lively interchange have fallen flat. They come away from the same conversations increasingly convinced that American students are uninformed, apathetic, and not very interesting.

This description is based on an article written by Heidi Byrnes (1986), a Georgetown University professor who has worked with many college students preparing for and returning from study-abroad programs in her native Germany. According to Dr. Byrnes, these mutual frustrations and stereotypes between American and German students are common. Although the German students speak English and the American students speak German, they have very different assumptions about how to use language when they talk to each other, and it does not occur to them that they are exercising culturally learned linguistic habits. They believe they are simply trying to talk to each other in ways that are self-evidently appropriate.

Everyone knows that those who live in different countries speak different languages. But as American students quickly learn when they go abroad, knowing the vocabulary and grammar of the language is only a starting point for successful communication. Members of different cultures not only speak different languages but also have different ways of using the languages they speak – different assumptions about what's appropriate to say and how to go about saying it. In fact, people who live in the same country and speak the same language can also have different assumptions about what to say and how to say it, depending on their ethnic and class backgrounds, geographic region, gender, and many other influences.

The ways of speaking that characterize *how* you say what you mean, which distinguish the Germans' and Americans' use of language in our example, occur at every level of language use, from such obvious elements as what it is appropriate to talk about to less obvious aspects of speech like intonation (the musical lilt of language) and turn-taking (how to get the floor). When we talk to each other, we tend to focus on what we want to say, and we automatically make these and many other linguistic choices that communicate how we mean what we say. These choices tend to differ from one culture to another. Here are some of the linguistic elements that characterize and distinguish the German and American students' use of language in the situation described above:

> ***Topic*** (what to talk about). Is it appropriate to discuss politics and religion with someone you have just met? To many Germans it is; to many Americans it is not. As a result, the German students come across to the American students as intrusive and rude, while the Americans strike the Germans as ignorant or apathetic.

> ***Agonism*** (using an adversarial format to accomplish goals other than literal fighting). Is it appropriate to oppose the ideas of someone you have just met? If so, how strongly? For many Germans, strong expressions of opposition make for lively interchange; many Americans regard such levels of opposition as unacceptably belligerent, so they withdraw, giving the impression to the German students that they have nothing to say.

> ***Amplitude, pitch, and tone of voice*** (levels of loudness and pitch combined with voice quality). How loud or soft, high-pitched or low-pitched, should your voice be, to indicate emotions or other stances toward what is said? The loudness and assertive voice quality that for many Germans connotes enthusiasm and passionate commitment can seem overbearing, angry, and even intimidating to Americans; this too encourages them to back off or withdraw from the conversation.

> ***Intonation*** (the music of language). To most Americans, when an utterance ends with rising pitch, it sounds like a question or like an invitation for the listener to signal understanding or agreement (such as *mhm* or *uhuh*). When an utterance ends with falling intonation (that is, the pitch goes down), it sounds like a statement or even a demand. German speakers often use falling intonation where Americans would use rising intonation, so the Americans may come away with the impression that their German conversational partners were peremptory or curt. Conversely, Americans' tendency to end sentences with flat or rising intonation may give Germans the impression that they are tentative or uncertain.

Overlap vs. interruption (speaking at the same time). When does talking at the same time as another speaker constitute **interruption** (taking the floor away) and when is it a **cooperative overlap** (talking along to show interest and enthusiasm)? Germans often start speaking while others are speaking in order to show eager involvement in the conversation. To an American who believes that only one person should be speaking at a time, this overlap comes across as an interruption, an attempt to take the floor before the American has finished. The American will probably yield the floor, feeling interrupted, convinced that the German wants only to speak, not to listen. But the German who intended the overlap as a show of enthusiasm will conclude that the American has no more to say or is unwilling to contribute ideas to the conversation.

Turn-taking (how speakers determine who has, gets, or relinquishes the floor). Conversation is a two-party or multi-party enterprise: one person speaks, then another speaks, and so on. Speakers use many linguistic elements to signal when they are done talking, wish to speak, or are taking the floor. We have just seen how differing habits regarding overlap can disrupt turn-taking. All the other elements play a role here, too: topic (Does the speaker seem to have finished? Is the second speaker introducing a new subject?); agonism (Is the second speaker agreeing or disagreeing, and in how strong terms?); amplitude (Does the level of loudness give the impression a second speaker is trying to shout down the first? Is the level so quiet that the first speaker doesn't know the second wants to say something?); and intonation (How peremptory or tentative does a speaker sound?).

Indirectness (communicating meaning implicitly rather than explicitly). What should be stated directly, and what should be implied? If meaning is not explicit, what indirect locutions are appropriate to convey it? Americans might use indirectness by sending out feelers to discover whether new acquaintances share their political views before speaking passionately in support of those views. German students' direct expression of their political views strikes the American students as overly blunt, whereas Americans' subtle indications of their political views are likely to be missed by German speakers altogether, leading them to conclude that American students don't have any.

Framing (how ways of speaking signal what speakers think they are doing by talking in a particular way in a particular context). All the aspects of conversational style described above, along with others, "frame" the interaction by signaling to listeners how they should interpret what is said: Are we having a chat? An argument? Are you teasing? Angry? The American and German students perceive different frames. What the Germans regard as a lively conversation, the Americans regard as an unpleasant argument or verbal attack.

All these ways of speaking operate whenever people talk to each other. They are simply the linguistic elements that we use to communicate how we mean what we say and what we think we are doing at each moment in a conversation. They tend to be invisible, because we take the meaning of these linguistic elements for granted; we find them self-evident. When conversationalists share expectations about these linguistic elements, there is no reason to pay attention to them. But when habits and expectations regarding their use are not shared, we need to pay attention to them, first because listeners may misinterpret how we mean what we say, and second because these ways of speaking also form the basis for judgments we make about each other's intentions and abilities.

The above discussion could give the impression that all Germans share the same communicative habits and all Americans share a different set of communicative habits. But this is not the case. No two individuals have exactly the same ways of using language. "Culture" is a highly complex and multifaceted phenomenon. Each individual has a unique personality, and there are many other "cultural" influences as well, such as geographic region (think of New England, the Midwest, the South, and all the smaller geographic regions within these areas); ethnic groups (among Americans, these include the influence of the countries from which their ancestors came); social class; gender; profession (think of an accountant as compared to a psychologist); sexual orientation; and so on. These and other cultural influences can affect the words, expressions, intonation patterns, turn-taking habits, and other linguistic aspects of how speakers say what they mean. At the same time that these ways of speaking communicate ideas, they also communicate what you think you are doing in a particular conversation, the relationship you have or want to have with the person you are speaking to, and what kind of person you are. Since these linguistic elements vary by cultural influence, they affect what happens when speakers of different cultural backgrounds talk to each other.

In what follows, we will look more closely at how linguistic elements work together to communicate meaning and negotiate social relationships in interaction; how their use can differ from one cultural group to another; and how these differences affect the outcome when speakers of varying cultural backgrounds talk to each other.

Language, culture, and framing

Let's start with the concept of framing, because it governs all the other linguistic signals we will discuss. Framing is the way speakers communicate what they think they are doing in a particular interchange, and therefore how to interpret what they say.

Anthropologist Gregory Bateson ([1955]1972) developed the idea of framing during a visit to a zoo, where he watched two young monkeys playing. Bateson asked himself how the monkeys (and the zoo visitors) knew that although they were behaving aggressively (for example, biting each other), they were not really fighting, but just playing. In other words, "playing" and "fighting" are alternate frames that determine how the bites are to be interpreted. Bateson concluded that whereas the bite was the message (the literal meaning of the action) the monkeys simultaneously communicated to each other a **metamessage** ("This is play") that signaled how the bites were meant. A metamessage signals a frame – what the monkeys were *doing* when they bit each other – within which bites are understood as playful.

In conversations between human beings, every utterance is framed by a metamessage that signals how that utterance is intended (for example, literally or sarcastically, angrily or teasingly). The metamessage signals what people think they are *doing* when they speak particular words in particular ways in particular contexts. Everything said in a conversation includes clues to how listeners should interpret the words spoken, so that participants understand not only what is *said* but also what is *going on*. Metamessages are signaled by *how* you say what you mean – that is, all the linguistic elements that we listed above, such as tone of voice, rate of speech, loudness, intonational patterns, and so on. For example, in American English, sarcasm is often signaled by flat intonation and exaggerated stress on key words – <u>Nice</u> one after a missed basketball shot, or *Thanks a lot* when a speaker does not really appreciate what another has said or done. Idiomatic words and phrases can also signal how a remark is intended. For example, the phrase *Did you hear the one about . . .* would alert many Americans that a joke will follow. Anyone who has a dictionary and a grammar book could potentially understand what the words mean, but in order to understand how to interpret those words a conversationalist needs to know how the linguistic features frame the utterance.

> *Contrasting impressions of metamessages and the frames they signal are also ubiquitous in intracultural communication. For example, a young woman was preparing salad when her mother asked, "Are you going to quarter those tomatoes?" She replied, "Well I was. Is that wrong?" Her mother said, "No, it's just that personally, I would slice them." The daughter sliced the tomatoes, but she thought to herself, "Can't I do anything without my mother letting me know she thinks I should do it some other way?"*
>
> *The daughter heard her mother's question as criticism, framed as such by the metamessage that the tomatoes should be sliced, whereas the mother truly believed that her question bore no such metamessage, but was framed as a request for information, pure and simple. Similarly, the remark "Those pants don't flatter you" can be heard as criticism by a daughter whereas her mother genuinely intends it to be helpful. In both examples, mother and daughter agree on what the words mean (the message) but disagree on what they imply – that is, the metamessage indicating the speaker's intentions.*

The concept of framing shows that language and culture are inseparable: you cannot communicate or interpret meaning through language without signaling metamessages – how you mean what you say – and the way metamessages are signaled varies from culture to culture. Imagine, for example, visitors to the United States who speak the language but are unfamiliar with the culture. When asked *How are you?* they may begin to describe a health problem and be surprised and offended when the person who asked this question does not listen to the answer. (When this happens repeatedly, they may conclude that Americans are insincere.) The visitors understood the question but not the frame; the question *How are you?* was a routine greeting, not a request for information.

Every group of people has culturally agreed-upon ways of greeting each other that are not meant literally. Those who are unfamiliar with the routine are likely to interpret the greeting literally. In Burma, a routine greeting is *Have you eaten yet?* Americans visiting Burma, when asked this question, may think they are being invited to lunch and feel snubbed when their negative reply is ignored. They miss the framing of this question as a greeting. A typical Javanese greeting is the question, *Where are you going?* The expected routinized reply is *Over there*. A visitor unfamiliar with this routine may miss the frame "greeting" and wonder, "What business is it of yours where I'm going?" Any time people talk to each other, being able to understand the language and therefore interpret the message – the literal meaning of what others say – is a start, but it is not sufficient. To really understand what is said, a listener must be able to interpret the metamessages that identify the frame – how the words are meant, what the speaker is *doing* by saying these words in this way in this context. To do this, one needs to be familiar not only with the language but also with the culture.

Every utterance must be said in some intonational pattern, at some rate of speech, with some combination of pitch and loudness, and so on. But habits for and assumptions about using these linguistic elements to frame utterances differ among members of different cultural groups. Indeed, these ways of framing utterances are a large part of how speakers identify each other as members of particular cultural groups. Culture is constituted in part by ways of using language, and language exists only as it is shaped in particular cultures.

Crosscultural miscommunication

How do such features as intonation and loudness signal the frame for interpreting utterances, and what are the consequences when habits regarding the use of these linguistic features differ? Let's look at a specific case analyzed by anthropological linguist John Gumperz (1982), the founder of **interactional sociolinguistics**, a subdiscipline of linguistics that examines how language creates meaning in interaction. (Interactional sociolinguistics is a type of discourse analysis.) Gumperz tape-recorded and analyzed real conversations that took place among speakers of different social and cultural backgrounds, and traced some of the problems in the interactions to culturally different habits for using the linguistic features we have discussed. Gumperz calls these linguistic features **contextualization cues**, because they signal, or "cue," the context in which speakers intend their utterances. Note that "context" in this sense is comparable to the notion of "frame," because it refers to what speakers think they are doing when they speak, and how they intend their words to be interpreted.

Gumperz's particular goal was to understand how cultural differences in language use can lead to discrimination against members of minority groups and social inequality. Here is one example of a situation he studied and how he discovered that language was part of the problem. In the 1970s, Gumperz was asked to address a thorny employment situation in London, England. The staff cafeteria at a British airport had recently hired food servers from India and Pakistan for the first time, and both supervisors and customers were complaining that these new employees were "surly and uncooperative." For their part, the South Asian employees were complaining that they were being discriminated against. To figure out what was going on, Gumperz used the research methods of interactional sociolinguistics. First, he tape-recorded interactions that took place while customers were getting food on the cafeteria line. He then listened to the audiotapes and identified a contrast in the intonation patterns of British and South Asian food servers that helped explain both complaints. When customers chose a meat course, the server asked whether or not they wanted gravy. Both British and South Asian servers made this offer by uttering a single word, *Gravy*. But the British servers said this word with rising intonation while the South Asian servers said it with falling intonation. This tiny difference in intonation – whether the pitch went up or down at the end of a single word – resulted in very different impressions. To British ears, *Gravy?* said with rising intonation sounded like a question roughly paraphrased as *Would you like gravy?* In stark contrast, *Gravy*, said with falling intonation, was heard by the British as a statement which might roughly be paraphrased, *This is gravy. Take it or leave it.*

Next, Gumperz played segments of the interactions back to both British and South Asian employees. The British cafeteria workers pointed to the South Asians' responses as evidence that they were rude to customers. The South Asian cafeteria workers felt that they had caught their British colleagues displaying discrimination and prejudice, since they were being criticized for saying exactly the same thing as their British co-workers. It was only when their supervisor and English teacher explained how the different intonation patterns resulted in different meanings that the South Asian servers understood the negative reactions they had been getting. Indeed, they recognized that intonation patterns used by their British co-workers had struck their ears as odd. At the same time, the supervisors learned that for speakers of South Asian languages, the falling intonation was simply the normal way of asking a question in that context.

Such uses of contextualization cues are not unconscious; a speaker will readily recognize them when they are pointed out. But they are automatic; we use them without thinking about or focusing on them. In other words, the use of contextualization cues, linguistic elements that frame meaning, is *conventionalized* – associated by longstanding habit with a given intention. In British English, a single word uttered with rising intonation is conventionally associated with a question, and the hearer fills in the missing parts: *Happy?* is likely to be interpreted as *Are you happy?* And *Hurt?* would be interpreted as *Does it hurt?* Although this seems natural to speakers of British English, the link between rising intonation and asking a yes/no question (and the contrasting link between falling intonation and making a statement) is neither logically necessary nor universal. In many South Asian languages, yes/no questions end with falling intonation. When learning and using a new language, we typically concentrate on choosing the appropriate words and on getting the grammar right, but we may automatically use the intonational pattern we would use when speaking our native language. Since we're focusing on the message, we may be completely unaware of the metamessage that is conveyed by the way we said it. This was the case with the South Asian cafeteria workers and their British counterparts.

This example shows how the tiny linguistic features that frame utterances can play a large part in conveying meaning and in negotiating relationships between individuals and between cultural groups. It also demonstrates that differing habits with regard to linguistic signals can contribute to the perception and the reality of social inequality and discrimination. Of course, linguistic processes are not the only factors at play when a minority group

---

BOX 10.1 THE CONSEQUENCES OF CULTURAL DIFFERENCES IN SCHOOL

Crosscultural differences in linguistic behavior can have significant negative consequences when the communicative style that children learn in their home communities differs from that expected by their teachers. Susan Philips (1983) has documented this for children on the Warm Springs Indian Reservation who have Anglo teachers. Jeffrey Shultz, Susan Florio, and Frederick Erickson (1982) have described a similar case with an Italian-American child in a Boston elementary school.

Philips shows, for example, that Native American children often remain silent in classrooms run by Anglo teachers, because the teachers call on children to speak in front of the class as a whole, and they expect children to claim the floor by raising their hands. These formats for speaking require students to behave in ways that are considered inappropriate in the Native American community, where children are discouraged from drawing attention to themselves by acting as if they know more than or are better than their peers. (The Native American children, however, outshine their Anglo classmates when the teacher allows students to work unsupervised in small groups.)

Shultz, Florio, and Erickson also found that the child suffers when expectations for regulating talk differ at school and at home. They videotaped conversation in an Italian-American child's home and discovered that the child was encouraged to pipe up with his own comments while adults were speaking. Children in this family were not instructed that only one voice should be heard at a time. When the boy spoke up in class much as he did at home, he was chastised for misbehavior and identified as a problem child.

---

faces discrimination and social inequality; many other factors, such as economics and politics, play a role as well, as does outright prejudice. But it is important to acknowledge that linguistic elements may be part of the problem, as these elements are often invisible and therefore overlooked. A particular irony is that, unless the effect of linguistic differences is recognized, when individuals of differing cultural background spend more time together, the result may be more rather than less prejudice against members of a cultural group. Until Gumperz raised their awareness about their differing uses of intonation, the South Asian and British servers who worked together did not learn to like and understand each other better. Instead their negative impressions of the other group were reinforced repeatedly, like those that arose between the German and American students in our first example.

Politeness and interaction

The concept of framing helps explain the relationship between language and culture, but so far we have discussed only how words are spoken, not the ideas that those words express. *What* you choose to say to a particular person in a particular situation is just as important in communicating and negotiating social relationships. Norms and expectations about who can say what, to whom, and when, may vary across cultures as well. To explain the interactive goals that account for what people choose to say, linguists use the term **politeness**. This term is used in a technical sense, different from the everyday meaning when we say someone is "polite" or "impolite." In linguistic terms, politeness refers to a way of balancing several competing interactive goals. Cultural differences in politeness norms help to explain some of what happens when people of different cultural backgrounds talk to each other.

Linguist Robin Lakoff ([1975] 2004) identified three **Rules of Rapport** that speakers try to follow when they interact:

1 Don't impose
2 Give options
3 Maintain camaraderie

Emphasizing different Rules of Rapport leads to different styles of politeness.

Let's see how these politeness rules can shape a simple speech activity (making and receiving an offer of a beverage) and how the emphasis of one rule over the others is part of a culture's characteristic style of politeness. Imagine that someone comes to visit you in your home, and you ask, *Would you like something to drink?*

- A visitor who replies, *No thanks*, despite being thirsty, is applying Rule 1, "Don't impose."
- A visitor who replies, *I'll have whatever you're having*, is applying Rule 2, "Give options."
- A visitor who replies, *Yes, thanks. Have you got a Diet Coke?* is applying Rule 3, "Maintain camaraderie."

Many variations on these replies are possible, each representing slightly different balancings of the three politeness rules. For example, a good friend might not wait for you to offer but might ask, *I'm really thirsty. Have you got anything to drink?* That would evince even more camaraderie. In some cultures, a very close friend or family member might go right to your refrigerator and take a Diet Coke without asking – an even stronger expression of camaraderie.

Language provides many ways of negotiating a simple offer of a drink. But assumptions and habits about the right way to conduct this exchange vary across cultures. When people learn a new language, they usually use it to say what they would say in their native language, and this could make a very different impression than it would in their home culture. For example, in Greece (and in many other parts of the world) it is considered rude to accept food or drink the first time it is offered. Even a second offer is typically deflected. Only on the third offer is it appropriate to accept. In the United States, however, it is typical to accept on the first offer, so the decline of a first offer is taken literally, and second and third offers may never be made. Many a visitor to the US has gone hungry or thirsty because of these different applications of the politeness rules! They are applying Rule 1, "Don't impose," whereas the American expectation is Rule 3, "Maintain camaraderie." In all cases, the goal is politeness in the technical sense: ways of honoring human needs to display camaraderie and to avoid imposing. Saying *No thanks* when you are thirsty and heading straight for the refrigerator are both ways of being polite in this technical sense. However, when the participants in an interaction apply differing politeness norms, each may judge the other impolite (in the everyday sense). Someone who expects Rule 1, "Don't impose," will judge a visitor who asks for a drink to be impolite, but by the same token, someone who expects Rule 3, "Maintain camaraderie," may judge a visitor who refuses to accept an offer of a drink to be cold and unfriendly.

BOX 10.2 ETHNIC DIFFERENCES: THE LINE BETWEEN TALKING AND FIGHTING

Thomas Kochman (1981) identifies cultural differences that tend to distinguish the styles of American whites and African Americans. For example, he observes that most whites tend to regard verbal aggressiveness as threatening, whereas many blacks value it as a sign of engagement. He gives an example of a confrontational meeting that took place between university faculty and community representatives. At one point, a black male faculty member pointed a finger at a white female colleague and angrily accused, "Professor___, you need to know something. You can't make me over into your image. Do you understand that? You can't make me over into your image." When he saw that the woman appeared frightened, he assured her, "You don't need to worry; I'm still talking. When I *stop* talking, then you might need to worry." Kochman goes on:

When the meeting was over, she accused the black faculty member of having "threatened" her. He was astonished by her accusation. His comment to me afterward was, "All I did was *talk* to her. Now how can that be threatening?"

(p. 44)

Kochman explains that whites tend to regard "fighting" as having begun as soon as violence seems imminent, an impression they may get from the intensity of anger expressed verbally and the use of insults. In contrast, blacks do not deem a fight to have begun until someone makes a provocative movement. As a result, whites may try to prevent a fight by curtailing verbal disputes, whereas blacks "conceive the danger of violence as greater when people are not communicating with each other than when they are, no matter how loud, angry, or abusive their arguments may become" (p. 58).

Growing up in the same country and speaking the same language does not necessarily mean two speakers have grown up in the same "culture." Americans who grow up in different parts of the country, or have different ethnic or class backgrounds, also have different habits and expectations about how to use language to accomplish social goals, with the result that one speaker could do or say something intended to be friendly (Rule 3) that another interprets as rude (a violation of Rule 1). For example, Americans of Greek background may expect that food will be accepted only after several offers – and be put off by Americans of East European background who think it is a heart-warming gesture of close friendship to help themselves from a good friend's refrigerator.

High-involvement and high-considerateness styles

In my own work (Tannen [1984] 2005), I have combined the concepts of framing and of politeness phenomena to describe how Americans of different backgrounds use language, and how these differences lead to problems. The first two Rules of Rapport, "Don't impose" and "Give options," are closely related, both serving people's need for independence – that is, not to be imposed on. The third Rule of Rapport, "Maintain camaraderie," serves the need for involvement – that is, to be connected to others. Any two people can have different ideas about which goal to focus on, and how to use language to do so. In our opening example of an American student in Germany, the German student who launches into an animated political argument is focusing on the need to show involvement, using a "high-involvement" conversational style. The American student who resists talking about politics or religion is focusing on the need to avoid imposition, using a "high-considerateness" style.

Let's look at how several of the linguistic elements we discussed at the beginning of this chapter can characterize either "high-involvement" or "high-considerateness" styles among speakers who come from obviously different cultures as well as among Americans of different ethnic or regional backgrounds.

Overlap

We saw earlier that all speakers have assumptions and expectations about conversational overlap, that is, two (or more) speakers talking at once. Avoiding overlap honors the need not to be imposed on, so it is associated with a "high-considerateness" style. Embracing overlap as a show of enthusiasm and interest honors the need to be connected, so it is part of a "high-involvement" style. Both styles can work well among speakers who share assumptions about conversational overlap. High-involvement speakers enjoy talking over each other and have no trouble getting or keeping the floor when they want it and saying what they want to say while someone else talks along. The same is true for conversations among high-considerateness speakers: they take turns and get to say what they want. But when speakers using the two styles interact, their impressions of each other may be the opposite of what each intends. High-involvement speakers might chime in to show their enthusiasm, but high-considerateness speakers tend to think that anyone who begins talking before they are finished is trying to interrupt them. They will probably stop speaking in order to avoid an unpleasant and unacceptable situation, yielding the floor but resenting the interruption. High-considerateness speakers who wait for their turn at talk may find few opportunities to join the conversation and give the impression that they are not interested.

This is just what happened when American women living in Paris spoke to French women, in a study conducted by Molly Wieland (1991). Wieland tape-recorded four separate dinner parties attended by native French women and Americans who had lived in France for at least two years. The American women all spoke French fluently, but when they took part in the conversations, they applied their American norms for turn-taking and overlap. The American women believed that only one voice should be heard at a time, so when two American women's talk overlapped, one quickly gave way to the other. In contrast, the French women frequently overlapped each other, with both speakers continuing to talk until they had finished what they had to say. Each regarded the other's overlap as supportive and cooperative. Because of their different attitudes toward overlap, whenever a French and American woman started to speak at the same time, it was almost always the American who gave way, and they frequently regarded the French women as rude for interrupting. Furthermore, the French women frequently talked along with another speaker as a way to contribute, while the Americans awaited their turn. As a result, the American women had a hard time getting a word in edgewise. The French women told Wieland that they got the impression the American women were uninterested and thinking of other things when they listened silently (and from the American point of view, attentively).

Not all Americans share an overlap-resistant style of speaking, as my own research (Tannen [1984] 2005) indicates. I tape-recorded a Thanksgiving dinner conversation which included, in addition to me, four other Americans and one British woman. After transcribing the entire conversation and analyzing the transcript, I found that the three speakers who had grown up in New York City (I was one) tended to talk along with others to show enthusiasm; for us, overlap was cooperative. In contrast, the two speakers from southern California and the British woman tended to stop speaking when someone else started; they interpreted overlap as interruption. (Differing assumptions about overlap were part of an array of linguistic features that distinguished the New Yorkers' style as high-involvement and the others' style as high-considerateness.)

When speakers use – and interpret – overlap differently, conversations between them can have unintended outcomes. In the conversation I analyzed, the New Yorkers' overlaps were interpreted as interruption *only by the Californians and the British speaker*. When a New Yorker overlapped with a Californian, the Californian usually hesitated or stopped speaking, and the conversation became halting and awkward. When New Yorkers overlapped other New Yorkers, talking-along had the opposite effect; it greased the conversational wheels rather than causing them to grind to a halt.

Crosscultural misunderstandings like these are not the result of any individual's conversational style; rather, such misunderstandings result from the *interaction* of participants' differing styles. New Yorkers' overlapping habits appeared interruptive only when they interacted with overlap-resistant speakers. However, the two-way nature of crosscultural differences typically eludes participants in the throes of conversation. A speaker who stops talking because another has begun is unlikely to think, "I guess we have different attitudes toward cooperative overlap." Instead, such a speaker will probably think, "You are not interested in hearing what I have to say," or even "You are a boor who only wants to hear yourself talk." And the cooperative overlapper is probably concluding, "You are unfriendly and are making me do all the conversational work here" or even "You are a bore who has nothing to say."

Back-channel cues

The tendency to overlap as a way of showing enthusiastic listenership has been documented for speakers in many cultures, including Germany (Straehle 1997), Antigua (Reisman 1974), and Japan (Hayashi 1988), though the forms of overlap and their frequency are not always the same. Linguists call the verbalizations speakers make to show that they're listening **back-channel cues**. In Japan, according to Japanese linguist Haru Yamada, listeners typically provide very frequent back-channel cues, called *aizuchi*, that are typically accompanied by rhythmic head nods. Yamada, who grew up in both Japan and the United States, had external evidence that *aizuchi* is more frequent in Japanese than it is in English. A friend told her that he can always tell from a distance whether she is speaking English or Japanese, because when she speaks English, she nods occasionally, but when she's speaking Japanese, her head jerks up and down constantly. *Aizuchi* may range from the repetition of a single word *hai*, which functions rather like the English expressions *mhm* and *uhuh*, to entire sentences, such as *Nn, Nn, Nn, tashika ni soo desu yo ne*, which Yamada (1997: 97) translates as 'Yeah, yeah, yeah, that's exactly right.' This apparent agreement means only 'I'm listening and I'm following,' not 'I agree,' but Americans often take these expressions of attention literally and feel misled if it turns out that their Japanese interlocutor does not in fact agree.

Misunderstandings resulting from different uses of back-channel cues can also occur among Americans who have different norms for their use. For example, researchers who recorded cross-sex conversations (Fishman 1978, Hirschman 1994) discovered that women tend to say *mhm*, *uhuh*, and *yeah* frequently during a conversational partner's stream of talk, whereas men typically offer fewer back-channel cues and are more likely to offer them only at the end of another's turn. Especially problematic are the different ways these back-channel cues tend to be used: women typically use them to indicate 'I'm listening,' whereas for men they tend to mean 'I agree.' As a result, just as with Americans and Japanese, an American man might feel misled when a woman has (from the man's point of view) indicated agreement with what he was saying, and then turns out to disagree. Here too, the result can lead to negative stereotypes of the other group: you can't trust women; when you talk to them, you don't know where you stand. At the same time, the lack of back channels from men helps give women the impression that men are not listening to them.

Americans of different backgrounds can also have divergent expectations about how loud and expressive a listener response should be. The New Yorkers in my study often showed appreciation of another's comment with expressive reactions such as *Wow!* or *That's incredible!* This often gave the non-New Yorkers the impression that they were overreacting to, or even doubting the veracity of, what they had heard. Similar confusion – from different expectations regarding how extreme listener reactions should be – caused trouble for a woman who grew up in New York City but raised her own children in Vermont. When her daughters came home from school and told their mother about something that had happened during the day, their mother might exclaim *Wow!* or *Oh-my-god!* The daughters would look around to see what had frightened their mother. When they realized that she was simply reacting to what they had said, they accused her of overreacting. Not realizing that their mother's reaction was a standard enthusiastic response in the high-involvement style their mother had learned growing up, they thought they were witnessing a quirk (if not a pathology!) of her personality.

In this, as in all cross-style encounters, it is always the relative difference that matters, not absolute style. The level of enthusiasm that seems too extreme to one listener may seem too understated to another. The same woman who thinks a man is not listening because he provides fewer back-channel cues than she expects, may feel that a Japanese speaker is rushing her along, because he is providing more back-channel cues than she expects. Any time expectations regarding back-channel cues differ, speakers can come away with the wrong impression – of whether the other person agrees or not and of whether the other person was interested or even listening.

Turn-taking

Overlap and listener response, along with rate of speech and pausing, work together to accomplish the exchange of turns in a conversation. Those who value overlap as a show of involvement often leave shorter pauses between turns, perhaps because long pauses would give them the impression that the conversation is foundering. Those who avoid overlap because it seems intrusive often leave longer pauses between turns, perhaps to be certain that the previous speaker won't be inadvertently interrupted. Whenever two speakers have differing senses of how long a pause between turns should be, the speaker who expects longer pauses has a hard time getting the floor, because the shorter-pauser is likely to begin speaking while the longer-pauser is still waiting for the right amount of pause. This is exactly what happened in the Thanksgiving dinner conversation that I analyzed. The Californians rarely started speaking when a New Yorker was speaking, and often stopped speaking if a New Yorker overlapped. The New Yorkers expected shorter pauses between conversational turns and therefore frequently claimed the floor before the Californians had a chance to start talking.

Here's an example (Tannen [1984] 2005: 93) of the three New Yorkers talking companionably, overlapping each other's talk without interrupting. Steve was trying to explain the precise location of a building that housed a radio station with the call letters WINS. The two other speakers are Steve's brother Peter and his best friend, Deborah (that's me). Left brackets indicate overlap.

1 Steve: Remember where WINS used to be?
2 Deborah: No
3 Steve: Then they built a big huge skyscraper there?
4 Deborah: No. Where was that?
5 Steve: Right where Central Park West met Broadway. That
              ⌈building shaped like that.
6 Peter: └Did ⌈I give you too much?
7 Deborah: └By Columbus Circle? … that Columbus Circle?
8 Steve: └Right on Columbus Circle.
              Here's Columbus Circle, ⌈here's Central Park West,
9 Deborah: └Now it's
              the Huntington Hartford Museum.
10 Peter: └That's the Huntington Hartford, right?

As you can see from the brackets and the placement of the lines of dialogue, two people were speaking at once for much of this segment, and there is no indication that the overlaps annoy or interfere with the speakers. In lines 5–7, all three were speaking at the same time: Steve was describing the building he had in mind: line 5 *That building shaped like that*. (He made a pyramid with his hands to illustrate the shape.) Peter was serving turkey: line 6 *Did I give you too much?* I was suggesting the location Steve was describing: line 7 *By Columbus Circle?* My comment did not cause Steve to stop or slow down, so his ratification in line 8 *Right on Columbus Circle* overlapped with my overlap. As Steve continued his description: *Here's Columbus Circle, here's Central Park West*, I overlapped to offer another guess about the location: line 9 *Now it's the Huntington Hartford Museum*.

The next overlap is a particularly good example of a high-involvement style. In line 10 Peter spoke almost at the same time that I did, offering the same guess: *That's the*

Huntington Hartford, right? But it turned out that we were wrong. Steve replied with three *No*'s in quick succession: *Nuhnuhno*. Now, think of an exam in which two students who sat next to each other wrote the same answer. If that answer happens to be wrong, the teacher may well suspect that one copied from the other. And this is precisely what happened in this conversation. When I played the segment back to Peter, he said that he had had no idea of the location his brother was referring to, but had assumed I did. So Peter had piggybacked on my overlap, talking at the same time that I did by repeating what I said just a split second behind me. Because he shared expectations regarding overlap and pacing, Peter was thus able to participate in the conversation even when he did not have much knowledge of what we were talking about. In contrast, the other three dinner guests were not able to participate, even when they had the knowledge and ideas to contribute, because they were not comfortable talking-along and rarely encountered the pause they needed to begin speaking.

BOX 10.3 INTERACTIONAL SOCIOLINGUISTIC METHODOLOGY

The practice of analyzing interactions in which the researcher participated has a long history in discourse analysis; it is similar to the practice of participant observation in the field of anthropology. Interactional sociolinguists acknowledge that there are disadvantages as well as advantages in analyzing conversations they themselves took part in. For example, if the goal is understanding conversation among friends, recording at a natural social gathering makes available for study patterns of language use that do not emerge among strangers and would be inhibited by the presence of an outside researcher – patterns such as playful routines, irony and allusion, or reference to familiar jokes and assumptions. Furthermore, people who regularly interact with each other create a special language between and among themselves, a language that is called upon and built upon in their continuing interactions. Awareness of this history of the discourse is necessary to truly understand what is going on, and is available only to those who have shared in that history.

Analyst participation is related to another aspect of interactional sociolinguistics. The objection is inevitably raised, "How do you know this is what is really going on? It is just your interpretation." To this the interactional sociolinguist replies, "That's right." Interactional sociolinguistics is a hermeneutic discipline; all analysis in this paradigm is essentially interpretive. But, as with interpretation in such fields as literary analysis and psychology, any interpretation posed is offered as one among many, not a definitive one. Furthermore, interpretations are based on internal and external evidence. Since all interpretation has a subjective character, acknowledging and correcting for subjectivity is, in the end, less dangerous than assuming an impossible objectivity. Another way of addressing the danger of subjectivity is playback. Segments of the interaction that are identified for analysis are played back to those who participated (as well as to others), and their interpretations – of what they meant and understood – are elicited. Such comments are not taken at face value, but offer further material for analysis as well as a potential corrective to the analyst's interpretations.

There is a final paradox inherent in recording conversation for analysis; the researcher is committed both to collecting natural data and to securing the informed consent of participants. So long as participants are aware of the presence of the tape recorder, their talk may not be completely natural. Sociolinguists argue, however, that if there is a relatively large number of participants who have ongoing social relationships, they soon forget the tape recorder. But if they forgot they were being taped, was their consent not effectively canceled? In my own work, I correct for this by allowing participants to see what I plan to write about them before it goes into print, to make sure that I do not inadvertently expose any aspect of their lives that they would prefer to keep private.

Asking questions

Along with rate of speech and turn-taking, a high-involvement style includes habits regarding asking questions – when, how many, how quickly, what about – that differ from those of high-considerateness style speakers. The New Yorkers in the Thanksgiving dinner conversation asked more questions, and the questions they asked often came quickly, with marked high pitch, one after another. These questions could catch the Californians and the British woman off guard, impeding their flow of speech and even puzzling them. For these high-involvement speakers, questions indicate enthusiastic listening, and speakers are not obligated to stop mid-sentence to answer them – nor even to answer them at all.

For example, Steve was telling about having lived in Quonset huts when he and Peter were children, after their father returned from military service in the Second World War. (Quonset huts were a form of temporary housing that the government had constructed to accommodate the many returning veterans.) When this segment begins, Steve had just commented that there were rats in the Quonset huts.

1 Steve: Cause they were built near the swamp … We used to go …
             hunting frogs ⌐in the swamps.
2 Deborah: ⌐Where was it. Where were yours?
3 Steve: In the Bronx
4 Peter: ⌐In the Bronx. In the East Bronx?
5 Deborah: How long did you live in it?⌐
6 Steve: ⌐Near the swamps? … Now
             there's a big cooperative building.
7 Peter: ⌐Three years.
8 Deborah: Three years?

My first question (line 2) *Where was it. Where were yours?* overlapped Steve's explanation in line 1 that the Quonset huts had rats because there were swamps nearby. He answered my question in line 3 *In the Bronx,* and Peter answered as well, again overlapping: line 4 *In the Bronx. In the East Bronx?* But my second question, line 5 *How long did you live in it?* never got an answer from Steve, who simply went on with his explanation of where the Quonset huts were located: line 6 *Now there's a big cooperative building.* (Peter overlapped Steve to answer my question in line 7: *Three years.*) The high-involvement habits regarding overlap and questions worked together. This example shows that part of the reason a high-involvement questioner can throw out questions exuberantly is that a high-involvement speaker is under no obligation to stop what he's saying and answer them.

Indirectness

Another important element of conversational style is indirectness – conveying meaning without saying it explicitly. It is not possible to articulate everything we mean in every utterance. Some of the meaning must always be "read between the lines," based on past conversations and expectations about what will be said, and from culturally agreed-upon meanings that are associated with particular expressions. Cultures differ in how much indirectness is expected, when it is expected, and what form it will take. For example, Americans who travel to Japan, even those who speak Japanese well, find it difficult to interpret what Japanese speakers mean, because Japanese culture places great value on indirectness. Haru Yamada explains that the Japanese have a word, *sasshi*, for the guess-work that is expected and valued, by which listeners fill in unstated meaning. She gives an example (1997: 37–38) from a conversation between two Japanese bank executives, Igarishi and Maeda. Igarishi asks Maeda's opinion about a proposal, and Maeda responds, *Sore wa chotto . . .* ('That's a little . . .'). He says no more, but Igarishi understands that Maeda does not approve of the proposal, and he tells another colleague as much on another occasion (and even infers why Maeda disapproves).

Although this level of indirectness is more extreme than is typically found in American conversations, we all use forms of indirectness in conversation. For example, two American college roommates were frustrated by a third who habitually left her dirty dishes in the sink. Reluctant to tell her outright that she should wash her dishes, the two neatniks put up a sign, *We love a clean sink.* In another case, a student was annoyed that one of her roommates habitually left her hair dryer in the bathroom. Rather than telling her to please keep her hair dryer in her room, she asked, *Is that your hair dryer?* In both instances the indirect communications were effective: the dirty dishes disappeared from the kitchen sink, and the hair dryer disappeared from the bathroom. These indirect requests honored the roommates' need not to be imposed on (even while imposing on them).

> *A young woman, Jen, knew that her roommates planned a party on a night she needed to be writing a paper. When the day came, Jen found herself walking beside one of her roommates, whom she asked, "What are you doing tonight?" Her roommate replied, "I'm not sure. We were thinking of having a party. What are you up to?" Jen said she had a paper due the next day. "Oh, in that case we won't have a party," her roommate said. Jen said it would be fine but the roommate repeated that they definitely wouldn't, and that time Jen didn't protest. Indirectness worked well to solve this problem. Rather than making a direct demand that would seem selfish, Jen let her roommate know the situation and decide on her own to be considerate. Had her roommate taken literally Jen's assurance that it would be fine to have a party, then indirectness would have failed. In that case, Jen would have done better to state her preference directly.*
>
> *Can you think of conversations you've had in which indirectness either succeeded or failed, or different assumptions about indirectness led to misunderstanding or hurt feelings?*

When assumptions regarding the use of indirectness are not shared, the result can be miscommunication. This happened to a young man in one of my classes named Scott. While at home during winter break, Scott was sitting with his mother at the kitchen table. Looking out the window, his mother remarked on how much snow had fallen during the night and how long it would take to shovel it. Scott agreed – then finished his breakfast and went to his room to watch television. Later his mother angrily chided him for lounging around while she was busy cleaning the house, and she added that the least he could have done was to shovel the snow as she had asked him to. Scott was incensed because he was certain she had not asked him to do anything, and he would have been glad to help her out if she had asked him. Neither realized that different uses of indirectness were at fault. Scott truly believed he had not been asked to shovel the snow because he had interpreted his mother's observations literally. His mother believed she had asked him to shovel the snow, and it never occurred to her that he had missed her meaning.

Differences in assumptions about indirectness can lead to accusations of dishonesty or manipulativeness. Thus a journalist who traveled to Japan asked his Japanese host whether he could see a particular robot and was told. *That might be possible.* He was fairly optimistic that if it was possible, it would be arranged, so he felt misled when he later discovered not only that he could not see the robot, but that there had never been any possibility that he could. But a Japanese person would have known that *That might be possible* is a considerate and polite way to say *No.* In parts of India, it is considered rude to ask for something directly, so an accepted way of requesting something is to compliment it. Conversely, a person who receives a compliment on a possession is expected to offer it as a gift. An American woman who married an Indian man had no idea of this cultural convention by which compliments are an indirect way of making requests. When her husband's mother came to the United States for a visit, the American woman helped her mother-in-law unpack and ooh'd and aah'd over the beauty of her saris and her jewelry. Her mother-in-law later asked her own daughter (an Indian who also lived in the United States), *What kind of woman did he marry? She wants everything!*

Mutual stereotyping

When participants in a conversation have different norms for using language, they often come away with negative impressions of the other person. When speakers see others as members of identifiable cultural groups, the result often is cultural stereotyping. Understanding high-involvement style goes a long way toward explaining why natives of New York City are often stereotyped as pushy and aggressive. And understanding high-considerateness style might explain why many New Yorkers regard Americans from other parts of the United States as somewhat dull and uninteresting.

Around the world, members of groups who tend to speak more slowly tend to be negatively stereotyped (by faster speakers, of course) as dull. For example, Finns tend to speak more slowly and to be silent more often than Swedes. Finnish linguists Jaakko Lehtonen and Kari Sajavaara (1985) suspected that this difference might have something to do with the negative stereotyping of Finns as slow and dull by neighboring Swedes. Moreover, they suspected that such differences might account for ethnic and regional stereotypes in other parts of the world as well. They found similar patterns of stereotyping in country after country where one ethnic or regional group tends to speak more slowly than others: in German stereotypes of East Frisians, in French stereotypes of Belgians, and in Swiss stereotypes of residents of Berne or Zurich. Even Finns themselves stereotype their more deliberate compatriots from a region called Häme (pronounced hah-may) as dull. As we saw in the work of John Gumperz with South Asian speakers in London, such negative stereotypes can have important social consequences, affecting decisions about educational advancement, job hiring, and even social policies on a national scale.

The ritual nature of conversation

Within the United States, women and men often have different habits with regard to indirectness when it comes to deciding what to do. For example, a woman and a man were riding in a car. The woman turned to the man and asked, *Are you thirsty? Would you like to stop for a drink?* The man wasn't particularly thirsty, so he answered *No*. Later he was perplexed to learn that she was annoyed with him because she had wanted to stop for a drink. He became annoyed in turn, wondering why she didn't just say so. He assumed that her question was an indirect way of expressing her desire to stop for a drink, and this could have been the case. But there is a more complex – and more likely – explanation. When the woman asked, *Would you like to stop for a drink?* she did not expect a yes/no answer. Rather, she expected the man to respond by saying something like, *I don't know. Do you want to?* She then might have said, *I don't know. What do you want?* After they had both expressed their inclinations and preferences, they might or might not stop for a drink. Either way, she would feel satisfied because the decision had been made taking both their preferences into account. In other words, her frustration was not because she did not get her way, but because her question had shown that she was considering what he wanted, whereas his peremptory response indicated he was not interested in what she wanted.

Culturally learned conventions for using language to communicate are not simply a matter of the meaning of words and utterances but also a matter of **conversational rituals**: how you expect an interaction to go in its totality, how you expect utterances to follow in sequence. In this interchange, the woman's question was meant to begin an exchange – a conversational ritual by which a general question leads to mutual expressions of inclinations and preferences, leading to a decision. The purpose of this ritual is as much to share perspectives as it is to come to a decision. But when the man answered *No*, the ritual sequence the woman expected was short-circuited. The man had not expressed an interest in her preferences (or worse, he had revealed a lack of interest in them) and, on top of that, it seemed to her that he had made a unilateral decision that they would not stop.

Of course, the man had a conversational ritual of his own in mind. According to his self-report, his reply meant that he wasn't thirsty, not that he was averse to stopping for a drink if she wanted to. He assumed that if she wanted to stop for a drink, she would say so, even though he had said he was not thirsty. The conversational ritual he expects is that one person throws out a possible decision and anyone who is differently inclined states an alternative option. He therefore interpreted the woman's subsequent silence as agreement, whereas she had become silent because she was annoyed.

Language and gender

Misunderstandings like this occur frequently between women and men. There is ample evidence that many American women are more inclined than most American men to use indirectness when it comes to making a decision or expressing preferences about what to do. This doesn't mean American women are always more indirect, however. There are other contexts in which many men are inclined to be more indirect than women. One such context is apologizing. For example, a neighbor of mine once wrote me a note saying, "I guess I wasn't much help" when he owed me an apology. I took this to be an indirect way of giving me one. Robin Lakoff (2001) describes an indirect apology that she received from her father. When he sent her a copy of *The Portable Curmudgeon*, she understood it to mean, "I'm just an old curmudgeon; please forgive me."

Expectations about how men and women tend to speak (that is, gender norms) vary across cultures, as do norms regarding the use of indirectness. For example, among a small community of Malagasy speakers in Madagascar, indirectness is the norm. It is unacceptable, for example, to express anger directly, though it can be expressed to an intermediary who passes the sentiment on. It is men, however, who observe this norm; women typically break it, expressing anger and criticism directly. The linguistic anthropologist who studied this community, Elinor Keenan (1974), notes that when she and her co-worker encountered a couple walking while they were riding in a car, it was the woman who flagged them down, requested a ride, and asked directly for sensitive information such as where they were going, where they had been, and how much things had cost. Women also are the ones who criticize inappropriate behavior in the community. It is interesting to note that whereas indirectness is associated with women in the United States, and directness is associated with women among the Malagasy, in both cases the style of speaking associated with men is more highly valued. In Malagasy culture, women's directness – though relied upon to get important social tasks done – is disparaged, while men's indirectness is admired as verbal skill. This is similar to the way that Japanese admire those who are skilled in *sasshi* – the ability to guess at others' meaning that has not been put into words. In contrast, in the United States, indirectness is often associated with dishonesty and manipulation, so many women who use indirectness feel guilty about it when it is called to their attention.

Gender differences in ways of speaking can create problems at work. Many women in authority are seen as less confident and competent than they are, while men may be seen by women as arrogant or belligerent. A college president who said to her secretary, "Could you do me a favor and type this?" was misjudged as insecure by a board member who interpreted her question literally rather than as ritually polite. A manager who asked her subordinates for their input was heard as asking them to make decisions for her. Conversely, a woman thought her colleague disliked her because he teased her mercilessly, when in fact his teasing meant that he liked and accepted her. And a man who argued with a colleague in the constructive spirit of playing devil's advocate was misheard as genuinely thinking her ideas were weak – and therefore she was.

BOX 10.4 **GENDER DIFFERENCES GROW UP**

The idea that conversation between women and men can be regarded as crosscultural communication traces to anthropologists Daniel Maltz and Ruth Borker (1982). Maltz and Borker combined the research findings of anthropologists and sociologists who had studied how boys and girls, and men and women, use language, with the theoretical framework of John Gumperz, and concluded that Gumperz's framework could account for some of the frustrations that arise in cross-sex conversations. Studies of children at play had revealed that boys and girls tend to play in sex-separate groups; that their play follows very different rules and patterns; and that these differences account for some of the differing habits and assumptions that lead to frustration when women and men talk to teach other. Researchers like Marjorie Harness Goodwin (1990) found that girls tend to play in small groups or pairs, and their friendships are formed through talk. Girls discourage behavior that seems to put one on a higher footing than another. Boys play in larger groups; their groups are more hierarchically organized, and they use language to assert dominance and to attract and hold attention.

These differences explain, for example, why women ask more questions: they regard questions as a way to keep conversation going, something they want to do because they value conversation as a sign of friendship. They also explain why women often discuss problems with each other, matching experiences, and expressing understanding – and why they are frustrated when men hear the statement of problems as requests for solutions. Discussing and matching problems is a way for women to maintain talk and also maintain the appearance of equality. Giving advice, on the other hand, frames men as experts.

Complementary schismogenesis

In many of the preceding examples, you might be wondering why people who talk to each other frequently, such as family members and roommates, don't come to understand each other's styles and adapt to them. Sometimes they do. But sometimes the opposite happens; the more two people with differing styles interact, the more frustrated they become. Things seem to get progressively worse rather than better. Often, what happens is complementary schismogenesis – a process by which two speakers drive one another to more and more extreme expressions of divergent ways of speaking in an ever-widening spiral. What begins as a small difference becomes a big one, as each speaker tries harder to do more of what seems obviously appropriate. Here is a hypothetical example. An American man asks a Japanese woman directly if she'd like to go to lunch. She does not want to, so she declines the invitation by saying, *That's a very nice idea, maybe we could have lunch one day*. Because she has left the door open, he asks again. This time she replies even more indirectly: *That's an idea … lunch is nice …* Befuddled by this ambiguous response, he tries to pin her down: *Are you trying to tell me you never want to have lunch with me, or should I keep asking?* He regards this as the best way to cut through the ambiguity. However, given her conviction that it would be unacceptable to reply directly, her next reply is even more indirect: *Gee, well, I don't know, lunch, you know…* Her talking in circles confuses him even more; he has no idea that it was the directness of his question that drove her to these extreme circumlocutions. For her part, his continuing to pester her after she has made her lack of interest clear reinforces her determination to avoid having lunch with him. She has no idea that her refusals were not clear to him, and that his increasing directness was provoked by her indirectness.

> ### Box 10.5 PERSONAL SPACE AND COMPLEMENTARY SCHISMOGENESIS
>
> There are spatial correlates to the linguistic elements we have discussed. The anthropologist Edward T. Hall has written many books on **proxemics**, the study of how people use space "as a specialized elaboration of culture" (Hall 1969: 1). One of Hall's (1959: 205) examples of proxemics corresponds to what happens when speakers have different expectations about the appropriate amount of pause between turns. Hall notes that each person has a sense of the appropriate conversational distance between strangers. If someone you're talking to gets too close, you automatically back up to adjust the space between you. If someone stands too far away, you automatically move in. But our sense of conversational distance varies by culture. Hall notes that he has seen an American and a foreigner inch their way down a long corridor as the foreigner tries to get comfortable by closing the space between them, and the American keeps backing up to adjust the distance between them to what is comfortable for him.
>
> The gradual trip down the corridor is another example of complementary schismogenesis. Each person ends up in a place he had no intention of going as he reacts to the other's behavior without realizing that the behavior is a reaction to his own.

The term "complementary schismogenesis" was coined by Gregory Bateson ([1935] 1972) to describe what happens when divergent cultures come into contact: each reacts to the other's differing pattern of behavior by doing more of the opposing behavior. As an example, Bateson describes a hypothetical situation in which a culture that favors assertiveness comes into contact with a culture that favors submissiveness. The submissive group will react to aggressive behavior with submissiveness, to which the first group will react with more aggressiveness, and so on, until each is exhibiting far more aggressiveness and submissiveness, respectively, than they normally would. This pattern is one of the most surprising and frustrating aspects of crosscultural communication. We would like to believe that exposure to people from a different culture would lead to mutual understanding and accommodation. Sometimes it does, but at other times, initial differences become exaggerated, so that the other ends up doing more of the behavior we dislike, and we find ourselves acting in ways we would not otherwise act and may not even like in ourselves. This is what happens when, for example, speakers differ with regard to how long a pause they regard as normal between turns. What begins as a small difference ends up as a big one, with one person talking nonstop and the other silent. We rarely stop and question whether the other's behavior is in part a reaction to our own. Though each believes the other chose that form of behavior, both may be frustrated with the resulting imbalance. You might say it is the inseparability of language and culture that is the culprit driving complementary schismogenesis.

Language and cultural relativity

Our discussion so far has shown that language and culture are inseparable, because language is learned and used in a cultural context.

In order to emphasize the inseparability of language and culture, linguistic anthropologist Michael Agar (1994) refers to them collectively by a single term, **languaculture**.

It helps to have a single word because the phrase "language and culture" creates the notion of two separate entities; in other words, the language itself shapes the way we think about things. Moreover, language gives the world a sense of coherence by providing ways to order the many objects, people, and experiences we encounter.

The claim that language shapes thinking is referred to as the **Sapir–Whorf hypothesis**, named for its original proponent, Benjamin Lee Whorf, and his teacher, the anthropological linguist Edward Sapir. Some scholars make a distinction between strong and weak forms of this hypothesis. The strong form is called **linguistic determinism**: the idea that the language you speak is like a straitjacket that determines how you think. According to linguistic determinism, you can never *really* conceive of culture and language as one because your language does not give you a single word to represent them. Few linguists believe in linguistic determinism. In contrast, the weak form of the Sapir–Whorf hypothesis, **linguistic relativity**, claims that a language makes it easier to conceive of ideas for which it has words or obligatory grammatical categories, but it is still possible to think in other ways; it just takes more effort. Agar explains linguistic relativity this way:

> Language isn't a prison; it's a room you're comfortable with, that you know how to move around in . . . But familiarity doesn't mean you can't ever exist in another room; it does mean it'll take a while to figure it out, because it's not what you're used to.

In other words, learning a particular language while growing up in a given culture provides ways of representing the world that come to seem natural; later, learning a different language which is associated with a different culture pulls you up short and makes you realize that there are other ways of conceptualizing the world. A language frames the way you see the world.

> *An influential linguist who argued that language and culture are inseparable was Dell Hymes, who founded the field known as the ethnography of speaking. Hymes's concept of communicative competence was patterned on Chomsky's notion of linguistic competence and founded on the claim that "a theory of language use" is every bit as crucial as "a theory of grammar." Thus the goal of ethnography of speaking (or, alternatively, ethnography of communication) is "to discover and explicate the competence that enables members of a community to conduct and interpret speech" (Hymes 1972: 52). The foundational text in this field is the collection of essays gathered by Gumperz and Hymes (1972), followed shortly by a second collection edited by Hymes's students Richard Bauman and Joel Sherzer (1974). Each essay in these volumes demonstrates the cultural knowledge necessary to make sense of language use in a given cultural community.*

Anyone who has tried to translate from one language to another quickly encounters words in the original language for which there is no counterpart in the other. Equally significant, though perhaps less immediately obvious, in translating you have to add words for which there was no counterpart in the original. Citing the Spanish philosopher José Ortega y Gasset, the anthropological linguist A. L. Becker (1995) refers to these liabilities of translation as **exuberances and deficiencies**. "Exuberances" are the many meanings that are added by the translation which do not exist in the original language. "Deficiencies" are the many meanings that are lost in translation because the second language does not have words or grammatical categories to express them.

Exuberances and deficiencies between languages go much deeper than the challenge of finding words in one language to correspond to words in another. The very grammatical structure of a language provides what Becker calls a **coherence system** by which speakers learn to view and order the world. For example, in English, as in other western languages, verbs come in forms that indicate tense. So when they utter verbs, English speakers *must* indicate whether the action denoted *takes* place in the present, *took* place in the past, or *will take* place in the future. The language itself forces English speakers to pay attention to temporality, and we come to take it for granted that temporality is fundamental to understanding events in the world. Temporal causality provides a "coherence system" for native speakers of English – a way of making sense of, and ordering, the world. In contrast, South Asian languages such as Burmese, Malay, and Javanese do not have grammatical tense. A speaker may well use a verb without indicating whether the action occurred in the past, occurs in the present, or will occur in the future. Therefore, Becker says, "a common Western exuberance in translating Southeast Asian texts is to add temporal causality, the basic coherence system in tense-marking languages" (p. 226). This exuberance – what gets added in a translation – alters the world created by the original text.

At the same time, Becker shows that "[t]he deficiencies of the translation – those things in the Burmese that have no counterpart in the translation – include things at the core of the Burmese system of discourse coherence" (p. 236). For example, just as English verbs must indicate tense, Burmese nouns must have linguistic particles called classifiers that distinguish the universe of discourse. In Burmese, when you refer to a river, you must classify the river as a place (the destination for a picnic), a line (on a map), a section (fishing areas), a distant arc (a passage to the sea), a connection (tying two villages), a sacred object (in mythology), or a conceptual unit (rivers in general) (Becker 1975). Just as verbs in English *require* linguistic markings that indicate tense, nouns in Burmese *require* classifiers that characterize the context in which the noun is being used. The categories identified by these classifiers provide a coherence system by which Burmese speakers order the world, just as we tend to order the world by temporal sequence.

In addition to the exuberances and deficiencies introduced by grammatical categories and words that are particular to a given language, another way in which language is inseparable from culture is that much of the meaning we glean from an utterance comes from how those words have been used in the past, what Becker calls **prior text**. Thus a cowboy movie is about prior cowboy movies more than it is about events that occurred on the American frontier. A viewer who had never before seen a western would miss many layers of meaning that would be obvious to a viewer who had seen many. Memories of prior text are necessary for all but the most rudimentary understanding of a language, and it is this memory – or the lack of it – that is the biggest barrier when speakers talk to each other across cultures. You might say that the reason an American does not realize that *Have you eaten yet?* is a greeting, not a literal question, and that a Burmese doesn't realize that *How are you?* is a greeting, not a literal question, is that they lack the prior text that a native speaker has.

Box 10.6 **TRANSLATING CULTURE**

A survey of 1,000 translators and interpreters has identified a word from Tshiluba, a language spoken in southeastern DR Congo, as the world's most difficult word to translate. The word *ilunga* means 'a person who is ready to forgive any abuse for the first time, to tolerate it a second time, but never a third time.' In second place was *shlimazl*, which is Yiddish for 'a chronically unlucky person.' Third was *Naa*, used in the Kansai area of Japan to emphasize statements or agree with someone.

The definitions seem pretty straightforward, but the problem is trying to convey the cultural experiences and assumptions surrounding these words. This is even more difficult to do at the speed of simultaneous interpretation. Interpreters also have difficulty with the technical jargon of politics, business or sport. For example, *googly* is a cricket term for 'an off-breaking ball disguised by the bowler with an apparent leg-break action.' If you don't understand cricket, it won't be easy to appreciate a good *googly*. Naa!

(From BBC News Online, Tuesday, June 22, 2004)

Understanding what is lost and what is added when texts are translated from one language to another reveals a few of the many ways that a language both reflects and creates a world. Similarly, the linguistic elements that vary from one culture to another are the very elements by which language works to create meaning. There is simply no way to speak without making choices about level of loudness, voice quality, words and grammatical structures, how to get the floor, how to frame the words to signal what you think you're doing when you speak, and so on – and all these choices vary depending on the culture in which the language was learned. That is why it is misleading even to speak of "language and culture"; the very words imply that the two can be separated.

CHAPTER SUMMARY

This chapter has explored the relationship between language and culture. As the term "languaculture" implies, language and culture are inseparable, because language is composed of linguistic elements that vary by culture. Speakers use a range of linguistic elements to convey meaning in conversation, but the appropriate ways to use these elements vary from culture to culture. These cultural differences affect encounters between speakers from different countries as well as between Americans of different cultural and regional backgrounds, and even between women and men. Crosscultural encounters provide insight into how language works to create meaning and how language shapes the way a speaker perceives and orders the world.

The relationship between language and culture has been illustrated by real-life examples of conversations, including an opening anecdotal example of German and American college students, as well as detailed analysis of tape-recorded conversations that took place between Americans of different regional and ethnic backgrounds. Linguistic phenomena that vary by culture include topic, intonational patterns, turn-taking, attitudes toward and uses of overlap, and indirectness. Systematic differences in uses of these linguistic phenomena have real-world consequences, as the interactional sociolinguistic work of John Gumperz demonstrates. To the extent that speakers use language and expect language to be used in predictable, culturally coherent ways and sequences, conversation can be said to have a ritual nature. When conversational rituals are shared, the result is not only successful communication, but also a satisfying sense of coherence in the world.

Exercises

EXERCISE 10.1

Linguist Roger Shuy (1993: 8–9) gives the following example of a crosscultural encounter with very significant consequences. A Japanese industrial engineer was prosecuted for allegedly trying to buy industrial secrets from someone representing an American company who was actually an undercover FBI agent. The tape-recorded evidence against the Japanese engineer included the following conversation:

Agent:	You see, these plans are very hard to get.
Engineer:	Uh-huh.
Agent:	I'd need to get them at night.
Engineer:	Uh-huh.
Agent:	It's not done easily.
Engineer:	Uh-huh.
Agent:	Understand?
Engineer:	Uh-huh.

The prosecution claimed that the agent's statements made it clear that the information the engineer was requesting was secret, and that the engineer's affirmative responses proved that he was aware of this and sought to obtain them illegally. What role do the linguistic features, indirectness and back-channel responses, play in this conversation? How are crosscultural differences relevant in assessing whether or not the evidence proves the engineer's guilt?

EXERCISE 10.2

Record and analyze a naturally occurring conversation, following the methods discussed in Box 10.3 on "Interactional sociolinguistic methodology." This recording must not be secret. Prior to recording your friends or anybody else, you must obtain their informed consent. Listen to the recording and identify a small segment (about a minute or two) to transcribe. You may choose a segment in which some problem or misunderstanding arose, or a segment which went especially smoothly, or just a segment in which you noticed one of the features discussed in the chapter. You may look for any aspects of the conversation that relate to linguistic elements mentioned in the chapter, including but not limited to:

intonational contours and tone of voice
turn-taking

cooperative overlapping or interruption
what's appropriate to talk about
loudness and pitch
indirectness
framing

EXERCISE 10.3

Do linguistic field work in your own life. Think of a conversation you had in which a speaker (maybe you) used indirectness. Was it effective? Was there any misunderstanding? Did the participants in the conversation seem to appreciate or resent the indirectness? Negotiations with roommates or family members about accomplishing chores are often a rich source of examples.

EXERCISE 10.4

Experiment with conversational space. Without getting yourself into a threatening situation, try standing a little closer or a little farther away than you normally do when talking to someone, and note how the other person responds as well as how you yourself respond.

EXERCISE 10.5

Experiment with pacing, pausing, and turn-taking. If you are in a conversation in which you're doing more than your share of talking, try counting to seven before you begin speaking and see whether the other person begins to speak. If you are finding it hard to get a word in edgewise, push yourself to begin speaking before it feels comfortable and see whether the other person stops and cedes you the floor.

EXERCISE 10.6

The New York Times, January 26, 2005 (p. A17) reported a controversy involving the president of Harvard University, Lawrence Summers. According to the article, many Harvard professors felt that the president had "created a reservoir of ill will with what they say is a pattern of humiliating faculty members in meetings, shutting down debate, and dominating discussions." In an interview, President Summers said that "his propensity to debate and challenge 'sometimes leaves people thinking I'm resistant to their ideas when I am really trying to engage with their ideas.'"

Bearing in mind the experience of the American student studying in Germany, discuss how ways of using language discussed in this chapter might be playing a role in this controversy.

SUGGESTIONS FOR FURTHER READING

Agar, Michael 1994, *Language shock: understanding the culture of conversation*, New York: Morrow. This book is a highly readable and nuanced presentation of the concept of languaculture. Agar draws on his own research and experiences in India, Greece, Austria, and Mexico, as well as in the United States with junkies and long-distance truckers.

Fasold, Ralph W. 1990, *The sociolinguistics of language*, Oxford and Malden, MA: Blackwell. This introductory textbook covers numerous topics that pertain to how language works in cultural context.

Kiesling, Scott F. and Bratt Paulston, Christina, (eds,) 2005, *Intercultural discourse and communication: the essential readings*, Oxford and Malden, MA: Blackwell. This volume brings together many key essays that address various aspects of the relationship between language and culture.

Tannen, Deborah 1986, *That's not what I meant!: How conversational style makes or breaks relationships*, New York: Ballantine. This short book lays out the elements of language that make up conversational style and how they work in everyday interactions. It also shows how conversations can go awry when there are differences in speakers' habits and assumptions regarding use of these linguistic features.

Tannen, Deborah 2001, *I only say this because I love you: talking to your parents, partner, sibs and kids when you're all adults*, New York: Ballantine. This book examines how the linguistic phenomena discussed in this chapter affect conversations that take place among adult family members and consequently their relationships.

11 The politics of language

CHAPTER PREVIEW

In incident after incident around the world, controversies arise as governments try to control what languages or forms of languages are allowed to be taught or used for certain purposes. Often the issues involved might seem hardly worth the attention they get, yet what is behind them is actually quite serious. We start by describing a number of such cases. In order to understand them, we take a look at the relationship between language and identity, reviewing some of the concepts introduced by the sociologist of language Joshua Fishman. We then reconsider our introductory cases and see why they are controversial. This leads us to a discussion of how linguists and nonlinguists view language standardization and analyses of nonstandard language varieties, such as Ebonics. One kind of social organization of varieties of a language into more and less formal categories has some unique properties. This phenomenon is called **diglossia**. Once we've looked at disapproved varieties, we discuss the difference between a language and a dialect, and find that the difference is extraordinarily difficult to pin down. In fact, we'll see that whether what you speak is a language or a dialect is as much a political phenomenon as a linguistic one; some languages have gone from being languages to being dialects and back again, all depending on the political environment. Next, we examine one more case of the politics of language – the effort to make English the official language of the United States. This case is puzzling because English is so thoroughly dominant in American political and social life, so we will examine the political currents behind the movement. Finally, we take up two issues about the content of speech and the political response to them: (1) blasphemy and cursing, and (2) hate speech.

GOALS
The goals of this chapter are to:

- explain the role of identity in political actions concerning language
- offer insight into selected cases of the politics of language
- make clear the concept of language standardization from the linguistic perspective
- present "diglossia" as a unique way that communities organize and evaluate the varieties of the language they speak
- present the difficulties in distinguishing "languages" and "dialects" and the political issues that arise from this difficulty
- provide a detailed description of the movement to make English official in the United States
- present the politics of speech content control, using two representative issues

Identity politics and language

Until 1991, it you were caught singing in Kurdish in southeastern Turkey, you could be arrested. In that year the strict ban on the use of Kurdish was lifted, but there are still restrictions. In 2002, students were taken into police custody while trying to present petitions to university officials to allow Kurdish to be taught.

In China, the television cartoon show featuring Tom and Jerry, the warring cat and mouse, was a big hit. Until 2004, Tom and Jerry spoke local dialects, like Shanghainese; then the Beijing government put a stop to it, insisting that television programming in local dialects must end, to be replaced by Mandarin (*putonghua*), the official language. Complicating matters is the fact that Chinese dialects are so different from each other that they might be considered separate languages in other parts of the world. For example, 'Thank you' is *xie xie* in *putonghua*, *do jey* in *guongdonghua* (Cantonese), and *sha zha* in Shanghainese. These days Tom and Jerry are not as easy to understand (and maybe not as funny) in some regions of China.

In 2002, the government of Singapore put a rating of NC-17 on a comedy motion picture consisting of excerpts from the lives of four ordinary Singaporeans. A rating of NC-17 means that no one younger than seventeen is allowed to see it. The movie contained no violence, no sex, no profanity, but the dialogue included too much of what the government considered bad grammar. Voters in the state of Alaska in the United States overwhelmingly passed an initiative amending the state's constitution to make English the state's only official language. The local government of the village of Tuntutuliak promptly passed a resolution requiring that all local government business be conducted in Yup'ik, despite the fact that most of its 380 residents also speak English.

Considering these cases might well make you want to ask why. Why does the government of Turkey care what languages are or are not taught in schools and universities? Why should the government of China care how a cartoon cat and mouse speak? How does "bad grammar" in a movie dialogue earn an NC-17 rating? Why should the Tuntutuliak government require the use of Yup'ik when most of its people can speak English perfectly well? And why on earth should the government of Turkey care whether people sing in Kurdish in public?

Identity in language

No doubt the most crucial part of the answer to these questions can be summed up in one word – **identity**. A judge who originally issued an injunction against the Alaskan official English amendment (the amendment was later reinstated by the Alaska Supreme Court) said that legislating against the use of certain languages is wrong because, "language is the beginning, it is part of who we are" (Rosen 2002). We've seen in Chapter 9 that dialect differences are used to distinguish groups of people. Differences among languages accomplish the same thing. (In fact, we'll soon see that the difference between what are called "languages" and what are called "dialects" is a lot fuzzier than you might think.) Everyone knows that people use language to get ideas across to other people, but it's also true that whenever we speak in one language or dialect rather than another we are displaying an affinity with one social group and distancing ourselves from others. This identity-marking function of speech is at least as important as the communicative one. Social identity is tied to loyalty, and governments are very much concerned with where the loyalties of their citizens lie. Hence, language is often a very big part of politics. As we go along, we will see how identity issues influenced each of the above cases.

> Most linguists agree that animals in the wild do not use language in the sense of human language (but see the discussion of animal language in Chapter 13) but they do use "dialects" in much the same way that humans do – to help mark social divisions. White-crowned sparrows have "clear" and "buzzy" varieties of their basic bird-songs that are sung by groups in the north and south part of Point Reyes in Marin County, California (Baker and Cunningham 1985: 87–95). Humpback whales similarly have distinct versions of their underwater songs associated with different pods (Rendall and Whitehead 2001: 312–313). So you might say that the social identity function of language is more basic than its communicative function, since it is shared with nonhuman species.

Key concepts

To see more clearly how language works its way into politics, we'll have to understand some basic concepts explained by the sociologist of language Joshua Fishman (1972). Fishman takes terms from everyday discourse and gives them technical definitions. One such term is **nationality**. A nationality is a social group with a relatively complex level of organization. It is keenly aware of its distinctive customs and values and acts to preserve and strengthen them. A nationality may or may not control territory as a sovereign nation. The Basques in Spain are an example of a nationality living within the borders of a state under the control of another nationality, with only limited territorial autonomy of its own. The Kurds in Iraq are another such example. Portugal, on the other hand, would be an example of a state under the control of a single nationality; hence, it is a **nation**.

Fishman's definitions also distinguish nationalities from **ethnic groups** because their concerns go beyond local affairs. Ethnic groups are concerned primarily with their own local affairs and don't have much interest in other social entities, except possibly their closest neighbors. In extreme cases, ethnic groups do not even know what country they live in. Nationalities, on the other hand, are very much concerned with their status in relation to other social groups around them. They are keenly aware of the political forces at work in the country they live in and are eager to extract concessions from their governments that will give them political advantages. In many cases, nationalities insist on some level of autonomy over their own territory. In the ultimate situation, a nationality has as a goal the establishment of its own sovereignty, to become a new country in its own right. A number of nationalities in Europe and elsewhere have succeeded in this goal over the past quarter century. The countries that were formed out of the former Soviet Union are prime examples.

Although I have defined the difference between nationalities and ethnic groups as if they were completely different from each other, nationalities and ethnic groups can better be thought of as end points on a continuum. Some nationalities are more like ethnic groups in not being very demanding of the governments that control them, and some ethnic groups behave something like nationalities by making certain demands of the government. There are always some groups in the middle of the continuum that defy classification as a nationality or an ethnic group with any confidence.

Fishman also distinguishes a nation from a **state**. Oversimplifying, a state can be understood as an area on a world map that is a different color from the areas around it. A state is a political unit with control over and responsibility for all the people that live within it. A nation is a state that is "largely or increasingly" under the control of one particular nationality (Fishman 1972: 4). This definition is a bit fuzzy because of the use of the adverbs "largely" and "increasingly" – how extensive and how rapidly increasing does the nationality's control have to be? It is clear that this means that far fewer of the world's countries are nations than ordinary usage of the term would suggest. Instead, a large number, probably most, of the world's countries are not technically nations at all, but rather **multinational states**. A multinational state is a country with more than one nationality within its borders. Among the very few clear examples of nations by Fishman's definition are Iceland, North and South Korea, and probably Portugal. It is less clear whether such large countries as France, Germany, and the United States are nations by the technical definition. And it's quite clear that other major countries, like Canada, the United Kingdom, China, and Russia (even after the dissolution of the Soviet Union), are not.

Hypothetically a country could have multiple distinct social groups within its borders and still be a nation, if they were all ethnic groups rather than nationalities. Such a country would be a **multiethnic nation** rather than a multinational state. A moment's reflection will show that, by allowing both extent of control and status as a nationality to be matters of degree, Fishman makes his concepts much clearer in abstraction than in actual application.

So what does all this have to do with language? One characteristic of being a nationality is the importance of symbols of the national identity. Three of the most important symbols of national identity are religion, territory, and language. Language is very often of critical importance to nationalities, and they defend their languages with great energy. Of course, ethnic groups speak languages too, but groups at this end of the continuum do not see their language as critical to their identity, and they often give up their languages over several generations in favor of another language that seems more politically or economically advantageous. This is a major mechanism for language loss around the world. The loss of scores of indigenous languages in North and South America over the course of the past two centuries, as their speakers replaced them with English or Spanish, is an example.

Fishman throws the nature of language as a symbol for nationalities into stark relief with his distinction between **nationalism** and **nationism**. Nationalism, akin to nationality, concerns the identity of a people, their awareness of themselves as a people unified among themselves and distinct from others. Nationism has to do with the nuts and bolts of governing. A nationalist (or national) language emphasizes the symbolic. A nationist language (also called an **official language**) is the language used to carry out government tasks – printing tax forms, debating in the legislature, running the military, educating children. Nationist concerns have led many countries, particularly in Africa and Asia, to use the language of a former colonial power as at least one of their official languages. The language of a former colonial ruler makes no sense as a national language (symbol of national identity), but in a situation where there are several important nationalities within a country's borders, each with its own language, nationist concerns make the colonial language a reluctant best choice as an official language. To choose the language of one of several nationalities as the country's national language is bound to offend the others and risk political instability. If Nigeria, for example, were to choose one of its three major languages, Hausa, Igbo or Yoruba, as a national language, there would be severe repercussions from the other two. The official language of Nigeria is English.

A national language is like the national flag. Its value is more symbolic than functional. A nationist or official language is comparable to the national railroad. A railroad's primary purpose is functional, getting people and goods from one part of the country to another. In the extreme, the national language does not even have to be spoken, as long as it represents the identity of the people. The official language does not have to be loved, as long as it does its job, making it possible for the government to function. Of course, national languages are almost always spoken, and countries are no doubt best off if the official language is loved – that is, if the national and official languages are the same.

An example of a national language that is loved but not spoken is Manx Gaelic, the historic language of the Isle of Man. The last native speaker of Manx Gaelic died in 1974, although more than 1,000 people have learned the language as a second language. Manx Gaelic was declared a limited "official" language along with English by the Tynwald (Parliament) in 1985. The law uses the word "official," but it is clear that the function of Manx Gaelic is as a national language, in Fishman's terms. It is used ceremoniously on Tynwald Day, a national holiday, and some members of the Tynwald address the body using some Manx Gaelic along with English, but the language has very little further official function. There are members of the Tynwald who vigorously urge increased official use.

Interpreting some of the cases

We are now in a position to understand some of the cases that introduced this chapter. The Kurds are among the most nationalistic of all the world's nationalities that do not control their own state. Kurds live in parts of Turkey, Syria, and Iraq and would very much like to establish their own state, which would be called Kurdistan. Not surprisingly, the states that control the territory that would make up Kurdistan are not willing to give that territory up. These states, including Turkey, want to damp down Kurdish nationalist fervor as much as possible. One way to do this is to weaken the status of the Kurdish language, a strong symbol of Kurdish nationality. At one time, the Turkish government went so far as to forbid the public use of Kurdish, even singing in it. That proved to be too provocative, but the government still does not want to see the language strengthened by being taught at a university in Turkey.

The case of the Yup'ik speakers in Alaska is quite easy to understand in Fishman's terms. Although they are a small population, probably an ethnic group in most respects, they acted very much like a nationality in insisting on using Yup'ik for local government. The language used by the local legislature ordinarily would be decided on nationist grounds, with English at least as satisfactory functionally as Yup'ik. But under the perceived threat to the survival of their language represented by the official English vote at the state level, the citizens of Tuntutuliak were motivated to nationalistically defend the linguistic symbol of their group identity.

Language standardization

In order to understand the cases concerning dialects in China and Singapore, we will have to first take up another issue in the politics of language, **language standardization**. Language standardization is a policy response to one of the most fundamental properties of language: it varies and it changes. As we saw in Chapter 9, speakers of languages typically differ in their pronunciation, grammar, and vocabulary, and in some languages these differences are quite extensive. For some purposes, like education and the language of government publications, some countries feel a need to determine which of these variants are considered appropriate. Some countries have established language academies to standardize and guide the development of their languages. L'Académie française for French and La Real Academia Española for Spanish are two of the best known, but academies also exist for such non-European languages as Hebrew (in Israel) and Quechua (in Peru).

Governments make language standardization decisions, but individuals and institutions in the private sector make them as well. Newspapers, magazines, and news agencies often produce editorial guidelines on how language is to be used within their pages. These standards are enforced by the editors and proof-readers and go on to have a broad indirect influence on the thousands of readers of the publication. In fact, what you are reading in this book has undergone the standardizing influence of the editors and proof-readers at Cambridge University Press! Individuals can contribute to language standardization, too. The English publisher William Caxton owned one of the very few printing presses in

England in the latter half of the fifteenth century and, through his editorial control, was able to enforce his own standards on a large proportion of what was published at the time (which in turn influenced the language that followed). Two individuals constructed very influential English dictionaries – Samuel Johnson in England and Noah Webster in the United States. If you are annoyed at seeing spellings like *standardize* and *behavior* in these pages, you can blame Noah Webster for his quite successful effort to distinguish the spelling of English in the United States from the conventions in England.

So far, I have described language standardization as the process of selecting from the variation that is the essence of any language in order to achieve uniformity in some uses of the language. But the notion of a standard language, like much that we have been discussing, has symbolic dimensions that go beyond such pragmatic considerations. Most people unquestioningly believe that the language presented by language academies and in dictionaries and grammar books is correct and the other varieties are incorrect. For example, *She is not ready* is included in standard English while another commonly used variant, *She ain't ready*, is not. Virtually every English speaker – even those who actually say *She ain't ready* – is convinced, not only that the latter form is not appropriate for use in formal speech and writing, but that it is incorrect English and should not be used at all, by anyone, under any circumstances. Furthermore, most people who speak English (or any other standardized language) are sure that somewhere, someone has determined that the standard forms are correct *in an absolute sense* – that it would not be possible for any reasonable person, if they were expert enough and followed scholarly principles, to find that the standard language could be anything different from what it is. To fail to use standard forms is to fail to use the real language.

Linguistic research has led to an entirely different conclusion. When language is examined closely, it turns out that standard forms are no better than other forms. There is no scientific reason to prefer *She is not ready* over *She ain't ready*; as far as communicating propositions, one will do quite as well as the other. English speakers are so sure that *She is not ready* is correct and *She ain't ready* is incorrect only because it is customary to disparage the form *ain't*. This custom is reinforced by the instruments of standardization – grammar books, dictionaries, and the teaching of language usage in schools. Linguists call this **prescriptive linguistics** and contrast it with their own approach to language, which is more like the way a chemist would study chemical structures. Linguists study how language works in its natural settings, and the use of language by educated people is not considered either more or less significant than usage by less educated people.

Convention determines what is accepted in languages. The use of "double negatives" is not allowed in standard English. It is generally condemned on the grounds that two negatives make a positive, so it is illogical to say, *The guy doesn't know nothing* unless you mean that he does know something. But the argument from logic simply does not hold up. In standard Spanish, two negatives are required; there is no other way to say the sentence.

El   tipo   no   sabe   nada.
The   guy   not   knows   nothing
'The guy doesn't know anything.'

This is simply the normal, correct way to say *The guy doesn't know anything* in standard Spanish. Now, the fundamental rules of logic, like the rules of arithmetic, are universal – if they hold for English, they should hold for Spanish – so logic has nothing to do with the syntax of negatives in natural languages. English and Spanish just have different conventions for handling negative sentences, just as basketball and baseball managers have different customary ways of dressing for games. In fact, at different points in their histories, both languages have had the opposite conventions. At points in its history, Spanish did *not* allow two negative forms in a negative sentence, and there were times when English *did*. For example, Chaucer had no qualms about writing:

| He | nevere | yet | no | vileynye | ne | sayde. |
| He | never | yet | no | rudeness | not | said |

'He never spoke rudely.'

Today, of course, you would be criticized if you used a double (in Chaucer's case triple) negative where standard English was expected. But that would be like the criticism a basketball head coach would get if he showed up in a player's uniform. It would not be because you are not using a genuine form in English; it would be because you are using it in a situation where social conventions do not allow it.

> *An example might make this point clearer. In major professional sports in the United States, there are different conventions for how the team coach or manager dresses during games. The coaches of an American football team will dress casually, wearing slacks, a casual shirt, a jacket if the weather calls for it, and perhaps a baseball-style cap. The manager of a baseball team wears a uniform styled just like the players' uniforms. In basketball or hockey, the coach wears a dress shirt, tie, and suit. To ask which sport has the correct convention doesn't make sense. Each convention is correct within its own context. Of course, it would be incorrect for a basketball coach to show up for a game wearing shorts and a sleeveless shirt like his players do, and he would be laughed at if he did. Similarly, a baseball manager who came out on the field wearing a suit and tie would also look ridiculous. But these styles are only "incorrect" because the various sports have developed different traditions.*

Coded and alternative standards

The term "standard" itself is not as straightforward as it may seem. Standards may be coded or uncoded. Coded standards are those that have been explicitly formulated. Uncoded standards are in force despite not having been deliberately specified. Our example of the game-day attire of US sports team coaches is an example of an uncoded standard. No one has published regulations that say basketball coaches should wear suits and ties (indeed, a few do not), or that American football coaches cannot. Yet the dress standards are by-and-large followed.

There are numerous examples of coded standards. For example, government transportation departments typically designate upper limits on how fast it is permissible to drive a car. In the United States, speed limits are set by the individual states. Speed limits on the interstate system (motorways) currently vary from 60 miles per hour (about 97 km/h) in

Hawai'i to 80 mph (about 129 km/h) in a few sparsely populated parts of Texas, with most states having maximum speed limits of 70 mph (about 113 km/h) or 75 mph (about 121 km/h). In Europe, several countries allow speeds up to 130 km/h (about 81 mph) on motorways. Speed limits, then, are coded standards (they are stipulated in traffic laws). They also have two other properties: (1) they are measured – technically, you are speeding in France if you are driving at 130.1 km/h on a motorway, although the standard wouldn't be enforced that closely, and (2) they are alternative standards. You cannot determine if a given car is speeding unless you know what speed limit applies where the car is being driven. In fact, if you cross the state line from Idaho to Oregon driving at 70 mph on Interstate 84, you are suddenly speeding, though you weren't, on the same road, in Idaho. The interstate speed limit in Idaho is 75 mph while it is 65 mph in Oregon. Whether or not you are following the standard depends on which standard is in force.

Some coded standards are not measured. The rules in a book of etiquette are coded, unmeasured standards. One of these might be whose name is mentioned first if a man and a woman are introduced. Another would be the placement of silverware on a dining table. These are thought of as standards that people ought to follow. If they don't, then their behavior is considered incorrect. Uncoded standards are almost always unmeasured, like how a coach in US sports dresses on game days.

Standards as minimums. An interesting phenomenon connected with unmeasured standards, especially unmeasured coded standards is that they are popularly thought of as if they were measured standards with a set minimum value (unlike speed laws where the set standard is a maximum). In the US, the minimum hourly wage was set at $7.25 in July 2009. If a worker is paid less than that, she or he is being paid a *subminimum* wage (which is legal for categories of workers not covered by the federal minimum wage law). It is common to use similar terminology for violations of unmeasured standards, including language. So expressions like "substandard," "not up to standard," "below standard" can be found in discussions of unmeasured coded standards.

Language standards. Most people take language standards to be unmeasured coded standards, coded by a plethora of grammar books and usage guides. For English, there is substantial agreement among these various sources, though they may differ in what the standard might be in the case of small details. Any use of language that violates these rules but generally sounds like English is thought of as substandard – not good enough to be used. Of course there are alternative standards; English grammar standards do not apply to Dutch, and the standards differ even for language varieties as similar as British and American English. Most people would tell you that coded language standards are the only ones, but sociolinguists recognize *uncoded* language standards. These are usages found in the speech of respected members of a society even though they don't conform to the coded standards. For American English, at least, the coded-standard insistence that prepositions not be stranded at the end of their clauses and that *whom* be used where it is the object of a preposition can safely be ignored in speech. Respected speakers can say *Who are you getting that birthday card for?* with impunity. Actually, the coded-standard *For whom are you getting that card?* would be avoided by most standard American English speakers as too stiffly formal, even though they would readily admit that it is "correct." A newer feature that is becoming established in uncoded standard American English is the use of *I* in coordinated noun phrases, instead of *me*, in object position. US President Barack Obama once said, "Well, President Bush *graciously invited Michelle and I* to meet with him and First Lady Laura Bush." He was roundly criticized by language purists, but the *Michelle and I* kind of usage is quite common and goes unnoticed most of the time. Many sociolinguists would tell you that *Who are you getting that card for?* and *President Bush graciously invited Michelle and I...* conform to uncoded American English standards even though they violate the coded standards. And for sociolinguists the uncoded standards are more interesting and important because they are the standards that are actually followed by standard-setting speakers.

Once the difference between coded and uncoded language standards is recognized, we can consider the possibility of *alternative* uncoded standards. We can find examples of what I mean in the lyrics of particular genres of music. The lyrics of a country music song sung by Jimmy Martin include:

> Another man he stole my darlin from me
> And there ain't nobody gonna miss me when I'm gone

And from the hiphop group Dirty Money, lyrics from "Hello Good Morning," performed by group member, Dawn Richards:

> all these broads won't give me my props
> 25 on the bank I be stuntin on their ass
> and they mad cause the bitch won't stop

Jimmy Martin could hardly sing, "And there isn't anybody who is going to miss me when I'm gone." and Dawn Richards couldn't make it "And they are mad because this girl won't stop." (The line, "I be stuntin on their ass," in fact, can't be translated into standard English except very awkwardly.) This is, of course, because those lyrics wouldn't sound authentic to their respective genres. But why not? The reason is that the artists are conforming to the uncoded language standards of the communities they are part of and represent. In these communities, the uncoded standards, without regard to how far they depart from the coded or uncoded standard English rules, call for precisely these grammatical forms. The standards these artists are conforming to are uncoded standards that are alternatives to standard English. They do not fail to "come up" to the standards of prestigious English – whether coded or not – they just follow different standards.

Nonstandard language: Ebonics

You were introduced to African American English, also called Ebonics, in Chapter 9. AAE has periodically become politicized, most recently in 1996 when a local school district in the United States declared that it would use Ebonics in the classroom in the process of teaching standard English. This created a brief national reaction, and the majority of Americans, including many African Americans, objected that Ebonics was bad English, substandard, and had no place in the education of children. Linguists who have studied the structure of Ebonics found this reaction to be not unexpected, but discouraging nonetheless. Under careful analysis, it actually turns out that some aspects of Ebonics allow finer distinctions in verbal expression than standard English does. For example, standard English has two forms that describe action that includes the present, exemplified by:

She works
She is working

> The Oxford English Dictionary *implicitly takes the point of view of linguistics that its duty is to report how people are using the language, not dictate how people should use it. Accordingly, in recent years such items as* doh *(popularized by Homer Simpson from* The Simpsons *television show),* gangsta, *and* bling-bling *have been added to the prestigious dictionary.*

Ebonics has three contrasting forms for the same area of meaning:

She work
She workin
She be workin

She work in Ebonics is a close approximation of the meaning of *She works* in standard English: 'She is the sort of person who characteristically works'; in some contexts it might mean 'she has a job.' *She workin* in Ebonics means much the same as *She is working* in standard English; at the moment of utterance, the person referred to as *she*

BOX 11.1 **MORE EBONICS**

Some other features of the grammar and pronunciation of Ebonics that emerge in these examples are the pronunciation [ɪn] for the suffix standardly spelled -*ing*, the inflection of present-tense verbs with third-person subjects without an -*s* suffix, and the use of a present participial form like *writin* without a form of *be* as in *She writin*. Each of these is a structured part of Ebonics, not a failure to speak English correctly. The suffix [ɪn] is an alternate pronunciation used surprisingly often in standard English, even by the best-educated speakers; in Ebonics it is the dominant pronunciation and so it makes the best sense to spell it without *g*. The present-tense third-person form is a continuation of a process of suffix-regularization in English that is complete in Ebonics, but has not as yet been completed in standard English. In standard English, only the third-person singular has a suffix:

Singular	Plural
I walk	We walk
You walk	You walk
She walks	They walk

In Ebonics, third-person singular verbs are regularized to match the rest of the paradigm. Forms like *She writin* most likely represent a continuation of the contraction process. In standard English, it is possible to say *She is writing*, or to contract *is* by removing the vowel spelled with *i*, yielding *She's writing*. Ebonics has both these forms also, but has an additional process by which the remaining consonant is removed as well, giving *She writin*.

could be observed to be working. As you saw in Chapter 2, how a language morphologically indicates tense or aspect is completely arbitrary, so neither the Ebonic nor standard forms are superior. However, Ebonics syntax gives its speakers an extra verbal aspect not available in standard English. *She be workin* is generally taken – by people who do not understand Ebonics syntax – to be a corrupted form of *She is working*. In fact, in Ebonics *She be workin* means something quite different from *She workin*. It means she's at work sometimes, at other times she isn't, then she is again, then she stops again. At the moment of the utterance, she may or may not actually be working. *She be workin*, with the meaning of intermittent action, is totally missing from the standard English verb system. If a standard English speaker needs to express that meaning, he or she must resort to an adverbial form, like *sometimes* or *usually* or *off and on*.

Ebonics has another verb form that standard English lacks, the form *been* with stress, pronounced something like *bín*. If an Ebonics speaker says something like *She bín married*, a standard English speaker hears it as a (slightly incorrect) version of *She's been married*. But the two forms have vastly different implications in some contexts. John Rickford (1999: 23–25) asked 25 African American and 25 white American speakers the following question:

> Someone asked, "Is she married?" and someone else answered, "She bín married."
> Do you get the idea that she is married now?

Of the 25 African American respondents, 23 answered "Yes." All but 8 of the white respondents answered "No." While the standard English form *She's been married*, even with stress, *might* mean that she was married in the past and still is, it generates the implicature (Chapter 4) that she no longer is. It does so via Grice's second maxim of quantity, which says you are to say no more than is necessary at a given point in the conversation. If she still is married, it would be most cooperative to simply answer "Yes." If the response is *She's béen married*, most hearers would assume that the speaker must have had some reason for giving the longer, more specific answer, and conclude that the reason is that she isn't married any more. But the hearer does not *have to* take this implicature, so it's not surprising that a minority of the white speakers do not.

But the Ebonics form *She bín married* exploits the unique remote-time aspect marker, stressed *bín*, that standard English simply doesn't have. The use of the remote-time aspect in Ebonics means the speaker is representing the action or state as having begun long in the past, so long ago that it is foolish to question it, and as still in force. Sometimes this is more a rhetorical stance the speaker takes than a literal commitment to the distant past. In any case, here it would mean, in standard English, something like: 'Are you serious? She's been married so long I thought everybody knew it.'

I have gone into this much detail about Ebonics to demonstrate that even a language variety that is widely assumed to be incorrect and "substandard," on closer inspection can be shown to have structures that allow expressive possibilities a standard language might well envy.

> "I be stuntin on their ass" from "Hello Good Morning," is hard to render in standard English because of vocabulary (stuntin – 'showing off one's wealth'), the ass camouflage construction – widespread and possibly originating in Ebonics – where 'X's ass' refers to X, expressing a degree of contempt for X, and the uninflected be verbal aspect discussed in the text. A standard English rendition like "You'll often find me showing off my wealth in front of these contemptible women" would minimally touch on the nuances in the original, but far less efficiently or completely than in Ebonics.
>
> The ass camouflage construction has received detailed technical analysis by syntacticians, e.g. Levine (2010), showing that uncoded standard varieties like Ebonics are a source of data for linguistic analysis that is just as good as coded standard varieties.

Language issues in China and Singapore

The case of the Beijing government forbidding Tom and Jerry television cartoons to be dubbed into dialects is actually a combination of identity concerns and standard language concerns. It was mentioned earlier that the Chinese "dialects" are very different from each other, as different as linguistic systems considered separate languages in other parts of the world. When the central Chinese government continues its long-running policy of promoting *putonghua* as the standard language for the whole country, it is only partly because *putonghua* is taken as correct Chinese. The various nonstandard Chinese dialects are associated with social groups which are somewhere in the middle of the continuum between ethnic groups and nationalities. Just as the government in Ankara discourages the use of Kurdish, the Beijing government wants to promote *putonghua* as a symbol of national unity and to reduce the power of the dialects as symbols of potentially competing group identities. (Not surprisingly, *putonghua* is based on the Mandarin dialect spoken in Beijing.) At the same time though, the government said that it was requiring television programming to be in *putonghua* because it wanted to provide a favorable linguistic environment for children; using *putonghua* (and Mandarin Chinese on which it is based) is considered evidence of education and good breeding.

The action of the government of Singapore when it placed an NC-17 rating on the movie, citing the poor grammar of the characters, was more clearly based on considerations of standards and "correctness." In the government's view, the "Singlish" portrayed in the film is bad language and bad for Singapore's image as a commercial and financial center. For some years now, it has been conducting a Speak Good English Movement (SGEM) to encourage standard English. According to the prime minister at the initiation of SGEM, Singlish makes Singaporeans seem less intelligent.

The politics of standardization

So far, language standardization looks like a rather innocuous matter of style and convention: some kinds of speech, and especially writing, require that users of a language all agree on one set of variants, so that all language in those genres will be understood by everyone

BOX 11.2 SINGLISH

Singlish is the kind of English that provoked the NC-17 movie rating from the government of Singapore. The following is part of the story of Little Red Riding Hood, in a very marked kind of Singlish.

> *Little Led Liding Hoot*
> Once upon a time hor, got one girl little led liding hoot. She
> want to go to Ah Mah's house. Morning alleady she go out
> one, she got take come one basket to put flower. She "do
> want" to walk long-long so go take shot cut. Wah!!! she dono
> got one animal follow her one hor! She happy-happy walk
> until she come to Ah Mah house.
>
>   (*Singlish Jokes*)

You can see that there are numerous departures from standard English. If you speak the standard English of one of the natively English-speaking countries, you might sympathize with the government of Singapore. But if we take note that Singlish developed in contact with dialects of Chinese, it is easy to see the origin of many of its features. Chinese doesn't have a phonological distinction between [l] and [r]. The sound spelled *r* in English has a pronunciation that is quite unusual among the world's languages and non-native speakers learning English find it difficult. So it is not surprising that Singlish has pronunciations like *led* and *solly*. Some languages, again Chinese is included, do not require morphemes to mark tense. So we should not be surprised to find the same thing in Singlish; for example, *She want to go to Ah Mah's house* where standard English would have *wanted*. The expressive particles *lah* and *leh* are typical of this kind of English and provide nuances that are impossible to translate. The form *hor*, pronounced [hɔ] is another expressive particle for calling the listener's attention or assent to what is being said. In some contexts (not all), it could be roughly translated 'Right?' Linguists look at the language of "Little Led Liding Hoot," find it fascinating, and set about figuring out how it works. Speakers of Singlish, for their part, would feel hopelessly constricted if they were forced to give up their colorful variety and speak only the standard kind of English.

and everyone will find these (spoken or written) texts esthetically pleasing. But it is possible to see language standardization efforts as having a more sinister side. It is clear that the controlling segments of a society are the ones who get to decide what is standard and what is not, and invariably the standard form is very close to the language the decision-makers use anyway. We might ask why some people get to decide how everybody has to use the same language, or why people should be told, "If you want to get anywhere, you have to learn to use language more or less the way I do." But if it were simply a matter of being asked to conform to certain conventions in a particular context – like a basketball coach being expected to wear a suit and tie to games whether he wants to or not – language standardization would be pretty innocuous. Sure, powerful people get to set the standards, but, if there are going to be standards, someone has to decide what they are. But, as we've seen, it goes beyond a simple arbitrary choice. It's not just that Singlish and Ebonics speakers are at a disadvantage because their everyday English is farther from accepted standards in Singapore and the United States than the everyday language of more privileged speakers. Singlish, Ebonics, and Chinese dialects like Shanghainese are treated as not just different from, but *beneath* the standard language. These kinds of English or Chinese are treated not only as being out of style, but as being a corruption and degradation of the standard language. In short, the standards of language are treated as *minimum* standards, instead of the *arbitrary* standards they actually are.

Diglossia

Some communities have found a way to have a formal, standard form of their language alongside a more colloquial form, without the colloquial variety being held in contempt. This phenomenon is called diglossia. It was first described by Charles Ferguson in 1959, and the idea has recently been further developed by Alan Hudson (2002). Ferguson noticed that there were some communities that had two noticeably distinct versions of their language, which he called the **high dialect** and the **low dialect**. The low dialect is the ordinary spoken language that people learn at home, in their families and neighborhoods. The high dialect is used for formal speaking purposes and most writing. It is typically quite different from the low dialect, although the two are linguistically related. The high dialect is no one's first language. In most cases, people have to be taught the high dialect in school. What is special about low dialects in diglossic communities is that they are not disparaged. Even the highest-status people in the community always use the low dialect for everyday communication. The critical difference between attitudes toward high dialects and standard languages is that no one ever imagines that everyone should avoid the low dialect and speak the high dialect. The high dialect is seen as purer and more correct than the low dialect, but everyone understands that it is not appropriate for everyday speech. People who do not actually learn the high dialect still consider it in some sense "theirs," but they are not ashamed that they speak only the low dialect.

Two clear examples of diglossia are found in German-speaking Switzerland and in the Arab world. The Swiss German dialects are substantially different from standard German, and every Swiss citizen from the German-speaking cantons grows up speaking one of these low dialects. Most Swiss later learn standard German in school, but they never give up their low dialect, which for most is a source of considerable pride. In Arabic-speaking countries, Classical Arabic is the high dialect, and the spoken dialects of each country are the low dialects. Classical Arabic is markedly different from the spoken varieties, and relatively few people learn to speak it fluently. It is used for religious and literary purposes, and in other formal settings. As in Switzerland, Arabic speakers do not regard their spoken language as a corruption of Classical Arabic or as something to be ashamed of, although they regard Classical Arabic as more pure. Whether they speak Classical Arabic or not, all Arabic speakers regard it as theirs.

There are numerous other cases of diglossia in the world. In all of these communities, the high dialect is regarded as in some senses better than the low dialect, but no one thinks speaking the low dialect is a sign of a lack of intelligence and no one ever advocates giving up the low dialect in favor of the high dialect for all purposes. The existence of diglossic communities shows that it is possible to reserve a variety of a language for formal uses without considering the generally spoken varieties as bad language that should be eliminated.

Singaporean English and Singlish
Standard Singaporean English and Singlish are linguistically related to each other more or less the way high and low dialects are. But they do not constitute a case of diglossia. In a diglossic community, something like a Speak Good English Movement would be unthinkable.

"Languages" and "dialects"

At the beginning of the chapter, you read that the Chinese dialects were different enough from each other so that they might be considered separate languages in other parts of the world. Part of the justification given for restricting the teaching of Kurdish in Turkey is that Kurdish is too primitive and not a real language. Singlish and Ebonics are also accused of not being real languages. The high and low dialects in diglossia are said to be distinctively different, but are called dialects, not separate languages. You might well ask what the difference is between languages and dialects.

This question is addressed in Chapter 9, but it will be useful to amplify the discussion here. One criterion that immediately suggests itself is mutual intelligibility. People can understand a different dialect from the one they speak, but they can't understand a different language. But this criterion turns out not to work at all. First, how do we define "understand"? If I understand 80 percent of what you say, do you and I speak different dialects of the same language? What if I understand 75 percent or 50 percent? Understanding varies depending on how fast people are speaking, how familiar the topic being talked about is, and whether one is listening to someone speak or reading something. If this were not bad enough, there are some cases in which speakers of Variety A can understand speakers of Variety B, but B-speakers cannot understand A. Then there is the phenomenon of **dialect chains**. In a dialect chain, speakers of Dialect A can understand Dialect B and speakers of Dialect C can understand B, but they can't understand A. Are A and C dialects of the same language? Dialect chains are not hypothetical; they are common in many parts of the world. So mutual intelligibility doesn't distinguish between languages and dialects perfectly.

Another, quite distinct, notion of the difference between languages and dialects is the idea that dialects are less developed than languages. If a linguistic variety has been standardized and has a literary tradition associated with it, then it is a language; otherwise it is a dialect. This definition is frequently used in the media when someone writes about the number of "languages and dialects" in a certain part of the world. Many linguists find this approach undesirable, because they know there are hundreds of languages with intricate and fascinating grammatical and pronunciation properties, comparable with anything you would find in the commonly studied European languages. They would be loath to deny these systems status as languages simply because no one has yet written a grammar or dictionary for them, or produced books of poetry or literary prose. In any case, this criterion faces the same sort of problem as mutual intelligibility. For example, a 31-page Shiwiar–Spanish dictionary was published in 2002. (Shiwiar is an indigenous language of the Amazon region of South America.) Is Shiwiar now a language when it was a dialect in

2001? Perhaps a dictionary is not enough; perhaps a language also needs other standardizing devices like grammar books and maybe literary works as well. But how many of these elements have to be present before an erstwhile dialect achieves language status? It is hard to imagine how any of these questions can be answered other than arbitrarily.

The German linguist Heinz Kloss (1967) combined the criterion of mutual intelligibility with the criterion of development. He claimed that some languages are so different from other languages that their status as languages is not in dispute. He called these languages by **separation** (German: *Abstand*). Other languages are languages by **development** (German: *Ausbau*). These languages are similar enough to other languages that their differences wouldn't guarantee them language – rather than dialect – status, but they have been deliberately developed by their communities – via standardization and literary usage – and achieve language status that way. Swedish and Norwegian, for example, would be languages by development, so would Spanish and Portuguese. Some languages, like French and English, are separate languages by separation, but qualify as different languages by development as well.

Linguists generally work with a loose version of the first concept of language and dialect – the (imperfect) criterion of mutual intelligibility – to (roughly) distinguish languages and dialects. In other words, there are groups of linguistic varieties whose speakers understand each other reasonably well. At the same time, they don't understand speakers of other linguistic varieties very well, or at all. These are "languages." Within each of these languages are linguistic subsystems. Speakers of the language generally understand speakers of other subsystems of that language, but also notice that their speech is peculiar, or in any case different from their own. These are "dialects." Linguists recognize that it is impossible, in many cases, to determine if a particular linguistic variety is a "dialect" of another variety or a separate language. In spite of more than a century of effort, linguists have never found a definition of mutual intelligibility or separation that can unambiguously tell us if we are looking at a language or a dialect. Nevertheless, they find this way of distinguishing languages and dialects sufficient for most of their work.

The politics of languages and dialects

The lack of definitive criteria for deciding what is or is not a language allows people to decide what is or is not a language for political reasons. Sometimes this is done using criteria that award language status only when the linguistic system has sufficient standardization and literary development. We have seen that some Turks regard Kurdish as not quite a language because they think it is not developed enough in this way. In similar fashion, when Francisco Franco held power in Spain, he declared Basque – a language completely different from Spanish and often cited as a clear example of a language by separation – to be a mere peasant dialect. The reason given was again the supposed lack of development, but it is also true that the Basques were a restive nationality with a strong sense of identity who desired territorial autonomy, as many Basques do today.

Franco hoped to reduce their sense of independence by reducing the status of their language, a strong symbol of their identity.

Sometimes the ambiguity of similarity or mutual intelligibility between linguistic varieties as a criterion also allows for decisions to be made on political grounds. China has long considered the related linguistic systems within its borders to be dialects rather than languages in spite of the considerable separation among them. This reduces the danger of the development of regional nationalisms, by emphasizing linguistic similarity over difference, even to the point of controlling how Tom and Jerry speak Chinese on television. Arab unity is a strong value in the Arab world, so the various kinds of spoken Arabic are never considered separate languages although, like the Chinese case, there is quite marked separation among some of them.

In South Africa, the decision went somewhat the other way. When the apartheid system was ending, a proposal was offered to simplify the way that languages would be dealt with officially, by considering the four languages of the Nguni group and the three languages of the Sotho group as single languages for some purposes. There is relatively little separation among the languages within each of these two groups and a high level of mutual intelligibility. Nevertheless, this proposal never got off the ground, partly because the individual languages are symbols of different group identities. Today, there are eleven official languages in post-apartheid South Africa, including the seven Nguni and Sotho languages.

Sometimes a linguistic system can go from being a language to being a dialect and back to being a language again, depending on the political environment. One particularly dramatic example of this is the case of Serbian and Croatian. For the past 150 years or more there has been controversy over whether Serbian and Croatian are separate languages or whether they are varieties of a single Serbo-Croatian language. It is clear that there is very little separation between the two – mostly some vocabulary differences and different writing systems; Croatian is almost always written in the Latin alphabet, while Serbian is mostly written in Cyrillic. During the nineteenth and early twentieth centuries, the two were undergoing deliberate separate development. Then the Federal People's Republic of Yugoslavia was formed after World War II under Josep Broz Tito. Unity throughout the new Yugoslavia was considered desirable and decisions about language were made accordingly. A 1954 agreement called for the publication of a unified "Serbo-Croatian/ Croato-Serbian" orthography and dictionary, and people began to speak of a Serbo-Croation language. With the dissolution of Yugoslavia at the end of the twentieth century and the formation of Serbia-Montenegro and Croatia as separate states, Serbian and Croatian are again considered separate languages.

Official English

In the United States, one manifestation of the politics of language is the movement to amend the constitution or at least pass a federal law making English the official language of the United States. Two facts about the United States partially shape debates about language. First, there is no legislatively designated official language. In practice, English is the functioning official language for the vast majority of the activities of the federal government, but there is no law at the federal level that says English is official. This means that there are no legislated language rights, either; it is not against the law for anyone in the private sector, or any agency of the government, to discriminate against people on the basis of language alone. Second, the United States does not have a sense of nationality based on membership of a single ancestral group. It prides itself on being "a nation of immigrants" that welcomes people from other countries, but they are then expected to give up allegiances to their countries of origin or to any identity other than American. Since there is no historic sense that Americans are all descended from the same ancestors, or that Americans share the same religion, there is a tendency to seek another symbol of nationality. For some, the English language is that symbol.

Toleration for the widespread maintenance of languages other than English varies with historical circumstances. Large influxes of immigrants spark an emphasis on the necessity for immigrants to learn English. An emphasis on Americanization, including learning English, was strong around 1900, when there was a perceived influx of immigrants from eastern and southern Europe. In the 1960s and early 1970s, there was a greater tolerance for identity diversity. People were more inclined to look to their roots and take on hyphenated identities like Italian-American and Polish-American, as well as African American (though that term was not widely used then), associated with the civil rights movement that went on at the same time. This was sometimes accompanied by more-or-less desultory attempts to learn the language of their immigrant ancestors. Congress passed the Bilingual Education Act providing federal funding for the education of bilingual children. These funds were largely used for transitional bilingual education programs, in which bilingual children were taught subjects in their first (non-English) language while they were learning English. Congress also passed the Voting Rights Act, which provided for ballots in languages other than English under some circumstances.

As immigration seemed to grow again at the end of the twentieth century, emphasis on being American and speaking English increased also. Every year since the early 1970s legislation has been introduced to make English the official language of the United States. So far no federal official language legislation has passed, but 28 of the 50 states have legislation or constitutional amendments making English official in those states. The majority of state official language legislation has been passed since 1980. One of these, Hawai'i, has two official languages, English and Hawai'ian. Illinois passed a law in 1923 making "American" the state's official language. In 1969, that law was repealed and English was made official in Illinois.

Most Americans are quite content for native peoples to keep using their languages for whatever purposes they choose, even official ones. Note that Hawai'i has made its indigenous language explicitly official. As we saw, it is possible for the government of Tuntutuliak, in spite of Alaska's official English amendment, to conduct town business in Yup'ik. Even supporters of the official English law in Alaska say they intend that it should exempt indigenous languages and apply only to immigrant languages. This was not always the case. Well into the last century, official policy was severely oppressive of native American languages. But in 1990, Congress passed the Native American Languages Act, preserving the right of Native American peoples to use and develop their languages and requiring that state official language laws must be consistent with the Native American Languages Act. The law passed by a voice vote in both Houses of Congress without opposition and was signed into law by President George H. W. Bush. However, no funding for programs to preserve indigenous languages was provided by the law.

Language rights in the United States

With very few exceptions (the Native American Languages Act is one), there are no laws preserving language rights in the United States. As a result, the private sector responds in various ways to the presence of speakers of languages other than English. In the Washington, DC area some companies and government agencies that employ considerable numbers of Central American immigrants are asking their monolingual English supervisors to learn at least some words and phrases in Spanish. Other employers have been known to fire workers for speaking in a language other than English, not only when they are carrying out their jobs or talking with clients or customers, but when talking to each other on breaks or even on the street as they are leaving work. People who feel they are discriminated against based on language technically have no legal recourse. One strategy is to argue that the discrimination is not really about language, but based on their national origin, which is against the law. Whether this strategy will be successful in a particular case is uncertain. The Equal Employment Opportunity Commission (EEOC), an agency of the Executive Branch of the government, has historically opposed blanket rules requiring that only English be used at the workplace on the grounds that it violates prohibitions against discrimination based on national origin. The courts, on the other hand, have upheld such rules when employers have legitimate business reasons for the rules, and the employees are fully competent in English, even though they speak another language. No test case has yet reached the Supreme Court, so case law is not definitive.

Another basis for resisting English-only policies is the constitutional guarantee of freedom of speech. The Arizona State Supreme Court (not the United States Supreme Court) cited freedom of speech as one reason why an earlier Arizona official English amendment (not the one in force today) was not allowed to stand; the current amendment underwent revisions to meet freedom-of-speech concerns. At one point a judge in Alaska also ruled that the Alaska official-English law was not constitutional because it violated freedom of speech. It is still not clear the degree to which requiring the use of English is legally a violation of freedom of speech.

Bilingualism

It's obvious that English is not threatened by any other language in the United States. Why, then, do some Americans want to enforce the use of English to the exclusion of other languages? Where English has been proposed as the only official language of government, nationist reasons are generally cited. Producing official documents, printing ballots, and providing services in multiple languages is inefficient and expensive. Multilingual public education is expensive, and opponents say the stated ultimate goal of producing children fluent in English is not being achieved. Private-sector employers justify requiring only English at work on the grounds that the use of other languages lowers the morale of monolingual English speakers, who suspect they are being ridiculed in languages they can't understand, that it might interfere with safety, or that it drives away customers. These arguments have merit, but it seems that nationalist identity is what drives the movement at a gut level.

One problem is that bilingualism is not widely viewed as a possible solution. The majority of Americans speak only English, and monolingualism seems normal to them. Many Americans have studied foreign languages in high school or college, but have not become proficient in them, even though they may have received high grades in language classes. This leaves Americans with the vague idea that most people can have only one language at a time. Of course, everyone knows that there are people who speak two or more languages well, but they are usually seen as exceptionally intelligent. If pressed, no doubt most Americans could be convinced that it would be possible for people to learn English well and still be fluent speakers of their heritage language, but the vague assumption persists that learning English well entails forgetting any other language you might know. If you know an individual Latino is a fluent speaker of Spanish, for instance, you are likely to assume that he/she is not a fluent speaker of English. A picture of America with large communities of bilingual speakers of Spanish and English, Vietnamese and English, or Navajo and English just doesn't occur to most Americans, and if it does, it presents a threat to national identity. To be fluent in a non-English, language seems to mean you aren't fluent in English, and that means you have not fully accepted an American identity, a disturbing thought if a strong American national identity is important to you.

In fact, the vast majority of immigrants to the United States *do* become monolingual in English within three generations. Furthermore, this applies as well to more recent immigrants from Latin America or Asia as it did to immigrants from Europe around 1900.

Bilingual maintenance: continuing immigration

In order to understand this better, we should think about what it takes to maintain a community of speakers of a language other than English in the United States. It is certainly a huge advantage to know and use English in the US, so to maintain another language must require particular circumstances and motivation. One of these is continuing immigration. Continuing immigration supplies new speakers of a non-English language as the descendants of previous generations switch to English. In that way, there are always people who speak a non-English language in the United States, but most of them weren't born there. This is like a lake that is fed by one stream while being drained by another stream at the other end. The lake always has water in it, it's just not the same water.

A second circumstance motivating bilingual maintenance is for a group of people to have a sense of identity more characteristic of a nationality than an ethnic group, and for language to be a crucial symbol of that nationality. They may have a dual national identity, thinking of themselves as American as well as something else. This context also requires a cohesive community that is somewhat separated from other Americans, either

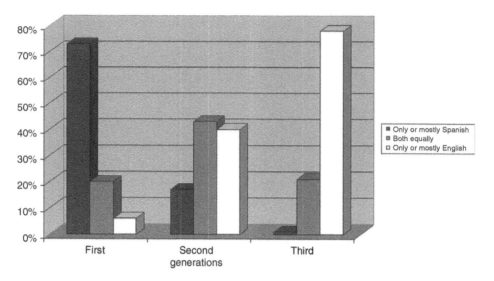

Figure 11.1 Use of English and Spanish: 1999 survey of Latinos

geographically or socially. Such a community will use the non-English language within their own community, but speak English for interactions with the wider community.

The most prominent social group in the United States that speaks a language other than English are Latinos. More than half of those Americans who speak a non-English language at home speak Spanish. For the most part, Spanish persists in Latino communities because of continuing immigration. Just like other immigrants before them, Latinos who settle in the United States become fluent in English in the second generation and lose Spanish by the third generation. Calculations from data in the 2000 US Census show that over 95 percent of the population eighteen years old or older is fluent in English. "Fluent" speakers are people who speak only English (the vast majority), or people who speak some other language at home, but report that they can also speak English "well" or "very well." The percentage of fluent speakers is even higher for people aged five to seventeen, over 97 percent. Clearly, most immigrants are rapidly picking up English.

More direct evidence of the rapid transition from Spanish to English comes from two telephone surveys of Latinos in the United States. The first was conducted by the *Washington Post*, the Henry J. Kaiser Family Foundation, and Harvard University in the summer of 1999 (Goldstein and Suro 2000). It found that 73 percent of first-generation Latino immigrants spoke only Spanish or more Spanish than English at home and 6 percent spoke only or mostly English (the rest used both languages equally). Yet 78 percent of third-generation descendants of Latino immigrants used all or mostly *English* and only 1 percent used all Spanish or more Spanish than English.

In 2002, the Pew Hispanic Center and the Henry J. Kaiser Family Foundation conducted a similar telephone survey that essentially replicated those results (Pew Hispanic Center / Henry J. Kaiser Family Foundation 2004: 3). It found that 72 percent of first-generation Latino immigrants were Spanish-dominant while 4 percent claimed to be English-dominant.

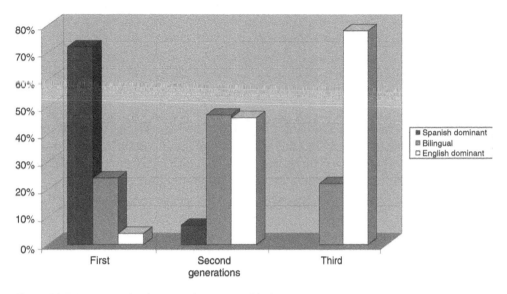

Figure 11.2 Language dominance: 2002 survey of Latinos

The remainder were bilingual. A full 78 percent of the third generation or beyond said they were English-dominant, with no respondents claiming Spanish dominance.

It seems clear that the maintenance of Spanish in the United States is mostly due to continuing immigration, not a reluctance on the part of Latinos born in the United States to switch to English. If you think having bilingual citizens is an advantage to a country, the speed with which Latinos lose Spanish might be the problem, not that they might not learn English.

Bilingual maintenance: group identity

The other kind of bilingual maintenance community is much rarer. Some indigenous populations maintain their non-English languages because they have a strong sense of ethnic identity. One example we have already encountered are Yup'ik-speaking communities in Alaska. However, indigenous languages have been dying out at a rapid pace over the past 100 years or more, as their speakers reduce the importance of a non-English community language as an identity symbol. Other examples are communities based on religious faith. Old Order Amish have been living in what is now the United States since before the American Revolution. They reject modern conveniences, such as electricity and automobiles, and are friendly in their dealings with outsiders, but keep themselves carefully separate from them. Amish communities have maintained bilingualism over the generations. They use a variety of German commonly called "Pennsylvania Dutch" in their homes and for worship. They use English, not only for contacts outside the community, but also as the language of education. These communities operate their own parochial schools because they are suspicious of the values their children would learn in public schools. Although the schools are run by the community for their own children, the medium of instruction is English.

Another faith-based group, found particularly in New York City, are the Haredi Jews, close-knit religious communities with a strong awareness of their unique identity. They use Yiddish as a home and school language, as well as for aspects of worship. Although they use English for outside contacts, they are careful to limit external influences. The Haredi Jewish communities have maintained stable Yiddish–English bilingualism over generations.

In general, Americans admire people who know more than one language. An American from an English-speaking background who becomes fluent in another language (even if he/she speaks with an accent) is considered intelligent. Americans are happy to have their children study foreign languages in high school and college, and even study abroad for part of their college career. On the other hand, an American from a Spanish-speaking back-ground who learns English, but continues to speak Spanish within the family and local community is viewed with suspicion. Why should bilingualism only be admired if English is the first language? Perhaps the answer is an intuitive realization of the relationship between language and nationalist identity. Americans who appear to maintain a language other than English within their communities, no matter how well they speak English, are suspected of holding a dangerously divided loyalty. The genuine cases of nationality-based bilingual maintenance by indigenous populations, like the Old Order Amish and Haredi Jews, are tolerated because the communities are small, isolated, and maybe a bit quaint. But many mainstream Americans do not distinguish "transitory" bilingualism due to continu-ing immigration from bilingualism maintained as a symbol of group identity. The real question may be whether Americans can accept stable bilingualism if the price is allowing people to think of themselves as being something else in addition to being American. That seems to be what it would take to achieve continuing crossgenerational bilingualism.

Controlling the content of speech

So far, we've discussed the political treatment of languages and dialects, like the push to make English official in the United States and the restrictive NC-17 rating on the movie with Singlish dialogue in Singapore. Regulating what languages or dialects people speak or discouraging nonstandard language has to do with trying to control social identity, or projecting a desirable national image. But the *content* of speech sometimes becomes a political issue as well. Two such language-content issues are (1) **blasphemy** (insults against sacred individuals or items) and cursing (irreverent use of religious terms or use of terms considered obscene), and (2) **hate speech** (threats or intimidation against individuals or groups based on social characteristics like race). Cursing is related to lan-guage standardization. It is a violation of social standards, like saying *ain't*, but more serious. But this is only part of it. Governments try to control blasphemy and cursing or hate speech, not to encourage desired identities, but to protect the public from affronts to important values. In both issues, there is political tension between freedom of speech and the social harm that might come from allowing some kinds of speech in public.

Blasphemy and cursing

The power of blasphemous expression to inflict pain on and infuriate the faithful is great. Just how great became apparent in 2005 when the Danish newspaper *Jyllands-Posten*, concerned about self-censorship elsewhere in Europe where Islam was involved, commissioned illustrators to create cartoon caricatures of the Prophet Muhammad (may peace be with him). The Qur'an can be interpreted as forbidding the production of any images of Muhammad, but depictions of the Prophet have appeared in the past without incident. Not all the cartoons were deliberately negative, but some were, particularly one in which a bomb appears in the Prophet's turban. Muslims around the world took deep offense and there were attacks on Danish embassies and other sites associated with the West, resulting in scores of deaths, as well as a largely ineffective boycott of Danish products.

Although the blasphemy in this case involved pictures rather than words, it highlighted a sharp difference in values about expression in the West and in the Muslim world. Muslims felt that an attack on their religion was being willfully condoned. The Danish and other western governments took the position that a more primary value was to defend the right to freedom of expression, no matter how offensive. There are blasphemy laws in the West; English common law has made blasphemy illegal in the United Kingdom since Henry VIII established the Church of England in the sixteenth century, and it is technically in force today. Blasphemy has been against the law in several states in the United States, but these laws have been enforced only rarely. The last blasphemy prosecution in the United States took place in the 1970s. A more effective deterrent in the cartoon case was the threat of violence. In the United States, for example, Yale University Press decided not to include the cartoons in a book called *The Cartoons that Shook the World*, when specialists it consulted agreed that the threat of physical attacks would be severe. The American animated television cartoon *South Park*, known for its irreverent and often insulting treatment of admired people and topics, heavily censored an episode in which Muhammad was a subject, although he would never have been actually represented. This happened after a veiled threat appeared on an Islamic website based in New York. On the other hand, Denmark declined to pressure *Jyllands-Posten* to apologize and the cartoons were republished in Norway in support of the Danish newspaper. In spite of all this, it is generally true that in much of the western world, the harm caused by blasphemy is now considered less damaging than the limitations to free speech that would result if governments tried to prevent it.

The conclusion has not been quite so clear when it comes to the public use of curse words. In two different incidents in the state of Michigan in the US, men were convicted of cursing in public. One man had fallen out of a canoe and responded with a string of curse words in a place where children could hear him. He was fined and required to work several days in a child-care program. The other man was accused of cursing a school bus driver who he thought had mistreated his daughter. He was also charged with assault and disturbing the peace, and was sentenced to ninety days in jail. In both cases, judges found the century-old state law against cursing constitutional, apparently considering the harm caused by children hearing the cursing to override the right to freedom of speech as it might have applied in these cases. At the University of Maryland, university officials were outraged by students who uttered profanities while taunting their team's opponents at basketball games. University officials tried to persuade students to change their behavior, in part because people from the community brought young children to the games, but these attempts failed. The university then asked for a ruling from the state attorney general's office on whether it would be constitutional for them to officially ban cursing at these sports events. A preliminary ruling was that the university would not violate the constitution if it did. It seems that, in the United States at least, the harm caused, particularly to children, by cursing in public is sometimes considered greater than the damage that might be done by limiting people's freedom to curse in public.

In 2010, Google, Inc. marketed a mobile telephone, the Nexus One, that enabled users to send text messages by speaking, using speech recognition technology. Users were startled when they discovered that any four-letter words they spoke while composing text messages were replaced by sequences of "#" in the written version. Was Google trying to clean up its customers' offensive language? No, the company said, it was afraid that its imperfect speech recognition algorithms might interpret innocent expressions as obscenity or profanity when none was intended. Google discontinued marketing the Nexus One six months later for unrelated reasons.

Hate speech

What kinds of speech you think should be limited or protected tends to depend on your overall political viewpoint. Generally, people of conservative political leanings find that limiting freedom of speech to prevent swearing (and maybe blasphemy) is justified, but tend to feel differently about hate speech. On the other hand, liberals are more likely to defend restrictions on hate speech and see serious violations of the right to free speech when swearing is prohibited. In 2005, the pastor of an evangelical protestant church in Sweden was arrested for delivering a sermon in which he condemned homosexuality. He was found guilty of violating Sweden's strict hate speech laws and was sentenced to thirty days in prison. Hate speech is generally defined as speech that is intimidating towards people on the basis of social characteristics such as race, national origin, religion, sex, or, as in this case, sexual orientation. This case highlights the trade-off between harmful versus free speech. The Swedish clergyman sees his arrest (which he apparently took some steps to provoke) as infringing on his right to preach his religious convictions. His critics say that religious freedom or freedom of speech does not extend to speech intimidating historically persecuted minority groups, like homosexuals.

Hate speech laws in Europe are more likely to make speech against groups illegal. The stance in the United States has been that a crime must have occurred in order for there to be a legal penalty. It might be illegal, for example, to intimidate an individual Buddhist on account of his/her religion, because a specific person has suffered harm. To speak against all Buddhists, on the other hand, is constitutionally protected speech.

The difference in political orientation with respect to hate speech is perhaps most clear in the case of hate speech regulations at universities. State-funded universities in the US are more limited by law in restricting hate speech than private universities are because the government is forbidden to take actions that might limit freedom of speech. Private institutions have more latitude in conducting their business. It is not uncommon for private US universities to prohibit harassing speech against a particular list of groups if such speech at least foreseeably might cause a hostile environment for members of those groups. Critics of hate speech codes argue that a university ought to be the first place where people should be free to express unpopular ideas. Hate speech codes might protect some people from hostile environments, but create a hostile environment for those with views that run afoul of the codes. Proponents of hate speech codes agree that minority viewpoints certainly should be allowed if rationally expressed, but claim that hate speech is inherently irrational since it consists of blanket condemnations of whole groups. Furthermore, they say that harassing speech is much more harmful to minorities who have experienced a history of oppression than it would be to members of more powerful groups who don't have such a history; having to endure a harassing environment would disrupt the education of a minority student in a discriminatory way.

It is clearly far from simple to attempt to balance a desire to defend freedom of speech against the harm some kinds of speech might cause. Governments have an obligation to protect people's freedoms, but they also have a responsibility to protect them from harm. They sometimes have to do less of one to do more of the other. How you evaluate these trade-offs is inevitably colored by your general political views.

CHAPTER SUMMARY

If you think of language as a means of communicating ideas from one person to another, it might seem strange that language should be the source of political controversy. But when you speak, you also display who you are in society. The language you speak – your dialect and accent, even the way you construct your sentences – helps shape your identity. This means that those with political power are going to be tempted to control language in an attempt to guide people's identities in desired directions. Government agencies and powerful people try to stipulate what languages can be used for what purposes, what forms of the language are acceptable, and even what is or is not a language. Beyond control over language form, people in power sometimes try to restrict the sorts of things you can say when you speak. All of these efforts to control the form and use of language, and people's reaction to them, add up to the politics of language. Language, for reasons that are not always obvious, turns out to have a surprisingly prominent place as a political issue.

Exercises

EXERCISE 11.1

South Tirol is an Italian province that was once part of Austria. Most of the population of South Tirol (68 percent) is German-speaking and the province is officially bilingual. The German-speaking population – a majority in South Tirol but a minority in Italy – resents the fact that names of towns, rivers, valleys, and other locations are officially in Italian, though they are locally referred to by their German names by German speakers and by their Italian names by Italian speakers. It became a contentious issue, for example, whether or not the official name of the town traditionally known as Innichen should be allowed to remain officially San Candido. Given what you know about language and identity, try to explain why place names in South Tirol became an emotional issue.

EXERCISE 11.2

The owners of an antique store near Monréal were fined 500CND in 1999 because the letters naming the store were the same size in French and in English instead of being larger in French, as the law requires. The Québec Superior Court ruled against the owners and the Supreme Court of Canada refused to hear the case. Why is the size of letters on a store sign taken so seriously in Québec? Relate your answer to language and identity. It may be helpful to gather information on Québec language laws from the internet.

EXERCISE 11.3

Do you consider your country a **nation** or a **multinational state** by Fishman's definitions? Give reasons for your answer.

EXERCISE 11.4

The text mentions the Alaskan native village of Tuntutuliak, which passed a law requiring village government business to be conducted in Yup'ik. The same year, the town of El Cenizo, Texas, on the Mexican border, began conducting city council business in Spanish. There were numerous newspaper and television stories and commentaries about the El Cenizo case but hardly any discussion of the Tuntutuliak case. (1) Did these decisions involve official or national language? (2) Why did the El Cenizo case incite so much more indignation than the Tuntutuliak case? (3) In your opinion, should either or both localities be required to conduct government business in English? Explain.

EXERCISE 11.5

Which of the following is probably a coded standard and which is an uncoded standard?
a. Dogs are kept on a leash when walked in public areas.
b. Shoppers in Japan leave wet umbrellas outside or cover them in plastic sheaths.
c. In Washington, DC, bicycles are taken onto subway train cars only through doors at the far ends of cars, never through the center doors.
d. Men are not expected to wear high-heeled shoes, but women may.
e. Stand to the right on the escalator and pass on the left.
   Find two other real-life examples of coded standards and two of uncoded standards.

EXERCISE 11.6

Consider the following examples:
a. You are not so smart as I.
b. You are not as smart as me.
c. You ain't as smart as me.
d. You ain't so smart as I.

(1) Identify which one is an example of conformity to a coded English standard and which represents conformity to an uncoded English standard. Which one are you more likely to say when you are with student friends? Why wouldn't you use the other one?

(2) Of the remaining two examples, one is not likely to be used at all, by anyone. Which one is it? Speculate on why it would not be used, even by speakers who do not totally follow English standards, coded or uncoded.

(3) Discuss the remaining example as a case of conformity to an alternative standard rather than a violation of a traditional standard (coded or uncoded). In your opinion, is it preferable to treat it as a violation, as a standard, or as conformity to an alternative standard?

EXERCISE 11.7

In the novel *The Color Purple*, the father of the main character, Celie, offers her as a wife to a man she hardly knows. Alice Walker has Celie narrate the scene in one of her letters to God, in Ebonics:

> She ugly. He say. But she ain't no stranger to hard work. And she clean. And God done fixed her.
> You can do everything just like you want to and she ain't gonna make you feed it or clothe it.
>   Mr._____still don't say nothing. I take out the picture of Shug Avery. I look into her eyes. Her eyes say Yeah, it *bees* that way sometime. (p. 18)

Explain why Walker has the father say *She ugly* instead of *She be ugly*, and why the picture of Shug Avery (Celie's friend) seems to say *It bees that way sometime* rather than *It is that way sometime*.
Hint: since *She ugly* does not involve a verb with the *-in* suffix, it should be compared to the simple present-tense *She write* in the example in the text, rather than to *She writin*.
Hint: treat *bees* as a variant of *be*.

EXERCISE 11.8

In 1923, the US state of Illinois declared "American" as the state's official language, not "English." (This decision was reversed in 1969.) What would it take for "American" to become a language distinct from "English"?

EXERCISE 11.9

Here is another exercise like 11.7. Later on in Dirty Money's "Hello Good Morning" the following line appears:

> I just be like hello hello but I never could salute them.

Based on your understanding of the Ebonics verb system, explain why the line is not:

> I'm just like hello hello but I never could salute them.

Be sure you mention the meaning difference, not just whether or not traditional or alternative standards are being followed.

EXERCISE 11.10

At the January 2003 Golden Globes award, U2 band member Bono made the comment, "This is (expletive) brilliant!" His comment was broadcast on television during prime-time hours. The United States Federal Communications Commission, which is responsible for enforcing federal decency standards on the public airwaves, originally decided that an adjectival use of the expletive that Bono used was not indecent, and did not impose a penalty. A few months later, the FCC reversed itself and warned that future offenses of that kind would be penalized. Given that the airwaves belong to the public and therefore are supposed to be regulated in the public interest, do you think the FCC was right the first time, when it declined to impose a penalty, or the second time, when it said in essence that it should have? Give reasons for your answer.

EXERCISE 11.11

Suppose your college or university had the technology to remove blasphemy or cursing from students' email messages sent through the school's email system. Would you support using the technology? What if it were used only to remove language that disparaged minority groups, but allowed blasphemy or cursing? Would you support it then? Explain your position, whether or not it is the same in the two cases.

SUGGESTIONS FOR FURTHER READING

Fishman, Joshua A. 1972, *Language and nationalism*, Rowley, MA: Newbury House. Two essays by Joshua Fishman elaborating his basic concepts concerning language and politics.

Milroy, James and Milroy, Lesley 1998, *Authority in language: investigating standard English*, 3rd edition, London: Routledge. An authoritative study of standardization and "correctness" in English by highly respected scholars.

Ricento, Thomas (ed.) 2005, *An introduction to language policy theory and method*, Oxford and Malden, MA: Blackwell. A collection of studies by scholars working in the field of language and politics from contemporary perspectives.

Rickford, John Russell and Rickford, Russell John 2000, *Spoken Soul*, New York: John Wiley. An easy-to-read treatment of Ebonics, which the authors call Spoken Soul, by a father–son, linguist–journalist team. History, usage, and politics are covered, as well as linguistic structure.

Schmidt, Ronald, Jr. 2000, *Language policy and identity politics*, Philadelphia: Temple University Press. Coverage of the politics of language in the United States, with emphasis on issues of identity.

Spolsky, Bernard 2004, *Language policy*, Cambridge University Press. A detailed treatment of major topics in the politics of language with examples taken from around the world.

12 Writing

CHAPTER PREVIEW

As preceding chapters have shown, a fundamental characteristic of language is that it varies; different speech communities develop different languages, and different groups within those speech communities develop their own dialects. Speech communities also vary their use of their language to serve different purposes and different situations. People speak to friends differently than they speak to their bosses. People use different language in a church versus in a bar. Someone giving a report at work speaks differently than that same person telling a joke at a party. And when they write, people use language in different ways than when they speak. Different ways of using language to meet the communicative and social needs of different situations are called **registers**.

Writing is perhaps the clearest example of the adaptation of language to serve different purposes and situations, so we will examine the different writing systems of the world and how they developed. Describing the different kinds of writing systems with examples from three East Asian languages and Arabic, we'll show how each system is suited to its spoken language and its culture. Then we'll trace the history of writing from Egyptian **hieroglyphics** to the Latin **alphabet**, a story which demonstrates the two-way relationship between writing and the development of human culture. Finally, we'll take a look at the role that writing has played in more recent European history.

GOALS

The goals of this chapter are to:

- compare the functional strengths of speaking and writing
- describe how different writing systems developed to fit the structure of different languages and the communicative needs of different cultures
- sketch the development of writing from prehistoric protowriting to the Latin alphabet
- explain how technological advances have combined with the development of writing to facilitate cultural changes in Europe

Writing and speaking

Most of linguistics – and most of this book – focuses on spoken language, and with good reason. For several reasons, speech is more basic than writing. Spoken language existed tens of thousands of years before writing was invented (around 6,000 years ago). Every society has spoken language, but only some societies have writing systems; literacy is valuable to human societies, but not necessary. Speech is part of our human birthright: children learn to speak without trying but have to be taught to read and write. Writing is a social skill, not a biological attribute: every normally developed person in a society that uses writing learns to speak, but not all learn to read and write.

However, as we saw in Chapter 8, the tool of language is constantly being adapted to meet the changing needs of its users. One of the most important functional adaptations of language has been the development of writing. Many of the benefits of language to human beings have been amplified by the invention and development of writing.

- With spoken language, people can talk about their lives; with writing, they can record them in detail, analyze and fictionalize them, and share them with people they will never meet.
- With spoken language, people can communicate complex information to other people near them; with writing, they can communicate that information to others far away or yet to be born, who can then compare and combine it with information in other written documents.
- Speaking allows people to share experiences with those near them; writing (especially in its digitized forms) allows people to search huge stores of information, to experience (at least vicariously) the full range of the human condition.

Writing allows us to leap the barriers of space and time (and even mortality)! Writing has its costs and limitations, however:

- In most cases, people speaking to each other can rely on a shared context when they are producing their utterances and interpreting what other people are saying. Writers cannot rely on a shared context with their readers, so they have to construct the relevant context more explicitly in their text.
- People speaking to each other can use facial expressions, gestures, and eye gaze (and other paralinguistic cues) to express more than what they actually say. Writers must rely almost

exclusively on their language; they can't wink to show that they are being ironic, for example.

- Speakers usually have the immediate opportunity to check to see if they have understood each other. Writers must anticipate and try to avoid possible sources of misunderstanding. Readers typically can't ask the writer of a text what he/she meant and must "read between the lines" without confirmation that they have correctly inferred the writer's meaning.

- Once a text is written and published (shared formally or informally), it is fixed, and the written record can be referred to and analyzed; we may argue about what the text meant, but not about what the text actually said. It is much easier to deny saying something (or at least having said particular words, in a particular way) as well as an interpretation of an utterance.

But some of the costs of writing contain a silver lining. For example, Plato argued that writing would destroy memory, but writing preserves texts more reliably than a bard's memory. Writing extends access to texts to many more people, even across generations. Ironically, by preserving the past, writing also freed the human species from its tyranny. By freeing people from the time and effort required to memorize past texts, writing enabled them to look forward, develop new ideas, and create new texts.

The advantages and limitations of writing have had a profound effect on the speech communities that developed and came to rely on writing. As Florian Coulmas points out:

> It is not risky to call writing the single most consequential technology ever invented. The immensity of written record and the knowledge conserved in libraries, databanks, and multilayered information networks makes it difficult to imagine an aspect of modern life unaffected by writing ... Writing not only offers ways of reclaiming the past, but is a critical skill for shaping the future.
>
> (2003: 1)

So just what is writing? It turns out that defining writing is not easy, and definitions of writing raise a number of important questions. In *The Blackwell Encyclopedia of Writing Systems*, Florian Coulmas defines a writing system as:

> a set of visible or tactile signs used to represent units of language in a systematic way, with the purpose of recording messages which can be retrieved by everyone who knows the language in question and the rules by virtue of which its units are encoded in the writing system.
>
> (1989: 560)

Coulmas characterizes writing in terms of its mode of representation (visual or tactile), its relation to spoken language, and its purpose. Most writing systems use visible signs; nowadays these signs are printed on paper or pixillated on a computer screen, but in the past other materials – bones, wood, stone, and clay – were used. Braille, with its raised patterns of bumps for blind readers, is a tactile system. The central characteristic of a writing system is that it systematically "represents units of language"; it systematically encodes spoken (audible) language into a visible (or tactile) form. Crucially, this means that written symbols directly represent forms (sounds, syllables, and/or words) in a spoken language. Writing represents the world only indirectly, through the spoken language. The general purpose of writing – recording and retrieving messages – has been applied to a broad array of communicative situations, facilitating the development of complex societies and creating a virtual library (the internet) of enormous size.

Types of writing systems

Writing systems, or scripts, can be classified by which units of language are graphically represented. In logographic systems, each **grapheme**, or individual written symbol, represents a particular morpheme or word. In syllabic systems, each symbol represents a particular syllable. And in alphabetic systems, each letter represents a particular sound or phoneme. Of course, these categories are simplifications of a more complex reality! Logographic systems often have some phonetic elements which refer to sounds in the spoken language. Syllabic scripts frequently "cheat" by using **diacritics** to indicate consonant quality or vowel length. Alphabets sometimes treat vowels differently from consonants, and no alphabet has a perfect one-to-one correspondence between letter and phoneme. Most scripts do not neatly fit into one particular category, in part because they are evolving systems, adapted from and influenced by the scripts of surrounding speech communities.

In this section, we will exemplify four different writing systems, showing how each is formally suited to the spoken language it transcribes and how each functionally reflects the history of its culture. Later in this chapter we'll trace the development of writing leading to the Latin alphabet as used by most European languages today, so in this section we'll look at the scripts of three culturally related East Asian languages (Chinese, Japanese, and Korean) and then examine the consonantal alphabetic system of written Arabic. To give you a sense of what each orthography, or standardized version of a language's writing system, looks like, a sample text is presented in each script described below – the translation into each language of the first two sentences of Article 1 of the Universal Declaration of Human Rights:

> All human beings are born free and equal in dignity and rights. They are endowed with reason and conscience and should act towards one another in a spirit of brotherhood.

(This idea was borrowed from Coulmas (2003), using graphics, by permission, from www. omniglot.com.)

Logographic systems

In a logographic system, like Chinese, each written sign, called a logogram, represents a morpheme in the spoken language. Although signs can be combined to create signs with related or compound meanings, the number of logograms in a logographic system is typically very large. The most comprehensive dictionaries of Chinese list as many as 50,000 different logograms (called *hanzi*), but most represent words that are used rarely. To read a newspaper in Chinese, for example, one must know approximately 3,500 written characters, while reading specialized or technical texts requires recognition of perhaps another 3,000 *hanzi*. While this may seem like a lot of individual characters to memorize, the 1,000 most frequently used logograms account for around 90 percent of all writing in Chinese publications aimed at general readers. Users of alphabetic systems are often shocked at the need to memorize several thousand characters in the Chinese logographic system, but it is important to remember that alphabetic systems make their own demands on memory. For example, while the twenty-six letters of the English alphabet make it possible to "sound out" the *pronunciation* of an unknown word (although not always accurately), the *meaning* of the word must still be learned – and English dictionaries have as many as 500,000 entries!

Many monosyllabic words in Chinese are represented by a single symbol. For example, 'horse,' pronounced [mǎ] (with a rising tone) in Mandarin Chinese, is written 馬. However, most Chinese words (about 98 percent) are represented by characters that have two parts – a **phonetic determinative** and a **radical**. The phonetic determinative (often simply called the 'phonetic') gives a clue to the pronunciation of the character, while the radical gives clues to the meaning of the character. A symbol like 馬 can be used as a phonetic determinative – that is, combined with other words whose spoken form includes the syllable [ma]. For example, 馬 is in the following characters (and many more, as well):

罵 [mà] 'to swear'

嗎 [ma] '?' (a particle indicating that an utterance is a question)

螞 蟻 [mǎyǐ] 'ant'

媽 媽 [māma] 'mother'

In the character 媽 媽 [māma] 'mother,' for example, the 馬 symbol represents the syllable [ma], not the meaning 'horse.' It is combined with the radical (see below) 女, meaning 'woman.'

Because of sound changes in the spoken language and because of its many homophones, phonetic determinatives typically represent only part of the pronunciation of a syllable. Two characters containing the same phonetic determinative may have different tones or different syllable-initial or syllable-final sounds. (For example, 馬 [mǎ] 'horse,' is pronounced with a rising tone, 罵 [mà] 'to swear' is pronounced with a falling tone, and 嗎 [ma] '?' is pronounced with a level tone.) As a result, phonetic determinatives are only partially helpful in determining the meaning of a character and are almost always combined with a semantic component called a radical.

A radical is a symbol which is used in a variety of more complex characters to indicate aspects of those characters' meanings. Radicals were originally used to label semantic categories in dictionaries. The current set of 214 radicals has been in use since 1633 and its categories are of varying classificatory value and transparency. For example, there are radicals for 'human' and 'thing,' as well as 'earth,' 'fire,' and 'water,' but also for 'pig's head' and 'melon.' The character for 'horse' is used as a radical in the following characters:

馮 [píng] 'to gallop'

駕 [jià] 'to ride, drive, pilot'

駝 [túo] 'camel'

In 馮 [píng] 'to gallop,' the symbol for 'horse' is combined with a phonetic determinative 冫 [ping] suggesting a galloping sound. In 駕 [jià] 'to ride, drive, pilot,' it is combined with a phonetic determinative 加口, meaning 'yoke.'

In most characters, the semantic contribution of the radical is not so direct. For example, the character for 'horse' is also used as a radical in the following characters:

騙 [piàn] 'to cheat, deceive'

騷 [sāo] 'to disturb, worry'

驚 [jing] 'to startle, alarm'

While the meaning of 騷 [sāo] 'to disturb, worry' makes some sense if you know that the phonetic determinative 蚤攵 derives from the character for 'flea', the other phonetic determinatives have no such helpful associations.

You may have heard Chinese referred to as an "ideographic" writing system – in which symbols represent ideas. However, as these examples show, Chinese written characters also represent units of the spoken language, so Chinese writing is not purely ideographic. While neither phonetic determinatives nor radicals give unambiguous clues to the meaning of most characters, the combination of the two helps readers to narrow the range of possible interpretations. However, even highly educated native speakers of Chinese cannot predict what the written character for an unknown spoken word might look like. This can more easily be done with alphabetic writing systems. Chinese readers rely heavily on memorization of individual characters.

Because they represent morphemes and words, logographic writing systems are best suited to a language like Chinese which does not have lots of inflectional morphology. Recall that inflectional morphemes add grammatical information (tense, aspect, number, gender, and case) to a root morpheme – like the verb suffixes *-ed* and *-ing* and the plural marker *-s* in English, or suffixes to indicate gender on verbs in Italian. Imagine the complexity of Chinese characters if, in addition to phonetic determinatives and radicals, they also had one or more elements for various inflectional morphemes!

人人生而自由，在尊严和权利上一律平等。他们赋有理性和良心，并应以兄弟关系的精神互相对待。

Figure 12.1 Chinese sample text (simplified script): beginning of Article 1 of the Universal Declaration of Human Rights

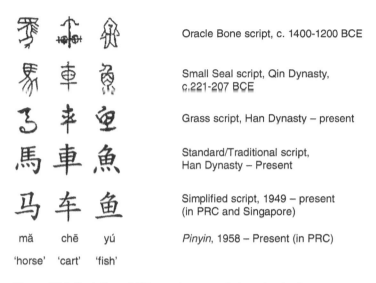

Oracle Bone script, c. 1400-1200 BCE

Small Seal script, Qin Dynasty,
c.221-207 BCE

Grass script, Han Dynasty – present

Standard/Traditional script,
Han Dynasty – Present

Simplified script, 1949 – present
(in PRC and Singapore)

Pinyin, 1958 – Present (in PRC)

mǎ   chē   yú

'horse'   'cart'   'fish'

Figure 12.2 Evolution of Chinese characters (selected scripts)

History of Chinese writing

Legend holds that the inventor of Chinese writing was Ts'ang Chieh, who recorded the history of the court of Emperor Huang Ti, the first emperor of China. According to the legend, Ts'ang Chieh was inspired by the lines and shapes in the footprints of birds and animals. True or not, the pictographic origins of Chinese characters can be seen in the evolution of the characters for 'horse,' 'cart,' and 'fish,' in Figure 12.2.

Early **pictograms**, which visually depicted their referents, became increasingly stylized by occasional script simplifications, which typically eliminated "unnecessary" brush strokes. The Chinese culture has a long tradition of reverence for writing, evident in the importance of calligraphy as an art form, and several earlier scripts have been preserved, in limited domains of use. For example, the Small Seal script is still used to write names on chops (ink stamps of one's name), business cards, and stationery. The Grass script is a cursive script (that is, each character is written with one continuous stroke) still used in calligraphy. In more recent times, the Standard script (which is referred to also as Traditional Chinese) is used in Taiwan, Hong Kong, Macau, and among many overseas Chinese communities. The Simplified script was adopted in the People's Republic of China in 1949 as part of a universal literacy effort. The use of pinyin, a spelling system which uses the Latin alphabet, in such domains as tourism (for example, street signs), reflects China's increasing interdependence with the western world.

Although many early writing systems (like Mesopotamian cuneiform and Egyptian hieroglyphics) were initially logographic, the Chinese script is the only logographic system to survive to modern times. Chinese logographic writing has survived in large part because it is a good marriage of form and function. For thousands of years, Chinese emperors ruled over huge territories in which many different languages were spoken. Development of a logographic writing system meant that even if members of two different speech communities pronounced a word (say, for 'horse') differently, they could *read* the same

> ### BOX 12.1 **THE NUSHU SCRIPT: FOR WOMEN ONLY**
>
> Nushu (Chinese for 'women's writing') is a syllabic script that was created and used exclusively by women in the Jiang Yong Prefecture of Hunan Province, China, for at least 400 years. Denied formal education, the women of Jiang Yong developed the Nushu script in order to communicate with one another in a male-dominated world. They embroidered the script into cloth and wrote it in books and on paper fans. Mothers taught the Nushu script to their daughters (often by singing and transcribing songs), and men were excluded from the code.
>
> Girls of the Jiang Yong area observed a custom of *jiebai zimei*, or 'sworn sisterhood' – strong bonds with female friends who were not blood relatives. Marriage typically meant leaving their sworn sisters and moving to an unfamiliar village to serve a husband and mother-in-law, often under difficult conditions. The separation of sworn sisters appears to have motivated the creation and development of the Nushu script. Cloth-bound booklets given by women to their sworn sisters when they were married contained songs wishing happiness in marriage and expressing sorrow at being separated. They were called *San Chao Shu*, or 'Third Day Missives,' because they were delivered on the third day after the recipient's marriage. Nushu was also used to write letters to a woman's sworn sisters about abusive marriages, the isolation of arranged marriages, and the liberation of widowhood.
>
> Nushu manuscripts are extremely rare because by custom they were burned or buried with their owners.
>
> (You can learn more about Nushu at the "World of Nushu" website (www2.ttcn.ne.jp/~orie/home. htm), constructed by Orie Endo, a sociolinguistics professor at Bunkyo University, Japan.)

word symbol. Written Chinese had a unifying effect as the lingua franca of government, the arts, and the sciences.

Syllabic systems

In a syllabic writing system, each written symbol represents a syllable of the spoken language. "Pure" syllabic systems are rare, however; most use additional diacritics, or additional markings on the basic written symbols, to indicate phonetic information like vowel length and voicing, or gemination (doubling) of consonants.

The Japanese writing system is actually a hybrid of Chinese logograms and two different syllabic systems – a compromise between Japan's historical ties to Chinese culture and the demands of its language. The first writing in Japan came from China during the fourth century CE and consisted of Chinese characters (called *kanji* in Japanese). However, Japanese is a highly inflected language (from a different language family than Chinese), so some Chinese characters were used to represent Japanese inflectional affixes, which are mostly monosyllables. Over time the former *kanji* logograms which had come to represent Japanese syllables were regularized into two syllabic scripts: *hiragana* and *katakana*. *Hiragana* are used to write native Japanese words, while *katakana* are used to write non-Chinese loan words.

Japanese has a very simple syllable structure. Most syllables are open, consisting of a consonant (C) followed by a vowel (V). Just as languages (like Chinese) with little inflection are well suited to logographic systems, languages with simple syllables (and a limited

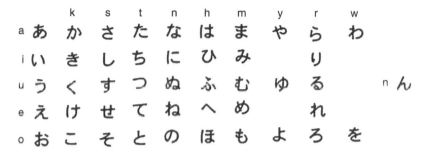

Figure 12.3 *Hiragana*

syllable inventory) are formally well suited to syllabic scripts. This is particularly evident with *hiragana*, in which most syllabic graphemes, called *kana*, can be represented in a two-dimensional table, like Figure 12.3.

Japanese has a basic inventory of fifteen sounds (nine consonants and five vowels, plus a nasal). Combinations of nearly all of the consonants and vowels are represented by a unique *kana*, so [ka] = か, [sa] = さ, [ki] = き, and so on. The vowels and the syllable-final nasal have their own *kana*. (*Hiragana* and *katakana* also use diacritics, marks placed over syllabic *kana* symbols, to indicate changes in consonant quality and vowel length.)

All Japanese words can be written syllabically, using *hiragana*, but most Japanese texts use approximately 1,000 Chinese characters (*kanji*) to represent root morphemes and *hiragana* to add affixes, as shown in (1).

(1)　犬に当る男の子は私の兄弟である。

inuobuttaotokonokowaotootoda

inuo	butta	otokonokowa	otootoda
dog+OBJ	hit+PAST	boy+SUBJ	younger-brother+be-PRES

'The boy who hit the dog is my brother.'

Hiragana are sometimes used exclusively to make some texts more accessible – for example, children's books, textbooks, animation, video games, and comic books.

Japanese also has a separate **syllabary**, called *katakana*, used to write non-Chinese loan words.

Figure 12.4 *Katakana*

すべての人間は、生まれながらにして自由であり、かつ、尊厳と権利とについて平等である。人間は、理性と良心を授けれてあり、互いに同胞の精神をもって行動しなければならない。

Figure 12.5 Japanese sample text: beginning of Article 1 of the Universal Declaration of Human Rights

The aggregation of Japanese scripts reflects Japanese history and culture. Strong early influences of Chinese philosophy and religion are reflected in the use of *kanji*, which is adapted to Japanese grammar with *hiragana* affixes. Japan's cultural homogeneity and long history of isolation from the western world is reflected in the use of *katakana*, to graphically and symbolically mark foreign loan words. In recent years, the Latin alphabet (called *romaji*) has been used for many borrowed English words, marking these words (and the things or concepts they refer to) as particularly non-Japanese. For example, in Japanese advertisements *sexy* and *my house* often appear in *romaji*, making the underlying concepts of eroticism and private ownership more exotic. In the same ad, more assimilated foreign words/concepts might be represented in *katakana* while traditional values are represented by a *kanji* character (with *hiragana* affixes)! Having several scripts might seem confusing to an outsider, but it is actually quite functional in signaling Japanese cultural values and boundaries.

Japanese scripts also bear traces of the culture's history of gender relations. *Hiragana* originally were used by women (who were not allowed to learn *kanji*) and scorned by literate men (who wrote in *kanji* and *katakana*). However, beginning with *The Tale of Genji*, written by a noblewoman during the Heian era (795–1192 CE), much Japanese literature was written in *hiragana*, and it became a widely used script. Even today, *hiragana* are sometimes used to write words which would normally be written with *katakana* to make them appear more "feminine," particularly in comic books and cartoons for young girls.

Hiragana and *katakana* are particularly simple syllabaries. The syllabic script of the Vai people of Liberia has 280 symbols, and the Ethiopic syllabary, used to write Amharic, has 251 symbols. Perhaps the largest syllabic script in current use is used by the speakers of Yi, a Tibeto-Burman language. The Yi script contains 756 syllabic symbols (and 63 more graphemes for Chinese loan words). To complicate matters, many characters have separate forms to represent the three different tones of spoken Yi.

English spelling

The spelling of many English words does not consistently correspond to their pronunciation, in part because English spelling was established before the Great Vowel Shift (see Chapter 8) changed the pronunciation of many English words. In fact, English spelling diverges from the phonemic principle in just about every way possible:

- *A language may represent a given phoneme with a combination of letters (digraphs): e.g. ship, chin*
- *A language may represent one phoneme with different letters or combinations of letters: e.g. home, boat, though*
- *A language may represent different phonemes with the same letter or combination of letters: e.g. read (present tense), read (past tense)*

- *A language may retain unpronounced letters from earlier pronunciations: e.g. "silent e" (*home, ripe, tame*) and "silent k" (*knight, kneel*).*
- *Different dialects of a language may pronounce different phonemes for the same word: e.g. the different pronunciations of* neither *and* either.

Alphabetic systems

In an alphabet, the written symbols represent the phonemes – both consonants and vowels – of the spoken language. (In the next section we will discuss consonantal alphabets, like Arabic and Hebrew, in which only consonants are represented by letters.) The smallest known alphabets are those for Mura-Piraha, spoken in the Amazon region of Brazil (10 letters) and for Rotokas, spoken in New Guinea (11 letters). Not surprisingly, these two languages also have the smallest inventories of phonemes of the world's languages. Armenian has the largest currently used alphabet, with 38 letters.

Alphabetic systems are organized, more or less, according to the **phonemic principle** of a one-to-one relationship between letter and phoneme. In an alphabet which followed the phonemic principle perfectly, the phonemes of the spoken language and letters of the alphabet would correspond perfectly in both directions: a writer could accurately spell every word from its pronunciation, and a speaker could pronounce every word from its spelling. Most languages fall short of phonemic accuracy, for several reasons. In many cases, languages adapted alphabets from another language. Also, the spoken form of a language tends to change more rapidly than its writing system (although alphabetic writing systems do tend to slow down sound change in their languages). Spanish comes close to a one-to-one correspondence between phonemes and letters. It is possible to pronounce words accurately from their spellings, but some phonemes are represented by more than one letter, so it is not possible to predict the spelling of every word from its pronunciation.

Because readers of this textbook are very familiar with the English alphabet, we will take a closer look at Hangul, the Korean alphabet. Northern Korea was occupied by China from 108 BCE to 313 CE, and Koreans wrote in Chinese from the fifth century CE forward. Korean, like Japanese, has a variety of verbal inflections and various adaptations of Chinese characters were devised to represent them until the middle of the 1400s when King Sejong commissioned a new writing system, which was called Hangul (literally, 'Korean letters'). Since 1949, most Korean literature and nontechnical publications have used Hangul, but in South Korean academic papers and official documents Korean words of Chinese origin are still sometimes written in Chinese characters.

ㄱ	ㄲ	ㄴ	ㄷ	ㄸ	ㄹ	ㅁ	ㅂ	ㅃ
k, g	kk	n	t, d	tt	l, ɭ	m	p, b	pp

ㅅ	ㅆ	ㅇ	ㅈ	ㅉ	ㅊ	ㅋ	ㅌ	ㅍ	ㅎ
s	ss	ŋ	ç, ɟ	çç	ç'	k'	t'	p'	h

Figure 12.6 Hangul consonants

Hangul is highly systematic in its representation of Korean phonemes. There are 24 letters: 14 consonants and 10 vowels. The letters representing the consonants show that the team of scholars who devised the alphabet in 1444 were very familiar with phonetics; the shapes of some consonants, like /k/ ㄱ, /n/ ㄴ, /s/ ㅅ, /m/ ㅁ and /ŋ/ ㅇ, represent the shapes of the vocal tract in making those sounds. Other consonants were created by adding lines to the basic shapes, representing their phonetic relationship; for example, consider the relation between /n/ ㄴ, /t/ ㄷ, and /ɹ/ ㄹ, or between /m/ ㅁ, and /p/ ㅂ.

The doubled signs indicate that the consonants are glottalized (that is, the throat is tensed, as in the negative grunt *unh-unh*). In addition, Hangul adds a diacritic apostrophe to some consonants to indicate that they are aspirated.

The letters for Korean consonants demonstrate application of the phonemic principle very clearly. In Korean, some consonantal phonemes are pronounced differently depending on where they appear in a word. For example, the phoneme /k/ has two allophones: unvoiced [k] and voiced [g]. Similarly, the phoneme /ɹ/ has two allophones: [ɹ] and [l]. It would be inefficient for an alphabet to represent all the allophones of a language; an alphabet attempting to create a one-to-one relationship between *sounds* and letters would require many more letters than an alphabet representing only *phonemes*. It would also be unnecessary; just as speakers of Korean automatically "translate" an allophone (for example, [g]) into its underlying phoneme (/k/), so too Korean readers know that the velar stops [k] and [g] are represented by the single letter ㄱ and that the liquids [ɹ] and [l] are represented by the single letter ㄹ.

The letters for Korean vowels were based on three elements: man (a vertical line), earth (a horizontal line), and heaven (originally a dot which evolved into a short line). Like the letters for consonants, the letters for related vowels and dipthongs are similar; for example, consider the letters representing [a], [æ], [ja], and [jæ].

Unlike alphabets derived from the Greek alphabet, the Korean alphabet iconically reflects the categorical difference between consonants and vowels. The vowel letters are constructed from a different set of strokes and shapes than the consonant letters. This makes alternating consonant and vowel symbols more visually discernible, as does the way the letters are arranged into words.

When writing words in Hangul, letters are grouped by syllables into blocks. Notice that the letters for some Hangul vowels, such as /o/, /u/, /ɨ/, are laid out horizontally, while others, such as /i/, /a/, /e/, are made of one or more vertical lines. Most Korean syllables consist of a consonant followed by a vowel (CV) or a consonant-vowel-consonant (CVC).

Figure 12.7 Hangul vowels and diphthongs

모든 인간은 태어날 때부 터 자유로우며 그 존엄과 권리에 있어 동등하다. 인간은 천부 적 으로 이성과 양심을 부여받았으며 서로 형제애의 정신으로 행동하여야한다.

Figure 12.8 Korean sample text: beginning of Article 1 of the Universal Declaration of Human Rights

In syllables with a "vertical" vowel, the first consonant and the vowel are placed side by side, as in (2a) below. If there is a consonant following the vowel, it is placed below the first two letters, as in (2b). In syllables with a "horizontal" vowel, the first consonant is placed above the vowel, as in (2c), and any following consonant is placed below the vowel, as in (2d).

(2)   Hangul syllable writing

사   간   모   존

sa   kan   mo   çon

(a)   (b)   (c)   (d)

Spaces are placed between words, which can be written in vertical columns running from top to bottom and right to left, or in horizontal lines running from left to right.

Hangul combines the strengths of an alphabet and a syllabary. The relatively small inventory of graphic symbols, with systematically related shapes and strong phonemic transparency, is easy to learn, while the grouping of those letters into syllable blocks provides a structural segmentation (not found in strictly linear alphabets) which makes reading easier.

Consonantal alphabetic systems

In some writing systems (like the Arabic and Hebrew scripts), only consonants are represented by letters; vowels are indicated by changes to or diacritics on the consonants. These consonantal alphabets are sometimes called **abjads**. (Just as alphabets are named for the first two letters of the Greek alphabet (*alpha* and *beta*), abjads are named for four letters in the Arabic consonantal alphabet which correspond to A, B, J, and D.)

The Arabic alphabet consists of twenty-eight basic letters representing Arabic consonants and long vowels. The three long vowels /a:/, /i:/, and /u:/ are written in words, but the short vowels are usually omitted; they are normally only indicated – using diacritic lines and points above and below other letters – in the Qur'an and other classical texts, and occasionally in texts for children or foreigners. Arabic is written right to left, and most letters are connected cursively to any preceding or following letters within a word. Because of these cursive connections, the shape of each letter varies slightly when connected to a preceding or following letter, as shown in Figure 12.9.

A consonantal alphabet is well suited to representing spoken Arabic because of its "root-and-template" morphology. Recall from Chapter 2 that lexical roots in Arabic are bound morphemes consisting of only consonants, which must be completed with vowels to

IPA	Roman	Name	Final	Medial	Initial	Isolated
[k]	k	kāf̌	كاف	ـك	ـكـ	كـ	ك
[t]	t	tā'	تاء	ـت	ـتـ	تـ	ت
[b]	b	bā'	باء	ـب	ـبـ	بـ	ب

Figure 12.9 Letters for selected Arabic consonants

يولد جميع الناس أحرارًا متساوين في الكرامة والحقوق. وقد وهبوا
عقلاً وضميرًا وعليهم ان يعامل بعضهم بعضا بروح الإخاء.

Figure 12.10 Arabic sample text: beginning of Article 1 of the Universal Declaration of Human Rights

derive a word. For example, the root *ktb* in Arabic has the general meaning 'write' but the sequence of sounds *ktb* must be filled in with specific vowels in specific patterns in order to derive different words. All three words in (3) below would be written with the same consonantal letters: ك ت ب ([k], [t], and [b], respectively, in their isolated forms). Example (3) shows them written from right to left and cursively connected. Figure 12.10 shows a longer sample of written Arabic.

(3)   *Arabic*

[kataba]	'wrote'	كتب
[kitaab]	'book'	كتاب
[kaatib]	'clerk'	كاتب

Mny rdrs f nglsh thnk tht rdng cnsnntl lphbt wld b dffclt, bt s ths sntnc shws, mny nglsh wrds cn b rd wtht thr vwls. This is in part because proficient readers (of any script) read "whole words"; they don't sound out each letter. Everyday texts in Arabic rarely use diacritics to mark short vowels. Arabic readers read the consonant template, associate it with a particular semantic set (for example, writing) and then use the surrounding context to figure out any further meaning that might be necessary.

There are over thirty different colloquial dialects of Arabic throughout the Middle East and North Africa. Some dialects (for example, Palestinian Arabic and Levantine Arabic, spoken in Lebanon and Syria) are mutually intelligible, but other, more geographically distant dialects (like Magrebi, spoken in Morocco, and Najdi, spoken in Saudi Arabia, Iraq, Jordan, and Syria) are not. As described in Chapter 11, Arabic has developed a system of diglossia, in which speakers of many local "low" dialects share one "high" dialect – and one writing system. A consonantal alphabet, like the logographic script of Chinese, is well suited to the challenge of spanning varying pronunciations across many local dialects. As we saw in Chapters 8 and 9, vowels are particularly susceptible to change over time, and therefore many dialectal differences in the pronunciation of words are vowel differences.

The Arabic writing system is closely related to the spread of Islam. Around the fourth century CE, the Arabic script evolved from the Aramaic script, from which the Phoenician and Greek (and eventually Latin) alphabets also developed. In the seventh century CE, the Qur'an was written in the Arabic script, and the religion and the writing system together have served as a unifying cultural force in the Middle East and North Africa ever since. As Islamic armies in the Middle Ages conquered North Africa and modern-day Spain and moved east toward Asia, the Arabic script was adapted to many indigenous languages. Languages from Africa (e.g. Berber, Somali, and Swahili) to the Middle East (e.g. Farsi) and Asia (e.g. Urdu, Pashto, and Malay) developed scripts based on the Arabic script.

All writing systems tend to be conservative; once the conventions for representing a spoken language have been accepted widely throughout a speech community, it takes a lot of effort to change even the spelling of particular words. Broader changes and innovations usually take place when one language adapts the writing system of another language. The Arabic script – with its strong connection to the Qur'an, a sacred text – has changed very little over the centuries, while the spoken dialects have developed dramatically and diversified to meet the changing needs of their speakers. The diglossia of the Arabic speech community, then, is in part due to the conservatism of its writing system.

Spelling and reading

Consider the following email exchange:

Forwarded message: Aoccdrnig to a rschreearch at Cmabrigde Uinervtisy, it deosn't mttaer in waht oredr the ltteers in a wrod are, the olny iprmoetnt tihng is taht the frist and lsat ltteer be at the rghit pclae. The rset can be a total mses and you can sitll raed it wouthit porbelm.

Tihs is bcuseae the huamn mnid deos not raed ervey lteter by istlef, but the wrod as a wlohe.

Amzanig huh?
Response: I've hraed that this is a web mtyh, but yroue rhigt, it wrkos! I'll hvae to tnhik auobt tihs. Smees taht it's llragey a mtaetr of rudceed cbtmroiananl pssbltoiieis. Ntoe how it only mtatres in wrdos of fuor lttrees or mroe, and rllaey dsnoet mkae mcuh dffrnciee ulnses the wrod is lngeor than fvie lterets (like 'cbtmroianail pssbltoiieis'!). I'm plnyaig wtih lndaoig all the mddlie cnsntoaos in the frnot of the wrod veusrs puitntg the veowls fisrt; wichh do you tinhk is more diuifflct to uaednrtsnd?

Writing culture

A script can reflect the culture of its speech community in many ways. In medieval times, Islamic law prohibited the representation of humans or animals in art. As a result, Muslim artists often resorted to "arabesque" designs (based on geometrical forms or patterns of leaves and flowers) or to calligraphy (which literally means 'beautiful writing') for decoration. For example, basmalahs *are phrases from the Qur'an. Those below present the opening words of the Qur'an: "In the name of Allah, the Merciful, the Compassionate." Large* basmalahs *are often hung in mosques or other public places.*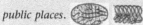

BOX 12.2 **THE POLITICS OF WRITING**

Chapter 11 discussed how one's language is an important part of one's national and ethnic identity. Writing systems are also symbols of identity, and therefore are contested territory. The history of the Arabic scripts provides examples of the politics of writing from four continents:

- In the Middle Ages, indigenous languages spoken from Spain to India adopted the Arabic script, facilitating the spread of Islam.
- While Spain was occupied by the Moors in the Middle Ages, an Arabic script, called Aljamiado, was developed for writing Spanish. The Moriscos, former Muslims who had been forcibly converted to Christianity in 1492, continued to secretly use the Arabic script (even though they had forgotten Arabic) until their expulsion from Spain in 1609.
- Turkey abolished the Arabic script in 1928, replacing it with a modified Latin alphabet, as part of Turkish leader Ataturk's campaigns to spread literacy and westernize the country.
- For hundreds of years, Indian languages like Kashmiri, Punjabi, and Sindhi were written in scripts adapted from the Arabic script. Since India's independence in 1947, the Arabic script has been largely replaced by the (Indian) Devanagari alphabet.
- Hausa, the lingua franca spoken by over 50 million West Africans, was written for centuries in Ajami – a script adapted from the Arabic alphabet. In the early twentieth century, Christian missionary schools and European colonial administration succeeded in "re-scripting" Hausa into a Latin alphabet, although some Islamic texts are still written in Ajami.

The development of writing

The historical development of writing systems is a process of discovering and elaborating the capacities of graphic symbols to represent the spoken language, combined with the invention and refinement of physical media for producing, storing, and (eventually) reproducing writing. In the following section, we will see how these three elements – linguistic, material, and social – came together to produce a dramatic spiral of cultural development. This is the story of what became the "Latin" alphabet used today by many European languages. It is important to remember that other scripts around the world have their own histories – weaving together their own linguistic and cultural contexts.

Protowriting

In many ancient societies, myths often attributed the invention of writing to the gods and recognized the dependence of many social institutions on writing. In ancient Egypt, the god Thoth was given credit for inventing writing. Thoth was the scribe and historian of the gods, responsible for keeping the calendar and (not coincidentally) for inventing art and science. The power of writing to preserve information was seen as a supernatural tool. Thoth could transform speech into material objects, and ancient Egyptians believed that to become immortal a person's name must be written somewhere forever. They called their hieroglyphic script "god's words." Writing was frequently represented as a way of communicating with the gods, and written texts often were believed to express divine truth.

In ancient China, for example, inscribed oracle bones used for divination served as a medium for communication between heaven and earth. Many contemporary religions claim divine provenance for their written texts, as well.

Archaeological finds from 100,000 years ago show that our early ancestors used graphic symbols and mnemonic (memory) tools to store information. Graphic symbols (for example, of human figures, flowers, animals, and the sun) were used to represent various kinds of human experience. At least 30,000 years ago, human beings were painting pictures, called **petroglyphs**, on cave walls. These cave paintings are pictograms – literal representations of objects in the world. A pictogram makes a direct connection between the symbol and its referent; it doesn't refer to the spoken word for the referent. This is sometimes called **primary symbolization**. Interpreting a pictogram does not require the viewer to "go through" the spoken language. For example, the simple line drawing in (4) represents a fish, but it doesn't require you to use the word *fish* to know what it means.

(4)

A pictogram also does not give you any clues to what the word for the referred-to object might be, or how it is pronounced; (4) could just as easily be called a *fish, poisson,* or *pesce*.

The creators of petroglyphs also referred to the animals in their paintings with words. These cave paintings were the first step toward writing – a visual link between a word and the thing it refers to.

Early protowriting systems used pictograms to *directly* represent objects (and ideas). A surviving pictographic writing system is used by the Naxi, a Tibeto-Burman-speaking people in China's Yunnan province. The Naxi have a pictographic writing system which helps the Dongba (shamans) recite ritual texts during religious ceremonies. Ninety percent of the 1,400 symbols in the Naxi Dongba script are pictograms, which directly represent objects in the world, rather than words or other forms in the Naxi language. For this reason, you can probably get a general idea of some of the legend related in Figure 12.11.

Figure 12.11 Example of Naxi script. (Lo, Lawrence. 2012, March 29. Naxi. Ancient Scripts.com. Retrieved April 3, 2014 from http://www.ancientscripts.com/naxi.html.)

However, while you might guess that  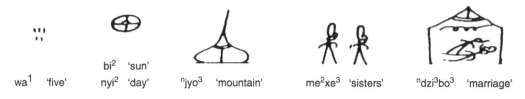 and  are both mammals of some kind, you probably wouldn't know that the former is an otter and the latter is a tiger, and your comprehension of the story would suffer. Likewise,  allows for quite a range of interpretations. (See Exercises 12.1–2 for further tests of the universality and ambiguity of pictograms.)

> *The US Nuclear Regulatory Commission is responsible for storing dangerous nuclear waste with a radioactive half-life of 10,000 years. In the 1980s, it commissioned research to devise a universal warning that would be interpretable by anyone, even after 10,000 years. A report, written in part by linguist Thomas Sebeok, concluded that there was no message, code, and channel of communication that could be guaranteed to bridge ten millennia of language and culture change. You can read his reasons in Chapter 13 of his book* I Think I am a Verb: More Contributions to the Doctrine of Signs *(1986).*

Even pictograms for more abstract notions represent things in the real world, as shown in Figure 12.12. (The numbers refer to tones in the spoken language.)

Because this large inventory of graphic signs must be memorized, it can take over fifteen years to become proficient in the Naxi Dongba script.

A small percentage of Naxi signs do represent the spoken language. These are rebuses, where a symbol for one concept also represents another concept because the two words sound alike. For example, the words for 'food' and 'sleep' are both pronounced xa^3, so the symbol for 'food' (which looks like a pot) is also used for 'sleep.'

wa^1 'five' bi^2 'sun' nyi^2 'day' $^n jyo^3$ 'mountain' $me^2 xe^3$ 'sisters' $^n dzi^3 bo^3$ 'marriage'

Figure 12.12 Naxi pictograms (superscripted numbers refer to pronunciation)

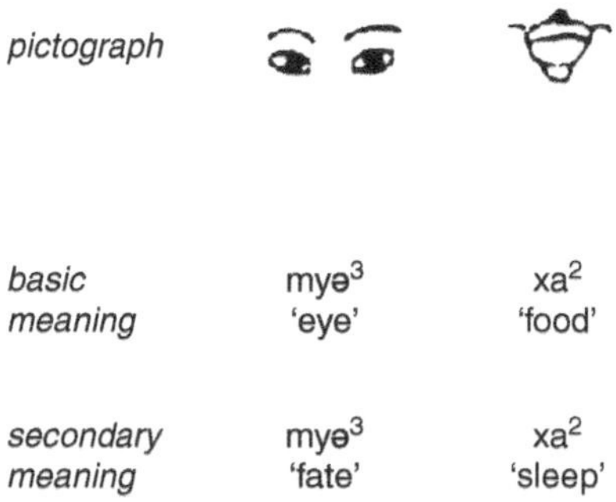

pictograph		
basic meaning	mye^3 'eye'	xa^2 'food'
secondary meaning	mye^3 'fate'	xa^2 'sleep'

Figure 12.13 Naxi rebuses

The words and written symbols for 'food' and 'sleep' are linked only by their common pronunciation – and a pot does not represent sleep pictorially – so knowledge of spoken Naxi (specifically, that 'food' and 'sleep' share the same spoken form) is required to understand the meaning of 'sleep.' The link between [symbol] and 'food' could be guessed at without knowing any Naxi. But the link between [symbol] and 'sleep' is necessarily mediated through the language. This is sometimes called **secondary symbolization**, and is the distinguishing characteristic of a writing system; the written forms directly represent some units of the language (phonemes, syllables, or words), and *only through those linguistic units* do the written forms refer to objects and concepts in the world.

Beer and literature

Writing serves and reflects the needs of its users. Early agrarian societies were organized around the cultivation, storage, and exchange of grain. Beer is fermented grain. It is no surprise, then, that some of the oldest written Sumerian inscriptions record the daily beer ration allotted to each citizen. The world's oldest literature has been found on Sumerian tablets as well, including the five-poem Gilgamesh cycle.

Cuneiform

Writing seems to have been invented independently in several places (including China, Mexico, and possibly Egypt), but the best-documented case of the invention of writing is in Mesopotamia (modern-day Iraq). The development of writing began as human beings evolved from hunter–gatherer tribes to more permanent agrarian societies. The greater stability of agricultural life led to greater social and economic complexity. People exchanging grain, livestock, and land needed to record their transactions, and rulers and priests needed to record taxes, for which they began to use incised clay "counting tokens," as early as 8000 BCE. Clay was a great improvement over cave walls for transactional communication. It was easy to inscribe, easy to erase, easy to preserve (by baking), and portable. The counters were not quite pictograms, since they typically held only a few stylized lines, but they were not yet a writing system.

The transition to secondary symbolization probably took place around 3500 BCE, perhaps inspired by a very mundane need of its users. Carrying large numbers of individual tokens around could be cumbersome, so Sumerians started carrying them in small clay envelopes, called *bullæ*. Eventually, the *bullæ* themselves were inscribed with the number and kind of tokens enclosed (Schmandt-Besserat 1992). The *bullæ* inscriptions were *symbols of symbols*. Around the same time, the Sumerians began to record the same information (number and kind of commodity) on clay tablets, using a reed stylus to make wedge-shaped marks.

The Sumerians now were ready for the next step toward a full-fledged writing system. When Sumerians used tokens for flour in transactions, for example, they might say the Sumerian word for 'flour' [zid]. Over time, the symbol would have become loosely associated with the sound of the word. As clay inscriptions were used in more and more contexts, more and more symbols had to be devised for more referents. But the medium of clay and stylus limited the number of different kinds of symbols one can invent (especially for abstract concepts), and memory limited how many of these could be remembered. At some point, a Sumerian scribe discovered a shortcut – the **rebus**. When the graphic symbol for one word was firmly associated with the sounds of that word, it could then be used to represent another word with the same pronunciation (its homophone). For example, the Sumerian word [im] is a homophone meaning both 'clay' and 'wind'; both words were represented by the grapheme . Ambiguity – which of the two homophones the grapheme represented in a particular instance of use – could usually be resolved from the context of use.

The use of rebuses makes a script more efficient (representing more words with fewer graphemes). But a writing system really develops when the secondary symbolization of the rebus – the grapheme directly representing a sound or sequence of sounds and then the referents of those sounds – is applied systematically to all sounds. In Sumerian, the first rebuses were probably single-syllable words. Having made the grapheme–syllable connection, scribes looking for shortcuts then discovered that they could combine graphemes (each representing a single syllable) to represent words made of combinations of those syllables:

[ka] 'gate'   + [ba] 'to distribute, give as a gift'   = [ka ba] 'to talk'

[ka] 'gate'   + [bad] 'to open'   = [ka bad] 'to open the mouth'

[zid] 'flour'   + [baba]   = [zidbaba] 'porridge'

(Sumerian cuneiform symbols from *Pennsylvania Sumerian Dictionary*: http://psd.museum. upenn.edu/epsd/)

Sumerian cuneiform was a mostly syllabic writing system (with some nonphonetic graphemes probably derived from pictograms), but once the link between visual symbol and sound symbol had been established, it was just a matter of time before someone invented the alphabet. The link between grapheme and sound also freed the graphemes from having to somehow visually represent their referents, and they became more abstract, stylized, and arbitrary. For example, early cuneiform was written in columns from top to bottom, but during the third millennium BCE the signs were rotated 90 degrees and written from left to right.

By 2500 BCE schools were established to train sons of the Sumerian upper classes to be scribes for religious and government bureaucracies and to record legal and business transactions. Libraries were established to store records, allowing laws and business contracts to be referred to as precedent. Spoken Sumerian died out around 1800 BCE, but with centuries of history, law, business, and religion recorded in the Sumerian script, it continued to be used as a "learned" written language (much like Latin was during the Middle Ages in Europe) for more than a thousand years.

The word "cuneiform" derives from Latin *cuneus*, meaning 'wedge,' so any script made of wedge-shaped signs can be called cuneiform. Cuneiform was adapted by a number of speech communities in the Middle East and Asia Minor, including the Akkadians (who spoke a Semitic language) around 2350 BCE, and the Hittites (who spoke an Indo-European language) around 1800 BCE. The leap to systematic phoneticization made cuneiform highly adaptable to other languages. Where another language had syllables similar to Sumerian, it could adopt Sumerian graphemes; where it had different syllables, it could invent new graphemes.

> **Translators needed**
>
> *Fired clay tablets are virtually indestructible. Only a fraction of the thousands of tablets that have been found have been translated. In 1975, 15,000 tablets were discovered in Syria, the remains of a library that burned in 2300 BCE, and it is estimated that many thousands more remain to be discovered.*

Egyptian hieroglyphs

The word "hieroglyph" comes from the Greek *hieros* 'sacred' plus *glypho* 'inscriptions.' The earliest known examples of writing in Egypt date to 3300 BCE. (Because of the similar dates of the earliest records of Egyptian hieroglyphs and Sumerian cuneiform, scholars disagree on whether the two scripts were invented independently or not.) Like early Sumerian cuneiform, early Egyptian writing was apparently motivated by economics. The earliest archaeological finds record deliveries of linen and oil paid as taxes.

Like cuneiform signs, hieroglyphs started out as pictograms, but they evolved into a complex script combining **logograms** (representing morphemes), **phonograms** (representing one, two, or three consonants), and **determinatives** (semantic classifiers). Many logograms reflected their pictographic origins. For example, the glyph for 'house' is ⌐ ⌐

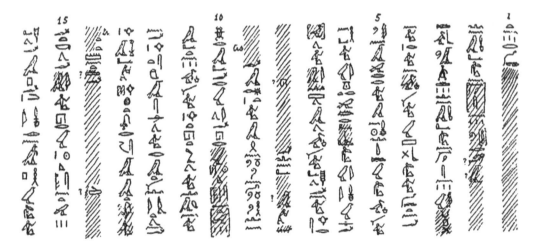

Figure 12.14 Excerpt from transcription of Berlin Papyrus no. 3024 (R.O. Faulkner, "The man who was tired of life," *Journal for Egyptian Archeology*, 42 (1956): 22–26)

and the glyph for 'sun' is ☉. From such pictographic symbols, Egyptian scribes derived the world's first alphabet by the principle of **acrophony**, in which a hieroglyph for a word came to represent the first consonant of that word. So, for example, the Egyptian word for 'owl' began with an [m] sound, so the glyph for 'owl' 🦉 became the letter *m*. Similarly, the word for 'foot' began with a [b] sound, so the glyph 𓃀 became the letter *b*. There were 26 uniconsonantal glyphs and numerous bi- and triconsonantal glyphs. Vowels were not represented. With the 26 uniconsonantal glyphs it was possible to write every Egyptian word, but this was only done in graffiti. Determinatives are glyphs that were added at the end of a word to clarify its meaning. Determinatives were necessary because, as with the Arabic consonantal alphabet, several different words may be spelled with the same sequence of consonants.

Hieroglyphic script was written in horizontal lines running either from left to right or from right to left, or in vertical columns running from top to bottom. The direction of any piece of hieroglyphic writing is easy to figure out; the animals and people always face the beginning of the line.

There were three different versions of the Egyptian script used over the course of four thousand years – hieroglyphic, hieratic, and demotic – but though they differed in appearance, they were the same writing system. Hieroglyphic (3300 BCE – 400 CE) was used mainly for formal inscriptions on stone monuments. Hieratic (3100–650 BCE) was a cursive form of hieroglyphic writing for everyday use – government, business, and religious documents – written in ink on papyrus. The demotic script (650 BCE – 450 CE) replaced hieratic for everyday use, although hieratic continued to be used for religious writing. In the late fourth century CE, the Roman emperor Theodesius I ordered all pagan temples throughout the Roman empire to be closed, and knowledge of the hieroglyphic script was buried for fourteen hundred years.

Early alphabets

Long before it fell into disuse, the Egyptian hieroglyphic script had launched a new writing system, the ancestor of the Latin alphabet. The evolution from hieroglyphics to the Latin alphabet would be carried by several successive dominating cultures: the Phoenicians, the Greeks, and the Romans.

Around 2000 BCE, Canaanite scribes working for the Egyptians realized that the Egyptian consonantal alphabet could be adapted to represent the thirty consonants of their own language. Because alphabetic graphemes represent individual phonemic segments, alphabets can add or drop letters as they are adapted to new spoken languages. This made alphabets much easier to adapt to other languages than logographic or even syllabic writing systems. If Language B were adapting an alphabet from Language A, Language B could use letters from Language A for sounds which the two languages shared. For sounds in Language B that Language A didn't have, Language B could make

Box 12.3 **THE ROSETTA STONE: KEY TO EGYPTIAN HIEROGLYPHIC**

The Rosetta Stone, currently in the British Museum in London, provided the key to deciphering Egyptian hieroglyphs. It was found in 1799 by Napoleon's troops, while fighting in Egypt. The Rosetta Stone has three different scripts. The center text is written in the Egyptian demotic script. The bottom text is written in koine Greek, spoken throughout the eastern Mediterranean in the three centuries BCE. The broken top is in Egyptian hieroglyphic.

When the Rosetta Stone was carved in 196 BCE, three scripts were being used in Egypt. Hieroglyphic was used for important monuments; demotic was the everyday script; and Greek was the language of the rulers of Egypt at the time. The text of the Rosetta Stone honors the Egyptian pharaoh Ptolemaios V, listing his accomplishments for the priests and people of Egypt.

Jean-François Champollion deciphered hieroglyphs in 1822. He already knew the Greek and demotic Egyptian scripts, recognized that the middle and lower texts were identical, and guessed that the hieroglyphs above represented the same text as well. He began by matching seven known demotic signs to their hieroglyphic counterparts. With these seven hieroglyphs as "anchors," he was able to guess the meaning of neighboring signs, and his deciphering went from there. Champollion also used his knowledge of Coptic (the language of Christian descendants of ancient Egyptians) to discover that hieroglyphs have phonetic values as well as symbolic meaning.

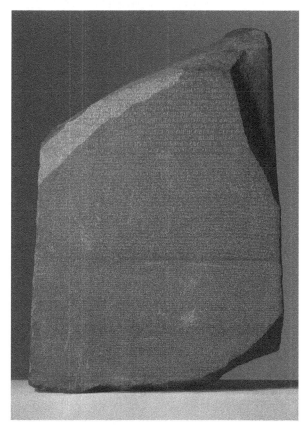

The Rosetta Stone. © The Trustees of the British Museum

up new letters (since the particular form of a letter didn't matter). Often speakers of Language B would "recycle" letters from Language A's alphabet to represent new sounds in their own language. For example, the sound [n] in the Egyptian uniconsonantal alphabet was represented by the symbol for water ~~~~~, since the Egyptian word for water started with [n]. Early Canaanite alphabets borrowed this symbol, stylized it to just a few waves, and used it to represent the sound [m]. Our letter *m* is the descendant of those waves.

Over the next two thousand years, the consonantal alphabet spread from language to language. Proto-Canaanite evolved into the Aramaic script (the script of early biblical texts), from which both Hebrew and Arabic evolved. (The Aramaic script also may have been the source of most Indian scripts.) The Proto-Canaanite script also evolved into the Phoenician script (*c.* 1000 BCE), which was spread widely by that trading culture. Each time, a few letters would be lost, a few added, and a few assigned to new consonants. The form of letters changed somewhat as well.

Around 900 BCE, the Greeks began to adapt the Phoenician script to their language. They faced a problem. In Semitic languages, all words begin with consonants, so a consonantal alphabet works well. However, Greek words often start with vowels, and many Greek words include two vowels in sequence. Writing Greek words using only consonantal letters would not work. The solution was to extend the phonemic principle to vowels – to assign letters to vowels as well as consonants. The letters for Phonenician consonants which did not exist in Greek were "recycled" to represent Greek vowels. For example, as Figure 12.15 shows, Phoenician ✿, which represented a glottal stop not used in Greek, was assigned to the vowel [a]. Similarly, the Phoenician ⇒, representing the glottal fricative [h], was assigned to the vowel [e]. Greek scribes also added several new signs (probably recycled from a Minoan syllabary) for consonants which Phoenician did not have.

Greece's military, economic, and cultural domination of the Mediterranean world in the first millennium BCE further spread the alphabet. The flexibility of an alphabet including letters for both vowels and consonants made it easily adaptable to each language that was exposed to it. The Etruscans of the Italic peninsula adapted the Greek script around 700 BCE, dropping letters for sounds which were not phonemic in spoken Etruscan. The Etruscan alphabet was adapted in turn by the Romans around 600 BCE. The Latin alphabet used by most European languages today evolved from that script.

Figure 12.15 Evolution of the Latin alphabet (Adapted from the Professor Robert Fradkin's "Evolution of alphabets" webpage, at www.wam.umd.edu/~rfradkin/alphapage.html. Go there to see an animation of these changes.)

The consequences of literacy

So far, we have seen that writing evolved in response to the developing needs of increasingly complex societies. The power of writing to preserve information made it a valuable tool for governing. Writing helped rulers keep records of taxes and tributes, maintain agricultural and religious calendars, and administer far-flung and complex empires. For these reasons, writing was (and still is) a form of social capital – a skill that offers access to social and economic resources.

Conservatism

Because of its permanency, writing is a conservative tool; it allows "repeated inspection, verification, and comment" (Coulmas 2003: 225). It selectively preserves certain information (while unwritten information fades), as recognized in the old adage that "History is written by the victors." What gets written (and reproduced) becomes a part of the culture – its history, literary canons, religious doctrine, and civil laws.

Writing plays a role in the organization of societies. On the one hand, it can create new social classes. Scribes in ancient Sumeria, Egypt, and China were members of a privileged class, as were monks during the Middle Ages, who were largely employed copying texts in scriptoria. On the other hand, the distribution of literacy – who gets to read and write – has been a tool of social engineering for centuries. Slaves in most societies were denied literacy because of the empowerment it offered. In the American South in the first half of the twentieth century, literacy tests were used to deny African Americans their voting rights.

Through the Middle Ages, the ability to write and read was a valuable skill, restricted to those who controlled society – members of the church, the government, and the social and economic elite. Controlling access to literacy helped rulers to control populations. The church controlled who learned to speak and write Latin. Because bibles were printed only in Latin (not in the local vernacular, or spoken language), the priest had to intercede between local churchgoers and God, and in this way the church maintained its political power. For example, the beautiful frescoes in Italian churches were visual aids, comic-book bibles, used by priests to educate an illiterate populace to behave correctly. Elaborate visions of hell, with specific tortures associated with particular sins, were a form of social control. Likewise, gigantic murals in palaces and town halls, depicting the deeds of kings and dukes, were works of propaganda, designed to remind the people of the might and protection of their rulers.

Democratization

Technologies of writing, especially the invention of the printing press and moveable type, played an important role in the democratization of literacy. Through the Middle Ages, scrolls and books could only be reproduced by hand. Illuminated manuscripts (mostly of religious texts) were copied in monasteries, which also served as repositories of knowledge. However, the emphasis was on preservation of knowledge, not discovery of new knowledge. The church's monopoly on knowledge was challenged by the rise of universities in the twelfth and thirteenth centuries, which created a demand for secular knowledge. Elizabeth Eisenstein, a historian of the impact of print on European culture, points out that as universities began to build libraries, information grew because books could be compared (Eisenstein 1983). Scholars could examine a range of opinions at one time. Knowledge did not have to come from direct experience of the world, but could come from books as well.

The late Middle Ages also saw the rise of the merchant class and a related rising interest in the outside world, but the cost of reproducing books constrained the spread of secular knowledge. Even the influx of new texts, brought back from the Middle East by returning crusaders (and later from explorations around the world), had limited impact because they had to be copied by hand.

The invention of the printing press (1436) and especially moveable type (1452), by Johannes Gutenberg, and the spread of paper mills in the 1400s, radically reduced the cost of reproducing texts. This, in turn, radically affected what got printed and who got to write and read texts. By 1500 there were 1,000 printing shops in Europe, which had produced 20 million copies of 35,000 different texts. Books were no longer restricted to reproducing old knowledge; new information and theories about the world – fueled by the discoveries of the age of exploration – could be distributed widely. The ruling establishment's grip on writing – and on knowledge – was dramatically weakened.

The Protestant Reformation, beginning in the early 1500s, was the first revolutionary mass movement, made possible in part by printed propaganda. Martin Luther's "Ninety-Five Theses" (1517) protested the selling of indulgences by priests and disputed the Roman Catholic Church's role as intercessor between people and God. Interestingly, Luther's "Theses" were an invitation to a discussion, offered in writing so "that those who are unable to be present and debate orally with us, may do so by letter." The rapid spread of the Protestant Reformation was certainly motivated by the social conditions of the time, but it was facilitated by inexpensively printed pamphlets proclaiming the Protestant message.

Standardization

Writing is also an important tool for language standardization. Writing systems are inherently conservative; the effort to establish conventional pairings between an inventory of graphemes and the sounds (or syllables or morphemes) they represent is considerable, and changes face stiff resistance. For example, despite its many irregularities (see the box below on "Spelling reform"), attempts to reform English spelling have been unsuccessful. Major innovations typically have occurred when one speech community borrowed the writing system of another, free of much of its prior cultural baggage.

Ironically, writing played an important role in the rise of the "vernacular languages" in Europe. After the fall of the Roman Empire in 476 CE, the versions of Latin spoken in Spain, France, and Italy drifted farther and farther apart. In the late 700s, in an effort to stem the "corruption of Latin," the Holy Roman Emperor Charlemagne decreed that Latin should be pronounced *as it is written*. Because only a small fraction of the population of the

Holy Roman Empire was literate, the "Carolingian reform" actually contributed to a widening of differences between written Latin and its vernaculars. When vernacular words could no longer be related to their written Latin forms, they were transcribed (more or less phonetically) as "new" words of what eventually became the Spanish, French, and Italian languages.

Europe maintained a diglossic system for most of the Middle Ages. Latin was the "high dialect" throughout Europe, its script used for academic, religious, and governmental writing. Luther wrote his "Ninety-Five Theses" in Latin, but Protestant pamphlets were soon printed in a range of vernacular languages, further fueling its dissemination. The increase of texts printed in vernacular languages helped democratize education, once Latin was not the only literate language, which further spurred the spread of literacy throughout widening circles of society. In 1500, Europe was publishing around 200,000 volumes per year. In the year 2000, the world published about 10 billion books and 8,000 daily newspapers and over 70,000 weekly and monthly magazines – 50 pounds of paper per person (Man 2000). This does not include the World Wide Web, which grows so fast – and has so many redundant pages – that a meaningful count is problematic.

Technologies of writing played their role in freezing English orthography as well. When William Caxton set up the first printing press in England in 1476, he faced a dilemma: how should he spell English words? The phonemic principle sounds easy in principle, but English had (and still has) many dialects, some of them virtually mutually unintelligible. Caxton made a sound business decision; he spelled most words according to the dialect of his customers, most of whom were from London and its surrounding counties. The orthography used by Caxton and other early British printers was spread so quickly and became so firmly entrenched that 500 years – and a Great Vowel Shift – later many English words are still spelled as they were pronounced by literate Londoners in the fifteenth century.

Spelling reform (satire)

The European Commission has just announced an agreement whereby English will be the official language of the European Nation rather than German, which was the alternative possibility. As part of the negotiations, Her Majesty's Government conceded that English spelling had some room for improvement and has accepted a five-year phase-in plan that would become known as "Euro-English."

In the first year, s will replace the soft c. Sertainly, this will make the sivil servants jump with joy. The hard c will be dropped in favour of k. This should klear up konfusion, and keyboards kan have one less letter. There will be growing publik enthusiasm in the sekond year when the troublesome ph will be replaced with the f. This will make words like fotograf 20 percent shorter.

In the third year, publik akseptanse of the new spelling kan be expekted to reach the stage where more komplikated changes are possible.

Governments will enkourage the removal of double letters which have always ben a deterent to akurate speling. Also, al wil agre that the horibl mes of the silent e in the languag is disgrasful and it should go away.

By the fourth yer peopl wil be reseptiv to steps such as replasing th with z and w with v. During ze fifz yer, ze unesesary o kan be dropd from vords kontaining ou and after ziz fifz yer, ve vil hav a reil sensibl riten styl. Zer vil be no mor trubl or difikultis and evrivun vil find it ezi tu understand ech oza. Ze drem of a united urop vil finali kum tru.

Box 12.4 **WRITING AND STANDARDIZATION: THE CASE OF ITALIAN**

If you want to know how a word is spelled in Italian, you ask how it "is written" (*scriversi*). The *standard* pronunciation of an Italian word follows nearly exactly from its spelling. The relation of the standard spoken dialect and Italian spelling goes back nearly 800 years, and illustrates the relation of writing, prestige, power, and language standardization.

Although its history goes back to the Romans and the Etruscans before them, Italy is a relatively young nation, formed in the 1860s from dozens of city-states whose citizens spoke many different dialects of Italian. To this day, the regions of Italy have their own dialects, some of which are almost mutually unintelligible.

Written Italian played an important role in the creation of a national language. In the Middle Ages, Italian was a spoken vernacular and most writing was done in Latin. During the thirteenth century, the popular writers Dante Alighieri, Petrarch, and Boccaccio helped popularize the Tuscan dialect of Florence as the literary language of Italy. The artistic eminence of Florence during the Renaissance (and the financial and political dominance of Florence's ruling Medici family) cemented Florence's cultural leadership, and the Tuscan dialect became the language of politics and culture throughout Italy. Leon Battista Alberti published the first grammar of Italian, entitled "Rules of the Florentine language," in 1495, and during the fifteenth and sixteenth centuries, Italian (spelled according to Tuscan pronunciation) slowly replaced Latin in most domains of writing. When the independent regions of Italy were united in the 1860s, *la lingua Fiorentina* became the official national language, a choice made easier by the dialect's literary pedigree and long history as the written standard.

Relative advantage

In the nineteenth and twentieth centuries, some social scientists claimed that writing was a distinguishing characteristic of civilization, but it is important to recognize that many complex societies never developed writing systems. Some, like the Incas, used a series of ropes with knots (called a *quipu*) for record keeping and wove complex tapestry calendars. Others, like the Mississipians in the American Midwest, built complex cities but apparently had no record-keeping system at all.

There is also a tendency, especially among users of the Latin alphabet, to proclaim the superiority of alphabetic writing systems over syllabic and logographic systems, and even over consonantal alphabets. However, just as there is no one "best" language, there is no one "best" writing system. Chinese logographs are more complex than alphabetic letters, but they also encode more information. Syllabic systems and consonantal alphabets are as suited to the structure of their languages and the needs of their speech communities as is the Latin alphabet. And in case you've forgotten, the spellings of some 50 percent of English words need to be memorized, despite its use of a "complete" alphabet!

In addition, the question is not just the relative efficiency of a writing system to process information; a person's writing system, like his/her language or dialect, is a symbol of identity, and therefore not easily changed. It took 500 years for Koreans to accept the straightforward Hangul alphabet, despite the complexity of Chinese *hanzi*. The Japanese have two syllabaries, each capable of representing their language, but continue to use *kanji* to symbolize cultural heritage and values.

CHAPTER SUMMARY

Writing is a tool which extends and amplifies many of the functions of spoken language. Just as archaeologists can learn a lot about a culture by analyzing its tools, we can learn a lot about cultures and their languages by understanding their writing systems. Writing systems developed within the constraints of the structure of their spoken language to meet the communicative needs of their speech community. Each kind of writing system – logographic, syllabic, alphabetic, and consonantal alphabetic – is the product of a complex balance between form and function. As speech communities have developed, so too have their writing systems, responding to new needs and facilitating or hastening some social changes.

Logographic systems, in which each written sign represents a morpheme in the spoken language, are formally appropriate to languages, like Chinese, with little inflectional morphology. They help to unify speech communities with broad dialect variation; even when speakers of mutually unintelligible dialects pronounce a word very differently, they can read the same word symbol. In syllabic writing systems, each written symbol represents a syllable of the spoken language, though most syllabic systems use additional diacritic symbols to indicate additional phonetic information. Syllabic systems are particularly well suited to languages, like Japanese, with simple syllables (and a limited syllable inventory). In alphabetic systems, like Hangul and English, the written symbols represent the phonemes of the spoken language. (In consonantal alphabets, like Arabic, only consonants are represented by letters.) Because they represent the smallest meaningful units of meaning, alphabetic systems were easily adapted to new languages.

Writing developed from pictograms which were direct representations of objects in the world, using primary symbolization. With the leap to secondary symbolization in Sumerian cuneiform, written forms directly represented some units of the spoken language (phonemes, syllables, or words), and referred to objects and concepts in the world only through the spoken language. Over centuries, Egyptian hieroglyphics developed a consonantal alphabet which successive dominant cultures – the Phoenicians, the Greeks, and the Romans – adapted to their own languages.

Writing has played a profound role in the development of literate human cultures – although its effects sometimes seem contradictory. On one hand, writing exerts a conservative force – sustaining social orders by preserving their histories, laws, and values. For centuries, controlling access to literacy preserved a monopoly on most domains of knowledge for the privileged few. Writing has even slowed language change, by freezing earlier pronunciations and setting prescriptive grammatical standards. On the other hand, increasing literacy in many speech communities has facilitated social change. And the knowledge preserved in writing has been distributed more and more widely by new technologies – first print and more recently the computer and the internet.

Perhaps the most profound effect of writing on modern cultures has been the way we think about knowledge itself. As Douglas Biber (1988; 3) has pointed out, "The permanency of writing ... confronts us with the incorrect 'knowledge' of earlier generations and thereby fosters a critical attitude towards knowledge." Writing has fostered the advance of knowledge by forcing us to confront prior conceptions and continually question our own beliefs.

Exercises

EXERCISE 12.1

You might think that pictograms – representing a referent directly and nonarbitrarily and not being linked to the forms of a language – would be universal. Based on this assumption, pictograms are often used in signs for international travelers. But even very recognizable pictograms, like those used to indicate restrooms for men and women, are partially conventional, their meaning fixed by frequent use over time. In fact pictographic systems tend to leave a good bit of room for interpretation because the pictorial representation of an object varies by culture. Consider the Aztec pictograms below. What does each represent? Check your answers against the meanings listed below. How many did you interpret correctly? Try to figure out why you got some wrong.

miquiztli   mazatl   calli   atl   xochitl

EXERCISE 12.2

Here's another test of the universality of pictograms:

Make a list of 5–10 referents, some physical objects (like 'tree') and some nonphysical concepts (like 'sickness').

Ask two friends to *independently* draw simple pictograms representing each of the referents on your list. (They should be simple enough that someone else could easily reproduce them.)

Compare your friends' pictograms: are they the same? Are their pictograms for the physical objects more similar than those for concepts?

Have your friends explain their pictograms. Are their "theories" systematic (explaining all or even several of their pictograms) or is the logic behind each pictogram different?

Your list probably contained only or mostly nouns, so ask your pictographers to try to compose some sentences using only their pictographs (and without telling you the meaning of those sentences). Can you interpret their pictographic sentences accurately? What is missing? What would pictograms of those missing elements look like?

Try this experiment with two people from different speech communities/cultures. Consider what your results say about the efficiency of pictograms – their accuracy and range of expression – for communicating.

EXERCISE 12.3

Here's another test of the universality of pictograms. Test yourself and a friend on the meanings of the icons in a computer program (like on the Windows or Mac desktop). Analyze their misinterpretations; do they reflect your test-taker's ignorance of computer "culture"?

EXERCISE 12.4

Try writing the following English sentences using Hangul "syllabic squares." How well does English orthography – and syllable structure – fit into syllabic squares? What does this tell you about the relation between a language's phonology and its orthography?

L	th	s	fl	bl
e	a	ou	a	ow	e	oo
t		nd		rs	m

Example: Let a thousand flowers bloom.

a. The quick brown fox jumped over the lazy dog.
b. Colourless green ideas slept furiously.
c. Up the Establishment!
d. John's sister's dog chased an ambulance.

EXERCISE 12.5

While discussing Arabic, we noted that it is relatively easy to read consonantal alphabets. In contrast, notice that it is impossible to read an alphabet representing only vowels. (See if you can translate the following sentence: *a eae o Ei I a eai a ooaa aae ou e iiu, u a i eee o, a Ei o a e ea iou oe.*) Think of at least three reasons why a vowel-only alphabet can't work for English. Would it work better for a language like Hawai'ian? (Hint: many of the reasons can be found in Chapter 1, "The sounds of language.")

EXERCISE 12.6

Compare the impact on human life of the following technological developments of the twentieth century with the impact of writing: nuclear power, air conditioning, the automobile, the internet. How are their influences similar to and different from those of writing?

EXERCISE 12.7

Compare the effects of the printing press on Renaissance Europe with the effects of the internet on life today. Who gets to publish on the internet? Who are its consumers? What gets published? Are there rules or conventions for how information may be presented?

Answers to Exercise 12.1: *miquiztli* 'death,' *mazatl* 'deer,' *calli* 'house,' *atl* 'water,' *xochitl* 'flower'

SUGGESTIONS FOR FURTHER READING

Coulmas, Florian 1989, *The writing systems of the world*, Oxford and Malden, MA: Blackwell. An engaging overview of writing from a linguistic perspective.

Daniels, Peter T. and Bright, William (eds.) 1996, *The world's writing systems*, New York: Oxford University Press. Encylopedic reference volume, with articles by experts on every known script.

Eisenstein, Elizabeth L. 1983, *The printing revolution in early modern Europe*, New York: Cambridge University Press. Very readable social history linking the printing press to the Renaissance, the Reformation, and the rise of modern science.

Robinson, Andrew 1999, *The story of writing: alphabets, hieroglyphs and pictograms*, London: Thames and Hudson. An accessible, illustrated overview focusing on ancient scripts and decipherment, but with a section on major current writing systems.

Sole, Robert and Valbelle, Dominique 2002, *The Rosetta Stone: the story of the decoding of hieroglyphics*, New York: Four Walls Eight Windows. Written by a novelist and an Egyptologist.

13 Second language acquisition

CHAPTER PREVIEW

As we saw in Chapter 6, first language acquisition is a complicated but relatively rapid process through which children become competent and proficient users of their communities' language(s). However, for those of us who start learning a language after childhood – for example, by enrolling in a foreign language course or moving to a new country – the process of learning a non-native language is far more difficult and much less likely to end in complete mastery/fluency. Adult language learners usually take years to reach a level of proficiency that most children attain easily in their first languages before they are three, and few adults achieve complete native-like mastery of languages they have tried to learn after the end of childhood. What can explain these differences? Why do so many people claim the title of "worst language learner in the world" for themselves? Do adults learn second languages in the same way as children learning their first? If not, what kinds of instruction or learning contexts are most effective for them? These questions are central to the field of second language acquisition (SLA) – broadly defined as the formal study of the learning processes and teaching practices related to the acquisition of non-native languages.

Although scholars have been intrigued by these kinds of general questions about language learning for centuries, SLA as a formally defined field of research is relatively young. From the 1940s onwards, scholars began to propose a number of different theories to explain how people learn non-native languages. The first section of this chapter introduces the theories that have been influential in SLA – from traditional behaviorist approaches to universal grammar-based claims to more recent hypotheses about the roles of input and interaction. We examine how research is carried out in each of these paradigms. Next, we review some of the factors that impact SLA, including learners' first languages, age, gender, motivation, working memory capacity, and the context for their second language learning. This leads us to a discussion of some of the cognitive processes involved in SLA, including attention, typical patterns of second language development, and fossilization or stabilization. We discuss the methodologies of second language research. Finally, we discuss second language pedagogy and how current research findings are being applied to teaching practice.

GOALS
The goals of this chapter are to:

- introduce some of the main theories of second language acquisition with an overview of several research methodologies
- discuss the ways in which the second language learning processes of individuals vary
- outline second language pedagogy and its connections with SLA theory

Theories of second language acquisition

What exactly is second language acquisition? Broadly speaking, a second language (L2) refers to any language learned after one's first language (L1), no matter how many others have been learned. However, some linguists also make a distinction between *second* language learning and *foreign* language learning. **Second language learning** refers to the process of acquiring a non-native language that is spoken by the community where the learner is living (for example, when a native speaker of Japanese comes to the US to learn English), while **foreign language learning** refers to the process of acquiring a non-native language that is *not* spoken by the surrounding community (for example, when a native speaker of English takes a Japanese class in the US). The learning processes may be different depending on the context. For example, foreign language learners hear and speak the foreign language in the classroom, but have little exposure to it outside the classroom. Second language learners have access to the language both in and out of the classroom. In the field of SLA, most researchers tend to use "second language learning" as an umbrella term covering all non-native language learning, a practice we will follow in this chapter as well.

Behaviorism

As described in Chapter 6, early researchers attempted to apply behaviorist theories and research to understanding first language acquisition. Behaviorist theories were also applied to second language learning, and the approach was widely influential in the 1950s and 1960s. Behaviorists believed that second language learners – like children learning their native tongues (or any other skill for that matter) – acquired the appropriate language behaviors (or "habits") through repetition and reinforcement. For example, they believed that learners of English as a second language (ESL) would learn the plural -*s* form most effectively by producing it repeatedly in their own speech. As such, in classrooms, teachers often required learners to repeat linguistic forms in production drills (e.g. *two cats, three dogs, five cows, seven pigs*, and so on) without necessarily paying much attention to meaning. Though it has never been proven that any students died from this pattern practice, the exercise of repeating phrases ad infinitum (and, at times, perhaps ad nauseam!) became known as "drill and kill."

Behaviorists also claimed that errors produced by the second language learner (such as mistakes in word order) could be attributed to **interference** from the learner's first language. They argued that existing L1 knowledge or "habits" that differed from those of the L2 could interfere with second language development. For example, a native speaker of Japanese, a language that has no distinction between *r* and *1* sounds, would tend to have problems pronouncing *r* and *1* in English – leading, for example, to jokes about restaurants that serve "flied lice" with the meal. Differences between the learner's L1 and the L2 were thought to be the main source of difficulty for L2 learners, and the phonology and grammatical structures of languages were compared to predict areas of difficulty. This became formally known as the **contrastive analysis hypothesis (CAH)**.

While a comparison of languages to predict grammatical errors has some commonsense appeal and people can sometimes recall anecdotal evidence in favor of the idea, later research has shown that language differences do not reliably predict language learning difficulty. Studies have indicated that very few of the errors produced by L2 learners can be traced to their L1. Instead, many errors are due to developmental processes common to all learners regardless of L1 background. Just because grammatical structures in two languages are different, this does not necessarily mean that the second language learner will find them difficult. Interestingly, though, one area where contrastive analysis continues to be used and useful is in predicting pronunciation problems. We can easily tell when a person's accent does not sound native-like, and many people can make a reasonable guess at the first language. For example, native Spanish speakers are sometimes known to add an extra vowel onto the beginning of words with consonant clusters in English, as in *eschool* and *estudy*, while native speakers of French might substitute a *z* for a *th* sound as in *zis school*.

During the 1970s, much of the rationale behind behaviorist teaching methods was called into question following the impact of Noam Chomsky's ideas about generative grammar in the field of theoretical linguistics. At this time, there was a general move away from behaviorist theories and toward approaches that focused on the various learner-internal mechanisms involved in language acquisition – a move that led to the emergence of new theories of second language acquisition, which will be discussed in the sections below.

Comprehensible input and the natural order hypothesis

Beginning in the 1970s, another view of L2 learning became popular. Rather than treating language as a series of mechanical habits that are learned through reinforcement, researchers began to view language learning as a more complex interaction of internal and external factors. One example of this approach can be found in the work of Stephen Krashen, who believed that L2 learners needed to be exposed to a special kind of input in order to learn the target language.

Krashen recognized the importance to language learning of **comprehensible input**, that is, input in the target language that is understandable in a particular context of use but slightly more advanced than the learner's current level of ability. Comprehensible input is often abbreviated as "i+1," where "i" refers to the learner's current level and "+1" denotes the slightly more advanced input. Through exposure to this input, L2 acquisition was believed to progress automatically and in the same fashion as L1 acquisition – but only if the learner's **affective filter** (or emotional barrier) was sufficiently low. In other words, if the learner was anxious or harbored negative emotions toward the target language, its speakers, or the learning context, comprehensible input could be "filtered out."

Krashen also argued that there is a natural order of acquisition; in other words, he claimed that all learners, regardless of their L1, progress through the same stages of second language development and in the same order. This "natural order hypothesis" was based on a series of studies known as the **morpheme order studies** (see Box 13.1). Together, Krashen's hypotheses and the morpheme order studies suggested to teachers and researchers that if second language learners were simply exposed to the right kind of input and had the right attitude, the target language would emerge naturally in a particular predetermined order.

Although Krashen's hypotheses were subject to criticisms on both theoretical and methodological grounds, his model was influential. One basic problem addressed by researchers, for example, was the difficulty of spelling out the current level ("i") and corresponding level of comprehensible input ("i+1") for a particular learner. However, subsequent work building on Krashen's model was able to locate learners' levels more specifically with respect to certain grammatical forms in clear-cut, empirically verifiable developmental sequences. Researchers also recognized the value to L2 learners of receiving feedback on problematic utterances and having their attention drawn to linguistic form. Such processes play central roles in the interaction hypothesis, and it is to this idea that we turn next.

The interaction hypothesis

The **interaction hypothesis**, stemming from the work of Michael Long and Susan Gass, suggests that second language development can be facilitated when learners attempt to communicate with other speakers in the L2, experience difficulties, and engage in further interaction with their interlocutors to resolve their problems. As part of this process, learners often need to seek help in order to comprehend the input they receive (e.g. by using clarification requests such as "Could you say that again?"). For instance, in example (1) below, the learner (the non-native speaker, or NNS) fails to understand the native speaker's (NS) utterance. By using a clarification request, she is able to obtain input that is more comprehensible and perhaps better suited to her language learning needs.

BOX 13.1 **MORPHEME ORDER STUDIES**

(From *The Bilingual Syntax Measure*, © Harcourt Brace Jovanovich, Inc. 1975.)

Following research on how children acquire their native languages, second language researchers Dulay and Burt sought to determine whether there was a similar order of acquisition for second language learners of English. In their 1974 study, for example, they investigated whether children from two different first language backgrounds (Chinese and Spanish) acquired eleven different English morphemes in a similar order. (The morphemes were pronoun case, articles, the copula, the present progressive -*ing*, plural forms, auxiliary verbs, past regular and irregular forms, long plurals, possessives, and the third-person singular -*s*.) They used the Bilingual Syntax Measure to gather the data, eliciting samples of children's natural L2 speech by showing them pictures like the one above and asking a series of questions (e.g. *What is the fat man doing?*). The questions were constructed to require certain morphemes; for example, the morpheme -*ing* would be obligatory to answer the previous question since a sentence such as *The fat man is eat* is ungrammatical.

Dulay and Burt reasoned that there was a correspondence between how accurately a morpheme was used and how early it was acquired. Thus, they calculated each child's accuracy score for each morpheme based on whether it was used correctly in obligatory contexts. Then they ranked the morphemes by their accuracy scores and equated these rankings with the order in which the morphemes were acquired. Using this procedure, Dulay and Burt found similar orders of morpheme acquisition for both groups of children learning English. Since Chinese and Spanish are unrelated first languages, they argued that the only way to explain the similar acquisition orders was through universal processing mechanisms. In other words, regardless of their L1 background, children would acquire the morphemes in the same sequence because of innate language learning processes.

Unfortunately, such morpheme order studies involved several methodological problems. For example, accuracy rankings may not in fact reflect the order in which morphemes are learned. Also, second language production involves more than using correct forms in obligatory contexts; it involves

---

BOX 13.1 (cont.)

not using forms in inappropriate contexts as well. That is, it is also possible to produce utterances that are grammatically correct but pragmatically odd. Furthermore, the study's limited database, consisting of learners from only two L1 backgrounds, undermines claims about the universality of these processes. Finally, the similarities found in accuracy orders may have been the result of other nonbiological factors. For example, given that the children were all receiving ESL instruction, the results might have been influenced by the pedagogy or by the textbooks the children were using. However, building on the valuable notion of universal stages in language acquisition, research on developmental sequences has continued to evolve, as we will see in the example of question-formation stages discussed later in this chapter.

---

(1)	NS:	there's there's just a couple more things	
	NNS:	a sorry? Couple?	← *clarification request*
	NS:	couple more things in the room only just a couple	
	NNS:	couple? What does it mean couple?	← *clarification request*
	NS:	like 2 2 things 2 or 3 things	
	NNS:	more	
	NS:	yeah	

(From Mackey and Philp 1998: 339)

During interaction, learners also need to produce output that is comprehensible to others. In example (2), the NNS produces an utterance that is incomprehensible to her partner. In this case, she must draw upon her linguistic knowledge (of English phonology or syntax, for example) to make herself understood; this process is known as producing **modified output**.

(2)	NNS:	the windows are crozed	
	NS:	the windows have what?	
	NNS:	crosed?	
	NS:	crossed? I'm not sure what you're saying there	
	NNS:	windows are closed	← *modified output*
	NS:	oh the windows are closed oh OK sorry	

(From Pica 1994: 514)

Through processes such as obtaining comprehensible input and producing modified output, interaction is believed to help draw learners' attention to problematic differences between their **interlanguage** (i.e. their current knowledge of the target language) and the native form of the target language. When learners receive feedback on their L2 production (e.g. through clarification requests), their attention can be drawn to "gaps" – that is, to areas in their linguistic knowledge that need improvement. For instance, in example (3) the student makes an error in subject–verb agreement, and the teacher provides

corrective feedback in the form of a **recast** in her subsequent utterance. A recast is a more targetlike way of expressing what is perceived to be a learner's intended meaning, changing the form but not the content of the utterance.

(3) S: The boy have many flowers in his basket.
     T: Yes, the boy has many flowers in his basket.   *recast*
                                                              (corrective feedback)

(From Nicholas, Lightbown, and Spada 2001: 721)

In summary, then, interactionists claim that interaction provides *opportunities* for learning, although interaction is not the only force driving learning. Related to this is the question of whether interaction itself *is* learning, which is the claim made by socioculturalists, discussed below. Researchers working within the interactionist framework are currently carrying out qualitative, quantitative, and descriptive research on interaction-driven L2 learning. An example of an experimental study appears in Box 13.2.

Socioculturalism

Whereas interactionists focus on the cognitive mechanisms (such as attention) that are facilitated by interaction, socioculturalists, as their name implies, focus on the relationship between interpersonal and social aspects of interaction and language learning. Sociocultural theory posits that all cognitive development (including language) stems from interactions between individuals. One type of interaction that has received research attention in sociocultural studies of second language learning is the interaction between a less skilled L2 learner and a more expert "other" – a teacher, tutor, or more proficient fellow learner. The expert can provide the learner with a form of scaffolding, the co-construction of an utterance. That is, by simplifying the task, controlling the learner's frustration, modeling solutions, and bringing the learner's attention to important features of the task, the expert can provide the learner with the opportunity to develop and practice a particular linguistic skill, enabling the learner to accomplish more in collaboration with others than she could by herself.

Sociocultural research often includes careful and detailed analysis of the social and linguistic context of the participants in a communicative exchange – for example, the relationship between the learners and their understanding of the task at hand. An example of this sort of study appears in Box 13.3.

Universal Grammar

In contrast to both the interactionist and socioculturalist approaches to language acquisition, researchers working within a Universal Grammar framework have focused on the innate linguistic knowledge, or **Universal Grammar (UG)**, believed to guide all language learning. This approach is broadly known as **nativism** and is derived from the work of Noam Chomsky. UG SLA researchers address questions such as, "What is the nature of the linguistic knowledge with which learners begin the SLA process?" and "To what extent are learners' first language grammars and UG available to them as they learn additional languages?"

BOX 13.2 EXAMPLE OF AN INTERACTIONIST STUDY

(From P. Ur (1981), *Discussions that work: task-centered fluency practice*, © Cambridge University Press. Reproduced by permission.)

One example of an empirical study investigating the effects of interaction (and, in particular, recasts) on second language development is Mackey and Philp (1998). In this study, the researchers sought to determine whether learners of English as a second language who received recasts during conversational interaction produced more advanced question forms than those who did not receive recasts.

Thirty-five ESL learners from beginning and lower-intermediate classes in Australia were first divided into two proficiency groups (high and low) based on an independent pre-test measure of proficiency. The learners were then randomly assigned to either an Interactor group, Recast group, or Control group. The Interactor group participated in task-based activities with a native speaker of English, but did not receive recasts on their linguistic errors. (In the spot-the-differences task, shown above as an example of one such activity, the learner and native speaker were given slightly different pictures of the same scene and had to compare the contents of their pictures verbally without looking at the other's picture.) The recast group participated in the same activities, but they differed from the Interactor group in that they did receive recasts on their errors. The Control group, meanwhile, only completed the pre- and post-tests.

The researchers assessed the impact of the recasts by looking at changes in the production of question forms from the pre-test to the post-test. (See Box 13.8 for more information on the developmental sequence for questions.) They found that the learners who participated in conversational interaction with recasts showed a greater increase in the development of question forms, with higher-level learners showing the greatest increase. The study thus provides support for the interaction hypothesis and its claims that recasts can facilitate second language development.

It should be noted, however, that this study addressed only a very small aspect of what constitutes learning, the development of a selected type of question forms in ESL. While narrowly defining development like this is sometimes necessary to test theory, it leaves open questions about other linguistic forms.

> ### BOX 13.3 **EXAMPLE OF A SOCIOCULTURAL STUDY**
>
> In an interesting study based on the socioculturalist approach to language learning, Swain and Lapkin (1998) studied the language of two grade 8 French immersion students, Kim and Rick, as they worked collaboratively on a classroom activity. The students' task was to construct a story orally from a sequence of pictures and then put the story into writing. Before the task, the learners were given a pre-test on adjective–noun agreement in French, and one week after the task, they were given a post-test.
>
> Arguing that interaction not only provides *opportunities* for learning (which is the general claim made by interactionists), but that interaction itself *is* learning, Swain and Lapkin conducted a close analysis of the speech of these two students in order to find evidence of learning. To this end, they focused on "language-related episodes," or instances where the students talked about the language they were producing, questioned each other's and their own language use, or provided corrections. For instance, in the example below, neither Kim nor Rick is confident of the correct French translation of *alarm clock*. However, together, the two learners are able to "construct a **scaffold**," that is, to piece together their collective knowledge to arrive at the correct answer.
>
> Kim: *Du réveille-matin qui sonne?* Does that sound OK?
>   Of the alarm clock that rings? Does that sound OK?
> Rick: Or what about... *Jacqueline se lève à cause du ... du réveille-...* yeah, *qui sonne.*
>   Or what about... Jacqueline [the girl in their story] gets up because of the ... of the alarm-... yeah, that rings.
> Kim: OK. Or you can say *du réveille-matin* or *du sonnement du réveille-matin.*
>   OK. Or you can say of the alarm clock or of the ring of the alarm clock.
> Rick: No, *réveille-matin qui sonne.*
>   No, alarm clock that rings.
>
> Through this kind of close examination, Swain and Lapkin argue that the learners jointly constructed knowledge during their dialogue. Post-test scores further indicate that the knowledge was retained. This study thus provides evidence for socioculturalist claims that interaction involving some kind of scaffolding or co-construction can be a source of linguistic development.
>
> The focus of some sociocultural research on the learner, as opposed to learning processes and outcomes, has sometimes been criticized for not being helpful in testing claims about linguistic development. In Swain and Lapkin's research, only two learners were studied, but the claims made were appropriately cautious, and the learning connections were clear.

As discussed in Chapter 6, nativists use Universal Grammar to help explain what they call the "logical problem" of first language acquisition. They point out that the input that children hear is full of false starts, hesitancies, and other dysfluencies, and that it does not contain all the sentences that children come to produce. Nativists argue that it is not possible for children to deduce from this "impoverished" input the complex linguistic knowledge that they so quickly and effortlessly acquire in just a few years. Nor, they claim, can children learn much of their linguistic knowledge from the limited (and inconsistent) instruction that parents offer. Hence, nativists posit that the only logical explanation for children's language acquisition is an innate language endowment guiding the process, a **language acquisition device (LAD)** in the brain.

Some nativists claim that a logical problem exists for second language acquisition as well. More specifically, they maintain that the complex linguistic knowledge that second language learners eventually attain cannot simply be gleaned from the input or from instruction and therefore must be obtained from universal grammar. Other nativists point out that many learners (especially adult L2 learners) do not obtain a very complex level of L2 knowledge. Their claim is that UG is no longer available after a certain age. Such researchers argue that once a learner has passed a **critical** (or **sensitive**) **period** for language acquisition (typically placed around the age of puberty), the language acquisition device "atrophies" and the knowledge it contains (i.e. UG) is no longer directly available to help guide the second language learning process. Instead, learners must rely on general learning mechanisms such as memorization to make what progress they can. To investigate whether, and until what age, universal grammar may be available to L2 learners, nativists have often relied on **acceptability** (or **grammaticality**) **judgment tests**. In these tests, L2 learners are asked to evaluate the acceptability of various sentences in the L2 (see Box 13.4 below).

Frequency-based approaches

Whereas Universal Grammar is claimed to consist of categorical linguistic rules that guide the language acquisition process, proponents of frequency-based approaches argue that this innate endowment may be more like an emergent, bottom-up result of frequencies and regular patterns of actions, events, and objects (both linguistic and nonlinguistic) that language learners perceive in their environment. In other words, L1 and L2 learners experience and unconsciously keep track of a vast array of linguistic information, including whether or not particular sounds occur together, the orderings of particular words, and even discourse characteristics of language. Learning how to use articles in English (i.e. *a*, *the*, *an*), for instance, may involve learning through simple associative processes where they occur frequently (e.g. before nouns and adjectives) and where they occur infrequently or not at all (e.g. after nouns). Thus, the knowledge that *the cat* is grammatical while *cat the* is highly unusual, or that *I saw the cat* is more well-formed than *I saw cat*, is something that learners deduce based on their mostly unconscious sensitivity to frequencies and patterns in the language they hear.

Researchers claim that a range of cognitive systems, such as working memory and perceptual representations, as well as attentional resources, are involved in forming such associations and applying regularities to first and second language acquisition. However, unconscious analysis of frequencies and patterns in input may not be the only mechanism leading to second language learning. For example, adult language learning is typically more conscious and directed than child language acquisition, and for many adult language learners, input is limited to materials used in the language classroom.

It is interesting to note that questions about the role of frequency in second language learning were raised many years ago. Beginning in the 1950s, as discussed above, some behaviorists argued that language learning was the (explicitly learned) acquisition of patterns. With the decline of behaviorism, this line of argument was not pursued; however, frequency-based approaches are enjoying something of a renaissance at the moment, with

BOX 13.4 **ACCEPTABILITY JUDGMENT TESTS**

In a study relying on acceptability judgment tests, Schachter (1989) tested three groups of English language learners (native speakers of Indonesian, Chinese, and Korean) on an aspect of grammar known as *subjacency*, which refers to how far a wh-word can be separated from its referent. These languages were chosen because they behave very differently with respect to subjacency. Schachter hypothesized that if all three groups of learners behaved similarly by correctly indicating that English sentences that violated subjacency were ungrammatical, it could be argued that they still had access to Universal Grammar. In other words, since they would not be able to derive knowledge of subjacency from their native languages (as their native languages differed from English with respect to this rule), some innate linguistic knowledge would have to be guiding their acceptability judgments.

To test this hypothesis, Schachter gave her learners an acceptability judgment test like the one below in the example, in which learners were asked to indicate how acceptable they thought the given sentences or questions were. In Schachter's study, half of the test items dealt with subjacency, while the other half were distractors, meaning that they did not deal with subjacency but were of similar length and/or complexity. This latter type was included to determine whether the learners could handle grammatically complex sentences.

1 = completely ungrammatical; 5 = completely grammatical

	1	2	3	4	5
Is the boy who standing over there is happy?					
I read a book of which my professor had recommended the style.					
Yesterday I saw a girl of whom I have forgotten the name.					
This is a book of which I hate the title.					
How many did you buy of the books?					

Schachter found that most of the participants got the distractor items right (that is, they correctly indicated which ones were grammatical and which ones were not), but they did not properly reject the subjacency violations. In other words, they marked items acceptable even when they were actually ungrammatical because they violated subjacency. Based on these results, she concluded that late second language learners, like those in her study, did not have access to Universal Grammar. Subsequent researchers have expressed reservations about some uses of acceptability judgment tests and the assumptions underlying them; however, the investigation of whether advanced language learners have access to innate linguistic knowledge in the second language acquisition process has been an important line of research in SLA.

questions about the role of frequency being currently addressed by SLA researchers and psycholinguists. Such work is becoming popularized though the research of Nick Ellis, who has argued that frequency-based approaches make sense because, unlike UG, they engage with other approaches to first and second language acquisition and are consistent with cognitive neuroscience research into the measurable processes going on in the brains of second language learners. Innovative technology, such as functional magnetic resonance

BOX 13.5 **EXAMPLE OF A FREQUENCY-BASED STUDY**

In contrast to nativist researchers, connectionist researchers emphasize that although it is possible to describe language behavior as rule-like, this does not mean that it is governed by rules. They argue that generalizations from simple associative learning mechanisms can lead to novel language. Computational modeling lets researchers assess how well linguistic regularities can be acquired through the extraction of probabilistic patterns. Since frequency-based models are neurally inspired, dynamic, and data-driven, some researchers have argued that they are biologically more plausible than the language acquisition device of nativist accounts.

To address the question of whether it is necessary to postulate rules or whether it is possible to understand the learning of morphology in terms of associative processes, Ellis and Schmidt (1997) carried out a laboratory study of SLA in which they controlled for prior knowledge and frequency of exposure to linguistic input by having both adult humans and a computational associative learning system acquire an artificial language. The participants first learned twenty new lexical items and were then exposed to their plural forms. Because prior research had used differing frequency effects to argue that regular and irregular past-tense morphological forms are learned differently (i.e. by rule generation and associative memory, respectively), half of the items were regular, while the other half had unique (irregular) plural affixes. In each of these groups, half of the plurals were presented five times more frequently than the others.

Ellis and Schmidt measured both accuracy and reaction time, finding an advantage for regular plurals and high-frequency items. They also found that the frequency effect was larger for irregulars, especially in the middle stages of learning. Their results differed from previous research, however, in that the early stages of acquisition showed frequency effects for regular items as well as irregulars. The sizes of these effects decreased as the learners learned more, with the size of the frequency effect on irregular items diminishing more slowly. According to Ellis and Schmidt, these findings show that the power law of practice (which states that the amount of improvement decreases as a function of increasing practice) applies to the acquisition of morphosyntax. Combining this with the finding that their connectionist model simulated the humans' course of acquisition quite accurately when exposed to the same materials as the system at the same frequencies, they concluded that it is *not* in fact necessary to postulate underlying rules. Rather than there being a hybrid system of learning in which some forms are rule-generated and others are learned by associative memory, they claimed that all of the effects could be explained as a natural result of simple associative learning. Naturally, these conclusions are challenged by those working within the UG perspective, but findings such as these – taken together with work on pattern recognition in children's language learning discussed in Chapter 6 – are hard to dispute.

imaging (fMRI), is beginning to provide investigators with the means of examining the acquisition and processing of language in the brain. Although these neurobiological functions are complex and little understood at present, the recent advances in brain imaging research, together with sophisticated computer modeling strategies, are likely to lead to significant advances in our understanding of SLA processes in the future. An example of a frequency-based study is described in Box 13.5.

Summary

The relatively young field of second language acquisition includes a variety of approaches to explaining second language learning. While a comprehensive theory is clearly the central goal of most SLA research, each of the current theories views the problem of explaining the second language learning process from a slightly different angle. Most theories have built on previous research and, in their gradual development, have provided us with an emerging view of the L2 learning process. With researchers increasingly taking advantage of insights from related disciplines and approaches, the process of theory development and testing is ongoing, and this is one reason why SLA is such an exciting field.

Individual differences in second language acquisition

While the theories described above were developed primarily to account for the universal features of learning second languages – that is, the processes and stages characteristic of *all* learners – there are also many differences among L2 learners. In first language acquisition by children, individual differences (e.g. across genders or the languages being learned) are largely overshadowed by striking similarities in terms of natural stages and ultimate attainment. However, in second language acquisition, individual differences have more of an impact on the L2 learning process, and their role has thus received considerable attention in recent years. We now turn to a discussion of six important areas of difference among L2 learners: L1, age, gender, working memory, motivation, and context.

First language (L1)

The language learner's first language (L1) was one of the first individual differences to receive serious scholarly attention. The strong form of the contrastive analysis hypothesis – which claimed that all L2 errors could be attributed to differences between the L1 and L2 – was largely discredited (as discussed above in relation to behaviorism). However, recent research has suggested that while characteristics of the L1 do not strongly predict L2 errors, they do influence the development of the L2 in subtle and complicated ways. Researchers point out that learners often *consciously* **transfer** or employ their knowledge about the L1 in their attempts to communicate in the L2, especially early in the learning process. Learners are more likely to transfer L1 knowledge when they believe the L1 and L2 are similar or related. The L1 may also influence what learners notice in the L2. For example, rules for adverb placement in French and English are similar but not identical, and mistakes made by French learners of English in this regard are unlikely to cause major communication difficulties. It is possible, for instance, to understand a French learner who says *I ate slowly the apples*. If he/she does not receive negative evidence indicating that this word order is disallowed in English, the learner may not initially be aware that it is ungrammatical from the simple fact of its nonoccurrence.

Age

Another individual difference that is believed to play a key role in second language learning is age. It is commonly thought that younger language learners are more successful, and indeed researchers have found a relationship between age of acquisition and ultimate attainment in at least some aspects of the L2, with age showing itself to be the strongest predictor of success.

One proposal that has been offered to explain children's apparent advantage in language learning is the **critical period hypothesis**. Originally discussed in the late 1960s by Eric Lenneberg, this hypothesis states that language acquisition must occur before puberty in order for the speaker to reach native-like fluency. Since then, a number of neurological changes that are believed to coincide with puberty have been set forth as possible reasons for the critical period. These include lateralization (a process whereby the left hemisphere becomes dominant for language) and myelinization (a process whereby neurons become encased in a myelin sheath, resulting in less rapid firing). UG researchers have also discussed deactivation, by which they mean a loss of complete access to Universal Grammar. There are several problems with neurological proposals, however, including mismatches in time frames (lateralization is believed to occur around the age of five; puberty usually begins in the pre-teen years) and the fact that some individuals do achieve native-like fluency even though they began their studies of the L2 later on in life. For these reasons, researchers have also proposed that there must be social and other nonbiological factors involved, such as learners' attachment to their own language and culture, different types of motivation, and the amount and type of input that children and adults receive (for example, children may have more opportunities to use the L2 outside the home – in school and playing with peers – than their adult counterparts).

Along with this increasing recognition of social factors, researchers have also distinguished between the *rate of attainment* and the *ultimate level of success*. In particular, they have noted that even though adults and adolescents may initially be faster at learning an L2, children generally outperform them in the long run. In addition, they have argued that the label "critical period" may be a misnomer. Because some adult learners *do* achieve native-like proficiency in the L2, some researchers have argued for use of the term **sensitive period** to reflect the fact that while success in acquiring a second language may be much *more likely* for children, it is still *possible* for adults.

Recent research has also investigated whether age-related differences in language learning ability hold for *all* aspects of language or only a subset of features. Younger learners do appear to have an advantage in L2 phonology. Nonetheless, there is growing consensus that even late learners (that is, people who started learning a non-native language after puberty) can achieve a mastery of L2 syntax that is nearly indistinguishable from that of native speakers. (Box 13.6 provides an example of some recent thinking about age within the field of second language acquisition.)

Gender

Another individual difference that may impact L2 development is the gender of the learner. It has been found, for instance, that females tend to use a greater variety of language learning strategies than males and that they use them more frequently. Other

BOX 13.6 **AGE AND SLA**

Researchers have long debated the notion of a critical period for second language learning, noting that some adult learners of a second language can actually become highly proficient, even native-like, in a second language. While some researchers believe that these learners provide evidence against a critical period, Bley-Vroman (1990) has proposed the Fundamental Difference Hypothesis – that the method of learning of an adult is fundamentally differently from that of a child. While it is not impossible to become fluent in a second language as an adult, it can be more difficult since over time our brain loses the ability to learn structures implicitly from a large amount of data. Some researchers have suggested that there are two critical periods where fast implicit learning slows down, around ages 6–7 and again around 16–17. According to this hypothesis, adult learners benefit more from explicit learning strategies and can learn salient structures (such as basic word order, gender in pronouns, and *do*-support in English yes/no questions) faster than child learners do implicitly.

However, the ability to learn subtle differences in grammatical structure (such as use of determiners and adverb placement) slows for adults.

DeKeyser (2000) conducted a study of Hungarian learners of English who had lived in the US for over ten years and whose age of immigration (i.e. first exposure to English) ranged from a 1 to 50 years. He asked the learners for grammaticality judgments on 200 sentences that tested various salient or subtle grammatical structures in English. He found that all those who arrived before age 17 attained a high level of grammaticality in English. However, as the age of arrival increased, proficiency level decreased. Only adult learners with a high degree of verbal or analytical abilities were able to attain a high level of proficiency in the second language. His data demonstrate that adult learners can indeed attain high proficiency in a second language with the right skill set, attention to grammar, and motivation (see Box 13.9 for studies on motivation).

studies have shown that females usually have more positive attitudes toward learning an L2 and may be more motivated. In terms of performance, however, findings have been contradictory; some research suggests that female students outperform males, while other studies suggest the opposite. Psycholinguistic studies looking at frequency effects (as discussed above in Box 13.5) suggest that males and females process language differently, with females using (and having an advantage in) some types of memory and males using different memory strategies. Gender can also influence classroom dynamics and potentially affect the second language learning process. For example, research on interactions between non-native speakers shows that:

- both males and females work harder to achieve mutual comprehension in mixed-gender pairings than in matched-gender pairings;
- males indicate nonunderstanding more often than females;
- males, when interacting with females, tend to talk more and dominate the conversation.

Since gender is expressed differently across cultural groups, identifying gender effects in second language learning is a complex task. However, because interaction is a crucial aspect of second language learning, evidence of unequal distribution of talk may have ramifications for language development. Box 13.7 provides some information about a recent study of gender and language learning.

BOX 13.7 **GENDER DIFFERENCES IN SECOND LANGUAGE LEARNING TASKS**

Ross-Feldman (2007) studied the conversation of second language learners working in pairs as they carried out communicative tasks such as spot-the-difference activities, and found that the gender of the learners influenced language-related episodes (LRE). LREs are episodes in which learners interrupt their own conversations in order to clarify questions of grammar, lexical choice, or meaning. Such episodes increase the potential for overall learning. In the study, when either a male or female was paired with a female there were more language-related episodes. This is related to general findings that women tend to play a more supportive role in interactions and attend to the needs of their conversational partners, allowing the other learner more opportunities to stop the conversation and ask questions.

In a mixed-gender setting (i.e. male and female learners working together), Ross-Feldman found that when males initiated the LRE their questions were resolved (taken up) in the direction of the correct answer significantly more often than those initiated by females. Below is an example from the study of a resolved LRE initiated by a male during a story-writing task.

Example 1

Female: Okay. Okay, um the dishrag, dishrag is. . .
Male: Dishrag?
Female: Dishrag, is the fabric, the fabric that you use for clean, for drying the dish.
Male: Ah, ok. Where is?

Compare the male-initiated LRE with the following female-initiated LRE:

Female: Interchange their bags. What is the word? I don't know.
Male: After that they. . .
Female: Their bags.
Male: They went to the cafeteria and drink cup of coffee.

The LREs initiated by females in a mixed-gender pairing were more likely to be ignored and left unresolved. This finding is in line with research that men's topic initiations in conversation are more often discussed and developed while women's topic changes can be ignored or interrupted by men. It is important to understand that when studying gender behavior the results only demonstrate tendencies and that there is considerable variation within genders and also some overlap in behaviors between the genders. However, second language teachers can use this information to construct environments and tasks that can benefit all learners in the classroom.

Working memory

Another important way in which learners differ is in their working memory capacities – that is, in their ability to store and process information at the same time. Working memory (WM) is thought to differ from short-term memory in that it involves some sort of processing as well as storage, rather than a verbatim repetition of the information. A working memory test might ask a learner to recall the last word of sentences presented aurally or repeat back in reverse order numbers presented visually. Research suggests that working memory plays a role in first language acquisition, language processing (e.g. disambiguating sentences), and language loss (e.g. in Alzheimer's patients). In light of these findings, researchers have begun to investigate the relationship between working memory and second language acquisition. For example, researchers have found that learners' working memory capacities affect their ability to learn L2 vocabulary and grammatical rules, as well as their L2 reading ability and listening proficiency. Studies such as these have provided evidence that working memory may help predict differences in the rate of L2 learning.

In one such study, Mackey *et al.* (2010) found a significant relationship between L2 performance and higher-WM capacity in delayed test results. Interestingly, learners with lower-WM capacity appeared to do well on the immediate post-tests, but did not maintain this development on delayed post-tests. In contrast, the higher-WM learners did not tend to demonstrate initial progress, but did show improvement on the delayed post-tests. The authors suggested that the learners with higher-WM capacity may have been better able to make cognitive comparisons between the feedback given in the target language and their interlanguage, with lasting effects for L2 development. On the other hand, the low-WM learners may not have processed the feedback in a sufficiently elaborative way so that encoding in long-term memory could occur.

Assessing WM is not always straightforward; the type of data and processing involved in a WM test may affect a learner's scores. Phonological short-term memory (PSTM), often measured by ability to remember nonsense words, has been shown to be related to vocabulary acquisition as well as grammatical learning. The method of presentation of the data (aural versus visual) and type of data (language-related versus numerically based) may affect learners' WM scores. There is also the potential for circularity in the definition of WM and its correlation with SLA; since sentence-span tests of WM involve language processing in the first place, learners' demonstrated ability on such tasks should naturally predict their language. In summary, it is important to understand that while working memory has various implications for language learning there are likely to be various subcomponents of WM and nuanced abilities that affect different areas of second language learning.

Motivation

Motivation is another characteristic that varies considerably across L2 learners. The commonsense view is that motivated language learners, who are willing to devote more time and energy to achieving fluency in the target language, are more successful. Some researchers have even claimed that motivation is the single most important individual difference impacting SLA. Motivation is not monolithic, however; it is a complex, multidimensional construct. Studies making use of Robert Gardner's socio-educational model of motivation have focused not only on **integrative motivation** (involving the learner's attitudes toward the target language group and the desire to integrate into the target language community), but also on **instrumental orientations**, which refer to more practical reasons for language learning, such as gaining some social or economic reward through L2 achievement.

Distinctions have also been made between extrinsic and intrinsic bases of motivation. Intrinsic motivation often involves the desire to communicate and socialize with the people of the second language being learned, and is often associated with very advanced proficiency in the language. It makes sense that those who have an affinity for the second language culture would seek out more experiences and communication opportunities in order to attain this advanced level of proficiency. Dörnyei and Csizér (2002) give an extreme example of how extrinsic versus intrinsic motivation and language attitudes can affect language learning. In Hungary, Russian, the language of the former USSR, was seen as the language of an oppressive power. Although all Hungarian students had to study Russian for ten years, the proportion of Hungarians who actually spoke Russian decreased from 2.9% in 1979–1982 to only 1% in 1994. These statistics demonstrate that an extrinsic motive by itself, such as the language being a local lingua franca, does not necessarily motivate and promote language learning. There must also be an integrative aspect or positive attitude toward the L2 in order for successful acquisition to occur.

Although SLA researchers are still debating whether motivation *causes* language learning (e.g. by putting learners in contact with more input) or whether success in language learning gives rise to motivation, some recent studies do suggest that motivation helps to predict the level of proficiency that an L2 learner ultimately attains. Studies also show that motivation can change during the learning process, varying from day to day and even from task to task. A learner's motivation additionally appears to be affected by such factors as group dynamics, the learning environment, the learner's self-image, and even the learner's conversational *partner's* motivation. Research has further provided evidence for what savvy students and teachers have already figured out: varied and challenging instructional activities help learners to stay focused and engaged in learning and facilitate the second language learning process. (For two examples of studies of motivation, see Box 13.9.)

Context of second language learning

There are two different ways in which the term context is used in SLA. It is used to refer to the environmental context in which the learning occurs – in an immersion program, during study abroad, at home with an audiotape, in a university classroom, and so on. It is also used to refer to linguistic context, such as the topic of the conversation, the meanings that can be gleaned from surrounding discourse, and (more socially) the person with whom the learner is interacting. There is increasing evidence that all sorts of contextual factors may affect the second language learning process.

In order to investigate the role of context in SLA, recent research by Collentine and Freed (2004) has compared the relative linguistic gains made by two groups of native English-speaking students learning Spanish. One group studied at a university in the US, while the other took part in a study-abroad program in Spain, living with Spanish families. Students' language abilities were measured before and after the course of their studies, using oral interviews (among other measures) in order to determine proficiency. The study-abroad group significantly outperformed the US learners on oral fluency and also made greater improvements in their narrative abilities. On the other hand, the US learners experienced more lexico-grammatical growth than did their study-abroad counterparts. Although both groups improved over the course of their studies, however, neither improved significantly in their production of intervocalic voiced fricatives in such words as *todo* 'all,' *pagar* 'to pay,' and *vaya* 'go' (some of the most difficult sounds of Spanish for non-native speakers to produce). It is interesting to note that while these studies do not suggest that one context is superior to another for *all* language skills, they do show the influence that context can have on the development of particular aspects of the L2. Students learning an L2 in a second language context (for instance, learning English in the US) are likely to develop strengths and weaknesses which differ from those developed by L2 learners in a foreign language context (for instance, learning English in their home country).

SLA processes

In addition to investigating theories about how second languages are learned and how second language learners may vary in terms of individual differences, researchers also seek to understand various process-related factors that learners have in common. To this end, SLA researchers have focused on the psycholinguistics of second language learning – studying, for example, the roles of attention, developmental patterns, and fossilization in L2 acquisition. We now turn to a discussion of each of these processes.

Attention

What is the role of attention in language learning? When acquiring their first language, children often seem to be unaware of their own mistakes and of the corrections occasionally made by their parents. Research and anecdotal evidence have suggested that children frequently disregard the difference between what they say (e.g. *I holded the baby ducks*) and the models that are offered to them (*I held the baby ducks*); yet they still acquire their native languages with remarkable speed and accuracy. For second language learners, however, it has been hypothesized that conscious attention to linguistic form in the target language input is necessary for learning to occur. This is the central claim of the **noticing hypothesis** of SLA, put forward by Richard Schmidt (2001). According to this hypothesis, subliminal or unconscious learning is impossible. In other words, those features of the L2 that are not noticed do not get stored in the short-term memory system and thus are not learned. Schmidt's hypothesis further claims that since learners are exposed to much more language input than they can process, some kind of mechanism (attention) is necessary to help them sort through the large volume of language data and eventually to encode the data into memory (that is, to learn).

Research seeking to test this hypothesis and explore the role of attention in L2 learning has faced difficulties in clearly defining exactly what attention is and obtaining accurate measurements of it; however, some researchers are currently using more direct methods of measuring awareness. One way is through innovative applications of research methodologies originally used in other fields such as philosophy and psychology. Think-aloud protocols, for example, ask learners to verbalize their thought processes while they perform a task. Another method asks the learner to comment on a task or interaction after it has taken place, often using a stimulus such as a videotape of the original interaction. This is known as "stimulated recall" and is an increasingly popular method of uncovering information about what learners were attending to or noticing during language tasks. Two learners may derive the same answer through very different methods, and these introspective narrations provide insight into their internal processes. These verbalizations, whether online or retrospective, allow the researcher to understand how attention is drawn to particular forms in the second language during a task. Many studies carried out using such methods are finding increasing evidence that attention is one of the key cognitive processes underlying L2 development.

Developmental sequences

A major goal of SLA research has been to determine whether there are regular **developmental sequences** that are common to all second language learners. A developmental sequence is a series of identifiable stages that L2 learners pass through in acquiring the second language. Research approaches in this vein have included identifying when specific linguistic features are learned and examining how errors change over time (error analysis). This research shows that second language learners acquire the non-native language in a regular, systematic fashion, much like learners acquiring their native languages. For example, regardless of their L1 and the type of input they receive, learners of English pass through similar sequences of developmental stages when learning negation and question formation. Research suggests that instruction can speed up passage through a developmental sequence, but it cannot alter the order of the learning stages. These interesting findings have led some researchers to conclude that learning a second language involves psycholinguistic processes that are only minimally influenced by contextual factors and the learner's L1. Box 13.8 illustrates a well-researched developmental sequence in SLA.

Fossilization

Even though there are regular developmental patterns, one of the most salient (and frustrating) traits of second language learning is that L2 learners often do not sound like native speakers even after many years of study and practice. It has been argued that language learning typically fossilizes and remains permanently at a level short of native-like speech. More recently, some researchers have pointed out the difficulty of determining whether language learning has truly ceased or simply hit a temporary plateau. They have thus suggested the term **stabilization** is more appropriate than fossilization.

A wide variety of explanations have been offered to account for this phenomenon. As discussed earlier, one proposal is that the language acquisition mechanisms and processes that work so well in childhood may work less effectively for older learners, resulting in incomplete L2 development. There may also be sociolinguistic factors behind language

BOX 13.8 **DEVELOPMENTAL SEQUENCES**

Question formation is one of the best understood developmental sequences in the acquisition of English as a second language. Most researchers have found that second language learners of English typically pass through similar stages in learning how to form questions in English and that they do so in the same order (see the table below, which is based on research by Pienemann and Johnston 1986). If the development of question formation were influenced by one's native language, a native speaker of Chinese would have a noticeably different pattern of question development than would a native speaker of Spanish, for example. However, researchers have found that this is not the case; such processes are not affected by the learner's L1 or the amount and type of input they receive, suggesting that underlying psycholinguistic processes common to all human beings are the driving force behind SLA.

Proposed stages of question formation

Stage 1	*Single words or sentence fragments* (learners use question intonation with less than a complete clause)	One astronaut outside the spaceship?
Stage 2	*Canonical word order* (learners use a complete clause with question intonation)	It's a monster in the right corner? The boys throw the shoe? He have two house in the front?
Stage 3	*Wh-fronting and* do-*fronting* (direct questions with main verbs and question words, e.g. *do, are,* at the beginning of the question)	How many planets are in this picture? Where the little children are? What color the dog? Do you have a shoes on your picture? Does in this picture there is four astronauts?
Stage 4	*Pseudo-inversion* (in yes/no questions an auxiliary or modal is placed at the beginning of the question; in wh-questions, the subject and the copula change positions)	Where is the sun? The ball is it in the grass or in the sky?
Stage 5	Do/*Aux-second* (auxiliary verbs and modals are placed in second position to wh-words and before the subject)	Why did you leave? Where does your friend live?
Stage 6	*Question tag* *Negative question* *Subordinate clause*	You live here, don't you? Doesn't your wife speak English? Can you tell me where the station is?

(Adapted from Spada and Lightbown 1993)

learning stabilization: older learners, who may be more attached to their own social and linguistic identities than children, may find it less important to sound like native speakers of an L2. Furthermore, learners often seem to stabilize at a point where they are communicatively competent and therefore are no longer receiving feedback on their nontargetlike

BOX 13.9 **LONGITUDINAL VERSUS CROSS-SECTIONAL APPROACHES TO RESEARCH**

The main differences between longitudinal and cross-sectional studies concern the role of time in what is being investigated. In general, longitudinal studies involve collecting data from the same individuals or groups at different points in time, with the researcher collecting data regularly over many weeks, months, or even years to examine how a particular individual or group changes over time. A typical longitudinal study might seek to compare one group of learners' performance or knowledge of a particular linguistic structure at times A, B, and C. In cross-sectional research, on the other hand, data are typically collected at a single point in time, with the researcher looking for relationships or patterns in the data. For example, a cross-sectional study might examine learners' knowledge of a linguistic structure by looking at data collected at one point in time from beginning, intermediate, and advanced learners. In cross-sectional research, data can also be collected from comparable groups of learners that differ in a variable of interest to the researcher, such as the length of exposure to a particular language teaching approach. To illustrate some of the differences between longitudinal and cross-sectional research, we will first consider two studies that used questionnaires and surveys to investigate motivation in second language learning, and then consider a third study that examined differences in motivation and rate of acquisition among learners of different age groups.

In a study that adopted a longitudinal approach, Dörnyei and Csizér (2002) examined data collected from 8,593 Hungarian language learners, once in 1993 and again in 1999, comparing the two data sets in order to see how the learners' views had changed and evolved with respect to the learning of five target languages (English, German, French, Italian, and Russian) in light of the significant sociocultural changes that took place in Hungary in the 1990s. Dörnyei and Csizér found that there was an overall decline in the students' motivation to learn foreign languages, except in the case of English. They interpreted these data as reflecting what they called a "language globalization" process, whereby the study of the global language (i.e. English) and that of the other foreign languages showed an increasingly deviating pattern in terms of learners' motivations for

study. (Indeed, English – and other local lingua francas – have become a threat to many languages across the globe at an alarmingly increasing rate. See Nettle and Romaine 2000 for a further discussion on environmental and economic effects on language learning and loss.)

Using a cross-sectional design, Clément, Dörnyei, and Noels (1994) gathered information about Hungarian high school students' attitudes towards learning English. They administered a one-time survey to 301 students, finding a relationship between the students' attitudes toward learning the language and their self-confidence, motivational patterns, and the learning environment, and further observing that linguistic self-confidence is an important component of L2 motivation.

In an example of a different sort of cross-sectional study, Cenoz (2003) collected data from 135 primary and secondary students in Spain to find out whether (1) the rate of acquisition of a third language (English) was higher for older or younger children when learning time was held constant, (2) attitudes and motivation were more or less positive when the target language was taught from an early age, and (3) younger children tended to mix languages more often than older children. All participants had had 600 hours of instruction in English, but they had started learning at different ages (four, eight, and eleven years old). Cenoz found that the oldest group of learners obtained significantly higher results on most tests of language proficiency, but that the youngest learners showed more positive attitudes and motivation for learning English than the older groups. There were no significant differences between the groups in terms of code-switching on an oral production task. The study also, however, demonstrated the difficulty involved in making cross-sectional comparisons of groups of learners at different ages. It is possible that the older students' cognitive maturity and better developed test-taking strategies could help to explain their higher levels of linguistic development. In relation to both the students' reported motivation and the nature of the proficiency testing, it may also be of consequence that the older learners had received more traditional instruction, with grammar and writing practice, whereas the teaching methods for the younger children were more oral-based and active.

utterances. However, only very recently have researchers begun to conduct the necessary longitudinal studies of L2 development to investigate the factors behind plateaus in language learning. (See Box 13.9 below on the differences between longitudinal and cross-sectional studies.)

Instruction

The relationship between second language acquisition theory and second language pedagogy is the focus of much discussion in the field. Some SLA researchers have concentrated on the psycholinguistic aspects of second language acquisition, aligning themselves with researchers in formal linguistics and cognitive science. These researchers typically maintain that there need be no relationship between SLA and L2 pedagogy. Other SLA researchers believe that the results of SLA studies can be helpful if applied cautiously to language pedagogy. For example, research indicates that learners of English will acquire the third-person singular *s (She sings, he walks)* at a relatively late stage in the learning process. However, most introductory textbooks present this form in early chapters as part of the simple present tense. This mismatch between what teachers teach and what learners are ready to learn can be easily corrected if the teacher is aware of SLA research findings and can adapt the textbook accordingly. Some language teachers are eager to find out everything that research can tell them in order to optimize instructional practices, while others are cautious about applying the results of studies that do not appear to be relevant to their own classrooms and teaching contexts. Over the years, a number of attempts have been made to bring SLA research and language pedagogy together. In the section that follows, we will discuss some of the methodologies for L2 teaching and report where some of them have drawn on theories of learning.

Teaching methods

Language teaching methodologies reflect ideas about the processes and purposes of language learning. One of the earliest teaching methods for foreign language learning was the **Grammar Translation** approach. Traditionally used to teach Greek and Latin, it was based on the premise that the main purpose for studying these languages was as a tool for literary translation and research, as an effortful intellectual exercise in logic and deduction, and as evidence of the learners' erudition. The end goal was not oral communication; rather, learners were expected to develop explicit knowledge of language structure with constant reference to the L1. Accordingly, the Grammar Translation approach used classical literary texts to teach the vocabulary and grammar of the target language. Success was measured by students' ability to translate sentences (in writing) from the L2 into the L1 (and vice versa), and these sentences served mainly as exemplars of particular grammatical points as opposed to carriers of real-world meanings.

With an increase in the demand for oral proficiency in other foreign languages, this approach gradually fell out of favor. It was replaced by a more "natural" approach called the **Direct Method** (associated with the work of Charles Berlitz), which held that non-native languages, just like native languages, could be learned without translation and detailed grammar explanations. Teachers and researchers at the time had been noticing the ease with which children learn languages and concluded that an approach emphasizing the importance of understanding and conveying meaning could be useful for adults as well. Thus, as in first language learning, spontaneous oral interaction in a modern conversational style of the target language was seen as crucial; the approach to grammar was inductive, and concrete, everyday vocabulary was emphasized. Proponents of the Direct Method argued that if teachers presented all information in the L2, using actions or pictures when necessary, the second language learner could acquire the L2 naturally and directly.

The period from the 1950s to the 1980s has been referred to as "The Age of Methods" because a number of quite detailed proposals for teaching approaches emerged during this time. The **Audiolingual Method** emphasized spoken language and maintained that grammar should be taught inductively, with little or no explicit grammar explanation. Based on the principles of behaviorism and drawing on contrastive analyses of the L1 and L2, the Audiolingual Method claimed that language learning was essentially habit formation, requiring mimicry, rote memorization, teacher feedback, extensive drills, and over-learning to form habits. There was not much emphasis on meaning; rather, structures were presented one at a time in sequence, and it was seen as important to provide positive reinforcement for learners' correct responses while suppressing their errors.

After behaviorism fell out of favor in the 1960s, a new approach to foreign language teaching known as **Community Language Learning** began to receive more attention. L2 teachers and innovators made use of research insights in the fields of cognitive and educational psychology (e.g. by Vygotsky and Piaget), which led them to develop more humanistic methods focusing on the social interaction and affective and interpersonal factors in learning. In this method, teachers were seen as counselors rather than instructors, providing a warm, empathic, and nonthreatening environment where their clients (the students) could shed their insecurities and anxieties about learning a new language. In this way, the learners were gradually supposed to become more independent in using the L2 to express their own thoughts.

Around the same time, another method called the **Silent Way** (developed by Caleb Gattegno) also became more widespread. In contrast to Community Language Learning, however, the rationale behind this approach was more concerned with cognition than with affect. In this method, which viewed learning language as problem-solving, the teacher spoke only when necessary, thus encouraging students to figure out the rules of the language by themselves instead of relying on the teacher to model and guide the process. It was seen as important for students to raise their awareness about the L2 and become autonomous learners. To this end, props such as color-coded charts were used extensively to stimulate student analysis and use of the target language.

In the early 1980s, the **Natural Approach** became popular. Based on the Input and Natural Order Hypotheses discussed above, it was believed that if learners had a low enough affective filter, they would automatically acquire the target language when exposed to comprehensible input slightly above their current proficiency level. While the Natural Approach did not use any unique techniques, borrowing freely instead from other methods, it was innovative in its focus on meaningful communication within a

---

BOX 13.10 EXAMPLE OF A ROLE-PLAYING ACTIVITY BETWEEN A NATIVE SPEAKER AND A NON-NATIVE SPEAKER

Below is a conversation between a native speaker (NS) and a non-native speaker (NNS). The native speaker asks the non native speaker whether or not she would like to have her ears pierced. The non native speaker refuses and is able to practice negotiation and culturally appropriate refusal methods.

NS: yeah. y'd I-wouldja like to get your ears pierced like that?
NNS: oh yes. (NOD)
NS: you'd like to? good I'll call my girlfriend, my g-see see what my girlfriend did to my ears? all these studs?
NNS: NOD
NS: I'm gonna call my girlfriend right now. ok? all right?
NNS: wait a minute
NS: what what?
NNS: I want to pierce my ears but mm someday, mm NOD
NS: oh but she can do it right now, she does it really well, she see see what she said I mean it doesn't hurt it just hurts y'know it's a little sting? and then it's all over? she does it really well,
NNS: oh no, but uh
NS: my ears were only infected for three months (laughs)
NNS: but I uh nn I'm not determined yet, nn
NS: you're not determined yet
NNS: umm yeh NOD
NS: . . . I can call my girlfriend (.) right away,
NNS: oohh nn no thank you very much
NS: are you sure?
NNS: NOD
NS: sure? I c'n we c'n just do it and it just takes twenty minutes, it doesn't take a long time
NNS: ohhh no hh
NS: I can call her
NNS: no thank you
NS: ok, ok, all right,
NNS: NOD

(From Gass and Houck 1999)

---

nonthreatening classroom environment. However, with increasing criticism of Krashen's theories of language acquisition, the natural approach began to give way to Communicative Language Teaching (CLT), which is now one of the most commonly employed approaches in classrooms today.

Like the Natural Approach, CLT also highlights communication as a means of facilitating language development. However, whereas the Natural Approach focused almost exclusively on speaking and paying attention to meaning (with little attention to matters of form), CLT addresses all four skills (speaking, listening, reading, and writing). It also incorporates recent insights about the importance of active learner participation and the development of communicative competence, emphasizing that students need to be able to *produce* language in linguistically and culturally appropriate ways to carry out certain functions. For example, two students could work together on a map activity to figure out the correct route to a restaurant from the school. One learner would have a set of directions from *MapQuest* with half of them blanked out, and the other learner would have the actual map. Without seeing each other's pictures, they would have to work together using locative constructions, questions, and negatives in order to complete the task successfully with language that is sufficiently fluent and accurate. In CLT, the teacher's role is not so much to provide comprehensible input, but rather to act as an advisor and facilitator, answering questions and creating learning situations in which students can engage in purposeful communication (through games, role plays, problem-solving activities, and the like). These activities typically focus on a particular communicative function with a meaningful purpose, such as making an invitation or offering advice in an unrehearsed context. Box 13.10 provides an example of a typical activity within the communicative approach.

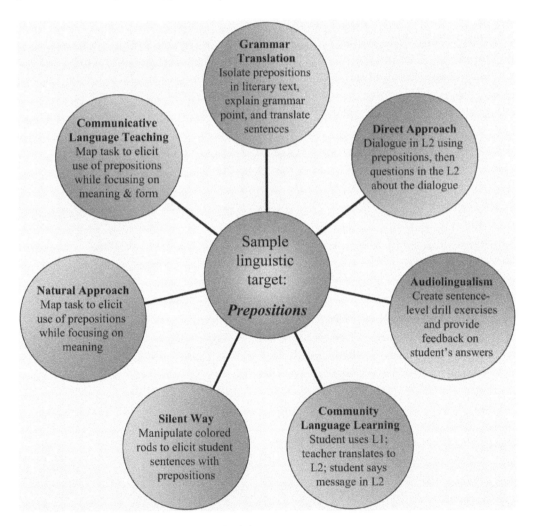

Figure 13.1 Selected ESL/EFL teaching methodologies

It is important to remember that today most language teachers do not adhere strictly to one method or another, but instead use a combination of approaches, depending upon the goals of the lesson, the characteristics of their learners, and institutional factors, among other things. Instead of thinking of **Communicative Language Teaching** as a concrete method, it may make more sense to view it as an overall approach reflecting theories about the nature of the processes and purposes for language learning. Figure 13.1 gives an example of how one linguistic target, prepositions, might be taught under each of the approaches discussed in this section.

Bridging the theory–pedagogy gap

Advances in SLA research and linguistic theory have influenced how languages are thought to be learned and taught. Current SLA research suggests that in selecting a method, teachers also need to consider their learners' backgrounds and the context and institutional constraints within which they are working, as well as their own experience and intuitions about what does and does not work for their learners in the L2 classroom. SLA theory should not dictate what happens in the classroom, but it can provide language teachers with information about classroom possibilities and ideas that they can evaluate for their own adaptation. For example, ideas about how to teach prepositions are currently emerging from cognitive linguistics, which suggests that the ideal instructional strategy would be to explain from a cognitive linguistic standpoint how prepositions might be related to each other in spatial terms, and then to provide learners with communicative activities to apply their understanding. If research provides evidence for this idea, then another circle entitled "Cognitive Linguistics Instruction" can be added to Figure 13.1. Another idea that is currently popular with SLA researchers and L2 teachers alike is task-based language teaching, which we will discuss in more detail below.

Task-based language teaching and learning

Task-based language teaching is grounded in the interactionist approach to second language learning, which as we saw earlier, suggests that L2 acquisition is facilitated when language learners negotiate for comprehensible input, receive feedback, and modify their output. Task-based language teaching uses authentic, real-world communicative activities that allow learners to interact with each other to resolve linguistic problems and achieve defined goals. These tasks focus on meaning and real-world communication, but at the same time encourage learners to pay attention to linguistic forms that cause comprehension or production problems. The approach thus contrasts with traditional methods of language teaching in which the teacher explicitly draws the learners' attention to formal aspects of the language (as in the Grammar Translation approach reviewed above).

When learners experience breakdowns of communication while engaged in the communication of meaning, they often give and receive feedback on each other's utterances. This, in turn, can draw their attention to non-native uses of linguistic forms (e.g. in pronunciation and syntax) that may otherwise go unnoticed in everyday conversation, and language learning can occur as learners reformulate their utterances in order to make themselves understood. In addition, through encouraging conversational interaction, tasks allow learners to practice speaking and hearing the language. This cluster of events has the potential to improve L2 production and development and is supported by at least fifty empirical studies as well as six syntheses and meta-analyses so far. (A meta-analysis summarizes, compares, and takes into account a number of different types of experiments and research findings.)

Looking more closely at the idea of a language teaching task, we can ask what it means for learners to interact together in resolving a linguistic problem while achieving a defined goal. Tasks can involve various activities, such as arriving at a single, correct solution, arriving at a group consensus, or even creating a picture or a second language text. Crucially, the learners must use the target language in order to complete the task, and oftentimes particular linguistic forms are necessary for successful task completion. For example, in picture story jigsaw tasks, learners work in pairs; each learner receives one half of a picture story, and the learners are required to put the story together by describing their pictures to each other. Since they cannot show each other their pictures, the only way for the learners to complete the task successfully is through communicating with each other using language.

In classifying different types of tasks, it is useful to point out that they vary along a number of dimensions, including:

- The flow of information (Does one person hold all the information, or do both partners have different information which they must share?)
- The open or closed nature of the task goal (Is there one correct solution, or are learners relatively free to come up with their own solution?)
- The degree of task complexity (Does the task follow an expected series of events, or are learners unsure about the next event? For example, do the learners have to order a series of pictures depicting a restaurant meal, or do they have to work out the logic behind a Mr. Bean TV episode, where the main character often does seemingly inexplicable things, such as placing a dog inside the glove compartment of a very small car?)
- The availability and length of planning time (including concerns such as whether the planning is directed by the teacher and whether notes are allowed)

Amidst a growing consensus that task-based learning can facilitate second language acquisition, researchers are currently investigating which types of tasks are the most effective and under what conditions. This is as it should be: ultimately, the relationship between teaching and research should be a two-way street, with research informing teaching practice and teaching informing research agendas.

CHAPTER SUMMARY

Second language acquisition is a broad, complex, dynamic, and exciting field of inquiry that is relevant to real-world concerns. For very practical reasons, many instructors and students wonder about the issues of why individuals learn differently and how they can teach and learn languages efficiently. Many questions are also more theoretical in nature, related to how the brain and language work. Despite significant advances over the past forty years, there is much that remains to be uncovered. SLA is a relatively young field, and many areas are ripe for well-founded and potentially rewarding research.

SLA researchers have a number of available sources of insight from which to draw theoretical foundations for studies of language learning. This chapter introduced some of the most prominent theories and hypotheses about how languages are learned, including early ideas drawing on behaviorist psychology as well as the more recent viewpoints put forward by interactionists, socioculturalists, and frequency researchers. Researchers operating in these various paradigms have a variety of methodological tools – including studies of natural learning sequences, analyses of interaction employing recasts, sociocultural studies of how learning unfolds in learner–learner collaboration, UG studies using acceptability judgment tests, frequency-based studies making use of connectionist modeling, and studies of motivation using survey data. An important source of knowledge – theoretical and practical – lies in the individual differences between learners that have been found to play a role in SLA: learners' L1s, age, gender, working memory, different aspects of motivation, and the learning context. Cognitive factors such as attention, developmental sequences, and fossilization also play important roles in SLA.

Finally, this chapter introduced a number of language teaching methodologies, and their connections to SLA theory. Grammar Translation, the Direct Method, Audiolingualism, Community Language Learning, the Silent Way, the Natural Approach, and Communicative Language Teaching all represent significant trends in the second language teaching field, and the current use of Task-based Language Teaching, with its grounding in interactionist research, can be seen as bridging the gap between theory and practice. This mutual influence – along with the variety of approaches, hypotheses, and interdisciplinary insights that SLA researchers have at their disposal – makes SLA a fascinating field of inquiry with a promising outlook in the drive towards a comprehensive theory of second language acquisition.

Exercises

EXERCISE 13.1

Examine the following extracts of conversation between a learner and her native-speaker partner. Identify the following elements of the interaction: (a) a clarification request, (b) a recast, and (c) modified output.

Is the modified output more or less targetlike? Refer to examples (1)–(3) in this chapter for similar data. Do you find any evidence of (d) scaffolding in this conversation?

A.

NS:	There's there's a a pair of reading glasses above the plant.
NNS:	A what?
NS:	Glasses, reading glasses to see the newspaper?
NNS:	Glassi?
NS:	You wear them to see with, if you can't see. Reading glasses.
NNS:	Ahh ahh glasses glasses to read you say reading glasses.
NS:	Yeah.

(From Mackey 1999: 558–559)

B. Recall that some researchers include think-alouds or retrospective recalls from the learners to shed light on the thought processes of learners. Examine the following interaction. Determine the elements of the interaction as in A. How does the learner's recall shed light on the interaction and thought process?

NNS:	We don't know the truth until we tried it itself.
NS:	We don't know the truth until we have tried it ourselves.
NNS:	Right.
NNS recall:	Well, I thought what I said was grammatically incorrect. But … well … I didn't know where was wrong.

(From Kim and Han 2007: 283)

EXERCISE 13.2

Take a look at the following acceptability judgment test that was provided as an example on p. 455. In addition to marking your own answers, ask two non-native speakers of English to take the test as well. Do their answers agree with each other? Do their answers match yours? Consider how you might modify this test to gain more insight into the learners' language. For example, you could ask them how confident they are in their answers.

	1	2	3	4	5
Is the boy who standing over there is happy?					
I read a book of which my professor had recommended the style.					
Yesterday I saw a girl of whom I have forgotten the name.					
This is a book of which I hate the title.					
How many did you buy of the books?					

EXERCISE 13.3

Make a note of the six individual learner differences discussed in this chapter. Using a recent second language learning or teaching experience of your own, explain how two of these individual differences may have influenced your experience.

EXERCISE 13.4

Read Box 13.7 on gender differences in language learning. Try and think of a recent mixed-gender learning experience and comment on how gender could have affected the interaction. Can you think of other differences between men and women's conversational styles that may affect language learning in mixed-gender pairings? Take a look at the section on language and gender in Chapter 10 for a closer look at gender and conversation. How might culture and cultural expectations for different genders affect learning in mixed-gender interactions?

EXERCISE 13.5

Second language learners' motivation appears to be influenced by group dynamics, the learning environment, and one's classroom partners, among other things. In L2 classrooms, research suggests that teachers can help learners to stay focused and engaged with instructional content by making use of varied and challenging instructional activities. Describe an example of a classroom language teaching activity that you believe could positively influence instrumental motivation and explain why.

EXERCISE 13.6

In the table below, assign the questions asked by second language learners to developmental stages based on the Pienemann–Johnston sequence from Box 13.8.

Stage	Question
	What is in the bag?
	Haven't you been to Japan?
	Where does your friend live?
	Does in this room there is computer?
	Your notebook is blue?

Ask a fellow student who is learning English as a second language to interview you. Record his or her questions and see where they fit in the Pienemann–Johnston sequence.

EXERCISE 13.7

Assume you are a language teacher with a class of fifteen beginning-level English learners who are college students from a range of L1 backgrounds. You have two aims for a 50-minute class: (a) to teach third-person singular s *(She walks, he sings)*, and (b) to teach the class something about American culture, specifically, the upcoming Thanksgiving holiday. Design activities that fit with three of the methods presented in the table below. Each activity should provide grammar teaching within a culture-based context, as in the example provided below for Communicative Language Teaching. Compare your teaching activities with those designed by your classmates.

Approach	Task activity	Linguistic form	Thanksgiving cultural content
Communicative Language Teaching	*Picture-ordering activity where each learner holds half the pictures and they have to figure out the order by explaining to each other what the Smith family are doing on Wednesday and Thursday*	*3SG s: shops, cooks, sets, carves, eats, talks, watches*	*Typical elements in the family meal, typical pre- and post-meal activities*
Grammar Translation			
Direct Method			
Audiolingualism			
Silent Way			
Community Language Learning			
Natural Approach			
Task-based Language Teaching			

SUGGESTIONS FOR FURTHER READING

Ellis, R. 1997, *The study of second language acquisition*, Oxford University Press. This 824-page book covers virtually every aspect of L2 learning, and the information is presented in a highly readable manner.

Lardiere, D. 2006, *Ultimate attainment in second language acquisition: a case study*, Mahwah, NJ: Lawrence Erlbaum. This book examines the various reasons behind why some adult second language learners do not seem to progress in their L2s.

Larsen-Freeman, D. 2000, *Techniques and principles in language teaching*, Oxford University Press. This book provides a succinct discussion of the main methods and approaches in second language teaching.

Mackey, A. 2007, *Conversational interaction in second language acquisition*, Oxford University Press. This book is a collection of studies on individual, social, and cognitive factors in conversational interaction and the effect of interactional feedback on second language learning.

Mackey, A. and Gass, S. 2005, *Second language research: methodology and design*, Mahwah, NJ: Lawrence Erlbaum. This book describes the various methods and techniques for collecting and analyzing data from second language learners.

Philp, J., Adams, R., and Iwashita, N. 2014, *Peer interaction and second language learning*, New York and London: Routledge. This readable book provides a fascinating and up-to-date account of the increasingly popular topic of how learners can learn from each other.

Tomasello, M. 1995, "Language is not an instinct," *Cognitive Development* 10: 131–156. This article challenges the nativist approach to second language acquisition.

14 Computational linguistics

CHAPTER PREVIEW

The goal of having a computer understand and communicate in a human language has long been a dream of science fiction. In recent years part of this dream has become reality as scientists have developed computer programs that can understand and learn aspects of human languages, in both written and spoken form. These systems are also capable, to varying degrees, of translating between languages. The methods these programs use derive from both linguistics and computer science, and they reveal a relationship between the patterns found in human languages and in mathematical languages. These programs can sift through large online samples of everyday language (called corpora), counting how often particular forms actually occur in everyday use. This allows linguistic rules to be weighted based on such statistics, and these weights are used by the programs to identify more likely linguistic analyses of ambiguous utterances. The success of such programs also suggests that humans might learn by induction based on statistical regularities in their experience. The practical tools developed by computational linguists can be used to carry out linguistic analyses on a larger scale than ever before. Even more significantly, these tools can radically change the way we acquire and communicate information. All these factors make computational linguistics an intellectually lively, exciting, and influential area of study.

GOALS

The goals of this chapter are to:

- describe some of the linguistic problems that computational linguists work on
- provide examples of the methods they use
- outline some important applications of computational linguistics
- characterize some of the intellectual debates in the field
- discuss the major challenges facing computational linguists today

The computational perspective

The idea of computers "doing" linguistics might at first seem strange, since we have traditionally associated language primarily with humans, but this chapter will show that working within the framework of computational linguistics is actually a very natural way to understand language.

First, a definition: computational linguistics seeks to develop the computational machinery needed for an agent to exhibit various forms of linguistic behavior. By "agent," we mean both human beings and artificial agents such as computer programs. By "machinery," we mean computer programs as well as the linguistic knowledge that they contain.

What does it mean for a computer to communicate in or interpret a human language? After all, computers have no inherent intelligence. Their linguistic capabilities derive from programs that are written for them. Computational linguistics therefore involves designing and developing programs to carry out linguistic tasks. These programs are based mainly on methods developed by computer scientists, but they use linguistic knowledge developed by linguists. So computational linguistics integrates ideas from linguistics and computer science.

The connection between these two fields is hardly an accident. Language involves complex symbol systems, and computers are very fast mechanical symbol-processors. There are natural connections between linguistic processing and computation, between the complexity of linguistic patterns and the complexity of mathematical models of computation. These connections raise important questions about how human beings represent and process linguistic knowledge.

Since the 1990s, computers have become steadily faster and have provided access to increasing quantities of online linguistic data (the Web being a prime example). Methods based on statistical analyses of such data have dramatically improved the accuracy with which systems carry out tasks like understanding the syntactic structure of a sentence. The success of such methods has raised questions about how language is represented and processed by the human mind, and particularly about the role of statistics in language understanding. It also suggests that humans might learn from experience by means of induction using statistical regularities.

In addition to pushing the envelope of linguistic theory, applications of computational linguistics have yielded practical tools that can benefit society tremendously. Most people who use computers are familiar with tools such as spelling and grammar checkers, as well as Web search engines such as Google, without realizing that they involve aspects of computational linguistics. Here are some other activities that natural language processing (NLP) systems can do:

- **speech processing:** *getting flight information or booking a hotel over the phone*
- **information extraction**: *discovering names of people, organizations, and places from a collection of documents*
- **machine translation**: *translating a document from one human language into another*
- **question answering:** *finding answers to natural language questions in a collection of texts or a database*
- **summarization:** *generating a short biography of someone from one or more news articles*

In the following sections, we will examine the application of computational linguistics methods to a range of linguistic phenomena, illustrating the problems and approaches. We begin with words, focusing on the use of computers to analyze the internal structure, or morphology, of words. We then move on to the grammatical structure of sentences, discussing syntactic processing. Next, we discuss semantic processing – that is, using computers to extract meaning from sentences. We then briefly overview the automatic generation of text by computers, before discussing the role of linguists in computational linguistics system development, the issue of categorical (all-or-nothing) rules versus probabilistic rules, and examples of interesting explorations of linguistic data that computational linguistic tools make possible. We then introduce various applications like speech recognition and synthesis and machine translation, before concluding with an assessment of the major challenges facing the field.

Morphological processing

Morphology is the study of the structure of words. The task of an automatic morphological analyzer is to take a word in a language and break it down into its stem form along with any affixes that it may have attached to that stem. In processing a sentence such as *Husain reads well*, the analyzer should be able to identify *Husain* as a proper name, *reads* as the third-person singular present form of the verb *read* (*read* + *s*), and *well* as either an adverb or a singular noun.

Notice that the morphological analyzer will not be able to identify the syntactic roles of words – for example, that *Husain* is the subject of *reads*. This is the subsequent task of a syntactic parsing program. An important strategy in computational linguistics is to treat language as modular, or composed of different subsystems, and to develop and integrate modules for different subsystems. As we've seen in previous chapters, this is similar to linguists' theories of human language as well.

Tokenization

Usually, the first step in morphological analysis is to identify separate words, a process called **tokenization**. This can be fairly simple in languages like English, where words are delimited by spaces and punctuation characters, and where sentences start with capital letters. But even in English, ambiguous punctuation can cause tokenization problems. For example, periods may be part of an abbreviation (*U.K. products*) or may indicate sentence-final punctuation; a tokenizer needs to be able to automatically distinguish these.

In languages where the orthography, or written form, doesn't mark word boundaries with spaces or punctuation, tokenization is a more challenging problem. In some of these languages, the notion of what a word is may not be clear. Consider the following Japanese sentence containing Chinese *kanji* and Japanese *hiragana* characters:

(1)   犬に当る男の子は私の兄弟である。

inuobuttaotokonokowaotootoda

inuo	butta	otokonokowa	otootoda
dog+OBJ	hit+PAST	boy+SUBJ	younger-brother+be-PRES

'The boy who hit the dog is my brother.'

With Chinese *kanji* characters, in particular, there is a genuine ambiguity as to how certain common multi-character words are to be segmented, and different morphological analyzers sometimes differ in their segmentation decisions.

Morphological analysis and synthesis

An automatic morphological analyzer takes a word and breaks it down into its component morphemes (stems and affixes). Sometimes, instead of a full morphological analysis, a simple **stemming** algorithm is used which strips off suffixes to arrive at a stem form. Stemming is used in applications like search engines, which are perfectly happy to find *love* when given the search word *loved*, but it is less useful in situations where in-depth syntactic and semantic analyses are needed.

Another strategy is to use a fully inflected lexicon, which (ideally) includes all the possible affixed forms of every word in the language. The analyzer simply looks up the word in the list. Such lists are almost inevitably incomplete, and they can become too large and unwieldy for computers to handle. For example, Tamil has about 2,000 inflected forms *per verb*, while the number of inflected forms for a given Turkish stem (Hankamer 1989) may be in the millions! Real morphological analysis and disambiguation – rather than shortcuts like stemming algorithms or fully inflected lexicons – are necessary when dealing with such languages.

Language learners are familiar with textbooks that teach a rule (a regular pattern in the target language like "To form the past tense of a verb in English, add -*ed*") and then teach all the "exceptions" to the rule (for example, irregular verbs like *bring* and *come*). One approach to a full morphological analysis is to store only exceptional forms in the lexicon, and handle the regular patterns with morphological rules. A typical strategy for applying morphological rules is the **pattern–action** approach. A computer program identifies words that match the rule's pattern; it then records that word's morphological components, as specified by the rule's action.

Here is an example of a pattern–action morphological rule with an exception (from the system of Minnen, Carroll, and Pearce 2001):

(2) $\{V|C\}^+\{C\}ied => $ string-transform $(3, y + ed)$
      boogied $=> $ string-transform $(1, + ed)$

Each rule has a pattern on the left-hand side (also called a "regular expression"), and an action on the right. The first rule says that a word made up of one or more alphabetic characters {in the set of vowels V or consonants C} followed by a consonant character {in the set C} and followed by *ied* is transformed by removing the last three characters (*ied*), and replacing them with *y* followed by +*ed*. Thus, *cried* is analyzed as a form consisting of the morpheme *cry* followed by the past morpheme + *ed*: *cried* = *cry* + *ed*.

Now, if we applied this rule to *boogied* (whose stem is *boogie*), it would produce an incorrect analysis: *boogied* = *boogy* + *ed*. To address exceptions like this, more specific rules (like the second rule in (2)) are listed below general rules. As a processing strategy, all the rules are applied in order to the input word, using the analysis produced by the last rule which succeeds.

The task of an automatic morphological *synthesizer* is to produce a word, given the stem form along with the affixes. The rules shown in (2) are used for analysis; different rules are required for synthesis. For example, to produce *cried* from *cry* and + *ed*, we could use the pattern $\{V|C\}^+\{C\}y + ed => $ string-transform $(4, ied)$.

Having separate rules written for analysis and synthesis, even though they are clearly related, can be awkward. Having separate rules for each direction also seems unnatural; we humans, at least, must tap into the same linguistic knowledge whether we are understanding or producing language. Since operations like "string-transform" are invoked in a different way in analysis compared to synthesis, one way to address this is to remove any references to such processing strategies within morphological rules. The result is a representation that is declarative, i.e. that doesn't make reference to procedures or processing strategies. Computational linguists like to have declarative representations of linguistic information, because these representations clearly separate the linguistic data from the processing strategies (computer programs) that operate on the data. A more declarative representation than (2), which could be used in both analysis and synthesis, would specify a mapping between surface forms (e.g. *cried*) and the underlying forms (e.g. *cry* + *ed*). An example of such a mapping is shown in (3a).

(3)   a. (<c, c>, <r, r>, <i, y>, <e, +>, <d, ed>)

(3a) states that a *c* as the first symbol in the surface form maps to a *c* as the first symbol in the underlying form, that an *r* as the second symbol in the surface form maps to an *r* as the second symbol in the underlying form, and so forth, with finally the *d* in the surface form mapping to *ed* in the underlying form. The mapping doesn't assume anything about the direction of processing and, as we shall see, can be used for both analysis and synthesis.

To process inputs and produce outputs, the mappings expressed in (3a) are used by a program called a **finite-state transducer**. This is shown in (3b).

(3)   b.

Let's walk through the example of the computer analyzing *cried* using the transducer representation in (3b). It starts in the initial "state" (labeled "1" in (3b)). On seeing *c* in its input (above the arrow), the transducer prints *c* as its output (below the arrow), and advances to state 2. Next, on seeing *r* in its input, it prints *r* as its output, and advances to state 3. Then, on seeing *i* in its input, it prints *y* in its output, advancing to state 4. On seeing *e* in its input, it prints "+" in its output, advancing to state 5. Finally, on seeing "*d*" in its input, it prints *ed* in its output, and thus reaches the final state (labeled ●). Thus, given *cried* as input, the transducer yields *cry* + *ed* as output. Since transducers are bidirectional, they can be used in both morphological analysis and synthesis. In morphological synthesis, starting with *cry* + *ed* as the input, the transducer yields *cried* as the output.

The finite-state transducer in (3b) is called "finite-state" because it uses just a finite number of states (six, in this case), and the number of states is predetermined before it starts any processing. (A device which is not finite-state, by contrast, may require its memory to grow as it processes its input.) One nice property of finite-state transducers is that they can be strung together in various ways. This property allows very complex finite-state devices to be assembled in a modular fashion from simpler "building block" finite-state devices, rather like Lego blocks are put together to create a complex structure. Finite-state methods used in morphological analysis are widely used in phonology as well.

> **Quick comprehension check**
> By now, you should understand how computer programs can analyze and synthesize words in a language, even one with a rich inflectional morphology. Test your understanding by solving Exercise 14.1!

Syntactic processing

In this section, we will introduce the problem of trying to get a computer to characterize the grammatical structure of a sentence. Given a set of linguistic rules that describe how elements of a sentence can be put together (a grammar), a computer program called a syntactic parser will try to find the best grammatical analysis of a sentence. If the sentence is ambiguous (that is, if it has more than one possible grammatical structure), the syntactic parser will produce all analyses. Consider this short sentence:

(4)   I can fish.

This sentence could mean that I know how to fish, or that I habitually put fish in cans. In the first reading, *can* is a modal auxiliary verb; in the second sentence, *can* is the main verb. These two different meanings correspond to distinct syntactic structures.

Context-free grammars

We can describe the structure of sentences like (4) in terms of a grammar, expressed as a system of rules. These rules, called phrase structure rules, break up a sentence into its constituent parts, consisting of syntactic phrases or words. Such a grammar is shown in (5).

(5)

S → NP VP	V → can
VP → Aux V	V → fish
VP → V NP	V → dance
VP → V	Aux → can
VP → Aux V NP	D → the
NP → D N	N → fish
NP → N	N → dance
NP → Pronoun	Pronoun → I

We will call this kind of partial, simplified grammar a "toy" grammar, since it "handles," somewhat awkwardly, only a tiny fragment of the language. To improve processing speed, computational linguists often use simplified grammars, representing only those elements of syntactic structure that are required for a particular application.

This toy grammar recognizes four different kinds of VPs (Aux V, V NP, V, and Aux V NP) and three kinds of NPs (D N, N, and Pronoun). The categories to the left of the arrow in the left-hand column (S, NP, and VP) are structural categories; they can be expanded into other categories, but not directly into words. So here a sentence (S) is made up of a noun phrase followed by a verb phrase. Another way to put this is that a sentence (S) can be rewritten as, or expanded into, a noun phrase followed by a verb phrase. The categories to the left of the arrow in the right-hand column are lexical categories (or parts of speech); they map to particular words. All the categories to the left of the arrow (in either column) are called "nonterminals," since they rewrite to other categories or words. Words, in turn, don't rewrite to anything, and are therefore called "terminals."

Our toy grammar covers only three different verbs, one auxiliary verb, one determiner, two nouns, and one pronoun, but even so it can describe quite a variety of sentences. Grammars written in this format are called **context-free grammers**.

"Toy grammar" abbreviations
Symbol Meaning

Aux	Auxiliary (e.g. 'can')
D	Determiner (e.g. 'the')
N	Noun
NP	Noun Phrase
S	Sentence
V	Verb
VP	Verb Phrase
→	(right arrow) "is made up of"

This toy grammar represents the structure of a set of sentences which have a similar syntactic structure – in this case, declarative sentences of the form "NP VP." A real grammar would need to be extended to add parts of speech like adjectives and adverbs, and to handle syntactic structures like questions, imperatives, and relative clauses. It also would need to handle things like subject–verb agreement, as in *He cans tuna*, and much more.

Although incomplete, even our toy grammar can represent a variety of syntactic forms: *I fish, I can dance, I can the fish, I can can fish*, etc. Just adding more words to the lexicon (the right-hand column of (5)) will allow a large number of sentences to be covered, without making the grammar more complex.

Parsing

Now, how can we get a computer to analyze the syntactic structure of a sentence like *I can fish* (4)? A computer program which does this is called a parser. A *parser takes* an input sentence and produces one or more syntactic representations of it. It produces a single representation if the sentence is syntactically unambiguous, but more than one representation if there is syntactic ambiguity (as in *I can fish*). One way to represent the hierarchical syntactic structure of a sentence is called a **parse tree**. Here are the two parse trees for (4): the parser takes *I can fish* as input and processes it using the grammar in (5) to produce parse trees (6) and (7) as output.

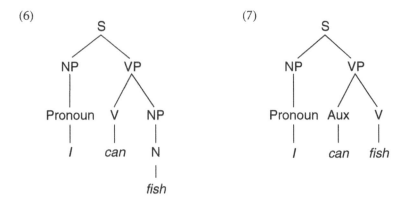

There are several types of parsers. A top-down parser, as you might expect, builds the parse trees from the top down. Given the grammar in (5), the top of the parse tree is always "S," so a top-down parser would start with the rules for S and expand each constituent a step at a time.

Here is how top-down parsing works, using the grammar in (5) applied to *I can fish*. The grammar starts with one rule, which amounts to "Assume a sentence (S)." Applying this rule produces a small tree of the form shown in (8a). Applying the S rule (S → NP VP), the parser produces the parse tree in (8b).

There are two nodes in the parse tree (8b) that the parser could expand: NP and VP. The parser is designed to expand the left-most nonterminal node (on the right-hand side of the rule) first. So in this case the parser will choose the node NP, shown with a circle in (8b), and try to expand, or further specify, what that NP node contains. The grammar in (5) states three possible expansions for NP (NP → D N, NP → N, NP → Pronoun). The parser will generate three possible partial parse trees, shown in (8c).

(8)   **a.**   (i)

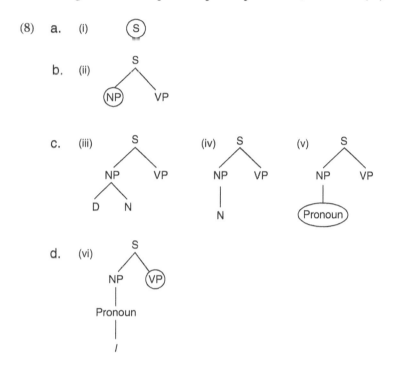

b.   (ii)

c.   (iii)   (iv)   (v)

d.   (vi)

Expanding the first tree (iii) in (8c) will not be possible, because according to the NP → D N rule, the first nonterminal should be a determiner (D), and according to the grammar, D expands to the word *the*, which doesn't match the start of the input (*I*). So, the parser finds that tree (iii) is a dead-end and tries the next possible expansion of NP.

The second tree (iv) in (8c) has a similar problem; the NP → N rule predicts a noun, but the only nouns in the grammar (*fish* and *dance*) don't match the first word of the input sentence *I can fish*, which is *I*. This leads the parser to check the third NP expansion rule (NP → Pronoun). The grammar states that the lexical category Pronoun can be expanded to *I*, which matches the start of the input, so the parser expands Pronoun to *I*, as shown in (8d). I is a terminal category, so the parser, having expanded the NP node as far as it can, turns to the "new" left-most nonterminal (VP) and uses the grammar to expand it.

The process continues until all the words in the input are covered. Describing the process takes a long time, but computers can run through it in a fraction of a second!

In contrast to working top-down, a parser could proceed bottom-up, somewhat as structures were built in Chapter 3. In the first steps, each input word is associated with a lexical category. For example, *I* would be associated with a Pronoun node. Then, the lexical category nodes are connected to their parent nodes using the rules of the grammar, so that, for example, Pronoun will be a child of NP. Bottom-up parsers may waste time building structures that don't lead to an S, while top-down parsers may, as we have seen, waste time expanding structures that don't lead to a match with the input. More advanced parsing strategies, like chart parsing, combine top-down and bottom-up approaches.

> **Quick comprehension check**
> This is a good time to pause and confirm that you have understood how a parser, given a grammar, can syntactically analyze a sentence in a language. In fact, you should be able to mimic the steps the computer takes in carrying out a top-down parse of a sentence. Exercises 14.2 and 14.3 will further consolidate your understanding.

Part-of-speech tagging

As we have seen, a word (like *can* and *fish*) can have different possible parts of speech. Instead of having the parser consider all parts of speech of an ambiguous word, it is possible to reduce the ambiguity prior to parsing, by running a program called a **part-of-speech tagger** before parsing. To each word that has more than one part of speech, the tagger assigns the most likely part of speech. This is done based on context-based rules derived by human intuition (for example, after *the*, *fish* is likely to be a noun), as well as rules derived by machines that learn from a collection of example sentences that have been tagged already with parts of speech. (See the Box 14.3 on "The changing role of linguists" for more information about how linguists help develop automatic part-of-speech tagging programs.)

While part-of-speech tagging can reduce ambiguity due to parts of speech, it cannot reduce other kinds of syntactic ambiguity, such as deciding, given the sentence *The astronomer saw the planet with a telescope*, whether the prepositional phrase *with a telescope* modifies the VP *saw the planet* or the NP *the planet* (a decision which humans can easily make!).

Beyond context-free grammars

One problem with context-free grammars is that they require many rules. For example, if we want to add subject–verb agreement to the grammar, so that we get a successful parse for *I dance* and *he dances* (but not *he dance* or *I dances*), we would have to create two S rules, one which combines ThirdPersonSingularNP with ThirdPersonSingularVP, and another which combines NonThirdPersonSingularNP with NonThirdPersonSingularVP. In addition, we would have to create separate rewrite rules for each of these more specific NP and VP categories. And, as we added new types of Ss to cover questions and imperatives, we would have to create corresponding "agreement" branches in them as well. This approach may yield a descriptively adequate grammar, but it is not very elegant or efficient.

Instead, it is possible to augment a grammar like (5) with features – for example, agreement features like number and person, or grammatical relations like subject and object. The parser then has to ensure that the agreement features of the NP and the VP match, a process known as unification. The cost of the increased expressiveness in the linguistic representation is a slowing down of the parsing process, due to the need to carry

BOX 14.1 DECLARATIVE VERSUS PROCEDURAL GRAMMARS

A variety of syntactic theories have been developed based on unification-based grammars, including Lexical Functional Grammar (LFG) (Kaplan and Bresnan 1982), Head-Driven Phrase Structure Grammar (HPSG) (Pollard and Sag 1994), and Unification Categorial Grammar (Zeevat, Klein, and Calder 1991). These unification-based theories differ in one crucial way from transformational theories of syntax, like the theory presented in Chapter 3. Transformational theories make use of *movement rules* that transform a deep (or underlying) structure into a surface structure by moving constituents, sometimes over a long distance. For example, in the transformational account of sentence (i) below, the constituent *which dog* is moved by a rule from the position marked "_" to the front of the sentence:

(i) Which dog did Husain ask Mary to tell Peter to buy_?

This account is a **"procedural" representation** of the relationship between *which dog* and *to buy*, explaining that structural relationship by a procedure involving movement. In syntax, as in morphology, computational linguists like to have declarative descriptions of linguistic data because they help keep the linguistic data distinct from the computer programs that operate on the data. Unification-based theories use a declarative representation, based on sharing feature values across the two structural positions (for example, sharing agreement between subject NPs and VPs), without committing to any particular processing strategy or derivation from an underlying structure.

Unification-based theories have proven more attractive to computational linguists for a variety of reasons, including the need for detailed linguistic description, efficient processing, and because, being declarative, unification-based grammars can be used for both generation and parsing. Good overviews of unification-based approaches are found in Sells (1985) and Shieber (1986).

out this additional matching. Grammar formalisms based on such additional sets of features are called **unification-based grammars**.

In languages with relatively free word order, such as Sanskrit, Turkish, or Czech, the ordering information present in phrase structure rules has less of an influence on syntactic analysis. This in turn has called for a variety of different syntactic theories (as well as different parsing strategies) such as Dependency Grammar (Mel'čuk 1979) and Tree Adjoining Grammar (Joshi and Schabes 1996).

Statistical parsing

So far, we have discussed linguistic rules which have been designed "by hand" by linguists. It is also possible to train a machine to discover the rules from examples of linguistic analyses. For example, in the case of syntax, the linguist may provide only the parse trees, from which the computer can "discover" the grammar by "studying" examples of parse trees. To do this, linguists need to decide on the phrase structure rules (the sets of nonterminal structural categories and terminal lexical categories) that will be included in (and allowed by) the grammar. The linguists then take a collection of texts called a **corpus** (ideally a representative sample of the language), and analyze and "mark up" the sentences in those texts with parse trees. Once a large corpus has been annotated in this way, creating a **treebank**, computers can be taught to induce grammars from it.

How can a computer "learn" a grammar from a treebank? First, a program counts how often each type of syntactic configuration is found in the annotated treebank. Each configuration is represented as a rule like the ones in our toy grammar, and each rule is "weighted" according to how often that configuration appears in the treebank. For example, if we had a tiny treebank consisting of just the two sentences in (6) and (7), the rules S → NP VP and NP → Pronoun would each occur twice, while the rules VP → V NP, VP → Aux V would each occur once. Since the rule S → NP VP is used every time an S is expanded in the treebank, the rule is weighted very high (given a probability of 1). Of the two times a VP is expanded in the treebank, the rule VP → V NP is used half the time (once), and the rule VP → Aux V is used the other time, so these latter two rules will be weighted equally (given a probability of 0.5). (Bear in mind, though, that such a tiny treebank is too small a sample of language to provide good estimates of probabilities!) These weighted rules would then be used in statistical parsing. For example, faced with two possible parse trees for a sentence like *The astronomer saw the planet with a telescope*, the statistical parser would search for the parse tree with the highest probability. The probability of a parse tree can be viewed as the probability of all the rules in that parse tree occurring together. Assuming that the probability of a rule in a parse tree is independent of (that is, not affected by) the presence of another rule in the parse tree, the parse tree probability is computed as the product (by multiplication) of probabilities of all the rules in the parse tree.

The need for human mark-up makes the construction of annotated corpora an expensive capital investment, of course, but once the statistical parser has been developed, it can very quickly parse (create syntactic representations of) an indefinite number of new sentences in the language with a measurable level of accuracy. Accuracy is measured by selecting test sentences and comparing the constituents in the statistical system's parse trees to the constituents (identified by humans) in the treebank's parse tree. Grammars induced by machines tend to perform at least as well as grammars developed "by hand" based on human intuitions. (This is not all that surprising, since the human intuitions about the language's structures that go into the annotated corpus are the basis of the statistical parser's model of the grammar.) Statistical parsers trained on context-free grammar parse trees from a treebank achieve about 90 percent accuracy on various test sets.

Both hand-crafted and corpus-induced grammars are widely used, especially when the grammars are in context-free form. In practical settings, parsing methods need to deal efficiently with long and/or syntactically ambiguous sentences. They also need to be able to represent fragments of sentences when the input is ill-formed (or informal and telegraphic, as in chat messages), or outside the scope of the system's grammar.

Semantic processing

How can a computer understand the meaning of an utterance? Since utterances are made up of words, we must first answer another question: how can a computer understand the meaning of a word?

BOX 14.2 **THE CHOMSKY HIERARCHY**

At the beginning of this chapter, we described some connections between computation and linguistics. Now that we've introduced finite-state methods and context-free grammars, we can discuss a fundamental connection between linguistic descriptions and computation. We have seen that languages are composed of structures of varying complexity. More complex structures require more complex, or more "expressive," grammars. The hierarchy of successively more expressive grammars is called the **Chomsky hierarchy** (Chomsky 1956).

The simplest grammars are called regular expressions. Regular expressions can model morphological phenomena, for example. Anything modeled by regular expressions can in turn be modeled by context-free grammars as well. However, there are phenomena (for example, center-embedded sentences like *The little puppy the boy the principal hated loved ran away*) that can't be modeled by regular expressions but can be modeled by context-free grammars. So context-free grammars are more expressive than regular expressions; they can model everything that regular expressions can model, and more.

In turn, there are phenomena in natural language that can't be accounted for by context-free grammars but can be handled by a context-sensitive grammar (Shieber 1985). Context-sensitive grammars can model everything a context-free grammar can express, and more. Context-sensitive grammars, in turn, cannot represent certain formal patterns which another class of grammars, the aptly named "unrestricted grammars," can express.

It turns out that for every level of grammatical expressiveness in the Chomsky hierarchy there is an analogous computing device, as shown in the figure below. Thus, regular expressions are equivalent to **finite-state machines**. Context-free grammars are equivalent to machines called push-down automata. Context-sensitive grammars are equivalent to machines called linear-bounded automata. And unrestricted grammars are equivalent to Turing Machines. The Church–Turing thesis, which has yet to be disproved, proposes that this is the limit to computable complexity.

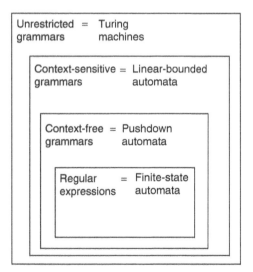

The Chomsky hierarchy with computational equivalent

Such a fundamental relationship between the complexity of linguistic patterns (arising from a long evolutionary process) and classes of computational models (arising from mathematical principles) is evidence of formal patterning in nature. It also shows that linguistic phenomena that can be captured in particular grammar formalisms can be automatically processed, thus guaranteeing the viability of computational approaches to linguistics.

Word meaning

Assume that we have carried out syntactic parsing of the utterance, and have obtained a parse tree for it. If we start with the parse tree, we can associate meanings with the words at the bottom of the tree, and use that information and the structure of the tree to provide a meaning for the sentence. For a syntactically unambiguous sentence, consisting of words which each have only one meaning, this would be relatively simple. Each word at the bottom of the tree would be "looked up" in a lexical database (essentially, a digital dictionary) and the meanings of words would be connected together according to the structural relations represented in the parse tree, to produce the meaning of the sentence.

However, things are rarely that simple! Words can be semantically ambiguous. Not only can a word have more than one part of speech, but even a word which is a given part of speech may have more than one meaning. For example, even if we leave out its several meanings as a verb, the noun *spot* could mean a particular location (*We found a nice spot for lunch*) or a stain (*Out, out, damned spot*) or, in British English, a small amount (*Would you like a spot of tea?*). How is a computer to decide which meaning is intended? A program called a word-sense disambiguator is used for this. A **word-sense disambiguator** (Kilgarriff and Palmer 2000) can use the context of neighboring words in the sentence as well as other words in the document to figure out which meaning of a given word is most likely. Like a part-of-speech tagger, it uses rules that depend on context, and these rules can be derived by human intuition or by training a machine learning program.

We now turn to how a word's syntactic and semantic properties are represented in the computer's digital lexicon. Consider the verb *cook*. A verb's meaning includes its syntactic subcategorization (the syntactic elements, or "arguments," it combines with) and its thematic roles (the semantic relations between a verb and its arguments). In (9), we show three different syntactic subcategorizations of the transitive verb *cook*. (We will use all capital letters to signify the meaning of a word.)

(9) a. COOK (Theme $_{NP}$)
     b. COOK (Recipient $_{NP}$, Theme $_{NP}$)
     c. COOK (Theme $_{NP}$, Recipient $_{for-PP}$)

The first syntactic subcategorization (9a) says that *cook* takes a single NP as its syntactic argument, and that NP is the theme, or thing cooked. So, if the computer saw *Husain cooked meatloaf*, the first meaning of *cook* would be recognized. The second meaning of *cook* in (9b) takes two NPs as its syntactic arguments – the first NP as recipient of something cooked, and the second NP as the theme, or thing cooked. So in processing a sentence like *Husain cooked Mary a great dinner*, the computer can use the knowledge that *Mary* and *a great dinner* are both NPs to recognize the second meaning. The third meaning of *cook* (9c) takes an NP and PP, the latter beginning with *for*, as its arguments – the first NP as theme, and the subsequent PP as recipient. If the program processes a sentence like *Husain cooked a great dinner for Mary*, it can use the identification of the NP and PP following *cook* to recognize the third meaning, where the recipient is to be found in the prepositional phrase.

Sentence meaning

Now that we have an idea of how to capture word meaning in a computer, we can turn to the problem of constructing a meaning for a sentence, based on the meanings of the words in it.

A common assumption underlying computational approaches to semantics is that the meaning of the whole is systematically composed of the meaning of the parts. A computer program based on compositional semantics puts together the sentence meaning from the meanings of the words and phrases that compose it. Thus, given the sentence *Husain cooks meatloaf*, which should have a parse tree similar in many respects to (6), the meaning (9a) for *cook* would be applicable, so that we have *cook* taking a single argument that is an NP. The meaning of the NP *meatloaf* would be supplied by the lexical database: MEATLOAF. Then, the meaning of the VP can be built up by combining the meaning of *cook* with the meaning of *meatloaf*. But how can a computer combine meanings?

One way to approach this is to have semantic rules that accompany syntactic rules in the grammar. Thus, the syntactic rule (10a) below is augmented with a semantic rule (10b) that says the VP's meaning is constructed by applying the V's meaning to the NP's meaning (Jurafsky and Martin 2000).

(10)   a. VP → V NP

   b. VP.*meaning* = Apply(V.*meaning*, NP.*meaning*)

In other words, just like a mathematical function (n +1) will take any number (n) and return the result of adding 1 to it, (10b) is a function that takes V's meaning and adds the meaning of the NP and returns a result (the meaning of the VP). The result in our example indicates that MEATLOAF is what is COOKED. This meaning is represented by the expression COOK(MEATLOAF).

Computational semantics is largely concerned with representing these kinds of semantic functions, the rules for assembling the semantics of larger phrases from smaller ones.

Natural language generation

Can a computer generate text? You're probably familiar with computers providing warnings or help messages, such as "File not found!" These are examples of "canned text" which the computer prints out in response to particular cases that it has been programmed to handle. Such systems do not use linguistic rules, and they cannot generate novel sentences. On the other hand, context-free grammars, like the one we saw in (5), tend to overgenerate, or produce sentences that are ungrammatical, such as *I can the dance*. This is a problem for natural language generation, where unacceptable or misleading utterances should not be generated. Natural language generation goes far beyond canned text, applying linguistic knowledge to a range of practical applications, including generating weather reports, reports from the stock market, and "personalized" marketing letters.

The generator starts with some information to be communicated, along with a communicative goal – for example, to inform the user about something or to request more

BOX 14.3 **THE CHANGING ROLE OF LINGUISTS**

The 1970s and 1980s saw much use of hand-created linguistic models in morphological, syntactic, and semantic processing of natural language input. A computational linguistics team would spend many person-years hand-crafting grammars and rules for a particular application. When it came time to put the various rules together and get the system to work on a demonstration task (processing a test corpus of natural language), the team would have to try various ad hoc tricks (or "heuristics") to ensure that "the right parse" emerged from a syntactic analyzer or "the right meaning" was produced by a semantic interpreter. A great deal of effort was spent "tuning" the system's rules, by using stipulations (like "When in doubt, have the program attach PPs 'low' to NPs rather than 'high' to VPs"), preferences derived from corpus statistics, or assumptions about what sample of sentences the system would be demonstrated on.

The 1990s saw a sea-change in computational linguistics toward corpus-based, statistical methods, which dominate the field to this day. In most areas, linguists now spend less time designing and tweaking linguistic rules and more time designing and implementing annotation schemes for marking up natural language corpora with linguistic information. Once an annotation scheme is developed, it is "debugged" to ensure that other linguists can be trained to reliably annotate a corpus of natural language. Having an annotation which can be faithfully reproduced by other annotators is important for several reasons. In any scientific methodology, being able to replicate results is crucial to verify any claims. Further, a system trained on data that reflect the biases and whims of an individual annotator would not fare well on a general sample of the language.

From a sufficiently large and broad corpus which has been annotated for particular linguistic information (for example, for parts of speech) computer programs can derive statistical patterns. These patterns, in turn, are used to develop programs for automatically annotating further texts in an ever-expanding corpus. The annotated texts are then available for various "real-world" applications like information extraction and text summarization.

When linguists annotate a large corpus, an automatic program first annotates the corpus, with the machine annotations being corrected by the linguists. In many problem areas, including part-of-speech tagging and parsing, this method is generally far more efficient and leads to better reliability among linguists compared to having them annotate the text from scratch!

information from the user. There are two main steps in natural language generation: deciding what to say (called **strategic generation**), and deciding how to say it (called **tactical generation**).

In strategic generation, the system must select specific content (abstract chunks of information called "message units") from a data set, and decide on the overall structure of the output, which can be as short as a phrase or as long as an entire document. The strategic generator specifies which message units will be included in the text and plans the structure, or discourse model, of the output text. For example, a business letter touting a new product might include information elements such as an update on the latest developments at the company, information about the new product, and comparisons with (and perhaps disparaging remarks about) competing products, followed by contact and purchasing information. Each of these elements will be represented as one or more message units.

In tactical generation, the system generates sentences from the abstract message units specified by the discourse model. In the simplest case, each message unit may be expressed in a single sentence, but multiple messages can be combined in a single sentence or a single message can be split across multiple sentences. The tactical generator applies information from the discourse model to make these kinds of sentence-building decisions.

To build a sentence, the tactical generator uses a semantic representation of the intended output and a grammar like a recipe for how to mix together the right ingredients in a grammatically possible order and structure. There will usually be many possible sentences that can be built from the semantic input. Since generation involves making a variety of syntactic and lexical choices, it helps to organize the grammar rules in terms of these choices. For example, in such a grammar, the choices may first involve deciding on the mood of the sentence (imperative, interrogative, or declarative), whether the voice is active or passive, which constituent will be in focus, and so on; these choices then constrain the semantic and syntactic choices for constructing the utterance. The Systemic Grammar approach of Halliday (1985), which organizes grammar in this fashion, has been widely used in tactical generation.

We have seen earlier that statistical approaches can be used for parsing. Why not use them for generation as well? Statistical methods have been used, in recent years, in tactical generation; one approach is to use the grammar to find the many ways in which a given input can be realized, and then select the most likely sentence given a corpus. For example, given the input COOK+PAST(HUSAIN, MEATLOAF), this could yield *Husain cooked meatloaf, Husain baked the meatloaf, The meatloaf was cooked by Husain, It was Husain who prepared the meatloaf*, etc. However, the particular sentences we enumerated just now may not be in the corpus. (In fact, it is extremely unlikely that we will find any particular sentence – like the one I'm writing right now – in any corpus (that is, other than one made from this book!) So, how are we to compute the probability of sentences which aren't in the corpus?

Consider the sentence (11):

(11)   The three young men went to a singles __.

The most likely word to fill the gap in (11) is *bar* or *club*. How did you guess that? The word *singles* was a good hint. This example suggests we may be able to get away with assuming that the probability of seeing a word depends on a context of just the previous one or two words. (In the former case, we assume a "bigram model" of syntax, in the latter case, a "trigram model" of syntax.) While a given sentence may not occur in the corpus, pairs or triples of words are more likely to occur. This means we can compute the probability of a sentence which isn't itself in the corpus based on the (bigram model) probability of each particular word in the sentence following the previous word (except of course for the first word in the sentence). In other words, we can count how often one particular word follows another.

Bigram- and trigram-based statistical approaches to generation are relatively inexpensive to build and have been used in a variety of systems. However, they do not address long-distance dependencies. For example, the sentence (12) below shows that the noun phrase *which goldfish* is an argument of the verb *feed*, though they are located far away from each other (a long-distance dependency).

(12)   Which goldfish did Hilary request John to tell Barack to feed?

Probabilistic theories

It should be clear by now that, given the success of statistical methods, we have at least two ways of building linguistic theories at this time: the traditional way of arriving at rules by hand, based on linguistic intuitions, and the (once unfashionable) way of deriving rules automatically based on statistical generalizations from a corpus. Which of these methods is better? And which of these representations are actually used by human minds?

Statistical analysis was initially discredited by most linguists. They argued that statistical methods are based on induction from small samples of an infinite language, and so they will misrepresent the language. These linguists also claimed that the utterances that speakers actually produce are insignificant "noise" which is not systematically related to the speaker's linguistic competence. Since language corpora model only performance, they said, statistical analyses of those corpora cannot represent linguistic competence. But many linguists don't find the competence–performance distinction to be clear-cut. Socio-linguists, in particular, have argued that the variability of linguistic performance is system-atic, predictable, and meaningful to speakers of a language. Grammatical theories vary in where they draw the line between competence and performance, with some grammars (such as Halliday's Systemic Grammar) organized as systems of functionally oriented choices. Computational linguistics, by its very nature, does process actual, messy, and incomplete data. However, insights gleaned from a large corpus may be valid for language beyond the corpus.

If statistical rules induced from examples perform just as well as rules derived from intuition, then this suggests that probabilistic statistical linguistic rules might help explain or model human linguistic behavior. It also suggests that humans might learn from experi-ence by means of induction using statistical regularities. A critical issue in these arguments is the nature of grammaticality. Is the grammaticality of a sentence an all-or-nothing judgment, or is it gradable, or even measurable along a continuum? Every linguist is aware of the fuzziness of certain grammatical distinctions.

For many years, corpus linguistic research rarely examined statistics above the level of words, due to the lack of availability of broad-coverage parsers and statistical models that could handle syntax and other levels of "hidden structure." The present climate, awash in tools and statistical models, should allow corpus linguistics to extend its descriptive and explanatory scope dramatically.

> **Quick comprehension check**
> At this point, you should have a general idea as to how statistics can be used to disambiguate sentence parsing. You should understand what role syntactically annotated corpora play in this process. You should also have an appreciation of how natural language generation can be carried out – and you can test your understanding of tactical generation in Exercise 14.5.

Related technologies

The impact of computational linguistics on society depends on the applications it makes possible. Computers have for many years been using more computational linguistics tools

> ### BOX 14.4 **FUN WITH CORPUS-BASED DISCOVERY**
>
> In addition to testing theoretical hypotheses using a language corpus, corpus-based approaches can be used to discover interesting patterns in the real world. This can be sheer fun using a computer, and terribly tedious to do without one!
>
> For example, what if we wanted to know how different occupations are described or characterized in the media? Imagine a program that is able to troll through thousands of pages of online newspapers, (i) finding people mentioned in them, and (ii) finding their occupations. Then, the program could (iii) identify verbs in sentences where people with that occupation are mentioned as the subject (for example, *Johnson*, the *game show host, promised* in court to *pay* back the . . .). Finally, (iv) the program could measure how frequently particular verbs (and the actions they refer to) are attributed to particular occupations.
>
> Computer programs can find people on the Web by identifying proper names and resolving pronominal and other references to people. Other computer programs can parse titles, appositive phrases, and relative clauses adjacent to the name, and extract the head nouns of these descriptive phrases to identify people's occupations. Still other computer programs can parse the sentences containing these names and identified occupations to identify subject–verb associations. A final set of programs can count how many times particular subjects and particular verbs co-occurred, and then assess the probability of that subject–verb pair occurring together. These components could be put together like Lego blocks, as we saw with finite-state transducers.
>
> The table below (from Schiffman, Mani, and Concepcion 2001) shows the results of this kind of analysis on nearly three years of wire service news reports from the Reuters news service (about 106 million words, drawn from the North American News Text Corpus). The occupations are shown in italic, and the verbs most strongly associated with particular subjects are shown.
>
> **Verbs that characterize subjects described with particular occupations**
>
> | *executive* | *police* | *politician* |
> | --- | --- | --- |
> | reprimand | shoot | clamor |
> | conceal | raid | jockey |
> | bank | arrest | wrangle |
> | foresee | detain | woo |
> | conspire | disperse | exploit |
> | convene | interrogate | brand |
> | plead | swoop | behave |
> | sue | evict | dare |
> | answer | bundle | sway |
> | commit | manhandle | criticize |

BOX 14.4 (*cont.*)

Verbs that characterize subjects described with particular occupations		
worry	search	flank
accompany	confiscate	proclaim
own	apprehend	annul
witness	round	favor

The verbs paint a revealing portrait of each occupation, don't they?! This sort of data can be very relevant in computational linguistic applications, such as generating biographical "dossiers" that track people in the news. It also can be of sociolinguistic interest. Are there particular verbs that characterize particular occupations, in the eyes of the news media? (For example, are stories about politicians largely focused on infighting?) Can we classify a particular media outlet as "conservative" or "liberal" based on the way it characterizes particular people? Statistical methods can be used to further explore and answer these sorts of questions in ways that were previously impossible – by linguistically analyzing the patterns hidden in billions of words of text.

in applications such as multilingual word processing, spelling correction, and grammar checking. In the last decade, the dramatic increase in speed of computers and the ability to inexpensively store vast amounts of information online has resulted in an exponential increase in the amount of information available to computers, with a lot of it being in natural languages. There is also a lot of information stored in structured form in databases; as a result, being able to convert from text to structured form (the job of information extraction technology) has become important. Since computers can search through documents in different languages and find information much faster than humans can, search engines that troll through web pages have become extremely useful. With the wide use of email and cellular phones, speech-enabled applications have started to become a presence in flight information and hotel reservation systems. These and other technologies provide opportunities to embed and apply computational linguistic methods. We focus on four related technologies here: **information extraction**, **automatic summarization**, **speech recognition**, **speech synthesis**, and **machine translation**.

Information extraction

Earlier, we considered computational approaches to representing word and sentence meaning. The application area of information extraction (which is now a commercially "hot" technology) tries to derive the semantic content of a document as a whole as it relates to particular types of events. Information extraction programs automatically fill out templates (or tables) from natural language input. For example, for terrorist events, the

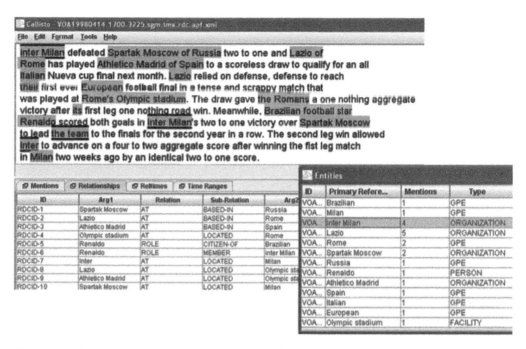

Figure 14.1 Annotating a document with entities and relations

event template slots to be filled may include the perpetrator, the victim, the type of event, and where and when it occurred. What is extracted here is not the meaning of individual sentences, but information about specific entities referenced in the text, such as events, people, organizations, locations, and times (these are called named entities) and particular relations between them. This summary information is collected together to represent document content. An information extraction program can extract the relevant content of hundreds of documents in the time it would take a human to read and extract the content of one.

Figure 14.1 shows an editing tool called Callisto that is used to insert tags into the text (in a way which does not damage or alter the original document) and then to view them. The window on the left shows, in the upper part, an English broadcast news article from a Voice of America radio program marked up by a human using an annotation scheme called Automatic Content Extraction (ACE). The window on the right shows entities of various types that were marked in the article, along with the number of mentions. For example, "Inter Milan" was highlighted and then marked as an *Organization*; it was mentioned four times (indicated with horizontal bars in the text): "Inter Milan," "Inter Milan," "the team," and "Inter." This grouping of mentions of an entity requires understanding coreference relationships in text above the level of the sentence, i.e. discourse-level inference. The bottom of the left window shows relationships that were found in the text, for example, the *Person* Renaldo is a *member of* the *Organization* (i.e. the soccer team) Inter Milan and a *citizen* of Brazil.

Once a collection of such documents is annotated, the computer is trained from the annotated data to reproduce the annotation, and the machine annotation for any test article can be compared against the human one and scored for accuracy. One of the key challenges for information extraction systems in tasks like this is having enough training examples for each kind of entity and relation, as well as the ability, in the case of tasks such as entity coreference, event templates, and relations, to integrate information from different parts of the text.

Automatic summarization

The goal of automatic summarization is to condense information from one or more documents, and then present that information to the reader in accordance with his or her needs. For example, a reader searching the web on a mobile phone may want to see just a few query-relevant snippets from each of the top text (or multimedia) documents that have been retrieved. A child perusing an advanced biology text may want a 200-word summary in plain English of the key concepts in the book; and a student reading a journal article on chemistry may want just the key findings and a precise description of the chemicals that were involved. A summary can take the form of an extract, i.e. a summary consisting entirely of material copied from the input, or an abstract, namely, a summary at least some of whose material is not present in the input (and, therefore, one that reflects some degree of assimilation of the source material's contents). For an example of an abstract and how it relates to the original source, see the short (less than 200-word) chapter summary at the end of this chapter.

Summarization can be viewed as somewhat analogous to natural language generation, in that the system has to decide what to say (based, in this case, on selecting what is relevant from the input) and then present it in a coherent manner. A crucial aspect of the selection phase is determining how the document structure and content help determine what is relevant. A headline news article, for example, will usually have the latest news at the beginning, while a scientific paper may have relevant information at the end, in the Results or Conclusion. Particular cues in the document may reveal key information, e.g. introduced with phrases like *in a nutshell, to summarize*, etc. Certain topics mentioned in the article, including those relevant to the reader's interests, are also likely to be important. In the case of multi-document summaries, the selection phase has to filter out redundant information that may be repeated across documents. Once information has been selected and weighted for importance, it must be organized. In the case of extraction, selecting sentences up to the target summary length in order of importance may result in their being out of order or having gaps in between. This can result in an incoherent summary, as will summary sentences that contain pronouns and other discourse-dependent references to information that isn't in the summary.

Automatic summarization has benefitted from the corpus-based approach used in other applications. Source documents along with reference summaries constructed by humans can be used to train a summarizer as to what to select, given a particular target length for the summary. Evaluation in this setting, as carried out in a series of annual evaluations called the Document Understanding Conference (DUC), has been based on comparing the system output against the reference summaries in terms of content, as well as judging the system summary for coherence. The content comparison can be carried out at the level of individual words (matching words and phrases that are in common), or else at a syntactic or semantic level. Note that summarizers which produce abstracts often reformulate material from the input, changing its syntactic structure and semantic content – for example, by shrinking sentences, or by paraphrasing content. Clearly, the comparison of content must take into account relations such as synonymy as well as paraphrase, since a system summary may or may not use the same words as a reference summary.

Speech recognition

Today, speech recognizers are an off-the-shelf commodity and are found embedded in a variety of day-to-day applications, including telephone access to business services, transcription of speech for the hearing-impaired, digital dictation, automatic multimedia information access (like searching of radio and TV news broadcasts), voice web search, and various uses in hands-busy environments.

You may have had the experience of interacting with a speech recognizer and been surprised that it understood you – or you may have come away annoyed at its inaccuracy after repeated attempts. The quality of speech recognition depends on a number of factors. For example, a system that recognizes digits spoken carefully into a high-quality microphone will perform much better than one that tries to recognize spontaneous speech in multiparty conversations in an office setting.

The problem of variation in how words are pronounced has been a major force behind the paradigm shift away from rule-based processing and toward statistical language processing in speech recognition. A speech recognizer uses a dictionary that lists pronunciations for words in its vocabulary, expressed as sequences of phonemes. Variant pronunciations are generated by phonological rules in the form of probabilistic (weighted) finite-state transducers. They take advantage of the rich statistical information obtainable from a corpus (like the frequencies of different pronunciations of words) to produce rules for recognizing a variety of combinations of sounds as one and the same word.

A speech recognizer uses several knowledge sources: an acoustic model, a pronunciation model, and a language model (the latter functions as a syntactic recognizer). The rules in the three models have their probabilities estimated from training data. The acoustic model predicts the likelihood of a particular input sound wave matching a particular sequence of phonetic segments. The pronunciation model uses the acoustic model's results to predict the likelihood of a particular sequence of phones matching a particular word. The language model then predicts the probability of each sequence of words identified by the pronunciation model.

Speech synthesis

Speech synthesis systems usually take written text as input and produce speech. Initial programs tokenize texts into words and preprocess them to detect proper names, numbers, abbreviations, and so on. Morphological disambiguation programs sort out words whose variants are spelled the same but pronounced differently, like *read* (past versus present tense). Some of this disambiguation can be helped by part-of-speech tagging, where the crucial distinction is between nouns and verbs (for example, *contrast*) and verbs and adjectives (for example, *intimate*). The output of the tokenization, preprocessing, lexical lookup, and morphological analysis programs is a phonetic transcription of the text. The next step is to transform this written representation into sequences of actual sounds. To do this, acoustic information from pronunciation models is processed along with mathematical procedures that calculate pitch, amplitude, and timing of the sound waveform expressing the sequence of phonetic elements.

Why do current speech synthesizers sound so "flat"? A crucial problem in speech synthesis is the generation of prosody – that is, accent, pitch, and intonation structure. In a sentence like *I can fish*, any of the three words could be stressed, depending on the focus of the utterance. This information, and a lot of other information related to prosody, simply isn't available to synthesizers. In a text-to-speech system, the computer doesn't know what it's talking about!

After some prosodic information is added (for example, standard patterns such as rising intonation for questions), the information in a text-to-speech system is fed to a signal processing module that produces the final audio output. Today, this module is based either on concatenative synthesis, where bits of prerecorded speech (pairs of sounds) are concatenated together, or on trigram models defined over phone units.

Speech synthesis is valuable in many applications, including telephone access to business services, aids for the disabled (blind people, as well as those who have difficulties speaking), education, toys, navigational systems, and weather and emergency bulletins.

Machine translation

The field of machine translation (MT) is the oldest application area of computational linguistics, dating back to the early years of the Cold War. One of the first demonstrations of a working Russian–English MT system was carried out in 1954 by a joint Georgetown–IBM system (Dostert 1955). There is a direct line of descent from work on that project to the Systran Babelfish system that is widely used on the Web to automatically translate web pages.

MT is one of the biggest application areas for computational linguistics, with millions of technical manuals, office materials, and other communications being translated daily. Unlike the translation of literary texts, where a considerable amount of creativity is required on the part of the translator, MT is focused on translations which preserve the information content of the source language as much as possible, while rendering it in a natural form in the target language. Its main advantages are economic, particularly when the volume of text is such that humans couldn't possibly translate it. Lower-accuracy translations may be sufficient for getting the gist of some foreign language source (such as a news headline, search engine result, or email message), whereas for higher-quality results, post-editing of the machine translation by humans is often necessary.

MT poses challenges to many areas of computational linguistics, since it involves understanding of utterances in one language and generation of utterances in the other. MT systems all tend to translate sentence-by-sentence, and, with a few exceptions, do so while ignoring discourse context. Usually, proper names, numbers, abbreviations and acronyms, dates, and times will be flagged and separately processed, as translating a proper name accidentally as a common word can produce embarrassing results, for example, translating a reference in a German document to the former German Chancellor "Kohl" as "cabbage."

There are three general approaches to MT.

- A direct approach looks up words from the source utterance in a bilingual dictionary, chooses the most appropriate word translations by some method, and then reorders the chosen word translations based on the target language word order. This string of words then undergoes morphological synthesis (adding necessary affixes). This approach is nowadays extended to one where instead of a bilingual dictionary, a parallel corpus of millions of source documents and their human translations is used to garner statistics for bilingual phrase translations.
- A transfer approach (which is the most widely used) builds an intermediate syntactic or semantic representation of the sentence in the source language, and then maps it to a syntactic or semantic representation in the target language, from which a target language sentence is generated. The transfer approach requires three components: source language analysis, transfer (involving grammar rules that map structures across the languages based on contrastive analyses of the two languages), and a target language generation component.
- An interlingual approach attempts to decompose the meaning of the source language utterance into a language-neutral conceptual representation, from which the target language sentence is directly generated. In an interlingual approach, either the system represents one concept for every word in each language, or else the system decomposes meanings into supposedly "universal" primitives.

  For example, Japanese has at least three words for rice: *gohan* for cooked rice (the default), *kome* for raw rice, and *raisu* for 'foreign-style' rice. An English–Japanese **interlingual MT** system will have to distinguish four kinds of rice concepts, corresponding to three words in Japanese and one word in English. Or it can choose to ignore the differences and map them all to a single "primitive" concept of 'rice,' or even a single primitive concept of 'foodgrain.'

  While an interlingual approach has the advantage of avoiding transfer modules for each pair of languages being translated, designing an interlingua of language-universal "primitives" is very difficult. Systems usually confine themselves to a "restricted interlingua" that is intended for a particular group of languages, focusing just on the semantic distinctions that the particular group of languages makes.

Most practical systems use a combination of a direct or transfer approach along with corpus statistics to achieve more robustness.

> **Quick comprehension check**
> You should now have a sense of various application areas of computational linguistics, and the very different ways linguistic knowledge is used in systems for speech processing, information extraction, summarization and machine translation. If you're ready, Exercises 14.7–14.9 await you!

Major challenges in computational linguistics

While computer algorithms are very well understood, getting computers to acquire some of the linguistic and world knowledge needed by those algorithms is a major challenge, even with the very large corpora now available. Many of the problems in processing semantics and pragmatics depend on the computer acquiring vast amounts of linguistic and world knowledge. To illustrate, let us consider a simple problem of natural language story understanding. Consider the short narrative in (13):

(13)   Yesterday, Holly was jogging when she twisted her ankle.
        David pushed her. The ankle hurt like hell.

A human being can tell when Holly was jogging, by using information from verb tense (the jogging was in the past, with respect to the narration) and context (when the narration was spoken) to resolve the specific time that *yesterday* refers to. He or she can also tell when the ankle twist occurred (during the jog), and that the pushing occurred before the twisting, that the pushing caused the twisting, and that the ankle started to hurt when she twisted it. Verb tense and aspect (the jogging, expressed linguistically as a progressive, was ongoing when the twisting happened) are clearly helpful, but in addition the human makes inferences based on implicit information inferred from world knowledge. For example, world knowledge is needed to order the pushing with respect to the twisting, since there is no explicit linguistic "after" signal linking the pushing to the twisting.

A great deal of the linguistic knowledge about tense, aspect, and discourse relations needed just to understand a simple story like (13) can come by learning from annotated corpora. For example, an annotation scheme called TimeML (Pustejovsky *et al.* 2005) annotates events and their temporal relations in stories. However, the costs of constructing such annotated corpora are high. One strategy of current research is to balance quantity and quality of information: information from large corpora that are unannotated or automatically annotated without human supervision (and therefore relatively inexpensive) is combined with information from smaller (but more expensive) sets of data that are annotated with human supervision.

Inferencing isn't easy for the computer, and general knowledge of the world, such as the principle that pushes cause falls, is hard for a computer to "learn" from corpora. "Commonsense" knowledge bases built by hand are very expensive to develop and must be meticulously enriched by hand for each new application area. Information extraction methods can acquire various facts (or "factoids") about the world, but acquiring a machine-interpretable knowledge base of commonsense knowledge (let alone specialized knowledge in areas like biology and medicine) is a formidable undertaking. Many of the remaining linguistic processing challenges facing computational linguistics are intimately tied to the problem of representing human beings' knowledge of the world. In meeting these challenges, we will learn much more about how humans represent and reason with such knowledge while communicating in natural language.

CHAPTER SUMMARY

This chapter has discussed a variety of methods for getting computers to process human languages. The field is motivated in part by the fundamental relationship between patterns found in human languages and mathematical models of systems that process artificial languages. Linguistic theories go hand-in-hand with computational representations and algorithms to address natural language problems

The current success of computational linguistics is due in large part to the availability of large quantities of online data that can be processed very quickly. This has led to the use of statistical approaches, displacing some of the earlier approaches that involved hand-created models of linguistic usage. The success of these statistical approaches – and the wealth of new empirical data they provide – pose fundamental questions for many current linguistic theories.

While computer algorithms and statistical models are very well understood, getting computers to acquire the vast amounts of linguistic and world knowledge needed remains a major challenge. Linguistic knowledge acquisition faces high annotation costs, while acquisition of world knowledge is still an almost entirely manual process.

Exercises

EXERCISE 14.1

Extend the mapping in (3a) to also handle *tried = try + ed* and *fried = fry + ed.*

EXERCISE 14.2

Draw the next set of expansions that the top-down parser discussed earlier will carry out on (8d). Which ones can be expanded? Do any lead to immediate dead ends?

EXERCISE 14.3

Here is a parse tree for the English translation of the Japanese sentence (1) mentioned at the start of this chapter. (Note that it is a little more complicated than the parse trees we saw before, because it includes a nonterminal category Nom as a component of NPs.)

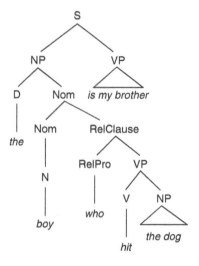

a. Induce a grammar from the parse tree. That is, state the phrase structure rules that a computer could build from the hierarchical relations of the tagged components of this sentence. (Hint: The first, or top-most, rule is S → NP VP.)

b. Modify the grammar in (a) to handle the Japanese sentence (1), reproduced below. (Use the same grammar nonterminals as in (a), except D and RelPro, which can be dropped.)

(1) 犬に当る男の子は私の兄弟である。

inuobuttaotokonokowaotootoda

inuo	butta	otokonokowa	otootoda
dog+OBJ	hit+PAST	boy+SUBJ	younger-brother+be-PRES

'The boy who hit the dog is my brother.'

c. Draw the parse tree for the Japanese sentence (1) using the grammar in (b).

EXERCISE 14.4

Provide three examples where translating a proper name accidentally as a common word can produce embarrassing results.

EXERCISE 14.5

See how many grammatical sentences you can generate from the context-free grammar in (5). Does it allow you to generate any ungrammatical sentences? Now add just three words to the grammar: N → *beans*, V → *eat*, Pronoun → *you*. How many more sentences can you generate? (Don't forget the many new combinations possible with the original words.)

EXERCISE 14.6

Why is a word list (or lexicon) for English likely to be incomplete? Give an example of a particular word or phrase and its part of speech that is not likely to be in most English lexicons.

EXERCISE 14.7

What linguistic information in the news story in Figure 14.1 could be used by a computer to infer that Renaldo is a citizen of Brazil? What information in the story would be pertinent to the computer inferring that he is a member of Inter Milan?

EXERCISE 14.8

Consider the following forty-five-word sentence:

> *A transfer approach (which is the most widely used) builds an intermediate syntactic or semantic representation of the sentence in the source language, and then maps it to a syntactic or semantic representation in the target language, from which a target language sentence is generated.*

Condense this sentence into one of no more than thirty words. What sorts of linguistic information did you remove, and what syntactic or semantic reorganization did you carry out?

EXERCISE 14.9

View a documentary on YouTube that provides an automatic transcript (e.g. via the 'transcript' icon). Can you detect errors in the automatic transcript and explain them in terms of speech recognition software? Which errors are most likely to be attributable to the acoustic model, to the pronunciation model, and to the language model?

SUGGESTIONS FOR FURTHER READING

Jurafsky, D. and Martin, J. H. 2000, *Speech and language processing: an introduction to natural language processing, computational linguistics, and speech recognition*, Saddle River, NJ: Prentice Hall. This is the standard textbook on computational linguistics, one of the best ever written. It is remarkable for its lively, detailed discussion of linguistic topics and depth of coverage of traditional rule-based as well as statistical approaches. It also provides useful historical discussion and summarizes relevant psycholinguistics work. Accessible to the beginner who has a basic mathematical background, but certainly not bedside reading.

Manning, C. and Schutze, H. 1999, *Foundations of statistical natural language processing*, Cambridge, MA: MIT Press. This is an excellent guide to the statistical approaches in use today. The presentation is stepwise and systematic. A neat feature of the book is its review of whatever mathematics is needed. Not always an easy read, but particular sections are very rewarding.

Mitkov, R. (ed.) 2003, *The Oxford handbook of computational linguistics*, Oxford University Press. This book is a collection of thirty-eight self-contained chapters introducing all the main areas of computational linguistics. An excellent, generally clearly written, and well-edited reference book, with a useful glossary and a wealth of references. Some of the chapters make for very easy reading by the beginner, others are a bit more specialized.

Shieber, S. M. 1986, *An introduction to unification-based approaches to grammar*, Stanford, CA: CSLI Publications. This book is a set of notes on various grammar formalisms such as Functional Unification Grammar, Definite-Clause Grammars, Lexical–Functional Grammar, Generalized Phrase Structure Grammar, and Head-Driven Phrase Structure Grammar. Although both Lexical–Functional Grammar and particularly Head-Driven Phrase Structure Grammar have evolved quite a bit since then, it remains a clear and indispensable introduction from a computational linguistics standpoint. Easy read.

Stork, D. G. (ed.) 1997, *HAL's legacy: 2001's computer as dream and reality*, Cambridge, MA: MIT Press. HAL was the artificially intelligent computer on board the spaceship in Stanley Kubrick's 1968 film *2001: A Space Odyssey*, whose screenplay was written by Kubrick and Arthur C. Clarke, based on a short story by Clarke. HAL was fluent in natural language, and was a key character in the film. This collection of articles by leading experts, published nearly thirty years later, with a foreword by Clarke, presents a highly upbeat account of how close we have come to realizing HAL. Full of glossy plates, it provides a lively introduction to present-day artificial intelligence capabilities. A great bedside read, but remember that we still have a way to go!

GLOSSARY

abjad: A writing system in which only consonants are represented by letters and vowels are optionally marked by diacritics (i.e. a consonantal alphabet).

ablaut: A vowel change in a root that signals a grammatical contrast, e.g. *speak/spoke*.

accent: Pronunciation, especially that associated with a particular regional or social group.

acceptability judgment tests: Tests given to both native and non-native speakers of a particular language, asking whether certain sentences are acceptable in that language.

accusative: The case of the direct object of a verb (sometimes the object of a preposition); who or what is having something done to it.

acetylcholine: A neurotransmitter that plays important roles in the hippocampus, in declarative memory, and in word learning.

acoustic phonetics: Study of the physical characteristics of sound waves.

acrophony: Derivation of a letter from the first sound of a word, logogram, or pictogram.

active articulators: Articulators that move in the vocal tract to create a constriction.

act structure: An ordered sequence of actions performed through speech (see speech acts).

acute: Acute lesions are those caused by sudden damage (e.g. from stroke or head trauma).

adaptation: The replacement of foreign sounds occurring in loan words by their nearest phonetic equivalents in the borrowing language.

adjacency pair: A pair of utterances in which the first part (e.g. a question, a greeting) sets up so strong an expectation for the next part (e.g. an answer, a second greeting) that something is "missing" if the next part does not occur.

adjunction: A type of merger by which phrases, other than heads, complements, or specifiers are added to other phrases. Adjunction involves expanding to two segments the phrasal node to which the modifiers are being added.

affective filter: The emotional "blocks" (such as self-consciousness or embarrassment) that can hinder the language acquisition process. According to Krashen, the affective filter must be "raised" (i.e. removed) in order for language learning to occur.

affix: A bound morpheme that attaches to a base to alter it in some way, e.g. in the word *dehumidifiers*, the affixes are *de-*, *-ify*, *-er*, and *-s*.

affricate: A sound that is comprised of a sequence of stop plus fricative.

African American English (AAE): The language variety spoken by many African Americans in the US. Also called Ebonics; although considered to be a very uniform dialect, AAE does show variation across regional, social class, gender, and age groups, as well as across different speech styles.

age-graded features: Language features used temporarily during a particular life stage, for example, the heavy use of slang by teenagers and young adults who have not yet entered the workforce.

agrammatism: Impairments of grammar. Agrammatic speech is syntactically and morphologically simplified. Patients with agrammatic speech often also have receptive agrammatism, i.e. difficulties using syntactic structure to understand the meaning of sentences.

agreement: A grammatical matching relation in which the form of one or more words is inflected to signal a correspondence with one or more features of another word, e.g. in the Spanish noun phrase *una amiga americana* 'a (female) American friend' both the determiner *una* and adjective *americana* are inflected to agree with the feminine gender and singular number of the noun *amiga*.

allomorph: A variant pronunciation of a morpheme that appears in a particular conditioning environment, e.g. the English negative prefix *in-* may be pronounced as [ɪn], [ɪm], or [ɪŋ] depending on the first sound of the base it attaches to, e.g. *inescapable, impossible, incapable* (respectively).

allophone: A contextually determined variant pronunciation of a phoneme.

allophonic change: A sound change that produces only allophones and does not change the structural organization of the phonemic inventory of sounds.

alphabet: A script consisting of symbols for the consonants and vowels of a spoken language.

alternation: Correspondence between two allophones revealed when the same morpheme is pronounced in different ways depending on the context.

alveolar: Sound made with a constriction of the tongue tip or blade against the alveolar ridge.

alveolar ridge: The bony rise just behind the teeth.

Alzheimer's disease: A neurodegenerative disease marked by severe memory loss, and also resulting in language and other cognitive deficits.

ambiguity: A word, phrase, or sentence is ambiguous if it has multiple meanings.

amelioration: See **pejoration**.

analogy: The modification or creation of linguistic forms by (over)generalization of an existing pattern.

anaphor: A word that does not have its own reference but derives its meaning from a preceding word or phrase; in Binding Theory, an expression, like *herself*, that is required to refer to the subject of its clause.

anaptyxis or svarabhakti: The insertion of a vowel between two consonants.

anatomical structures: Distinct physical structures in the brain.

antecedent: The word or phrase from which an anaphor derives its meaning.

anterior: Toward the front of the head and brain.

anterograde amnesia: The inability to form new long-term memories, resulting in a lack of awareness of what has occurred since the onset of the condition.

antonym: Words that have opposite meanings are antonyms of each other.

aphasia: The loss of expressive and/or receptive language abilities following brain damage.

apparent-time data: Language data from different generations of speakers in a given community at a single moment in time; can often be used to infer language changes in progress.

approximant: A speech sound in which the articulators narrow the vocal tract, but not so much so that fricative noise is created.

apocope: A kind of deletion or loss of a sound, usually a vowel, at the end of a word.

arbitrary standard: A socially agreed-on system of measurement or way of behaving that could as easily be otherwise.

argument: A word or phrase which saturates a predicate; a subject, object, or indirect object.

arbitrariness: A fundamental property of human language whereby there is no intrinsic relationship between the form of a word (how it sounds) and its meaning.

articulatory phonetics: Study of how the vocal tract produces speech sounds.

aspect: A grammatical category that indicates some temporal property of an action or state such as whether it is completed, ongoing, habitual, or iterative. One basic distinction is between **perfective** (temporally bounded, completed) and **imperfective** (unbounded, ongoing) expressions. In English, for example, the so-called "progressive" form (a kind of imperfective aspect) is marked on the verb by the suffix -ing, as in *John was painting the kitchen*.

aspectual class: A classification of sentences in terms of how the situation they describe unfolds in time.

aspiration: Extra airflow, due to the larynx remaining open, after the release of closure for a stop consonant.

assimilation: 1. A phonological alternation in which two sounds that are different become more alike. 2. A diachronic process by which a sound changes in the direction of a nearby sound, in which two sounds become more alike. Dissimilation is the opposite of assimilation, in which two sounds become less alike.

Audiolingual Method: An approach to teaching second languages, based on the principles of behaviorism, which claimed that language learning was essentially habit formation, requiring mimicry, rote memorization, and extensive drills with lots of correction from teachers.

autism: A developmental disorder that appears early in life and is marked by a range of deficits, including problems with language and social interaction.

automatic summarization: The process of reducing a text to a coherent summary of its most important points.

autosegmental representation: Phonological formalism in which features are treated as autonomous from the string of segments.

auxiliary *be*: The use of *to be* as part of a progressive verb form, as in *She is running* or *We were eating*.

babble: Prelinguistic vocal behavior produced by infants beginning at about four months of age; typically consists of simple syllables (e.g. *ma ma*) and later by sequences of different syllables (e.g. *ma ba da*).

back channels: Verbalizations with little (or no) semantic content, such as *mhm* and *uhuh*, by which listeners signal that they are listening, paying attention, and/or willing to continue ceding the floor to a speaker.

back formation: The formation of a shorter word by removing an affix from a longer word.

back vowel: Vowel sound for which the tongue body moves back in the mouth.

balanced bilinguals: Individuals who have identical and native competence in all areas of both languages.

basal ganglia: A group of highly interconnected structures deep in the brain. These structures include the putamen, the caudate nucleus, the globus pallidus, and the substantia nigra. The basal ganglia are usually associated with motor functions but are also involved in language.

base: Any form to which a morphological operation applies, such as affixation, reduplication, etc. to yield another form, e.g. *humid* is the base (and also the **root**) for the derived word *humidify*, and *humidify* is in turn the base (but not the root) for the derived word *humidifier*, which in turn is the base for the inflected form *humidifiers*. The base for inflected forms is also often called a **stem**.

behavioral genetics: The study of the genetic basis of behavior.

bilabial: Sound made by bringing together the upper and lower lips.

bilaterally: Taking place on both sides, i.e. in both hemispheres of the cerebrum or the cerebellum.

Binding Theory: A set of three principles that determine permitted and forbidden coreference patterns for anaphors, pronouns, and names.

biochemical: Relating to chemicals involved in biological functions (e.g. neurotransmitters).

biocognitive: Relating to the various biological (genes, molecules, neurons, brain structures, and so on), cognitive, and computational correlates of mental functions.

biotemporal dynamics: The pattern of biological activity (e.g. of genes, neurotransmitters, neurons, brain structures, etc.) during the real-time processing of a given task or cognitive function. The visual representation of biological activity through time during mental processing.

blasphemy: Insulting or mocking what the faithful consider sacred.

bootstrap: Process of learning language in which the child uses skills in one area of language to develop competencies in other areas.

borrowing: The adoption of elements from one language or dialect into another.

bound: Applied to morphemes, a term indicating that a morpheme must be attached to a base, e.g. an affix such as -*ing* in the word *singing*.

broadening: An increase in the range of meaning of a word. The reverse of this is **narrowing**, in which the range of meaning of a word decreases and becomes less general.

Broca's aphasia: A type of aphasia marked by agrammatism, and associated with damage to Broca's *region* (though not with damage limited to Broca's *area* alone).

Broca's area: A classical brain language area consisting of the opercular part and the triangular part of the inferior frontal gyrus – which in turn correspond largely to Brodmann's areas 44 and 45, respectively. The area is named for the French scientist Paul Broca, who first suggested its involvement in language.

Broca's region: A brain region that plays important roles in language. It is generally taken to comprise Broca's area and certain nearby regions, including the orbital part of the inferior frontal gyrus (Brodmann's area 47) and the frontal operculum.

Brodmann's area (BA): One of the brain areas from the cytoarchitectonic map developed by Korbinian Brodmann in the early 1900s.

case: A grammatical category marked on nouns and pronouns that indicates their role in a sentence such as subject, direct object, or indirect object, or in relation to another noun, as, for example, its possessor. Case marking appears on pronouns in English – distinguishing, for example, the forms *I*, *me*, and *my*.

central vowel: Vowel sound for which the tongue body moves neither forward nor back.

cerebellum: The part of the brain beneath the back of the cerebrum. Although the cerebellum has long been implicated in movement, it is now clear that it also underlies memory, language, and other functions.

cerebrum: The large, main part of the brain, made up of two hemispheres.

chain shift: A series of sound changes which are connected and depend upon one another.

child-directed speech (CDS): The special type of speech that is directed towards infants and children, which includes exaggerated intonation, simpler sentence structures, and an emphasis on the "here and now."

Chomsky hierarchy: An ordering of formal languages in terms of a complexity hierarchy.

cilia: Hair cells in the cochlea, connected to nerve cells, stimulation of which results in hearing.

circumfix: A type of affix that surrounds a base (appearing as both a prefix and suffix), e.g. the German past participle form *ge-t* in the word *ge-zeig-t* 'shown.'

classifier: A morpheme that is used to grammatically individuate mass nouns or specify a subclass of nouns in a language, often on the basis of some semantic property of the noun.

In the Mandarin Chinese examples *wŭ -ge rén* 'five persons' and *nèi -zhāng zhĭé* 'that (sheet of) paper,' the suffixes *-ge* and *-zhang* are classifiers which specify units of people and paper, respectively.

cochlea: The inner ear.

coda: The consonants in a syllable that follow the nucleus.

coda constraint: Restriction on the type or number of consonants that can occur in the coda.

code-mixing: Speakers' switching from one language to another during a conversation seemingly without discrimination.

code-switching: The intentional use of more than one language by bilinguals for symbolic, strategic, or communicative purposes.

cognates: Words in two or more sister languages which are descended from a common word in the parent language.

coherence: The overall sense of a discourse that results from relationships (a) within a sequence of utterances and (b) between those utterances and their context.

coherence system: The way language orders the world.

cohesion: A sense of unity within a text that results from language that connects a current point in the text to a prior point in the text.

cohesive ties: Aspects of language (e.g. pronouns, repetition, ellipsis) that presuppose a relationship with some prior part of a text.

common ground: The set of propositions which the participants in a conversation treat as uncontroversially true.

communicative competence: The knowledge people have, most of it below the level of awareness, of what is and is not a culturally appropriate way to carry out a communicative task in their native language and culture.

Communicative Language Teaching: One of the most commonly employed approaches to teaching second languages today, highlighting communication as a means of facilitating language development of all four skills (speaking, listening, reading, and writing) and emphasizing that students need to be able to *produce* language in linguistically and culturally appropriate ways to carry out communicative functions with meaningful purposes.

Community Language Learning: An approach to teaching second languages which focuses on social interaction and affective and interpersonal factors in learning; teachers act as counsellors to help learners become more independent in using the target language to express their own thoughts.

comparative method: A method employed in the reconstruction of a protolanguage from a comparison and analysis of cognates.

compensation: A reliance on brain structures not usually involved in a function, in order to perform that function, as a result of damage to those parts of the brain that normally underlie the function. By analogy, if you lose your hands, you may compensate by using your feet to grasp, etc.

compensatory lengthening: The lengthening of a vowel to compensate for the loss of another segment.

complement: A branch of a phrase, with a category determined by its head, into which another phrase is merged. The complement completes the meaning of the head of the phrase of which it is the complement.

complementary distribution: Predictable, nonoverlapping distribution.

complementary schismogenesis: The process by which each speaker's linguistic behavior drives the other to increasingly exaggerated forms of an opposing behavior, in an ever-widening spiral.

complementizer: An element, such as *that* in English, that introduces a clause, often an embedded clause.

Complementizer Phrase (CP): A phrase headed by a complementizer and taking an Inflection Phrase as its complement.

compositionality: The principle of grammar by which phrases and clauses are made up of other phrases and clauses, the smallest of which are projected from words drawn from the mental lexicon.

compositional semantics: An approach to representing meaning where the meaning of the whole is a function of the meaning of the parts. Thus, the meaning of a sentence is a mathematical function of the meaning of its constituents, down to the meanings of the individual lexical items.

compound: The combining of two or more words to derive a new word, e.g. *toenail*.

comprehensible input: Originally introduced by Krashen, this refers to the input (i.e. language addressed to the learner) that the learner can understand.

conceptual-semantics: Having to do with the meanings of concepts, including concepts associated with words (e.g. living thing, furniture, hammer).

conditional: The mood of a verb that expresses a hypothetical or uncertain state or event, dependent upon some other circumstance.

conjugation: One of two or more classes of verbs distinguished by a set of inflectional forms that differs in some respect from that of verbs in another class. In Spanish, for example, verbs are grouped into three main classes reflected in the infinitive suffixes *-ar* (first conjugation, e.g. *trabajar* 'to work'), *-er* (second conjugation, e.g. *comer* 'to eat'), or *-ir* (third conjugation, e.g. *abrir* 'to open').

connectionism: An approach used in the study of the mind and brain that models language and other mental functions as emerging from statistical learning that takes place over multiple interconnected units.

constative: A sentence whose function is to describe a fact; compare with **performative**.

constituent: A natural grouping of words that act like a unit.

contamination: The reshaping of a word on the basis of frequent association with some other word belonging to the same semantic field.

content words: Words that play a primary role in expressing meaning in a sentence, such as nouns, verbs, and adjectives.

context-free grammars: A family of grammars where each grammar rule is of the form A → B, where A is a single nonterminal and B is a sequence of zero or more terminals and nonterminals. Context-free grammars can represent the structure of center-embedded sentences, such as *The little puppy the boy the principal hated loved ran away*.

context of use: The linguistic or social environment in which a word, phrase, or sentence is produced.

contextualization cues: The paralinguistic and prosodic features that signal how the words spoken are to be interpreted.

contrastive: Creating a contrast in meaning.

contrastive analysis hypothesis (CAH): The hypothesis that difficulties in language learning may be attributed to differences between the L1 and L2.

converging evidence: Evidence from two or more approaches or methods resulting in similar conclusions (e.g. fMRI imaging and lesion studies implicating the same brain region in a particular language function).

conversational rituals: The sequence of utterances that speakers in a given culture expect conversation to follow.

cooing: Vowel-like sounds of very young infants which are generally interpreted as signs of pleasure and playfulness.

cooperative overlap: Two speakers talking at once in a conversation where the second speaker talks along in order to show enthusiastic listenership, not to interrupt.

coordination: A recursive device allowing the linking of words, phrases, or clauses at the same level of structure, using coordinators like *and* and *but*.

Cooperative Principle: The idea, suggested by Grice, that people understand language in light of the assumption that the speaker is behaving rationally and cooperatively.

copula *be*: The use of *to be* as a linking verb, as in *He is nice* or *They are hungry*.

corpus (*plural*: corpora): A collection of linguistic data created as a sample with particular linguistic characteristics.

corrective feedback: An interlocutor's provision of the correct form in response to a learner's non-targetlike utterance.

cortex: The outermost layer of the cerebrum, consisting largely of neuronal cell bodies.

creole: A language that arises from contact between different languages, often in situations of unequal power between the groups of speakers who use the languages. A pidgin which over time becomes grammatically more complex and becomes the mother language of a speech community.

criterion of plurality: A strategy for reconstructing forms in a protolanguage which selects an analysis or a reconstruction of sounds which is supported by cognates in a majority of related languages.

critical period hypothesis: The hypothesis that language learning must occur before a certain age (usually puberty) in order for the language to be learned to a native-like level.

cross-sectional: A type of study in which the researcher investigates different subjects simultaneously and comparatively (e.g. males and females, or English and Japanese speakers).

cuneiform: A script consisting of symbols made by combinations of wedge-shaped impressions in soft clay.

cursing: The irreverent or frivolous use of religious terms or the use of taboo expressions related to sexual or scatological functions.

cytoarchitectonics: The cellular makeup – i.e. the types and distribution of neurons – of a brain area.

dative: The case of the recipient of something given.

declarative memory: The memory system for knowledge of facts and personal experiences. Evidence suggests that this knowledge is largely, though not completely, available to conscious awareness.

declarative representation: A computational strategy that refers to linguistic data and not to procedures or processing strategies.

definiteness: When a noun has (a) particular referent(s) assumed to be identifiable by the listener; in English indicated by the article *the*.

deixis: A word or phrase whose referent cannot be understood without additional contextual information; for example, the referent of *I* depends on who is speaking.

deletion: 1. The removal of an element in a grammatical structure, sometimes the copy of an element left behind by movement. Deletion is tightly restricted by Universal Grammar. 2. Diachronic loss of segments from a word.

dense network: A social network in which everyone knows everyone else.

dental: Sound made by bringing the tongue tip or blade into contact with the upper teeth.

deontic: Modality having to do with what possibilities are better than others according to rules, morality, etc.

derivation: 1. Application of a sequence of phonological rules to convert an underlying representation into a surface representation. 2. The process of forming a new word by modifying an existing base via affixation, reduplication, compounding, etc. The derived word may belong to another lexical category or have a different meaning, or both; e.g. the verb *humidify* is derived from the adjective *humid* by the affixation of *-ify*.

derivational morphology: The creation of new words from existing ones (e.g. the noun *toughness* from the adjective *tough*).

descriptive: An empirical approach which observes and analyzes how language is actually spoken.

determinatives: Symbols in hieroglyphic systems that were added at the end of a word to clarify its meaning.

determiner: A syntactic category that limits the reference of a noun; includes articles, demonstratives, possessive pronouns, and the possessive morpheme *'s*.

Determiner Phrase: A phrase headed by a determiner, such as *the* or *a* in English, taking a Noun Phrase as its complement.

development (*Ausbau*): A criterion for status as a language rather than a dialect based on conscious efforts to standardize, and encourage literary activity in, a linguistic variety.

developmental sequences: A series of identifiable stages that L2 learners pass through in acquiring the second language.

diachronic linguistics: The discipline of linguistics which seeks to explain how languages change over time. Also known as historical linguistics.

diacritic: A mark added to a phonetic symbol to further specify its value (e.g. to indicate the vowel(s) in a syllable or consonantal template).

dialect: 1. One of several distinguishable varieties, generally (but not always) mutually intelligible, of a language. A dialect has features on all levels of language, including lexical, phonological, morphosyntactic, and pragmatic. Linguists use this term to refer to any language variety, regardless of its social status. 2. A linguistic variety without standardization or published literature.

dialect chain: A series of dialects such that speakers of each dialect can understand the next dialect in the series, but speakers of the first dialect in the series may not understand the last.

diaphragm: The large muscle that separates the chest cavity from the stomach; contraction of the diaphragm draws air into the lungs.

diglossia: A social organization of dialects of the same language so that one is seen as more pure and is used for formal purposes (including writing), while others are used for everyday purposes. Diglossic communities take pride in both.

diphthong: A vowel that combines two different tongue positions in sequence.

Direct Method: An approach to teaching second languages which held that non-native languages, just like native languages, could be learned without translation and detailed grammar explanations, and therefore emphasized inductive learning of grammar through spontaneous oral interaction in the target language using concrete, everyday vocabulary.

direct MT: Machine translation based on mapping words in a source-language sentence to words in a target language, without constructing an explicit syntactic or semantic representation of the source-language sentence.

discourse: Language use above the sentence (text) and beyond the sentence (context).

Discourse: The beliefs, values, and practices associated with the use of language.

discourse analysis: The branch of linguistics that focuses on language use above and beyond the sentence, how language is used in context. Discourse analysis relates the forms of language (sounds, morphemes, words, and sentences) to units of language use larger than sentences and to aspects of the world in which language is used.

discourse markers: Small words with little (or no) overt semantic content, often occurring at the beginning of utterances, that display connections among utterances as well as between an utterance and its context. Examples: *well, but.*

discreteness: A fundamental property of human language whereby a continuous range of possible sounds or forms is divided into individual, bounded units. For example, different languages divide the continuous "space" of possible speech sounds into different inventories of phonemes.

dissimilation: 1. A phonological alternation in which two sounds that are similar become more different. 2. A diachronic process by which two sounds become less alike.

dissociation: A stronger association of a brain area or other biological substrate (e.g. neurotransmitter type) with one mental process than another.

distinctive feature: Formal representation (originally as a plus or minus distinction) of a phonetic dimension relevant to phonological contrast and alternation.

divergence: Linguistic differences among related speech communities.

domain-specificity: The degree to which a brain area or other biological substrate subserves only one cognitive function (i.e. the degree to which it is domain-specific as opposed to domain-general).

dominant: If the two hemispheres (of the cerebrum or cerebellum) play unequal roles in a given function, the dominant hemisphere is that which plays the more important role.

donor/recipient language: A language from which elements are borrowed is called the donor, and the borrowing language is called the recipient language.

dorsal: Toward (or generally at) the top of the brain.

double articulation: Sound that combines two places of articulation, such as a labiovelar.

double dissociation: Situation in which one function is associated with one biocognitive substrate, while another function is associated with another substrate. For example, one brain region may show more activation during grammatical than lexical processing, while another region shows greater activation for lexical than grammatical processing.

double modals: The use of two modal verbs – that is, verbs indicating permission or ability (e.g. *may, can, will, might, could, would, should*) – in a single verb phrase, for example, *I might could do it.*

dual: See **number**.

duality: A fundamental property of human language whereby a single sequence of sounds can have more than one meaning.

dyslexia: A developmental disorder in which reading is impaired, although language (in particular aspects of phonological processing) is also affected.

Ebonics: A language variety, part of English or related to English, with its own grammatical structure, that has been developed by communities of people of African descent.

EEG (electroencephalogram): Scalp-based recording of the brain's ongoing electrical activity.

electrochemical: Relating to electrical activity emanating from chemical changes.

ellipsis: A semantic change in which a word occurring in a phrase takes on the meaning of the whole phrase.

epenthesis: The insertion of a sound into a word.

epenthetic r: The insertion of *r* in certain word positions, for example in *warsh* for *wash* or *idear* for *idea*.

epiglottis: Flap of tissue that covers the larynx during swallowing.

epistemic: Modality having to do with knowledge.

ERP component: A characteristic ERP waveform (e.g. the N400) that is found consistently under particular experimental conditions.

ethnic group: A social group with primarily local interests.

evidentiality: A grammatical category indicating the evidence or source (and indirectly, the reliability) of a speaker's utterance. In languages which morphologically mark evidentiality, a typical distinction encodes firsthand or "eyewitness" knowledge (more reliable) vs. secondhand or "hearsay" knowledge (less reliable).

exchange structure: An ordered sequence of turns and the procedures that allow for turn exchange.

excrescence: A kind of epenthesis in which a consonant is inserted between other consonants.

explicit: Available to conscious awareness.

extensional: Aspects of meaning having to do with actual, current facts; meaning that is not **intensional**.

exuberances and deficiencies: The meanings that are necessarily added or lost in the process of translation, because the second language has no lexical or grammatical counterpart to elements in the first or requires grammatical elements that do not exist in the first.

feature: In the morphology–syntax interface, an abstract grammatical property that is realized by (free or bound) grammatical morphemes, e.g. [plural] is a number feature that is realized by various morphological means in English: by the suffix -/z/ and its phonologically conditioned allomorphs for regular nouns (*books*, *papers*), or ablaut (*geese*, *men*), or irregular suffixes such as -*en* (*oxen*) or zero (*deer*).

finite-state machine: A computer program that processes a sequence of input symbols by representing the processing in terms of a network consisting of a finite, prespecified set of states and labeled transition between states. The program starts in an initial state and, on seeing a particular symbol in the input, transitions to another state. The program is said to *accept* its input if it reaches a state designated as a final state on processing all of its input. Finite-state machines are equivalent to regular expressions.

finite-state transducer: A finite-state network where the labels of transitions are pairs of symbols. The transducer can be viewed as mapping sequences of symbols (or strings) in an upper language to strings in a lower language (this is a form of analysis), or vice versa (a form of generation). The program starts in an initial state and, on seeing a particular symbol in the upper language and a corresponding symbol in the lower language, transitions to another state. When it reaches a final state, it has processed a pair of strings defined in the mapping.

fixed stress: System in which stress is predictable based on position in the word.

flouting: Saying something which appears to violate a Gricean maxim, but which in an indirect way conforms to the maxim.

folk etymology/reanalysis: Creation of new forms or a new interpretation of existing forms through misinterpretation of the constituents of a word.

foot: Grouping of a stressed syllable and adjacent unstressed syllables.

foreign language learning: Learning a non-native language in a context where the language is not widely spoken by the community (e.g. learning English in Japan).

formal semantics: The approach to semantics which is especially interested in using tools drawn from logic to understand how the meanings of phrases are composed from their parts.

formant: A resonance of the vocal tract, determinative of vowel quality; a component frequency of high amplitude.

fortition: An alternation in which a speech sound becomes articulatorily stronger, as in the change from a fricative to a stop.

fossilization: The state when a foreign language learner reaches a plateau and remains at a level of proficiency short of native-like mastery. See also **stabilization**.

fragmentation: A way of packaging information in which a unit of language (typically a tone unit in spoken language) presents roughly one idea at a time.

framing: A superordinate message that communicates how utterances are meant and what speakers think they are doing when they speak in a given context.

free: Applied to morphemes, a term indicating that a morpheme may stand freely on its own without having to be attached to a base, e.g. *book, and, about*.

frequency: Rate of vibration, measured in cycles per second, or Hertz (Hz). The perceptual correlate of frequency is pitch.

fricative: Manner of articulation in which the articulators are brought close together but not closed completely, so that the stream of air that is forced between them becomes turbulent and noisy.

front vowel: Vowel sound for which the tongue body moves forward in the mouth.

functional category: A class of "words" (lexical items), and the phrases they project, with relatively weak meaning, but an important structural role. Functional categories, despite their name, are part of formal theories of syntax.

functional neuroanatomy: The anatomical bases of language and other cognitive functions in the brain.

Functional Syntax: The study of principles of grammar derived from aspects of their use by speakers and writers.

function words: Words that serve grammatical functions in a sentence, such as determiners, auxiliaries, and prepositions.

fundamental frequency: Basic rate of vibration of a complex sound, correlated with pitch.

geminate: A long, or double, consonant.

gender: 1. A system of categories (also referred to as **noun classes**) into which the nouns of a language are placed. 2. A grammatical category that distinguishes two or more classes of nouns with which other words such as determiners, adjectives, or verbs must agree. For example, in the Spanish noun phrase *una amiga americana* 'a (female) American friend' both the determiner *una* and adjective *americana* are inflected to agree with the feminine gender of the noun *amiga*.

generation: Automatic production of expressions in a language.

genre: A text whose form and use characterize a particular type (e.g. prayer, narrative, essay).

glide: An approximant, such as [j] and [w], with a high tongue position and constriction just slightly narrower than that of a high vowel.

glottal stop: Sound made by closing the vocal folds, stopping the airflow at the larynx.

Grammar Translation: An approach to teaching foreign languages (particularly Greek and Latin) that focused on explicit instruction of grammar and vocabulary with constant reference to and translation from the learner's L1.

grammatical: A grammatical sentence of a language X is a sentence that speakers of X consider an acceptable sentence of X.

grammatical competence: The knowledge people have, most of it below the level of awareness, of what is and is not a well-formed structure of their native language, in terms of sound, grammatical form, and meaning.

grammatical morpheme: A free or bound morpheme containing little to no lexical content that expresses one or more grammatical properties, such as person, number, or gender agreement, tense, aspect, case, etc.

grapheme: A symbol in a writing system.

Great Vowel Shift: A sound change in which long vowels of Middle English were unconditionally but systematically raised in early Modern English.

Grimm's Law: Jacob Grimm's description of the systematic shift of PIE consonants into Germanic.

group-exclusive: Features that are unique to a single language variety, for example, the use of *gumband* for *rubberband* in Pittsburgh, PA.

group-preferential: Features that are prevalent in one language variety but used to an extent in others, for example, the deletion of copula *be* in African American English, which is used to a more restricted extent in US Southern White vernacular varieties.

gyrus (*plural*: gyri): A ridge or plateau on the surface of the brain.

haplology: A sound change in which a repeated sequence of sounds is reduced to a single occurrence.

hard palate: The roof of the mouth.

harmonics: Component frequencies present in a complex sound wave.

hate speech: Threatening or intimidating discourse aimed at individuals or groups defined by such social characteristics as race, national origin, gender, religion, or sexual orientation.

head: 1. A key "word" (lexical item) from which a phrase of the same category is projected. 2. The part of a derived word (especially in compounds) that constitutes the superordinate semantic category or determines the lexical category (or both) of the overall word, e.g. a *shortlist* is a kind of list whose meaning is narrowed by the lexeme *short* (vs. a *wait(ing) list*, a *black list* or a *hit list*), and the Noun category of *list* determines the overall category of the entire compound (vs. the Adjective category of *short*); thus *list* is the head of the compound.

"heavy" DP movement: The process by which long, extensively modified Determiner Phrases are moved to the rightmost end of their clauses. Like all movements it is tightly restricted by Universal Grammar.

hemisphere: One of the two halves of the cerebrum or cerebellum.

hemodynamic: Concerned with the characteristics of blood flow.

hieroglyphics: An Egyptian writing system which combined logograms, consonantal symbols, and semantic class indicators.

high amplitude sucking paradigm (HASP): An experimental procedure used to assess a young infant's perception of different sounds (among other things) by measuring the duration and strength of sucking responses.

high dialect: The language variety in diglossia that is usually learned by formal study and is used for more formal purposes.

high vowel: Vowel sound in which the tongue body moves up from a neutral position.

hippocampus: A structure in the medial temporal lobe that underlies learning in declarative memory. Evidence also suggests that this structure underlies word learning.

holophrastic stage: The stage of linguistic development in which children produce one-word utterances to carry the meaning of what an adult would express in a longer sentence.

hormone: A molecule that is made in one part of the body but affects another (e.g. estrogen).

Huntington's disease: An inherited neurodegenerative disease marked by characteristic jerking movements (chorea), as well as a number of language and other cognitive deficits.

hypercorrection: A kind of analogical change, in which a changed form is mistakenly assumed to be more correct than a correct form, which it replaces.

hypernym: A word whose referent stands in the relation of class to subclass of another word/ referent; for example, *bird* is the hypernym of *sparrow*.

hyponym: A word whose referent is included within that of another word (its hypernym); for example, *sparrow* is a hyponym of *bird*.

IPA: International Phonetic Alphabet.

idea structure: An ordered sequence of ideas within sentence and text.

identity: In the context of the politics of language, an awareness of membership in a particular social group.

idiom: A phrase whose literal meaning does not follow from principles of semantics.

illocutionary act: A speech act of communication, such as asserting or asking something.

imperative: See **mood**.

imperfect(ive): The aspect of a verb which expresses ongoing, habitual or repeated actions or states.

implicature: Speaker's meaning which comes about because of the cooperative principle.

implicit: Not available to conscious awareness.

indexical: A morpheme or word which depends for its meaning on the context of use.

indicative: See **mood**.

indirectness: Communicating without putting all the meaning into the literal meaning of the words spoken.

individual differences: Differences between individual subjects or groups of subjects that are not well characterized by studies that examine only general patterns.

inferior: Toward the bottom of the head and brain.

infinitive: The untensed expression or form of a verb which is often used as a citation form. For example, English may use the bare verb or the special infinitive marker *to* as in *to sleep*, whereas German (and many other languages) mark the infinitive form with a particular suffix, e.g. *schlaf-en* 'to sleep.'

infix: A type of affix that appears inside the base to which it's applied, e.g. Tagalog past-tense infixation: *tulong* 'help' → *t-um-ulong* 'helped.'

inflection: 1. In morphology, the process of modifying the form of a lexeme to signal a grammatical contrast as required by the syntax of a language. For example, many languages require their verbs to be inflected for agreement with the person and number features of their subjects, e.g. Italian *(noi) lavor-iamo* 'we're working' vs. *(loro) lavor-ano* 'they're working.' 2. In syntax, an element, like a tense or an auxiliary, that is central to the structure of a sentence and contributes to its verbal meaning.

Inflection Phrase (IP): The "scaffold" of a sentence. Inflection Phrases have a required specifier, containing the subject of the sentence, and a complement, containing the main Verb Phrase, and are headed by an inflection.

inflectional morphology: The modification of a word to fit its grammatical role (e.g. *sang* and *walked* are past-tense inflected forms of *sing* and *walk*).

information extraction: The process of automatically filling templates (or tables) from natural language input, including information about specific entities referenced in the text, such as events, people, organizations, locations, and times (these are called named entities) and particular relations between them.

information state: The distribution of knowledge (as new or old information) among people interacting with one another.

inherent variability: Variability between items in a single language variety, for example, variability between *r* and *ø* in certain word and sentence positions in *r*-less dialects (see **r-lessness**). Such variability is inherent in all languages and language varieties and shows regular patterns according to linguistic and social factors.

instrumental orientation: A desire to obtain something practical or concrete from learning a another language.

integration: A way of packaging information in which a unit of language (typically a sentence) presents and syntactically integrates several ideas.

integrative motivation: A desire to identify with the target language community.

intensional: Aspects of meaning having to do with possibilities that may not be actually true at the present time. Examples include modality and tense.

interactional sociolinguistics: A subfield of linguistics in which the social consequences of interactions are traced to linguistic phenomena.

Interaction Hypothesis: The hypothesis that interacting with either a native or non-native speaker of the L2 can facilitate the development of the L2.

interactive: A type of mental processing in which individual subprocesses interact interdependently and largely concurrently.

interference: The knowledge of one language (e.g. one's first language) negatively impacting on the development, production, or comprehension of another (e.g. one's second language).

interlanguage: The learner's rule-based L2 system, which may possess characteristics of both the L1 and L2; the use of a pattern or rule from one's native language in learning an L2, resulting in an error.

interlingual MT: Machine translation based on analyzing an utterance in a source language into a representation that is *language-neutral*, i.e. devoid of any features specific to a particular natural language, and generating a target language utterance from the language-neutral representation.

internal reconstruction: Reconstruction of an earlier form of a language which relies on the analysis of forms within a single language. Since many morphophonemic changes leave noticeable traces, by analyzing these traces one can reconstruct earlier forms and the changes that led to their current forms.

interrogative: See **mood**.

interruption: As distinguished from **overlap**, an attempt to wrest the conversational floor from another speaker.

intonation: The use of pitch to convey meaning at the sentence or discourse level.

invasive: Potentially causing harm or discomfort to a subject, specifically as a result of introducing a foreign instrument or substance into the body.

irregular: Not following the regular linguistic pattern. For example, English irregular past-tense forms (e.g. *dug* from *dig*) do not follow the regular past-tense pattern of adding the *-ed* suffix to the verb.

jargon: A set of lexical items associated with a particular sphere of activity, such as a profession or a hobby, for example, computer jargon or sports jargon.

labiodental: Sound made by bringing the lower lip into contact with the upper teeth.

languaculture: Term used to express the inseparability of language and culture.

language: A language variety acknowledged to have social and political importance, generally (but not always) not mutually intelligible with other languages.

language acquisition device (LAD): The proposed innate area of the brain that is dedicated to language and which makes language acquisition possible.

language acquisition support system (LASS): The daily interactions and relationships the child has with his/her caregivers which support the acquisition of language.

language by development: (German: *Ausbau*) A language that is similar enough to other languages that its differences wouldn't guarantee it language – rather than dialect – status, but that has been deliberately developed by its speech community – via standardization and literary usage – as a distinct language.

language by separation: (German: *Abstand*) A language that is so different from other languages that its status as a language is not in dispute.

language family: A group of languages evolved from a common source.

language organ: The aspect of the human brain which encompasses an individual's language capacity. It is an "organ" in the sense that it is identifiable as a distinct element of cognition, such as real-world knowledge, perceptual mechanisms, and various aesthetic components.

language standardization: Deliberate specification of the forms of a language that are acceptable for certain prestigious purposes, often taken as defining the "correct" forms of a language.

laryngeal: Sound made with the larynx as the only active articulator.

larynx: Cartilaginous structure at the top of the trachea that contains the vocal folds.

lateral: 1. An [l] sound; a sound that is made with one or both sides of the tongue lowered. 2. Toward the outside of the brain on either side (i.e. toward either side of the head).

Latin rhotacism: The change which occurred in Latin about 600 BCE, in which Latin /s/ changed to /r/ between vowels.

lax: Produced with relaxation of the tongue root. Lax vowels are slightly shorter and lower than their tense counterparts.

lenition: An alternation in which a sound becomes articulatorily weaker, as in the change from a stop to a fricative or a fricative into an approximant.

lexeme: A lexical morpheme, that is, a vocabulary entry typically belonging to one of the major lexical categories Noun (N), Verb (V) or Adjective (A), and capable of being inflected for use in particular grammatical contexts, e.g. *dance, danced, dances,* and *dancing* are all words based on the lexeme DANCE.

lexical category: A class of "words" (lexical items), and the phrases they project, with relatively rich meaning and a relatively less important structural role. Lexical categories overlap substantially with traditional "parts of speech."

lexical entry: A representation in the mental lexicon that contains information about a given word. It is typically thought to include (at least) idiosyncratic information about its syntactic roles (e.g. whether it is a noun or a verb), as well as information about the word's meaning and phonological form.

lexical semantics: The study of the meanings of morphemes and words.

lexical stress: System in which stress is an unpredictable property of individual lexical items.

lexical variation: Variation in lexical items or vocabulary that occurs across or within dialects, for example, the use of *lift* in British English vs. *elevator* in American English.

lexicon: The "mental dictionary" of a speaker comprising knowledge of lexical items, including their pronunciation, meaning, and grammatical properties.

linguistic determinism: The strong form of the Sapir–Whorf hypothesis by which language is believed to determine how individuals think about what they talk about.

linguistic relativity: The more commonly held weak form of the Sapir–Whorf hypothesis by which language is believed to influence how individuals think about what they talk about.

liquids: Rhotics and laterals.

loan shift/loan translation: The adoption of material already present in the borrowing language for the objects and concepts belonging to the donor language.

loan words: Lexical items borrowed from another language.

localize: To determine the brain location(s) of biological substrates, in particular of substrates that underlie a given mental process.

locative: The case referring to some location in space, often by a noun's form or by a preposition.

locutionary act: An act of saying (or writing) a word, phrase, or sentence.

Logical Form (LF): A level of syntactic structure which represents semantic information such as scope.

logogram: A writing symbol which represents a morpheme or word in a language.

longitudinal: A type of study in which the researcher investigates the same subjects over an extended period of time (typically many months or years).

low dialect: The language variety in diglossia that is learned first in childhood and subsequently used for everyday purposes by everyone in the community.

low vowel: Vowel sound in which the tongue body moves down from a neutral position.

machine translation: Automatic translation between languages using a computer program with or without human interaction.

manner of articulation: The type of constriction that is made for a speech sound: stop, fricative, affricate, approximant, vowel.

marked: Relatively uncommon crosslinguistically, or relatively more difficult to hear or to say.

mass (or noncount) noun: A noun that denotes a nonindividuatable substance, activity, or quality that is not typically counted or pluralized, e.g. *milk*, *gardening*, *carelessness*.

maxims: Four principles of communication which fall under Grice's Cooperative Principle.

mean length of utterance (MLU): A measure of a child's linguistic development by calculating the average number of morphemes per sentence.

medial: Towards the middle of the brain (i.e. where the hemispheres meet).

merger: 1. The process by which phrases are included in larger phrases. 2. The falling together over time of two or more phonemes into one.

message and metamessage: The message is the meaning of the words spoken; the metamessage identifies the frame in which the words are intended – how to interpret the words.

metalinguistic awareness: Conscious awareness of the characteristics of the language itself and how it works.

metanalysis/recutting: When the structural analysis of an older form is analogically replaced by an analysis which makes "more sense" to a speaker.

metaphor: A perception of similarity between two things or situations which leads one to treat something as if it were something else.

metathesis: 1. A synchronic switching of the order of speech sounds. 2. A diachronic process in which the positions of sounds are transposed.

metonymy: A broadening of meaning, in which a word referring to a single item of a semantic domain is used to represent the entire domain.

mid vowel: Vowel sound in which the tongue body remains at a neutral, intermediate height.

minimal pair: Two distinct words that differ only in a single sound in the same position, such as [pʰæt] and [bæt].

minimum standard: A point on some specified scale below which the item to which the minimum standard applies is deemed not fit for use.

modality: Aspects of meaning having to do with possibilities which may not be actual; modals include words like *must* and *can*.

modified output: After learners receive feedback on a non-targetlike utterance (e.g. an utterance that was ungrammatical), they may change their original utterance (i.e. produce modified output) in an attempt to be more comprehensible to their interlocutors.

monomorphemic: Containing a single morpheme.

mood: A grammatical category that expresses a speaker's belief, opinion, or attitude about the content of an utterance, such as whether a proposition is likely or doubtful to be true, or something he/she wonders about, or hopes or wishes for. Some common mood distinctions include **indicative** (for assertions), **interrogative** (for questions), **imperative** (for commands), and **subjunctive** (for the expression of desire, hope, doubt, etc.).

morpheme: The smallest meaningful unit of language. Words are made up of one or more morphemes, e.g. the word *roses* is made up of two morphemes – the lexeme *rose* plus the plural suffix (realized in this case by the allomorph [əz]).

morpheme order studies: A group of studies designed to investigate the order in which learners of English as a second language acquire particular morphemes in English.

morphology: The branch of linguistics that is concerned with the analysis of internal word structure, including the categories and processes for producing and interpreting the possible words of one's language.

morphophonology: Having to do with the phonological structure, properties, and relations of morphologically complex words.

morphosyntactic: Having to do with the correspondence of morphological structure and properties on the one hand, and those of syntax on the other (such as how morphological affixes for past-tense and other types of inflection are represented as categories in syntactic structure).

morphosyntactic variation: Variation in how words are put together into sentences, for example, the use of *gotten* vs. *got* as the past participle form of *get* in American vs. British English, respectively (e.g. *She has gotten used to it* vs. *She has got used to it*).

motivation: The degree of effort a learner makes to acquire a particular skill.

multiethnic nation: A state which includes a number of ethnic groups, but only one nationality.

multinational states: A state which includes two or more nationalities, none of which is largely or increasingly in control.

multiplex network: A **social network** in which people interact with one another in more than one capacity, for example, a neighbor, workmate, and friend.

multi-word stage: Stage of language development in which children begin to produce phrases of three or more words; at approximately two years of age.

name: A "full" noun phrase, not a pronoun or anaphor, required by the Binding Theory not to refer to any subject to the left within its sentence.

narrative: A recapitulation of a past experience by telling about what happened in temporal order.

narrowing: See **broadening**.

nasal: Produced with an open velum, and thus nasal airflow.

nation: A state that is largely or increasingly under the control of a single nationality.

nationalism: Feelings and actions in favor of one's nationality that are symbolic rather than pragmatic.

nationality: A social group that is aware of, and desirous of preserving or increasing, its place with respect to other nationalities. A nationality may not control its own territory, but may aspire to territorial autonomy.

nationism: The desire to make a state function well at a practical level.

nativism: An approach to language acquisition, derived from the work of Noam Chomsky, which assumes that innate linguistic knowledge, or **Universal Grammar (UG)**, guides all language learning.

Natural Approach: An approach to teaching second languages which was based on the belief that in a relaxed learning environment, motivated learners would automatically acquire the target language when exposed to comprehensible input slightly above their current proficiency level.

natural class: A group of sounds that has one or more phonetic properties in common.

naturalness: A characteristic of language data when they are similar to the language used in everyday life.

need-filling motive: See **prestige motive**.

negative concord: The phenomenon in some languages by which two or more negative forms appear, agreeing with one another, without affecting the negative force of the sentence. For example, French *Je ne sais pas* ('I don't know', lit. 'I don't know not'), Spanish *No veo nada* ('I don't see anything', lit. 'I don't see nothing'), or nonstandard English *He won't do nothing.*

neocortex: The main type of cortex found in the human cerebrum. Neocortex is important for most cognitive functions, including language.

neurocognitive: Relating to the neural, cognitive, and computational correlates of mental functions.

neurodegenerative disease: A disease involving the progressive loss of brain tissue.

neuroimaging: The construction of images that display information from actual brains. Using different methods (e.g. MRI, fMRI, PET, etc.), different types of images can be created, containing different types of information. These include "structural images" (which show anatomical structures) and "functional images" (which show brain activity during cognitive processing).

neuron (nerve cell): The cells in the brain and the rest of the nervous system that underlie movement, perception, cognition, and other mental processes.

neurotransmitters: Molecules that pass between one neuron and another, allowing the two neurons to communicate.

nominative: The case of the subject of a verb; who or what is "doing something."

nonstandard variety: A variety of language other than the most socially favored variety or varieties in a particular society. Nonstandard dialects are not imperfect approximations of a standard but rather have their own internal consistency and can be used to express any idea or concept that can be expressed by a standard variety. A nonstandard variety could become the standard language if the political, social, or economic situation were to change.

noticing hypothesis: The claim that input must be noticed in order to be converted into intake (i.e. learned).

nucleus: The sonority peak of a syllable, usually the vowel.

number: A grammatical property of nouns and pronouns which contrasts a basic quantity of countable entities, such as **singular** ('one') or **plural** ('more than one'), and may require agreement by other elements such as determiners, adjectives, or verbs, e.g. *student* vs. *students.* Some languages have a three-way contrast between singular, **dual** ('two'), and **plural** ('more than two').

observational studies: A type of study in which the researcher observes (and often audio- or videotapes) individual children interacting in natural contexts.

obstruent: A speech sound that is made audible by obstruction of the airflow in the vocal tract: oral stops, fricatives, and affricates.

official language: The language used to carry out the practical functions of a state, such as publishing official documents, conducting the business of the legislature, or operating the military.

onset: The consonants in a syllable that precede the nucleus.

oral: Produced with a closed velum, and thus no nasal airflow.

orthography: The standardized version of a language's writing system.

ossicles: The bones of the middle ear.

other-repair: See **repair**.

oval window: The membrane of the inner ear.

overextension: The child's use of a word to cover more referents than an adult would; for example, referring to all four-legged creatures as "dogs."

overgeneralization: Misapplying a rule to an exceptional case, such as saying "goed" instead of "went."

overlap: Speaking at the same time as another speaker.

palatal: Sound made with a constriction of the tongue body and blade against the hard palate.

paradigm: A set of inflectional contrasts, defined in relation to one or more grammatical features, such as the set of person and number agreement inflectional contrasts for verbs of a particular conjugation class in a particular tense.

paradigmatic stress: System in which stress depends on the morphological properties of a word.

Parallel Distributed Processing (PDP): An information processing approach which makes associations based on regularities detected in the input and also works with many levels of information simultaneously (rather than sequentially, as in serial processing).

parental diaries: Detailed personal records of a child's language development, typically written by the parent or guardian of the child.

Parkinson's disease: A neurodegenerative disease leading to motor impairments, including tremor, as well as language and other cognitive dysfunctions. The degeneration takes place primarily in the basal ganglia.

parse tree: A graphic representation of the hierarchical syntactic structure of a sentence.

parsing: Automatically constructing a structural analysis of a sequence of symbols in an input language, usually based on a grammar for that language.

parsimony: The logical principle that the simplest explanation is preferred. Sometimes referred to as "Occam's razor," after the fourteenth-century philosopher, William of Occam.

part-of-speech tagging: The process of mapping each word in an input sentence to its most likely part of speech.

pattern–action rules: A strategy for applying morphological rules: a computer program identifies words that match the rule's pattern; it then records that word's morphological components, as specified by the rule's action.

participation framework: The ways that people organize and maintain an interaction by adapting roles, identities, and ways of acting and interacting.

passive articulators: Structures in the vocal tract toward which the active articulators move in order to create a constriction.

pejoration/amelioration: Pejoration is a semantic change in which a word acquires a negative value. Its opposite is amelioration, in which a word acquires a more positive value.

perfect(ive): The aspect of a verb which describes an action or process as a whole, without internal structure.

performative: A sentence whose function is to affect the world; compare to **constative**.

perlocutionary act: A speech act which affects the world in a way that goes beyond pure communication.

person: A grammatical property of nouns and pronouns that distinguishes entities referred to in an utterance in relation to their role as speaker ("first" person), addressee ("second" person), or everything else ("third" person), and that may require agreement by other words in a clause, such as verbs.

petroglyphs: Prehistoric paintings on cave walls.

pharmacological: Relating to the action or effects of drugs in the body.

pharynx: The open area in the back of the throat, between the larynx and the velum.

pharyngeal: Sound made with constriction of the tongue body toward the back wall of the pharynx.

phoneme: One of the contrastive sounds of a language; a label for a group of sounds that are perceived by the speaker to be the same.

phonemic principle: The ideal of a one-to-one relationship between the phonemes of a language and the letters of its alphabet.

phonetic alphabet: A system for writing speech sounds.

phonetic determinative: Part of a Chinese character which indicates how the corresponding morpheme is pronounced.

phonetic plausibility: The requirement in reconstruction of protolanguage forms that a posited sound change must be phonetically likely.

phonetics: The study of speech sounds as physical objects.

phonetic transcription: Writing down sounds using a phonetic alphabet.

phonogram: A written symbol which represents a sound unit (phoneme or syllable) of the spoken language.

phonological rule: Formal statement, using distinctive features, of a phonological alternation, in the form "A becomes B in context C."

phonological variation: Variation in pronunciations, for example, the pronunciation of *c* and *z* as [θ] in Castilian Spanish vs. [s] in Spanish varieties in the Americas.

phonology: The study of how languages organize sounds into different patterns.

phonotactic constraints: Restrictions on the types of sounds that are allowed to occur next to each other or in particular positions in a word.

phrase structure rules: Rules that describe the structure of phrases and sentences in a language.

pictogram: A written symbol which resembles and nonarbitrarily represents an object or idea.

pidgin: A rudimentary contact or trade language which has a basic vocabulary and grammar.

pinna: The visible shell of the ear.

pitch track: A graph of changes in fundamental frequency over time.

place of articulation: The area of the vocal tract at which a constriction is made.

plasticity: Brain plasticity refers to changes in brain organization in response to experience, such as changes as to which brain structures subserve a function after brain damage (see **compensation**).

plural: See **number**.

politeness: A technical term for the norms in a culture for balancing the competing interactive needs of personal freedom and belonging to a group.

polysemy: The situation of a word having multiple related meanings.

possible world: A way that the universe could be; the real universe is a possible world, called the actual world, as are all other hypothetical possibilities.

postalveolar: Sound made with a constriction of the tongue blade against the roof of the mouth just behind the alveolar ridge.

posterior: Toward the back of the head and brain.

postposition: A lexical item in some languages that is like a preposition in English, except that it occurs *after* its complement.

poverty of the stimulus: The argument that the ability speakers demonstrate in conforming to the restrictions of natural grammar exceeds what could be learned from their experience with language, hence supporting the existence of a language organ (Universal Grammar).

pragmatic variation: Variation in conventions for language use, for example, variation in whether pauses are expected between turns in conversation and, if so, how long these pauses are expected to be.

pragmatics: The field of linguistics which studies meaning in particular contexts of use.

predicate: The verb phrase of a sentence.

prefix: An affix that precedes the base to which it is bound, e.g. *un-* in the word *unhappy*.

prescriptive: An approach which claims some uses of language are more correct than others.

prestige/need-filling motive. When elements are borrowed from a culturally or politically dominant language, the motive is prestige. The motive becomes need filling when the recipient language borrows new objects and concepts along with their names.

presupposition: A proposition which a speaker must take for granted if what he/she says is to be appropriate in the context of use.

primary symbolization: Direct (pictorial) representation of an object or idea, without reference to language.

principle of compositionality: The principle which states that the meaning of a word, phrase, or sentence can be computed from the meanings of its parts and the way they are put together.

prior text: Previous instances of language use without which current instances of language cannot be interpreted.

procedural memory: The memory system that underlies the learning and control of motor and cognitive skills such as riding a bicycle. This knowledge seems to be entirely implicit. The system is rooted in brain circuits passing through the basal ganglia and frontal cortex.

procedural representation: A computational strategy that refers to procedures or processing strategies, as well as linguistic data.

productive: Productive affixes, such as *-ed* or *-ness*, can be used to create new word forms. For example, one can add such affixes to made-up or borrowed words.

productivity: A fundamental property of human language whereby an infinite number of new meanings can be constructed by combining existing forms according to the rules of a given language. For example, new words can be coined by creating novel combinations of existing morphemes.

progressive: The aspect of a verb which expresses incomplete state or continuing action at a given point in time.

projection: The process by which a phrase is created from a "word" (lexical item). The phrase is of the same category as the "word" and may have structure into which a complement and/or a specifier phrase is to be merged.

pronoun: A type of noun phrase, with little intrinsic meaning, used to refer to an already-known entity, and required by the Binding Theory *not* to refer to the subject of its own clause.

property: An unsaturated proposition, denoted by a predicate.

proposition: A complete thought, which can be true or false.

prosody: The timing, rhythm, and intonation of speech.

prosthesis: The insertion of a sound at the beginning of a word.

protoconversations: An exchange between an infant and caregiver that resembles a conversation, in which the caregiver responds to the infant's smiles, burps, and babbling as if the infant was communicating a message.

protolanguage: A (reconstructed) parent language from which related languages are derived.

proxemics: The study of the meaning and arrangement of space (between people and among elements of the physical setting) within and across cultures.

psycholinguistic: Relating to the mental processes underlying language production and comprehension, or to the mainly behavioral methods used to examine these processes.

pulmonic egressive airstream mechanism: Air moving out from the lungs as a source of sound.

push chain/pull chain: In a push chain, a sound moves into the articulatory space of another sound. In a pull chain, a sound fills an articulatory space by pulling another sound from somewhere else.

quantifier: A word or phrase which serves to make a statement about quantities or amounts of things. For example, *nobody* can be used to state that no person has a certain property.

radical: Part of a Chinese character which indicates the semantic category of its corresponding morpheme.

rate of speech: How quickly or slowly a speaker utters words in sequence.

real-time data: Language data from a particular community at two or more different time periods, typically used to examine language change.

reanalysis: See **folk etymology**.

rebus: The extension of a pictogram for one referent to phonetically represent a homophone of that referent (e.g. the use of a circle pictographically representing the sun to also represent a son).

recast: A more targetlike reformulation of a learner's non-targetlike utterance.

receptor: A molecule on the surface of a neuron that receives a specific type of neurotransmitter.

recipient design: The process whereby a speaker considers the informational and social needs of the addressee of what he/she is saying.

recipient language: See **donor language**.

recursion: The property of natural grammar which allows grammatical processes to be applied repeatedly, making infinitely long sentences hypothetically possible.

recutting: See **metanalysis**.

reduplication: The copying of all or part of a base to signal a grammatical or meaning change, e.g. Tagalog *tawag* 'call' → *ta-tawag* 'will call,' in which the first syllable of the base is copied and prefixed to the base to indicate future tense.

reference: The relationship between a word or phrase and the thing(s) in the world which it describes; the extensional meaning of a word, phrase, or sentence.

referent: An entity (person, place, or thing) that can be evoked by language.

register: A way of using language that is functionally adapted to and reflects different facets its context of use (e.g. participants, goals, setting).

regular: The default linguistic pattern. For example, in English past-tense formation, the regular pattern (adding the *-ed* suffix to the verb, as in *walked*) applies to most English verbs, as well as to new verbs entering the language (e.g. *googled*).

reinforcement: A response to a behavior which increases the likelihood that the behavior will occur.

relative chronology: The chronological order of changes which occurred in the history of a language.

repair: The process whereby a person, having noticed that something problematic has been said, alters it; **self-repair** is directed to one's own speech; **other-repair** is directed to another's speech.

representativeness: A characteristic of language data when they are representative of the language used by the child everyday or by the general population under investigation.

restrictor: The part of a quantifier expressing the set of things relevant to the meaning of the quantifier.

retroflex: Sound made with the tongue tip curled back toward the palato-alveolar region.

rhotic: An [r] sound.

rhyme: The nucleus and coda of a syllable.

***r*-lessnessness:** The systematic production of *r* as a vowel or ∅ after vowels, as in [fiᵊ] for *fear*, [wœk] for *work*, or [brʌθ] for *brother*.

root: The most basic form of a lexical morpheme before any morphological operation has applied to it, e.g. the adjective lexeme *humid* is the root of the complex word *dehumidifier*. In Italian, the bound form *lavor-* 'work' is the verb root from which all its inflected forms are derived by affixation, and in Arabic the triconsonantal sequence *d-r-s* 'study' is the bound verb root from which all its related forms are derived by affixation and vowel infixation.

round: Made with rounded lips.

Rules of Rapport: Lakoff's term to describe the principles underlying speaker's choices of ways to express meaning while honoring others' interactional needs.

Sapir–Whorf hypothesis: The hypothesis that what we think is strongly affected by the language we speak.

scaffolding: Supportive interaction, typically between an expert (such as a teacher or a more experienced peer) and a learner, or between caregivers and children, which allows a learner or child to first practice skills in collaboration with another.

scale: An ordered set of values for some property, important for the semantics of adjectives.

schema: A set of structured expectations about an experience (e.g. events, people, setting).

schwa: An unstressed mid central vowel.

scope: The part of a sentence over which a word or phrase has a semantic effect. Also used more specifically to refer to the part of a sentence which, in combination with a quantifier, describes a quantity or amount of things.

scope ambiguity: The type of ambiguity which can arise when a sentence contains two phrases which have scope, such as quantifiers.

script: The set of symbols of a given writing system.

secondary symbolization: Indirect representation of an object or idea, through the direct representation of some unit of spoken language (phoneme, syllable, or morpheme).

second language learning: Learning a non-native language in a context where the language is widely spoken by the community (e.g. learning English in the US).

self-repair: see **repair**.

semantic dementia: A neurodegenerative disease that mainly affects the temporal lobes, and results in a progressive loss of lexical and semantic abilities.

semantic meaning: The literal meaning of a word, phrase, or sentence.

semantics: The field of linguistics which studies literal meaning; the study of those aspects of meaning which are determined within the linguistic system.

sense: The intensional meaning of a word, phrase, or sentence.

sensitive period: The time frame in which language acquisition should most likely occur (i.e. before puberty) in order for native-like levels of mastery to be reached.

separable: Relying on independent biological, cognitive, or computational substrates.

separate systems hypothesis: The proposal that bilingual children begin with two grammar and lexical systems from the earliest stages of language acquisition.

separation (*Abstand*): A criterion for status as a language rather than a dialect based on substantial structural differences from other linguistic varieties.

serial: A type of mental processing in which individual subprocesses act in succession (one after the other), and are substantially independent of one another.

sibilant: a class of noisy, strident sounds which in English consist of the following: /s, z, ʃ, ʒ, tʃ, dʒ/.

Silent Way: An approach to teaching second languages which focused on learning language through problem-solving; teachers spoke only when necessary, using props like colored wooden rods to stimulate student use and analysis of the target language.

singular: See **number**.

sister languages: Languages derived from a single language.

slang: Lexical items that carry non-neutral connotations and are typically considered to be short-lived.

social network: A network of individuals who interact in some way; networks in which people interact frequently may be characterized as *dense* and/or *multiplex*.

sociolinguistic interview: An informal interview designed to approximate a natural conversation and to yield a large amount of naturalistic speech data which can then be analyzed to reveal regular patterns of variation.

sociolinguistics: The study of language in its social setting.

soft palate: The velum.

sonorant: A speech sound that is made audible by resonance of air in the vocal tract, rather than by obstruction of airflow: vowels, glides, nasals, and some liquids.

sonority: Relative openness of the vocal tract.

sound change: A change in the way members of a speech community pronounce particular sounds, which in turn may result in changes to the phonology of the language (the set of sounds used by the language and its organization).

sound wave: A pressure wave that propagates from a sound source.

source-filter theory of speech production: Conception of speech sounds as a combination of a sound source (the larynx) and a sound filter (the resonances of the vocal tract).

spatial resolution: The degree of accuracy (e.g. of a research method) in localizing activity within the brain.

spatiotemporal dynamics: The pattern of realtime brain activation for a given task or cognitive function. The visual representation of brain activity through time during mental processing.

speaker's meaning: What a speaker intends to communicate though his or her language.

species-specificity: The degree to which a function is specific to a particular species (e.g. language in humans).

Specific Language Impairment (SLI): A developmental language disorder associated with syntactic and other language impairments, as well as a range of motor and other nonlanguage deficits.

specifier: A part of phrasal structure, two levels above the head and branching in the opposite direction from the complement. For example, subjects of sentences are located in the specifier position of Inflection Phrases.

speech act: An action performed by one person using language. It can be labeled by a noun that names the act. The speaker intends to communicate the act and that intention is recognized by the recipient. Examples: greeting, request, warning.

speech event: An interaction between two or more people in which more than one speech act occurs. Examples: greetings, request and compliance.

speech perception: The process of using acoustic information to recognize speech sounds in a message.

speech recognition: The automatic transcription of a speech signal into natural language text.

speech situation: A social occasion with more than one speech event. During the occasion, speech contributes to what happens, but it is not necessarily *all* that happens. Examples: a classroom, a party.

speech synthesis: The automatic transformation of a natural language text into a speech signal.

split: The breaking up over time of a single phoneme into two or more phonemes.

stabilization: When learning of the second language temporarily or permanently plateaus.

standard: A socially favored variety of a language.

state: An autonomous territory all of which is considered to be under the control of the same political authority.

statistical parsing: A computational approach in which linguists train a computer to discover syntactic rules from examples of linguistic analyses in an annotated corpus, and use the probabilities of occurrence of different structures to parse new input.

stem: A form which serves as the base for further inflection. In Italian, the bound form *lavor-* 'work' is both the root and the stem from which the present-tense form *lavorano* 'they work' is derived; the form *lavorav-* is the stem (but not the root) from which the imperfective form *lavoravano* 'they were working/used to work' is derived.

stemming: Automatically stripping off morphological inflections from a word to arrive at a normalized form of it.

stop: A manner of articulation in which the flow of air from the lungs is interrupted by the closing of the vocal tract (at some point of articulation).

strategic generation: A step in natural language generation where the system selects abstract chunks of information called "message units" from a data set and decides on the discourse model of the output text.

stress: A prominence relation between syllables. Certain syllables may be longer, louder, higher-pitched, and more clearly articulated than those around them.

structure-building: The process of constructing a complex linguistic structure from its parts (e.g. constructing a phrase from its words, or the past-tense form *walked* from *walk* and *-ed*).

subcortical structures: Anatomical structures situated beneath the cortex (e.g. the basal ganglia).

subject: The first noun phrase under the S node in a sentence.

subjunctive: See **mood**.

suffix: An affix that follows the base to which it is bound, e.g. *-ness* in the word *happiness*.

sulcus (*plural*: sulci): A valley lying between gyri or lobes on the surface of the brain.

superior: Toward the top of the head and brain.

superstratum/substratum languages: In a multilingual community, a culturally or politically dominant language is a superstratum language, while those of lesser status are the substratum languages.

suppletion: The partial or total substitution of one lexical stem for another to indicate a grammatical contrast, e.g. *go/went* (total suppletion in the past-tense form) and *bring/brought* (partial suppletion).

suprasegmentals: Aspects of speech that influence stretches of sound longer than a single segment: length, tone, intonation, syllable structure, and stress.

surface representation: The way a phoneme or morpheme is actually pronounced.

syllabary: The inventory of written symbols representing the syllables of a language.

synapse: The tiny space between two neurons, across which they communicate via neurotransmitters.

syncope: Deletion of segments from the interior of a word.

synonym: Words that have shared meaning are synonyms of each other. Absolute synonyms have identical meanings in all contexts of use. Partial synonyms have identical meanings in only some contexts of use.

syntactic category: Where a word can appear in a sentence; sometimes referred to as "part of speech."

syntactic tree: A way to represent the structure of a sentence in a hierarchically organized diagram, generated by phrase structure rules.

syntax: The rule-governed combination of words into phrases and sentences.

tactical generation: A step in natural language generation where the system generates sentences from the abstract message units in the discourse model specified by the strategic generator.

task-based instruction: Using communicative activities in which participants must exchange or seek information to accomplish a (generally nonlinguistic) goal.

telegraphic speech: Speech in which function words are absent, common in the early stages of child language development.

temporal resolution: The degree of accuracy (e.g. of a research method) in determining the time course of a given neurocognitive process.

tense: A grammatical category that situates an event or state in relation to a reference point in time, typically the moment of speaking.

tense (vowel): Produced with stiffening of the tongue root. Tense vowels are slightly higher and longer than their lax counterparts.

thematic grid: The list of thematic roles associated with a word.

thematic role: A part of a word's meaning which indicates the role that some individual plays in the action which that word describes. Examples are *agent*, *patient*, and *theme*.

tokenization: Automatically identifying word and sentence boundaries in a text.

tone: The use of pitch to distinguish lexical items.

tone units: A cluster of words that form a perceptible unit. Typically it has one main stress, a complete intonation contour, a consistent prosody and/or ends with a pause.

tongue blade: The surface of the tongue a few centimeters behind the tongue tip.

tongue body: The main mass of the tongue, also known as the tongue dorsum.

tongue front: An active articulator encompassing the tongue tip and blade.

tongue root: The lowest part of the tongue, in the pharynx.

tongue tip: The frontmost few centimeters of the tongue.

trachea: The windpipe; cartilaginous tube connecting the lungs to the pharynx.

transcription: The process and product of writing details of speech.

transfer: The knowledge of one language (e.g. one's first language) impacting on the development, production, or comprehension of another (e.g. one's second language).

transition zones: Areas at the borders between dialect regions in which language features from the different regions may coexist or intermediate forms may be found.

truth conditions: The way that things would have to be in order to make a sentence true. Truth conditions are often understood in terms of possible worlds.

treebank: A corpus of sentences in a language that has been analyzed into parse trees.

turn at talk: A period of time in which one person is heard as a speaker.

turn continuers: Nonverbal and verbal devices (see **back channels**) produced by someone not currently holding a turn at talk; these devices allow current speaker to continue, or if current speaker opts not to, the other may begin a turn.

turn-transition place: A location in a current turn, often indicated by intonation, pause, prosody, meaning or form at which a current speaker may yield a turn to a next speaker.

two-level morphology: A morphological representation for natural language that is declarative and can be used for both analysis and generation. It is implemented with finite-state transducers.

two-word stage: The stage of language development characterized by use of phrases which are not more than two words; at approximately two years of age.

umlaut: The process or the result of assimilating a vowel to one in the following syllable.

underextension: The child's use of a word to cover less referents than would an adult; for example, only using the word *dog* to refer to the family dog but to no other canines.

underlying representation: The basic form of a morpheme as it is stored in the mental lexicon.

ungrammatical: An ungrammatical sentence of a language X is a sentence that speakers of X do not consider to be an acceptable sentence of X.

unification-based grammars: Grammars where linguistic information is expressed in the form of constraints involving matching of linguistic feature representations. The matching of such representations is called unification. In contrast to Chomskyan approaches to grammar, unification-based grammars are declarative, and can be used in both understanding and generation.

unitary system hypothesis: The proposal that bilingual children begin with just one grammar and lexical system that later become differentiated as they learn to distinguish between the two languages.

Universal Grammar (UG): The set of principles that determine the properties of the natural grammars of all languages, with which human children appear to be born and which is thought to guide children's acquisition of their native languages. The same as **language organ** in its initial state, except abstract principles are emphasized more than biology.

unmarked: Relatively common crosslinguistically, or relatively easier to hear or to say.

unproductive: Unproductive affixes, such as *-ity* and *-ation*, cannot usually be used to create new forms. For example, one cannot generally add such affixes to made-up or borrowed words.

unround: Not having the lips in a rounded position.

utterance: The realization of a sentence within a context.

uvula: The pendulous tip of the velum.

uvular: Sound made with a constriction of the tongue body against the uvula.

vagueness: The property of having a general meaning which is made more specific in a particular context of use.

velar: Sound made with a constriction of the tongue body against the velum.

velum: A muscular flap that regulates the opening in the back of the mouth that connects the mouth and nose. Also called the soft palate.

ventral: Toward (or generally at) the bottom of the brain.

vernacular: See **nonstandard variety**.

vocabulary spurt: At the end of the second year, the rapid development of the child's productive vocabulary.

vocal tract: The structures of the lungs, trachea, larynx, mouth, and nose used to create speech sounds.

vocal folds: Flaps of tissue inside the larynx which may vibrate as air passes over them, producing voicing.

voiced: Produced with vocal fold vibration.

voiceless: Produced without vocal fold vibration.

vowel harmony: A type of assimilation, in which all vowels in a certain domain, usually the word, must agree in some phonological feature, such as roundness or backness.

waveform: A graph of pressure variations in a sound wave, where the x-axis indicates time and the y-axis indicates amplitude.

Wernicke's area: A classical language area generally taken to correspond to the posterior portion of the superior temporal gyrus. The area is named for the German scientist Carl Wernicke, who first suggested its involvement in language.

wh-movement: The process by which wh-phrases, headed by "words" with meanings like *who*, *what*, *where*, *why*, and *how* are moved from their original position to the specifier position of Complementizer Phrases. Like all movements it is tightly restricted by Universal Grammar. Not all languages have wh-movement.

wh-question: A question that cannot be answered by *yes* or *no* often contains a wh-word.

wh-word: Word that starts with *wh-* that is found in questions, e.g. *what, when, where, who, why*.

Williams syndrome: A hereditary developmental disorder marked by a characteristic facial deformity as well as certain cognitive impairments. It has been argued that language – in particular, aspects of grammar – may be spared in Williams syndrome.

word: An abstract sign that is the smallest grammatically independent unit of language.

word-sense disambiguation: The process of mapping each word in an input sentence to its most likely meaning (or "sense").

working memory: The ability to store and process information simultaneously in real time.

zero derivation: The shifting of a word from one lexical category to another without altering the form of the word in any way, e.g. *cook* (V) → *cook* (N) ('someone who cooks').

BIBLIOGRAPHY

Agar, Michael 1994, *Language shock: understanding the culture of conversation*, New York: Morrow.

Akinlabi, A. To appear, "Sonorant nasalization in Yoruba deverbal nouns," in *Proceedings of the 3rd World Congress of African Linguistics*. [Paper downloaded from www.rci.rutgers.edu/~akinlabi/ Sonorant–nasal.pdf]

Akmajian, A., Demers, R. A., Farmer, A. K., and Harnish, R. M. 1995, *Linguistics: an introduction to language and communication*, 4th edition, Cambridge, MA: MIT Press.

Algeo, John 1972, *Problems in the origins and development of the English language*, New York: Harcourt Brace.

Alim, Samy 2004, "Hip hop nation language," in Edward Finegan and John R. Rickford (eds.), *Language in the USA*, Cambridge University Press, pp. 387–409.

Al-Wer, Enam 1997, "Arabic between reality and ideology," *International Journal of Applied Linguistics* 7: 251–65.

Anderson, Stephen R. and Lightfoot, David W. 2002, *The language organ: linguistics as cognitive physiology*, Cambridge University Press.

Anttila, Raimo 1972, *An introduction to historical and comparative linguistics*, New York: Macmillan.

Appleyard, David 1995, *Colloquial Amharic: a complete language course*, New York: Routledge.

Austin, J. 1962, *How to do things with words*, Cambridge, MA: Harvard University Press.

Baker, C. 2001, *Foundations of bilingual education and bilingualism*, 3rd edition, Clevedon, UK: Multilingual Matters.

Baker, Myron Charles and Cunningham, Michael A. 1985, "The biology of bird-song dialects," *Behavioral and Brain Sciences* 8: 85–99.

Barson, J. 1981, *La grammaire à l'œuvre*, 3rd edition, New York: Holt, Rinehart & Winston.

Bates, E. and Devescovi, A. 1989, "Crosslinguistic studies of sentence production," in B. MacWhinney and E. Bates (eds.), *The crosslinguistic study of sentence processing*, Hillsdale, NJ: Lawrence Erlbaum, pp. 225–253.

Bates, E., Devescovi, A., and Wulfeck, B. 2001, "Psycholinguistics: a cross-language perspective," *Annual Review of Psychology* 52: 369–396.

Bates, E. and Goodman, J. 1997, "On the inseparability of grammar and the lexicon: evidence from acquisition, aphasia, and real-time processing," *Language and Cognitive Processes* 12(5/6): 507–584.

Bateson, Gregory [1935] 1972, "Culture contact and schismogenesis," in *Steps to an ecology of mind*, New York: Ballantine, pp. 61–87.

Bateson, Gregory [1955] 1972, "A theory of play and fantasy," in *Steps to an ecology of mind*, New York: Ballantine, pp. 177–193.

Bauer, L. 2002, *An introduction to international varieties of English*, Edinburgh University Press.

Bauer, L. 2003, *Introducing linguistic morphology*, 2nd edition, Washington, DC: Georgetown University Press.

Bauman, R. and Sherzer, J. (eds.) 1974, *Explorations in the ethnography of speaking*, Cambridge University Press.

Beard, R. 1995, *Lexeme–morpheme base morphology*, Albany, NY: SUNY Press.

Becker, A. L. 1975, "A linguistic image of nature," *International Journal of the Sociology of Language* 5: 109–121.

Becker, A. L. 1995, *Beyond translation: essays toward a modern philology*, Ann Arbor: University of Michigan Press.

Beesley, K. R. and Karttunen, L. 2003, *Finite state morphology*, Stanford, CA: CSLI Publications.

Bell, Allan 1984, "Language style as audience design," *Language in Society* 13: 145–204.

Berko, J. 1958, "The child's learning of English morphology," *Word* 14: 150–177.

Berko Gleason, J. and Bernstein Ratner, N. 1998, "Language acquisition," in J. Berko Gleason and N. Bernstein Ratner (eds.), *Psycholinguistics*, Belmont, CA: Wadsworth/Thomson Learning, pp. 347–407.

Berman, R. A. 1997, "Modern Hebrew," in R. Hetzron (ed.), *The Semitic languages*, New York: Routledge, pp. 312–333.

Bialystok, E. 1997, "The structure of age: in search of barriers to second-language acquisition," *Second Language Research* 13: 116–137.

Biber, Douglas 1988, *Variation across speech and writing*, Cambridge University Press.

Bickerton, Derek 1981, *The roots of language*, Ann Arbor, MI: Karoma.

Bickerton, Derek 1984, "The language bioprogram hypothesis," *Behavioral and Brain Sciences* 7: 173–203.

Bickerton, Derek 1990, *Language and species*, University of Chicago Press.

Birdsong, D. (ed.) 1999, *Second language acquisition and the critical period hypothesis*, Mahwah, NJ: Lawrence Erlbaum.

Bittner, Maria and Hale, Ken 1995, "Remarks on definiteness in Warlpiri," in Emmon Bach, Eloise Jelinek, Angelika Kratzer, and Barbara Partee (eds.), *Quantification in natural language*, Dordrecht: Kluwer Academic Publishers, pp. 81–105.

Bley-Vroman, R. 1990, "The logical problem of foreign language learning," *Linguistic Analysis* 20: 3–49.

Bloomfield, Leonard 1933, *Language*, New York: Holt.

Bolton, Whitney F. 1982, *A living language: the history and structure of English*, New York: Random House.

Bortfeld, H., Morgan, J. L., Golinkoff, R. M., and Rathbun, K. 2005, "*Mommy* and me: familiar names help launch babies into speech stream segmentation," *Psychological Science* 16: 298–304.

Bowerman, S. 2004, "White South African English: morphology and syntax," in B. Kortmann *et al.* (eds.), *A handbook of varieties of English*, vol. 2: *Morphology and syntax*, Berlin: Mouton de Gruyter, pp. 948–61.

Boysson-Bardies, B., Sagart, L., and Durand, C. 1984, "Discernible differences in the babbling of infants according to target language," *Journal of Child Language* 11: 1–15.

Braine, M. 1971, "On two types of models of the internalization of grammars," in D. I. Slobin (ed.), *The ontogenesis of grammar: a theoretical symposium*, New York: Academic Press.

Breitenstein, Caterina, Jansen, Andreas, Deppe, Michael, Foerster, Ann-Freya, Sommer, Jens, Wolbers, Thomas, and Knecht, Stefan 2005, "Hippocampus activity differentiates good from poor learners of a novel lexicon," *Neuroimage* 25(3): 958–968.

Brodmann, K. (ed.) 1909, *Vergleichende Lokalisationslehre der Grosshirnrinde in ihren Prinzipien dargestellt auf Grund des Zeelenbaues*, Leipzig: Barth.

Brown, R. 1973, *A first language: the early stages*, Cambridge, MA: Harvard University Press.

Bruner, J. 1983, *Child's talk: learning to use language*, New York: Norton.

Burnham, D., Kitamura, C., and Vollmer-Conna, U. 2002, "What's new pussycat? On talking to babies and animals," *Science* 296: 1435.

Byrnes, Heidi 1986, "Interactional style in German and American conversations," *Text* 6: 189–206.

Camaj, M. 1984, *Albanian grammar*, Wiesbaden: Harrassowitz.

Campbell, Lyle 1999, *Historical linguistics: an introduction*, Cambridge, MA: MIT Press.

Cardie, C. 1997, "Empirical methods in information extraction," *AI Magazine* 18: 65–79.

Caselli, M. C., Bates, E., Casadio, P., Fenson, J., Fenson, L., Sanderl, L., and Weir, J. 1995, "A cross-linguistic study of early lexical development," *Cognitive Development* 10: 159–199.

Cedergren, Henrietta 1973, "The interplay of social and linguistic factors in Panama," PhD dissertation, Cornell University.

Cenoz, J. 2003, "The influence of age on the acquisition of English: general proficiency, attitudes and code-mixing," in M. P. García-Mayo and M. L. García Lecumberri (eds.), *Age and the acquisition of English as a foreign language*, Clevedon, UK: Multilingual Matters, pp. 77–93.

Chafe, Wallace 1982, "Integration and involvement in speaking, writing, and oral literature," in D. Tannen (ed.), *Spoken and written language: exploring orality and literacy*, Norwood, NJ: Ablex, pp. 35–53.

Chomsky, Noam [1955] 1975, *The logical structure of linguistic theory*, University of Chicago Press.

Chomsky, N. 1956, "Three models for the description of language," *IRI Transactions on Information Theory* 2: 112–124.

Chomsky, Noam 1957, *Syntactic structures*, The Hague: Mouton.

Chomsky, Noam 1981, *Lectures on Government and Binding*, Dordrecht: Foris.

Chomsky, Noam 1995, *The Minimalist Program*, Cambridge, MA: MIT Press.

Chomsky, N. 1999, "On the nature, use and acquisition of language," in W. Ritchie and T. Bhatia (eds.), *Handbook of child language acquisition*, New York: Academic Press, pp. 33–54.

Chomsky, Noam and Halle, Morris 1968, *The sound pattern of English* (reprinted 1991), Cambridge, MA: MIT Press.

Clark, E. V., Hecht, B. F., and Mulford, R. C. 1986, "Coining complex compounds in English: affixes and word order in acquisition," *Linguistics* 24: 7–29.

Clément, R., Dörnyei, Z., and Noels, K. A. 1994, "Motivation, self-confidence, and group cohesion in the foreign language classroom," *Language Learning*, 44: 417–448.

Collentine, J. and Freed, B. F. 2004, "Learning context and its effects on second language acquisition: introduction," *Studies in Second Language Acquisition* 26: 153–171.

Comrie, Bernard 1976, *Aspect*, Cambridge University Press.

Comrie, Bernard 1985, *Tense*, Cambridge University Press.

Corbett, G. G. 1991, *Gender*, Cambridge University Press.

Corina, David P., Gibson, E. K., Martin, R., Poliakov, A., Brinkley, J., and Ojemann, G. A. 2005, "Dissociation of action and object naming: evidence from cortical stimulation mapping," *Human Brain Mapping* 24: 1–10.

Cottrell, G. and Plunkett, K. 1991, "Learning the past tense in a recurrent network: acquiring the mapping from meaning to sounds," *Proceedings of the 13th Annual Conference of the Cognitive Science Society*, Hillsdale, NJ: Lawrence Erlbaum, pp. 328–333.

Coulmas, Florian 1989, *The writing systems of the world*, Oxford and Malden, MA: Blackwell.

Coulmas, Florian 1996, *The Blackwell encyclopedia of writing systems*, Oxford and Malden, MA: Blackwell.

Coulmas, Florian 2003, *Writing systems: an introduction to their linguistic analysis*, New York: Cambridge University Press.

Coupland, Nikolas 1980, "Style-shifting in a Cardiff work-setting," *Language in Society* 9: 1–12.

Crain, S. and Thornton, R. 1998, *Investigations in universal grammar: a guide to experiments on the acquisition of syntax and semantics*, Cambridge, MA: MIT Press.

Curtiss, S. 1977, *Genie: a psycholinguistic study of a modern-day "wild child,"* New York: Academic Press.

Daniels, Peter T. and Bright, William (eds.) 1996, *The world's writing systems*, New York: Oxford University Press.

Darcy, N. T. 1953, "A review of the literature on the effects of bilingualism upon the measurement of intelligence," *Journal of Genetic Psychology* 82: 21–57.

Davidson, D. 1967, "The logical form of action sentences," in N. Rescher (ed.), *The logic of decision and action*, University of Pittsburgh Press, pp. 81–120.

DeGraff, Michel 1999, "Creolization, language change and language acquisition: an epilogue," in Michel DeGraff (ed.), *Language creation and language change: creolization, diachrony and development*, Cambridge, MA: MIT Press, pp. 473–543.

DeKeyser, R. 2000, "The robustness of critical period effects in second language acquisition," *Studies in Second Language Acquisition* 22: 499–534.

Dhond, Rupali P., Marinkovic, Ksenija, Dale, Anders M., Witzel, Thomas, and Halgren, Eric 2003, "Spatiotemporal maps of past-tense verb inflection," *Neuroimage* 19: 91–100.

Dörnyei, Z. and Csizér, K. 2002, "Some dynamics of language attitudes and motivation: the results of a longitudinal nationwide survey," *Applied Linguistics* 23: 421–462.

Dostert, L. 1955, "The Georgetown–IBM experiment," in *Machine translation of languages: fourteen essays*, Cambridge, MA: MIT Press, pp. 124–135.

Dronkers, N., Wilkins, David P., Van Valin Jr., Robert D., Redfern, Brenda B., and Jaeger, J. J. 2004, "Lesion analysis of the brain areas involved in language comprehension," *Cognition* 92(1–2): 145–177.

Dulay, H. and Burt, M. 1974, "Natural sequences in child second language acquisition," *Language Learning* 24: 37–53.

Dutoit, T. 1997, *An introduction to text-to-speech synthesis*, Dordrecht: Kluwer.

Dutoit, T. and Stylianou, Y. 2003, "Text-to-speech synthesis," in R. Mitkov (ed.), *Handbook of computational linguistics*, Oxford University Press, pp. 323–338.

Eckert, Penelope 1988, "Adolescent social structure and the spread of linguistic change," *Language in Society* 17: 183–207.

Eckert, Penelope 1989, *Jocks and burnouts: social categories and identity in the high school*, New York: Teachers College Press.

Eckert, Penelope 2000, *Linguistic variation as social practice*, Malden, MA: Blackwell.

Eimas, P., Siqueland, E., Jusczyk, P., and Vigorito, J. 1971, "Speech perception in infants," *Science* 171: 303–306.

Eisenberg, A. R. 1986, "Teasing: verbal play in two Mexicano homes," in B. B. Schieffelin and E. Ochs (eds.), *Language socialization across cultures*, New York: Cambridge University Press, pp. 182–198.

Eisenstein, Elizabeth L. 1983, *The printing revolution in early modern Europe*, New York: Cambridge University Press.

Eliot, L. 2000, *What's going on in there? How the brain and mind develop in the first five years of life*, New York: Bantam Books.

Ellis, N. C. and Schmidt, R. 1997, "Morphology and longer distance dependencies: laboratory research illuminating the A in SLA," *Studies in Second Language Acquisition* 19: 145–171.

Elman, J. 2001, "Connectionism and language acquisition," in M. Tomasello and E. Bates (eds.), *Language development: essential readings*, Oxford and Malden, MA: Blackwell, pp. 295–306.

Elman, Jeffrey L., Bates, E. A., Johnson, M. H., Karmiloff-Smith, A., Parisi, D. and Plunkett, K. 1996, *Rethinking innateness: a connectionist perspective on development*, Cambridge, MA: MIT Press.

Fasold, Ralph W. 1968, "A sociolinguistic study of the pronunciation of three vowels in Detroit speech," unpublished ms.

Fenson, L., Bates, E., Dale, P., Goodman, J., Reznick, J. S. and Thal, D. 2000, "Measuring variability in early child language: don't shoot the messenger. Comment on Feldman *et al.*," *Child Development* 71: 323–328.

Ferguson, Charles A. 1959, "Diglossia," *Word* 15: 325–40.

Ferguson, C. A. 1978, "Talking to children: a search for universals," in J. H. Greenberg, C. A. Ferguson, and E. A. Moravcsik (eds.), *Universals of human language,* vol. 1: *Method and theory,* Stanford University Press, pp. 203–224.

Fillmore, C. 1968, "The case for case," in E. Bach and R. T. Harms (eds.), *Universals in linguistic theory,* New York: Holt, Rinehart, and Winston, pp. 1–88.

Finegan, Edward and Besnier, Niko 1989, *Language: its structure and use,* New York: Harcourt Brace.

Fischer, John N. L. 1958, "Social influences on the choice of a linguistic variant," *Word* 14: 47–56.

Fischer, Steven R. 2001, *A history of writing,* London: Reaktion Books.

Fishman, Joshua A. 1972, *Language and nationalism,* Rowley, MA: Newbury House.

Fishman, Pamela M. 1978, "Interaction: the work women do," *Social Problems* 5(4): 397–406.

Fodor, Jerry A. 1983, *The modularity of mind: an essay on faculty psychology,* Cambridge, MA: MIT Press.

Fox, Anthony 1995, *Linguistic reconstruction: an introduction to theory and method,* New York: Oxford University Press.

Frege, G. 1892, "Über Sinn und Bedeutung," *Zeitschrift für Philosophie und philosophische Kritik,* 100: 25–50. Translated as "On sense and reference" by M. Black in P. Geach and M. Black (eds.), *Translations from the philosophical writings of Gottlob Frege,* Oxford: Blackwell, 1980.

Friederici, A. 2002, "Towards a neural basis of auditory sentence processing," *Trends in Cognitive Science* 6(2): 78–84.

Friederici, A. D. 2004, "The neural basis of syntactic processes," in Michael S. Gazzaniga (ed.), *The cognitive neurosciences,* Cambridge, MA: MIT Press, pp. 789–801.

Fry, D. B. 1979, *The physics of speech,* Cambridge University Press.

Gallaway, C. and Richards, B. J. 1994, *Input and interaction in language acquisition,* Cambridge University Press.

Gass, S. and Houck, N. 1999, *Interlanguage refusals: a cross-cultural study of Japanese-English,* Berlin: Mouton de Gruyter.

Geach, P. 1962, *Reference and generality,* Ithaca, NY: Cornell University Press.

Gee, J. P. 1999, *An introduction to discourse analysis,* London: Routledge.

Genesee, F., Boivin, I., and Nicoladis, E. 1996, "Talking with strangers: a study of bilingual children's communicative competence," *Applied Psycholinguistics* 17: 427–442.

Genesee, F., Nicoladis, E., and Paradis, J. 1995, "Language differentiation in early bilingual development," *Journal of Child Language* 22: 611–631.

Givón, Talmy 1993, *English grammar: a function-based introduction,* vol. 2, Amsterdam and Philadelphia: John Benjamins.

Gleason, H. 1955, *Workbook in descriptive linguistics,* New York: Holt, Rinehart, and Winston.

Glinert, L. 1989, *The grammar of modern Hebrew,* New York: Cambridge University Press.

Goldsmith, John 1976, "An overview of autosegmental phonology," doctoral dissertation, MIT. Reprinted in J. Goldsmith (ed.), *Phonological theory: the essential readings.* Oxford: Blackwell.

Goldstein, Amy and Suro, Roberto 2000, "A journey in stages," *The Washington Post,* January 16, 2000, A1.

Goodwin, Marjorie Harness 1990, *He-said-she-said: talk as social organization among black children,* Bloomington: Indiana University Press.

Gopnik, A. and Choi, S. 1995, "Names, relational words, and cognitive development in English- and Korean-speakers: nouns are not always learned before verbs," in M. Tomasello and

W. Merriman (eds.), *Beyond names for things: young children's acquisition of verbs*, Hillsdale, NJ: Lawrence Erlbaum, pp. 63–80.

Gordon, P. 1996, "The truth-value judgment task," in D. McDaniel, C. McKee, and H. S. Cairns (eds.), *Methods for assessing children's syntax*, Cambridge, MA: MIT Press, pp. 211–231.

Grammont, M. 1902, *Observations sur le langage des enfants*, Paris: Mélanges Meillet.

Green, Lisa 2002, *African American English: a linguistic introduction*, Cambridge University Press.

Grice, H. P. 1957, "Meaning," *Philosophical Review* 66: 377–388.

Grice, H. P. 1975, "Logic and conversation," in P. Cole, and J. L. Morgan (eds.), *Syntax and semantics*, vol. 3: *Speech acts*, New York: Academic Press, pp. 41–58.

Grishman, R. and Sundheim, B. 1997, "Message understanding conference–6: a brief history," in *Proceedings of the 16th International Conference on Computational Linguistics*, New Brunswick, NJ: Association for Computational Linguistics, pp. 466–471.

Grodzinsky, Y. 2000, "The neurology of syntax: language use without Broca's area," *Behavioral and Brain Sciences* 23(1): 1–71.

Gruber, J. 1965, "Studies in lexical relations," PhD dissertation, MIT (published as *Lexical structures in syntax and semantics*, Amsterdam: North-Holland, 1976).

Gumperz, J. J. 1982, *Discourse strategies*, Cambridge University Press.

Gumperz, J. J. and Hymes, D. (eds.) 1972, *Directions in sociolinguistics: The ethnography of communication*, New York: Holt, Rhinehart, and Winston.

Gutiérrez-Clellen, V. F. and Kreiter, J. 2003, "Understanding child bilingual acquisition using parent and teacher reports," *Applied Psycholinguistics* 24: 267–288.

Haas, Mary R. and Subhanka, Heng R. 1945, *Spoken Thai*, New York: Henry Holt and Company.

Haeri, Niloofar. 1994, "A linguistic innovation of women in Cairo," *Language Variation and Change* 6: 87–112.

Haeri, Niloofar 1997. *The sociolinguistic market of Cairo: gender, class and education*, London and New York: Kegan Paul International.

Halgren, E., Dhond, Rupali P., Christensen, Natalie, Van Petten, C., Marinkovic, K., Lewine, Jeffrey D., and Dale, A. M. 2002, "N400-like magnetoencephalography responses modulated by semantic context, word frequency, and lexical class in sentences," *Neuroimage* 17: 1101–1116.

Hall, Edward T. 1959, *The silent language*, New York: Doubleday.

Hall, Edward T. 1969, *The hidden dimension*, New York: Doubleday.

Hall Jr., Robert A. 1964, *Introduction to linguistics*, Philadelphia: Chilton Books.

Halliday, M. A. K. 1985, *An introduction to functional grammar*, London: Edward Arnold.

Halliday, M. and Hasan, R. 1976, *Cohesion in English*, London: Longman.

Hamers, J. F. and Blanc, M. H. A. 2000, *Bilinguality and bilingualism*, 2nd edition, Cambridge University Press.

Hankamer, J. 1989, "Morphological parsing and the lexicon," in W. Marslen-Wilson (ed.), *Lexical representation and process*, Cambridge, MA: MIT Press, pp. 392–408.

Hart, B. and Risley, T. R. 1995, *Meaningful differences in the everyday experience of young American children*, Baltimore, MD: Paul H. Brookes.

Hauser, M. D., Chomsky, N., and Fitch, W. T. 2002, "The faculty of language: what is it, who has it, and how did it evolve?" *Science* 298(5598): 1569–1579.

Hayashi, Reiko 1988, "Simultaneous talk—from the perspective of floor management of English and Japanese speakers," *World Englishes* 7: 269–288.

Hayes, Bruce 1995, *Metrical stress theory: principles and case studies*, University of Chicago Press.

Heath, S. B. 1983, *Ways with words: language, life and work in communities and classrooms*, Cambridge University Press.

Hickok, G. and Poeppel, D. 2004, "Dorsal and ventral streams: a framework for understanding aspects of the functional anatomy of language," *Cognition* 92(1–2): 67–99.

Himmelmann, N. 2004, "Tagalog," in G. Booij, C. Lehmann, and J. Mugdan (eds), *Morphology: a handbook on inflection and word formation*, vol. 2, Berlin: de Gruyter, pp. 1473–1489.

Hillyard, S. A. and Kutas, M. 1983, "Electrophysiology of cognitive processing," *Annual Review of Psychology* 34: 33–61.

Hirschman, Lynette 1994, "Female–male differences in conversational interaction," *Language in Society* 23: 427–442.

Hirsh-Pasek, K. and Golinkoff, R. M. 1997, *The origins of grammar: evidence from early language comprehension*, Cambridge, MA: MIT Press.

Hirsh-Pasek, K. and Treiman, R. 1982, "Doggerel: motherese in a new context," *Journal of Child Language* 9: 229–237.

Hockett, C. F. 1958, *A course in modern linguistics*, New York: Macmillan.

Hornberger, N. H. 1988, *Bilingual education and language maintenance: a southern Peruvian Quechua case*, Berlin: Mouton de Gruyter.

Horvath, Barbara 1985, *Variation in Australian English: the sociolects of Sydney*, Cambridge University Press.

Hudson, Alan 2002, "Outline of a theory of diglossia," *International Journal of the Sociology of Language*, 157: 1–48.

Hutchins, W. J. and Somers, H. L. 1992, *An introduction to machine translation*, New York: Academic Press.

Hyltenstam, K. and Abrahamsson, N. 2001, "Age and L2 learning: the hazards of matching practical 'implications' with theoretical 'facts'," *TESOL Quarterly* 35(1): 151–170.

Hyltenstam, K. and Abrahamsson, N. 2003, "Maturational constraints in SLA," in C. J. Doughty and M. H. Long (eds.), *Handbook of second language acquisition*, Oxford and Malden, MA: Blackwell, pp. 539–588.

Hymes, D. 1972, "Models of the interaction of language and social life," in J. Gumperz and D. Hymes (eds.), *Directions in sociolinguistics: the ethnography of communication*, New York: Holt, Rhinehart, and Winston, pp. 35–71.

Hymes, Dell 1974, *Foundations in sociolinguistics: an ethnographic approach*, Philadelphia: University of Pennsylvania Press.

Indefrey, P., Hellwig, F., Herzog, H., Seitz, R. J., and Hagoort, P. 2004, "Neural responses to the production and comprehension of syntax in identical utterances," *Brain and Language* 89: 312–319.

International Dialects of English Archive website: http://web.ku.edu/~idea/IDEA (last accessed August 5, 2010).

Jackendoff, R. 1987, "The status of thematic relation in linguistic theory," *Linguistic Inquiry* 18(3): 369–411.

Jackendoff, R. 1990, *Semantic structures*, Cambridge, MA: MIT Press.

Jakobson, Roman 1960, "Closing statement: linguistics and poetics," in T. Sebeok (ed.), *Style in language*, Cambridge, MA: MIT Press, pp. 350–377.

Jakobson, R. 1968, *Child language, aphasia, and phonological universals*, The Hague: Mouton.

Jakobson, Roman, Fant, Gunnar, and Halle, Morris 1952, *Preliminaries to speech analysis: the distinctive features and their correlates*, reprinted 1961, Cambridge, MA: MIT Press.

Johnson, Keith 2003, *Acoustic and auditory phonetics*, 2nd edition, Oxford and Malden, MA: Blackwell.

Joshi, A. K. and Schabes, Y. 1996, "Tree-adjoining grammars," in G. Rosenberg and A. Salomaa (eds.), *Handbook of formal languages*, vol. 3, New York: Springer, pp. 69–123.

Julien, M. 2002, *Syntactic heads and word formation*, New York: Oxford University Press.

Jurafsky, D. and Martin, J. H. 2000, *Speech and language processing: an introduction to natural language processing, computational linguistics, and speech recognition*, Saddle River, NJ: Prentice Hall.

Jusczyk, P. W., Friederici, A. D., Wessels, J. M. I., Svenkerud, V., and Jusczyk, A. M. 1993, "Infants' sensitivity to the sound pattern of native-language words," *Journal of Memory and Language* 32: 402–420.

Kager, René 1999, *Optimality theory*, Cambridge University Press.

Kaplan, R. M. and Bresnan, J. 1982, "Lexical-functional grammar: a formal system for grammatical representation," in J. Bresnan (ed.), *The mental representation of grammatical relations*, Cambridge, MA: MIT Press, pp. 173–281.

Kastenholz, R. 1987, "Das Koranko," PhD dissertation, University of Cologne.

Katamba, Francis X. 2003, "Bantu nominal morphology," in Derek Nurse and Gérard Phillipson (eds.), *The Bantu languages*, London: Routledge, pp. 103–120.

Katamba, F. and Stonham, J. 2006, *Morphology*, 2nd edition, New York: Palgrave Macmillan.

Keenan, Elinor 1974, "Norm-makers, norm-breakers: uses of speech by men and women in a Malagasy community," in Richard Bauman and Joel Sherzer (eds.), *Explorations in the ethnography of speaking*, Cambridge University Press, pp. 125–143.

Kenstowicz, Michael 1994, *Generative phonology*, Oxford: Blackwell.

Kilgarriff, A. and Palmer, M. 2000 (eds.), "Computers and the humanities: special issue on SENSEVAL," *Computers and the Humanities* 34: 1–2.

Kim, J. H., and Han, Z-H. 2007, "Recasts in communicative EFL classes: do teacher intent and learner interpretation overlap?" in A. Mackey (ed.), *Conversational interaction in second language acquisition: a collection of empirical studies*, Oxford University Press, pp. 269–300.

King, K. A. and Melzi, G. 2004, "Intimacy, imitation and language learning: Spanish diminutives in mother–child conversation," *First Language* 24(2): 241–261.

Kloss, Heinz 1967, "Abstand languages and Ausbau languages," *Anthropological Linguistics* 9: 29–41.

Kochman, Thomas 1981, *Black and white styles in conflict*, University of Chicago Press.

Labov, William 1963, "The social motivation of a sound change," *Word* 19: 273–307.

Labov, William 1966, *The social stratification of English in New York City*, Washington, DC: Center for Applied Linguistics.

Labov, William 1972, *Sociolinguistic patterns*, University of Pennsylvania Press.

Labov, William, Ash, Sharon, and Boberg, Charles 2006, *Atlas of North American English*, Berlin: Mouton de Gruyter.

Ladd, D. R. 2000, *Intonational phonology*, Cambridge University Press.

Ladefoged, Peter 2001 *A course in phonetics*, 4th edition, Oxford and Malden, MA: Blackwell.

Ladefoged, Peter and Maddieson, Ian 1996, *The sounds of the world's languages*, Oxford and Malden, MA: Blackwell.

Laine, M., Rinne, J. O., Krause, B. J., Teras, M., and Sipila, H. 1999, "Left hemisphere activation during processing of morphologically complex word forms in adults," *Neuroscience Letters* 271(2): 85–88.

Lakoff, G. 1987, *Women, fire, and other dangerous things*, University of Chicago Press.

Lakoff, Robin [1975] 2004, *Language and woman's place: text and commentaries*, revised and expanded edition, ed. Mary Bucholtz, New York: Oxford University Press.

Lakoff, Robin Tolmach 2001, "Nine ways of looking at apologies: the necessity for interdisciplinary theory and method in discourse analysis," in Deborah Schiffrin, Deborah Tannen, and Heidi E. Hamilton (eds.), *The handbook of discourse analysis*, Oxford and Malden, MA: Blackwell, pp. 199–214.

Languages of the world 7: African language families. Retrieved March 10, 2005 from the University of Hong Kong, Department of Linguistics website: www.hku.hk/linguist/program/world7.html

Lanza, E. 1992, "Can bilingual two-year-olds code-switch?" *Journal of Child Language* 19: 633–658.

Lavric, Aureliu, Pizzagalli, Diego, Forstmeier, Simon, and Rippon, Gina 2001, "A double-dissociation of English past-tense production revealed by event-related potentials and low-resolution electromagnetic tomography (LORETA)," *Clinical Neurophysiology* 112: 1833–1849.

Lecarme, J. 2002, "Gender 'polarity': theoretical aspects of Somali nominal morphology," in P. Boucher (ed.), *Many morphologies*, Somerville, MA: Cascadilla Press, pp. 109–141.

Lehiste, Ilse 1970, *Suprasegmentals*, Cambridge, MA: MIT Press.

Lehmann, Winfred P. 1973, *Historical linguistics: an introduction*, New York: Holt, Rinehart, and Winston.

Lehtonen, Jaakko and Sajavaara, Kari 1985, "The silent Finn," in Deborah Tannen and Muriel Saville-Troike (eds.), *Perspectives on silence*, Norwood, NJ: Ablex, pp. 193–201.

Leney, T. 1993, *Finnish: a complete course for beginners*, London: Hodder.

Lenneberg, E. 1967, *Biological foundations of language*, New York: Wiley.

Leopold, W. F. 1939, *Speech development of a bilingual child: a linguist's record*, vol. 1: *Vocabulary growth in the first years*, Evanston, IL: Northwestern University Press.

Leopold, W. F. 1947, *Speech development of a bilingual child: a linguist's record*, vol. 2: *Sound learning in the first years*, Evanston, IL: Northwestern University Press.

Leopold, W. F. 1949a, *Speech development of a bilingual child: a linguist's record*, vol. 3: *Grammar and general problems*, Evanston, IL: Northwestern University Press.

Leopold, W. F. 1949b, *Speech development of a bilingual child: a linguist's record*, vol. 4: *Diary from age two*, Evanston, IL: Northwestern University Press.

Levine, Robert D. 2010, "The ass camouflage construction: masks as parasitic heads," *Language* 86: 265–301.

Leyendecker, B., Lamb, M., Schölmeric, A. and Fracasso, M. 1995, "The social worlds of 8 and 12-month-old infants: early experiences in two subcultural contexts," *Social Development* 4(2): 194–208.

Li, C. and Thompson, S. 1981, *Mandarin Chinese: a functional reference grammar*, Berkeley, CA: University of California Press.

Lieberman, P. 2002, "On the nature and evolution of the neural bases of human language," *American Journal of Physical Anthropology* 35: 36–62.

Lightfoot, David W. 2006, *How new languages emerge*, Cambridge University Press.

Long, M. H. 1990, "Maturational constraints on language development," *Studies in Second Language Acquisition* 12: 251–285.

Macaulay, Ronald K. S. 1976, "Social class and language in Glasgow," *Language in Society* 5: 173–88.

Mackey, A. 1999, "Input, interaction, and second language development: an empirical study of question formation in ESL," *Studies in Second Language Acquisition* 21: 557–587.

Mackey, A. (ed.) 2007, *Conversational interaction in second language acquisition: a collection of empirical studies*, Oxford University Press.

Mackey, A. and Philp, J. 1998, "Conversational interaction and second language development: recasts, responses, and red herrings?" *The Modern Language Journal* 82: 338–356.

Mackey, A., Adams, R., Stafford, C., and Winke, P. 2010, "Exploring the relationship between modified output and working memory capacity," *Language Learning*, 60: 501–533.

MacWhinney, B. 2000, *The CHILDES project: tools for analyzing talk*, 3rd edition, Mahwah, NJ: Lawrence Erlbaum.

MacWhinney, B. and Leinbach, J. 1991, "Implementations are not conceptualizations: revising the verb learning model," *Cognition* 40: 121–157.

Maling, Joan 1984, "Non-clause-bounded reflexives in modern Icelandic," *Linguistics and Philosophy* 7: 211–241.

Maltz, D. and Borker, R. 1982, "A cultural approach to male-female miscommunication," in John J. Gumperz (ed.), *Language and social identity*, Cambridge University Press, pp. 196–216.

Man, J. 2000, *Alpha Beta: how 26 letters shaped the western world*, New York: Wileys.

Maneva, B. and Genesee, F. 2002, "Bilingual babbling: evidence for language differentiation in dual language acquisition," *The Proceedings of the 26th Boston University Conference on Language Development*, pp. 383–392.

Mani, I., Pustejovsky, J., and Gaizauskas, R. (eds.) 2005, *The language of time: a reader*, New York: Oxford University Press.

Manning, C. D. 2003, "Probabilistic syntax," in R. Bod, J. Hay, and S. Jannedy (eds.), *Probabilistic linguistics*, Cambridge, MA: MIT Press, pp. 289–341.

Marinova-Todd, S. F., Marshall, D. B., and Snow, C. E. 2000, "Three misconceptions about age and L2 learning," *TESOL Quarterly* 34(1): 9–34.

Marinova-Todd, S. F., Marshall, D. B., and Snow, C. E. 2001, "Missing the point: a response to Hyltenstam and Abrahamsson," *TESOL Quarterly* 35(1): 171–176.

McClelland, J. L., Rumelhart, D. E., and the PDP Research Group 1986, *Parallel distributed processing: explorations in the microstructure of cognition*, Cambridge, MA: Bradford Books/MIT Press.

McClelland, J. L. and Patterson, K. 2002, "Rules or connections in past-tense inflections: what does the evidence rule out?" *Trends in Cognitive Sciences* 6(11): 465–472.

McCrum, R., Cran, W., and MacNeil, R. 1986, *The story of English*, New York: Viking Penguin.

Mchombo, S. A. 1998, "Chichewa (Bantu)," in A. Spencer and A. M. Zwicky (eds.), *The handbook of morphology*, Oxford and Malden, MA: Blackwell, pp. 500–520.

McDaniel, D., McKee, C., and Cairns, H. S. 1996, *Methods for assessing children's syntax*, Cambridge, MA: MIT Press.

McWhorter, John 1998, *Word on the street: debunking the myth of "pure" standard English*, New York: Basic Books.

Mel'čuk, I. A. [1958] 1974, "Statistics and the relationship between the gender of French nouns and their endings," in V. Ju. Rozencvejg (ed.), *Essays on lexical semantics*, Stockholm: Skriptor, pp. 11–42.

Mel'čuk, I. A. 1979, *Studies in dependency syntax*, Ann Arbor: Karoma.

Mehler, J., Jusczyk, P., Lambertz, G., Halsted, N., Bertoncini, J., and Amiel-Tison, C. 1988, "A precursor of language acquisition in young infants," *Cognition* 29: 143–178.

Meisel, J. M. 2001, "Early differentiation of languages in bilingual children," in L. Wei (ed.), *The bilingualism reader*, London: Routledge, pp. 344–369.

Melchers, G. and Shaw, P. 2003, *World Englishes*, London: Arnold.

Melzi, G. 2000, "Cultural variations in the construction of personal narratives: central American and European-American mothers' elicitation discourse," *Discourse Processes* 30(2): 153–177.

Melzi, G. and King, K. A. 2003, "Spanish diminutives in mother–child conversations," *Journal of Child Language* 30(2): 281–304.

Miles, C., Green, R., Sanders, G., and Hines, M. 1998, "Estrogen and memory in a transsexual population," *Hormones and Behavior* 34(2): 199–208.

Milroy, J. and Milroy, L. 1978, "Belfast: change and variation in an urban vernacular," in Peter Trudgill (ed.), *Sociolinguistic patterns in British English*, London: Arnold, pp. 19–36.

Milroy, L. 1987, *Language and social networks*, 2nd edition, Oxford: Blackwell.

Minnen, G., Carroll, J., and Pearce, D. 2001, "Applied morphological processing of English," *Natural Language Engineering* 7(3): 207–223.

Mitkov, R. (ed.) 2003, *The Oxford handbook of computational linguistics*, New York: Oxford University Press.

Montague, R. 1974, *Formal philosophy: selected papers of Richard Montague*, ed. R. H. Thomason, New Haven: Yale University Press.

Morris, H. F. and Kirwan, B. E. R. 1972, *A Runyankore grammar*, Nairobi: East African Literature Bureau.

Mottaghy, F. M., Hungs, M., Brugmann, M., Sparing, R., Boroojerdi, B., Foltys, H., Huber, W., and Topper, R. 1999, "Facilitation of picture naming after repetitive transcranial magnetic stimulation," *Neurology* 53(8): 1806–1812.

Nettle, D. and Romaine, S. 2000, *Vanishing voices: the extinction of the world's languages*. Oxford University Press.

Nicholas, H., Lightbown, P. M., and Spada, N. 2001, "Recasts as feedback to language learners," *Language Learning* 51: 719–758.

Nobre, A. C., Allison, T., and McCarthy, G. 1994, "Word recognition in the human inferior temporal lobe," *Nature* 372: 260–263.

Nylund, A. and Seals, C. 2010, "'It's not that big (of) a deal': The sociolinguistic conditioning of inverted degree phrases in Washington, DC." *University of Pennsylvania Working Papers in Linguistics* 16(2) (Selected papers from NWAV 38): 133–140.

Ochs, Elinor 1979, "Transcription as theory," in Elinor Ochs and Bambi B. Schieffelin (eds.), *Developmental pragmatics*, New York: Academic Press, pp. 43–72.

Ochs, E. 1983, "Cultural dimensions in language acquisition," in E. Ochs and B. B. Schieffelin (eds.), *Acquiring conversational competence*, London: Routledge and Kegan Paul, pp. 185–191.

Ochs, E. 1997, "Cultural dimensions of language acquisition," in N. Coupland and A. Jaworski (eds.), *Sociolinguistics: a reader*, New York: St. Martin's Press, pp. 430–437.

Ochs, E. and Schieffelin, B. B. 1984, "Language acquisition and socialization: three developmental stories," in R. Shweder and R. Levine (eds.), *Culture theory: essays on mind, self and emotion*, New York: Cambridge University Press, pp. 276–320.

Opitz, B., and Friederici, A. D. 2007, "Neural basis of processing sequential and hierarchical syntactic structures." *Human Brain Mapping* 28: 585–592.

Palmer, F. R. 1986, *Mood and modality*, New York: Cambridge University Press.

Patterson, M. L. and Werker, J. F. 2003, "Two-month-old infants match phonetic information in lips and voice," *Developmental Science* 6(2): 191–196.

Peal, E. and Lambert, W. E. 1962, "The relationship of bilingualism to intelligence," *Psychological Monographs* 76(27): 1–23.

Pearson, B. Z., Fernandez, S. C., Lewedeg, V., and Oller, D. K. 1997, "The relation of input factors to lexical learning by bilingual infants," *Applied Psycholinguistics* 18: 41–58.

Pew Hispanic Center/The Henry J. Kaiser Family Foundation 2004, *Survey brief: assimilation and language*, Publication No. 7052, Washington, DC: Pew Hispanic Center.

Philips, Susan U. 1983, *The invisible culture: communication in classroom and community on the Warm Springs Indian Reservation*, London: Longman.

Pica, T. 1994, "Research on negotiation: what does it reveal about second language learning, conditions, processes, outcomes?" *Language Learning* 44: 493–527.

Pienemann, M. and Johnston, M. 1986, "An acquisition based procedure for second language assessment (ESL)," *Australian Review of Applied Linguistics* 9: 92–122.

Pienemann, M., Johnston, M., and Brindley, G. 1988, Constructing an acquisition-based procedure for second language assessment," *Studies in Second Language Acquisition* 10: 217–224.

Pierce, A. 1992, *Language acquisition and syntactic theory: a comparative analysis of French and English child grammars*, Dordrecht: Kluwer Academic Publishers.

Pinker, S. 1999, *Words and rules: the ingredients of language*, New York: Basic Books.

Pinker, S. and Prince, A. 1988, "On language and connectionism: analysis of a parallel distributed processing model of language acquisition," *Cognition* 28: 73–193.

Pinker, S. and Ullman, M. T. 2002, "The past and future of the past tense," *Trends in Cognitive Sciences* 6(11): 456–463.

Plunkett, K. and Nakisa, R. 1997, "A connectionist model of the Arabic plural system," *Language and Cognitive Processes* 12(56): 807–836.

Plunkett, K. and Marchman, V. 1991, "U-shaped learning and frequency effects in a multi-layered perceptron: implications for child language acquisition," *Cognition* 38: 43–102.

Plunkett, K. and Marchman, V. 1993, "From rote learning to system building: acquiring verb morphology in children and connectionist sets," *Cognition* 48: 21–69.

Pollard, C. and Sag, I. A. 1994, *Head driven phrase structure grammar*, University of Chicago Press.

Postle, Bradley R. and Corkin, Suzanne 1998, "Impaired word-stem completion priming but intact perceptual identification priming with novel words: evidence from the amnesic patient H.M.," *Neuropsychologia* 15: 421–440.

Prince, Alan and Smolensky, Paul 2004, *Optimality theory*, Oxford: Blackwell.

Prokosch, Edward 1939, *A comparative Germanic grammar*, Philadelphia: Linguistic Society of America, University of Pennsylvania.

Pustejovsky, J., Ingria, B., Sauri, R., Castano, J., Littman, J., Gaizauskas, R., Setzer, A., Katz G., and Mani, I. 2005, "The specification language TimeML," in I. Mani, J. Pustejovsky, and Gaizauskas, R. (eds.), *The language of time: a reader*, New York: Oxford University Press.

Putnam, H. 1975, "The meaning of 'meaning'," in *Mind, language, and reality*, Cambridge University Press, pp. 215–271.

Pyles, Thomas and Algeo, John 2004, *The origins and development of the English language*, 5th edition, New York: Heinle.

Reisman, Karl 1974, "Contrapuntal conversations in an Antiguan village," in Richard Bauman and Joel Sherzer (eds.), *Explorations in the ethnography of speaking*, Cambridge University Press, pp. 110–124.

Reiter, E. and Dale, R. 2000, *Building natural language generation systems*, Cambridge University Press.

Rendall, Luke and Whitehead, Hal 2001, "Culture in whales and dolphins," *Behavioral and Brain Sciences* 24: 309–323.

Rhee, J., Pinker, S., and Ullman, M.T. 1999, "A magnetoencephalographic study of English past tense production," *Journal of Cognitive Neuroscience* Supplement: 47.

Rickford, John R. 1986, "The need for new approaches to social class analysis in sociolinguistics," *Language and Communication* 6(3): 215–21.

Rickford, John R. 1999, *African American Vernacular English*, Oxford and Malden, MA: Blackwell.

Rosen, Yereth 2002, "Judge strikes down Alaska's official English law," *Reuters News Service*, March 26, 2002.

Ross-Feldman, L. 2007, "Interaction in the L2 classroom: does gender influence learning opportunities?" in A. Mackey (ed.), *Conversational interaction in second language acquisition: a collection of empirical studies*, Oxford: Oxford University Press, pp. 56–78.

Rubino, C. 2002, "Reduplication: form, function, distribution," Paper presented at the Graz Reduplication Conference, University of Graz, Austria, November 3–6, 2002.

Rumbaut, R. G., Massey, D. S., and Bean, F. D. 2006, "Linguistic life expectancies: immigrant language retention in Southern California," *Population and Development Review* 32: 447–460.

Rumelhart, D. and McClelland, J. 1986, "On learning the past tenses of English verbs: implicit rules or parallel distributed processing?" in J. McClelland, D. Rumelhart, and the PDP Research Group (eds.), *Parallel distributed processing: explorations in the microstructure of cognition*, Cambridge, MA: MIT Press, pp. 216–271.

Sampson, Geoffrey 1985, *Writing systems: a linguistic introduction*, Stanford University Press.

Sánchez, L. 2003, *Quechua–Spanish bilingualism: interference and convergence in functional categories*, Amsterdam: John Benjamins.

Sandler, W. and Lillo-Martin, D. 2006, *Sign language and linguistic universals*. Cambridge University Press.

Sankoff, Gillian and Cedergren, Henrietta 1971, "Some results of a sociolinguistic study of Montreal French," in R. Darnell (ed.), *Linguistic diversity in Canadian Society*, Edmonton: Linguistic Research, Inc., pp. 61–87.

Sankoff, Gillian and Thibault, Pierrette 1980, "The alternation between the auxiliaries avoir and être in Montréal French," in Gillian Sankoff (ed.), *The social life of language*, University of Pennsylvania Press, pp. 311–345.

Sankoff, Gillian and Vincent, Diane 1977, "L'emploi productif du *Ne* dans le Français parlé à Montréal," *Le Français Moderne* 45: 243–256.

Sapir, Edward 1933, "The psychological reality of phonemes," *Journal de Psychologie Normale et Pathologique* 30: 247–265.

Schachter, J. 1989, "Testing a proposed universal," in S. Gass and J. Schachter (eds.), *Linguistic perspectives on second language acquisition*, Cambridge University Press, pp. 73–88.

Schachter, P. and Otanes, F. 1972, *Tagalog reference grammar*, Berkeley, CA: University of California Press.

Schieffelin, B. B. and Ochs, E. (eds.) 1986, *Language socialization across cultures*, Cambridge University Press.

Schieffelin, B. B. and Eisenberg, A. 1984, "Cultural variations in children's conversations," in R. Schiefelbusch and J. Rickar (eds.), *The acquisition of communicative competence*, Maryland: University Park Press, pp. 379–418.

Schiffman, B., Mani, I., and Concepcion, K. J. 2001, "Producing biographical summaries: combining linguistic knowledge with corpus statistics," in *Proceedings of the 39th Annual Meeting of the Association for Computational Linguistics*, New Brunswick, NJ: Association for Computational Linguistics, pp. 450–457.

Schiffrin, Deborah 1987, *Discourse markers*, Cambridge University Press.

Schmandt-Besserat, Denise 1992, *Before writing*, Austin: University of Texas Press.

Schmidt, R. 2001, "Attention," in P. Robinson (ed.), *Cognition and second language instruction*, Cambridge University Press, pp. 3–32.

Sebeok, Thomas A. 1986, *I think I am a verb: more contributions to the doctrine of signs*, New York: Plenum Press.

Seidenberg, Mark S. 1997, "Language acquisition and use: learning and applying probabilistic constraints," *Science* 275: 1599–1603.

Sells, P. 1985, *Lectures on contemporary syntactic theories: an introduction to Government-Binding Theory, Generalized Phrase Structure Grammar, and Lexical-Function Grammar*, University of Chicago Press.

Shibatani, M. and Kageyama, T. 1988, "Word-formation in a modular theory of grammar: postsyntactic compounds in Japanese," *Language* 64: 451–484.

Shieber, S. M. 1985, "Evidence against the context-freeness of natural language," *Linguistics and Philosophy* 8: 333–343.

Shieber, S. M. 1986, *An introduction to unification-based approaches to grammar*, Stanford, CA: CSLI Publications.

Shughrue, P. J., Scrimo, P. J., and Merchenthaler, I. 2000, "Estrogen binding and estrogen receptor characterization (ERalpha and ERbeta) in the cholinergic neurons of the rat basal forebrain," *Neuroscience* 96(1): 41–49.

Shultz, Jeffrey, Florio, Susan, and Erickson, Frederick 1982, "Where's the floor? Aspects of the cultural organization of social relationships in communication at home and at school," in Perry Gilmore and Alan Glatthorn (eds.), *Ethnography and education: children in and out of school*, Washington, DC: Center for Applied Linguistics, reprinted Norwood, NJ: Ablex, pp. 88–123.

Shuy, Roger 1993, *Language crimes: the use and abuse of language evidence in the courtroom*, Oxford: Blackwell.

Shuy, Roger W., Wolfram, Walt, and Riley, William K. 1967, "Linguistic correlates of social stratification in Detroit speech," USOE Final Report No. 6–1347.

Sihler, Andrew I. 2000, *A language history: an introduction*, Amsterdam: John Benjamins.

Singlish Jokes, retrieved May 31, 2005 from Koulern's website: http://home1.pacific.net.sg/~kuolern/singlish.html

Skinner, B. F. 1959, *Verbal behavior*, New York: Appleton-Century-Crofts.

Slobin, D. 1985, "Crosslinguistic evidence for the language-making capacity," *The Crosslinguistic Study of Language Acquisition* 2: 1157–1256.

Slobin, D. 1985–1997, *The crosslinguistic study of language acquisition*, vols. 1–5, Hillsdale, NJ: Lawrence Erlbaum.

Smyth, Herbert Weir 1974, *Greek grammar*, Cambridge, MA: Harvard University Press.

Sneddon, J. N. 1996, *Indonesian: a comprehensive grammar*, New York: Routledge.

Solan, Lawrence 2002, "Should criminal statutes be interpreted dynamically?" *Issues in Legal Scholarship: Dynamic Statutory Interpretation Art. 8*. Available online at www.bepress.com/ils/iss3/art8.

Spada, N. and Lightbown, P. 1993, "Instruction and the development of questions in the L2 classrooms," *Studies in Second Language Acquisition* 15: 205–224.

Spencer, A. 1991, *Morphological theory: an introduction to word structure in generative grammar*, Oxford and Malden, MA: Blackwell.

Spencer, Andrew 1996, *Phonology*, Oxford and Malden, MA: Blackwell.

Sproat, R. 1993, *Morphology and computation*, Cambridge, MA: MIT Press.

Stalnaker, R. 1974, "Pragmatic presupposition," in M. Munitz and P. Unger (eds.), *Semantics and philosophy*, New York University Press, pp. 197–213.

Stalnaker, R. 1978, "Assertion," in P. Cole (ed.), *Syntax and semantics,* vol. 9: *Pragmatics*, New York: Academic Press, pp. 315–332.

Stevens, Kenneth 1998, *Acoustic phonetics*, Cambridge, MA: MIT Press.

Straehle, Carolyn 1997, "German and American conversational styles: a focus on narrative and agonistic discussion as sources of stereotypes," PhD dissertation, Georgetown University.

Streeter, L. A. 1976, "Language perception of two-month-old infants shows effects of both innate mechanisms and experience," *Nature* 259: 39–41.

Stromswold, K., Caplan, D., Alpert, N., and Rauch, S. 1996, "Localization of syntactic comprehension by positron emission tomography," *Brain and Language* 52: 452–473.

Swain, M. and Lapkin, S. 1998, "Interaction and second language learning: two adolescent French immersion students working together," *Modern Language Journal* 82(3): 320–337.

Talmy, L. 2000, *Towards a cognitive semantics*, 2 vols., Cambridge, MA: MIT Press.

Tannen, Deborah [1984] 2005, *Conversational style: analyzing talk among friends*, 2nd edition, New York: Oxford University Press.

Tannen, Deborah 1989, *Talking voices: repetition, dialogue, and imagery in conversational discourse*, Cambridge University Press.

Tarski, A. 1944, "The semantic conception of truth," *Philosophy and Phenomenological Research* 4: 341–375.

Thomason, Sarah G. 2001, *Language contact: an introduction*, Washington, DC: Georgetown University Press.

Thompson-Schill, S. L., D'Esposito, M., Aguirre, G. K., and Farah, M. J. 1997, "Role of left inferior prefrontal cortex in retrieval of semantic knowledge: a reevaluation," *Proceedings of the National Academy of Science USA* 94(26): 14792–14797.

Thornton, R. 1996, "Elicited production," in D. McDaniel, C. McKee, and H. S. Cairns (eds.), *Methods for assessing children's syntax*, Cambridge, MA: MIT Press, pp. 77–102.

Tomasello, M. 1995, "Language is not an instinct," *Cognitive Development* 10: 131–156.

Tomasello, M. 1998, "The return of constructions" (book review), *Journal of Child Language* 25: 431–432.

Trager, George L. and Smith Jr., Henry Lee 1951, *An outline of English structure. studies in linguistics: occasional papers*, reprinted 1957, Washington DC: American Council of Learned Societies.

Trudgill, Peter 1974, *The social differentiation of English in Norwich*, Cambridge University Press.

Tsuchida, Ayako 1996, "Phonetic and phonological vowel devoicing in Japanese," PhD dissertation, Cornell University.

Tucker, G. R., Lambert, W. E., and Rigault, A. A. 1977, *The French speaker's skill with grammatical gender: an example of rule-governed behavior*, The Hague: Mouton.

Tyler, A. and Evans, V. 2003, *The semantics of English prepositions: spatial scenes, embodied meaning, and cognition*, Cambridge University Press.

Ullman, Michael T. 2001, "A neurocognitive perspective on language: the declarative/procedural model," *Nature Reviews Neuroscience* 2: 717–726.

Ullman, Michael T. 2004, "Contributions of memory circuits to language: the declarative/ procedural model," *Cognition* 92(1–2): 231–270.

Ullman, Michael T., Corkin, Suzanne, Coppola, Marie, Hickok, Gregory, Growdon, John H., Koroshetz, Walter J., and Pinker, Steven 1997, "A neural dissociation within language: evidence that the mental dictionary is part of declarative memory, and that grammatical rules are processed by the procedural system," *Journal of Cognitive Neuroscience* 9(2): 266–276.

Ullman, M. T., Miranda, R. A., and Travers, M. L. 2008, "Sex differences in the neurocognition of language," in J. B. Becker, K. J. Berkley, N. Geary, E. Hampson, J. Herman, and E. Young (eds.), *Sex on the brain: from genes to behavior*, New York: Oxford University Press, pp. 291–309.

Ullman, M. T., and Pierpont, E. I. 2005, "Specific language impairment is not specific to language: the procedural deficit hypothesis," *Cortex* 41(3): 399–433.

Ur, P. 1981, *Discussions that work: task-centered fluency practice*, Cambridge University Press.

van der Lely, Heather K. J. 2005, "Domain-specific cognitive systems: insight from grammatical-SLI," *Trends in Cognitive Sciences* 9(2): 53–59.

Vannest, J., Polk, T. A., and Lewis, R. L. 2005, "Dualroute processing of complex words: new fMRI evidence from derivational suffixation," *Cognitive, Affective and Behavioral Neuroscience* 5(1): 67–76.

Villafana, Christina 2006, "Consonant Weakening in Florentine Italian: an acoustic study of gradient and variable sound change," PhD dissertation, Georgetown University.

Wagner, Jane 1986, *The search for signs of intelligent life in the universe*, New York: Harper & Row.

Wahlster, W. 2000, *Verbmobil: foundations of speech-to-speech translation*, Berlin: Springer-Verlag http://verbmobil.dfki.de/overview-us.html

Walenski, M., Tager-Flusberg, H., and Ullman, M. T. 2006, "Language in autism," in Steven O. Moldin and John L. R. Rubinstein (eds.), *Understanding autism: from basic research to treatment*, New York: CRC Press.

Walker, Alice 1982, *The color purple*, New York: Washington Square Press.

Watt, Dom 2002, "'I don't speak with a Geordie accent, I speak, like, the Northern accent': contact-induced levelling in the Tyneside vowel system," *Journal of Sociolinguistics* 6(1): 44–63.

Watt, Dom and Milroy, Lesley 1999, "Patterns of variation and change in three Tyneside vowels: is this dialect leveling?" in Paul Foulkes and Gerry J. Docherty (eds.), *Urban voices*, London: Arnold; New York: Oxford University Press, pp. 25–46.

Webster's unabridged dictionary of the English language 1989, New York: Portland House.

Werker, J. F., Gilbert, J. H., Humphrey, K., and Tees, R. C. 1981, "Developmental aspects of cross-language speech perception," *Child Development* 52: 359–355.

Wieland, Molly 1991, "Turn-taking structure as a source of misunderstanding in French-American cross-cultural conversation," in Lawrence Bouton, and Yamuna Kachru (eds.), *Pragmatics and language learning*, vol. 2, Urbana-Champaign: Division of English as an International Language, pp. 101–118.

Wierzbicka, A. 1996, *Semantics, primes, and universals*, Oxford University Press.

Wikipedia: the free encyclopedia (Tok Pisin page). Retrieved April 6, 2005 from Main Page–Wikipedia: http://tpi.wikipedia.org/wiki/Main_Page.

Wolfram, Walt 1969, *A linguistic description of Detroit Negro speech*, Washington, DC: Center for Applied Linguistics.

Wolfram, Walt and Schilling-Estes, Natalie 1997, *Hoi Toide on the Outer Banks: the story of the Ocracoke brogue*, University of North Carolina Press.

Wolfram, Walt, and Schilling-Estes, Natalie 2006, *American English: dialects and variation*, 2nd edition, Oxford and Malden, MA: Blackwell.

Woolner, Alfred C. 1966, *Introduction to Prakrit*, Varanasi: Bhartiya Vidya Publishers.

Yamada, Haru 1997, *Different games, different rules: why Americans and Japanese misunderstand each other*, Oxford University Press.

Yip, Moira 2002, *Tone*, Cambridge University Press.

Zeevat, H., Klein, E., and Calder, J. 1991, "Unification categorial grammar," *Lingua e Stile* 26: 499–527.

Zentella, A. C. 1997, *Growing up bilingual: Puerto Rican children in New York*, Oxford and Malden, MA: Blackwell.

INDEX